# IMPORTANT:

## HERE IS YOUR REGISTRATION CODE TO ACCESS
## YOUR PREMIUM McGRAW-HILL ONLINE RESOURCES.

For key premium online resources you need THIS CODE to gain access. Once the code is entered, you will be able to use the Web resources for the length of your course.

If your course is using **WebCT** or **Blackboard**, you'll be able to use this code to access the McGraw-Hill content within your instructor's online course.

Access is provided if you have purchased a new book. If the registration code is missing from this book, the registration screen on our Website, and within your WebCT or Blackboard course, will tell you how to obtain your new code.

## Registering for McGraw-Hill Online Resources

TO gain access to your MCGraw-Hill web resources simply follow the steps below:

1. USE YOUR WEB BROWSER TO GO TO:  **http://www.mhhe.com/collins**

2. CLICK ON **FIRST TIME USER**.

3. ENTER THE REGISTRATION CODE* PRINTED ON THE TEAR-OFF BOOKMARK ON THE RIGHT.

4. AFTER YOU HAVE ENTERED YOUR REGISTRATION CODE, CLICK **REGISTER**.

5. FOLLOW THE INSTRUCTIONS TO SET-UP YOUR PERSONAL UserID AND PASSWORD.

6. WRITE YOUR UserID AND PASSWORD DOWN FOR FUTURE REFERENCE.
KEEP IT IN A SAFE PLACE.

**TO GAIN ACCESS** to the McGraw-Hill content in your instructor's **WebCT** or **Blackboard** course simply log in to the course with the UserID and Password provided by your instructor. Enter the registration code exactly as it appears in the box to the right when prompted by the system. You will only need to use the code the first time you click on McGraw-Hill content.

Thank you, and welcome to your MCGraw-Hill online Resources!

0-07-301973-9  T/A  COLLINS: DATA STRUCTURES AND THE JAVA COLLECTIONS FRAMEWORK, 2E

## REGISTRATION CODE

**1JFW-1NDQ-GZRR-I54W-ZGRB**

# Data Structures and the Java Collections Framework

**Second Edition**

William J. Collins
*Lafayette College*

 **Higher Education**

Boston   Burr Ridge, IL   Dubuque, IA   Madison, WI   New York   San Francisco   St. Louis
Bangkok   Bogotá   Caracas   Kuala Lumpur   Lisbon   London   Madrid   Mexico City
Milan   Montreal   New Delhi   Santiago   Seoul   Singapore   Sydney   Taipei   Toronto

## Higher Education

DATA STRUCTURES AND THE JAVA COLLECTIONS FRAMEWORK, SECOND EDITION

Published by McGraw-Hill, a business unit of The McGraw-Hill Companies, Inc., 1221 Avenue of the Americas, New York, NY 10020. Copyright © 2005, 2002 by The McGraw-Hill Companies, Inc. All rights reserved. No part of this publication may be reproduced or distributed in any form or by any means, or stored in a database or retrieval system, without the prior written consent of The McGraw-Hill Companies, Inc., including, but not limited to, in any network or other electronic storage or transmission, or broadcast for distance learning.

Some ancillaries, including electronic and print components, may not be available to customers outside the United States.

This book is printed on acid-free paper.

1 2 3 4 5 6 7 8 9 0 QPF/QPF 0 9 8 7 6 5 4

ISBN 0–07–282379–8

Publisher: *Elizabeth A. Jones*
Sponsoring editor: *Kelly H. Lowery*
Managing developmental editor: *Emily J. Lupash*
Marketing manager: *Dawn R. Bercier*
Senior project manager: *Sheila M. Frank*
Lead production supervisor: *Sandy Ludovissy*
Lead media project manager: *Audrey A. Reiter*
Media technology producer: *Eric A. Weber*
Senior coordinator of freelance design: *Michelle D. Whitaker*
Cover designer: *Rokusek Design*
(USE) Cover image: *© Mark Segal/Index Stock Imagery*
Compositor: *Lachina Publishing Services*
Typeface: *10/12 Times Roman*
Printer: *Quebecor World Fairfield, PA*

### Library of Congress Cataloging-in-Publication Data

Collins, William J. (William Joseph)
 Data structures and the Java collections framework / William J. Collins. — 2nd ed.
  p.   cm.
 Includes bibliographical references and index.
 ISBN 0–07–282379–8 (hard copy : alk. paper)
 1. Java (Computer program language).  2. Data structures (Computer science).  I. Title.

QA76.73.J38C657   2005
005.7'3—dc22                                    2004003590
                                               CIP

www.mhhe.com

**To my students, for all they have taught me.**

W.J.C.

# BRIEF CONTENTS

# CONTENTS

**CHAPTER 7**

**Linked Lists**   239

**CHAPTER 8**

**Stacks and Queues**   305

**CHAPTER 9**

**Binary Trees   365**

**CHAPTER 10**

**Binary Search Trees   389**

**CHAPTER 11**

**Sorting   445**

**APPENDIX** 1
## Java Review   707

**APPENDIX** 2
## Mathematical Background   725

**APPENDIX** 3
## Additional Features of the Java Collections Framework   743

# PREFACE

This book is intended for an object-oriented course in data structures and algorithms. The implementation language is Java, and it is assumed that students have taken an introductory course with that language. That course should have covered the fundamental statements and data types, as well as arrays. Appendix 1 has a review of that material.

## THE JAVA COLLECTIONS FRAMEWORK

One of the distinctive features of this text is its emphasis on the Java Collections Framework, part of the java.util package. Basically, the framework is a hierarchy with interfaces at each level except the lowest, and collection classes that implement those interfaces at the lowest level. The collection classes implement most of the data structures studied in a second computer-science course, such as a resizable array class, a linked-list class, a balanced binary-search-tree class, and a hash-map class.

There are several advantages to using the Java Collections Framework. First, students will be working with code that has been extensively tested; they need not depend on modules created by the instructor or textbook author. Second, the framework is available for later courses in the curriculum, and beyond! Third, although the primary emphasis is on *using* the Java Collections Framework, the framework classes are not treated simply as "black boxes." For each such class, the heading and fields are provided, and one method definition is dissected. This exposition takes away some of the mystery that would otherwise surround the class, and allows students to see the efficiency and succinctness of professionals' code.

The version of the Java Collections Framework we will be working with includes type parameters. Type parameters, sometimes called "generic types," "generics," or "templates," were added to the Java language starting with Java 2 Standard Edition (J2SE), version 1.5. With type parameters, there is no need to downcast the return value from a collection, and many errors can be detected at compile-time that previously were discoverable only at run-time.

To complement generics, three other features have been added: boxing, unboxing, and an enhanced **for** statement. The elements in collections must be (references to) objects, often from a wrapper class such as Integer. If a primitive value appears where a wrapper element is called for, ***boxing*** automatically converts the primitive value to the corresponding wrapper element. Conversely, if a wrapper-class element appears where a primitive value is needed, ***unboxing*** automatically converts that element to the corresponding primitive value. Finally, the enhanced **for** statement has a sleek structure for iterating through a collection. The net effect of these new features of Java is to improve productivity by relegating to the compiler many of the "boiler-plate" details related to casting and iterating.

## OTHER IMPLEMENTATIONS CONSIDERED

As important as the Java Collections Framework implementations are, they cannot be the exclusive focus of such a fundamental course in data structures and algorithms. Approaches that differ from those in the framework deserve consideration. For example, the HashMap class utilizes chaining, so there is a separate section on open addressing, and a discussion of the trade-offs of one design over the other. Also, there is coverage of data structures (such as a Network class) and algorithms (such as Heap Sort) that are not yet included in the Java Collections Framework.

Sometimes, the complexity of the framework classes is mitigated by first introducing simpler versions of those classes. For example, the SinglyLinkedList class—not in the Java Collections Framework—helps to pave the way for the more powerful LinkedList class, which is in the framework. And the BinarySearchTree class prepares students to understand the framework's TreeMap class, based on red-black trees.

This text satisfies another important goal of a data structures and algorithms course: students have the opportunity to develop their own data structures. There are programming projects in which data structures are either created "from the ground up" or extended from examples in the chapters. And there are many other projects to develop or extend applications that *use* the Java Collections Framework.

## PEDAGOGICAL FEATURES

This text offers several features that may improve the teaching environment for instructors and the learning environment for students. Each chapter starts with a list of objectives, and most chapters conclude with several major programming assignments. Each chapter also has a variety of exercises, and the answers to all of the exercises are available to the instructor.

Each data structure is carefully described, with the specifications for each method given in javadoc notation. Also, there are examples of how to call the method, and the results of that call. To reinforce the important aspects of the material and to hone students' coding skills in preparation for programming projects, there is a suite of 23 lab experiments. The organization of these labs is described later in this preface.

## SUPPORT MATERIAL

The website for all of the support material is

*www.mhhe.com/collins*

That website has links to the following information for students:

- An overview of the labs and how to access them
- The source code for all classes developed in the text
- PowerPoint Slides for each chapter

■ Applets for projects that have a strong visual component

Additionally, instructors can obtain the following from the website:

■ Instructors' options with regard to the labs
■ Answers to every exercise and lab experiment

## SYNOPSES OF THE CHAPTERS

Chapter 1 focuses on the fundamentals of object-oriented programming. The String class serves as a vehicle for some background material on constructors and references. Then encapsulation, inheritance, and polymorphism are introduced. For a concrete illustration of these topics, an interface is created and implemented, and the implementation is extended. The relationship between abstract data types and interfaces is explored, as is the corresponding connection between classes and data structures. The Universal Modeling Language provides a design tool to depict the interrelationships among interfaces, classes, and subclasses.

Chapter 2 introduces some additional features of the Java language. For example, there are sections on exception handling, file input and output, and the Java Virtual Machine. There is also a section on the Object class's equals method, why that method should be overridden, and how to accomplish the overriding.

Chapter 3, "Analysis of Algorithms," starts by defining functions to estimate a method's execution-time requirements, both in the average and worst cases. Big-O notation provides a convenient tool for estimating these estimates. Because Big-O notation yields environment-independent estimates, these results are then compared with actual run-times, which are determined with the help of the Random class and currentTimeMillis method in the System class.

Chapter 4 outlines the Java Collections Framework. We start with some preliminary material on collection classes in general, type parameters, and the iterator design-pattern. The remainder of the chapter presents the major interfaces (Collection, List, Set, Map) and their implementations. Special attention is given to comparing those implementations, for example, ArrayList versus LinkedList and TreeMap versus HashMap.

Chapter 5, on recursion, represents a temporary shift in emphasis from data structures to algorithms. There is a gradual progression from simple examples (factorial and decimal-to-binary) to more powerful examples (binary search and backtracking). The mechanism for illustrating the execution of recursive methods is the execution frame. Backtracking is introduced, not only as a design pattern, but as another illustration of creating polymorphic references through interfaces. And the same BackTrack class is used for maze-searching, eight queens, and knight's tour!

In Chapter 6, we study the Java Collections Framework's ArrayList class. An ArrayList object is a smart array: automatically resizable, and with methods to handle insertions and deletions at any index. The design starts with the method specifications for some of the most widely used methods in the ArrayList class. There follows a brief outline of the implementation of the class. The application of the

ArrayList class, high-precision arithmetic, is essential for public-key cryptography. This application is extended in a lab and in a programming project. There is another programming project to develop a Deque class from scratch.

Chapter 6 also introduces a "theme" project: to develop an integrated web browser and search engine. This project, based on a paper by Newhall and Meeden (2002), assumes some familiarity with graphical user interfaces. The project continues through five of the remaining chapters, and clearly illustrates the practical value of understanding data structures.

Chapter 7 presents linked lists. A discussion of singly linked lists leads to the development of a primitive SinglyLinkedList class. This serves mainly to prepare students for the framework's LinkedList class. LinkedList objects are characterized by linear-time methods for inserting, removing, or retrieving at an arbitrary position. This property makes a compelling case for *list iterators:* objects that traverse a LinkedList object and have constant-time methods for inserting, removing, or retrieving at the "current" position. The framework's design is doubly linked and circular, but other approaches are also considered. The application is a small line editor, for which list iterators are well suited. This application is extended in a programming project.

Stacks and queues are the subjects of Chapter 8. A PureStack interface, with several simple implementations, allows us to bypass the framework's Stack class. The fatal flaw in the Stack class is that elements can be inserted or removed anywhere in a Stack object. There are two applications of stacks: the implementation of recursion by a compiler, and the conversion from infix to postfix. This latter application is expanded in a lab, and forms the basis for a project on evaluating a condition.

The Java Collections Framework has a Queue interface, but that interface allows the removal of any element from a queue! Because this violates the definition of a queue, we instead create a simple PureQueue interface that corresponds to the abstract data type queue. Several implementations are developed and analyzed. The specific application, calculating the average waiting time at a car wash, falls into the general category of *computer simulation.*

Chapter 9 focuses on binary trees in general, as a prelude to the material in Chapters 10 through 13. The essential features of binary trees are presented, including both botanical (root, branch, leaf) and familial (parent, child, sibling) terms. Binary trees are important for understanding later material on AVL trees, decision trees, red-black trees, heaps, and Huffman trees.

In Chapter 10, we look at binary search trees, including a BinarySearchTree class, and explain the value of balanced binary search trees. Rotations are introduced as the mechanism by which rebalancing is accomplished, and AVL trees are offered as examples of balanced binary search trees. An AVLTree class, as a subclass of BinarySearchTree, is outlined; the crucial methods, fixAfterInsertion and fixAfterDeletion, are given as programming projects.

Sorting is the topic of Chapter 11. Estimates of the lower bounds for comparison-based sorts are determined. A few simple sorts are defined, and then we move on to two sort methods provided by the framework. Quick Sort sorts an array of a primitive type, and Merge Sort works for an array of objects and for implementations of the List interface. A lab experiment compares all of these sort algorithms on randomly generated integers.

The central topic of Chapter 12 is how to use the TreeMap class. A *map* is a collection in which each element has a unique key part and also a value part. In the TreeMap implementation of the Map interface, the elements are stored in a red-black tree, ordered by the elements' keys. There are labs to guide students through the details of restructuring after an insertion or removal. The application consists of searching a thesaurus for synonyms. The TreeSet class has a TreeMap field in which each element has the same, dummy value-part. The application of the TreeSet class is a simple spell checker.

Chapter 13 introduces the PurePriorityQueue interface, which is not yet part of the Java Collections Framework. A heap-based implementation allows insertions in constant average time, and removal of the smallest-valued element in logarithmic worst time. The application is in the area of data compression: given a text file, generate a minimal, prefix-free encoding. The project assignment is to convert the encoding back to the original text file.

Chapter 14 investigates hashing. The Java Collections Framework has a HashMap class for elements that consist of unique key/value pairs. Basically, the average time for insertion, removal, and searching is constant! This average speed is exploited in an application to create a simple symbol table. The implementation, using chained hashing is compared to open-address hashing.

The most general data structures—graphs, trees, and networks—are presented in Chapter 15. There are outlines of the essential algorithms: breadth-first traversal, depth-first traversal, finding a minimal spanning tree, and finding a shortest or longest path between two vertices. The only class developed is the Network (that is, WeightedDiGraph) class, with an adjacency-list implementation. Other classes, such as UndirectedGraph and UndirectedNetwork, can be straightforwardly defined as subclasses of Network. The Traveling Salesperson problem is investigated in a lab, and there is a programming project to complete an adjacency-matrix version of the Network class. Another backtracking application is presented, with the same Back Track class that was introduced in Chapter 5.

With each chapter, there is an associated Web page that includes all programs developed in the chapter, and applets, where appropriate, to animate the concepts presented.

## APPENDIXES

Appendix 1 has a review of Java topics assumed in the rest of the text: primitive types, the StringTokenizer class, console-oriented input, and arrays. There are also several programming exercises to reinforce the material presented.

Appendix 2 contains the background that will allow students to comprehend the mathematical aspects of the chapters. Summation notation and the rudimentary properties of logarithms are essential, and the material on mathematical induction will lead to a deeper appreciation of the analysis of binary trees.

Appendix 3 has two additional features of the Java Collections Framework. Each of the collection classes in the framework is *serializable,* that is, an instance of the class can be conveniently stored to an output stream, and the instance can later be reconstituted from an input stream (deserialization). Framework iterators are *fail-fast:* During an iteration through a collection, there should be no insertions into or removals from the collection except by the iterator. Otherwise, the integrity of that iterator may be compromised, so an exception will be thrown as soon as the iterator's unreliability has been established.

## ORGANIZATION OF THE LABS

There are 23 Web labs associated with this text. For both students and instructors, the initial Uniform Resource Locator (URL) is

*www.mhhe.com/collins*

The labs do not contain essential material, but provide reinforcement of the text material. For example, after the ArrayList and LinkedList classes have been investigated, there is a lab to perform some timing experiments on those two classes.

The labs are self-contained, so the instructor has considerable flexibility in assigning the labs:

1.   They can be assigned as closed labs.
2.   They can be assigned as open labs.
3.   They can be assigned as ungraded homework.

In addition to the obvious benefit of promoting active learning, these labs also encourage use of the scientific method. Basically, each lab is set up as an experiment. Students *observe* some phenomenon, such as creating a greedy cycle to solve the Traveling Salesperson Problem. They then formulate and submit a *hypothesis*—with their own code—about the phenomenon. After *testing* and, perhaps, revising their hypothesis, they submit the *conclusions* they drew from the experiment.

## ACKNOWLEDGMENTS

Joshua Bloch of Sun Microsystems gave valuable insights into the new features of J2SE 1.5 and their impact on the Java Collections Framework. The following focus-group members encouraged a solidly object-oriented approach:

Mikhail Brikman, Salem State University
Robert Cohen, University of Massachusetts, Boston
Art Lee, University of Utah
Bina Ramamurthy, State University of New York, Buffalo
John Ramirez, University of Pittsburgh
Michael Scott, University of Texas, Austin

I am especially grateful for Derek Lindner's scrutiny of the java code. Many helpful suggestions were also made by other reviewers:

Dennis R. Bahler, North Carolina State University
Natasha Bozovic, San Jose State University
Vladimir Drobot, San Jose State University
Matthew Evett, Eastern Michigan University
Ralph Grayson, Oklahoma State University
Harold C. Grossman, Clemson University
Anselmo Lastro, University of North Carolina
Cary Laxer, Rose-Hulman Institute of Technology
Mark Llewellyn, University of Central Florida
Marian Manyo, Marquette University
Kenneth E. Martin, University of North Florida
Robert Pastel, Michigan Technological University
Lawrence Peterson, Texas A& M University
Matthew Suderman, McGill University
Christopher C. Taylor, Milwaukee School of Engineering
Alex Thornton, University of California, Irvine
Ken Vollmar, Southwest Missouri State University
Zhigang Xiang, Queens College

I am thankful for the encouragement and support I got from McGraw-Hill, especially from Emily Lupash, Kelly Lowery, and Sheila Frank.

Several students from Lafayette College made important contributions. Matthew Hokanson converted the labs to run under J2SE 1.5. Eric Panchenko created all of the applets and many of the driver programs. Prashant Poddar helped with the development of solutions to the lab experiments. Finally, I am indebted to all of the students at Lafayette College who participated in the class testing of the book and endured earlier versions of the labs.

## CHAPTER 1

# Object-Oriented Concepts

This is a book about programming: specifically, about understanding and using data structures and algorithms. The Java Collections Framework has a considerable number of data structures and algorithms. Subsequent chapters will focus on what the framework is and how to use the framework in your programs. For this information to make sense to you, you will need to be familiar with certain aspects of object-oriented programming that we present in this chapter. Some of what follows may be a review for you; some may be brand new. All of the material is needed, either for the framework itself or to enable you to use the framework in your programming projects. ■

## CHAPTER OBJECTIVES

1. Learn (or review) the fundamentals of classes, objects, and messages.

2. Be able to use javadoc in writing method specifications.

3. Compare a developer's view of a class with a user's view of that class.

4. Understand how inheritance promotes code reuse.

5. Understand how polymorphic references can be useful.

6. Be able to create class diagrams in the Unified Modeling Language.

## 1.1 | CLASSES

In addition to primitive types such as **int** and **char**, Java provides programmers with the ability to create powerful new types called "classes." Given a problem, we develop classes—or utilize already existing classes—that correspond to components of the problem itself.

A *class* consists of variables, called *fields,* together with functions, called *methods,* that operate on those fields. A class combines the passive components (fields) and active components (methods) into a single entity. This grouping increases *program modularity:* the separation of a program into components that are coherent units. Specifically, a class is isolated from the rest of the program, and that makes the whole program easier to understand and to modify.

In Section 1.1.1, we investigate the class concept in more detail by looking at the String class, the most widely used of Java's predeclared classes.

### 1.1.1 The String Class

To start with a simple example, we consider the String class. Actually, the String class is somewhat intricate, with several fields and dozens of methods. But as we will focus on *using* the String class, we will ignore the fields and look at only a few of the methods. In Section 1.3.2, we will introduce a new class and investigate its fields as well as its methods.

An *object* is an instance of a class; in other words, an object is a variable that contains fields and can call methods. In the context of using the String class, an object can be thought of as a variable that contains a *string*—a sequence of characters—and can call the String class's methods. This gives rise to two questions:

1. How are String objects declared?
2. How do String objects call String methods?

The answer to the first question is somewhat surprising: String objects, in fact, objects of any class, cannot be declared in Java! Instead, we declare variables, called *reference variables,* that can contain the address of an object. For example, we can declare

```
String s1;
```

Then s1 is not a String object, but a variable that can contain the *address* of a String object.[1] In order for s1 to actually contain such a reference, the space for a String object must be allocated, then the fields in that newly created String object must be initialized, and finally, the address of that String object must be assigned to s1. We combine these three steps into a single assignment statement. For example, if we want s1 to be a reference to an empty String object, we write:

```
s1 = new String( );
```

---

[1]In the languages C and C++, a variable that can contain the address of another variable is called a *pointer variable*.

The right-hand side of this assignment statement accomplishes several tasks. The **new** operator allocates space in memory for a String object, calls a special method known as a constructor to initialize the fields in the object, and returns the address of that newly created object. That address is assigned to s1. A *constructor* is a method whose name is the same as the class's name and whose purpose is to initialize the object's fields. In this example, the fields are initialized to the effect that the newly created String object represents an empty string, that is, a string that contains no characters.

The constructor called above has no parameters, and is called the *default constructor.* The String class also has a constructor with a String-reference parameter. Here is the heading of that constructor:

```
public String (String original)
```

The parameter original is of type reference-to-String. When this constructor is called, the argument—inside the parentheses—will be assigned to the parameter, and then the body of the constructor (the statements inside the braces) will be executed. For an example of a call to this constructor, the following statement combines the declaration of a reference variable and the assignment to that variable of a reference to a newly constructed String object:

```
String s2 = new String ("transparent");
```

When this statement is executed, the space for a new String object is allocated, the fields in that newly created String object are initialized to the effect that the new String object represents the string "transparent", and the address of that new String object is assigned to the String reference s2.

Now that s1 and s2 contain live references, the objects referenced by s1 and s2 can invoke any String method.[2] For example, the length method takes no parameters and returns the number of characters in the calling object, that is, the object that invokes the length method. We can write

```
System.out.println (s1.length( ));
```

The output will be 0. If, instead, we write

```
System.out.println (s2.length( ));
```

then the output will be 11 because the calling object contains the string "transparent".

The default constructor and the constructor with a String-reference parameter have the same name, String, but have different parameter lists. In general, Java allows *method overloading*: the ability of a class to have methods with the same method identifier, but different parameter lists.

---

[2]Except String constructors, which are invoked by the **new** operator. For that reason, and the fact that constructors do not have a return type, the developers of the Java language do not classify a constructor as a method [see Arnold (1996)]. But for the sake of simplicity, we lump constructors in with the methods of a class.

### 1.1.2 Using javadoc **Notation for Method Specifications**

The String class has a method that returns a copy of a specified substring—a contiguous part of—the calling string object. To make it easier for you to understand this method, we will supply the method's specification. A ***method specification*** is the explicit information a user will need in order to write code that invokes the method.

The method specification will include javadoc notation. ***javadoc*** is a program that converts Java source code and a specially formatted block of comments into Application Programming Interface (API) code in Hypertext Markup Language (HTML) for easy viewing on a browser. Because javadoc is available on any system that has Java, javadoc format has become the standard for writing method specifications. Each comment block starts with "/**", each subsequent line starts with "*", and the final line in a block has "*/". The complete specification consists of the javadoc comments and the method heading:

```
/**
 * Returns a copy of the substring, between two specified indexes, of this String
 * object.
 *
 * @param beginIndex – the starting position (inclusive) of the substring.
 * @param endIndex – the final position (exclusive) of the substring.
 *
 * @return the substring of this String object from indexes beginIndex (inclusive)
 *       to endIndex (exclusive).
 *
 * @throws IndexOutOfBoundsException – if beginIndex is negative, or if
 *             beginIndex is greater than endIndex, or if endIndex is greater than
 *             length( ).
 *
 */
public String substring (int beginIndex, int endIndex)
```

The first sentence in a javadoc comment block is called the ***postcondition:*** the effect of a legal call to the method. The comment block also indicates parameters (starting with @param), the value returned (@return), and what exceptions can be thrown (@throws). An ***exception,*** such as IndexOutOfBoundsException, is an object created by an unusual condition, typically an attempt at invalid processing. Section 2.2 covers the topic of exceptions, including how they are thrown and how they are caught. To avoid confusing you, we will omit @throws comments for the remainder of this chapter.

To illustrate the effect of calls to this method, here are several calls in which the calling object is either an empty string referenced by s1 or the string "transparent" referenced by s2:

```
s1.substring (0, 0)   // returns reference to an empty string
s1.substring (0, 1)   // error: 2nd argument > length of calling object
s2.substring (1, 4)   // returns reference to copy of "ran", a 3-character string
```

s2.substring (5, 10) // returns reference to copy of "paren", a 5-character string

s2.substring (5, 11) // returns reference to copy of "parent", a 6-character string

There are several points worth mentioning about the javadoc comment block. In the postcondition and elsewhere, "this String object" means the calling object. What is returned is a reference to a copy of the substring. And the last character in the designated substring is at endIndex − 1, not at endIndex.

The javadoc comment block given above is slightly simpler than the actual block for this substring method in the String class. The actual javadoc comment block includes several html tags: <pre>, <blockquote>, and <code>. And if you viewed the description of that method from a browser—that is, after the javadoc program had been executed for the String class—you would see the comments in an easier-to-read format. For example, instead of

   * @return the substring of this String object from indexes beginIndex (inclusive)

   *     to endIndex (exclusive).

you would see

**Returns:**

     the substring of this String object from indexes beginIndex (inclusive)

     to endIndex (exclusive).

The on-line Java documentation is generated with javadoc. And the documentation about a method in one class may include hyperlinks to another class. For example, the heading for the nextToken( ) method in the StringTokenizer class is given as

    **public** String nextToken( )

So if you are looking at the documentation of the nextToken( ) method and you want to see some information on the String class, all you need to do is click on the String link.

Throughout the remainder of this text, we will regularly use javadoc to provide information about a method. You should use javadoc to describe your methods.

## 1.1.3 Equality of References and Equality of Objects

Reference variables represent an advance over the pointer mechanism of Java's predecessors, C and C++. A pointer variable could be assigned any memory address, and this often led to hard-to-find errors. In contrast, if a reference variable contains any address, that must be the address of an object. To indicate that a reference variable does not contain an address, we can assign to that variable a special value, indicated by the reserved word null:

    String s3 = **null**;

At this point, s3 does not contain the address of a String object, so it would be illegal to write

    s3.length( )

In object-oriented parlance, when a method is invoked, a ***message*** is being sent to the calling object. The term "message" is meant to suggest that a communication is being sent from one part of a program to another part. For example, the following message returns the length of the String object referenced by s2:

```
s2.length( )
```

This message requests that the object referenced by s2 return its length, and the value 11 is returned. The form of a message consists of a reference followed by a dot—called the ***member-selection operator***—followed by a method identifier followed by a parenthesized argument list.

Make sure you understand the difference between a **null** reference (such as s3), and a reference (such as s1) to an empty string. That distinction is essential to an understanding of Java's object-reference model.

The distinction between objects and references is prominent in comparing the equals method and the == operator. Here is the method specification for equals:

```
/**
 * Compares this String object to a specified object.
 * The result is true if and only if the argument is not null and is a String object
 * that represents the same sequence of characters as this String object.
 *
 * @param anObject – the object to compare this String against.
 *
 * @return true – if the two String objects are equal; false otherwise.
 *
 */
public boolean equals (Object anObject)
```

The parameter's type suggests that the calling object can be compared to an object of any type, not just to a String object. Of course, **false** will be returned if the type is anything but String. The Object class is discussed in Section 1.4.3.

The == operator simply compares two *references*: **true** is returned if and only if the two references contain the same address or both contain **null**. So if str1 and str2 are referencing identical String objects that are at different addresses,

```
str1.equals (str2)
```

will return **true** because the String objects are identical, but

```
str1 == str2
```

will return **false** because str1 and str2 contain different addresses.

Finally, you can create a String object without invoking the new operator. For example,

```
String str3 = "yes",
        str4 = "yes";
```

Because the underlying strings are identical, only one String object is constructed, and both str3 and str4 are references to that object.

**Figure 1.1** I Illustration of the effect of the equals method and == operator.

```
String s4 = new String ("restful"),
       s5 = new String ("restful"),
       s6 = new String ("peaceful"),
       s7 = s4,
       s8 = "restful",
       s9 = "restful";

System.out.println (s4.equals (s5));     // the output is "true"
System.out.println (s4.equals (s6));     // the output is "false"
System.out.println (s4 == s5);           // the output is "false"
System.out.println (s4 == s7);           // the output is "true"
System.out.println (s4 == s8);           // the output is "false"
System.out.println (s8 == s9);           // the output is "true"
```

Figure 1.1 has several examples, and contrasts the String method equals with the reference operator ==.

The reason the output is different for the first and third examples in Figure 1.1 is that the equals method compares strings and the == operator compares references. Recall that each time the **new** operator is invoked, a new String object is created. So, as shown in Figure 1.2, s4 is a reference to a String object whose value is "restful", and s5 is a reference to a *different* String object whose value is also "restful".

The preceding view of the String class is the user's perspective: what information about the String class is needed by users of that class? A *user* of a class writes

**Figure 1.2** I An internal view of the references and objects in Figure 1.1.

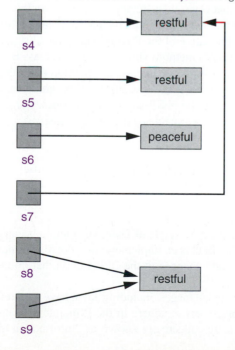

code that includes an instance of that class. Someone who simply executes a program that includes an instance of a class is called an ***end-user.*** A ***developer*** of a class actually creates fields and method definitions. In Section 1.2, we will look at the developer's perspective and compare the two perspectives.

## 1.2 | DATA ABSTRACTION

So far, we have concentrated on method specifications (that is, ***what*** a class provides to users), rather than on the class's fields and method definitions (that is, ***how*** the class is defined by developers). This separation—called ***data abstraction***—of what from how is an essential feature of object-oriented programming. For example, programmers who use the String class will not care about the fields that represent a string or how the methods are defined. Such details would be of no help when you are trying to develop a class that *uses* the String class, but were essential to the developers of the String class.

In general, suppose you are a programmer who is developing class A and, during development, you decide that you will need the services of class B. If someone else has already completed the definition of class B, you should simply use that class rather than reinventing the wheel. But even if you must define the class B yourself, you can simply create the method specifications for class B and postpone any further work on class B until after you have completed the development of class A. By working with class B's method specifications, you increase the independence of class A: its effectiveness will not be affected by any changes to class B that do not affect the method specifications of class B.

When users focus on what a class provides to users rather than on the implementation details of that class, they are applying the ***Principle of Data Abstraction:*** a user's code should not access the implementation details of the class used.

One important application of the Principle of Data Abstraction is that if class A uses class B, then class A's methods should not access class B's fields. In fact, class B's fields should be accessed only in class B's method definitions. This turns out to be a benefit to users of class B because they will be unaffected if the developer of class B decides to replace the old fields with new ones. For example, suppose the following definition is made outside of the String class:

```
String name;
```

Currently, one of the fields in the String class is an int field named count. But an expression such as

```
name.count
```

would be a violation of the Principle of Data Abstraction because whether or not the String class has a count field is an implementation detail. The developer of the String class is free to make any changes to the String class that do not affect the method specifications.

Most programming languages, including Java, have features that enable a developer of a class to force users to adhere to the Principle of Data Abstraction. These enforcement features are collectively known as "information hiding." We will discuss information hiding in Section 1.5 after we have introduced several of the relevant features.

We noted earlier that the Principle of Data Abstraction is a benefit to users of a class because they are freed from reliance on implementation details of that class. This assumes, of course, that the class's method specifications provide all of the information that a user of that class needs. The developer of a class should create methods with sufficient functionality that users need not rely on any implementation details. That functionality should be clearly spelled out in the method specifications. In particular, the user should be told under what circumstances a method call will be legal, and what the effect of a legal call will be.

In a method specification, the information relating to the legality of a method call is known as the ***precondition*** of the method. The precondition may be stated explicitly in sentences that follow the postcondition (for example, "The array must be sorted prior to making this call.") or implicitly from the exception information (for example, any call that throws an exception is illegal). The interplay between a method's precondition and postcondition determines a ***contract*** between the developer and the user. The terms of the contract are as follows:

> If the user of the method ensures that the precondition is true before the method is invoked, the developer guarantees that the postcondition will be true at the end of the execution of the method.

We can summarize our discussion of classes so far by saying that from the **developer's** perspective, a class consists of fields and the definitions of methods that act on those fields. A **user's** view is an abstraction of this: a class consists of method specifications.

The Java Collections Framework is, basically, a hierarchy of thoroughly tested classes that are useful in a variety of applications. The programs in this book will *use* the Java Collections Framework, so those programs will not rely on the definitions of the framework's methods. We will provide method specifications and an overview of most of the classes. Occasionally, to give you experience in reading the code of professional programmers, you will get to study the fields and method definitions.

In Section 1.3, we see the value of classes that have undefined methods.

# 1.3 | ABSTRACT METHODS AND INTERFACES

In Sections 1.1.2 and following, we used method specifications for the purpose of promoting data abstraction. In other words, a user should focus on the method specifications in a class and ignore the class's fields and method definitions. Some methods don't even have a definition, and it turns out that this can be helpful to programmers. For example, suppose we want to create classes for circles, rectangles, and other figures. In each class, there will be methods to draw the figure and to move the figure from one place on the screen to another place on the screen. The Circle class, for example, will have a draw method and a move method based on the center of the circle and its radius. Here are two method specifications and related constant identifiers that will apply to all of the figure classes:

```
final static int MAX_X_COORD = 1024;

final static int MAX_Y_COORD = 768;

/**
 * Draws this Figure object centered at the given coordinates.
 *
 * @param x – the X coordinate of the center point of where this Figure object
 *                 will be drawn.
 * @param y – the Y coordinate of the center point of where this Figure object
 *                 will be drawn.
 *
 */
public void draw(int x, int y)

/**
 * Moves this Figure object to a position whose center coordinates are specified.
 *
 * @param x – the X coordinate of the center point of where this Figure object
 *                 will be moved to.
 * @param y – the Y coordinate of the center point of where this Figure object
 *                 will be moved to.
 *
 */
public void move (int x, int y)
```

Each different type of figure will have to provide its own definitions for the draw and move methods. But by requiring that those definitions adhere to the above specifications, we introduce a consistency to any application that uses the figure classes. A user of one of those classes knows the exact format for the draw and move methods—and that will still be true for classes corresponding to new figure-types.

Java provides a way to enforce this consistency: the interface. Each method heading is followed by a semicolon instead of a definition. Such a method is called an *abstract method*. An **interface** is a collection of abstract methods and constant identifiers. There are no defined methods and no fields. For example, here is the interface for figures:

```
public interface Figure
{
        final static int MAX_X_COORD = 1024;

        final static int MAX_Y_COORD = 768;

        /**
         * Draws this Figure object centered at the given coordinates.
         *
         * @param x – the X coordinate of the center point of where this Figure
         *                 object will be drawn.
         *
```

```
     * @param y – the Y coordinate of the center point of where this Figure
     *                   object will be drawn.
     *
     */
    void draw (int x, int y);

    /**
     * Moves this Figure object to a position whose center coordinates are
     * specified.
     *
     * @param x – the X coordinate of the center point of where this Figure
     *         object will be moved to.
     * @param y – the Y coordinate of the center point of where this Figure
     *         object will be moved to.
     *
     */
    void move (int x, int y);

}//interface Figure
```

The **interface** Figure has two constant identifiers (MAX_X_COORD and MAX_
Y_COORD) and two abstract methods (draw and move). In any interface, all of the
methods and constant identifiers are public, so the declarations need not include the
visibility modifier **public**.

When a class provides method definitions for an interface's methods, the class
is said to *implement* the interface. The class may also define other methods. For
example, here is part of a declaration of the Circle class:

```
public class Circle implements Figure
{
    // declaration of fields:
    private int xCoord,
                yCoord,
                radius;

    // constructors to initialize x, y and radius:
    ...
    /** (javadoc comments as above)
     */
    public draw (int x, int y)
    {
        xCoord = x;
        yCoord = y;

        // draw circle with center at (xCoord, yCoord) and radius:
        ...
    } // method draw

    // definitions for move and any other methods:
```

...

```
} // class Circle
```

The reserved word **implements** signals that class Circle provides method definitions for the methods whose specifications are in the interface Figure. Interfaces do not include constructors because constructors are always class specific. For that reason, interfaces are not instantiable. For example, we cannot create a Figure object:

```
Figure myFig = new Figure( ); // illegal
```

In the method specifications in the Figure interface, the phrase "this Figure object" means "this object in a class that implements the Figure interface."

Of what value is an interface? In general, an interface provides a common base whose method specifications are available to any implementing class. Thus, an interface raises the comfort level of users because they know that the specifications of any method in the interface will be adhered to in any class that implements the interface. In practice, once a user has seen an interface, the user knows a lot about any implementing class. Unlike the interface, the implementing class will have constructors, and may define other methods in addition to those specified in the interface.

### 1.3.1 Abstract Data Types and Data Structures

An *abstract data type* consists of a collection of values, together with a collection of operations on those values. In object-oriented languages such as Java, abstract data types correspond to interfaces in the sense that, for any class that implements the interface, a user of that class can:

1. Create an instance of that class ("instance" corresponds to "value")
2. Invoke the public methods of that class ("public method" corresponds to "operation")

A *data structure* is the implementation of an abstract data type. In object-oriented languages, a developer implements an interface with a class. In other words, we have the following associations:

| general term | object-oriented term |
|---|---|
| abstract data type | interface |
| data structure | class |

A user is interested in abstract data types, given as interfaces, while a developer focuses on data structures, namely, classes. For example, one of the Java Collections Framework's interfaces is the List interface; one of the classes that implement that interface is LinkedList. When we work with the interface, we are taking a user's view of List as an abstract data type. But when we consider a specific choice of fields and method definitions in LinkedList, we are taking a developer's view of LinkedList as a data structure.

In Section 1.3.2, we introduce another interface, and utilize it and implementing classes as vehicles for introducing several object-oriented concepts.

## 1.3.2 An Interface and a Class That Implements the Interface

For another example of an interface, let's create a simple interface called Employee for the employees in a company. The information read in for each employee consists of the employee's name and gross pay. To lead into the method specifications, we first list the responsibilities of the interface, that is, the services provided to users of any class that implements the Employee interface. The responsibilities of the Employee interface are:

1. To determine if an employee's gross pay is greater than some other employee's gross pay

2. To convert an employee's name and gross pay to a string suitable for output

These responsibilities are refined into the following interface:

```
public interface Employee
{

    /**
     * Determines if this Employee object's gross pay is greater than
     * a specified Employee object's gross pay.
     *
     * @param otherEmployee – the specified Employee object whose
     *        gross pay this Employee object's gross pay is compared to.
     *
     * @return true – if this Employee object's gross pay is greater than
     *        otherEmployee's gross pay.
     *
     */
    boolean makesMoreThan (Employee otherEmployee);

    /**
     * Returns a String representation of this Employee object with the name
     * followed by a space followed by a dollar sign followed by the gross
     * weekly pay, with two fractional digits.
     *
     * @return a String representation of this Employee object.
     *
     */
    String toString( );

} // interface Employee
```

The Employee interface's method specifications are all that a user of any implementing class will need in order to invoke those methods. A developer of the class, on the other hand, must decide what fields to have and then define the methods. A convenient categorization of employees is full-time and part-time. Let's develop a FullTimeEmployee implementation of the Employee interface.

For example, a developer may well decide to have two fields: name (a String reference) and grossPay (a **double**). The complete method definitions are developed from the fields and method specifications. For example, here is a complete declaration of the FullTimeEmployee class; the next few sections of this chapter will investigate various aspects of the declaration. The import directives are also included. For general convenience, the entire collection of files that constitutes the package java.util is imported, even though for the FullTimeEmployee class, the only file needed from that package is StringTokenizer.java.

```java
import java.util.*;    // for StringTokenizer class
import java.text.DecimalFormat;

public class FullTimeEmployee implements Employee
{
        private String name;

        private double grossPay;

        /**
         * Initializes this FullTimeEmployee object to have an empty string for the
         * name and 0.00 for the gross pay.
         *
         *
         */
        public FullTimeEmployee( )
        {
                final String EMPTY_STRING = "";

                name = EMPTY_STRING;
                grossPay = 0.00;
        } // default constructor

        /**
         * Initializes this FullTimeEmployee object's name and gross pay from a
         * specified String object, which consists of a name and gross pay, with at
         * least one blank in between.
         *
         * @param s – the String object from which this FullTimeEmployee object
         *      is initialized.
         *
         */
        public FullTimeEmployee (String s)
        {
                StringTokenizer tokens = new StringTokenizer (s);
```

```
            name = tokens.nextToken( );
            grossPay = Double.parseDouble (tokens.nextToken( ));
     } // constructor with String parameter

     /**
      * Determines if this FullTimeEmployee object's gross pay is greater than
      * a specified Employee object's gross pay.
      *
      * @param otherEmployee – the specified Employee object whose
      *        gross pay this FullTimeEmployee object's gross pay is compared to.
      *
      * @return true – if otherEmployee is a FullTimeEmployee object, and
      *        the calling object's gross pay is greater than
      *        otherEmployee's gross pay. Otherwise, return false.
      *
      */
     public boolean makesMoreThan (Employee otherEmployee)
     {
            if (!(otherEmpoyee instanceof FullTimeEmployee))
                   return false;
            FullTimeEmployee full = (FullTimeEmployee)otherEmployee;
            return grossPay > full.grossPay;
     } // method makesMoreThan

     /**
      * Returns a String representation of this FullTimeEmployee object with the name
      * followed by a space followed by a dollar sign followed by the gross
      * weekly pay, with two fractional digits.
      *
      * @return a String representation of this FullTimeEmployee object.
      *
      */
     public String toString( )
     {
            final String DOLLAR_SIGN = " $";

            DecimalFormat d = new DecimalFormat ("0.00");

            return name + DOLLAR_SIGN + d.format (grossPay);
     } // method toString
} // class Employee
```

One noteworthy aspect of the definition of the makesMoreThan method is the appearance of grossPay all by itself on the left-hand side of operator >. Which object's grossPay field is being compared to the grossPay field of full's object? The grossPay field of the object that invoked the makesMoreThan method is being compared to the grossPay field of full's object. For example, suppose we have already created FullTimeEmployee objects referenced by employee and bestPaid. If we write

> employee.makesMoreThan (bestPaid)

then the comparison is between the employee object's grossPay and the bestPaid object's grossPay. The same rule applies if a method appears without a calling object. For example, here is the definition of the hasMoreTokens( ) method in String Tokenizer class:

```
public boolean hasMoreTokens( )
{
        newPosition = skipDelimiters(currentPosition);
        return (newPosition < maxPosition);
}
```

There is no calling-object reference specified for the invocation of the skipDelimiters method, and so the object assumed to be invoking skipDelimiters is the object that called hasMoreTokens( ). Similarly, newPosition, currentPosition, and maxPosition are fields in the calling object that called hasMoreTokens( ). Here is the general rule, where a *member* is either a field or a method:

> If an object has called a method and a member appears without an object reference in the method definition, you may assume that the member is part of the calling object.

Another interesting feature in the definition of makesMoreThan method is related to the problem that the Employee interface does not have a grossPay field (or any other field, for that matter). So the Java compiler would object to a statement such as the following:

> **return** grossPay > otherEmployee.grossPay; // compile-time error

According to the method specification, if otherEmployee is not a FullTimeEmployee object, **false** is returned. Java allows such a determination with the **instanceof** operator. The syntax is:

> object-reference **instanceof** class

**true** is returned if the object is an instance of the given class; otherwise, **false** is returned. So the appropriate test in the makesMoreThan method is

> **if**(!(otherEmployee **instanceof** FullTimeEmployee))
>         **return false**;

Even if **false** has not been returned at this point, the compiler will still not allow the expression otherEmployee.grossPay. But we can overcome this last hurdle with a *cast*: the temporary conversion of an expression's type to another type. The syntax for a cast is:

> (the new type)expression

Specifically, we will cast the type of otherEmployee to FullTimeEmployee:

> FullTimeEmpoyee full = (FullTimeEmployee)otherEmployee;

To put it anthropomorphically, we are saying to the compiler, "Look, I know that the type of otherEmployee is reference-to-Employee. But I promise that at run-time, the object referenced will, in fact, be a FullTimeEmployee object." The cast is enough to satisfy the compiler, and at run-time, the argument's type will be reference-to-FullTimeEmployee—unless **false** was returned after the **instanceof** test—so everything works out, and the calling object's gross pay is compared to full's gross pay.

### 1.3.3 Using the FullTimeEmployee Class

Suppose we want to determine the best-paid full-time employee in a company. We will create a Company class that uses the FullTimeEmployee class. The responsibilities of the Company class are to initialize a Company, to find the best-paid employee, and to print out that best-paid employee. We refine these responsibilities into method specifications for a constructor, findBestPaid and printBestPaid methods. Here is the complete Company class, including method definitions, and preceded by an **import** directive (the "**throws** IOException" clause after the heading of the findBestPaid method is discussed in Section 2.2):

```java
import java.io.*;

public class Company
{
        private FullTimeEmployee bestPaid;

        private boolean atLeastOneEmployee;

        /**
         * Initializes this Company object.
         *
         */
        public Company( )
        {
                bestPaid = new FullTimeEmployee( );
                atLeastOneEmployee = false;
        } // default constructor

        /**
         * Determines the best-paid full-time employee in this Company object.
         *
         */
        public void findBestPaid ( ) throws IOException // see Section 2.2
        {
                final String SENTINEL = "****";
                final String INPUT_PROMPT = "\nPlease enter a name (with no blanks) " +
                        "and gross pay, followed by the Enter key. The sentinel is"
                        + SENTINEL + " ";

                FullTimeEmployee employee;
```

```
                    String line;

                    BufferedReader reader = new BufferedReader
                            (new InputStreamReader (System.in));
                    while (true)
                    {
                            System.out.print (INPUT_PROMPT);
                            line = reader.readLine( );
                            if (line.equals (SENTINEL))
                                    break;
                            employee = new FullTimeEmployee (reader.readLine( ));
                            atLeastOneEmployee = true;
                            if (employee.makesMoreThan (bestPaid))
                                    bestPaid = employee;
                    }//while
            } // method findBestPaid

            /**
             * Prints out the best-paid full-time employee in the input, or an error
             * message if the only line of input is the sentinel.
             *
             */
            public void printBestPaid( )
            {
                    final String BEST_PAID_MESSAGE =
                            "\n\n\nThe best paid employee (and gross pay) is ";

                    final String NO_INPUT_MESSAGE =
                            "\n\n\nERROR: there were no employees in the input.";

                    if (atLeastOneEmployee)
                            System.out.println (BEST_PAID_MESSAGE + bestPaid);
                    else
                            System.out.println (NO_INPUT_MESSAGE);
            } // method printBestPaid

    } // class Company
```

We are not quite finished, because we still need a class that uses the Company class. Fortunately, we can accomplish this with a CompanyMain class whose only method is the main method that invokes the three Company methods. Here is the CompanyMain class (the "**throws** IOException" clause after the main method's heading is discussed in Section 2.2):

```
    import java.io.*;

    public class CompanyMain
    {
            /**
             * Finds and prints out the best-paid full-time employee in the input.
```

```
         *
         */
    public static void main (String[ ] args) throws IOException // see Section 2.2
    {
        Company company = new Company( );

        company.findBestPaid( );
        company.printBestPaid( );
    } // method main

} // class CompanyMain
```

All of the above code is available from the book's website.

As noted earlier, we should use existing classes whenever possible. What if a class has most, but not all, of what is needed for an application? We could simply scrap the existing class and develop our own, but that would be time-consuming and inefficient. Another option is to copy the needed parts of the existing class and incorporate those parts into a new class that we develop. The danger with that option is that those parts may be incorrect or inefficient. If the developer of the original class replaces the incorrect or inefficient code, our class would still be erroneous or inefficient. A better alternative is to use inheritance, explained in Section 1.4.

## 1.4 | INHERITANCE

We should write program components that are reusable. For example, instead of defining a method that calculates the average gross pay of 10 employees, we would achieve wider applicability by defining a method that calculates the average gross pay of any number of employees. By writing reusable code, we not only save time, but we also avoid the risk of incorrectly modifying the existing code.

One way that reusability can be applied to classes is through a special and powerful property of classes: inheritance. *Inheritance* is the ability to define a new class that includes all of the fields and some or all of the methods of an existing class. The previously existing class is called the *superclass*. The new class, which may declare new fields and methods, is called the *subclass*. A subclass may also *override* existing methods by giving them method definitions that differ from those in the superclass.[3] The subclass is said to *extend* the superclass.

As an example of how inheritance works, let's start with the class FullTime Employee defined in Section 1.3.2. Suppose that several applications use Full TimeEmployee. A new application involves finding the best-paid, full-time hourly employee who had no overtime, that is, did not work more than 40 hours in the past week. For this application, the input consists of the employee's name, hours worked (an int value) and pay rate (a double value). The gross pay is the hours worked times the pay rate.

---

[3]Don't confuse method overriding with method overloading (discussed in Section 1.1.1): having two methods in the same class with the same method identifier but different parameter lists.

We could alter FullTimeEmployee by adding hoursWorked and payRate fields and modifying the methods. But it is risky to modify, for the sake of a new application, a class that is being used successfully in existing applications. The underlying concept is known as the **Open-Closed Principle**: Every class should be open (extendible through inheritance) and closed (stable for existing applications).

Instead of rewriting FullTimeEmployee, we will create HourlyEmployee, a subclass of FullTimeEmployee. To indicate that a class is a subclass of another class, the subclass identifier is immediately followed by the reserved word **extends**. For example, we can declare the HourlyEmployee class to be a subclass of FullTimeEmployee as follows:

```
public class HourlyEmployee extends FullTimeEmployee
{
       ...
```

Each HourlyEmployee object will have the information from FullTimeEmployee— name and gross pay—as well as hours worked and pay rate.

The company we are working with now has hourly employees instead of employees who simply receive a flat gross pay. We still want to find the best-paid employee, but only of those hourly employees who worked at most 40 hours. So we will override the FullTimeEmployee class's makesMoreThan method. The toString method from the FullTimeEmployee class is inherited as is by HourlyEmployee. Constructors are never inherited, so the HourlyEmployee class will need its own constructors. For example, here is definition of the constructor-with-String-parameter:

```
/**
 * Initializes this HourlyEmployee object's name and gross pay from a
 * specified String object, which consists of a name, hours worked and
 * pay rate, with at least one blank between each of those three components.
 *
 * @param s – the String object from which this HourlyEmployee object
 *       is initialized.
 *
 */
public HourlyEmployee (String s)
{
        StringTokenizer tokens = new StringTokenizer (s);
        name = tokens.nextToken( );
        hoursWorked = Integer.parseInt (tokens.nextToken( ));
        payRate = Double.parseDouble (tokens.nextToken( ));

        grossPay = hoursWorked * payRate;
} // constructor with parameter
```

## 1.4.1  The protected Visibility Modifier

Notice that in the definition of the constructor-with-String-parameter for Hourly Employee, the name and grossPay fields from the FullTimeEmployee class are treated as if they had been declared as fields in the HourlyEmployee class. In order for this phenomenon to work, the visibility modifier for those fields in FullTime Employee are changed from **private** to **protected**:

```
protected String name;
protected double grossPay;
```

These declarations enable any subclass of FullTimeEmployee to access the name and grossPay fields as if they were declared within the subclass itself. This makes sense because an HourlyEmployee object *is a* FullTimeEmployee object as well. So the HourlyEmployee class actually has four fields: two inherited and two explicitly declared in HourlyEmployee.

The subclass HourlyEmployee can access all of the fields, from FullTime Employee, that have the **protected** modifier. Later on, if a subclass of Hourly Employee is created, we would want that subclass's methods to be able to inherit the HourlyEmployee fields—as well as the FullTimeEmployee fields. So the declarations of the HourlyEmployee fields hoursWorked and payRate should also have the **protected** modifier:

```
protected int hoursWorked;

protected double payRate;
```

The HourlyEmployee class's makesMoreThan method must override the Full TimeEmployee class's makesMoreThan method, which makes no mention of hours worked. The override can be accomplished easily enough: we copy the code from the makesMoreThan method in FullTimeEmployee, and add the test for overtime hours in the **return** statement:

```
if(!(otherEmployee instanceof FullTimeEmployee))
        return false;
FullTimeEmployee full = (FullTimeEmployeee)otherEmployee;
return hoursWorked <= 40 && grossPay > full.grossPay;
```

But, as noted at the end of Section 1.3.3, copying code is dangerous. Instead, the def-inition of makesMoreThan in the HourlyEmployee class will call the makesMoreThan method in the FullTimeEmployee class provided the hours worked is at most 40. To call a superclass method, use the reserved word **super** as the calling object:

```
return hoursWorked <= 40 && super.makesMoreThan (otherEmployee);
```

Here is the complete HourlyEmployee class:

```
import java.util.*;

public class HourlyEmployee extends FullTimeEmployee implements Employee
{
        protected int hoursWorked;

        protected double payRate;
```

```
/**
 *  Initializes this HourlyEmployee object to have an empty string for
 *  the name, 0 for hours worked, 0.00 for the pay rate and 0.00 for
 *  grossPay.
 *
 */
public HourlyEmployee( )
{
        hoursWorked = 0;
        payRate = 0.00;
} // default constructor

/**
 *  Initializes this HourlyEmployee object's name and gross pay from a
 *  a specified String object, which consists of a name, hours worked and
 *  pay rate, with at least one blank between each of those three
 *  components.
 *
 *  @param s – the String object from which this HourlyEmployee object
 *       is initialized.
 *
 */
public HourlyEmployee (String s)
{
        StringTokenizer tokens = new StringTokenizer (s);
        name = tokens.nextToken( );
        hoursWorked = Integer.parseInt (tokens.nextToken( ));
        payRate = Double.parseDouble (tokens.nextToken( ));

        grossPay = hoursWorked * payRate;
} // constructor with string parameter

/**
 *  Determines if this HourlyEmployee object's gross pay is greater than
 *  a specified Employee object's gross pay.
 *
 *  @param otherEmployee – the specified Employee object whose
 *       gross pay this Hourly Employee object's gross pay is compared to.
 *
 *  @return true – if this HourlyEmployee object did not work any overtime,
 *       otherEmployee is a FullTimeEmployee object, and this
 *       HourlyEmployee object's gross pay is greater than
 *       otherEmployee's gross pay. Otherwise, return false.
 *
 */
public boolean makesMoreThan (Employee otherEmployee)
{
        final int MAX_NORMAL_HOURS = 40;
```

```
            return hoursWorked <= MAX_NORMAL_HOURS
                && super.makesMoreThan (otherEmployee);
        }//method makesMoreThan
    } // class HourlyEmployee
```

Section 1.4.2 continues our discussion of inheritance by examining the interplay between inheritance and constructors.

## 1.4.2  Inheritance and Constructors

Constructors provide initialization for instances of a given class. For that reason, constructors are never inherited. But whenever a subclass constructor is called, the execution of the subclass constructor starts with an automatic call to the superclass's default constructor. This ensures that at least the default initialization of fields from the superclass will occur. For example, the FullTimeEmployee class's default constructor is automatically invoked at the beginning of any call to an HourlyEmployee constructor, and that is how the name and grossPay fields of any HourlyEmployee object are properly initialized.

What if the superclass has a constructor but no default constructor? Then the first statement in any subclass constructor must explicitly call the superclass constructor. A call to a superclass constructor consists of the reserved word **super** followed by the argument list, in parentheses. For example, suppose some class B's only constructor has an **int** parameter. If C is a subclass of B and C has a constructor with a String parameter, that constructor must start out by invoking B's constructor. For example, we might have

```
    public C (String s)
    {
            super (Integer.parseInt (s)); // explicitly calls B's int-parameter constructor

            ...
    } // class C
```

So if a superclass explicitly defines a default (that is, zero-parameter) constructor, there are no restrictions on its subclasses. Similarly, if the superclass does not define any constructors, the compiler will automatically provide a default constructor, and there are no restrictions on the subclasses. But if a superclass defines at least one constructor and does not define a default constructor, the first statement in any subclass's constructor must explicitly invoke a superclass constructor.

## 1.4.3  The Subclass Substitution Rule

Just as the Company class used Employee, the problem of finding the best-paid, non-overtime hourly employee requires that we create HourlyCompany, which uses the HourlyEmployee class. HourlyCompany, a subclass of the Company class described in Section 1.3.3, differs only slightly from the Company class. Specifically, the find BestPaid method is overridden because the object defined in HourlyCompany is

```
    hourly = new HourlyEmployee (line);
```

instead of

```
employee = new FullTimeEmpoyee (line);
```

Here is the HourlyCompany.java file:

```java
import java.io.*;

public class HourlyCompany extends Company
{
    /**
     * Initializes this HourlyCompany object.
     *
     */
    public HourlyCompany ( )
    {
    }

    /**
     * Determines the best-paid hourly employee in this HourlyCompany object.
     *
     */
    public void findBestPaid ( ) throws IOException // see Section 2.2
    {
        final String SENTINEL = "***";

        final String INPUT_PROMPT = "n\nPlease enter a name, with no " +
                "blanks, hours worked and pay rate. The sentinel is "
                + SENTINEL + " ";

        HourlyEmployee hourly;

        String line;

        BufferedReader reader = new BufferedReader
                (new InputStreamReader (System.in));

        while (true)
        {
            System.out.print (INPUT_PROMPT);
            line = reader.readLine( );
            if (line.equals (SENTINEL))
                    break;
            hourly = new HourlyEmployee (line);
            if (hourly.makesMoreThan (bestPaid)) {
                    atLeastOneEmployee = true;
                    bestPaid = hourly;} // if
        }//while
    }//findBestPaid

}//class HourlyCompany
```

Note that the visibility modifier for the bestPaid and atLeastOneEmployee fields in the Company class must be changed from **private** to **protected** so those fields can be accessed in HourlyCompany.

The findBestPaid method has a curious assignment:

```
bestPaid = hourly;
```

It seems that the types do not agree: the type of bestPaid is reference-to-FullTime Employee, but the type of hourly is reference-to-HourlyEmployee. Such an assignment is legal because an HourlyEmployee *is a* FullTimeEmployee. This is an application of the Subclass Substitution Rule:

> **Subclass Substitution Rule** Whenever a reference-to-superclass-object is called for in an evaluated expression, a reference-to-subclass-object may be substituted.

The Object class, declared in the file java.lang.Object.java, is the superclass of all classes. The Object class is a bare-bones class, whose methods are normally overridden by its subclasses. For example, here is the specification for the Object class's equals method:

```
/**
 * Determines if this Object object is the same as a specified Object object.
 *
 * @param obj – the Object object to be compared to the calling Object object.
 *
 * @return true – if the two objects are the same.
 *
 */
public boolean equals (Object obj)
```

The definition of this method compares *references,* not objects, for equality! So true will be returned if and only if the calling object reference contains the same address as the reference obj. For example, consider the following program fragment:

```
Object obj1 = new Object( ),
       obj2 = new Object( ),
       obj3 = obj1;

System.out.println (obj1.equals (obj2) + " " + obj1.equals (obj3));
```

The output will be

```
false true
```

For that reason, this method is usually overridden by the Object class's subclasses. We saw an example of this with the String class's equals method in Section 1.1.3. In that equals method, the parameter's type is Object, and so, by the Subclass Substitution Rule, the argument's type can be String, a subclass of Object.

For another illustration of the Subclass Substitution Rule, suppose that class Y is a subclass of class X. The following is legal:

```
X x = new X( );

Y y = new Y( );

x = y;
```

In this last assignment statement, a reference-to-X is called for in the evaluation of the expression on the right-hand side, so a reference-to-Y may be substituted: a Y **is-an** X.

But the reverse assignment is illegal:

```
X x = new X( );

Y y = new Y( );

y = x; // illegal
```

On the right-hand side of this last assignment statement, the compiler expects a reference-to-Y, so a reference-to-X is unacceptable: an X is not a Y. Note that the left-hand side of an assignment statement must consist of a variable, which is an expression. But that left-hand-side variable is not evaluated in the execution of the assignment statement, so the Subclass Substitution Rule does not apply to the left-hand side.

Now suppose we had the following:

```
X x = new X( );

Y y = new Y( );

x = y;
y = x;
```

After the assignment of y to x, x contains a reference to a Y object. But the assignment:

```
y = x;
```

still generates a compile-time error because the declared type of x is still reference-to-X. We can avoid a compile-time error in this situation with a cast (see Section 1.3.2). For example, we can cast x's type to Y as follows:

```
X x = new X( );

Y y = new Y( );

x = y;
y = (Y)x;
```

This last assignment passes muster with the compiler because the right-hand side now has type reference-to-Y. And there is no problem at run-time either because—from the previous assignment of y to x—the value on the right-hand side really is a reference-to-Y. But the following, acceptable to the compiler, throws a ClassCast Exception at run-time:

```
X x = new X( );

Y y = new Y( );

y = (Y)x;
```

The run-time problem is that x is actually pointing to an X object, not to a Y object.

The complete project, HourlyCompanyMain, is available from the book's website. Lab 1's experiment illustrates another subclass of FullTimeEmployee.

**Lab 1: The SalariedEmployee Class**

You are now prepared to do Lab 1.                    All Labs Are Optional

### 1.4.4 Is-a versus Has-a

You will often encounter the following situation. You are developing a class B, and you realize that the methods of some other class, A, will be helpful. One possibility is for B to inherit all of A; that is, B will be a subclass of A. Then all of A's nonprivate methods are available to B. An alternative is to define, in class B, a field whose class is A. Then the methods of A can be invoked by that field. It is important to grasp the distinction between these two ways to access the class A.

Inheritance describes an **is-a** relationship. An object in the subclass Hourly Employee is also an object in the superclass FullTimeEmployee, so we can say that an HourlyEmployee is-a FullTimeEmployee.

On the other hand, the fields in a class constitute a **has-a** relationship to the class. For example, the name field in the FullTimeEmployee class is of type (reference to) String, so we can say a FullTimeEmployee has-a String. Also, the bestPaid field in the Company class is of type (reference to) FullTimeEmployee, so we can say a Company has-an Employee.

Typically, if class B shares the overall functionality of class A, then inheritance of A by B is preferable. But if there is only one aspect of B that will benefit from A's methods, the better alternative will be to define an A object as a field in class B. That object can invoke the relevant methods from class A. Often, the choice is not clear-cut, so experience is your best guide. We will encounter this problem several times in subsequent chapters.

With an object-oriented approach, the emphasis is not so much on developing the program as a whole but on developing modular program-parts, namely, classes. These classes not only make the program easier to understand and to maintain, but they are reusable for other programs as well. A further advantage to this approach is that decisions about a class can easily be modified. We first decide what classes will be needed. And because each class interacts with other classes through its method specifications, we can change the class's fields and method definitions as desired as long as the method specifications remain intact.

The next section of this chapter considers the extent to which a language can allow developers of a class to force users of that class to obey the Principle of Data Abstraction.

## 1.5 | INFORMATION HIDING

The Principle of Data Abstraction states that a user's code should not access the implementation details of the class used. By following that principle, the user's code is protected from changes to those implementation details, such as a change in fields.

Protection is further enhanced if a user's code is *prohibited* from accessing the implementation details of the class used. **Information hiding** means making the implementation details of a class inaccessible to code that uses that class. The burden of obeying the Principle of Data Abstraction falls on users, whereas information hiding is a language feature that allows class developers to prevent users from violating the Principle of Data Abstraction.

As you saw in Section 1.4.1, Java supports information hiding through the use of the **protected** visibility modifier for fields. Through visibility modifiers such as **private** and **protected,** Java forces users to access class members only to the extent permitted by the developers. The term *encapsulation* refers to the grouping of fields and methods into a single entity—the class—whose implementation details are hidden from users.

There are three essential features of object-oriented languages: the *encapsulation* of fields and methods into a single entity with information-hiding capabilities, the *inheritance* of a class's fields and methods by subclasses, and *polymorphism,* discussed in Section 1.6.

## 1.6 | POLYMORPHISM

One of the major aids to code reuse in object-oriented languages is polymorphism. *Polymorphism*—from the Greek words for "many" and "shapes"—is the ability of a reference to refer to different objects. For a simple example of this surprisingly useful concept, suppose D is a subclass of A and that D overrides A's scan method. If reader is a reference to an already constructed BufferedReader object, we can write the following:

```
A a;          // a is of type reference-to-A

if (reader.readLine( ).equals ("Go with A"))
        a = new A( );        // a is a reference to an object of type A
else
        a = new D( );        // a is a reference to an object of type D, the subclass
a.scan ( );
```

Because the declared type of a is reference-to-A, it is legal to write

```
a = new A( );
```

So, by the Subclass Substitution Rule, it is also legal to write

```
a = new D( ):
```

Now consider the meaning of the message

```
a.scan( )
```

The version of the scan( ) method executed depends on the type of the object that a is referencing. If the input line consists of "Go with A", then a is assigned a reference to an instance of class A, so the A class's version of scan( ) is invoked. On the other hand, if the input string consists of anything other than "Go with A", then a is assigned a reference to an instance of class D, so the D class's version of scan( ) is invoked.

In this example, a is a polymorphic reference: the object referred to can be an instance of class A or an instance of class D, and this illustrates an important aspect of polymorphism:

> When a message is sent, the version of the method invoked depends on the *type of the object*, not on the type of the reference.

What is important here is that polymorphism allows code reuse for methods related by inheritance. We need not explicitly call the two versions of the scan( ) method.

The above code raises a question: how can the Java compiler generate the appropriate bytecode for a message such as a.scan( )? Another way to phrase the same question is this: how can the method identifier scan be *bound* to the correct version—in A or D—at compile time, when the necessary information is not available until run-time? The answer is simple: the binding cannot be done at compile-time, but must be delayed until run time! A method that is bound to its method identifier at run time is called a *virtual method.*

In Java, almost all methods are virtual. The only exceptions are for **static** methods (discussed in Section 2.1) and for **final** methods (the **final** modifier signifies that the method cannot be overridden in subclasses.) This delayed binding—also called *dynamic binding* or *late binding*—of method identifiers to methods is one of the reasons that Java programs execute more slowly than programs in most other languages.

Polymorphism is a key feature of the Java language, and makes the Java Collections Framework possible. We will have more to say about this in Chapter 4, when we take a tour of the Java Collections Framework.

Method specifications are method-level documentation tools. Section 1.7 deals with class-level documentation tools.

## 1.7 | THE UNIFIED MODELING LANGUAGE

For each project, we will illustrate the classes and relationships between classes with the *Unified Modeling Language* (UML). UML is an industry-standardized language, mostly graphical, that incorporates current software-engineering practices that deal with the modeling of systems. The key visual tool in UML is the class diagram. For each class, the class diagram consists of a rectangle that contains information about the class. The information includes the name of the class, its attributes and operations. For the sake of simplicity, we will regard the UML term *attribute* as a synonym for "field." Similarly, the UML term *operation* will be treated as a UML synonym for "method." For example, Figure 1.3 shows the class diagram for the FullTimeEmployee class from Section 1.3.2. For both attributes and operation parameters, the type follows the variable (instead of preceding the variable, as in Java).

In a class diagram, a method's parenthesized parameter-list is followed by the return type, provided the method actually does return a value. Visibility information is abbreviated:

**Figure 1.3** | A UML class-diagram for the FullTimeEmployee class

| FullTimeEmployee |
|---|
| # name: String<br># grossPay: **int** |
| + FullTimeEmployee( )<br>+ FullTimeEmployee(s: String)<br>+ makesMoreThan (otherEmployee: Employee): **boolean**<br>+ toString( ): String |

     +, for public visibility
     −, for private visibility
     #, for protected visibility

Inheritance is illustrated by a solid arrow, with a hollow head, from the subclass to the superclass. For example, Figure 1.4 shows the relationship between the HourlyEmployee and FullTimeEmployee classes in Section 1.4.

A dashed arrow illustrates the relationship between a class and the interface that class implements. For example, Figure 1.5 augments the class diagrams from Figure 1.4 by adding the diagram for the Employee interface.

**Figure 1.4** | In UML, the notation for inheritance is an arrow from the subclass to the superclass.

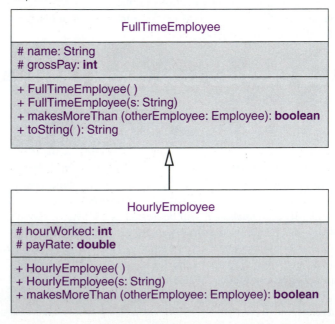

A noninheritance relationship between classes is called an ***association,*** and is represented by a solid line between the class diagrams. For example, Figure 1.6 shows an association between the Company and FullTimeEmployee classes in the find-best-paid-employee project in Section 1.3.3. In Figure 1.6, the symbol "*" at the bottom of the association line indicates a company can have an arbitrary number of employees. The number 1 at the top of the association line indicates that an employee works for just one company.

Sometimes, we want to explicitly note that the class association is a has-a relationship, that is, an instance of one class is a field in the other class. In UML, a has-a relationship is termed an ***aggregation,*** and is signified by a solid line between the classes, with a hollow diamond at the containing-class end. For example, Figure 1.7 shows that the Company class has a FullTimeEmployee field. To avoid clutter, the figure simply has the class name in each class diagram.

**Figure 1.5 I** A UML illustration of the relationship between an interface and an implementing class.

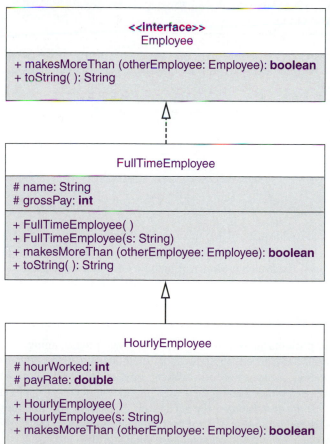

**Figure 1.6** I The UML representation of an association between two classes.

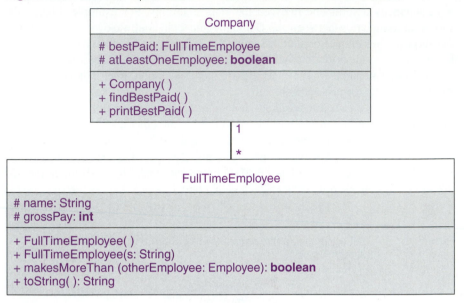

**Figure 1.7** I Aggregation in UML: the Company class has a FullTimeEmployee field.

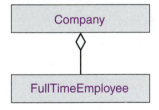

Graphical tools such as UML play an important role in outlining a project. We will be developing projects, starting in Chapter 5, as applications of data structures and algorithms. Each such project will include UML class diagrams.

## SUMMARY

This chapter presents an overview of object-oriented programming. Method *specifications*—what a user needs to know about methods—include comments written in javadoc notation, a consistent form that can be read from a browser. Our focus, on the use of classes rather than on their implementation details, is an example of data abstraction. *Data abstraction*—the separation of method specifications from field and method definitions—is a way for users of a class to protect their code from being affected by changes in the implementation details of the class used.

The three essential features of an object-oriented language are:

1.　*Encapsulation* of fields and methods into a single entity—the class—whose implementation details are hidden from users

2.　*Inheritance* of a class's fields and methods by subclasses

3.　*Polymorphism*: the ability of a reference to refer to different objects.

The Unified Modeling Language (UML) is an industry-standard graphical language that illustrates the modeling of projects.

# CONCEPT EXERCISES

**1.1**　Suppose Y and Z are subclasses of X, and we have:

```
X x = new X( );
Y y = new Y( );
Z z = new Z( );

x = z;
```

Which one of the following assignments would be legal both at compile-time and at run-time?

a.　z = (Z)x;

b.　z = x;

c.　z = (X)x;

d.　y = (Y)x;

Create a small project to validate your claim.

**1.2**　Assume that the classes below are all in the file PolyMain.java. Determine the output when the project is run.

```
public class PolyMain
{
        public static void main (String args [ ]) throws IOException
        {
                BufferedReader reader = new BufferedReader
                        (new InputStreamReader (System.in));
                A a;

                int code = Integer.parseInt (reader.readLine( ));

                if (code == 0)
                        a = new A ( );
                else            // non-zero int entered
                        a = new D ( );
                System.out.println (a); //same as System.out.println(a.toString( ));
        } // method main

} // class PolyMain

class A
```

```
        {
              public String toString ( )
              {
                    return "A";
              } // method toString

        } // class A

        class D extends A
        {
              public String toString ( )
              {
                    return "D";
              } // method toString
        } // class D
```

**1.3**   In the FullTimeEmployee class, modify the toString method so that the gross
pay is printed with a comma to the left of the hundreds digit. For example, if
the name is "O'Brien,Theresa" and the gross pay is 74400.00, the toString
method will return

O'Brien,Theresa $74,400.00

**1.4**   What can you infer about the identifier out from the following message?

System.out.println ("Eureka!");

What is the complete declaration for the identifier out? Look in
java.lang.System.java.

## PROGRAMMING EXERCISES

**1.1**   Here is a simple class—but with method specifications instead of method
definitions—to find the highest age in the input and to print out that age:

```
public class Age
{
        protected int highestAge;

        /**
         * Initializes this Age object.
         *
         */
        public Age ( )

        /**
         * Determines the highest age in the input.
         *                              *
         */
        public void findHighestAge ( ) throws IOException // see Section 2.2
```

```
        /**
         * Prints the highest age in the input.
         *
         */
        public void printHighestAge ( )
} // class Age
```

    **a.** Fill in the method definitions for the Age class.

    **b.** Test your Age class by developing a project and running the project.

**1.2** With the Age class in Programming Exercise 1.1a as a guide, develop a Salary class to read in salaries from the input until the sentinel ($-1.00$) is reached, and to print out the average of those salaries. The average salary is the total of the salaries divided by the number of salaries.

**1.3** This exercise presents an alternative to having **protected** fields. Modify the FullTimeEmployee class as follows: Change the visibility of the name and grossPay fields from **protected** to **private**, and develop **public** methods to get and set the values of those fields. A method that alters a field in an object is called a *mutator,* and a method that returns a copy of a field is called an *accessor.*

    Here are the method specifications corresponding to the name field:

```
/**
 * Returns this FullTimeEmployee object's name.
 *
 * @return the name of this FullTimeEmployee object.
 *
 */
public String getName ( )

/**
 * Sets this FullTimeEmployee object's name to a specified string.
 *
 * @param nameIn–the String object whose value is assigned to this
 *        FullTimeEmployee object's name.
 *
 */
public void setName (String nameIn)
```

## Programming Project 1.1

### Developing and Testing a CalendarDate Class

In this project, you will develop and test a CalendarDate class. Here are the responsibilities of the class, that is, the services that the class will provide to users:

1. To initialize a CalendarDate object to represent the date January 1, 2006.

2. To initialize a CalendarDate object from integers for the month, day-of-month, and year; if the date is invalid (for example, if the month, day-of-month, and year are 6, 31, and 2006, respectively), use 1, 1, 2006.

3. Return, in String form, the next date after this CalendarDate object; for example, if this CalendarDate object represents January 31, 2006, the return value would be "February 1, 2006".

4. Return, in String form, the date prior to this CalendarDate object; for example, if this CalendarDate object represents January 1, 2007, the return value would be "December 31, 2006";

5. Return, in String form, the day of the week on which this CalendarDate object falls; for example, if this CalendarDate object represents the date December 20, 2006, the return value would be "Wednesday."

### Part 1

Create method specifications for the above responsibilities.

### Part 2

Develop the CalendarDate class; that is, determine what fields to declare and then define the methods.

### Part 3

Create a project to test your CalendarDate class. Call each CalendarDate method at least twice.

# 2

# Additional Features of Java

In Chapter 1, the primary goal was to introduce object-oriented concepts, such as interfaces, inheritance, and polymorphism, in the context of the Java programming language. This chapter introduces more Java topics, and illustrates how they can aid your programming efforts. For example, Java's exception-handling mechanism provides programmers with significant control over what happens when errors occur. ■

## CHAPTER OBJECTIVES

1. Distinguish between static members and instance members.

2. Be able to create **try** blocks and **catch** blocks to handle exceptions.

3. Compare file input/output with console input/output.

4. Be able to develop a driver to test the methods in a class.

5. Understand the fundamentals of the Java Virtual Machine.

6. Be able to override the Object class's equals method.

7. Understand the interplay between packages and visibility modifiers.

# 2.1 | STATIC VARIABLES, CONSTANTS, AND METHODS

Recall, from Section 1.3.2, that a class member is either a field or method in the class.[1] Let's look at some of the different kinds of members in Java. There are two kinds of fields. An *instance variable* is a field associated with an object—that is, with an instance of a class. For example, in the FullTimeEmployee class from Chapter 1, name and grossPay are instance variables. Each FullTimeEmployee object will have its own pair of instance variables. Suppose we declare

```
FullTimeEmployee oldEmployee,
                 currentEmployee,
                 newEmployee;
```

Then the object referenced by oldEmployee will have its own copy of the instance variables name and grossPay, and the objects referenced by currentEmployee and newEmployee will have their own copies also.

In addition to instance variables, which are associated with a particular object in a class, we can declare *static variables,* which are associated with the class itself. The space for a static variable—also known as a *class variable*—is shared by all instances of the class. A field is designated as a static variable by the reserved modifier **static**. For example, if a count field is to maintain information about all objects in a class Student, we could declare the field count to be a static variable in the Student class:

**private static int** count = 0;

This static variable would be incremented, for example, whenever a Student constructor is invoked. Then the variable count will contain the total number of Student instances created.

To access a static member *inside* its class, the member identifier alone is sufficient. For example, the above static field count could be accessed in a method in the Student class as follows:

count++;

In order to access a static member *outside* of its class, the class identifier itself is used as the qualifier. For example, outside of the class Student, we could write:

**if** (Student.count == 0)

A class may also have constant identifiers, also called "symbolic constants" or "named constants." A *constant identifier* is an identifier that represents a constant, which is a variable that can be assigned to only once. The declaration of a constant identifier includes the reserved word **final**—indicating only one assignment is allowed—as well as the type and value of the constant. For example, we can write

**private final static int** SPEED_LIMIT = 65.0;

---

[1]In Section 2.6, we will see that a class may also have another class as a member.

Constant identifiers promote both readability (SPEED_LIMIT conveys more information than 65.0) and maintainability (because SPEED_LIMIT is declared in only one place, it is easy to change its value throughout the class). There should be just one copy of the constant identifier for the entire class, rather than one copy for each instance of the class. So a constant identifier should be declared as **static**. At the developer's discretion, constant identifiers may have **public** visibility. Here are the declarations for two constant, class identifiers:

```
public final static String NAME_SENTINEL = "****";

public final static double GROSS_PAY_SENTINEL = −1.00;
```

Here is the declaration for an often-used constant in the System class:

```
public final static PrintStream out = nullPrintStream( );
```

Because out is declared as static, its calls to the PrintStream class's println method include the identifier System rather than an instance of the System class. For example,

```
System.out.println ("Elections for the Young Anarchists Club are next week.");
```

The **static** modifier is used for any constant identifier that is defined outside of a class's methods. The **static** modifier is *not* available within a method. For example, in the definition of the toString( ) method in the FullTimeEmployee class, we had:

```
final String DOLLAR_SIGN = " $";
```

It would have been illegal to use the **static** modifier for this constant.

Java also allows static methods. For example, the Double class has a parseDouble method that takes a String argument and returns a **double**. We can write

```
double gpa = Double.parseDouble ("3.86");
```

When parseDouble is called, there is no calling object because the effect of the method depends only on the String argument. To signify this situation, the class identifier is used in place of a calling object when parseDouble is called. A method that is called without a calling object is known as a **static** method, as seen in the following heading

```
public static double parseDouble (String s)
```

The execution of every Java application (excluding applets, servlets, and so on) starts with a static main method. And static methods are not virtual; that is, static methods are bound to method identifiers at compile time, rather than at run time. The reason is that static methods are associated with a class itself rather than an object, so the issue of which object is invoking the method does not arise.

## 2.2 | EXCEPTION HANDLING

An *exception* is an object created by an unusual condition, typically, an attempt at invalid processing. When an exception object is constructed, the normal flow of control is halted; the exception is said to be ***thrown.*** Control is immediately trans-ferred to code—either in the current method or in some other method—that "han-dles" the exception. The exception handling usually depends on the particular excep-tion, and may involve printing an error message, terminating the program, taking other action, or maybe doing nothing!

A ***robust*** program is one that does not terminate unexpectedly from invalid user-input. We almost always prefer programs that—instead of "crashing"—allow recovery from an error such as the input of 7.o instead of 7.0 for a **double**. Java's exception-handling feature allows the programmer to avoid almost all abnormal terminations.

For a simple introduction to exception handling, let's start with a **static** method printHalf—in a class Numbers—that takes a String parameter consisting of an integer, and prints out one-half of that integer. Here is the method specification and definition:

```
/**
 * Prints one half of the value of the int in a specified String object.
 *
 * @param s – the String object that consists of an int.
 *
 * @throws NumberFormatException – if s is not a reference to a String
 *      object that represents an int value.
 *
 */
public static void printHalf (String s)
{
        System.out.println (Integer.parseInt (s) / 2);
} // method printHalf
```

The problem with this method, as currently defined, is that the execution of the pro-gram will terminate if the precondition is not satisfied, specifically, if the argument corresponding to the parameter s is not a reference to a String object that represents an **int** value.

To allow execution to continue even if NumberFormatException is thrown, we "try" to execute the call to println, and "catch" the given exception. The revised spec-ification and definition are

```
/**
 * Prints one half of the value of the int in a specified String object.
 *
 * @param s – the String object that consists of an int.
 *
 *
 */
public static void printHalf (String s)
{
        try
```

```
    {
         System.out.println ("Half of " + s + " is " + Integer.parseInt (s) / 2);
    } // try
    catch (NumberFormatException e)
    {
         System.out.println (e + " is not an int");
    } // catch

    System.out.println ("\n...continuing with the rest of the program");
} // method printHalf
```

In the execution of this method, the flow of control is as follows. The println method inside the **try** block is executed. If the execution of that statement throws a Number FormatException object, the **try** block is exited, and the statement inside the **catch** block is executed, and then execution continues with the first statement after the **catch** block. If the execution of the println method inside the **try** block does not throw a NumberFormatException object, the next statement executed is the one after the **catch** block.

In the **catch** block, the parameter e is a reference to the NumberFormatException object created during execution (of the println method inside the **try** block) if the argument to printHalf is not a reference to a String object that represents an integer.

Figure 2.1 shows several calls to the revised version of the printHalf method, and the output from those calls. The fact that "...continuing" is printed in each case indicates that the program does not terminate abnormally—as the original version of printHalf would—even if NumberFormatException is thrown.

In the specification for the revised printHalf method, we omit the @throws comment because the exception is caught within the printHalf method itself.

Immediately after a **try** block there must be at least one **catch** block. What if you had several possible exceptions in a block of code? No problem! You simply include several **catch** blocks. For example, here is a printSum method specification and definition. Note that there are no @throws specifications because the exceptions are handled within the method itself.

**Figure 2.1** I Several calls to the **printHalf** method, and output from those calls.

| Method Call | Output |
| --- | --- |
| Numbers.printHalf ("50") | Half of 50 is 25<br>...continuing with the rest of the program |
| Numbers.printHalf ("55") | Half of 55 is 27<br>...continuing with the rest of the program |
| Numbers.printHalf ("55.0") | java.lang.NumberFormatException: 55.0 is not an int<br>...continuing with the rest of the program |
| Numbers.printHalf (**null**) | java.lang.NumberFormatException: null is not an int<br>...continuing with the rest of the program |

```java
/**
 * Prints the sum of the two int values in a specified String object.
 *
 * @param s – the String object that consists of two int values.
 *
 */
public static void printSum (String s)
{
      try
      {
              StringTokenizer st = new StringTokenizer (s);
              int first = Integer.parseInt (st.nextToken ( ));
              int second = Integer.parseInt (st.nextToken ( ));
              System.out.println ("The sum of " + first + " and " +
                      second + " is " + (first + second));
      } // try
      catch (NullPointerException e1)
      {
              System.out.println (e1 + " because s is null");
      } // catch
      catch (NumberFormatException e)
      {
              System.out.println (e + " is not an integer");
      } // catch
      catch (NoSuchElementException e3)
      {
              System.out.println (e3 + " because there must be two ints");
      } // catch
      System.out.println ("...continuing with the rest of the program");
} // method printSum
```

NullPointerException will be thrown by the StringTokenizer constructor if the argument to that constructor is **null**. That exception is caught in the printSum method. We will see shortly, in Section 2.2.1, how this is accomplished.

An exception can be explicitly thrown by the programmer, who gets to decide which exception class will be instantiated and under what circumstances the exception will be thrown. For example, suppose we want a method to return the smaller of two **double** values that represent prices obtained by comparison shopping. If the prices are too far apart—say, if the difference is greater than the smaller price—we throw an exception instead of returning the smaller price. The mechanism for explicitly throwing the exception is the **throw** statement, which can be placed anywhere a statement is allowed. For example, the code may be as in the following smaller method (the Math class's **static** method abs returns the absolute value of its argument):

```java
public static void main (String[ ] args)
{
```

```
        System.out.println (smaller (2.00, 7.15));
} // method main

public static double smaller (double price1, double price2)
{
        if (Math.abs (price1 − price2) > Math.min (price1, price2))
                throw new ArithmeticException ("difference too large");
        return Math.min (price1, price2);
} // method smaller
```

If the given condition is true, the **throw** statement is executed, which creates a new instance of the exception class ArithmeticException and initializes that instance by calling the constructor that takes a String argument. The program will terminate with the message:

```
java.lang.ArithmeticException: difference too large
```

The choice of ArithmeticException as the exception class to be instantiated was somewhat arbitrary.

A user can even create new exception classes. For example,

```
public class ProcrastiManiaException extends RuntimeException
{
        public ProcrastiManiaException( )
        {
                System.out.println ("Start projects early!");
        } // default constructor
} // class ProcrastiManiaException
```

To throw this exception, we write:

```
throw new ProcrastiManiaException( );
```

This creates a new instance of the class ProcrastiManiaException. If there is no **catch** block to handle this exception, the program would terminate with the output:

```
Start projects early!
ProcrastiManiaException
```

The ProcrastiManiaException class is a subclass of RuntimeException. The RuntimeException class handles[2] some of the low-level details of exception-handling, such as keeping track of the method the exception occurred in, the method that called that method, and so on. Such a "call stack" sequence can help a programmer to determine the root cause of an error. The entire exception hierarchy is discussed in Section 2.2.1.

---

[2]Actually, RuntimeException consists of several constructors, each of which merely invokes the corresponding constructor in Exception, the superclass of RuntimeException. The Exception class passes the buck to its superclass, Throwable, where the low-level tasks are performed.

## 2.2.1 Propagating Exceptions

What happens if an exception, such as ArithmeticException, is thrown in a method that does not catch that exception? Then control is transferred back to the calling method: the method that called the method that threw the exception. This transferring of control is known as **propagating the exception.** For example, we can have the following:

```java
public void printAverage ( )
{
        try
        {
                System.out.println (getAverage( ));
        } // try
        catch (ArithmeticException e)
        {
                System.out.println (e);
        } // catch
} // method printAverage

public int getAverage ( )
{
        int sum = 35;

        int n = 0;

        return sum / n;
} // method getAverage
```

The exception is thrown in the method getAverage( ), but is caught in the method printAverage( ). The output will be:

```
java.lang.ArithmeticException: / by zero
```

If the calling method does not handle the exception, then the exception is propagated back to the method that called the calling method itself. Ultimately, if the exception has not been caught even in the main method, the program will terminate abnormally and a message describing the exception will be printed. The advantage to propagating an exception is that the exception can be handled at a higher level in the program. Decisions to change how exceptions are handled can be made in one place, rather than scattered throughout the program. Also, the higher level might have facilities not available at lower levels, such as a GUI window for output.

Exceptions related to input or output, such as when a file is not found or the end-of-file marker is encountered while input is being read, are the most common examples of checked exceptions. With a **checked exception,** the compiler checks that either the exception is caught within the method itself or—to allow propagation of the exception—that a **throws** clause is appended to the method heading. For an example of the latter, we might have

```java
public void sample( ) throws IOException
{
```

This indicates that the sample method might throw an IOException object. If so, the exception will be propagated back to the method that called sample. That calling method *must* either catch IOException or append the same **throws** clause to its method heading. And so on.

For example, here is a simple program that illustrates how checked exceptions can be handled:

```java
import java.io.*;
public class ExceptionMain
{
      public static void main (String [ ] args)
      {
             ExceptionHandling.try1( );
      } // method main
} // class ExceptionMain

class ExceptionHandling
{
      public static void try1( )
      {
             System.out.println ("start of try1");
             try
             {
                   try2( );
             } // try
             catch (IOException e)
             {
                   System.out.println (e + "something went wrong with IO");
             } // catch
             System.out.println ("end of try1");
      } // method try1

      public static void try2( ) throws IOException
      {
             System.out.println ("start of try2");
             try3( );
             System.out.println ("end of try2");
      } // method try2

      public static void try3( ) throws IOException
      {
             System.out.println ("start of try3");
              throw new IOException ("IO error in method try3: ");
      } // method try3
} // class ExceptionHandling
```

The IOException is explicitly thrown in try3 but not caught there. So the **throws** clause after try3's heading ensures that the exception is propagated back to try3's calling method: try2. Then try2 propagates the exception back to try1, which catches the exception. So the main method need not have either a **throws** clause or **try** and **catch** blocks.

The output of this program will be:

```
start of try1
start of try2
start of try3
java.io.IOException: IO error in method try3: something went wrong with IO
end of try1
```

At the end of the try2 method, there is a call to println. But that call is not executed because it comes after the call to try3, and the exception thrown in try3 is propagated back from try2 to try1.

A checked exception must be caught or must be specified in a **throws** clause, and the compiler "checks" to make sure this has been done. Which exceptions are checked, and which are unchecked? The answer is simple: run-time exceptions are not checked and all other exceptions are checked. But which are which? Figure 2.2 shows Java's exception hierarchy, including IOException with its subclasses (such as FileNotFoundException), and RuntimeException with its subclasses (such as Null PointerException).

Why are run-time exceptions not checked? The motivation behind this is that an exception such as NullPointerException or NumberFormatException can occur in almost any method. So appending a **throws** clause to the heading of such a method would burden the developer of the method without providing any helpful information to the reader of that method.

When an exception is thrown, the parameter classes of the subsequent **catch** blocks are examined, in order, until (unless) one is found for which the thrown exception is an instance of the class. So if you want to ensure that all run-time exceptions are caught in a method, you can insert the following as the last **catch** block:

```
catch (RuntimeException e)
{
      // code to handle the exception
} // catch RuntimeException
```

If you do have a **catch** block for RuntimeException, make sure that **catch** block is not followed by a **catch** block for a subclass of RuntimeException. For example, because NullPointerException is a subclass of RuntimeException, the following sequence of **catch** blocks will generate a compile-time error:

```
catch (RuntimeException e)
{
      // code to handle the exception
} // catch RuntimeException
catch (NullPointerException e)    //error!
{
      // code to handle the exception
} // catch NullPointerException
```

**Figure 2.2 I** The exception hierarchy. In the Unified Modeling Language, inheritance is represented with an arrow from a subclass to its superclass.

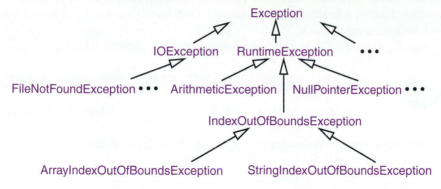

The error message will inform you that the second **catch** block is unreachable code.

## 2.2.2 The finally Block

Under normal circumstances, any code you place after the last **catch** block will be executed whether or not any exceptions were thrown in the **try** block. So you can place cleanup code—such as closing files—after the last **catch** block and be confident that the code will be executed no matter what happens. There are two drawbacks to this approach. First, there may be an exception thrown in the **try** block that is not caught in a **catch** block. Another danger is that one of the **catch** blocks may itself throw an exception that is not caught. Then the cleanup code will not be executed. To avoid these pitfalls, Java allows a **finally** block after the last **catch** block. We can write

```
try
{
        ... // code that may throw an exception
} // try
catch (NumberFormatException e)
{
        ... // code to handle NumberFormatException
} // catch NumberFormatException
catch (IOException e)
{
        ... // code to handle IOException
} // catch IOException
finally
{
        ... // clean-up code; will be executed even if there are uncaught
            // exceptions thrown in the try block or catch blocks.
} // finally
```

If your **try** or **catch** blocks may throw uncaught exceptions, you should include a **finally** block—otherwise, any code placed after the last **catch** block may not be executed. Finally, a **finally** block is required by the Java language if you have a **try** block without a **catch** block.

Lab 2 provides the opportunity for you to practice exception-handling.

 **Lab 2:** **Exception Handling**

You are now prepared to do Lab 2.                          All Labs Are Optional

The handling of input-output exceptions is one of the essential features of file processing, discussed in Section 2.3.

## 2.3 | FILE OUTPUT AND INPUT

We begin our study of file output and input with an introduction to file output, because a file must be created before it can be read.

### 2.3.1 File Output

File output is only slightly different from console output. We first associate a Print Writer reference with a file name. For example, to associate fileWriter with "scores.out":

```
PrintWriter fileWriter = new PrintWriter (new BufferedWriter
                          (new FileWriter ("scores.out")));
```

The PrintWriter object that is referenced by fileWriter can now invoke the print and println methods. For example,

```
fileWriter.println (line);
```

The output is not immediately stored in the file "scores.out". Instead, the output is stored in a *buffer:* a temporary storage area in memory. After all calls to print and println have been made by fileWriter's object, that object's close method must be called:

```
fileWriter.close( );
```

The close method flushes the buffer to the file "scores.out".

Here is a revised version of a main method from Section A1.5 of Appendix 1. The program calculates the sum of scores read in from the keyboard. In the new version, the output goes to a file. To enable someone reading that file to confirm that the result is correct for the given input, each score is written to the output file. IOException is caught for keyboard input and output-file creation. The corresponding **try** block encompasses the input loop. For the sake of simplicity, there is no **try** block to catch number-format exceptions (arising from input values that are not integers).

```
import java.io.*;

public class Scores2
```

```java
{
    public static void main (String [ ] args)
    {
        final String SENTINEL = "****";

        final String HEADING = "Here are the test scores:";

        final String PROMPT =
            "Please enter a test score, or " + SENTINEL + " to quit: ";

        final String RESULT = "\n\nThe sum of the scores is ";

        final String DONE = "The execution of this project has ended.";

        PrintWriter fileWriter = null;

        try
        {
            BufferedReader keyboardReader = new BufferedReader
                (new InputStreamReader(System.in));

            fileWriter = new PrintWriter (new
                BufferedWriter (new fileWriter("scores.out")));

            String line;

            int sum = 0;

            fileWriter.print(HEADING);
            while (true)
            {
                System.out.print(PROMPT);
                line = keyboardReader.readLine( );
                if (line.equals(SENTINEL))
                    break;
                fileWriter.print("\n" + line);
                sum += Integer.parseInt(line);
            } // while
            fileWriter.println (RESULT + sum);
        } // try for IOException
        catch (IOException e)
        {
            System.out.println (e);
        } // catch IOException
        finally
        {
            fileWriter.close( );
            System.out.println (DONE);
        } // finally
    } // method main
} // class Scores2
```

The simplification of ignoring number-format exceptions leads to an unfortunate consequence: If a number-format exception is thrown, the program will terminate without printing the final sum. The output file will be closed before the final sum is printed, and the NumberFormatException message—signifying abnormal termination—will be printed. We could add a **catch** block for NumberFormatException right after (or right before) the **catch** block for IOException. This change would not be much of an improvement: The program would still terminate without printing the final sum, but the termination will be normal!

To enable the program to continue after a number-format exception, we create a new **try** block and a corresponding **catch** block inside the **while** loop. Here is the revised **while** statement:

```java
while (true)
{
        System.out.print(PROMPT);
        line = keyboardReader.readLine( );
        if (line.equals(SENTINEL))
                break;
        fileWriter.print("\n" + line);
        try
        {
                sum += Integer.parseInt(line);
        } // try for NumberFormatException
        catch (NumberFormatException e)
        {
                fileWriter.print (" " + e);
        } // catch NumberFormatException
} // while
```

Here is a sample run of the resulting program, with input in boldface:

```
Please enter a test score, or *** to quit: 50
Please enter a test score, or *** to quit: x
Please enter a test score, or *** to quit: 80
Please enter a test score, or *** to quit: y
Please enter a test score, or *** to quit: ***
The execution of this project has ended.
```

The file scores.out will now contain the following:

```
Here are the test scores:
50
x java.lang.NumberFormatException: For input string: "x"
80
y java.lang.NumberFormatException: For input string: "y"
The sum of the scores is 130
```

The most important fact to remember about file output is that the file writer must be explicitly closed, or else the file will be incomplete, and probably empty (depending on whether there was an intermediate flushing of the buffer). As we will illustrate in Section 2.3.2, we can ensure that a file writer is closed when (if) a program terminates by encompassing the main method statements in a **try** block, which is followed by a **finally** block that closes the file writer.

## 2.3.2  File Input

Just as file output was similar to console output, file input is quite similar to console input. Instead of constructing a keyboard reader, we construct a file reader. For example, to read from the file "scores.in1", we start with

```
BufferedReader fileReader = new BufferedReader
                   (new FileReader ("scores.in1"));
```

*Warning:* This assumes that the file scores.in1 is in the expected directory. For some Integrated Development Environments, the input file is assumed to be in the directory that is one level up from the source-file directory. Sometimes, you may need to specify a full path, such as

```
BufferedReader fileReader = new BufferedReader
                   (new FileReader ("c:\\projects\\score_project\\scores.in1"));
```

Two backslashes are required because a single backslash would be interpreted as the escape character.

If the input file ends with a sentinel, then we simply replace the keyboard reader's call to the readLine method with the file reader's call to the readLine method, and the read-and-process loop is otherwise unchanged from before. But input files seldom end with a sentinel because it is too easy to forget to add the sentinel at the end of the file. Instead, reading continues until the end-of-file marker is reached during a call to the readLine method, and then the readLine method returns **null**. So for file input, we replace

```
if (line.equals (SENTINEL))
        break;
```

with

```
if (line == null)
        break;
```

For the sake of simplicity, if there is only one input file, we will not worry about closing that file at the end of the program: it will automatically be closed. And when it is reopened in a subsequent program, its contents will be unchanged. A program that leaves many input files unclosed can run out of file descriptors, and IOException will be thrown.

As noted in Section 2.3.1, closing an output file entails copying the final contents of the file buffer to the file, so we should explicitly close each output file before the end of a program. Of course, if the program does not terminate—because of an infinite loop, for example—the file buffer will not be copied (unless the file was closed before the infinite loop).

The following program combines file input and file output. Also, for the sake of generality, the program does not "hardwire" the file names (for example, "scores.in" and "scores.out"). In response to prompts, the end-user enters, from the keyboard, the names of the input and output files. If there is no input file with the given name, the IOException—file not found—is caught, an error message is printed and the end-user is re-prompted to enter the name of the input file. To allow this iteration, the **try** and **catch** blocks that involve throwing and handling IOException are placed in an outer **while** loop.

What if there is no file corresponding to the output file name? Normally, this is not a problem: an empty output file with that name will be created. But if a file name is too bizarre for your system, such as

    !@#$%^&*( )

an IOException object (specifically, a FileNotFoundException object) will be thrown.
The following program has three **try** blocks:

1.  An outermost **try** block followed by a **finally** block to close the file writer
2.  A **try** block/**catch** block sequence in an outer **while** loop to create the file reader and file writer from file names read in from the keyboard
3.  A **try** block/**catch** sequence block in an inner **while** loop to read each line from the input file and process that line, with output going to the file writer

Here is the program, whose general structure is the same for all file-processing programs (except that each **try** block would be in a separate method for the sake of modularity):

```
import java.io.*;

public class Scores3
{
        public static void main (String [ ] args)
        {
                final String IN_FILE_PROMPT =
                        "\nPlease enter the name of the input file: ";

                final String OUT_FILE_PROMPT =
                        "\nPlease enter the name of the output file: ";

                final String HEADING = "Here are the test scores:";

                final String RESULT = "\n\nThe sum of the scores is ";

                final String DONE = "\n\nThe execution of this project has ended.";

                BufferedReader keyboardReader,
                                fileReader;

                PrintWriter fileWriter = null;

                try
```

```
{
     boolean filesOK = false;
     while (!filesOK)
     {
          try
          {
               keyboardReader = new BufferedReader
                    (new InputStreamReader (System.in));

               System.out.print (IN_FILE_PROMPT);
               fileReader = new BufferedReader
                    (new FileReader (keyboardReader.readLine( )));

               System.out.print (OUT_FILE_PROMPT);
               fileWriter = new PrintWriter (new BufferedWriter
                    (new FileWriter (keyboardReader.readLine( ))));

               String line;

               int sum = 0;

               fileWriter.print (HEADING);
               while (true)
               {
                    line = fileReader.readLine ( );
                    if (line == null)
                         break;
                    fileWriter.print ("\n" + line);
                    try
                    {
                         sum += Integer.parseInt (line);
                    } // try
                    catch (NumberFormatException e)
                    {
                         fileWriter.print (" " + e);
                    } // catch NumberFormatException
               } // while more scores in input file
               fileWriter.println (RESULT + sum);
               filesOK = true;
               System.out.println (DONE);
          } // try
          catch (IOException e)
          {
               System.out.println (e);
          } // catch
     } // while files not OK
} // try
finally
```

```
              {
                      fileWriter.close( );
              } // finally
          } // method main
      } // class Scores3
```

Note that the message fileWriter.close( ) is not in a **catch** block because the relevant **try/catch** block is in a loop and fileWriter should not be closed until the termination of that loop.

Assume that the file "scores.in" consists of the following three lines:

```
82
77
99
```

Also, assume that there is no file named "scores.in1" or "scores3.in" in the working directory. Whether there is already a file named "scores.out" or not is irrelevant. Here is a sample keyboard session, with input in boldface:

Please enter the name of the input file: **scores.in1**
java.io.FileNotFoundException: scores.in1 (The system cannot find the file specified)

Please enter the name of the input file: **scores3.in**
java.io.FileNotFoundException: scores3.in (The system cannot find the file specified)

Please enter the name of the input file: **scores.in**

Please enter the name of the output file: **scores.out**

The execution of this project has ended.

The final contents of the file "scores.out" will be

Here are the test scores:
82
77
99

The sum of the scores is 258

With file input, it is not sufficient that the file exist in order to associate a file reader with that file. Your code must also account for the possibility that the file does not exist. The easy way to accomplish this is to include a **throws** IOException clause immediately after the heading of the method that associates a file reader with the file. The drawback to this approach is that if the file name is incorrect—either the file does not exist or the file name is misspelled—then the end-user will not have the opportunity to correct the mistake.

A better alternative, as we did in the program just shown, is to include a **try** block and **catch** block for FileNotFoundException or its superclass, IOException. To enable end-users to recover from incorrect file names, those blocks should be within a loop that continues until a correct file name has been entered.

For problems that entail the input or output of large quantities of data, files are essential. But, as we will see in Section 2.4, files are also useful for programs that are repeatedly executed.

## 2.4 | METHOD TESTING

A method is ***correct*** if it satisfies its method specification. After a developer has completed the definitions of all the methods in a class, the class is ready for testing. The purpose of testing is to discover errors, which are then removed. When—eventually— no errors are discovered during testing, that does not imply that the methods are correct, because there may be other tests that would reveal errors. In general, it is rarely feasible to run all possible tests, and so we cannot infer correctness on the basis of testing alone. As E. W. Dijkstra has wisely noted, *testing can reveal the presence of errors but not the absence of errors.*

The most popular technique for increasing confidence in the correctness of a method is to test the method with a number of sample values for the fields and parameters (and inputs, if the method includes any input statements). We then compare the actual results with the results expected according to the method's postcondition.

For example, suppose we want to test a next( ) method—in a CalendarDate class— that returns the date immediately following the calling object's date. Special care should be given to make sure that the method works properly for *boundary values* such as the last day of a month and the last month of the year. Here are some test data:

| Sample Value of Calling Object | | | Expected Value of Returned Object | | |
|---|---|---|---|---|---|
| day | month | year | day | month | year |
| 17 | 11 | 2006 | 18 | 11 | 2006 |
| 30 | 11 | 2006 | 1 | 12 | 2006 |
| 31 | 12 | 2006 | 1 | 1 | 2007 |
| 28 | 2 | 2000 | 29 | 2 | 2000 |
| 28 | 2 | 2006 | 1 | 3 | 2006 |
| 28 | 2 | 2008 | 29 | 2 | 2008 |
| 28 | 2 | 2100 | 1 | 3 | 2100 |

The last four lines reflect the fact that the earth travels around the sun in approximately 365.2425 days. A ***leap year*** is a year that is both evenly divisible by 4 and either not evenly divisible by 100 or evenly divisible by 400.

If the next( ) method passes these tests, our confidence in that method's correctness will increase. But we cannot yet be certain of the method's correctness because we have not tried all possible tests.

Another problem with testing is the objectivity of the person who constructs the test data. Programmers tend to view their work favorably, even glowingly ("a masterpiece," "a thing of beauty and a joy forever," "the eighth wonder of the world").

Therefore, programmers are ill suited to test their own methods because the purpose of testing is to uncover errors. Ideally the person who constructs test data should hope that the method will fail the test. In a classroom setting, the instructor may appear to satisfy this criterion!

If a class has a single method, we can set up a test regimen that deals with that method in isolation. More often, a class will have several methods. Each method should first be tested in isolation, and then the methods should be tested together. For example, we may need to test method m1( ) followed by method m2( ), and also to test method m2( ) followed by method m1( ). A *driver* is a program created specifically to test a class's methods in concert. A production-strength driver that permits many methods to be tested extensively is more complex than testing a single method.

The input from a driver will almost always come from a file, because otherwise, the test data would have to be reentered for each run of the driver. The output will always go to a file so that you (or others) will be able to look at the output later, or if your console-output window is not scrollable.

For example, suppose you want to create a driver, FullTimeEmployeeDriver, for the FullTimeEmployee class. Essentially, the driver consists of an input loop that continues until the end-of-file is reached. During each loop iteration, one line is read from the file, just as in the inner **while** loop of the file-processing program in Section 2.3.1. The code to replace that **while** loop is

```
while (true)
{
        line = fileReader.readLine ( );
        if (line == null)
                break;
        fileWriter.println (line);
        testMethod (line);
} // while more lines in input file
```

Each line will consist of the information needed to call one method from the FullTimeEmployee class. For example, here is a line for the constructor with a String parameter:

```
e1 FullTimeEmployee Jager 3500.00
```

This line corresponds to the assignment:

```
e1 = new FullTimeEmployee ("Jager 3500.00");
```

The testMethod method will tokenize the line. The first token represents the calling object, and the second token represents the method identifier: FullTimeEmployee, makesMoreThan or toString. If that token is FullTimeEmployee, there will be either two more tokens (for the constructor with a String parameter) or no more tokens (for the default constructor). Once the line has been parsed, a method call will be made, and the result of making the call will be printed.

For simplicity, the FullTimeEmployeeDriver class will have only two fields, e1 and e2, both of type FullTimeEmployee. In the testMethod method, the first token is

saved so that, for a constructor call, the appropriate field will be initialized. Here is
the definition of the testMethod method:

```
public void testMethod (String line)
{
        FullTimeEmployee callingObject,
                          argument;
        StringTokenizer st = new StringTokenizer (line);
        String temp = st.nextToken( );
        if (temp.equals ("e1"))
                callingObject = e1;
        else
                callingObject = e2;

        String method = st.nextToken( );
        if (method.equals ("FullTimeEmployee"))
        {
                if (st.countTokens( ) == 0)
                        callingObject = new FullTimeEmployee( );
                else
                        callingObject = new FullTimeEmployee (
                                        st.nextToken( ) + " " + st.nextToken( ));
                if (temp.equals ("e1"))
                        e1 = callingObject;
                else
                        e2 = callingObject;
        } // constructor
        else if (method.equals ("toString"))
                fileWriter.println (callingObject.toString( ));
        else if (method.equals ("makesMoreThan"))
        {
                if (st.nextToken( ).equals ("e1"))
                        argument = e1;
                else
                        argument = e2;
                        fileWriter.println (callingObject.makesMoreThan (argument));
        } // testing makesMoreThan
} // method testMethod
```

Here is a sample input file from one run of the driver program:

```
e1 FullTimeEmployee a 1000.00
e2 FullTimeEmployee b 2000.00
e1 makesMoreThan e2
e1 makesMoreThan e1
e2 makesMoreThan e1
```

```
e1 toString
e2 FullTimeEmployee *** -1.00
```

And here are the contents of the resulting output file:

```
e1 FullTimeEmployee a 1000.00
e2 FullTimeEmployee b 2000.00
e1 makesMoreThan e2
false
e1 makesMoreThan e1
false
e2 makesMoreThan e1
true
e1 toString
a $1000.00
e2 FullTimeEmployee *** −1.00
```

All of the relevant files are available in the Chapter 2 directory of the book's website.

A well-designed driver and a large input file can greatly increase your confidence in the correctness of your classes. The general format for driver programs is as follows—we assume that MyDriver (in a different class than the class with the main method) is the driver class and ClassToBeTested is the class whose correctness is being tested:

```java
public static void main (String[ ] args)
{
        PrintWriter fileWriter = null;

        try
        {
                MyDriver driver = new MyDriver( );

                fileWriter = driver.openFiles( );
                driver.testAllMethods( );
        } // try
        finally
        {
                fileWriter.close( );
        } // finally
} // method main

import java.io.*;

public class MyDriver
{
        // declare fields, define constructors, ...

        public PrintWriter openFiles( )
        {
                boolean filesOK = false;
```

```
            while (!filesOK)
            {
                    try
                    {
                            // try to read in file paths from the keyboard
                            // and open a file reader and a file writer
                    } // try
                    catch (IOException e)
                    {
                            System.out.println (e);
                    } // catch
            } // while files not OK
            return fileWriter;
    } // method openFiles

    public void testAllMethods( )
    {
            while (true)
            {
                    try
                    {
                            line = fileReader.readLine( );
                            if (line == null)
                                    break;
                            // based on line, call a ClassToBeTested method
                    } // try
                    // catch IOException, and exceptions thrown by methods
                    // in ClassToBeTested
            } // while
    } // method testAllMethods
} // class MyDriver
```

In this text, the term "driver" is used only when the output goes to a file and the methods of the class to be tested need not be executed in a fixed order. The (weaker) term "tester" is used if either the output is not sent to a file or if the methods must be tested in a fixed order.

In Lab 3, you will have the opportunity to develop a driver for the Hourly Employee class from Chapter 1, and store the output to a file. This will give you practice on testing with drivers.

 **Lab 3: The HourlyEmployeeDriver Class**

You are now prepared to do Lab 3.               All Labs Are Optional

Just as it is unusual for a class to have a single method, it is unlikely that a project will have a single class. For a multiclass project, which class should be tested first? In an object-oriented environment, bottom-up testing is the norm. With *bottom-up testing,* a project's low-level classes—those that are used by but do not use other classes—are tested and then integrated with higher-level classes and so on. After each of the component classes has satisfied its tests, we can perform *system testing,* that is, testing the project as a whole. Inputs for the first few system tests are created before the program is developed. If the project passes those tests we conduct additional tests until we are convinced the project is correct, that is, that it satisfies the specifications provided initially.

The purpose of testing is to detect errors in a program (or to increase confidence that no errors exist in the program). When testing reveals that there is an error in your program, you must then determine what brought about the error. This may entail some serious detective work. And the purpose of detection is correction. The entire process—testing, detection, and correction—is iterative. Once an error has been corrected, the testing should start over, because the "correction" may have created new errors.

## 2.5 | THE JAVA VIRTUAL MACHINE

Your Java classes are compiled into a low-level but machine-independent language called Java *bytecode.* For example, the bytecode version of the file Hourly Employee.java is stored in the file HourlyEmployee.class. The bytecode files are then interpreted and executed on your computer. The program that interprets and executes bytecode is the Java Virtual Machine. It is called a virtual machine because it executes what is almost machine-level code. There are several advantages to this arrangement

source code→bytecode→Java Virtual Machine

Instead of

source code→machine code

The main advantage is platform independence. It doesn't matter whether your computer's operating system is Windows, Linux, or something else, the results of running your Java program will be exactly (well, almost exactly) the same on all platforms. A second benefit is customized security. For example, if the bytecode file is coming from the web, the virtual machine will not allow the application to read from or write to the local disk. But such activities would be allowed for a local application. The Java Virtual Machine oversees all aspects of your program's run-time environment. In Sections 2.5.1 and 2.5.2, we investigate two tasks of the Java Virtual Machine.

### 2.5.1  Preinitialization of Fields

One of the Java Virtual Machine's duties is the initialization of fields just prior to the invocation of a constructor. For example, we might have the following:

**new** FullTimeEmployee ("Dilbert 345.00")

First, the **new** operator allocates space for a FullTimeEmployee object. Then, to ensure that each field has at least a minimal level of initialization, the Java Virtual Machine initializes all of the class's fields according to their types. Reference fields are initialized to **null**, integer fields to 0, floating-point fields to 0.0, **char** fields to the character at position 0 in the Unicode collating sequence, and **boolean** fields to **false**. Finally, the specified constructor is called.

There is an important consequence of this preinitialization by the Java Virtual Machine. Even if a default constructor has an empty body—such as the one supplied by the Java compiler if your class does not declare any constructors—all fields in the class will still get initialized.

Unlike fields, local variables are *not* automatically initialized. Section A1.6 has the details.

### 2.5.2 Garbage Collection

The memory for objects is allocated when the **new** operator is invoked, but what about deallocation? Specifically, what happens to the space allocated for an object that is no longer accessible? For example, suppose an object is constructed in a method, and at the end of the execution of that method, there are no references pointing to the object. The object is then inaccessible: *garbage,* so to speak. If your program generates too much garbage, it will run out of memory, which is an error condition. Errors, unlike exceptions, should not be caught, so an error will force the abnormal termination of your program. Are you responsible for garbage collection, that is, for deallocating inaccessible objects?

Fortunately, you need not worry about garbage collection. The Java run-time system includes a method that performs *automatic garbage collection.* This method will be invoked if the **new** operator is invoked but there is not enough memory available for the object specified. With the supersizing of memory in recent years, this is an increasingly rare occurrence. To free up unused memory, the space for any object to which there are no references can be deallocated. But if space is needed, the garbage collector will seek out big chunks of garbage first, such as an array. In any event, this is all taken care of behind the scenes, so your overall approach to the topic of garbage collection should be "Don't worry. Be happy."

Section 2.6 investigates the relationship between packages and visibility modifiers.

## 2.6 | PACKAGES

A *package* is a collection of related classes. For each such class, the file in which the class is declared starts with the package declaration. For example, a file in a package of classes related to neural networks might start with

    **package** neuralNetwork;

For another example, the StringTokenizer class, part of the package java.util, starts with

```
package java.util;
```

If a file includes an instance of the StringTokenizer class, that class can be "imported" into the file. This is done with an import directive, starting with the reserved word **import**:

```
import java.util.StringTokenizer;
```

The advantage of importing is convenience: A declaration such as

```
StringTokenizer st;
```

can be used instead of the fully qualified name:

```
java.util.StringTokenizer st;
```

Many of the classes you create will utilize at least one class from the package java.util, so you can simply import the whole package:

```
import java.util.*;
```

Occasionally, you may prefer to use the fully qualified name. For example, suppose your project uses two classes named Widget: one in the package com.acme and one in the package com.doodads. To declare (a reference to) an instance of the former, you would write

```
com.doodads.Widget myWidget;
```

Every Java file must have a class with the visibility modifier **public**. Also, the name of that public class must be the same as the name of the file—without the .java extension. At the beginning of the file, there are **import** directives for any package (or file) needed by the file but not part of the file. An exception is made for the package java.lang, which is automatically imported for any file.

A class member with no visibility modifier is said to have *default visibility.* A member with default visibility can be accessed by any object (or class, in the case of a static member) in the same package as the class in which the member is declared. That is why default visibility is sometimes referred to as "package-friendly visibility." All classes without a package declaration are part of an unnamed package. But there may be more than one unnamed package so, as a general rule, if your project contains more than one class file, you may want each file to include a package declaration.

Technically, it is possible for a Java file to have more than one class with public visibility; all but one of those classes must be *nested,* that is, declared within another class. The Java Collections Framework, part of the package java.util, has many nested classes. Except for nested classes, a Java file is allowed to have *only one* class with public visibility. Every other nonnested class must have default visibility.

Because of the way the Java language was developed, protected visibility is not restricted to subclasses. In general, if an identifier in a class has protected visibility, that identifier can be accessed in any class that is in the same package as the given class. For example, any class—whether or not a subclass—that is in the same package as FullTimeEmployee can access the name and grossPay fields of a FullTime Employee object.

In the Java Collections Framework, most of the fields have default visibility or **private** visibility; almost no fields have **protected** visibility. Subclassing across package boundaries is discouraged in the Java Collections Framework. Why? The main reason is philosophical: a belief that the efficiency to users of the subclass is not worth the risk to the integrity of the subclass if the superclass is subsequently modified. This danger is not merely hypothetical. In Java 1.1, there was a class in java.security that subclassed the Hashtable class. In Java 2, the Hashtable class was modified, and this opened a security hole in the subclass. The bottom line is that subclassing represents more of a commitment than mere use. So even if a class permits subclassing, it is not necessarily the wisest choice.

The bottom line is that protected visibility is even less restrictive than default visibility. This corruption of the meaning of protected visibility may make you reluctant to designate your fields as **protected**. An alternative is to designate the fields as **private**, but to create **public** methods to get and set the values of those **private** fields. As described in Programming Exercise 1.3, an *accessor* method returns a copy of a field, and a *mutator* method alters a field. The usefulness of this approach diminishes as the number of fields increases.

The final topic in this chapter looks at the importance of overriding the Object class's equals method, the barriers to overriding that method, and how those barriers are overcome.

## 2.7 | OVERRIDING THE Object CLASS'S equals METHOD

In Section 1.4.3, we saw the method specification for the equals method in the Object class, the superclass of all classes. Here is that specification:

```
/**
 * Determines if this Object object contains the same as a specified Object
 * object.
 *
 * @param obj – the Object object to be compared to the calling Object object.
 *
 * @return true – if the two objects are the same.
 *
 */
public boolean equals (Object obj)
```

This method, as with the other methods in the Object class, is intended to be overridden by subclasses, which can compare field values, for example. The object class has no fields, so what does it compare? It compares references, specifically, the calling object reference with the argument reference. Here is the definition:

```
public boolean equals (Object obj)
{
        return this == obj;
} // method equals
```

In any class, the reserved word **this** is a reference to the calling object. For example, suppose the call is

```
obj1.equals (obj2)
```

Then in the definition of the equals method, **this** is a reference to the object that is also referenced by obj1, and obj is a reference to the object that is also referenced by obj2.

Because the Object class's equals method compares references, any class with an equals method should define its own version of that method. For example, suppose we decide to add an equals method to the FullTimeEmployee class. The first question is, given

```
public boolean equals (FullTimeEmployee emp)
```

and

```
public boolean equals (Object obj)
```

should we overload (that is, define the former) or override (that is, define the latter for calling objects of type FullTimeEmployee)? Overloading equals—that is, having a different parameter list than the version inherited from the Object class—can be done fairly simply. Here is the definition:

```
public boolean equals (FullTimeEmployee emp)
{
        return name.equals (emp.name) && grossPay == emp.grossPay;
} // overloading method equals
```

This version compares objects, not references, and so the value true would be printed by the following:

```
System.out.println (new FullTimeEmployee ("a 100.00").equals
                (new FullTimeEmployee ("a 100.00")));
```

The overloaded version works well as long as the type of the calling object is known, at compile-time, to be FullTimeEmployee. Sadly, that is seldom the case. For example, many of the classes in the Java Collections Framework store a collection of objects. Those classes have a contains method to determine if a given object occurs in the collection. The contains method's heading is

```
public boolean contains (Object obj)
```

Typically, in testing for containment, the equals method is invoked, with obj as the calling object. For a given application, the collection may consist of FullTime Employee objects. But when the equals method—called by contains—is compiled, the only information available about the calling object is its type: Object. Therefore, the compiler generates bytecode for a call to the equals method in the Object class, which takes an Object parameter. At run-time, when the class of the object (referenced by) obj is available, the version of the Object-parameter equals method executed will be the one in the Object class unless that has been overridden.

For example, here is a short code segment to insert a FullTimeEmployee object in an instance of the Java Collection Framework's LinkedList class and then test to see if that employee is in the linked list:

```
FullTimeEmployee e1 = new FullTimeEmployee ("a 100.00");
LinkedList list = new LinkedList( );
list.add (e1);
System.out.println (list.contains (new FullTimeEmployee ("a 100.00")));
```

The value printed will be **true** if the FullTimeEmployee class has overridden (to compare objects) the Object class's equals method, and **false** if the FullTimeEmployee class has not overridden the Object class's equals method. Whether the FullTime Employee class has *overloaded* the equals method is irrelevant.

Now that we have established the importance of overriding the Object class's equals method, let's see how to do it. We will take the FullTimeEmployee class as an example. The basic idea is simple: if the type of the argument object is not Full TimeEmployee, return **false**. Otherwise, compare the name and gross pay of the calling object and the argument object. Here are some sample results:

```
System.out.println (new FullTimeEmployee ("a 100.00").equals
                    ("yes"));                                    // false
System.out.println (new FullTimeEmployee ("a 100.00").equals
                    (new FullTimeEmployee ("a 100.00")));        // true
System.out.println (new FullTimeEmployee ("a 100.00").equals
                    (new FullTimeEmployee ("b 100.00")));        // false
System.out.println (new FullTimeEmployee ("a 100.00").equals
                    (new FullTimeEmployee ("a 200.00")));        // false
```

The definition of the equals method follows the same structure as the definition of the makesMoreThan method of the FullTimeEmployee class in Chapter 1. Here is the full definition:

```
public boolean equals (Object obj)
{
        if(!(obj instanceof FullTimeEmployee))
                return false;
        FullTimeEmployee full = (FullTimeEmployee)obj;
        return name.equals (full.name) && grossPay == full.grossPay;
} // method equals
```

To summarize this section: Every class whose instances might be elements of a collection should have an equals method that overrides the Object class's equals method.

Programming Exercise 2.11 has even more information about the equals method.

## SUMMARY

The **static** modifier is used for identifiers that apply to a class as a whole, rather than to a particular instance of a class. Constants should be declared to be static, because then there will be only one copy of the constant, instead of one copy for each instance of the class. To access a static identifier outside of its class, the class identifier—rather than an object—is the qualifier.

An **exception** is an object that signals a special situation, usually that an error has occurred. An exception can be handled with **try/catch** blocks. The sequence of statements in the **try** block is executed. If, during execution, an exception is thrown (indicating that an error has occurred), the appropriate **catch** block is executed to specify what, if anything, is to be done.

File output is similar to console-oriented output, except that a PrintWriter object is explicitly created to write to the specified output file. The output is not immediately sent to the output file, but rather to a buffer. At the conclusion of file processing, the buffer is flushed to the output file by a call to the **close** method.

To increase a programmer's confidence that a method is correct—that is, satisfies the method's specifications—the method can be tested in a program that repeatedly invokes the method with a variety of argument values. For testing all of a class's methods in concert, a program called a **driver** is created. Testing is bottom-up: low-level classes are tested first; ultimately, the entire project is run against system tests.

The Java run-time, also known as the Java Virtual Machine, is a program that interprets and executes the bytecode output from a Java compiler. Among other tasks, the Java Virtual Machine is responsible for preinitialization of fields and deallocation of inaccessible objects.

A package is a collection of related classes. An identifier with no visibility modifier is said to have *default visibility.* Java is "package friendly." That is, an identifier with default visibility can be accessed by any object (or class, in the case of a static member) in the same package as the class in which the identifier is declared. If a given class's identifier has **protected** visibility, that identifier can be accessed in any subclass of the given class, even in a different package. Unfortunately, that identifier may also be accessed in any class—even if not a subclass—within the given package's class.

The equals method in the Object class should be overridden for any class C whose instances might become elements of a collection. The overriding method invokes the **instanceof** method to return **false** for any argument object that is not an instance of class C, and then casts the Object class to class C in order to make the appropriate comparisons.

## CONCEPT EXERCISES

**2.1**  Why should a class's constant identifiers be **static**? Should a method's constant identifiers be **static**? Explain.

**2.2** Create a **catch** block that will handle any exception. Create a **catch** block that will handle any input/output exception. Create a **catch** block that will handle any run-time exception.

**2.3** What is wrong with the following skeleton?

```
try
{
    ...
} // try
catch (IOException e)
{
    ...
} // catch IOException
catch (FileNotFoundException e)
{
    ...
} // catch FileNotFoundException
```

**2.4** Suppose fileReader is a BufferedReader object for reading from an input file, and fileWriter is a PrintWriter object for writing to an output file. What will happen if, at the end of a program, you forget to close fileReader? What will happen if, at the end of a program, you forget to close fileWriter?

**2.5** What does "bottom-up" testing mean with respect to the classes in a project? Why is bottom-up testing preferable to top-down testing?

**2.6** Suppose we create a two-dimensional array (literally, an array in which each element is an array). The following creates an **int** array with 5000 rows and 100000 columns:

```
int [ ][ ] a = new int [5000][100000];
```

If this code is executed, the program terminates abnormally, and the message is

```
java.lang.OutOfMemoryError
Exception in thread "main"
```

Why wasn't memory reallocated by the garbage collector? Can this abnormal termination be handled with a **try** block and **catch** block? Explain.

**2.7** Can a **protected** field be accessed outside of the class in which it is declared and outside of subclasses of that class? What does the following statement mean? "Subclassing represents more of a commitment than mere use."

**2.8** Arrays are strange objects because there is no array class. But an array object can call methods from the Object class. Determine and explain the output from the following code:

```
int [ ] a = new int [10];

int [ ] b = new int [10];
```

```
a [3] = 7;
b [3] = 7;
b [5] = 0;
System.out.println (a.equals(b));
```

# PROGRAMMING EXERCISES

**2.1**    Develop a main method to read in one line with three **double** values and print out the largest. Catch all possible exceptions.

**2.2**    Develop a main method to read in **double** values from a file and print out the largest. Handle all possible exceptions, including a reprompt for a nonexistent input file.

**2.3**    Create a driver for the FullTimeEmployee class that reads from an input file and writes to an output file.

**2.4**    Hypothesize what is wrong with the following method:

```
public static boolean isEven (int i)
{
      if (i % 2 == 0)
            return true;
      if (i % 2 != 0)
            return false;
} // method isEven
```

Test your hypothesis by calling this method from a main method. Can a **try** block and **catch** block handle the problem? Explain.

**2.5**    Hypothesize the output from the following:

```
System.out.println (null + "null");
```

Test your hypothesis with a one-line main method. Provide the code in the String class that explains why the output is what it is.

**2.6**    Give an example to show that **private** visibility is more restrictive than default visibility. Give an example to show that default visibility is more restrictive than **protected** visibility. Give an example to show that **protected** visibility is more restrictive than **public** visibility. In each case, test your code to make sure that the more restrictive choice generates a compile-time error message. No error message should be generated for the less restrictive choice.

**2.7**    Protectedness transfers across packages, but only within a subclass, and only for objects whose type is that subclass. For a bare-bones illustration, suppose we have class A declared in package APackage:

```
package APackage;
public class A
{
```

```
        protected int t;
} // class A
```

Also, suppose that classes C and D are subclasses of A and that C and D are in a different package from A. Then within class D, the t field is treated as if it were declared in D *instead of* in A. (Ditto for class C.) Here are possible declarations for classes C and D:

```
import APackage.*;

public class C extends A { }
```

Class D is declared in another file. For each of the four accesses of t in the following declaration of class D, hypothesize whether the access is legal or illegal:

```
import APackage.*;

public class D extends A
{
        public void meth( )
        {
            D d = new D( );
            d.t = 1;            // access 1
            t = 2;              // access 2
            A a = new A( );
            a.t = 3;            // access 3
            C c = new C( );
            c.t = 4;            // access 4
        } method meth

} // class D
```

Test your hypotheses by creating and running a project that includes the above files.

2.8 Redo Programming Exercise 1.2 to print out the number of above-average salaries. Use an array field to hold the salaries, and assume there will be at most 10 salaries in the input.

2.9 Study the specification of the arraycopy method in the System class, and then write a short program that uses the arraycopy method to copy all the elements of an array to another array. Output the elements in the destination array to make sure the copying actually occurred.

2.10 Redo Programming Exercise 2.8 if the input can contain an arbitrary number of salaries. *Hint:* Start with an array of length 10. Whenever the number of salaries in the input exceeds the current length of the array field, create a new array of twice that length, copy the old array to the new array—see Programming Exercise 2.9—and then assign the new array (reference) to the old array (reference).

**2.11** According to the full method specification in the Object class, any override of the Object class's equals method should satisfy the following five properties:

a.  *reflexivity,* that is, for any reference x,

   x.equals (x)

   should return **true**.

b.  *symmetry,* that is, for any references x and y,

   x.equals (y)

   should return the same result as

   y.equals (x)

c.  *transitivity,* that is, for any references x, y, and z if

   x.equals (y)

   returns **true**, and

   y.equals (z)

   returns **true**, then

   x.equals (z)

   should return **true**.

d.  *consistency,* that is, for any references x and y, multiple invocations of

   x.equals (y)

   should consistently return **true** or consistently return **false**, provided no information used in equals comparisons on the objects is modified.

e.  *actuality,* that is, for any nonnull reference x,

   x.equals (**null**)

   should return **false**.

For the FullTimeEmployee class's equals method (see Section 2.7), provide examples to support the claim that the equals method satisfies those five properties. You are not being asked to *prove* that the FullTimeEmployee class's equals method satisfies those properties.

# Analysis of Algorithms

As noted in Section 2.4, a ***correct*** method is one that satisfies its specification. In defining a method, the first goal is to make sure the method is correct. After testing has sufficiently increased our confidence in a method's correctness, we can then measure the method's efficiency. This chapter introduces two tools for measuring a method's efficiency. The first tool provides an estimate, based on studying the method, of the number of statements executed and number of variables used, in a trace of the method. The second tool entails a run-time analysis of the method. Both tools have some value, and they can complement each other. ■

## CHAPTER OBJECTIVES

1. Be able to use Big-O notation to estimate the time and space requirements of methods.

2. Be able to conduct run-time analyses of methods.

## 3.1 | ESTIMATING THE EFFICIENCY OF METHODS

The correctness of a method depends only on whether the method does **what** it is supposed to do. But the efficiency of a method depends to a great extent on **how** that method is defined. How can efficiency be measured? We could test the method repeatedly, with different arguments. But then the analysis would depend on the thoroughness of the testing regimen, and also on the compiler, operating system, and computer used. As we will see in Section 3.2, run-time analysis has blaring weaknesses, mainly due to the "noise" of other processes that are executing at the same time as the method being tested.

At this stage, we prefer a more abstract analysis that can be performed by directly investigating the method's definition. We will ignore all memory restrictions, and so, for example, we will allow an **int** variable to take on any integer value and an array to be arbitrarily large. Because we will study the method without regard to a specific computer environment, we can refer to the method as an *algorithm,* that is, a finite sequence of explicit instructions to solve a problem in a finite amount of time.

The question then is, how can we estimate the execution-time requirements of a method from the method's definition? We take the number of statements executed in a trace of a method as a crude measure of the execution-time requirements of that method. This measure will be represented as a function of the "size" of the problem. Given a method for a problem of size $n$, let *worstTime(n)* be the maximum (over all possible parameter/input values) number of statements executed in a trace of the method.

For example, let's determine worstTime($n$) for the following method, which returns the number of elements greater than the mean of an array of nonnegative **double** values. The nonnegative **int** n holds the number of elements in the array. In this example, the size of the problem is the value of the variable n; often, you will have to figure out the size of the problem from the context.

```java
public static int aboveMeanCount (double [ ] a, double mean, int n)
{
        int count = 0;

        for (int i = 0; i < n; i++)
                if (a [i] > mean)
                        count++;
        return count;
} // method aboveMeanCount
```

There are six statements that will be executed only once: the assignment of the arguments to the parameters a, mean, and n, the initialization of count and i, and the return of count. Within the **for** statement, i will be compared to $n$ a total of $n + 1$ times, i will be incremented $n$ times and the comparison of a [i] to mean will be made $n$ times. If $n - 1$ elements have the value 1.0 and the other element has the value 0.0, then a [i] will be greater than mean a total of $n - 1$ times, so count will be incremented $n - 1$ times. The total number of statements executed in the worst case, that is, worstTime($n$), is

$$6 + (n + 1) + n + n + (n - 1) = 4n + 6$$

Sometimes we will also be interested in the average-case performance of a method. We define ***averageTime(n)*** to be the average number of statements executed in a trace of the method. This average is taken over all invocations of the method, and we assume that each set of $n$ inputs for a call is equally likely. For some applications, that assumption is unrealistic, so averageTime($n$) may not be relevant.

In the **for** loop of the just completed example, a [i] will be greater than mean, on average, half of the time, so count will be incremented only $n/2$ times. Then averageTime($n$) is $3.5n + 7$.

Occasionally, especially in Chapters 5 and 11, we will also be interested in estimating the space requirements of a method. To that end, we define ***worstSpace(n)*** to be the maximum number of variables accessed in a trace of the method, and ***average Space(n)*** to be the average number of variables accessed in a trace of the method. For an array, we treat each element—that is, indexed variable—to be a separate variable. So an array of length $n$ would contribute $n$ variables.

### 3.1.1 Big-O Notation

We need not calculate worstTime($n$) and averageTime($n$)—or worstSpace($n$) and averageSpace($n$)—exactly, since they are only crude approximations of the time and space requirements of the corresponding method. Instead, we approximate those functions by means of "Big-O" notation, defined in the next paragraph. Because we are looking at the method by itself, independent of any specific computer environment, this "approximation of an approximation" is quite satisfactory for giving us an idea of how fast the method will be (or how much space will be allocated for its variables).

The basic idea behind Big-O notation is that we often want to determine an *upper bound* for the behavior of a function, that is, to determine how bad the performance of the function can get. For example, suppose we are given a function $f$. If some function $g$ is, loosely speaking, an upper bound for $f$, then we say that $f$ is Big-O of $g$. When we replace "loosely speaking" with specifics, we get the following definition:

> Let $g$ be a function that has nonnegative integer arguments and returns a nonnegative value for all arguments. A function $f$ is said to be $O(g)$ if for some pair of nonnegative constants $C$ and $K$,
>
> $$f(n) \le C \, g(n) \text{ for all } n \ge K$$

If $f$ is $O(g)$, pronounced "big-oh of $g$," we can also say "$f$ is of order $g$."

The idea behind Big-O notation is that if $f$ is $O(g)$ then $f$ is eventually bounded above by some constant times $g$, so we can use $g$ as a crude upper-bound estimate of the function $f$.

By a standard abuse of notation, we often associate a function with the value it calculates. For example, let $g$ be the function defined by

$$g(n) = n^3, \text{ for } n = 0, 1, 2, \dots$$

Instead of writing $O(g)$ we write $O(n^3)$.

## EXAMPLE 3.1

Let $f$ be the function defined as follows:

$$f(n) = n * (n + 3) + 4 \text{ for } n = 0, 1, 2, \dots$$

Show that $f$ is $O(n^2)$.

### ■ Solution

We need to find nonnegative constants $C$ and $K$ such that $f(n) \leq C * n^2$ for all $n \geq K$. We first rewrite the function definition:

$$f(n) = n^2 + 3n + 4 \text{ for } n = 0, 1, 2, \dots$$

We then show that each term in that definition is less than or equal to some constant times $n^2$ for $n \geq$ some nonnegative integer. Right away, we get:

$$n^2 \leq 1n^2 \text{ for } n \geq 0$$

$$3n \leq 3n^2 \text{ for } n \geq 0$$

$$4 \leq 4n^2 \text{ for } n \geq 1$$

So for any $n \geq 1$,

$$f(n) \leq n^2 + 3n^2 + 4n^2 = 8n^2$$

That is, for $C = 8$ and $K = 1$, $f(n) \leq C\, n^2$ for all $n \geq K$. This shows that $f$ is $O(n^2)$.

In general, if $f$ is a polynomial of the form

$$a_k n^k + a_{k-1} n^{k-1} + \cdots + a_1 n + a_0$$

then we can establish that $f$ is $O(n^k)$ by choosing $K = 1$, $C = |a_k| + |a_{k-1}| + \cdots + |a_1| + |a_0|$, and proceeding as in Example 3.1.

The next example shows that we can ignore the base of a logarithm when determining the order of a function.

## EXAMPLE 3.2

Let $a$ and $b$ be positive constants. Show that if $f$ is $O(\log_a n)$ then $f$ is also $O(\log_b n)$.

### ■ Solution

Assume that $f$ is $O(\log_a n)$. Then there are nonnegative constants $C$ and $K$ such that for all $n \geq K$,

$$f(n) \leq C \log_a n$$

By a fundamental property of logarithms (see Appendix 2),

$$\log_a n = (\log_a b)(\log_b n) \quad \text{for any } n > 0$$

Let $C_1 = C \log_a b$. Then for all $n \geq K$, we have

$$f(n) \leq C \log_a n = C \log_a b \log_b n = C_1 \log_b n$$

and so $f$ is $O(\log_b n)$.

The final example in this introduction to Big-O notation is a code segment.

**EXAMPLE 3.3**

Show that worstTime($n$) is $O(n^2)$ for the following nested loop:

```
for (int i = 0; i < n; i++)
    for (int j = 0; j < n; j++)
        System.out.println (i + j);
```

**■ Solution**

For this nested loop, every trace will entail the execution of the same number of statements. Therefore, for example, worstTime($n$) and averageTime($n$) will be equal. And that is frequently the case.

In the outer loop, the initialization of i is executed once, the continuation condition, i < n, is executed $n + 1$ times, and i is incremented $n$ times. So far, we have

$$1 + (n + 1) + n$$

statements executed. For each of the $n$ iterations of the outer loop, the initialization of j is executed once, the continuation condition, j < n, is executed $n + 1$ times, j is incremented $n$ times, and the output statement is executed $n$ times. That increases the number of statements executed by

$$n(1 + (n + 1) + n)$$

The total number of statements executed is

$$1 + (n + 1) + n + n(1 + (n + 1) + n) = 2n^2 + 4n + 2$$

Since the same number of statements will be executed in every trace, we have

$$\text{worstTime}(n) = 2n^2 + 4n + 2$$

By the same technique used in Example 3.1,

$$\text{worstTime}(n) \leq 8n^2 \text{ for all } n \geq 1$$

We conclude that worstTime($n$) is $O(n^2)$.

Note that Big-O notation merely gives an upper bound for a function. For example, if $f$ is $O(n^2)$, then $f$ is also $O(n^2 + 5n + 2)$, $O(n^3)$, and $O(n^{10} + 3)$. Whenever possible, we choose the *smallest* element from a hierarchy of orders, of which the most commonly used are shown in Figure 3.1. For example, if $f(n) = n + 7$ for $n = 0, 1, 2, \ldots,$ it is most informative to say that $f$ is $O(n)$—even though $f$ is also $O(n \log n)$ and $O(n^3)$. Similarly, we write $O(n)$ instead of $O(2n + 4)$ or $O(n - \log n)$, even though $O(n) = O(2n + 4) = O(n - \log n)$; see Concept Exercise 3.9.

Figure 3.2 shows some more examples of functions and where they fit in the order hierarchy.

The next section illustrates how easy it can be to approximate worstTime($n$)— or averageTime($n$)—with the help of Big-O notation.

## 3.1.2 Getting Big-O Estimates Quickly

By estimating the number of loop iterations in a method, we can often determine at a glance an upper bound for worstTime($n$). Let S represent any sequence of statements whose execution does not include a loop statement for which the number of iterations depends on $n$. The following method skeletons provide paradigms for determining an upper bound for worstTime($n$).

**1.**   worstTime($n$) is $O(1)$:

   S

Note that the execution of S may entail the execution of millions of statements! For example:

```
double sum = 0;
for (int i = 0; i < 10000000; i++)
        sum += Math.sqrt (i);
```

**Figure 3.1** | Some elements in the Big-O hierarchy. The symbol $\subset$ means "is contained in." For example, every function that is in $O(1)$ is also in $O(\log n)$.

$$O(1) \subset O(\log n) \subset O(n^{1/2}) \subset O(n) \subset O(n \log n) \subset O(n^2) \subset O(n^3) \subset \bullet \bullet \bullet \subset O(2^n) \bullet \bullet \bullet$$

**Figure 3.2** | Some sample functions in the order hierarchy.

| Order | Sample function |
|---|---|
| $O(1)$ | $f(n) = 3000$ |
| $O(\log n)$ | $f(n) = [n \log_2(n + 1) + 2]/(n + 1)$ |
| $O(n)$ | $f(n) = 5 \log_2 n + n$ |
| $O(n \log n)$ | $f(n) = \log_2 n^n$ (See Appendix 2) |
| $O(n^2)$ | $f(n) = n(n + 1)/2$ |
| $O(2^n)$ | $f(n) = 3500n^{100} + 2^n$ |

The reason that worstTime($n$) is $O(1)$ is that the number of loop iterations is constant and therefore independent of $n$. In fact, $n$ does not even appear in the code. In the remaining examples of this section, $n$ will be given explicitly for the sake of simplicity.

2. worstTime($n$) is $O(\log n)$:

```
while (n > 1)
{
        n = n / 2;
        S
} // while
```

Let $t(n)$ be the number of times that S is executed during the execution of the **while** statement. Then $t(n)$ is equal to the number of times that $n$ can be divided by 2 until $n$ equals 1. By Example 3 in Appendix 2, $t(n)$ is the largest integer $\leq \log_2 n$. That is, $t(n) = \text{floor}(\log_2 n)$.[1] Since floor($\log_2 n$) $\leq \log(n)$ for any positive integer $n$, we conclude that $t(n)$ is $O(\log n)$ and so worstTime($n$) is also $O(\log n)$.

The phenomenon of repeatedly splitting a collection in two will reappear time and again in the remaining chapters. Be on the lookout for the splitting: it signals that worstTime($n$) will be $O(\log n)$.

> **The Splitting Rule**  In general, if during each loop iteration, $n$ is divided by some constant greater than 1, worstTime($n$) will be $O(\log n)$.

3. worstTime($n$) is $O(n)$:

```
for (int i = 0; i < n; i++)
{
        S
} // for
```

The reason that worstTime($n$) is $O(n)$ is simply that the **for** loop is executed n times. It does not matter how many statements are executed during each iteration of the **for** loop: suppose the maximum is $k$ statements, for some positive integer $k$. Then the total number of statements executed is $\leq kn$.

4. worstTime($n$) is $O(n \log n)$:

```
int m;

for (int i = 0; i < n; i++)
{
        m = n;
```

---

[1] floor(x) returns the largest integer that is less than or equal to x.

```
            while (m > 1)
            {
                    m = m / 2;
                    S
            } // while
      } // for
```

The **for** loop is executed n times. For each iteration of the **for** loop, the **while** loop is executed floor($\log_2 n$) times—see Example 2 above—which is $\leq$ $\log_2 n$. Therefore worstTime(n) is $O(n \log n)$.

5.  worstTime(n) is $O(n^2)$:

a.   **for** (int i = 0; i < n; i++)

```
            for (int j = 0; j < n; j++)
            {
                    S
            } // for j
```

The number of times that S is executed is $n^2$. That is all we need to know to conclude that worstTime(n) is $O(n^2)$. In Example 3.3, we painstakingly counted the exact number of statements executed and came up with the same result!

b.   **for** (int i = 0; i < n; i++)

```
            for (int k = i; k < n; k++)
            {
                    S
            } // for k
```

The number of times that S is executed is

$$n + (n - 1) + (n - 2) + \cdots + 3 + 2 + 1 = \sum_{k=1}^{n} k$$

As shown in Example 1 of Appendix 2, the above sum is equal to

$$n (n + 1)/2$$

which is $O(n^2)$. That is, worstTime(n) is $O(n^2)$.

c.   **for** (int i = 0; i < n; i++)

```
      {
            S
      } // for i
      for (int i = 0; i < n; i++)
            for (int j = 0; j < n; j++)
            {
                    S
            } // for j
```

For the first segment, worstTime(n) is $O(n)$, and for the second segment, worstTime(n) is $O(n^2)$, so for both segments together, worstTime(n) is $O(n + n^2)$, which is equal to $O(n^2)$. In general, for the sequence

A
B

if worstTime($n$) is $O(f)$ for A and worstTime($n$) is $O(g)$ for B, then worstTime($n$) is $O(f + g)$ for the sequence A, B.

**6.** worstTime($n$) is $O(2^n)$:

```
int k = 1;

for (int i = 0; i < n; i++)
    k = 2 * k;
for (int i = 0; i < k; k++)
{

    S

}
```

The first loop is executed $n$ times. At the end of the execution of that **for** statement, $k$ has the value $2^n$. The second loop is executed $k$ times, that is, $2^n$ times, and so worstTime($n$) is $O(2^n)$.

### 3.1.3 Big-Omega, Big-Theta, and Plain English

In addition to Big-O notation, there are two other notations that you should know about: Big-Omega and Big-Theta. Whereas Big-O provides a crude upper bound for a function, Big-Omega supplies a crude lower bound. Here is the definition:

> Let $g$ be a function that has nonnegative integer arguments and returns a non-negative value for all arguments. We define $\Omega(g)$ to be the set of functions $f$ such that for some pair of nonnegative constants $C$ and $K$,
>
> $$f(n) \geq C\, g(n) \quad \text{for all } n \geq K$$

If $f$ is in $\Omega(g)$ we say that $f$ is "Big-Omega of $g$." Notice that the definition of Big-Omega differs from the definition of Big-O only in that the last line has $f(n) \geq C\, g(n)$ instead of $f(n) \leq C\, g(n)$, as we had for Big-O.

All of the Big-O examples from Section 3.1.1 are also Big-Omega examples. Specifically, in Example 3.1, the function $f$ defined by

$$f(n) = n\,(n + 3) + 4 \quad \text{for } n = 0, 1, 2, \ldots$$

is $\Omega(n^2)$: for $C = 1$ and $K = 0$, $f(n) \geq Cn^2$ for all $n \geq K$. Also, for all of the code skeletons in Section 3.1.2, we can replace $O$ with $\Omega$ as a bound on worstTime($n$).

Big-Omega notation is used much less frequently than Big-O notation because we are usually more interested in providing an upper bound than a lower bound for worstTime($n$) or averageTime($n$). That is, "can't be any worse than" is often more relevant than "can't be any better than." One exception occurs in Chapter 11, where we establish the important result that, for any sort method based on comparisons of $n$ elements, worstTime($n$) is $\Omega(n \log n)$.

A somewhat artificial example shows that Big-O and Big-Omega are distinct. Let $f$ be the function defined by

$$f(n) = n \quad \text{for } n = 0, 1, 2, \ldots$$

Clearly, $f$ is $O(n)$, and therefore, $f$ is also $O(n^2)$. But $f$ is not $\Omega(n^2)$. And that same function $f$ is clearly $\Omega(n)$, and therefore $\Omega(1)$. But $f$ is not $O(1)$. In fact, the Big-Omega hierarchy is just the reverse of the Big-O hierarchy in Figure 3.1. For example,

$$\Omega(n^2) \subset \Omega(n \log n) \subset \Omega(n) \subset \Omega(1)$$

In most cases the same function will serve as both a lower bound and an upper bound, and this leads us to the definition of Big-Theta:

> Let $g$ be a function that has nonnegative integer arguments and returns a nonnegative value for all arguments. We define $\Theta(g)$ to be the set of functions $f$ such that for some nonnegative constants $C_1$, $C_2$, and $K$,
>
> $$C_1\, g(n) \leq f(n) \leq C_2\, g(n) \quad \text{for all } n \geq K$$

The idea is that if $f$ is $\Theta(g)$, then eventually (that is, for all $n \geq K$), $f(n)$ is bounded below by some constant times $g(n)$ and also bounded above by some constant times $g(n)$. In other words, to say that a function $f$ is $\Theta(g)$ is exactly the same as saying that $f$ is both $O(g)$ and $\Omega(g)$. When we establish that a function $f$ is $\Theta(g)$, we have "nailed down" the function $f$ in the sense that $f$ is, roughly, bounded above by $g$ and also bounded below by $g$.

As an example of Big-Theta, consider the function $f$ defined by

$$f(n) = n\,(n + 3) + 4 \quad \text{for } n = 0, 1, 2, \ldots$$

We showed in Example 3.1 that $f$ is $O(n^2)$, and earlier in this section we showed that $f$ is $\Omega(n^2)$. We conclude that $f$ is $\Theta(n^2)$.

For ease of reading, we adopt plain-English terms instead of Big-Theta notation for several families of functions in the Big-Theta hierarchy. For example, if $f$ is $\Theta(n)$, we say that $f$ is "linear in $n$." Table 3.1 shows some English-language replacements for Big-Theta notation. We prefer to use plain English (such as "constant," "linear," and "quadratic") whenever possible. But as we will see in Section 3.1.4, there will still be many occasions when all we specify is a Big-O estimate of an upper bound.

**Table 3.1** | Some English-language equivalents to Big-Theta notation.

| Big-Theta | English |
| --- | --- |
| $\Theta(1)$ | Constant |
| $\Theta(\log n)$ | Logarithmic in $n$ |
| $\Theta(n)$ | Linear in $n$ |
| $\Theta(n \log n)$ | Linear-logarithmic in $n$ |
| $\Theta(n^2)$ | Quadratic in $n$ |

## 3.1.4 Growth Rates

In this section, we look at the growth rate of functions. Specifically, we are interested in how rapidly a function increases based on its Big-Theta classification. Suppose we have a method whose worstTime(n) is linear in n. Then we can write:

worstTime(n) $\approx Cn$   for some constant $C$ (and for sufficiently large values of n)

What will be the effect of doubling the size of the problem, that is, of doubling n?

$$worstTime(2n) \approx C2n$$
$$= 2Cn$$
$$\approx 2\ worstTime(n)$$

In other words, if we double n, we double the estimate of worst time.

Similarly, if a method has worstTime(n) that is quadratic in n, we can write:

worstTime(n) $\approx Cn^2$   for some constant $C$ (and for sufficiently large values of n)

Then

$$worstTime(2n) \approx C(2n)^2$$
$$= C4n^2$$
$$= 4Cn^2$$
$$\approx 4\ worstTime(n)$$

In other words, if we double n, we quadruple the estimate of worst time. Other examples of this kind of relationship are explored in Concept Exercise 3.7, Concept Exercise 11.5, and in later labs.

Figure 3.3 shows the relative growth rates of worstTime(n) for several orders of functions.

Figure 3.4 indicates why Big-Theta differences eventually dominate other factors in estimating the behavior of a function. For example, if n is sufficiently large, $t_1(n) = n^2/100$ is much greater than $t_2(n) = 100n \log_2 n$. But the phrase "if n is sufficiently large" should be viewed as a warning. Note that $t_1$ is *smaller* than $t_2$ for arguments less than 100,000. So whether Big-Theta (or Big-O or Big-Omega) is relevant may depend on how large the size of your problem might get.

Figure 3.4 has a concrete example of the differences between several families in the Big-Theta hierarchy. For a representative member of the family—expressed as a function of n—the time to execute that many statements is estimated when n equals 10 million.

Some of the differences shown in Figure 3.4 are worth exploring. For example, there is a huge difference between the values of $\log_2 n$ and n. In Chapter 9, we will study a data structure—the binary search tree—for which averageTime(n) is logarithmic in n for inserting, removing, and searching, but worstTime(n) is linear in n for those methods.

Another notable comparison in Figure 3.4 is between $n \log_2 n$ and $n^2$. In Chapter 11, on sort methods, we will see tangible evidence of this difference. Roughly speaking, there are two categories of sort methods: fast sorts, whose averageTime(n) is linear-logarithmic in n, and simple sorts, whose averageTime(n) is quadratic in n.

**Figure 3.3** I The graphs of worstTime($n$) for several families of functions.

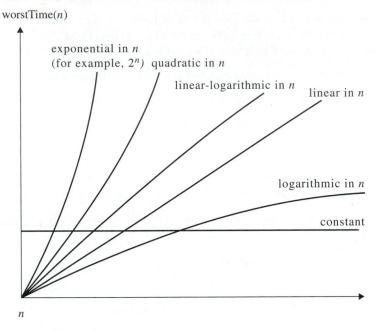

worstTime($n$)

exponential in $n$
(for example, $2^n$)   quadratic in $n$

linear-logarithmic in $n$

linear in $n$

logarithmic in $n$

constant

$n$

**Figure 3.4** I Estimated time to execute a given number of statements for various functions of $n$ when $n = 10,000,000$ and 10,000 statements are executed per second. For example, to execute $n \log_2 n$ statements takes approximately 7 hours.

| Function of $n$ | Time Estimate |
| --- | --- |
| $\log_2 n$ | 0.0024 seconds |
| $n$ | 17 minutes |
| $n \log_2 n$ | 7 hours |
| $n^2$ | 300 years |
| $2^n$ | Much longer than a trillion years |

The most glaring difference in Figure 3.4 is between $n^2$ and $2^n$, and this has important practical and theoretical consequences. A ***polynomial-time*** method is one for which worstTime($n$) is $O(n^k)$ for some positive integer $k$. For example, a method whose worstTime($n$) is $O(n^2)$ is a polynomial-time method. Similarly, a method whose worstTime($n$) is $O(n \log n)$ is polynomial-time because $O(n \log n) \subset O(n^2)$. When we try to develop a method to solve a given problem, we prefer polynomial-time methods whenever possible; otherwise, it will be infeasible to run the method for large values of $n$.

As you can see from Figure 3.4, a method whose worstTime($n$) is $\Theta(2^n)$ grows too rapidly to be useful for large values of $n$. Such methods are in the category of exponential-time methods. An ***exponential-time*** method is one whose worstTime($n$) is $\Omega(x^n)$ for some real number $x > 1.0$. Then we say worstTime($n$) is ***exponential in n.*** For example, a method whose worstTime($n$) is $\Omega(2^n)$ is an exponential-time method. Chapter 5 has an example of an exponential-time method, and Labs 7 and 9 have two more exponential-time methods. As you might expect, a polynomial-time method cannot also be exponential-time (Concept Exercise 3.10).

The existence of exponential-time methods gives rise to an interesting question: for a given exponential-time method, might there be a polynomial-time method to solve the same problem? In some cases, the answer is no. An ***intractable problem*** is one for which any method to solve the problem is an exponential-time method. For example, a problem that requires $2^n$ values to be printed is intractable because any method to solve that problem must execute $\Omega(2^n)$ statements. The problem in Chapter 5 for which an exponential-time method is supplied is an intractable problem. The problem in Lab 9 is also intractable, but the problem in Lab 7 has a polynomial-time solution.

Lab 23 investigates the traveling salesperson problem, for which the only known methods to solve the problem are exponential-time methods. The most famous open question in computer science is whether the traveling salesperson problem is intractable. There may be a polynomial-time method to solve that problem, but no one has found such a method, and most experts believe that no such method is possible.

If we are working on a single method only, it may be feasible to optimize that method's averageTime($n$) and worstTime($n$), with the intent of optimizing execution time. But for the management of an entire project, it is usually necessary to strike a balance. The next section explores the relevance of other factors, such as memory utilization and project deadlines.

### 3.1.5  Trade-Offs

In the previous section we saw how to estimate a method's execution-time requirements. The same Big-O (or Big-Omega or Big-Theta) notation can be used to estimate the memory requirements of a method. Ideally, we will be able to develop methods that are both fast enough *and* small enough. But in the real world, we seldom attain the ideal. More likely, we will encounter one or more of the following obstacles during programming:

1. The program's estimated execution time may be longer than acceptable according to the performance requirements. ***Performance requirements,*** when given, state the time and space upper bounds for all or part of a program.

2. The program's estimated memory requirements may be larger than acceptable according to the performance requirements. This situation frequently arises for hand-held devices.

3. The program may require understanding a technique with which the programmer is only vaguely familiar. This may create an unacceptable delay of the entire project.

Often, a trade-off must be made: a program that reduces one of the three obstacles may intensify the other two. For example, if you had to develop a project by tomorrow, you would probably ignore time and space constraints and focus on understanding the problem well enough to create a project. The point is that real-life programming involves hard decisions. It is not nearly enough that you can develop programs that run. Adapting to constraints such as those mentioned above will make you a better programmer by increasing your flexibility.

We can incorporate efficiency concerns into the correctness of a method by including performance requirements in the method's specification. For example, part of the specification for the push method in the PureStack interface of Chapter 8 is:

$$\text{The worstTime}(n) \text{ is } O(n).$$

Then for a definition of that method to be correct in an implementation of the PureStack interface, worstTime($n$) would have to be $O(n)$. Recall that the Big-O estimates provide *upper bounds* only. But the class developer is free to improve on the upper bounds for average time or worst time. For example, there is a way to implement the PureStack interface so that, for the definition of the push method, worstTime($n$) is constant.

We want to allow developers of methods the flexibility to improve the efficiency of those methods without violating the contract between users and developers. So any performance requirements in method specifications will be given in terms of upper-bounds (that is, Big-O) only. Here are three conventions regarding the Big-O estimates in method specifications:

1.  If a class stores a collection of elements, then unless otherwise noted, the variable $n$ refers to the number of elements in the collection.
2.  For many methods, worstTime($n$) is $O(1)$. If no estimate of worstTime($n$) is given, you may assume that worstTime($n$) is $O(1)$.
3.  Often, averageTime($n$) has the same Big-O estimate as worstTime($n$). When they are different, we will specify both.

When we analyze the time (or space) efficiency of a specific method definition, we will determine lower as well as upper bounds, so we will use Big-Theta notation—or the English-language equivalent: constant, linear-in-$n$, and so on.

Up until now, we have separated concerns about correctness from concerns about efficiency. According to the Principle of Data Abstraction, the correctness of code that uses a class should be independent of that class's implementation details. But the efficiency of that code may well depend on those details. In other words, the developer of a class is free—for the sake of efficiency—to choose any combination of fields and method definitions, provided the correctness of the class's methods does not rely on those choices. For example, suppose a class developer can create three different versions of a class:

A: correct, inefficient, does not allow users to access fields

B: correct, somewhat efficient, does not allow users to access fields

C: correct, highly efficient, allows users to access fields

In most cases, the appropriate choice is B. Choosing C would violate the Principle of Data Abstraction because the correctness of a program that uses C could depend on C's fields.

Big-O analysis provides a cross-platform estimate of the efficiency of a method. The following section explores the execution-time tools for measuring efficiency.

# 3.2 | RUN-TIME ANALYSIS

We have seen that Big-O notation allows us to estimate the efficiency of methods independently of any particular computing environment. For practical reasons, we may also want to estimate efficiency within some fixed environment. Why settle for estimates? For one thing,

> In multiprogramming environments such as Windows, it is very difficult to determine how long a single task takes.

Why? Because there is so much going on behind the scenes, such as maintaining the desktop clock, executing a wait-loop until a mouse click occurs, and updating information from your mailer and browser. At any given time, there might be dozens of such processes under control of the Windows Manager. And each process will get a time slice of several milliseconds. The bottom line is that the elapsed time for a task is seldom an accurate measure of how long the task took.

Another problem with seeking an exact measure of efficiency is that it might take a very long time—$O$(forever). For example, suppose we are comparing two sorting methods, and we want to determine the average time each one takes to sort some collection of elements. The time may depend heavily on the particular arrangement of the elements chosen. Because the number of different arrangements of $n$ elements is $n!$, it is not feasible to generate every possible arrangement, run the method for each arrangement, and calculate the average time.

Instead, we will generate a sample ordering that is in "no particular order." The statistical concept corresponding to "no particular order" is randomness. We will use the time to sort a random sample as an estimate of the average sorting time. We start with a discussion of timing because, as we will see later, one aspect of randomness depends on the result of a timing method.

## 3.2.1 Timing

To assist in the timing of methods, Java supplies currentTimeMillis( ), a static method in the System class of java.lang. This method returns a **long** whose value is the number of milliseconds—that is, thousandths of a second—elapsed since January 1, 1970, Greenwich Mean Time. For example, at 2:27 P.M. Eastern Standard Time on January 12, 2004, a project with the following line was run:

```
System.out.println (System.currentTimeMillis( ));
```

The output was 1073935526655, which indicates that about 1 trillion milliseconds— 1 billion seconds—had elapsed since January 1, 1970. To estimate how much execution time a task consumes, we calculate the time immediately before and immediately after the code for the task. The difference in the two times represents the elapsed time. (As noted above, elapsed time is a very, very crude estimate of the time the task consumed.) For example, the following code serves as a skeleton for performing timing tests:

```java
final String ANSWER_1 = "The elapsed time was ";

final double MILLI_FACTOR = 1000.0; // milliseconds per second

final String ANSWER_2 = " seconds.";

long startTime,
     finishTime,
     elapsedTime;

startTime = System.currentTimeMillis( );

// Perform the task:

. . .

// Calculate the elapsed time:
finishTime = System.currentTimeMillis( );
elapsedTime = finishTime − startTime;
System.out.println (ANSWER_1 + (elapsedTime / MILLI_FACTOR) + ANSWER_2);
```

This skeleton determines the elapsed time for the task in seconds, with fractional digits.

We will use the time to process a random sample of values as an estimate of the average processing time. Section 3.2.2 contains an introduction to—or review of—the Random class, part of the package java.util.

## 3.2.2 Overview of the Random Class

If each number in a sequence of numbers has the same chance of being selected, the sequence is said to be ***uniformly distributed.*** A number so selected from a uniformly distributed sequence is called a ***random number.*** And a method that, when repeatedly called, returns a sequence of random numbers is called a ***random-number generator.***

The Random class in java.util supplies several random-number generators. We will look at three of those methods. Strictly speaking, the sequence of numbers returned by repeated calls to any one of those methods is a *pseudo-random-number* sequence because the numbers calculated are not random at all—they are determined by the code in the method. The numbers *appear* to be random if we do not see how they are calculated. If you look at the definition of this method in the Random class, the mystery and appearance of randomness will disappear.

Here is the method specification for one of the random-number generators:

```java
/**
 * Returns a pseudo-random int in the range from 0 (inclusive) to a specified int
 * (exclusive).
 *
 * @param n – the specified int, one more than the largest possible value
 *        returned.
 *
 * @return a random int in the range from 0 to n − 1, inclusive.
 *
```

```
 *  @throws IllegalArgumentException – if n is less than or equal to zero, or
 *      greater than Integer.MAX_VALUE.
 *
 */
public int nextInt (int n)
```

For example, a call to nextInt (100) will return a pseudo-random integer in the range from 0 to 99, inclusive.

For another example, suppose we want to simulate the roll of a die. The value from one roll of a die will be an integer in the range 1 . . . 6, inclusive. The call to nextInt (6) returns an **int** value in the range from 0 to 5, inclusive, so we need to add 1 to that returned value. Here is the code to print out that pseudo-random die roll:

```
Random die = new Random( );

int oneRoll = die.nextInt (6) + 1;

System.out.println (oneRoll);
```

The value calculated by the nextInt (**int** n) method depends on the seed it is given. The variable seed is a **private long** in the Random class. The initial value of seed depends on the constructor called. If, as above, the Random object is created with the default constructor, then seed is initialized to System.currentTimeMillis( ). The other form of the constructor has a **long** parameter, and seed is initialized to the argument corresponding to that parameter. Each time the method nextInt (**int** n) is called, the current value of the seed is used to determine the next value of the seed, which determines the **int** returned by the method.

For example, suppose that two programs have

```
Random die = new Random (800);

for (int i = 0; i < 5; i++)
        System.out.println (die.nextInt (6) + 1);
```

The output from both programs would be exactly the same:

```
3
5
3
6
2
```

This repeatability can be helpful when we want to compare the behavior of programs, as we will in Chapters 5 to 15. In general, repeatability is an essential feature of the scientific method.

If we do not want repeatability, we use the default constructor. Recall that the default constructor initializes the seed to System.currentTimeMillis( ).

Here are two other random-number generators in the Random class:

```
/**
 * Returns a pseudo-random int in the range from Integer.MIN_VALUE to
```

```
     * Integer.MAX_VALUE.
     *

     *

     * @return a pseudo-random int in the range from Integer.MIN_VALUE to
     * Integer.MAX_VALUE.
     *

     */
    public int nextInt ( )

    /**
     * Returns a pseudo-random double in the range from 0.0 (inclusive) to
     * 1.0 (exclusive).
     *

     */
    public double nextDouble ( )
```

The following program combines randomness and timing in an extremely inefficient sorting algorithm:

```
import java.util.*;

import java.io.*;

public class Timing_Random
{

    public static void main (String[ ] args)
    {

        final String PROMPT = "Please enter the number of " +
                              " doubles to be sorted: ";

        final String ANSWER_1 = "The elapsed time was ";

        final double MILLI_FACTOR = 1000.0; // milliseconds per second

        final String ANSWER_2 = " seconds.";

        BufferedReader reader = new BufferedReader (
                        new InputStreamReader (System.in));

        Random r = new Random( ); // seed = System.currentTimeMillis( )
        long startTime,
             finishTime,
             elapsedTime;
        try
        {
            System.out.print (PROMPT);
            int n = Integer.parseInt (reader.readLine( ));
            double[ ] x = new double [n];
            for (int i = 0; i < n; i++)
                x [i] = r.nextDouble( );
```

```
startTime = System.currentTimeMillis( );

// Sort x into ascending order:
for (int i = 0; i < n − 1; i++)
        for (int k = i+1; k < n; k++)
            if (x [i] > x [k])
            {
                    double temp = x [i];
                    x [i] = x [k];
                    x [k] = temp;
            } // if

// Calculate the elapsed time:
finishTime = System.currentTimeMillis( );
elapsedTime = finishTime − startTime;
System.out.println (ANSWER_1 +
        (elapsedTime / MILLI_FACTOR) + ANSWER_2);
} // try
catch (IOException e)
{
        System.out.println (e);
} // catch
} // method main

} // class Timing_Random
```

The nested loop structure is virtually identical to the one in Example 5b of Section 3.1.2, so worstTime($n$) is $O(n^2)$. Since the number of iterations is the same for any arrangement of the $n$ elements, averageTime($n$) is $O(n^2)$. In fact, $n^2$ provides a crude lower bound as well as a crude upper bound, so averageTime($n$) is quadratic in $n$. Then we expect the average run time—over all possible arrangements of $n$ doubles—to be quadratic in $n$. As suggested in Section 3.2, we use the elapsed time to sort $n$ pseudo-random doubles as an approximation of the average run time for all arrangements of $n$ doubles.

The elapsed time gives further credence to that estimate: for $n = 50000$, the elapsed time is 19.985 seconds, and for $n = 100000$, the elapsed time is 80.766 seconds. The actual times are irrelevant since they depend on the computer used, but the relative times are significant: when $n$ doubles, the elapsed time quadruples (approximately). According to Section 3.1.4 on growth rates, that ratio is symptomatic of quadratic time.

Randomness and timing are also combined in the experiment in Lab 4: you are given the unreadable (but runnable) bytecode versions of the classes instead of source code.

 **Lab 4: Randomness and Timing of Mystery Classes**

You are now prepared to do Lab 4.                    All Labs Are Optional

## SUMMARY

Big-O notation allows us to quickly estimate an upper bound on the time/space efficiency of methods. Because Big-O estimates allow function arguments to be arbitrarily large integers, we treat methods as algorithms by ignoring the space requirements imposed by Java and a particular computing environment. In addition to Big-O notation, we also looked at Big-$\Omega$ notation (for lower bounds) and Big-$\Theta$ notation (when the upper bound and lower bound are roughly the same).

Run-time analysis allows methods to be tested on a specific computer. But the estimates produced are often very crude, especially in a multiprogramming environment. Run-time tools include the currentTimeMillis( ) method and several methods from the Random class.

## CONCEPT EXERCISES

**3.1**   Create a method, sample (**int** n), for which worstTime($n$) is $O(n)$ but worstTime($n$) is not linear in $n$.

*Hint:* $O(n)$ indicates that $n$ may be (crudely) viewed as an upper bound, but linear-in-$n$ indicates that $n$ may be (crudely) viewed as both an upper bound and a lower bound.

**3.2**   Study the following algorithm:

```
int i = 0;
while (!a [i].equals (element))
       i++;
```

Assume that a is an array of n elements and that there is at least one index k in 0 . . . n −1 such that a [k].equals (element).

Use Big-O notation to estimate worstTime($n$). Use Big-$\Omega$ and Big-$\Theta$ notation to estimate worstTime($n$). In plain English, estimate worstTime($n$).

**3.3**   Study the following:

```
// Make a [0. . .n − 1] sorted (in increasing order):
for (int i = 0; i < n − 1; i++)
{
       // Make a [0. . .i] sorted and ≤ a [i+1. . .n − 1]:
       int position = i;
       for (int j = i+1; j < n; j++)
              if (a [j] < a [position])
                     position = j;
       double temp = a [i];
       a [i] = a [position];
       a [position] = temp;
} // outer for
```

**a.**   For the inner **for** statement, when i = 0, j takes on values from 1 to n − 1, and so there are n − 1 iterations of the inner **for** statement when i = 0. How many iterations are there when i = 1? When i = 2?

    **b.** Determine, as a function of n, the total number of iterations of the inner **for** statement as i takes on values from 0 to n − 2.

    **c.** Use Big-O notation to estimate worstTime($n$). In plain English, estimate worstTime($n$)—the choices are constant, logarithmic in $n$, linear in $n$, linear-logarithmic in $n$, quadratic in $n$ and exponential in $n$.

**3.4** For each of the following functions $f$, where $n = 0, 1, 2, 3, \ldots$, estimate $f$ using Big-O notation and plain English:

    **a.** $f(n) = (2 + n)(3 + \log n)$

    **b.** $f(n) = 11 \log n + n/2 - 3452$

    **c.** $f(n) = 1 + 2 + 3 + \ldots + n$

    **d.** $f(n) = n(3 + n) - 7n$

    **e.** $f(n) = 7n + (n - 1) \log (n - 4)$

    **f.** $f(n) = \log n^2 + n$

    **g.** $f(n) = \dfrac{(n + 1) \log(n + 1) - (n + 1) + 1}{n}$

    **h.** $f(n) = n + n/2 + n/4 + n/8 + n/16 + \cdots$

**3.5** In the order hierarchy in Figure 3.1, we have $\ldots, O(\log n) \subset O(n^{1/2}), \ldots$. Show that, for integers $n > 16$, $\log_2 n < n^{1/2}$. ***Hint from calculus:*** Show that for all real numbers $x > 16$, the slope of the function $\log_2 x$ is less than the slope of the function $x^{1/2}$. Since $\log_2 16 = 16^{1/2}$, we conclude that for all real numbers $x > 16$, $\log_2 x < x^{1/2}$.

**3.6** For each of the following code segments, estimate worstTime($n$) using Big-O notation or plain English. In each segment, S represents a sequence of statements in which there are no $n$-dependent loops.

    **a.**
```
for (int i = 0; i * i < n; i++)
        S
```

    **b.**
```
for (int i = 0; Math.sqrt (i) < n; i++)
        S
```

    **c.**
```
int k = 1;
for (int i = 0; i < n; i++)
        k *= 2;
for (int i = 0; i < k; i++)
        S
```

    *Hint:* In each case, 2 is part of the answer.

**3.7**   **a.** Suppose we have a method whose worstTime($n$) is linear in $n$. Determine the effect of tripling $n$ on the estimate of worst time. That is, estimate worstTime($3n$) in terms of worstTime($n$).

    **b.** Suppose we have a method whose worstTime($n$) is quadratic in $n$. Determine the effect of tripling $n$ on the estimate of worst time. That is, estimate worstTime($3n$) in terms of worstTime($n$).

    **c.** Suppose we have a method whose worstTime($n$) is constant. Determine the effect of tripling $n$ on the estimate of worst time. That is, estimate worstTime($3n$) in terms of worstTime($n$).

**3.8**   This exercise proves that the Big-O families do not constitute a strict hierarchy. Consider the function $f$, defined for all nonnegative integers as follows:

$$f(n) = \begin{cases} n & \text{if } n \text{ is even} \\ 0 & \text{if } n \text{ is odd} \end{cases}$$

Define a function $g$ on all nonnegative integers such that $f$ is not $O(g)$ and $g$ is not $O(f)$.

**3.9**   Show that $O(n) = O(n + 7)$. **Hint:** Use the definition of Big-O.

**3.10**  Show that if $f(n)$ is polynomial in $n$, $f(n)$ cannot be exponential in $n$.

**3.11**  Suppose, for some method, worstTime$(n) = n^n$. Show that the method is an exponential-time method (that is, worstTime$(n)$ is $\Omega(x^n)$ for some real number $x > 1.0$). But show that worstTime$(n)$ is not $\Theta(x^n)$ for any real number $x > 1.0$.

## PROGRAMMING EXERCISES

**3.1**   In mathematics, the absolute value function returns a nonnegative integer for any integer argument. Develop a main method to show that the Java method Math.abs (**int** a) does not always return a nonnegative integer.

**3.2**   Assume that r is (a reference to) an object in the Random class. Show that the value of the following expression is not necessarily in the range 0 . . . 99:

Math.abs (r.nextInt( )) % 100

*Hint:* See Programming Exercise 3.1.

**3.3**   Develop a main method that initializes a Random object with the default constructor and then determines the elapsed time for the nextInt( ) method to generate 123456789.

# Programming Project 3.1

## Let's Make a Deal!

This project is based on the following modification—proposed by Marilyn Vos Savant—to the game show "Let's Make a Deal." A contestant is given a choice of three doors. Behind one door there is an expensive car; behind each of the other doors there is a goat.

After the contestant makes an initial guess, the announcer peeks behind the other two doors and eliminates one of them that does not have the car behind it. For example, if the initial guess is door 2 and the car is behind door 3, then the announcer will show that there is a goat behind door 1.

If the initial guess is correct, the announcer will randomly decide which of the other two doors to eliminate. For example, if the initial guess is door 2 and the car is behind door 2, the announcer will randomly decide whether to show a goat behind door 1 or a goat behind door 3. After the initial guess has been made and the announcer has eliminated one of the other doors, the contestant must then make the final choice.

Develop a program to determine the answer to the following questions:

1.  Should the contestant stay with the initial guess, or switch?
2.  How much more likely is it that an always-switching contestant will win instead of a never-switching contestant?

For the sake of repeatability, the following system tests used a seed of 100 for the random-number generator.

**System Test 1:**

Please enter the number of times the game will be played: 10000

Please enter 0 for a never-switching contestant or 1 for always-switching: 0

The number of wins was 3330

**System Test 2:**

Please enter the number of times the game will be played: 10000

Please enter 0 for a never-switching contestant or 1 for always-switching: 1

The number of wins was 6628

On the basis of the output, what are your answers to the two questions given above?

Suppose, instead of working with three doors, the number of doors is input, along with the number of times the game will be played. Hypothesize how likely it is that the always-switching contestant will win. Modify and then run your project to confirm or reject your hypothesis. (Keep hypothesizing, and modifying and running your project, until your hypothesis is confirmed.)

*Hint for Hypothesis:* Suppose the number of doors is $n$, where $n$ can be any positive integer greater than 2. For an always-switching contestant to win, the initial guess must be incorrect, and then the final guess must be correct. What is the probability, with $n$ doors,

*(continued on next page)*

*(continued from previous page)*

that the initial guess will be incorrect? Given that the initial guess is incorrect, how many doors will the always-switching contestant have to choose from for the final guess (remember that the announcer will eliminate one of those doors)? The probability that the always-switching contestant will win is the probability that the initial guess is incorrect times the probability that the final guess is then correct.

# The Java Collections Framework

The Java Collections Framework is an assortment of related interfaces and classes in the package java.util. For most of the classes in the Java Collections Framework, each instance is a collection, that is, each instance is composed of elements. The collection classes can have type parameters, a new feature of Java, so that a user can specify the type of the elements when declaring an instance of a collection class. In this chapter, we will take a brief tour of the Java Collections Framework's collection classes, along with the new features that enhance the use of those classes. ■

## CHAPTER OBJECTIVES

1. Understand what a collection is, and how contiguous collections differ from linked collections.

2. Be able to create and manipulate parameterized collections.

3. Identify several of the methods in the Collection interface.

4. Describe a design pattern in general, and the iterator design pattern in particular.

5. Compare the ArrayList and LinkedList implementations of the List interface.

6. Discuss the difference between a list and a set, and between a set and a map.

7. Be able to utilize boxing/unboxing and the enhanced **for** statement when working with collection classes.

## 4.1 | COLLECTIONS

A *collection* is an object that is composed of elements. The elements can be either values in a primitive type (such as **int**) or references to objects. For a familiar example, an *array* is a collection of elements, of the same type, that are stored contiguously in memory. *Contiguous* means "adjacent," so the individual elements are stored next to each other.[1] For example, we can create an array of five String elements as follows:

```
String [ ] names = new String [5];
```

Here the **new** operator allocates space for an array of five String references, (each initialized to **null** by the Java Virtual Machine), and returns a reference to the beginning of the space allocated. This reference is stored in names.

There is an important consequence of the fact that arrays are stored contiguously: an individual element in an array can be accessed without first accessing any of the other individual elements. For example, names [2] can be accessed immediately—we need not access names [0] and names [1] first in order to reach names [2]. This *random access* property of arrays will come in handy in several subsequent chapters. In each case we will need a storage structure in which an element can be accessed quickly given its relative position, so an array will be appropriate in each case.

There are several drawbacks to arrays. First, the size of an array is fixed: space for the entire array must be allocated before any elements can be stored in the array. If that size is too small, a larger array must be allocated and the contents of the smaller array copied to the larger array.

Another problem with arrays is that the programmer must provide all the code for operating on an array. For example, inserting and deleting in an array may require that many elements be moved. Suppose an array's indexes range from 0 to 999, inclusive, and there are elements stored in order in the locations at indexes 0 to 755. To insert an element into the location with index 300, we must first move the elements at indexes 300 to 755 into the locations at indexes 301 to 756. Figure 4.1 shows the effect of such an insertion.

In your programming career up to now, you have had to put up with the above disadvantages of arrays. Section 4.1.1 describes an alternative that is almost always superior to arrays: instances of collection classes.

### 4.1.1 Collection Classes

Most of what we will do from here on involves collection classes. A *collection class* is a class in which each instance is a collection of elements, and each element is (a reference to) an object. For example, a String object can be an element, or a Full TimeEmployee object can be an element. Values in a primitive type are not objects, so we cannot create an instance of a collection class in which each element is of type **int**. But for each primitive type, there is a corresponding class, called a *wrapper class*, whose purpose is to enable a primitive type to be represented by (that is,

---

[1] Actually, all that matters is that, to a user of an array, the elements are stored *as if* they were contiguous, so an element can be accessed directly from its index.

**Figure 4.1** | Insertion in an array: to insert "Kalena" at index 300 in the array on the left, the elements at indexes 300, 301, . . . , 756 must first be moved, respectively, to indexes 301, 302, . . . , 757.

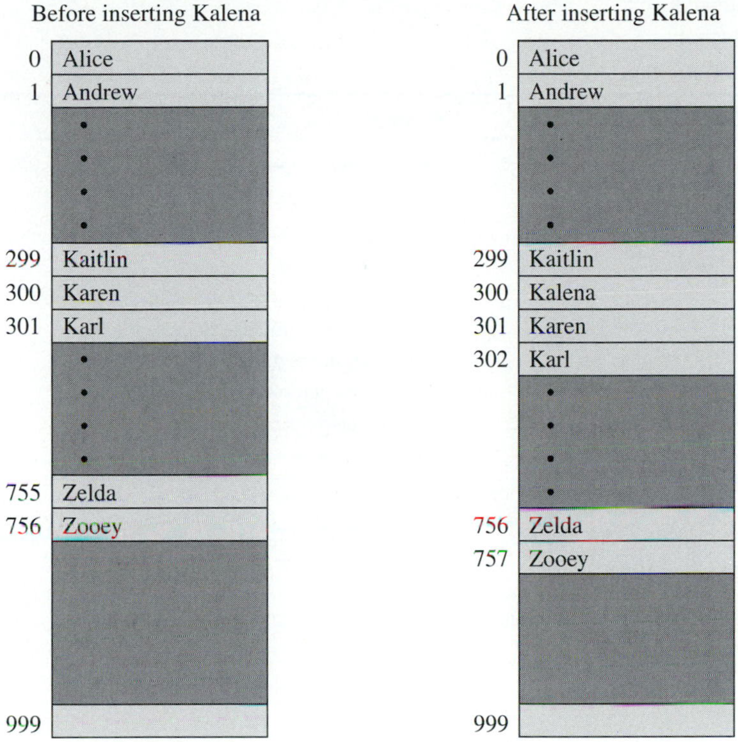

| Before inserting Kalena | | After inserting Kalena | |
|---|---|---|---|
| 0 | Alice | 0 | Alice |
| 1 | Andrew | 1 | Andrew |
| | • • • | | • • • |
| 299 | Kaitlin | 299 | Kaitlin |
| 300 | Karen | 300 | Kalena |
| 301 | Karl | 301 | Karen |
| | • • • | 302 | Karl |
| 755 | Zelda | | • • • |
| 756 | Zooey | 756 | Zelda |
| | | 757 | Zooey |
| 999 | | 999 | |

wrapped inside) a class. For example, there is an Integer class, and we can create an Integer object from an **int** j as follows:

> **new** Integer (j)

The **new** operator returns a reference to an Integer object. Table 4.1 provides several important conversions.

The Java Collections Framework includes a number of collection classes that have wide applicability. Those classes are ArrayList, LinkedList, TreeMap, TreeSet, HashMap, and HashSet. All of those collection classes have some common methods. For example, each collection class has an isEmpty method whose method specification is:

```
/**
 * Determines if this collection has no elements.
 *
 * @return true – if this collection has no elements.
 *
 */
public boolean isEmpty( )
```

**Table 4.1** I Some important conversion formulas.

**int** i;
Integer myInt;
String s;
Object obj;

| To Obtain | From | Example |
|---|---|---|
| Integer | **int** | myInt = **new** Integer (i);   // but see Section 4.2.2 |
| **int** | Integer | i = myInt.intValue( );   // but see Section 4.2.2 |
| String | **int** | s = Integer.toString(i); |
| String | Integer | s = myInt.toString( ); |
| Object | Integer | obj = myInt;   // by Subclass Substitution Rule |
| Object | String | obj = s;   // by Subclass Substitution Rule |
| **int** | String | i = Integer.parseInt (s); |
| Integer | String | myInt = **new** Integer (s); |
| Integer | Object | myInt = (Integer)obj; |
| String | Object | s = (String)obj; |

Suppose mySet is an instance of the collection class TreeSet, and mySet has four elements. The execution of

    System.out.println (mySet.isEmpty( ));

will produce output of

    false

Of course, a method specification does not indicate *how* the method's task will be accomplished. In subsequent chapters, we will investigate the details for several collection classes. But we can now introduce a simple classification of collection classes according to the way the elements are stored.

## 4.1.2 Storage Structures for Collection Classes

Instances of a collection class usually consume memory in proportion to the number of items in the collection. So the way such a collection is stored in memory can have a substantial impact on the efficiency of a program. One straightforward way to store a collection instance in memory is to store, in an array, a reference to each element in the collection. For example, an array could be a field in the collection class.

Such a class is called a *contiguous-collection class*. For example, the ArrayList class in Chapter 6 has an array field, and (a reference to) each element in an ArrayList instance is stored in that instance's array. So ArrayList is a contiguous-collection class. The Heap class in Chapter 13 is another example of a contiguous-collection class. For many applications of those classes, the random-access feature of an array is a great asset.

What about the disadvantages, cited earlier, of an array: the size of an array is fixed, and the programmer is responsible for writing all the code that works with the array? With a contiguous-collection class, those are problems for the developer of the class, *not* for users of the class. Basically, the developer of a contiguous-collection class writes the code—once—for methods that manipulate the array. Any user of that collection class simply invokes the appropriate methods for the given application. The user may not even be aware that there is an array field in the class, and by the Principle of Data Abstraction, would not rely on that field anyway.

You probably have not appreciated the random access feature of arrays. That's because you have probably not yet seen an alternative to arrays for storing a collection of elements in memory. We now describe a structure that competes with the array for storing the elements in a collection object.

Instead of a contiguous relationship, the elements are related by links. A *link* is another name for a reference. Basically, each element is housed in a special object called an *entry*—sometimes called a *node*. Within each entry object there will be at least one reference (called a *link*) to another entry object. In a linked-collection class, the elements in each instance are stored in entries. Figures 4.2 to 4.4 show parts of three linked collections. We will explore the details of linked collections in Chapters 7, 10, 12, and 14.

**Figure 4.2 |** Part of a linked collection—a **singly linked list**—in which each entry contains an element and a reference to the next entry in the linked collection.

**Figure 4.3 |** Part of a linked collection—a **doubly linked list**—in which each entry contains an element, a reference to the previous entry, and a reference to the next entry.

**Figure 4.4 |** Part of a linked collection—a **binary search tree**—in which each entry contains an element, and references to three other entries.

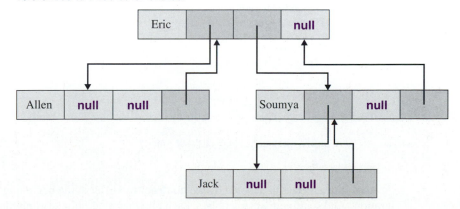

## 4.2 | OUTLINE OF THE JAVA COLLECTIONS FRAMEWORK

In this section we present, in broad strokes, the Java Collections Framework. The Java Collections Framework consists of a thoroughly tested assortment of interfaces and classes. The classes represent widely used data structures and algorithms. For most applications in which a collection is needed, the framework provides the appropriate class. By utilizing the framework classes, you improve your productivity by not "reinventing the wheel."

One of the impediments to understanding the framework is its sheer size; there are over 200 methods in the six classes we will study: ArrayList, LinkedList, TreeSet, HashSet, TreeMap, and HashMap. Fortunately, there is a lot of duplication. For example, as noted in Section 4.1.1, each of those classes has an isEmpty method. In fact, the definitions of many of the methods are the same in several classes. One of the unifying tools in the framework is the interface, which imposes method headings on implementing classes. Section 4.2.1 introduces another, similar, unifying tool: the abstract class.

### 4.2.1  Abstract Classes

An *abstract class* is a class that is allowed to have abstract methods as well as defined methods. The abstract methods *must* be defined in each subclass (unless the subclass is also abstract). Here is a bare-bones example of an abstract class:

```java
public abstract class Parent
{
    /**
     * Returns the String object "I am ".
     *
     * @returns "I am ".
     *
     */
    public String getPrefix( )
    {
        return "I am ";
    } // method getPrefix

    /**
     * Returns a String object.
     *
     * @return a String object.
     *
     */
    public abstract String getClassName( );

} // class Parent
```

An abstract class is denoted by the **abstract** modifier at the beginning of its declaration. And within an abstract class, each abstract method's heading must include the modifier **abstract** before the return type, and a semicolon after the method heading. Because the Parent class lacks a definition for one of its methods, we cannot instantiate the Parent class. That is, we cannot define a Parent object:

```
Parent p = new Parent ( ); // illegal because Parent is an abstract class
```

We can now declare two subclasses, Child1 and Child2, of Parent.

```
public class Child1 extends Parent
{
     /**
      * Returns the String object "Child1".
      *
      * @return the String object "Child1".
      *
      */
     public String getClassName( )
     {
          return "Child1";
     } // method getClassName

} // class Child1

public class Child2 extends Parent
{
     /**
      * Returns the String object "Child2".
      *
      * @return the String object "Child2".
      *
      */
     public String getClassName( )
     {
          return "Child2";
     } // method getClassName
} // class Child2
```

The main benefits of abstract methods are that they promote flexibility (defined methods may be, but need not be, overridden in subclasses) and consistency (abstract-class headings must be identical in subclasses). For example, we can now do the following:

```
Parent p;

int code;
// Get the value for code;

. . .

if (code == 1)
     p = new Child1( );
else
     p = new Child2( );
System.out.println (p.getPrefix( ) + p.getClassName( ));
```

The variable p is a polymorphic reference, so the version of the getClassName method called depends on the type—Child1 or Child2—of the object referenced by Parent. The output will be "I am Child1" or "I am Child2", depending on the value of the variable code.

The Java Collections Framework has quite a few abstract classes: Abstract Collection, AbstractList, AbstractSet, and others. Typically, one of these classes will declare as abstract any method whose definition depends on fields in the subclasses, and define any method whose definition does not depend on those fields. For now, a practical application of abstract classes is developed in Lab 5.

### Lab 5: A Class for Regular Polygons

You are now prepared to do Lab 5.                    All Labs Are Optional

Here are a few more details on the relationship between interfaces, abstract classes, and fully defined classes:

1. If a class implements some but not all of the methods in an interface, then the class would have to be declared as an abstract class—and therefore cannot be instantiated.

2. An interface can extend one or more other interfaces. For example, we could have:

   **public interface** Container **extends** Collection, Comparable
   { ...

   Container has abstract methods of its own, and also inherits abstract methods from the interfaces Collection and Comparable.

3. A class can extend at most one other class; by default, the Object class is the superclass of every class. *Multiple inheritance*—the ability of a class to have more than one immediate superclass—is illegal in Java. Multiple inheritance is illegal because of the danger of ambiguity. For example, viewing a teaching assistant as both a student and an employee, we could have a TeachingAssistant class that is the immediate subclass of classes Student and StaffMember. Now suppose classes Student and StaffMember each has its own getHolidays( ) method. If we define:

   TeachingAssistant teach = **new** TeachingAssistant( );

   which getHolidays( ) method does teach.getHolidays( ) invoke? There is no way to tell, and that is why Java outlaws multiple inheritance.

4. A class can implement more than one interface. For example, we could have:

   **class** NewClass **implements** Interface1, Interface2
   { ...

   This feature, especially when combined with feature 3, allows us to come close to achieving multiple inheritance. We can write:

```
class NewClass extends OldClass implements Interface1, Interface2
{
```

There is no ambiguity when a method is invoked because any methods in an interface are abstract, and any non-**final** superclass method can be explicitly *overridden*—that is, redefined—in the subclass. For example, suppose OldClass, Interface1, and Interface2 all have a writeOut( ) method, and we have

```
NewClass myStuff = new NewClass( );
...
myStuff.writeOut( );
```

Which version of the writeOut method will be invoked? Certainly not the version from Interface1 or Interface2, because those methods must be abstract. If NewClass implements a writeOut( ) method, that is the one that will be invoked. Otherwise, the version of writeOut defined in (or inherited by) OldClass will be invoked.

## 4.2.2 Parameterized Types

When collection classes were introduced in Section 4.1.1, we noted that the element type has to be a reference type: primitive types are not allowed. Starting with J2SE (that is, Java 2 Platform, Standard Edition) version 1.5, a class's element type is specified, in angle brackets, when an instance of the class is declared. For example, suppose we want to declare and initialize a LinkedList object to hold a collection of grade point averages in which each grade point average will be stored as a Double. You don't have to know the details of the LinkedList class; you will learn some of those in Chapter 7. The declaration and initialization of the LinkedList object is as follows:

```
LinkedList<Double> gpaList = new LinkedList<Double>( );
```

Only elements of type Double can be inserted into gpaList; an attempt to insert a String or Integer element will be disallowed by the compiler. As a result, you can be certain that any element retrieved from gpaList will be of type Double.

Let's see how elements can be inserted and retrieved from gpaList. In the LinkedList class, the add method inserts the element argument at the end of the LinkedList object. For example,

```
gpaList.add (new Double (2.7));
```

will append to gpaList a Double object whose **double** value is 2.7.

For retrievals, the get method returns the element in the LinkedList object at a specified index. So we can access the element at index 0 as follows:

```
Double gpa = gpaList.get (0);
```

Notice that we don't need to cast the expression on the right-hand side to Double because the element at position 0 of gpaList must be of type Double.

Now suppose we want to add that grade point average to a **double** variable sum, initialized to 0.0. The method doubleValue( ) in the Double class returns the **double** value corresponding to the calling Double object. The assignment to sum is

```
sum = sum + gpa.doubleValue( );
```

In this example, LinkedList<Double> is a parameterized type. A *parameterized type* consists of a class or interface identifier followed, in angle brackets, by a list of one or more class identifiers separated by commas. Typically, a parameterized type starts with a collection-class identifier, and the element type is enclosed in angle brackets. A parameterized type is sometimes called a "generic type," and the language feature permitting parameterized types is called "generics."

Parameterized collection classes improve your productivity as a programmer. You don't have to remember what the element type of a collection is, because that type is specified when the collection is declared, as we did with LinkedList<Double>. If you make a mistake and try to insert an element of type String for example, you will be notified at compile-time. Without parameterized types, the insertion would be allowed, but the assignment of gpaList.get (0) to gpa would generate a ClassCast Exception at run time. And this exception, if uncaught, could crash a critical program!

In the above example, the conversions from **double** to Double and from Double to **double** are annoyances. To simplify your working with parameterized collection classes, J2SE 1.5 automatically translates primitive values into wrapper objects: the technical term is *boxing*. For example, the above insertion into gpaList can be accomplished as follows:

```
gpaList.add (2.7);          // instead of gpaList.add (new Double (2.7));
```

*Unboxing* translates a wrapper object into its primitive value. For example, to increment the above **double** variable sum by the value of the Double object at index 0 of gpaList, we simply write

```
sum = sum + gpaList.get (0);
```

Unboxing eliminates the need for you to invoke the doubleValue( ) method, and that makes your code easier to read.

The general idea behind parameterized types and boxing/unboxing is to simplify the programmer's work by assigning to the compiler several tasks that would otherwise have to be performed by the programmer.

Section 4.2.3 introduces the backbone of the Java Collections Framework: the Collection interface.

### 4.2.3 The Collection Interface

The Java Collections Framework consists basically of a hierarchy. There are interfaces and abstract classes at every level except the lowest, and the lowest level has implementations of interfaces and extensions of abstract classes. At the top of the hierarchy are two interfaces, Collection and Map.

In this section, we will focus on the Collection interface. For the sake of specificity, Figure 4.5 presents the Collection interface in UML notation, with the meth-

**Figure 4.5 |** The Collection interface. In UML, a type parameter—in this case, E— is shown in a dashed rectangle in the upper right-hand corner of the interface or class.

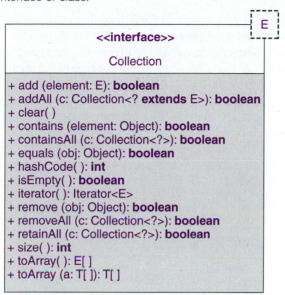

ods listed in alphabetical order. Don't worry if some of the methods are puzzling to you (or make no sense at all). You will learn all you will need to know in subsequent chapters, when we look at implementations of the interface.

As indicated in Figure 4.5, the Collection interface has E—for "element"—as the ***type parameter.*** That is, E is replaced with an actual class, such as Double or Full TimeEmployee, in the declaration of an instance of any class that implements the interface. For example, part of the LinkedList heading is

**public class** LinkedList $<$E$>$ **implements** Collection$<$E$>$ . . .

Here is an instance of the LinkedList class with FullTimeEmployee elements:

LinkedList$<$FullTimeEmployee$>$empList = **new** LinkedList $<$FullTimeEmployee$>$( );

In this example, FullTimeEmployee is the actual class of the elements: the class that replaces the type parameter E when the LinkedList class is instantiated.

In the heading of the addAll method in Figure 4.5, the type-parameter specification for the elements of c is $<$? **extends** E$>$. That means that when addAll is called, the type of the argument's elements can be any subclass of the actual class that replaced E when the calling object for the addAll method was instantiated. For example, suppose we have instantiated empList as in the previous declaration, and we also have

LinkedList$<$HourlyEmployee$>$ currentList = **new** LinkedList$<$HourlyEmployee$>$( );

We can insert all the elements of currentList to empList as follows:

    empList.addAll (currentList);

A class is considered to be a subclass of itself, so this invocation of addAll would still be legal if currentList were instantiated with FullTimeEmployee elements.

In the method heading for containsAll in Figure 4.5, the type-parameter specification for the elements of c is <?>. That means that type of the argument's elements can be any class.

As we will see in Sections 4.2.4 and 4.2.5, the Collection interface is extended by other interfaces (List and Set) and partially implemented by an abstract class (AbstractCollection). In fact, if you wanted to, you could create your own class that fully implements the Collection interface. That is, sort of, what happens in Lab 6. Only a few methods are realistically defined; the others just throw an exception. For example,

```
public int hashCode( )
{
        throw new UnsupportedOperationException( );
}
```

Such definitions satisfy the compiler, so the resulting class, ArrayCollection, is instantiable. That is, we can create and initialize an ArrayCollection object:

    ArrayCollection<Integer> coll = new ArrayCollection<Integer>( );

 **Lab 6: The ArrayCollection Class**

You are now prepared to do Lab 6.                    All Labs Are Optional

**Iterators**   The Collection interface provides a core of methods useful for applications. But each application will almost certainly have some specialized tasks that do not correspond to any method in the Collection interface. Here are some examples (Collection object means "object in a class that implements the Collection interface"):

1. Given a Collection object of students, print out each student who made the dean's list.
2. Given a Collection object of words, determine how many are four-letter words.
3. Given a Collection object of club members, update the dues-owed for each member.
4. Given a Collection object of full-time employees, calculate the average salary of the employees.

Surely, we cannot create a class that would provide a method for any task in any application—the number of methods would be limitless. But notice that in each of the four examples above, the task entails accessing each element in a Collection object. This suggests that we need to allow users of a Collection class to be able to construct a loop that accesses each element in a Collection object. As we will see when we look at classes that implement the Collection interface, developers can straightforwardly construct such a loop. Why? Because a developer has access to the fields in the class, so the developer knows how the class is organized. And that enables the developer to loop through each element in the instance.

According to the Principle of Data Abstraction, a user's code should not be able to access the implementation details of a Collection class. The basic problem is this: How can any implementation of the Collection interface allow users to loop through the elements in an instance of that class without violating the Principle of Data Abstraction? The solution is in the use of iterators. ***Iterators*** are objects that allow the elements of Collection objects to be accessed in a consistent way without accessing the fields of the Collection class.

Inside each class that implements the Collection interface, there is an iterator class that allows a user to access each element in the collection. Each iterator class must itself implement the following Iterator interface:

```
public interface Iterator<E>
{
      /**
       * Determines if this Iterator object is positioned at an element in
       * this Collection object.
       *
       * @return true – if this Iterator object is positioned at an element
       *        in this Collection object.
       *
       */
      boolean hasNext ( );

      /**
       * Advances this Iterator object, and returns the element this
       * Iterator object was positioned at before this call.
       *
       * @return the element this Iterator object was positioned at when
       *        this call was made.
       *
       * @throws NoSuchElementException – if this Iterator object is not
       *        positioned at an element in the Collection object.
       *
       */
      E next ( );

      /**
       * Removes the element returned by the most recent call to next( ).
       * The behavior of this Iterator object is unspecified if the underlying
       * collection is modified – while this iteration is in progress – other
       * than by calling this remove( ) method.
       *
       * @throws IllegalStateException – if next( ) had not been called
       *        before this call to remove( ), or if there had been an
       *        intervening call to remove( ) between the most recent
```

```
     *      call to next( ) and this call.
     *
     void remove ( );

} // interface Iterator<E>
```

For each class that implements the Collection interface, its iterator class provides the methods for traversing any instance of that Collection class. In other words, iterators are the behind-the-scenes workhorses that enable a user to access each element in any instance of a Collection class.

How can we associate an iterator object with a Collection object? The iterator( ) method in the Collection class creates the necessary connection. Here is the method specification from the Collection interface:

```
/**
 * Returns an Iterator object over this Collection object.
 *
 * @return an Iterator object over this Collection object.
 *
 */
Iterator<E> iterator( );
```

The value returned is (a reference to) an Iterator object, that is, an object in a class that implements the Iterator interface. With the help of this method, a user can iterate through a Collection object. For example, suppose that myColl is (a reference to) an instance of a Collection object with String elements, and we want to print out each element in myColl that starts with the letter "a." We first create an iterator object:

```
Iterator<String> itr = myColl.iterator( );
```

The variable itr is a polymorphic reference: it can be assigned a reference to an object in any class that implements the Iterator<String> interface. And myColl.iterator( ) returns a reference to an object that is positioned at the beginning of the myColl object.

The actual iteration is fairly straightforward:

```
String word;
while (itr.hasNext ( ))
{
      word = itr.next( );
      if (word.charAt (0) == 'a')
            System.out.println (word);
} // while
```

Incidentally, do you see what is wrong with the following?

```
// Incorrect!
while (itr.hasNext ( ))
      if (itr.next( ).charAt (0) == 'a')
            System.out.println (itr.next( ));
```

Because of the two calls to itr.next( ), each loop iteration will print out the word *following* a word that starts with the letter "a."

Very often, all we want to do during an iteration is to access each element in the collection. For such situations, J2SE 1.5 provides an ***enhanced* for** statement. For example, the above (correct) iteration through myColl can be abbreviated to the following:

```java
for (String word : myColl)
        if (word.charAt (0) == 'a')
                System.out.println (word);
```

The colon should be interpreted as "in," so the control part of this **for** statement can be read "For each word in myColl." The effect of this code is the same as before, but some of the drudgery—creating and initializing the iterator, and invoking the hasNext( ) and next( ) methods—has been relegated to the compiler.

Here is a complete example of iterating over a non-empty Collection object by using an enhanced **for** statement. You don't have to know the details of the Linked List class, the particular implementation of the Collection interface. You will learn those details in Chapter 7. The **import** directives (for java.io and java.util) must appear before the declaration of the class that contains the main method.

```java
public static void main (String [ ] args)
{
        final String PROMPT = "Please enter a GPA; to quit enter ";

        final String SENTINEL = "****";

        final String AVERAGE_MESSAGE = "\n\nThe average GPA is ";

        LinkedList <Double> gpaList = new LinkedList <Double> ( );

        BufferedReader reader = new BufferedReader (
                                        new InputStreamReader (System.in));

        String line;

        double sum = 0;

        try
        {
                while (true)
                {
                        System.out.println (PROMPT + SENTINEL);
                        line = reader.readLine ( );
                        if (line.equals (SENTINEL))
                                break;
                        gpaList.add (new Double (line));  // inserts in gpaList
                } // while
                for (Double gpa : gpaList)
                        sum += gpa;        //note unboxing
                System.out.println (AVERAGE_MESSAGE +
                                (sum / gpaList.size ( )));
```

```
        } // try
        catch (IOException e)
        {
                System.out.println (e);
        } // catch
    } // method main
```

The enhanced **for** statement simplifies your code, and that makes your programs easier to understand. So you should use an enhanced **for** statement whenever possible, namely, if you were to use an iterator instead, the only iterator methods invoked would be hasNext( ) and next( ). You cannot use an enhanced **for** statement if the collection may be modified during the iteration. For example, if you wanted to delete, from gpaList, each grade-point-average below 1.0, you would need to explicitly set up an iterator:

```
    Iterator<Double> itr = gpaList.iterator( );
    while (itr.hasNext( ))
        if (itr.next( ) < 1.0)
                itr.remove( );
```

**Design Patterns**    In the preceding section, we stated a problem, namely, how can the developer of a Collection class allow users to loop through one of the instances of that class without violating the Principle of Data Abstraction? The solution to the problem was to employ an iterator. The use of iterators is an example of a *design pattern:* a generic programming technique that can be applied in a variety of situations. As we will see in subsequent chapters, the iterator pattern plays an important role in an assortment of applications.

Throughout the text, we will identify several design patterns and corresponding applications. The basic idea is that each design pattern provides you with a problem that occurs frequently and the outline of a solution. You may have to tweak the solution for a particular instance of the problem, but at least you will not be reinventing the wheel!

In Section 4.2.4, we explore an extension of the Collection interface and two classes that implement that extension.

### 4.2.4  The List Interface

Java Collections Framework's List interface extends the Collection interface by providing some index-related methods. For example, there is a get method that returns the element at a given index. In any List object, that is, in any instance of a class that implements the List interface, the elements are stored in sequence, according to an index. For example, a List object pets might have the elements arranged as follows: "dog", "cat", "iguana", "gerbil", "cat". Here "dog" is at index 0, "gerbil" is at index 3. Duplicate elements are allowed: "cat" appears at index 1 and at index 4.

When viewed as a language-independent entity, a list is an abstract data type. Within Java, the List interface is abstract in the sense that it is not tied down to any particular implementation. In fact, in the Java Collections Framework, the List interface is not directly implemented. Instead, the abstract class AbstractList partially implements the List interface, and leaves the rest of the implementation to sub-classes, namely, ArrayList and LinkedList. See Figure 4.6.

The ArrayList class implements the List interface with an underlying array, and the LinkedList class implements the List interface with the underlying doubly-linked structure shown in Figure 4.3. We will get to the details in Chapters 6 and 7, respectively. To give you an idea of some of the methods in both classes, the following main method creates and manipulates a List of random Integer objects.

```java
public static void main (String[ ] args)
{
        final int SEED = 111;

        List<Integer> randList = new ArrayList<Integer>( );

        Random r = new Random (SEED);

        // Insert 10 random integers, in the range 0. . .99, into randList:
        for (int i = 0; i < 10; i++)
                randList.add (r.nextInt(100));        // insertion

        // Print out randList:
        System.out.println (randList);

        // See if 22 is in randList:
        if (randList.contains (22))
```

**Figure 4.6 |** Part of the Java Collections Framework hierarchy dealing with the List interface. In UML, an abstract-class identifier is italicized.

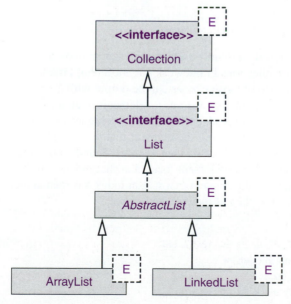

```
                System.out.println ("Yes, 22 is in randList.");
        else
                System.out.println ("No, 22 is not in randList.");

        // Print out the Integer at index 3:
        System.out.println (randList.get (3) + " is at index 3");

        // Remove the Integer at index 6:
        randList.remove (6);

        // Insert a new random Integer at index 5:
        randList.add (5, r.nextInt (100));

        // Print out randList.
        System.out.println (randList);

        // Remove all even Integers:
        Iterator<Integer> itr = randList.iterator( );
        while (itr.hasNext( ))
                if (itr.next( ) % 2 == 0)
                        itr.remove( );

        // Print out randList;
        System.out.println (randList);
    } // method main
```

The line

```
    System.out.println (randList);
```

is equivalent to

```
    System.out.println (randList.toString( ));
```

The toString method returns a String representation of randList. Every collection class in the Java Collections Framework has a toString( ) method, so all the elements in an instance of one of those classes can be output with a single call to println.

Because an ArrayList object stores its elements in an underlying array, when the element at index 6 is removed, each element at a higher index is moved to the location at the next lower index. So the element that was at index 7 is then at index 6, the element that was at index 8 is then at index 7, and so on. When a new element is inserted at index 5, each element located at that index or higher is moved to the next higher index. So the element that was at index 5 is then at index 6, the element that was at index 6 is then at index 7, and so on.

The output is

```
    [93, 70, 57, 97, 9, 20, 84, 12, 97, 65]
    No, 22 is not in randList.
    97 is at index 3
    [93, 70, 57, 97, 9, 60, 20, 12, 97, 65]
    [93, 57, 97, 9, 97, 65]
```

We could not use an enhanced **for** statement to iterate over randList because we needed to remove some of that object's elements, not merely access them.

In the program, randList is declared as a polymorphic reference and then immediately initialized as a reference to an ArrayList object. To re-run the program with a LinkedList object, the only change is the constructor call:

```
List<Integer> randList = new LinkedList<Integer>( );
```

How do the two versions compare? Part of the program—printing the Integer at index 3—is executed more quickly with an ArrayList object because of the random-access ability of the underlying array. And part of it—removing all even Integer elements—is executed more quickly with a LinkedList object. That's because an entry in a linked list can be removed by adjusting links: no movement of elements is needed. In general, there is no implementation of the List interface that is "best" for all applications.

## 4.2.5 The Set Interface

The Set interface extends the Collection interface by prohibiting duplicate elements. Practically speaking, this is not much of an extension, because the Set interface has the exact same 15 methods and method headings that the Collection interface has. As we did with the List interface, we can view the Set interface as defining an abstract data type, one that corresponds to the mathematical concept of a set.

The Set interface is partially implemented by the abstract class AbstractSet, which is extended by the TreeSet and HashSet classes. Figure 4.7 is the Set analogue of Figure 4.6.

**Figure 4.7** | Part of the Java Collections Framework hierarchy dealing with the Set interface.

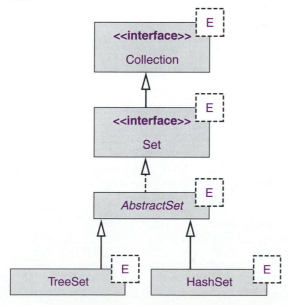

Figures 4.6 and 4.7 are intended to show you a little of the framework hierarchy. In fact, there are quite a few more details, even for these sections. For example, AbstractSet extends AbstractCollection, which provides a skeletal implementation of the Collection class, for methods in which the presence or absence of duplicates is irrelevant. Also, TreeSet implements the SortedSet interface, which extends Set by requiring that any iteration access the elements in "sorted" order.

A TreeSet object uses a sophisticated structure—a red-black tree—to store the elements in order, and for insertions, removals, or accesses, worstTime($n$) is logarithmic in $n$. A HashSet object uses an equally sophisticated structure—a hash table—to store the elements so when they are inserted, removed, or accessed, averageTime($n$) is constant!

The following main method is similar to the one in Section 4.2.4:

```java
public static void main (String[ ] args)
{
        final int SEED = 111;

        Set<Integer> randSet = new TreeSet<Integer>( );

        Random r = new Random (SEED);

        // Add 10 random integers, in the range 0. . .99, to randSet:
        int i = 0;
        while (i < 10)
                if (randSet.add (r.nextInt (100)))
                        i++;

        // Print out randSet:
        System.out.println (randSet);

        // See if 22 is in randSet:
        if (randSet.contains (22))
                System.out.println ("Yes, 22 is in randSet.");
        else
                System.out.println ("No, 22 is not in randSet.");

        // Print out randSet:
        System.out.println (randSet);

        // Remove all even Integers:
        Iterator<Integer> itr = randSet.iterator( );
        while (itr.hasNext( ))
                if (itr.next( ) % 2 == 0)
                        itr.remove( );

        // Print out randSet;
        System.out.println (randSet);
} // method main
```

This main method does not include the list-related methods that are in the main method in Section 4.2.4. And, because duplicates are not allowed, adding 10 random

Integer objects entails more than simply looping 10 times. Instead, i is initialized to 0 and a **while** loop continues until i = 10. The add method returns **false** if the element to be added is already in randSet, and in that case i is not incremented. The output is:

    [9, 12, 20, 57, 60, 65, 70, 84, 93, 97]
    No, 22 is not in randSet.
    [9, 12, 20, 57, 60, 65, 70, 84, 93, 97]
    [9, 57, 65, 93, 97]

Because randSet is a TreeSet object, the elements in randSet are printed in increasing order. Changing randSet to a HashSet object is easy:

    Set<Integer> randSet = **new** HashSet<Integer>( );

The output is then

    [9, 65, 97, 70, 60, 84, 20, 57, 93, 12]
    No, 22 is not in randSet.
    [9, 65, 97, 70, 60, 84, 20, 57, 93, 12]
    [9, 65, 97, 57, 93]

The contents of randSet do not appear to be in any discernible order. We will explain how hashSet objects are ordered in Chapter 14.

## 4.2.6 The Map Interface

A *map* is a collection[2] in which each element has two parts: a unique *key* part and a *value* part. The idea behind this definition is that there is a "mapping" from each key to the corresponding value. For example, we could have a map of social security numbers and names. The keys will be social security numbers and the values will be names. The social security numbers are unique: no two elements in the collection are allowed to have the same social security number. But two elements may have the same name. For example, we could have the following map, in which all of the social security numbers are unique, but two elements have the same name:

    123-45-6789 Builder, Jay
    222-22-2222 Johnson, Alan
    555-55-5555 Nguyen, Viet
    666-66-6666 Chandramouli, Soumya
    888-88-8888 Kalsi, Navdeep
    999-99-9999 Johnson, Alan

The Java Collections Framework has a Map interface that provides method headings for the abstract-data-type map. The Map interface does not extend the Collection interface because many Map methods are oriented toward the key-value relationship.

---

[2] Recall, from Section 4.1, that a *collection* is an object that is composed of elements. A collection is not necessarily a Collection object, that is, a collection need not implement the Collection interface. For example, an array is a collection but not a Collection object.

In fact, the type parameters are K (for the key class) and V (for the value class). As Figure 4.8 indicates, the Map hierarchy is quite similar to both the List and Set hierarchies: Map is partially implemented by AbstractMap, which is extended by the TreeMap and HashMap classes.

The Map interface has some standard methods such as size, equals, and clear. And the AbstractMap class defines toString. Here are specifications for two other methods in the Map interface:

**1.**    /**
    * Associates a specified key with a specified value in this Map object.
    *
    * @param key – the key with which the specified value is to be associated.
    * @param value – the value to be associated with the specified key.
    *
    * @return previous value associated with specified key, or null if there was
    *       no mapping for specified key (note that null could also be the
    *       previous value associated with the specified key).
    *
    */
**public** V put (K key, V value)

*Note:* The put method is somewhat more versatile than a typical add method would be because the put method handles replacement—of the value associated with a given key—as well as insertion of a new key-value pair.

**2.**    /**
    * Removes the mapping with a specified key from this Map object, if there
    * was such a mapping.
    *
    * @param key – the specified key whose mapping, if present, is to be

**Figure 4.8 I** Part of the Java Collections Framework hierarchy dealing with the List interface.

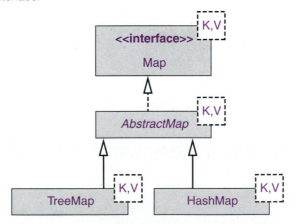

```
*          removed from this Map object.
*
*  @return the value to which the specified key is mapped, if there is such
*          a mapping; otherwise, return null.
*
*/
public V remove (Object key)
```

The following main method illustrates the creation and manipulation of a TreeMap object in which each element has a String key and a Double value:

```
public static void main (String[ ] args)
{
        Map<String, Double> students = new TreeMap<String, Double>( );

        students.put ("Bogan, James", 3.85);
        students.put ("Zawada, Matt", 3.95);
        students.put ("Balan, Tavi", 4.00);
        students.put ("Nikolic, Lazar", 3.85);

        System.out.println (students);

        System.out.println (students.remove ("Brown, Robert"));
        System.out.println (students.remove ("Zawada, Matt"));
        System.out.println (students.containsKey ("Tavi Balan"));
        System.out.println (students.containsKey ("Balan, Tavi"));
        System.out.println (students.containsValue (3.85));

        System.out.println (students);
} // method main
```

Just as with a TreeSet object, a TreeMap object is based on a red-black tree, and so the elements are stored in order of keys. The output from the program is

```
{Balan, Tavi=4.0, Bogan, James=3.85, Nikolic, Lazar=3.85, Zawada, Matt=3.95}
null
3.95
false
true
true
{Balan, Tavi=4.0, Bogan, James=3.85, Nikolic, Lazar=3.85}
```

We can easily make students an instance of a HashMap object:

```
Map<String, Double> students = new HashMap<String, Double>( );
```

The output is the same as above except students is no longer in order by keys:

```
{Nikolic, Lazar=3.85, Zawada, Matt=3.95, Bogan, James=3.85, Balan, Tavi=4.0}
null
3.95
false
```

true
true
{Nikolic, Lazar=3.85, Bogan, James=3.85, Balan, Tavi=4.0}

The great mystery of HashMap and HashSet objects, solved in Chapter 14, is the actual order the elements are stored in.

There is no iterator method for Map objects because there are three different kinds of iteration: over the keys, over the values, and over the key-value pairs. In Chapter 12 you will learn how to create iterators for each of those three options.

A TreeMap should be used instead of a TreeSet (and a HashMap instead of a HashSet) when each element can be decomposed into a key part and a value part, and the key-value relationship is important for the application.

## SUMMARY

A *collection* is an object that is composed of elements. The elements may be stored *contiguously*, that is, at consecutive locations in memory. Another option is a *linked* structure, in which each element is stored in a special object called an *entry* that also includes a reference to another entry.

A *collection class* is a class of which each instance is a collection. The Java Collections Framework, part of the package java.util, includes a number of collection classes that have wide applicability, including ArrayList, LinkedList, TreeMap, TreeSet, HashMap, and HashSet. Each of those classes can be *parameterized,* which means that the element class is specified when the collection-class object is created. And for any instance of one of those classes, an iterator can be defined. An *iterator* is an object that allows an instance of a collection class to loop through the elements in that class without violating the Principle of Data Abstraction.

To simplify the programmer's work of inserting elements into an instance of a parameterized class, J2SE 1.5 automatically boxes primitive values into the corresponding wrapper elements. Similarly, wrapper elements retrieved from a parameter-class instance are automatically unboxed into the corresponding primitive value. A further simplification of J2SE 1.5 is the *enhanced* **for** statement, which automates most of the routine code to access each element during an iteration.

The framework consists of two hierarchies, one rooted at Collection and one rooted at Map. The Collection interface consists of 15 method specifications for accessing and manipulating a Collection object. The Collection hierarchy is extended by the List and Set hierarchies.

The List interface adds several index-related methods to the Collection interface. The List interface is partially implemented by the AbstractList class, and fully implemented by the ArrayList and LinkedList classes.

The Set interface refines the Collection interface by allowing no duplicate elements. The Set interface is partially implemented by the AbstractSet class, and fully implemented in the TreeSet and HashSet classes.

A *map* is a collection in which each element has two parts: a unique *key* part and a *value* part. The Java Collections Framework's map hierarchy is rooted at the

Map interface, partially implemented in the AbstractMap class, and fully implemented in the TreeMap and HashMap classes.

## CONCEPT EXERCISES

**4.1**   What is a collection? What is a collection class? What is a Collection class? Give an example of a collection that is not an instance of a collection class. Programming Project 4.1 has an example of a collection class that is not a Collection class.

**4.2**   An array is a collection, even though there is no array class. But an array of objects can be converted into an instance of the ArrayList class. Look in the file Arrays.java in the package java.util to determine the generic algorithm (that is, static method) that converts an array of objects into an ArrayList of those objects. How can that ArrayList then be printed without a loop?

**4.3**   **a.**   Identify each of the following as either an interface or a class:

   Collection
   LinkedList
   Iterator
   AbstractSet
   Map

   **b.**   What is the difference between an interface and an abstract class?

   **c.**   Of what value is an abstract class? That is, to what extent can an abstract class make a programmer more productive?

**4.4**   Suppose that rateSet is a Set object of Double elements. Write the code to print each element in rateSet whose value is greater than 0.5.

**4.5**   What is a list? What is a set? What is a map?

## PROGRAMMING EXERCISES

**4.1**   For each of the following, create and initialize a parameterized instance, add two elements to the instance, and then print out the instance:

   **a.**   An ArrayList object, scoreList, of Integer elements.

   **b.**   A LinkedList object, salaryList, of Double elements.

   **c.**   A TreeSet object, wordSet, of String elements.

   **d.**   A HashSet object, employeeSet of FullTimeEmployee elements.

   **e.**   A TreeMap object, studentMap, with name keys and grade-point average values.

   **f.**   A HashMap object, tripMap, with flight-number keys and mileage values.

**4.2**   Develop a main method in which two ArrayList objects are created, one with String elements and one with Integer elements. For each list, add three elements to the list, remove the element at index 1, add an element at index 0, and print out the list.

**4.3**   Find an ArrayList method, other than a constructor, that is not also a method in the LinkedList class. Find a LinkedList method, other than a constructor, that is not also a method in the ArrayList class.

**4.4**   Suppose we have the following:

```
LinkedList<String> team = new LinkedList<String> ( );
team.add ("Garcia");
Iterator<String> itr = team.iterator( );
Integer player = itr.next ( );
```

What error message will be generated? When (at compile-time or at run-time)? Test your hypotheses.

**4.5**   Use the ArrayList class three times. First, create an ArrayList object, team1, with elements of type String. Add three elements to team1. Second, create team2, another ArrayList object with elements of type String. Add four elements to team2. Finally, create an ArrayList object, league, whose elements are ArrayList objects in which each element is of type team<String>. Add team1 and team2 to league.

**4.6**   Hypothesize the output from the following main method, and then test your hypothesis by building and running a project with that main method. Explain the result (that is, the output).

```
import java.util.*;

public static void main (String[ ] args)
{
        TreeSet<String> wordSet = new TreeSet<String>( );
        wordSet.add ("super");
        wordSet.add ("swell");
        wordSet.add ("swellegant");
        wordSet.add ("super");

        Iterator<String> itr = wordSet.iterator( );
        for (int i = 0; i < 4; i++)
                System.out.println (itr.next( ));
} // main
```

## Programming Project 4.1

### Wear a Developer's Hat and a User's Hat

In this project, you will get to be a developer of a parameterized class, and then become a user of that class. To start with, here are method specifications for the parameterized class, Sequence, with E the type parameter:

```
/**
 * Initializes this Sequence object to be empty, with an initial capacity of 10
 * elements.
 *
 */
public Sequence( )

/**
 * Initializes this Sequence object to be empty, with a specified initial
 * capacity.
 *
 * @param capacity – the initial capacity of this Sequence object.
 *
 * @throw IllegalArgumentException – if capacity is non-positive.
 *
 */
public Sequence (int n)

/**
 * Returns the number of elements in this Sequence object.
 *
 * @return the number of elements in this Sequence object.
 *
 */
public int size( )

/**
 * Appends a specified element to this Sequence object.
 * The worstTime(n) is O(n), where n is the number of
 * elements in this Sequence object, and averageTime(n) is constant.
 *
 * @param element – the element to be inserted at the end of this
 *          Sequence object.
 *
 */
public void append (E element)
```

*(continued on next page)*

*(continued from previous page)*

```
/**
 * Returns the element at a specified index in this Sequence object.
 * The worstTime(n) is constant, where n is the number of elements in this
 * Sequence object.
 *
 * @param k – the index of the element returned.
 *
 * @return the element at index k in this Sequence object.
 *
 * @throws IndexOutOfBoundsException – if k is either negative or less
 *               than or equal to the number of elements in this
 *               Sequence object.
 *
 */
public E get (int k)

/**
 * Changes the element at a specified index in this Sequence object.
 * The worstTime(n) is constant, where n is the number of elements in this
 * Sequence object.
 *
 * @param k – the index of the element returned.
 * @param newElement – the element to replace the element at index k in
 *               this Sequence object.
 *
 * @throws IndexOutOfBoundsException – if k is either negative or less
 *               than or equal to the number of elements in this
 *               Sequence object.
 *
 */
public void set (int k, E newElement)
```

## Part 1

Define the methods in the Sequence class. *Hint:* Use the following fields:

**protected** E [ ] data;
**protected int** size;   // the number of elements in the Sequence, not the
                          // capacity of the data array

*Note 1:* For the append method, if the data array is currently full, its capacity must be increased before the new element can be appended. See Programming Exercise 2.10 to see how to accomplish the expansion.

*Note 2:* For methods that may throw an exception, do not include **catch** blocks. Instead, the exception will be propagated, so the handling can be customized for the application.

**Part 2**

Create a driver to test your Sequence class. Create an input file that includes all methods, and throws all exceptions listed in Part 1.

# Recursion

One of the skills that distinguish a novice programmer from an experienced one is an understanding of recursion. The goal of this chapter is to give you a feel for situations in which a recursive method is appropriate. Along the way you may start to see the power and elegance of recursion, as well as its potential for misuse. Recursion plays a minor role in the Java Collections Framework: two of the sort methods are recursive, and there are several recursive methods in the TreeMap class. But the value of recursion extends far beyond these methods. For example, one of the applications of the PureStack class in Chapter 8 is the translation of recursive methods into machine code. The sooner you are exposed to recursion, the more likely you will be able to spot situations where it is appropriate—and to use it! ■

## CHAPTER OBJECTIVES

1. Recognize the characteristics of those problems for which recursive solutions may be appropriate.

2. Compare recursive and iterative methods with respect to time, space, and ease of development.

3. Trace the execution of a recursive method with the help of execution frames.

4. Understand the backtracking design pattern.

## 5.1 | INTRODUCTION

Roughly, a method is **recursive** if it contains a call to itself.[1] From this description, you may initially fear that the execution of a recursive method will lead to an infinite sequence of recursive calls. But under normal circumstances, this calamity does not occur, and the sequence of calls eventually stops. To show you how recursive methods terminate, here is the skeleton of a typical recursive method:

> **if** (simplest case)
>> solve directly
>
> **else**
>> make a recursive call with a simpler case

This outline suggests that recursion should be considered whenever the problem to be solved has these two characteristics:

1.  Complex cases of the problem can be reduced to simpler cases of the same form as the original problem.
2.  The simplest case(s) can be solved directly.

Incidentally, if you are familiar with the Principle of Mathematical Induction, you may have observed that these two characteristics correspond to the inductive case and base case, respectively. In case you are not familiar with that principle, Appendix 2 has a section on mathematical induction.

As we work through the following examples, do not be inhibited by old ways of thinking. As each problem is stated, try to frame a solution in terms of a simpler problem of the same form. Think recursively!

## 5.2 | FACTORIALS

Given a positive integer $n$, the **factorial** of $n$, written $n!$, is the product of all integers between $n$ and 1, inclusive. For example,

$$4! = 4 \cdot 3 \cdot 2 \cdot 1 = 24$$

and

$$6! = 6 \cdot 5 \cdot 4 \cdot 3 \cdot 2 \cdot 1 = 720$$

Another way to calculate 4! is as follows:

$$4! = 4 \cdot 3!$$

This formulation is not helpful unless we know what 3! is. But we can continue to calculate factorials in terms of smaller factorials (Aha!):

$$3! = 3 \cdot 2!$$
$$2! = 2 \cdot 1!$$

---

[1] A formal definition of "recursive" is given later in this chapter.

Note that 1! can be calculated directly; its value is 1. Now we work backwards to calculate 4!:

$$2! = 2 \cdot 1! = 2 \cdot 1 = 2$$
$$3! = 3 \cdot 2! = 3 \cdot 2 = 6$$

Finally, we get

$$4! = 4 \cdot 3! = 4 \cdot 6 = 24$$

For $n > 1$, we reduce the problem of calculating $n!$ to the problem of calculating $(n - 1)!$ We stop reducing when we get to 1!, which is simply 1. For the sake of completeness,[2] we define 0! to be 1. These observations lead to the following factorial method. The method is defined as a class method. Note that a class method has a **static** modifier in its heading (see Section 2.1). Why is factorial a class method? All the information needed by the method is provided by the parameter, and the only effect of a call to the method is the value returned. So a calling object would neither affect nor be affected by an invocation of the method.

```
/**
 * Calculates the factorial of a nonnegative integer, that is, the product of all
 * integers between 1 and the given integer, inclusive. The worstTime(n) is O(n),
 * where n is the given integer.
 *
 * @param n the nonnegative integer whose factorial is calculated.
 *
 * @return the factorial of n
 *
 * @throws IllegalArgumentException if n is less than 0.
 *
 */
public static long factorial (int n)
{
       if (n < 0)
              throw new IllegalArgumentException( );
       if (n <= 1)
              return 1;
       return n * factorial (n - 1);
} // method factorial
```

A driver for this function, and all recursive functions in this chapter, is available on the book's website.

Within the method factorial, there is a call to the method factorial, and so factorial is a recursive method. The parameter n has its value reduced by 1 with each recursive

---

[2] The calculation of 0! occurs in the study of probability: The number of combinations of $n$ things taken $k$ at a time is calculated as $n!/(k!(n - k)!)$. When $n = k$, we get $n!/(n! \cdot 0!)$, which has the value 1 because $0! = 1$. And note that 1 is the number of combinations of $n$ things taken $n$ at a time.

call. But after the final call with n = 1, the previous values of n are needed for the multiplications. For example, when n = 4, the calculation of n * factorial (n − 1) is postponed until the call to factorial (n − 1) is completed. When this finally happens and the value 6 [that is, factorial (3)] is returned, the value of 4 for n must be available to calculate the product.

Somehow, the value of n must be saved when the call to factorial (n − 1) is made. That value must be restored after the call to factorial (n − 1) is completed so that the value of n * factorial (n − 1) can be calculated. The beauty of recursion is that the programmer need not explicitly handle these savings and restorings; the compiler and computer do the work.

Notice that an exception is thrown if the argument's value is negative. This illustrates the robustness advocated in Chapter 1. Otherwise, the value returned for any negative argument would be incorrect, namely 1.

### 5.2.1 Execution Frames

The trace of a recursive method can be illustrated through *execution frames:* boxes that contain information related to each invocation of the method. Each execution frame includes the values of parameters and other local variables. Each frame also has the relevant part of the recursive method's code—especially the recursive calls, with values for the arguments. When a recursive call is made, a new execution frame will be constructed on top of the current one; this new frame is destroyed when the call that caused its creation has been completed. A check mark indicates either the statement being executed in the current frame or the statement, in a previous frame, whose recursive call created (immediately or eventually) the current frame.

At any time, the top frame contains information relevant to the current execution of the recursive method. For example, here is a step-by-step, execution-frame trace of the factorial method after an initial call of factorial (4):

| Step 0: | n = 4<br>✓ **return** 4 * factorial (3); | Frame 0 |
|---|---|---|
| Step 1: | n = 3<br>✓ **return** 3 * factorial (2); | Frame 1 |
| | n = 4<br>✓ **return** 4 * factorial (3); | Frame 0 |
| Step 2: | n = 2<br>✓ **return** 2 * factorial (1); | Frame 2 |
| | n = 3<br>✓ **return** 3 * factorial (2); | Frame 1 |
| | n = 4<br>✓ **return** 4 * factorial (3); | Frame 0 |

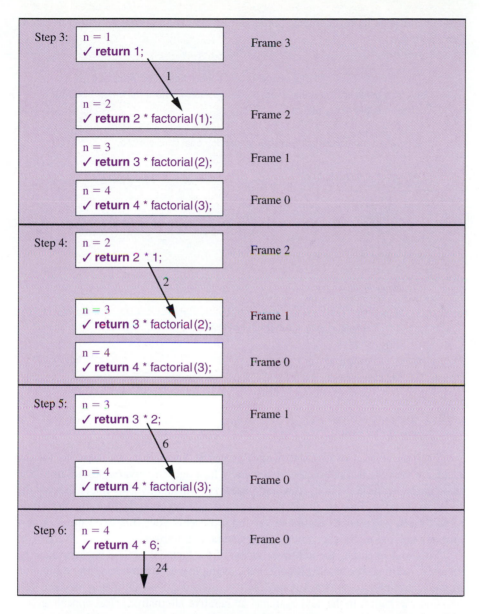

The analysis of the factorial method is fairly clear-cut. The execution-time requirements correspond to the number of recursive calls. For any argument n, there will be exactly n − 1 recursive calls. During each recursive call, the **if** statement will be executed in constant time, so worstTime($n$) is linear in $n$. Recursive methods often have an additional cost in terms of memory requirements. For example, when each recursive call to factorial is made, the return address and a copy of the argument are saved. So worstSpace($n$) is also linear in $n$.

Recursion can often make it easier for us to solve problems, but **any problem that can be solved recursively can also be solved iteratively.** An *iterative* method is one that uses a loop statement. For example, here is an iterative method to calculate factorials:

```
/**
 * Calculates the factorial of a nonnegative integer, that is, the product of all
 * integers between 1 and the given integer, inclusive. The worstTime(n) is O(n),
 * where n is the given integer.
 *
 * @param n the nonnegative integer whose factorial is calculated.
 *
 * @return the factorial of n
 *
 * @throws IllegalArgumentException if n is less than 0.
 *
 */
public static long factorial (int n)
{
        int product = n;

        if (n < 0)
                throw new IllegalArgumentException( );
        if (n == 0)
                return 1;
        for (int i = n−1; i > 1; i—)
                product = product * i;

        return product;
} // method factorial
```

For this version of factorial, worstTime(*n*) is linear in *n*, the same as for the recursive version. But no matter what value n has, only three variables are used in a trace of the iterative version, so worstSpace(*n*) is constant, versus linear in *n* for the recursive version. Finally, the iterative version follows directly from the definition of factorials, whereas the recursive version represents your first exposure to a new problem-solving technique, and that takes some extra effort.

So in this example, the iterative version of the factorial method is better than the recursive version. The whole purpose of the example was to provide a simple situation in which recursion was worth considering, even though we ultimately decided that iteration was better. In the next example, an iterative alternative is less appealing.

## 5.3 | DECIMAL TO BINARY

Humans count in base 10, possibly because we were born with 10 fingers. Computers count in base 2 because of the binary nature of electronics. One of the tasks a computer performs is to convert from decimal (base 10) to binary (base 2). Let's develop a method to solve a simplified version of this problem:

Given a nonnegative integer $n$, determine its binary equivalent.

For example, if $n$ is 25, the binary equivalent is $11001 = 1 \cdot 2^4 + 1 \cdot 2^3 + 0 \cdot 2^2 + 0 \cdot 2^1 + 1 \cdot 2^0$. For a large **int** value such as one billion, the binary equivalent will have about 30 bits: too big for an **int** or even a **long**. So we will store the binary equivalent in a String object. The method specification is:

```
/**
 *
 * Determines the binary equivalent of a nonnegative integer. The worstTime(n)
 * is O(log n), where n is the given nonnegative integer.
 *
 * @param n the nonnegative integer, in decimal notation.
 *
 * @return a String representation of the binary equivalent of n.
 *
 * @throws IllegalArgumentException if n is negative.
 */
public static String getBinary (int n)
```

There are several approaches to solving this problem. One of them is based on the following observation:

The rightmost bit has the value of $n \% 2$; the other bits are the binary equivalent of $n/2$. (Aha!)

For example, if $n$ is 12, the rightmost bit in the binary equivalent of $n$ is 12 % 2, namely, 0; the remaining bits are the binary equivalent of 12/2, that is, the binary equivalent of 6. So we can obtain all the bits as follows:

When the quotient is 1, the binary equivalent is simply 1. We concatenate (that is, join together) these bits from the bottom up, so that the rightmost bit will be joined last. The result would then be

1100

The following table graphically illustrates the effect of calling getBinary (12):

| n | n/2 | n % 2 | Output |
|---|-----|-------|--------|
| 12 | 6 | 0 | |
| 6 | 3 | 0 | |
| 3 | 1 | 1 | |
| 1 | | | |
| | | | 1 |
| | | | 1 |
| | | | 0 |
| | | | 0 |

This discussion suggests that we must perform all of the calculations before we return the result. Speaking recursively, we need to calculate the binary equivalent of *n/2 before* we append the value of *n % 2*. In other words, we need to append the result of *n % 2* to the result of the recursive call.

We will stop when *n* is 1 or 0, and 0 will occur only if *n* is initially 0. The method definition is:

```java
public static String getBinary (int n)
{
        if (n < 0)
                throw new IllegalArgumentException( );
        if (n <= 1)
                return Integer.toString (n);
        return getBinary (n / 2) + Integer.toString (n % 2);
} // method getBinary
```

We are assured that the simple case of n <= 1 will eventually be reached because, in each execution of the method, the argument to the recursive call is only half as big as the method parameter's value.

Here is a step-by-step, execution-frame trace of the getBinary method after an initial call of getBinary (12):

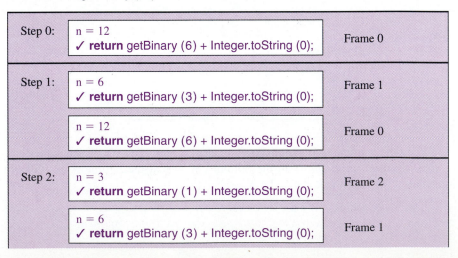

| Step 0: | n = 12<br>✓ **return** getBinary (6) + Integer.toString (0); | Frame 0 |
|---------|------------------------------------------------------------|---------|
| Step 1: | n = 6<br>✓ **return** getBinary (3) + Integer.toString (0); | Frame 1 |
| | n = 12<br>✓ **return** getBinary (6) + Integer.toString (0); | Frame 0 |
| Step 2: | n = 3<br>✓ **return** getBinary (1) + Integer.toString (0); | Frame 2 |
| | n = 6<br>✓ **return** getBinary (3) + Integer.toString (0); | Frame 1 |

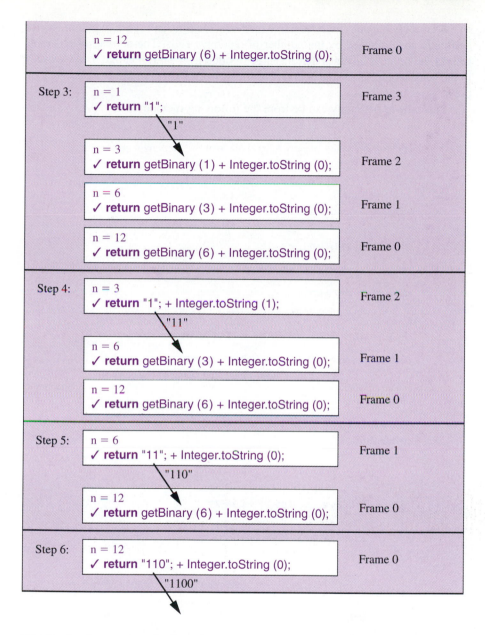

The final value returned is the string:

    1100

And that is the binary equivalent of 12.

As we noted earlier, the order of operands in the String expression of the last return statement in getBinary enables us to postpone the final return until *all* of the bit values have been calculated. If the order had been reversed, the bits would have been returned in reverse order. Recursion is such a powerful tool that the effects of slight changes are magnified.

As usually happens with recursive methods, the time and space requirements for getBinary are estimated by the number of recursive calls. The number of recursive calls is the number of times that $n$ can be divided by 2 until $n$ equals 1. As we saw in the last chapter, this value is floor($\log_2 n$), so worstTime($n$) and worstSpace($n$) are both logarithmic in $n$.

The calls to getBinary can be from the following method:

```java
/**
 *  Reads in nonnegative integers (until sentinel of "−1" reached) and
 *  prints out their binary equivalent.
 *
 */
public void readAndProcessInputs( )
{
       final String SENTINEL = "−1";

       final String SENTINEL_MESSAGE = "\nThe sentinel is " + SENTINEL + ".\n";

       final String PROMPT =
              "\nIn the Input line, please enter a nonnegative base−10 integer: ";

       final String RESULT_MESSAGE = "The binary equivalent is ";

       BufferedReader reader = new BufferedReader
                                     (new InputStreamReader (System.in));

       String line;

       System.out.println (SENTINEL_MESSAGE);
       while (true)
       {
              try
              {
                     System.out.print (PROMPT);
                     line = reader.readLine( );
                     if (line.equals (SENTINEL))
                            break;
                     System.out.println (RESULT_MESSAGE +
                                     getBinary (Integer.parseInt (line)));
              } // try
              catch (IOException e)
              {
                     System.out.println (e);
              } // catch
              catch (IllegalArgumentException e)
              {
                     System.out.println (e);
              }
       } // while
} // method readAndProcessInputs
```

This method will also catch an input error such as "seventeen" or "3.5" because NumberFormatException is a subclass of IllegalArgumentException.

You are invited to develop an iterative version of the getBinary method. (See Programming Exercise 5.1.) After you have completed the iterative method, you will probably agree that it was somewhat harder to develop than the recursive method. This is typical, and probably obvious: recursive solutions usually flow more easily than iterative solutions to those problems for which recursion is appropriate. Recursion is appropriate when larger instances of the problem can be reduced to smaller instances that have the same form as the larger instances.

**Lab 7: Fibonacci Numbers**

You are now prepared to do Lab 7.                    All Labs Are Optional

For the next problem, an iterative solution is *much* harder to develop than a recursive solution.

## 5.4 | TOWERS OF HANOI

In the Towers of Hanoi game, there are three poles, labeled *A*, *B*, and *C*, and several different-size numbered disks, each with a hole in the center. Initially, all of the disks are on pole *A*, with the largest disk on the bottom, then the next largest, and so on. Figure 5.1 shows the initial configuration if we started with four disks, numbered from smallest to largest.

The object of the game is to move all of the disks from pole *A* to pole *B*; pole *C* is used for temporary storage.[3] The rules of the game are:

1. Only one disk may be moved at a time.
2. No disk may ever be placed on top of a smaller disk.
3. Other than the prohibition of rule 2, the top disk on any pole may be moved to either of the other two poles.

**Figure 5.1** | The starting position for the Towers of Hanoi game with four disks.

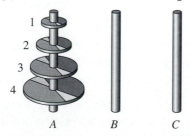

---

[3] In some versions, the goal is to move the disks from pole *A* to pole *C,* with pole *B* used for temporary storage.

**Figure 5.2 |** The game configuration for the Towers of Hanoi just before moving disk 4 from pole *A* to pole *B*.

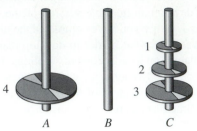

Let's try to play the game with the initial configuration given in Figure 5.1. We are immediately faced with a dilemma: Do we move disk 1 to pole *B* or to pole *C*? If we make the wrong move, we may end up with the four disks on pole *C* rather than on pole *B*.

Instead of trying to figure out where disk 1 should be moved initially, we will focus our attention on disk 4, the bottom disk. Of course, we can't move disk 4 right away, but eventually, disk 4 will have to be moved from pole *A* to pole *B*. By the rules of the game, the configuration just before moving disk 4 must be as shown in Figure 5.2.

Does this observation help us to figure out how to move four disks from *A* to *B*? Well, sort of. We still need to determine how to move three disks (one at a time) from pole *A* to pole *C*. We can then move disk 4 from *A* to *B*. Finally, we will need to determine how to move three disks (one at a time) from *C* to *B*.

The significance of this strategy is that we have reduced the problem from figuring how to move four disks to one of figuring how to move three disks. (Aha!) We still need to determine how to move three disks from one pole to another pole.

But the above strategy can be reapplied! To move three disks from, say, pole *A* to pole *C*, we first move two disks (one at a time) from *A* to *B*, then we move disk 3 from *A* to *C*, and finally, we move two disks from *B* to *C*. Continually reducing the problem, we eventually face the trivial task of moving disk 1 from one pole to another.

There is nothing special about the number 4 in the above approach. For any positive integer *n* we can describe how to move *n* disks from pole *A* to pole *B*: if $n = 1$, we simply move disk 1 from pole *A* to pole *B*. For $n > 1$,

**1.** First, move $n - 1$ disks from pole *A* to pole *C*, using pole *B* as a temporary.

**2.** Then move disk *n* from pole *A* to pole *B*.

**3.** Finally, move $n - 1$ disks from pole *C* to pole *B*, using pole *A* as a temporary.

This does not quite solve the problem because, for example, we have not described how to move $n - 1$ disks from *A* to *C*. But our strategy is easily generalized by replacing the constants *A*, *B*, and *C* with variables *origin*, *destination*, and *temporary*. For example, we will initially have

*origin* = *A*
*destination* = *B*
*temporary* = *C*

Then the general strategy for moving *n* disks from origin to destination is as follows:

If *n* is 1, move disk 1 from origin to destination.

Otherwise,

1. Move *n* − 1 disks (one at a time) from *origin* to *temporary*.
2. Move disk *n* from *origin* to *destination*.
3. Move *n* − 1 disks (one at a time) from *temporary* to *destination*.

The following recursive method incorporates the above strategy for moving *n* disks. If *n* = 1, the String representing the move, namely, "Move disk 1 from " + orig + " to " + dest + "\n" is simply returned. Otherwise, the String object returned consists of three String objects concatenated together, namely,

```
move (n−1, orig, temp, dest)
"Move disk " + n + " from " + orig + " to " + dest + "\n"
move (n−1, temp, dest, orig)
```

When the final return is made, the return value is the complete sequence of moves. This String object can then be printed to the console window, to a GUI window, or to a file.

```
/**
 * Determines the steps needed to move disks from an origin to a destination.
 * The worstTime(n) is O(2^n), where n is the number of disks to be moved.
 *
 * @param n the number of disks to be moved.
 * @param orig the pole where the disks are originally.
 * @param dest the destination pole.
 * @param temp the pole used for temporary storage.
 *
 * @return a String representation of the moves needed.
 *
 * @throws IllegalArgumentException if n is less than or equal to 0.
 */
public static String move (int n, char orig, char dest, char temp)
{
        final String DIRECT_MOVE =
                "Move disk " + n + " from " + orig + " to " + dest + "\n";
        if (n <= 0)
                throw new IllegalArgumentException( );
        if (n == 1)
                return DIRECT_MOVE;
        String result = move (n − 1, orig, temp, dest);
        result += DIRECT_MOVE;
        result += move (n − 1, temp, dest, orig);
        return result;
} // method move
```

It is difficult to trace the execution of this method because the interrelationship of parameter and argument values makes it difficult to keep track of which pole is currently the origin, which is the destination, and which is the temporary. In the following execution frames, the parameter values are the argument values from the call, and the argument values for subsequent calls come from the method code and the current parameter values. For example, suppose the initial call is:

```
move (3, 'A', 'B', 'C');
```

Then the parameter values at step 0 will be those argument values, so we have:

```
n = 3
orig = 'A'
dest = 'B'
temp = 'C'
```

Because n is not equal to 1, the recursive part is executed:

```
String result = move (n − 1, orig, temp, dest);
result += DIRECT_MOVE;
result += move (n − 1, temp, dest, orig) ;
return result;
```

The values of those arguments are obtained from the parameters' values, so the statements are equivalent to:

```
String result = move (2, 'A', 'C', 'B');
result = "Move disk 3 from A to B\n";
result = move (2, 'C', 'B', 'A');
return result;
```

Make sure you understand how to obtain the parameter values and argument values before you try to follow the trace given below.

Here is a step-by-step, execution-frame trace of the move method when the initial call is:

```
move (3, 'A', 'B', 'C');
```

| | Value of result |
|---|---|
| Step 0:  n = 3<br>orig = 'A'<br>dest = 'B'<br>temp = 'C'<br>✓ String result = move (2, 'A', 'C', 'B');<br>    result += "Move disk 3 from A to B\n";<br>    result += move (2, 'C', 'B', 'A');<br>**return** result; | |

Step 1:
```
n = 2
orig = 'A'
dest = 'C'
temp = 'B'
✓  String result = move (1, 'A', 'B', 'C');
   result += "Move disk 2 from A to C\n";
   result += move (1, 'B', 'C', 'A');
return result;
```

```
n = 3
orig = 'A'
dest = 'B'
temp = 'C'
✓  String result = move (2, 'A', 'C', 'B');
   result += "Move disk 3 from A to B\n";
   result += move (2, 'C', 'B', 'A');
return result;
```

Step 2:
```
n = 1
orig = 'A'
dest = 'B'
temp = 'C'
✓  return "Move disk 1 from A to B\n";
```

Move disk 1 from A to B

```
n = 2
orig = 'A'
dest = 'C'
temp = 'B'
✓  String result = move (1, 'A', 'B', 'C');
   result += "Move disk 2 from A to C\n";
   result += move (1, 'B', 'C', 'A');
return result;
```

```
n = 3
orig = 'A'
dest = 'B'
temp = 'C'
✓  String result = move (2, 'A', 'C', 'B');
   result += "Move disk 3 from A to B\n";
   result += move (2, 'C', 'B', 'A');
return result;
```

*continued*

Step 3:

```
n = 2
orig = 'A'
dest = 'C'
temp = 'B'
    String result = move (1, 'A', 'B', 'C');
✓   result += "Move disk 2 from A to C\n";
    result += move (1, 'B', 'C', 'A');
return result;
```

Move disk 1 from A to B
Move disk 2 from A to C

```
n = 3
orig = 'A'
dest = 'B'
temp = 'C'
✓   String result = move (2, 'A', 'C', 'B');
    result += "Move disk 3 from A to B\n";
    result += move (2, 'C', 'B', 'A');
return result;
```

Step 4:

```
n = 2
orig = 'A'
dest = 'C'
temp = 'B'
    String result = move (1, 'A', 'B', 'C');
    result += "Move disk 2 from A to C\n";
✓   result += move (1, 'B', 'C', 'A');
return result;
```

```
n = 3
orig = 'A'
dest = 'B'
temp = 'C'
✓   String result = move (2, 'A', 'C', 'B');
    result += "Move disk 3 from A to B\n";
    result += move (2, 'C', 'B', 'A');
return result;
```

Step 5:

```
n = 1
orig = 'B'
dest = 'C'
temp = 'A'
✓   return "Move disk 1 from B to C\n";
```

```
n = 2
orig = 'A'
dest = 'C'
temp = 'B'
    String result = move (1, 'A', 'B', 'C');
    result += "Move disk 2 from A to C\n";
✓   result += move (1, 'B', 'C', 'A');
return result;
```

Move disk 1 from A to B
Move disk 2 from A to C
Move disk 1 from B to C

n = 3
orig = 'A'
dest = 'B'
temp = 'C'
✓  String result = move (2, 'A', 'C', 'B');
   result += "Move disk 3 from A to B\n";
   result += move (2, 'C', 'B', 'A');
**return** result;

---

Step 6:  n = 3
orig = 'A'
dest = 'B'
temp = 'C'
   String result = move (2, 'A', 'C', 'B');
✓  result += "Move disk 3 from A to B\n";
   result += move (2, 'C', 'B', 'A');
**return** result;

Move disk 1 from A to B
Move disk 2 from A to C
Move disk 1 from B to C
Move disk 3 from A to B

---

Step 7:  n = 3
orig − 'A'
dest = 'B'
temp = 'C'
   String result = move (2, 'A', 'C', 'B');
   result += "Move disk 3 from A to B\n";
✓  result += move (2, 'C', 'B', 'A');
**return** result;

---

Step 8:  n = 2
orig = 'C'
dest = 'B'
temp = 'A'
✓  String result = move (1, 'C', 'A', 'B');
   result += "Move disk 2 from C to B\n";
   result += move (1, 'A', 'B', 'C');
**return** result;

n = 3
orig = 'A'
dest = 'B'
temp = 'C'
   String result = move (2, 'A', 'C', 'B');
   result += "Move disk 3 from A to B\n";
✓  result += move (2, 'C', 'B', 'A');
**return** result;

*continued*

Step 9:

```
n = 1
orig = 'C'
dest = 'A'
temp = 'B'
✓ return "Move disk 1 from C to A\n";
```

Move disk 1 from A to B
Move disk 2 from A to C
Move disk 1 from B to C
Move disk 3 from A to B
Move disk 1 from C to A

```
n = 2
orig = 'C'
dest = 'B'
temp = 'A'
✓ String result = move (1, 'C', 'A', 'B');
  result += "Move disk 2 from C to B\n";
  result += move (1, 'A', 'B', 'C');
return result;
```

```
n = 3
orig = 'A'
dest = 'B'
temp = 'C'
  String result = move (2, 'A', 'C', 'B');
  result += "Move disk 3 from A to B\n";
✓ result += move (2, 'C', 'B', 'A');
return result;
```

Step 10:

```
n = 2
orig = 'C'
dest = 'B'
temp = 'A'
  String result = move (1, 'C', 'A', 'B');
✓ result += "Move disk 2 from C to B\n";
  result += move (1, 'A', 'B', 'C');
return result;
```

Move disk 1 from A to B
Move disk 2 from A to C
Move disk 1 from B to C
Move disk 3 from A to B
Move disk 1 from C to A
Move disk 2 from C to B

```
n = 3
orig = 'A'
dest = 'B'
temp = 'C'
  String result = move (2, 'A', 'C', 'B');
  result += "Move disk 3 from A to B\n";
✓ result += move (2, 'C', 'B', 'A');
return result;
```

Step 11:

```
n = 2
orig = 'C'
dest = 'B'
temp = 'A'
  String result = move (1, 'C', 'A', 'B');
  result += "Move disk 2 from C to B\n";
✓ result += move (1, 'A', 'B', 'C');
return result;
```

```
n = 3
orig = 'A'
dest = 'B'
temp = 'C'
    String result = move (2, 'A', 'C', 'B');
    result += "Move disk 3 from A to B\n";
✓   result += move (2, 'C', 'B', 'A');
return result;
```

Step 12:
```
n = 1
orig = 'A'
dest = 'B'
temp = 'C'
✓  "Move disk 1 from A to B\n";
```

```
n = 2
orig = 'C'
dest = 'B'
temp = 'A'
    String result = move (1, 'C', 'A', 'B');
    result += "Move disk 2 from C to B\n";
✓   result += move (1, 'A', 'B', 'C');
return result;
```

Move disk 1 from A to B
Move disk 2 from A to C
Move disk 1 from B to C
Move disk 3 from A to B
Move disk 1 from C to A
Move disk 2 from C to B
Move disk 1 from A to B

```
n = 3
orig = 'A'
dest = 'B'
temp = 'C'
    String result = move (2, 'A', 'C', 'B');
    result += "Move disk 3 from A to B\n";
✓   result += move (2, 'C', 'B', 'A');
return result;
```

Notice the disparity between the relative ease in developing the recursive method and the relative difficulty in tracing its execution. Imagine what it would be like to trace the execution of move (15,'A','B','C')! Fortunately, you need not undergo such torture. Computers handle this type of tedious detail very well. You "merely" develop the correct program and the computer handles the execution. For the move method—as well as for the other recursive methods in this chapter—you can actually *prove* the correctness of the method. See Concept Exercise 5.5.

The significance of ensuring the precondition is illustrated in the move method. For example, let's see what would happen if no exception were thrown and a user called move with 0 as the first argument. Since n would have the value 0, the **else** part would be executed, including a call to move (−1, ...). Within that call, n would still be unequal to 1, so there would be a call to move (−2, ...) then to move (−3, ...), move (−4, ...), move (−5, ...), and so on. Eventually, saving all those copies of n would overflow an area of memory called the *stack*. This phenomenon is known as *infinite recursion.* A StackOverflowError—not an exception—is generated, and the execution of the project terminates. In general, infinite recursion is avoided if each recursive call makes progress toward a "simplest" case. And, just to be on the safe side, the method should throw an exception if the precondition is violated.

A recursive method does not explicitly describe the considerable detail involved in its execution. For this reason, recursion is sometimes referred to as "the lazy programmer's problem-solving tool." If you want to appreciate the value of recursion, try to develop an iterative version of the move method. Programming Project 5.1 provides some hints.

### 5.4.1  **Analysis of the** move **Method**

What about worstTime($n$)? In determining the time requirements of a recursive method, the number of calls to the method is of paramount importance. To get an idea of the number of calls to the move method, look at the tree in Figure 5.3.

As illustrated in Figure 5.3, the first call to the move method has n as the first argument. During that call, two recursive calls to the move method are made, and each of those two calls has n − 1 as the first argument. From each of those calls, we get two more calls to move, and each of those four calls has n − 2 as the first argument. This process continues until, finally, we get calls with 1 as the first argument.

To calculate the total number of calls to the move method, we augment the tree in Figure 5.3 by identifying levels in the tree, starting with level 0 at the top, and include the number of calls at each level. At level 0, the number of calls is 1 ($= 2^0$). At level 1, the number of calls is 2 ($= 2^1$). In general, at level $k$ there are $2^k$ calls to the move method. Because there are $n$ levels in the tree and the top is level 0, the bottom must be level $n − 1$, where there are $2^{n-1}$ calls to the move method. See Figure 5.4.

From Figure 5.4, we see that the total number of calls to the move method is

$$2^0 + 2^1 + 2^2 + 2^3 + \cdots + 2^{n-1} = \sum_{k=0}^{n-1} 2^k$$

By Example 6 in Appendix 2, this sum is equal to $2^n − 1$. That is, the number of calls to the move method is $2^n − 1$. We conclude that, for the move method,

**Figure 5.3** ❙ A schematic of the number of calls to the move method.

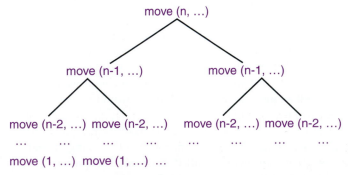

**Figure 5.4** I The relationship between level and number of calls to the move method in the tree from Figure 5.3.

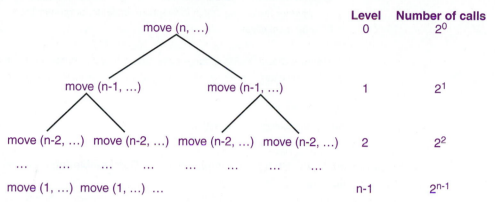

| | Level | Number of calls |
|---|---|---|
| move (n, ...) | 0 | $2^0$ |
| move (n-1, ...)  move (n-1, ...) | 1 | $2^1$ |
| move (n-2, ...)  move (n-2, ...)  move (n-2, ...)  move (n-2, ...) | 2 | $2^2$ |
| move (1, ...)  move (1, ...)  ... | n-1 | $2^{n-1}$ |

worstTime($n$) is exponential in $n$; specifically, worstTime($n$) is $\Theta(2^n)$. In fact, since *any* definition of the move method must return a string that has $2^n - 1$ lines, the Towers of Hanoi problem is intractable. That is, *any* solution to the Towers of Hanoi problem must take exponential time.

The memory requirements for move are modest because, although space is allocated when move is called, that space is deallocated when the call is completed. So the amount of additional memory needed for move depends, not simply on the number of calls to move, but on the maximum number of started-but-not-completed calls. We can determine this number from the execution frames. Each time a recursive call is made, another frame is constructed, and each time a return is made, that frame is destroyed. For example, if n = 3 in the original call to move, then the maximum number of execution frames is 3. In general, the maximum number of execution frames is n. So worstSpace($n$) is linear in $n$.

We now turn our attention to a widely known search technique: binary search. We will develop a recursive method to perform a binary search on an array. Lab 9 deals with the development of an iterative version of a binary search.

## 5.5 I SEARCHING AN ARRAY

Suppose you want to search an array for an element. We assume that the element class implements the Comparable interface (in java.lang):

```
public interface Comparable
{
      /**
       * Returns an int less than, equal to or greater than 0, depending on
       * whether the calling object is less than, equal to or greater than a
       * specified object.
       *
       * @param obj – the specified object that the calling object is compared to.
```

```
          *
          * @return an int value less than, equal to, or greater than 0, depending on
          *       whether the calling object is less than, equal to, or greater than
          *       obj, respectively.
          *
          * @throws ClassCastException – if the calling object and obj are not in the
          *       same class.
          *
          */
         public int compareTo(Object obj)
} // interface Comparable
```

For example, the String class implements the Comparable interface, so we can write the following:

```
String s = "elegy";

System.out.println (s.compareTo ("elapsed"));
```

The output will be greater than 0 because "elegy" is lexicographically greater than "elapsed"; in other words, "elegy" comes after "elapsed" according to the Unicode values of the characters in those two strings.

The simplest way to conduct the search is sequentially: start at the first location, and keep checking successively higher locations until either the element is found or you reach the end of the array. This search strategy, known as a *sequential search,* is the basis for the following generic algorithm (that is, static method):

```
/**
 * Determines whether an array contains an element equal to a given key.
 * The worstTime(n) is O(n), where n is the array length.
 *
 * @param a the array to be searched.
 * @param key the element searched for in the array a.
 *
 * @return the index of an element in a that is equal to key, if such an element
 *       exists; otherwise, −1.
 *
 * @throws ClassCastException, if the element class does not implement the
 *       Comparable interface.
 *
 */
public static int sequentialSearch (Object[ ] a, Object key)
{
        for (int i = 0; i < a.length; i++)
                if (((Comparable)) a [i].compareTo (key) == 0)
                        return i;
        return −1;
} // sequentialSearch
```

The sequentialSearch method is not currently included in the Java Collections Framework. But it is the basis for many of the method definitions in the ArrayList and LinkedList classes, which are in the framework.

For an unsuccessful sequential search of an array, the entire array must be scanned. So both worstTime($n$) and averageTime($n$) are linear in $n$ for an unsuccessful search. For a successful sequential search, the entire array must be scanned in the worst case. In the average case, assuming each location is equally likely to house the element sought, we probe about $n/2$ elements. We conclude that for a successful search, both worstTime($n$) and averageTime($n$) are also linear in $n$.

Can we improve on these times? Definitely! In this section we will develop an array-based search technique for which worstTime($n$) and averageTime($n$) are only logarithmic in $n$. And in Chapter 14, we will encounter a powerful search technique—hashing—for which averageTime($n$) is constant—but worstTime($n$) is still linear in $n$.

Given an array to be searched and a value to be searched for, we will develop a **binary search,** so called because the region searched is divided by two at each stage until the search is completed. Initially, the first index in the region is index 0, and the last index is at the end of the array. One important restriction is this: *A binary search requires that the array be sorted.*

The basic strategy is this: we compare the element at the middle index of the array to the key sought. If the middle element is less than the key, we recursively search the array from the middle index +1 to index last. If the middle element is greater than the key, we recursively search the array from index first to the middle index −1. If the middle element is equal to the key, we are done.

We assume, as above, that the array's element class implements the Comparable interface.

Our method will have four parameters:

1. a, the array being searched
2. first, the smallest index in the region of the array now being searched
3. last, the largest index in the region of the array now being searched
4. key, a reference to the object being sought

Here is the method specification, almost identical to one in the Arrays class in java.util:

```
/**
 * Searches the specified array for the specified object using the binary
 * search algorithm. The array must be sorted into ascending order
 * according to the <i>natural ordering</i> of its elements (as by
 * <tt>Sort(Object[ ]</tt>), above) prior to making this call. If it is
 * not sorted, the results are undefined. If the array contains multiple
 * elements equal to the specified object, there is no guarantee which
 * one will be found. The worstTime(n) is O(log n).
 *
 * @param a the array to be searched.
 * @param first the smallest index in the region of the array now being searched.
```

```
    * @param last the largest index in the region of the array now being searched.
    * @param key the value to be searched for.
    *
    * @return index of the search key, if it is contained in the array;
    *     otherwise, <tt>(−(<i>insertion point</i>) − 1)</tt>. The
    *     <i>insertion point</i> is defined as the point at which the
    *     key would be inserted into the array: the index of the first
    *     element greater than the key, or <tt>a.length</tt>, if all
    *     elements in the array are less than the specified key. Note
    *     that this guarantees that the return value will be &gt;= 0 if
    *     and only if the key is found.
    *
    * @throws ClassCastException if the array contains elements that are not
    *     <i>mutually comparable</i> (for example, strings and integers),
    *     or the search key is not mutually comparable with the elements
    *     of the array.
    * @see Comparable
    * @see #sort(Object[ ])
    */
   public static int binarySearch (Object[ ] a, int first, int last, Object key)
```

In javadoc, the html tag <tt> signifies code, <i> signifies italics, and &gt; signifies the greater-than symbol, >. The symbol > by itself would be interpreted as part of an html tag. The # in one of the @see lines creates a link to the given sort method in the document generated through javadoc; that line expands to

```
   See Also:
         sort(Object[ ])
```

Assume, for now, that first <= last. Later on we'll take care of the case where first > last. Following the basic strategy given earlier, we start by finding the middle index:

```
   int mid = (first + last) / 2;
```

The middle element is at index mid in the array a. We need to compare (the element referenced by) a [mid] to (the element referenced by) key. The compareTo method is ideal for the comparison, but that method is not defined in the element class, Object. Fortunately, the compareTo method is defined in any class that implements the Comparable interface. So we cast a [mid] to a Comparable object and then call the method compareTo:

```
   Comparable midVal = (Comparable)a [mid];
   int comp = midVal.compareTo (key);
```

If the result of this comparison is < 0, perform a binary search on the region from mid + 1 to last and return the result of that search. That is:

```
   if (comp < 0)
         return binarySearch (a, mid + 1, last, key);
```

Otherwise, if comp > 0, perform a binary search on the region from first to mid − 1 and return the result. That is,

```
if (comp > 0)
        return binarySearch (a, first, mid − 1, key);
```

Otherwise, return mid, because comp == 0 and so a [mid] is equal to key.

For example, let's follow this strategy in searching for "Frank" in the array names shown in Figure 5.5. That figure shows the state of the program when the binarySearch method is called to find "Frank".

The assignment:

```
mid = (first + last) / 2;
```

gives mid the value (0 + 9)/2, which is 4.

The middle element, "Ed", is less than "Frank", so we perform a binary search of the region from mid + 1 to last. The call is

```
binarySearch (a, mid + 1, last, key);
```

The parameter first gets the value of the argument mid + 1. During this execution of binarySearch, the assignment

```
mid = (first + last) / 2;
```

gives mid the value (5 + 9)/2, which is 7, so midVal is "Helen". See Figure 5.6.

**Figure 5.5 |** The state of the program at the beginning of the method call binarySearch (names, 0, 9, "Frank"). The parameter list is Object[ ] a, **int** first, **int** last, and Object key. (For simplicity, we pretend that names is an array of Strings rather than an array of references to Strings).

| first | mid | last | a[mid] | key |
|-------|-----|------|--------|-------|
| 0 | 4 | 9 | Ed | Frank |

| | |
|-------|------|
| Ada | a[0] |
| Ben | a[1] |
| Carol | a[2] |
| Dave | a[3] |
| Ed | a[4] |
| Frank | a[5] |
| Gerri | a[6] |
| Helen | a[7] |
| Iggy | a[8] |
| Joan | a[9] |

**Figure 5.6 |** The state of the program at the beginning of the binary search for "Frank" in the region from indexes 5 through 9.

| first | mid | last | a[mid] | key |
|-------|-----|------|--------|-----|
| 5 | 7 | 9 | Helen | Frank |

| | |
|------|------|
| Ada | a[0] |
| Ben | a[1] |
| Carol | a[2] |
| Dave | a[3] |
| Ed | a[4] |
| Frank | a[5] |
| Gerri | a[6] |
| Helen | a[7] |
| Iggy | a[8] |
| Joan | a[9] |

The middle element, "Helen", is greater than "Frank", so a binary search is performed on the region from indexes 5 through 6. The call is

    binarySearch (a, first, mid − 1, key);

The parameter last gets the value of the argument mid − 1. During this execution of binarySearch, the assignment

    mid = (first + last) / 2;

gives mid the value $(5 + 6)/2$, which is 5, so the middle element is "Frank". See Figure 5.7.

Success! The middle element is equal to key, so the value returned is mid, the index of the middle element.

The only unresolved issue is what happens if the array does not have an element equal to key. In that case, we want to return − insertionPoint − 1, where insertionPoint is the index where key could be inserted without disordering the array. The reason we don't return − insertionPoint is that we would have an ambiguity if insertionPoint were equal to 0: a return of 0 could be interpreted as the index where key was found.

How can we determine what value to give insertionPoint? If first > last initially, we must have an empty region, with first = 0 and last = −1, so insertionPoint should get the value of first. Otherwise we must have first <= last during the first call to binarySearch. Whenever first <= last at the beginning of a call to binarySearch, we have

    first <= mid <= last

So mid + 1 <= last + 1 and first − 1 <= mid − 1.

**Figure 5.7 |** The state of the program at the beginning of the binary search for "Frank" in the region from indexes 5 through 6.

| first | mid | last | a[mid] | key |
|-------|-----|------|--------|-----|
| 5 | 5 | 6 | Frank | Frank |

| | |
|-------|------|
| Ada | a[0] |
| Ben | a[1] |
| Carol | a[2] |
| Dave | a[3] |
| Ed | a[4] |
| Frank | a[5] |
| Gerri | a[6] |
| Helen | a[7] |
| Iggy | a[8] |
| Joan | a[9] |

If comp $<$ 0, we call

    binarySearch (a, mid + 1, last, key);

At the beginning of that call, we have

    first <= last + 1

On the other hand, if comp $>$ 0, we call

    binarySearch (a, first, mid − 1, key);

At the beginning of that call, we have

    first − 1 <= last

In either case, at the beginning of the call to binarySearch, we have

    first <= last + 1

So when we finally get first $>$ last, we must have

    first = last + 1

But any element with an index less than first must be less than key, and any element with an index greater than last must be greater than key, so when we finish, first is the smallest index of any element greater than key. That is where key should be inserted!

Here is the complete definition:

```
public static int binarySearch(Object[ ] a, int first, int last, Object key)
{
```

```
        if (first <= last)
        {
                int mid = (first + last) / 2;
                Comparable midVal = (Comparable)a [mid];
                int comp = midVal.compareTo (key);
                if (comp < 0)
                        return binarySearch (a, mid + 1, last, key);
                if (comp > 0)
                        return binarySearch (a, first, mid − 1, key);
                return mid; // key found
        } // if first <= last
        return −first − 1; // key not found; belongs at a[first]
} // method binarySearch
```

Here is a main method that allows an end-user to enter names for which a given array will be searched binarily:

```
public static void main (String[ ] args)
{
        final String ARRAY_MESSAGE =
                "The array on which binary searches will be performed is:\n" +
                "Ada, Ben, Carol, Dave, Ed, Frank, Gerri, Helen, Iggy, Joan";

        final String SENTINEL = "****";

        final String PROMPT =
                "\n\nPlease enter a name to be searched for in the array. The " +
                "sentinel is " + SENTINEL + ".\n";

        final String[ ] names = {"Ada", "Ben", "Carol", "Dave", "Ed", "Frank",
                                "Gerri", "Helen", "Iggy", "Joan"};

        final String FOUND = "That name was found at index ";

        final String NOT_FOUND = "That name was not found, but could be " +
                                "inserted at index ";

        String name;

        BufferedReader keyboardReader = new BufferedReader
                                (new InputStreamReader (System.in));

        int index;

        System.out.println (ARRAY_MESSAGE);
        while (true)
        {
                try
                {
                        System.out.print (PROMPT);
                        name = keyboardReader.readLine ( );
```

```
                    if (name.equals(SENTINEL))
                            break;
                    index = binarySearch (names, 0, names.length − 1, name);
                    if (index >= 0)
                            System.out.println (FOUND + index);
                    else
                            System.out.print (NOT_FOUND + (−index − 1));
            } // try
            catch (IOException e)
            {
                    System.out.println (e);
            } // catch
        } // while
    } // method main
```

Here is a step-by-step, execution-frame trace of the binarySearch method after an initial call of

```
binarySearch (names, 0, 9, "Dan");
```

Note that "Dan" is not in the array names.

| | | |
|---|---|---|
| Step 0: | a = ["Ada", "Ben", "Carol", "Dave", "Ed", "Frank", "Gerri", "Helen", "Iggy", "Joan"]<br><br>first = 0<br>last = 9<br>key = "Dan"<br>mid = 4<br>midVal = "Ed"<br>comp is > 0<br><br>**return** binarySearch (a, 0, 3, "Dan"); | Frame 0 |
| Step 1: | a = ["Ada", "Ben", "Carol", "Dave", "Ed", "Frank", "Gerri", "Helen", "Iggy", "Joan"]<br><br>first = 0<br>last = 3<br>key = "Dan"<br>mid = 1<br>midVal = "Ben"<br>comp is < 0<br><br>**return** binarySearch (a, 2, 3, "Dan"); | Frame 1 |

*continued*

a = ["Ada", "Ben", "Carol", "Dave", "Ed", "Frank",
      "Gerri", "Helen", "Iggy", "Joan"]

first = 0
last = 9
key = "Dan"
mid = 4
midVal = "Ed"
comp is > 0

**return** binarySearch (a, 0, 3, "Dan");

Frame 0

Step 2:  a = ["Ada", "Ben", "Carol", "Dave", "Ed", "Frank",
      "Gerri", "Helen", "Iggy", "Joan"]

first = 2
last = 3
key = "Dan"
mid = 2
midVal = "Carol"
comp is < 0

**return** binarySearch (a, 3, 3, "Dan");

Frame 2

a = ["Ada", "Ben", "Carol", "Dave", "Ed", "Frank",
      "Gerri", "Helen", "Iggy", "Joan"]

first = 0
last = 3
key = "Dan"
mid = 1
midVal = "Ben"
comp is < 0

**return** binarySearch (a, 2, 3, "Dan");

Frame 1

a = ["Ada", "Ben", "Carol", "Dave", "Ed", "Frank",
      "Gerri", "Helen", "Iggy", "Joan"]

first = 0
last = 9
key = "Dan"
mid = 4
midVal = "Ed"
comp is > 0

**return** binarySearch (a, 0, 3, "Dan");

Frame 0

Step 3:

a = ["Ada", "Ben", "Carol", "Dave", "Ed", "Frank",
    "Gerri", "Helen", "Iggy", "Joan"]

first = 3
last = 3
key = "Dan"
mid = 3
midVal = "Dave"
comp is > 0

**return** binarySearch (a, 3, 2, "Dan");

Frame 3

---

a = ["Ada", "Ben", "Carol", "Dave", "Ed", "Frank",
    "Gerri", "Helen", "Iggy", "Joan"]

first = 2
last = 3
key = "Dan"
mid = 2
midVal = "Carol"
comp is < 0

**return** binarySearch (a, 3, 3, "Dan");

Frame 2

---

a = ["Ada", "Ben", "Carol", "Dave", "Ed", "Frank",
    "Gerri", "Helen", "Iggy", "Joan"]

first = 0
last = 3
key = "Dan"
mid = 1
midVal = "Ben"
comp is < 0

**return** binarySearch (a, 2, 3, "Dan");

Frame 1

---

a = ["Ada", "Ben", "Carol", "Dave", "Ed", "Frank",
    "Gerri", "Helen", "Iggy", "Joan"]

first = 0
last = 9
key = "Dan"
mid = 4
midVal = "Ed"
comp is > 0

**return** binarySearch (a, 0, 3, "Dan");

Frame 0

*continued*

Step 4:

a = ["Ada", "Ben", "Carol", "Dave", "Ed", "Frank",
     "Gerri", "Helen", "Iggy", "Joan"]
first = 3
last = 2
key = "Dan"
**return** −3 −1;

Frame 4

−4 ↓

a = ["Ada", "Ben", "Carol", "Dave", "Ed", "Frank",
     "Gerri", "Helen", "Iggy", "Joan"]
first = 3
last = 3
key = "Dan"
mid = 3
midVal = "Dave"
comp is > 0
**return** binarySearch (a, 3, 2, "Dan");

Frame 3

−4 ↓

a = ["Ada", "Ben", "Carol", "Dave", "Ed", "Frank",
     "Gerri", "Helen", "Iggy", "Joan"]
first = 2
last = 3
key = "Dan"
mid = 2
midVal = "Carol"
comp is < 0
**return** binarySearch (a, 3, 3, "Dan");

Frame 2

−4 ↓

a = ["Ada", "Ben", "Carol", "Dave", "Ed", "Frank",
     "Gerri", "Helen", "Iggy", "Joan"]
first = 0
last = 3
key = "Dan"
mid = 1
midVal = "Ben"
comp is < 0
**return** binarySearch (a, 2, 3, "Dan");

Frame 1

−4 ↓

a = ["Ada", "Ben", "Carol", "Dave", "Ed", "Frank",
     "Gerri", "Helen", "Iggy", "Joan"]
first = 0
last = 9
key = "Dan"
mid = 4
midVal = "Ed"
comp is > 0
**return** binarySearch (a, 0, 3, "Dan");

Frame 0

−4 ↓

How long does the binarySearch method take? We need to make a distinction between an unsuccessful search, in which the element is not found, and a successful search, in which the element is found. We start with an analysis of an unsuccessful search.

During each execution of the binarySearch method in which the middle element is not equal to key, the size of the region searched during the next execution is, approximately, halved. If the element sought is not in the array, we keep dividing by 2 as long as the region has at least one element. Let $n$ represent the size of the region. The number of times $n$ can be divided by 2 until $n = 0$ is logarithmic in $n$—this is, basically, the Splitting Rule from Chapter 3. So for a failed search, worstTime($n$) is logarithmic in $n$. Since we are assuming the search is unsuccessful, the same number of searches will be performed in the average case as in the worst case, so averageTime($n$) is logarithmic in $n$ for a failed search.

The worst case for a successful search requires one less call to the binarySearch method than the worst case (or average case) for an unsuccessful search. So for a successful search, worstTime($n$) is still logarithmic in $n$. In the average case for a successful search, the analysis—see Concept Exercise 5.7—is more complicated, but the result is the same: averageTime($n$) is logarithmic in $n$.

During each call, a constant amount of information is saved: the entire array is not saved, only a reference to the array. So the space requirements are also logarithmic in $n$, for both successful and unsuccessful searches and for both the worst case and the average case.

In the Arrays class of the java.util package, there is an iterative version of the binary search algorithm. In Lab 8, you will conduct an experiment to compare the time to recursively search an array of **int**s, iteratively search an array of **int**s, and iteratively search an array of Integers. Which of the three do you think will be slowest?

 **Lab 8: Iterative Binary Search**

You are now prepared to do Lab 8.          All Labs Are Optional

Lab 9 introduces another recursive method whose development is far easier than its iterative counterpart. The method for generating permutations is from the delightful book *Thinking Recursively* (Roberts, 1986).

 **Lab 9: Generating Permutations**

You are now prepared to do Lab 9.          All Labs Are Optional

Section 5.6 deals with another design pattern (a general strategy for solving a variety of problems): backtracking. You have employed this strategy whenever you had to retrace your steps on the way to some goal. The BackTrack class also illustrates the value of using interfaces.

## 5.6 | BACKTRACKING

The basic idea with backtracking is this: From a given starting position, we want to reach a goal position. We repeatedly choose, maybe by guessing, what our next position should be. If a given choice is valid—that is, the new position might be on a path to the goal—we advance to that new position and continue. If a choice leads to a dead end, we back up to the previous position and make another choice. ***Backtracking*** is the strategy of trying to reach a goal by a sequence of chosen positions, with a retracing in reverse order of positions that cannot lead to the goal.

For example, look at the picture in Figure 5.8. We start at position P0 and we want to find a path to the goal state, P14. We are allowed to move in only two directions: north and west. But we cannot "see" any farther than the next position. Here is a strategy: From any position, we first try to go north; if we are unable to go north, we try to go west; if we are unable to go west, we back up to the most recent position where we chose north and try to choose west instead. We never revisit a position that has been discovered to be a dead end. The positions in Figure 5.8 are numbered in the order they would be tried according to this strategy.

Figure 5.8 casts some light on the phrase "retracing in reverse order." When we are unable to go north or west from position P4, we first back up to position P3, where west is not an option. So we back up to P2. Eventually, this leads to a dead end, and we back up to P1, which leads to the goal state.

When a position is visited, it is marked as possibly being on a path to the goal, but this marking must be undone if the position leads only to a dead end. That enables us to avoid revisiting any dead-end position. For example, in Figure 5.8, P5 is not visited from P8 because by the time we got to P8, P5 had already been recognized as a dead end.

We can now refine our strategy. To try to reach a goal from a given position, enumerate over all positions directly accessible from the given position, and keep looping until either a goal has been reached or we can no longer advance to another position. During each loop iteration, get the next accessible position. If that position may be on a path to a goal, so mark that position and, if it is a goal, the search has

**Figure 5.8** | Backtracking to obtain a path to a goal. The solution path is P0, P1, P8, P9, P10, P11, P12, P13, P14, P15.

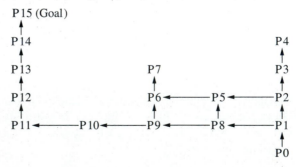

been successful; otherwise, attempt to reach a goal from that position, and mark the position as a dead end if the attempt fails.

Make sure you have a good understanding of the previous paragraph before you proceed. That paragraph contains the essence of backtracking. The rest of this section and Section 5.6.1 are almost superficial by comparison!

Instead of developing a backtracking method for a particular application, we will utilize a generalized backtracking algorithm from Wirth (1976, p. 138). We then demonstrate that algorithm on a particular application, maze searching. Two other applications, the eight queens problem and the knight's tour problem, are left as programming projects in this chapter. And Chapter 15 has another application of backtracking: a programming project for searching a network. Backtracking is a design pattern because it is a generic programming technique that can be applied in a variety of contexts.

The BackTrack class below is based on one in Noonan (2000). The details of the application class will be transparent to the BackTrack class, which works through an interface, Application. The Application interface will be implemented by the particular application.

A user (of the BackTrack class) supplies:

- The class implementing the Application interface. (***Note:*** To access the positions available from a given position, the iterator design-pattern is employed, with an inner iterator class.)
- A Position class to define what "position" means for this application.

The Application methods are generalizations of the previous outline of backtracking. Here is the Application interface:

```java
import java.util.*;

public interface Application
{
    /**
     * Determines if a given position is legal and not a dead end.
     *
     * @param pos – the given position.
     *
     * @return true if pos is a legal position and not a dead end.
     */
    boolean isOK (Position pos);

    /**
     * Indicates that a given position is possibly on a path to a goal.
     *
     * @param pos the position that has been marked as possibly being on a
     *       path to a goal.
     */
    void markAsPossible (Position pos);
```

```
/**
 * Indicates whether a given position is a goal position.
 *
 * @param pos the position that may or may not be a goal position.
 *
 * @return true if pos is a goal position; false otherwise.
 */
public boolean isGoal (Position pos);

/**
 * Indicates that a given position is not on any path to a goal position.
 *
 * @param pos the position that has been marked as not being on any path to
 *        a goal position.
 */
public void markAsDeadEnd (Position pos);

/**
 * Converts this Application object into a String object.
 *
 * @return the String representation of this Application object.
 */
public String toString( );

/**
 * Produces an Iterator object that starts at a given position.
 *
 * @param pos the position the Iterator object starts at.
 *
 * @return an Iterator object that accesses the positions directly available from pos.
 */
public Iterator<Position> iterator (Position pos);

} // interface Application
```

The BackTrack class has two responsibilities: to initialize a BackTrack object from a given application object, and to try to reach a goal position from a given position. The method specifications are

```
/**
 * Initializes this BackTrack object from an application.
 *
 * @param app the application
 */
public BackTrack (Application app)

/**
 * Attempts to reach a goal through a given position.
 *
```

```
    * @param pos the given position.
    *
    * @return true if the attempt succeeds; otherwise, false.
    */
public boolean tryToReachGoal (Position pos)
```

The only field needed is (a reference to) an **Application**. The definition of the con-structor is straightforward. The definition of the tryToReachGoal method is based on the outline of backtracking given above: To "enumerate over all positions accessible from the given position," we create an iterator. The phrase "attempt to reach a goal from that position" becomes a recursive call to the method tryToReachGoal. The com-plete BackTrack class, without any application-specific information, is as follows:

```
import java.util.*;

public class BackTrack
{
        protected Application app;
        /**
         * Initializes this BackTrack object from an application.
         *
         * @param app the application
         */
        public BackTrack (Application app)
        {
                this.app = app;
        } // constructor
        /**
         * Attempts to reach a goal through a given position.
         *
         * @param pos the given position.
         *
         * @return true if the attempt succeeds; otherwise, false.
         */
        public boolean tryToReachGoal (Position pos)
        {
                boolean success = false;

                Iterator<Position> itr = app.iterator (pos);

                while (!success && itr.hasNext( ))
                {
                        pos = itr.next( );
                        if (app.isOK (pos))
                        {
                                app.markAsPossible (pos);
                                if (app.isGoal (pos))
                                        success = true;
```

```
                                else
                                {
                                        success = tryToReachGoal (pos);
                                        if (!success)
                                                app.markAsDeadEnd (pos);
                                } // goal not reached yet
                        } // pos may be on a path to a goal
                } // while
                return success;
        } // method tryToReachGoal

    } // class BackTrack
```

Let's focus on the tryToReachGoal method, the essence of backtracking. We look at the possible choices of moves from the pos parameter. There are three possibilities:

1. One of those choices is a goal position. Then the **while** loop terminates and **true** is returned to indicate success.

2. One of those choices is valid but not a goal position. Then another call to tryToReachGoal is made, starting at the valid choice.

3. None of the choices is valid. Then the **while** loop terminates and **false** is returned to indicate failure to reach a goal position from the current position.

The argument to tryToReachGoal represents a position that has been marked as possibly being on a path to a goal position. Whenever a return is made from tryToReachGoal, the precall value of pos is restored, to be marked as a dead end if it does not lead to a goal position.

Now that we have developed a framework for backtracking, it is easy to utilize this framework to solve a variety of problems. One of these problems is presented in Section 5.6.1, two more in Programming Projects at the end of this chapter, and another in Chapter 15.

## 5.6.1 An A-maze-ing Application

For one application of backtracking, let's develop a program to try to find a path through a maze. For example, Figure 5.9 has a 7-by-13 maze, with a 1 representing a corridor and a 0 representing a wall. The only valid moves are along a corridor, and only horizontal and vertical moves are allowed; diagonal moves are prohibited. The starting position is in the upper left-hand corner and the goal position is in the lower right-hand corner.

A successful traversal of this maze will show a path leading from the start position to the goal position. We mark each such position with the number 9. Because there are two possible paths through this maze, the actual path chosen will depend on how the iterator class orders the possible choices. For the sake of specificity, assume the order of choices is north, east, south, and west. For example, from the position at coordinates (5, 8), the first choice would be (4, 8), followed by (5, 9), (6, 8), and (5, 7).

**Figure 5.9 |** A maze: 1 represents a corridor and 0 represents a wall. Assume the starting position is in the upper left-hand corner, and the goal position is in the lower right-hand corner.

```
1 1 1 0 1 1 0 0 0 1 1 1 1
1 0 1 1 1 0 1 1 1 1 1 0 1
1 0 0 0 1 0 1 0 1 0 1 0 1
1 0 0 0 1 1 1 0 1 0 1 1 1
1 1 1 1 1 0 0 0 0 1 0 0 0
0 0 0 0 1 0 0 0 0 0 0 0 0
0 0 0 0 1 1 1 1 1 1 1 1 1
```

From the initial position at (0, 0), the following positions are recorded as possibly being on a solution-path:

(0, 1) // moving east

(0, 2) // moving east

(1, 2) // moving south

(1, 3) // moving east

(1, 4) // moving east

(0, 4) // moving north

(0, 5) // moving east

This last position is a dead end, so we "undo" (0, 5) and (0, 4), backtrack to (1, 4) and then record

(2, 4) // moving south

(3, 4) // moving south

(3, 5) // moving east

From here we eventually reach a dead end. After we undo (3, 5) and retrace to (3, 4), we advance—without any further backtracking—to the goal position. Figure 5.10 shows the corresponding path through the maze of Figure 5.9, with dead-end positions marked with 2s.

**Figure 5.10 |** A path through the maze of Figure 5.9. The path positions are marked with 9s and the dead-end positions are marked with 2s.

```
9 9 9 0 2 2 0 0 0 2 2 2 2
1 0 9 9 9 0 2 2 2 2 2 0 2
1 0 0 0 9 0 2 0 2 0 2 0 2
1 0 0 0 9 2 2 0 2 0 2 2 2
1 1 1 1 9 0 0 0 0 1 0 0 0
0 0 0 0 9 0 0 0 0 0 0 0 0
0 0 0 0 9 9 9 9 9 9 9 9 9
```

For this application, a position is simply a pair: row, column. The Position class is easily developed:

```java
public class Position
{
        protected int row,
                        column;

        /**
         * Initializes this Position object to (0, 0).
         */
        public Position ( )
        {
                row = 0;
                column = 0;
        } // default constructor

        /**
         * Initializes this Position object to (row, column).
         *
         * @param row the row this Position object has been initialized to.
         * @param column the column this Position object has been initialized to.
         */
        public Position (int row, int column)
        {
                this.row = row;
                this.column = column;
        } // constructor

        /**
         * Determines the row of this Position object.
         *
         * @return the row of this Position object.
         */
        public int getRow ( )
        {
                return row;
        } // method getRow

        /**
         * Determines the column of this Position object.
         *
         * @return the column of this Position object.
         */
        public int getColumn ( )
        {
                return column;
        } // method getColumn

} // class Position
```

For this application, the Application interface is implemented in a Maze class. The only fields are a grid to hold the maze and a finish position to indicate when the goal has been reached. Figure 5.11 has the UML diagrams for the Maze class and Application interface.

Here is the complete Maze class, including the embedded MazeIterator class:

```java
import java.util.*;

public class Maze implements Application {

    protected static final byte WALL = 0;
    protected static final byte CORRIDOR = 1;
    protected static final byte PATH = 9;
    protected static final byte DEAD_END = 2;

    protected Position finish;

    protected byte[ ][ ] grid;

    /**
     * Initializes this Maze object.
     *
     * @param grid a two-dimensional array of bytes to hold the maze.
     * @param finish the Position that signifies the end of the maze.
     */
    public Maze (byte[ ][ ] grid, Position finish)
```

**Figure 5.11 |** The class diagram for the Maze class, which implements the Application interface and has a field (namely, finish) of type Position.

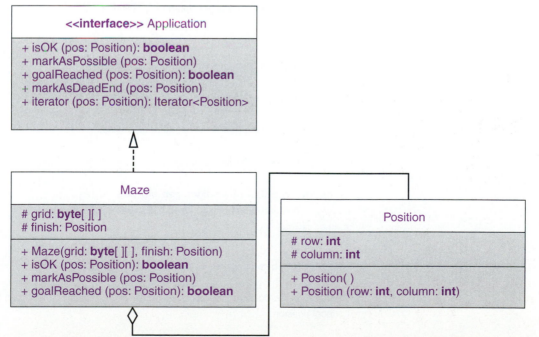

```
        {
                this.finish = finish;
                this.grid = grid;
        } // 2-parameter constructor

        /**
         * Determines if a given position is legal and not a dead end.
         *
         * @param pos – the given position.
         *
         * @return true if pos is a legal position and not a dead end.
         */
        boolean isOK (Position pos)
        {
                return pos.getRow( ) >= 0 && pos.getRow( ) < grid.length &&
                        pos.getColumn( ) >= 0 && pos.getColumn( ) < grid [0].length &&
                        grid [pos.getRow( )][pos.getColumn( )] == CORRIDOR;
        } // method isOK

        /**
         * Indicates that a given position is possibly on a path to a goal.
         *
         * @param pos the position that has been marked as possibly being on a path
         *       to a goal.
         */
        public void markAsPossible (Position pos)
        {
                grid [pos.getRow ( )][pos.getColumn ( )] = PATH;
        } // method markAsPossible

        /**
         * Indicates whether a given position is a goal position.
         *
         * @param pos the position that may or may not be a goal position.
         *
         * @return true if pos is a goal position; false otherwise.
         */
        public boolean isGoal (Position pos)
        {
                return pos.getRow( ) == finish.getRow( ) &&
                        pos.getColumn( ) == finish.getColumn( );
        } // method isGoal

        /**
         * Indicates that a given position is not on any path to a goal position.
         *
         * @param pos the position that has been marked as not being on any path to a
         *       goal position.
```

```
    */
    public void markAsDeadEnd (Position pos)
    {
            grid [pos.getRow( )][pos.getColumn( )] = DEAD_END;
    } // method markAsDeadEnd

    /**
     * Converts this Application object into a String object.
     *
     * @return the String representation of this Application object.
     */
    public String toString ( )
    {
            String result = "\n";

            for (int row = 0; row < grid.length; row++)
            {
                    for (int column = 0; column < grid [0].length; column++)
                            result += String.valueOf (grid [row][column]) + ' ';
                    result += "\n";
            } // for row = 0
            return result;
    } // method toString

    /**
     * Produces an Iterator object, over elements of type Position, that starts at a given
     * position.
     *
     * @param pos – the position the Iterator object starts at.
     *
     * @return the Iterator object.
     */
    public Iterator<Position> iterator (Position pos)
    {
            return new MazeIterator (pos);
    } // method iterator

    protected class MazeIterator implements Iterator<Position>
    {

            protected static final int MAX_MOVES = 4;
            protected int row,
                          column,
                          count;

            /**
             * Initializes this MazeIterator object to start at a given position.
             *
             * @param pos the position the Iterator object starts at.
```

```java
        */
       public MazeIterator (Position pos)
       {
             row = pos.getRow( );
             column = pos.getColumn( );
             count = 0;
       } // constructor

       /**
        *  Determines if this MazeIterator object can advance to another
        *  position.
        *
        *  @return true if this MazeIterator object can advance; false otherwise.
        */
       public boolean hasNext ( )
       {
             return count < MAX_MOVES;
       } // method hasNext

       /**
        *  Advances this MazeIterator object to the next position.
        *
        *  @return the position advanced to.
        */
       public Position next ( )
       {
             Position nextPosition = new Position( );
             switch (count++)
             {
                   case 0: nextPosition = new Position (row−1, column); // north
                           break;
                   case 1: nextPosition = new Position (row, column+1); // east
                           break;
                   case 2: nextPosition = new Position (row+1, column); // south
                           break;
                   case 3: nextPosition = new Position (row, column−1); // west
             } // switch;
             return nextPosition;
       } // method next

       public void remove ( )
       {
             // removal is illegal for a MazeIterator object
             throw new UnsupportedOperationException( );
       } // method remove

} // class MazeIterator
```

} // class Maze

The MazeTester class will read in a file with maze information and print out the result: either a solution or a statement that no solution is possible. The method specifications are

```
/**
 * Reads in the maze information.
 */
public void readMaze( )

/**
 * Prints the results of the maze search.
 */
public void printResults( )
```

The MazeTester class will have a Maze field (to hold the maze), a BackTrack field (to find a goal), and two Position fields (for the start and finish positions). Figure 5.12 has the UML class diagrams that illustrate the overall design. Because the Position class is quite simple and its diagram is in Figure 5.11, its class diagram is omitted.

The implementation of the MazeTester class is as follows:

```
import java.io.*;
import java.util.*;

public class MazeTester
{
        protected Maze maze;

        protected BackTrack backTrack;

        protected Position start,
                           finish;

        /**
         * Reads in the maze information.
         */
        public void readMaze( )
        {
        final String PROMPT =
                "\n\nPlease enter the path for the file whose first line contains the " +
                "number of rows and columns,\nwhose 2nd line the start row and column, " +
                "whose 3rd line the finish row and column, and then the maze, row-by-row: ";

        BufferedReader keyboardReader = new BufferedReader (
                                        new InputStreamReader (System.in));

        String fileName;

        BufferedReader fileReader;

        byte[ ][ ] grid = null;
```

**Figure 5.12** | The UML class diagrams for the maze-search project.

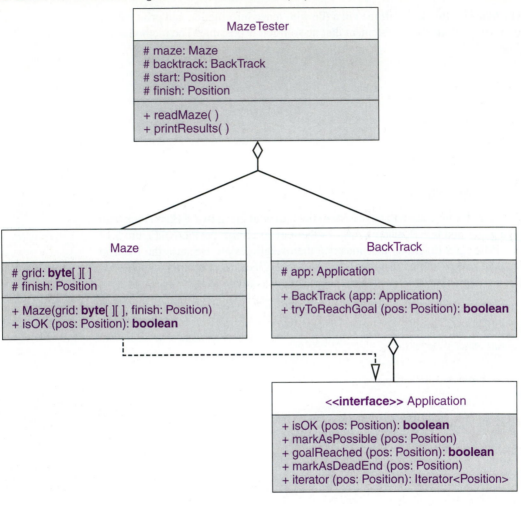

```
boolean fileFound = false;

while (!fileFound)
{
        try
        {
                System.out.print (PROMPT);
                fileName = keyboardReader.readLine( );
                fileReader = new BufferedReader (new FileReader (fileName));
                fileFound = true;

                StringTokenizer tokens;

                tokens = new StringTokenizer (fileReader.readLine( ));
```

```java
        int rows = Integer.parseInt (tokens.nextToken( )),
            columns = Integer.parseInt (tokens.nextToken( ));

        grid = new byte [rows][columns];

        tokens = new StringTokenizer (fileReader.readLine( ));
        start = new Position (Integer.parseInt (tokens.nextToken( )),
                              Integer.parseInt (tokens.nextToken( )));

        tokens = new StringTokenizer (fileReader.readLine( ));
        finish = new Position (Integer.parseInt (tokens.nextToken( )),
                               Integer.parseInt (tokens.nextToken( )));

        for (int i = 0; i < rows; i++)
        {
                tokens = new StringTokenizer (fileReader.readLine( ));
                for (int j = 0; j < columns; j++)
                        grid [i][j] = (byte)Integer.parseInt (tokens.nextToken( ));
                } // reading in maze entries
                fileReader.close( );
        } // try
        catch (IOException e)
        {
                System.out.print (e);
        } // catch IOException
    } // while
    maze = new Maze (grid, finish);
    backTrack = new BackTrack (maze);
} // method readMaze

/**
 * Prints the results of the maze search.
 */
public void printResults( )
{
        final String INITIAL_STATE =
                "\nThe initial state is as follows (0 = WALL, 1 = CORRIDOR):\n";

        final String START_INVALID = "The start position is invalid.";

        final String FINISH_INVALID = "The finish position is invalid.";

        final String FINAL_STATE =
                "The final state is as follows (2 = DEAD END, 9 = PATH):\n";

        final String SUCCESS =
                "\n\nA solution has been found:";

        final String FAILURE =
                "\n\nThere is no solution:";

        System.out.println (INITIAL_STATE + maze);
```

```
                    if (!maze.OK (start))
                            System.out.println (START_INVALID);
                    else if (!maze.OK (finish))
                            System.out.println (FINISH_INVALID);
                    else
                    {
                            maze.markAsPossible (start);
                            if (maze.isGoal (start) || backTrack.tryToReachGoal (start))
                                    System.out.println (SUCCESS);
                            else
                            {
                                    maze.markAsDeadEnd (start);
                                    System.out.println (FAILURE);
                            } // failure
                            System.out.println (FINAL_STATE + maze);
                    } // start and finish are valid
            } // method printResults

        } // class MazeTester
```

For the maze-search project, the main method simply constructs a MazeTester object and then invokes the readMaze( ) and printResults( ) methods. All of the files are available on the book's website.

How long does the tryToReachGoal method take? Suppose the maze has $n$ positions. In the worst case, such as in Figure 5.13 below, every position would be considered, so worstTime($n$) is linear in $n$. And with more than half of the positions on a path to the goal position, there would be at least $n/2$ recursive calls to the tryToReachGoal method, so worstSpace($n$) is also linear in $n$.

Projects 5.2 and 5.3 have other examples of backtracking. Because the above project separated the backtracking aspects from the maze traversing aspects, the BackTrack class and Application interface are unchanged! Coincidentally, the Position class for those two projects is the same Position class declared earlier.

**Figure 5.13 |** A worst-case maze: in columns 1, 4, 7, . . . , every row except the last contains a 0; every other position in the maze contains a 1. The start position is in the upper-left corner, and the finish position is in the lower-right corner.

```
1 0 1 1 0 1 1 0
1 0 1 1 0 1 1 0
1 0 1 1 0 1 1 0
.  .  .  .  .  .  .  .
.  .  .  .  .  .  .  .
.  .  .  .  .  .  .  .
1 0 1 1 0 1 1 0
1 0 1 1 0 1 1 0
1 1 1 1 1 1 1 1
```

We will revisit backtracking in Chapter 15 in the context of searching a network. And, of course, the BackTrack class and Application interface are the same as given above.

At the beginning of this chapter we informally described a recursive method as a method that called itself. Section 5.7 indicates why that description does not suffice as a definition and then provides a definition.

## 5.7 | INDIRECT RECURSION

Java allows methods to be indirectly recursive. For example, if method A calls method B and method B calls method A, then both A and B are recursive.

Because indirect recursion is legal, we cannot simply define a method to be recursive if it calls itself. To provide a formal definition of *recursive,* we first define *active.* A method is **active** if it is being executed or has called an active method. For example, consider a chain of method calls

$$A \longrightarrow B \longrightarrow C \longrightarrow D$$

That is, A calls B, B calls C, and C calls D. When D is being executed, the active methods are

D, because it is being executed

C, because it has called D and D is active

B, because it has called C and C is active

A, because it has called B and B is active

We can now define "recursive." A method is **recursive** if it can be called while it is active. For example, suppose we had the following sequence of calls:

$$A \longrightarrow B \longrightarrow C \longrightarrow D$$

Then B, C, and D are recursive because each can be called while it is active.

When a recursive method is invoked, a certain amount of information must be saved so that information will not be written over during the execution of the recursive call. This information is restored when the execution of the method has been completed. This saving and restoring, and other work related to the support of recursion, carry some cost in terms of execution time and memory space. Section 5.8 estimates the cost of recursion, and attempts to determine whether that cost is justified.

## 5.8 | THE COST OF RECURSION

We have seen that a certain amount of information is saved every time a method calls itself. This information is collectively referred to as an **activation record** because it pertains to the execution state of the method that is active during the call. In fact, an activation record is created whenever *any* method is called; this relieves the compiler of the burden of determining if a given method is indirectly recursive.

Essentially, an activation record is an execution frame without the statements. Each activation record contains:

1.  The return address, that is, the address of the statement that will be executed when the call has been completed.
2.  The value of each argument: a copy of the corresponding argument is made (if the type of the argument is reference-to-object, the reference is copied).
3.  The values of the method's other local variables.

After the call has been completed, the previous activation record's information is restored and the execution of the calling method is resumed. For methods that return a value, the value is placed on top of the previous activation record's information just prior to the resumption of the calling method's execution. The calling method's first order of business is to get that return value.

There is an execution-time cost of saving and restoring these records, and the records themselves take up space. But these costs are negligible relative to the cost of a programmer's time to develop an iterative method when a recursive method would be more appropriate. Recursive methods, such as move, tryToReachGoal, and permute (from Lab 9) are far simpler and more elegant than their iterative counterparts.

How can you decide whether a recursive method or iterative method is more appropriate? Basically, if you can readily develop an iterative solution, go for it! If not, you need to decide if recursion is appropriate for the problem. That is, if complex cases of the problem can be reduced to simpler cases of the same form as the original and the simplest case(s) can be solved directly, you should try to develop a recursive method.

If an iterative method is not easy to develop, and recursion is appropriate, how does recursion compare with iteration? At worst, the recursive will take about as long (and have similar time/space performance) as the iterative version. At best, developing the recursive method will take far less time than the iterative version, and have similar time/space performance. See, for example, the move, tryToReachGoal, and permute methods. Of course, it is possible to design an inefficient recursive method, such as the original version of fib in Lab 8, just as iterative methods can have poor performance.

In this chapter we have focused on what recursion is. We postpone to Chapter 8 a discussion of the mechanism, called a *stack,* by which the compiler implements the saving and restoring of activation records. As we saw in Chapter 1, this abstraction—the separation of what is done from how it is done—is critically important in problem solving.

## SUMMARY

The purpose of this chapter was to familiarize you with the basic idea of recursion so you will be able to understand the recursive methods in subsequent chapters and to design your own recursive methods when the need arises.

A method is *recursive* if it can be called while it is active—an *active* method is one that either is being executed or has called an active method.

If an iterative method to solve a problem can readily be developed, then that should be done. Otherwise, recursion should be considered if the problem has the following characteristics:

1. Complex cases of the problem can be reduced to simpler cases of the same form as the original problem.
2. The simplest case(s) can be solved directly.

For such problems, it is often straightforward to develop a recursive method. Whenever any method (recursive or not) is called, a new activation record is created to provide a frame of reference for the execution of the method. Each activation record contains

■ The return address, that is, the address of the statement that will be executed when the call has been completed.

■ The value of each actual parameter: a copy of the corresponding actual parameter is made (if the type of the argument is reference-to-object, the reference is copied).

■ The values of the method's other local variables.

Activation records make recursion possible because they hold information that might otherwise be destroyed if the method called itself. When the execution of the current method has been completed, a return is made to the address specified in the current activation record. The previous activation record is then used as the frame of reference for that method's execution.

Any problem that can be solved with recursive methods can also be solved iteratively, that is, with a loop. Typically, iterative methods are slightly more efficient than their recursive counterparts because far fewer activation records are created and maintained. But the elegance and coding simplicity of recursion more than compensates for this slight disadvantage.

A *backtracking* strategy advances step-by-step toward a goal. At each step, a choice is made, but when a dead end is reached, the steps are retraced in reverse order; that is, the most recent choice is discarded and a new choice is made. Backtracking was deployed for the maze-search application above, and can be used in Programming Projects 4.2 (eight queens) and 4.3 (knight's tour).

# CONCEPT EXERCISES

**5.1** What is wrong with the following method for calculating factorials?

```
/**
 * Calculates the factorial of a nonnegative integer, that is, the product of all
 * integers between 1 and the given integer, inclusive. The worstTime(n) is O(n),
 * where n is the given integer.
 *
 * @param n the nonnegative integer whose factorial is calculated.
 *
```

```
       * @return the factorial of n
       *
       * @throws IllegalArgumentException if n is less than 0.
       *
       */
    public static long factorial (int n)
    {
          if (n < 0)
                throw new IllegalArgumentException( );
          if (n <= 1)
                return 1;
          return fact (n+1) / (n+1);
    } // fact
```

**5.2**    Show the first three steps in an execution-frames trace of the move method after an initial call of

```
move (4, 'A', 'B', 'C');
```

**5.3**    Perform an execution-frames trace to determine the output from the following *incorrect* version of the recPermute method (from Lab 9) after an initial call to

```
permute ("ABC");
```

invokes

```
recPermute (['A', 'B', 'C'], 0);
```

```
/**
 * Finds all permutations of a subarray from a given position to the end of the array.
 *
 * @param c an array of characters
 * @param k the starting position in c of the subarray to be permuted.
 *
 * @return a String representation of all the permutations.
 *
 */
public static String recPermute (char[ ] c, int k)
{
      if (k == c.length − 1)
            return String.valueOf (c) + "\n";
      else
      {
            String allPermutations = new String( );

            char temp;

            for (int i = k; i < c.length; i++)
```

```
        {
                temp = c [i];
                c [i] = c [k + 1];
                c [k + 1] = temp;
                allPermutations += recPermute (String.valueOf (c).toCharArray( ),
                        k+1);
        } // for
        return allPermutations;
    } // else
} // method recPermute
```

**5.4** Perform an execution-frames trace to determine the output from the following *incorrect* version of the recPermute method (from Lab 9) after an initial call to

permute ("ABC");

invokes

recPermute (['A', 'B', 'C'], 0);

```
/**
 * Finds all permutations of a subarray from a given position to the end of the array.
 *
 * @param c an array of characters
 * @param k the starting position in c of the subarray to be permuted.
 *
 * @return a String representation of all the permutations.
 *
 */
public static String recPermute (char[ ] c, int k)
{
        if (k == c.length − 1)
                return String.valueOf (c) + "\n";
        else
        {
                String allPermutations = new String( );
                char temp;

                for (int i = k; i < c.length; i++)
                {
                        allPermutations += recPermute (String.valueOf (c).toCharArray( ),
                                k+1);
                        temp = c [i];
                        c [i] = c [k];
                        c [k] = temp;
                } // for
                return allPermutations;
```

```
    } // else
} // method recPermute
```

**5.5**   Use the Principle of Mathematical Induction (Appendix 2) to prove that the move method in the Towers of Hanoi example is correct; that is, for any integer n ≥ 1, move (n, orig, dest, temp) returns the steps to move n disks from pole orig to pole dest.

*Hint:* For $n = 1, 2, 3, \ldots$, let $S_n$ be the statement:

move (n, orig, dest, temp) returns the steps to move n disks from any pole orig to any other pole dest.

**a.**   Base case. Show that $S_1$ is true.

**b.**   Inductive case. Let *n* be any integer greater than 1 and assume $S_{n-1}$ is true. Then show that $S_n$ is true. According to the code of the move method, what happens when move (n, orig, dest, temp) is called and n is greater than 1?

**5.6**   In an execution trace of the move method in the Towers of Hanoi application, the number of steps is equal to the number of recursive calls to the move method plus the number of direct moves. Because each call to the move method includes a direct move, the number of recursive calls to the move method is always one less than the number of direct moves. For example, in the execution trace shown in the chapter, $n = 3$. The total number of calls to move is $2^n - 1 = 7$. Then the number of recursive calls is 6, and the number of direct moves is 7, for a total of 13 steps (recall that we started at Step 0, so the last step is Step 12). How many steps would there be for an execution trace with $n = 4$?

**5.7**   Show that, for the recursive binarySearch method, averageTime(n) is logarithmic in *n* for a successful search.

*Hint:* Let *n* represent the size of the array to be searched. Because the average number of calls is a nondecreasing function of *n*, it is enough to show that the claim is true for values of *n* that are one less than a power of 2. So assume that

$n = 2^k - 1$   for some positive integer k

In a successful search,

One call is sufficient if the item sought is half-way through the region to be searched;

Two calls are needed if the item sought is one-fourth or three-fourths of the way through that region;

Three calls are needed if the item sought is one-eighth, three-eighths, five-eighths, or seven-eighths of the way through the region;

and so on.

The total number of calls for all successful searches is

$$(1 \cdot 1) + (2 \cdot 2) + (3 \cdot 4) + (4 \cdot 8) + (5 \cdot 16) + \cdots + [k(2^k - 1)]$$

The average number of calls, and hence an estimate of averageTime($n$), is this sum divided by $n$. Now use the result from Exercise A2.3 of Appendix 2 and the fact that

$$k = \log_2(n + 1)$$

**5.8**  If a call to the binarySearch method is successful, will the index returned always be the smallest index of an item equal to the key sought? Explain.

## PROGRAMMING EXERCISES

**5.1**  Develop an iterative version of the getBinary method in Section 5.3. Test that method with a main method that reads in a decimal integer and then calls the getBinary method.

**5.2**  Develop an iterative version of the permute method (from Lab 9). Here is the method specification:

```
/**
 * Finds all permutations of a specified String.
 *
 * @param s – the String to be permuted.
 *
 * @return a String representation of all the permutations, with a line separator
 *         (that is, "\n") after each permutation.
 */
public static String permute (String s)
```

For example, if the original string is "BADCGEFH", the value returned would be

ABCDEFGH
ABCDEFHG
ABCDEGFH
ABCDEGHF
ABCDEHFG

and so on. Test your method with the project from Lab 9.

*Hint:* One strategy starts by converting s to a character array c. Then the elements in c can be easily swapped with the help of the index operator, [ ]. To get the first permutation, use the static method sort in the Arrays class of java.util. To give you an idea of how the next permutation can be constructed from the current permutation, suppose, after some permutations have been printed,

```
c = ['A', 'H', 'E', 'G', 'F', 'D', 'C', 'B']
```

What is the smallest index whose character will be swapped to obtain the next permutation? It is index 2, because the characters at indexes 3 through 7 are already in reverse alphabetical order: $G > F > D > C > B$. We swap E with F, the smallest character greater than E at an index greater than 2. After swapping, we have

c = ['A', 'H', 'F', 'G', 'E', 'D', 'C', 'B']

We then reverse the characters at indexes 3 through 7 to get those characters into increasing order:

c = ['A', 'H', 'F', 'B', 'C', 'D', 'E', 'G'],

the next higher permutation after 'A', 'H', 'E', 'G', 'F', 'D', 'C', 'B'.

Here is an outline:

```java
public static String permute (String s)
{
        int n = s.length( );

        boolean finished = false;

        char[ ] c = s.toCharArray( );

        String perms = "";

        Arrays.sort (c); // c is now in ascending order
        while (!finished)
        {
                perms += String.valueOf (c));

                // In 0 ... n−1, find the highest index p such that
                // p = 0 or c [p−1] < c [p].
                        . . .

                if (p == 0)
                        finished = true;
                else
                {
                        // In p ... n−1, find the largest index i such that c [i] > c [p−1].
                            . . .

                        // Swap c [i] with c [p−1].

                        // Swap c [p] with c [n−1], swap c [p+1] with c [n−2],

                        // swap c [p+2] with c [n−3], . . .
                            . . .
                } // else
        } // while
        return perms;
} // method permute
```

In the above example, p − 1 = 2 and i = 4, so c [p − 1], namely, E is swapped with c [i], namely, F.

Explain how strings with duplicate characters are treated differently in this method than in the recursive version.

**5.3**    Given two positive integers $i$ and $j$, the greatest common divisor of $i$ and $j$, written

gcd $(i, j)$

is the largest integer $k$ such that

$(i \% k = 0)$    and    $(j \% k = 0)$.

For example, gcd (35, 21) = 7 and gcd (8, 15) = 1. Develop a recursive method that returns the greatest common divisor of $i$ and $j$. Here is the method specification:

```
/**
 * Finds the greatest common divisor of two given positive integers.
 *
 * @param i – one of the given positive integers.
 * @param j – the other given positive integer.
 *
 * @return the greatest common divisor of i and j.
 *
 * @throws IllegalArgumentException – if either i or j is not a positive integer.
 *
 */
public static int gcd (int i, int j)
```

Test your method with a main method that reads in two positive integers and outputs their greatest common divisor.

**Big hint:** According to Euclid's algorithm, the greatest common divisor of $i$ and $j$ is $j$ if $i \% j = 0$. Otherwise, the greatest common divisor of $i$ and $j$ is the greatest common divisor of $j$ and $(i \% j)$.

**5.4**    A *palindrome* is a string that is the same from right to left as from left to right. For example, the following are palindromes:

ABADABA
RADAR
OTTO
MADAMIMADAM
EVE

For this exercise, we restrict each string to uppercase letters only. (You are asked to remove this restriction in the next exercise.)

Develop a method that uses recursion to test for palindromes. The only input is a string that is to be tested for palindromehood. The method specification is

```
/**
 * Determines whether a given string of upper-case letters is a palindrome.
 * A palindrome is a string that is the same from right-to-left as from left-to-right.
 *
 * @param s – the given string
 *
 * @return true – if the string s is a palindrome.
 *
 */
public static boolean isPalindrome (String s)
```

*Hint:* Make the above method a wrapper for the following overloaded, recursive method:

```
/**
 * Determines whether the substring of given string of upper-case letters is a
 * palindrome. A palindrome is a string that is the same from right-to-left as
 * from left-to-right.
 *
 * @param s – the given string
 * @param i – the starting index of the substring of s.
 * @param j – the ending index of the substring of s.
 *
 * @return true – if the substring of s between indexes i and j inclusive is a
 *          palindrome.
 *
 * @throws IllegalArgumentException – if either i or j is a negative integer.
 *
 */
public static boolean isPalindrome (String s, int i, int j)
```

If i >= j, the substring of s at indexes i through j is a (trivial) palindrome. Otherwise, that substring of s is a palindrome if and only if s.charAt (i) = s.charAt (j) and the substring of s at indexes i + 1 through j − 1 is a palindrome.

Test your method with a main method that reads in a string and outputs whether or not that string is a palindrome (and catches IllegalArgumentException).

5.5   Extend the recursive method developed in Programming Exercise 5.4 so that, in testing to see whether s is a palindrome, nonletters are ignored and no distinction is made between uppercase and lowercase letters. For example, the following are palindromes:

Madam, I'm Adam.

Able was I 'ere I saw Elba.

A man. A plan. A canal. Panama!

*Hint:* The toUpperCase( ) method in the String class returns the uppercase String corresponding to the calling object.

**5.6** **a.** Develop a recursive method power that returns the result of integer exponentiation. The method specification is

```
/**
    * Calculates the value of a given integer raised to the power of a second integer.
    * The worstTime(n) is O(n), where n is the second integer.
    *
    * @param i – the base integer (to be raised to a power).
    * @param n – the exponent (the power i is to be raised to).
    *
    * @return the value of i to the nth power.
    *
    * @throws IllegalArgumentException – if n is a negative integer.
    *
    */
public static long power (int i, Int n)
```

*Hint:* We define $0^0 = 1$, so for any integer $i$, $i^0 = 1$. For any integer $i$ and for any integer $n > 0$,

$$i^n = i \cdot i^{n-1}$$

**b.** Develop an iterative version of the power method.

**c.** Develop a recursive version of the power method for which worstTime($n$) is logarithmic in $n$.

*Hint:* If n is even, power (i, n) = power (i * i, n / 2); if n is odd, power (i, n) = $i \cdot i^{n-1}$ = $i$ * power (i * i, n / 2).

In all three cases, test your power method with a main method that converts an input line into integers $i$ and $n$ and outputs $i^n$ (and catches IllegalArgumentException).

**5.7** Develop a recursive method to determine the number of distinct ways in which a given amount of money in cents can be changed into quarters, dimes, nickels, and pennies. Each line of input contains an amount. For example, if the amount is 17 cents, then there are six ways to make change:

1 dime, 1 nickel, and 2 pennies

1 dime and 7 pennies

3 nickels and 2 pennies

2 nickels and 7 pennies

1 nickel and 12 pennies

17 pennies

Here are some input/output pairs. The first number in each pair is the amount, and the second number is the number of ways in which that amount can be changed into quarters, dimes, nickels, and pennies:

17 6

5 2

10 4

25 13

42 31

61 73

99 213

Here is the method specification:

```
/**
 * Calculates the number of ways that a given amount can be changed into
 * coins whose values are no larger than a given denomination.
 *
 * @param amount – the given amount.
 * @param denomination – the given denomination (1 = penny, 2 = nickel,
 *        3 = dime, 4 = quarter).
 *
 * @return 0 – if amount is less than 0; otherwise, the number of ways that
 *        amount can be changed into coins whose values are no larger than
 *        denomination.
 *
 */
public static int ways (int amount, int denomination)
```

For the sake of simplifying the ways method, develop a coins method that returns the value of each denomination. Thus, coins (1) returns 1, coins (2) returns 5, coins (3) returns 10, and coins (4) returns 25.

Test your ways and coins methods with a main method that reads in an integer amount in cents between 1 and 99, inclusive, and outputs the number of ways that amount can be changed into quarters, dimes, nickels, and pennies.

*Hint:* The number of ways that one can make change for an *amount* using coins no larger than a quarter is equal to the number of ways that one can make change for *amount* − 25 using coins no larger than a quarter plus the number of ways one can make change for *amount* using coins no larger than a dime.

**5.8**   Modify the maze-search application to allow an end user to enter the maze information directly, instead of in a file. Throw exceptions for incorrect row or column numbers in the start and finish positions.

**5.9**   Modify the maze-search application so that diagonal moves would be valid.

*Hint:* Only the MazeIterator class needs to be modified.

# Programming Project 5.1

## Iterative Version of the Towers of Hanoi

Develop an iterative version of the move method in the Towers of Hanoi game. Test that method with a main method that reads in the number of disks and then calls move.

*Hint:* We can determine the proper move at each stage provided we can answer the following three questions:

### 1. Which Disk Is to Be Moved?

To answer this question, we set up an *n-bit counter*, where $n$ is the number of disks, and initialize that counter to all zeros. The counter can be implemented as an $n$-element array of zeros and ones, or as an $n$-element array of **boolean** values. That is the only array you should use for this project.

    For example, if $n = 5$, we would start with

00000

Each bit position corresponds to a disk: the rightmost bit corresponds to disk 1, the next rightmost bit to disk 2, and so on.

    At each stage, the rightmost zero bit corresponds to the disk to be moved, so the first disk to be moved is, as you would expect, disk 1. After a disk has been moved, we increment the counter as follows: starting at the rightmost bit and working to the left, keep flipping bits (0 to 1, 1 to 0) until a zero gets flipped. For example, the first few increments and moves are as follows:

00000 // move disk 1
00001 // move disk 2
00010 // move disk 1
00011 // move disk 3
00100 // move disk 1
00101 // move disk 2

After 31 moves, the counter will contain all ones, so no further moves will be needed or possible. In general, $2^n - 1$ moves and $2^n - 1$ increments will be made.

### 2. In Which Direction Should that Disk Be Moved?

If $n$ is odd, then odd-numbered disks move clockwise:

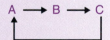

and even-numbered disks move counterclockwise:

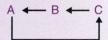

*(continued on next page)*

*(continued from previous page)*

If *n* is even, even-numbered disks move clockwise and odd-numbered disks move counterclockwise.

If we number the poles 0, 1, and 2 instead of *A*, *B*, and *C*, then movements can be accomplished simply with modular arithmetic. Namely, if we are currently at pole *k*, then

    k = (k + 1) % 3;

achieves a clockwise move, and

    k = (k + 2) % 3;

achieves a counterclockwise move. For the pole on which the just moved disk resides, we cast back to a character:

    **char** (k + 'A')

### 3. Where Is That Disk Now?

Keep track of where disk 1 is. If the counter indicates that disk 1 is to be moved, use the answer to question 2 to move that disk. If the counter indicates that the disk to be moved is not disk 1, then the answer to question 2 tells you where that disk is now. Why? Because that disk cannot be moved on top of disk 1 and cannot be moved from the pole where disk 1 is now.

# Programming Project 5.2

## Eight Queens

Develop and validate a program to place eight queens on a chess board in such a way that no queen is under attack from any other queen.

### Analysis

A chess board has eight rows and eight columns. In the game of chess, the queen is the most powerful piece: she can attack any piece in her row, any piece in her column, and any piece in either of her diagonals. See Figure 5.14.

The output should show the chess board after the placement of the eight queens. For example:

```
       0  1  2  3  4  5  6  7
   0 | Q|  |  |  |  |  |  |  |
   1 |  |  |  |  |  |  | Q|  |
   2 |  |  |  | Q|  |  |  |  |
   3 |  |  |  |  |  |  |  | Q|
   4 |  | Q|  |  |  |  |  |  |
   5 |  |  |  | Q|  |  |  |  |
   6 |  |  |  |  | Q|  |  |  |
   7 |  |  | Q|  |  |  |  |  |
```

*Hint:* There must be exactly one queen in each row and exactly one queen in each column. There is no input: start with a queen at (0, 0), and place a queen in each column. A valid position is one that is not in the same row, column, or diagonal as any queen placed in a previous column. The QueensIterator constructor should advance to row 0 of the next

**Figure 5.14** I Positions vulnerable to a queen in chess. The arrows indicate the positions that can be attacked by the queen Q in the center of the figure.

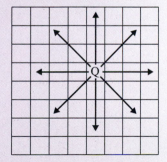

*(continued on next page)*

*(continued from previous page)*

column. The next method should advance to the next row in the same column. So the first time the tryToReachGoal method in the BackTrack class is called, the choices are:

(0, 1) // invalid: in the same row as the queen at (0, 0)

(1, 1) // invalid: in the same diagonal as the queen at (0, 0)

(2, 1) // valid

When the tryToReachGoal method is called again, the choices are:

(0, 2) // invalid: in the same row as the queen at (0, 0)

(1, 2) // invalid: in the same diagonal as the queen at (1, 2)

(2, 2) // invalid: in the same row as the queen at (1, 2)

(3, 2) // invalid: in the same diagonal as the queen at (1, 2)

(4, 2) // valid

# Programming Project 5.3

## A Knight's Tour

Develop and test a program to show the moves of a knight in traversing a chess board.

### Analysis

A chess board has eight rows and eight columns. From his current position, a knight's next position will be either two rows and one column or one row and two columns from the current position. For example, Figure 5.15 shows the legal moves of a knight at position (5, 3), that is, row 5 and column 3.

For simplicity, the knight starts at position (0, 0). Assume the moves are tried in the order given in Figure 5.15. That is, from position (row, column), the order tried is:

(row − 2, column + 1)
(row − 1, column + 2)
(row + 1, column + 2)
(row + 2, column + 1)
(row + 2, column − 1)
(row + 1, column − 2)
(row − 1, column − 2)
(row − 2, column − 1)

Figure 5.16 shows the first few moves.

**Figure 5.15** | For a knight (K) at coordinates (5, 3), the legal moves are to the grid entries labeled K0 through K7.

| | 0 | 1 | 2 | 3 | 4 | 5 | 6 | 7 |
|---|---|---|---|---|---|---|---|---|
| 0 | | | | | | | | |
| 1 | | | | | | | | |
| 2 | | | | | | | | |
| 3 | | | K7 | | K0 | | | |
| 4 | | K6 | | | | K1 | | |
| 5 | | | | K | | | | |
| 6 | | K5 | | | | K2 | | |
| 7 | | | K4 | | K3 | | | |

*(continued on next page)*

*(continued from previous page)*

For the nine moves, starting at (0, 0), in Figure 5.16, no backtracking occurs. In fact, the first 36 moves are never backtracked over. But the total number of backtracks is substantial: over 3 million. The solution obtained by the order of iteration from Figure 5.15 is:

|   | 0 | 1 | 2 | 3 | 4 | 5 | 6 | 7 |
|---|---|---|---|---|---|---|---|---|
| 0 | 1 | 38 | 55 | 34 | 3 | 36 | 19 | 22 |
| 1 | 54 | 47 | 2 | 37 | 20 | 23 | 4 | 17 |
| 2 | 39 | 56 | 33 | 46 | 35 | 18 | 21 | 10 |
| 3 | 48 | 53 | 40 | 57 | 24 | 11 | 16 | 5 |
| 4 | 59 | 32 | 45 | 52 | 41 | 26 | 9 | 12 |
| 5 | 44 | 49 | 58 | 25 | 62 | 15 | 6 | 27 |
| 6 | 31 | 60 | 51 | 42 | 29 | 8 | 13 | 64 |
| 7 | 50 | 43 | 30 | 61 | 14 | 63 | 28 | 7 |

Notice that the 37th move, from position (1, 3), does not take the first available choice—to position (3, 2)—nor the second available choice—to position (2, 1). Both of those choices led to dead ends, and backtracking occurred. The third available choice, to (0, 1), eventually led to a solution. In the system tests below, the input is in **boldface.**

## System Test 1

Enter the starting row and column: **0 0**

Starting at row 0 and column 0, the solution is

|   | 0 | 1 | 2 | 3 | 4 | 5 | 6 | 7 |
|---|---|---|---|---|---|---|---|---|
| 0 | 1 | 38 | 55 | 34 | 3 | 36 | 19 | 22 |
| 1 | 54 | 47 | 2 | 37 | 20 | 23 | 4 | 17 |
| 2 | 39 | 56 | 33 | 46 | 35 | 18 | 21 | 10 |
| 3 | 48 | 53 | 40 | 57 | 24 | 11 | 16 | 5 |
| 4 | 59 | 32 | 45 | 52 | 41 | 26 | 9 | 12 |
| 5 | 44 | 49 | 58 | 25 | 62 | 15 | 6 | 27 |
| 6 | 31 | 60 | 51 | 42 | 29 | 8 | 13 | 64 |
| 7 | 50 | 43 | 30 | 61 | 14 | 63 | 28 | 7 |

**Figure 5.16 |** The first few valid moves by a knight that starts at position (0, 0) and iterates according to the order shown in Figure 5.15. The integer at each filled entry indicates the order in which the moves were made.

|   | 0 | 1 | 2 | 3 | 4 | 5 | 6 | 7 |
|---|---|---|---|---|---|---|---|---|
| 0 | 1 |  |  | 3 |  |  |  |  |
| 1 |  |  | 2 |  |  | 4 |  |  |
| 2 |  |  |  |  |  |  | 10 |  |
| 3 |  |  |  |  |  |  | 5 |  |
| 4 |  |  |  |  |  | 9 |  |  |
| 5 |  |  |  |  |  | 6 |  |  |
| 6 |  |  |  |  | 8 |  |  |  |
| 7 |  |  |  |  |  |  | 7 |  |

*Note:* The lines are not part of the output; they are included for readability.

**System Test 2**

Enter the starting row and column: **3 5**

Starting at row 3 and column 5, the solution is

|   | 0 | 1 | 2 | 3 | 4 | 5 | 6 | 7 |
|---|---|---|---|---|---|---|---|---|
| 0 | 33 | 42 | 35 | 38 | 31 | 40 | 19 | 10 |
| 1 | 36 | 57 | 32 | 41 | 20 | 9 | 2 | 17 |
| 2 | 43 | 34 | 37 | 30 | 39 | 18 | 11 | 8 |
| 3 | 56 | 51 | 58 | 21 | 28 | 1 | 16 | 3 |
| 4 | 59 | 44 | 29 | 52 | 47 | 22 | 7 | 12 |
| 5 | 50 | 55 | 46 | 27 | 62 | 15 | 4 | 23 |
| 6 | 45 | 60 | 53 | 48 | 25 | 6 | 13 | 64 |
| 7 | 54 | 49 | 26 | 61 | 14 | 63 | 24 | 5 |

This solution requires 11 million backtracks. Some starting positions, for example (0, 1), require over 600 million backtracks. But for every possible starting position, there is a solution.

# Array-Based Lists

We begin this chapter by introducing the Java Collections Framework's List interface, which extends the Collection interface by providing some index-related methods. For example, there is a get method that returns the element at a given index. In any List object, that is, in any instance of a class that implements the List interface, the elements are stored in sequence, according to an index. For example, a List object pets might have the elements arranged as follows: "dog", "cat", "iguana", "gerbil". Here "dog" is at index 0, and "gerbil" is at index 3.

The main focus of this chapter is the user's view of the ArrayList class. We start by investigating the method specifications. We then briefly turn to the developer's view: The Java Collections Framework's ArrayList class implements the List interface with an underlying array that allows constant-time access of any element from its index. We finish up the chapter with an application in the area of public-key cryptography.

As with all of the other classes in the Java Collections Framework, the ArrayList class is parameterized, and the element class is the type parameter, so it would be more appropriate to refer to the class as ArrayList<E>. When a user creates an instance of the ArrayList<E> class, the user specifies the element type that will replace the type parameter E. For example, to create an ArrayList object whose elements must be of type (reference to) String, we write

```
ArrayList<String> myList = new ArrayList<String>( );
```

As we saw in Chapter 4, the element type cannot be a primitive type, such as **int** (but Integer is acceptable).

Chapter 7 covers another List implementation, the LinkedList class. The ArrayList and LinkedList classes have their own advantages and disadvantages: there is no "best" List implementation. A major goal of the two chapters is to help you recognize situations in which one of the classes would be preferable to the other. ∎

## CHAPTER OBJECTIVES

1. Recognize the methods in the List interface that are not in the Collection interface.

2. Understand the user's view of the ArrayList class.

3. Be able to decide when an ArrayList is preferable to an array—and vice versa.

4. Understand the VeryLongInt class from both the user's view and the developers' view.

## 6.1 | THE List INTERFACE

The List interface extends the Collection interface with methods that have an index as either a parameter or a return type. Here are thumbnail sketches of five of the methods. For each method below, E (for "element") is the type parameter.

**1.**    // Returns the element at position index in this List object.
     E get (**int** index);

**2.**    // Replaces the element that was at position index in this List object with the
     // parameter element, and returns the previous occupant.
     E set (**int** index, E element);

**3.**    // Returns the index of the first occurrence of element in this List object, if element
     // appears in this List object. Otherwise, returns −1.
     **int** indexOf (Object element);

**4.**    // Inserts element at position index in this List object; every element that
     // was at a position >= index before this call is now at the next higher position.
     **void** add (**int** index, E element);

**5.**    // Removes and returns the element at position index in this List object; every
     // element that was at a position > index before this call is now at the next lower
     // position.
     E remove (**int** index);

We do not include time estimates because different implementations of the interface may have different time estimates for the same method. Also, we cannot give examples of these methods because interfaces cannot be instantiated, but the above five methods should give you the idea that many of the methods in a List are index-based. Of course, we also have some holdovers from the Collection interface: the methods size, isEmpty, contains, clear, and so on.

Section 6.2 introduces the ArrayList class, which implements the List interface. We will emphasize the user's perspective of the ArrayList class by studying the method specifications. In Section 6.3, we take a quick look at the developer's perspective: the actual fields and method definitions in the Java Collections Framework. Then we return to the user's view with an application of the ArrayList class.

## 6.2 | THE ArrayList CLASS

An ArrayList object can be thought of as an improved version of the one-dimensional array. Like an array, the ArrayList class supports random access of its elements, that is, any element can be accessed in constant time, given only the index of the element. But unlike an array, an ArrayList object's size is automatically maintained during the execution of a program. Also, there are ArrayList methods for inserting and deleting at any index—if you insert or delete in an array, you must write the code to open up or close up the space. Finally, if you want to insert an element into an array that is already full, you must write the code (to create a new array, copy the old array to the new array, and so on). With an ArrayList object, such expansions are handled automatically.

Figure 6.1 has the big picture from the user's perspective: the method heading for each public method in the ArrayList class. Except for the constructors, the headings are in alphabetical order by method identifier. The type parameter E may appear as the return type as well as the element type of a parameter.

Section 6.2.1 has more detail: the method specifications, with examples, for several ArrayList methods.

## 6.2.1 Method Specifications for the ArrayList Class

The method specifications below use javadoc, and will yield specifications that are similar to, but shorter than, those provided with Sun's Application Programming Interface (API). You are strongly urged to consult that API to get the full details of each specification. The phrase "this ArrayList object" refers to the calling object.

**Figure 6.1** | Public methods in the class ArrayList<E>, where E is the type parameter. Except for the constructors, the method headings are in alphabetical order by method identifier.

1. **public** ArrayList (**int** initialCapacity)
2. **public** ArrayList( )
3. **public** ArrayList (Collection<? **extends** E> c)
4. **public boolean** add (E element)  // inserts at back
5. **public void** add (**int** index, E element)
6. **public boolean** addAll (Collection<? **extends** E> c)
7. **public boolean** addAll (**int** index, Collection<? **extends** E> c)
8. **public void** clear( )   // worstTime (n) is O (n)
9. **public** Object clone( )
10. **public boolean** contains (Object element)
11. **public boolean** containsAll (Collection<?> c)
12. **public void** ensureCapacity (**int** minCapacity)
13. **public boolean** equals (Object o)
14. **public** E get (**int** index)    // worstTime (n) is constant
15. **public int** hashCode( )
16. **public int** indexOf (Object element)
17. **public boolean** isEmpty( )
18. **public** Iterator<E> iterator( )
19. **public int** lastIndexOf (Object element)
20. **public** ListIterator<E> listIterator( )
21. **public** ListIterator<E> listIterator (**final int** index)
22. **public boolean** remove (Object element)
23. **public** E remove (**int** index)
24. **public boolean** removeAll (Collection<?> c)
25. **public boolean** retainAll (Collection<?> c)
26. **public** E set (**int** index, E element)
27. **public int** size( )
28. **public** List<E> subList (**int** fromIndex, **int** toIndex)
29. **public** Object[ ] toArray( )
30. **public** <T> T[ ] toArray (T[ ] a)
31. **public** String toString( )
32. **public void** trimToSize( )

Each method's time requirements are specified with Big-O notation because we are merely establishing an upper bound: a specific implementation of the method may reduce that upper bound. If no time estimate for a method is given, you may assume, that worstTime($n$) is constant. If a method's average-time estimate is the same as the worst-time estimate, only the worst-time estimate is given.

The following method specifications give you a user's of the ArrayList class. For each method, we include an example and a comparison with an array. The numbering of methods below is as given in Figure 6.1, but the order is different for the sake of the examples: the example of the two-parameter add method uses both the size and get methods.

**1.**   /**
    * Initializes this ArrayList object to be empty, with the specified initial capacity.
    *
    * @param initialCapacity the initial capacity of the list.
    *
    * @throws IllegalArgumentException–if the specified initial capacity is negative.
    *
    */
**public** ArrayList (**int** initialCapacity)

*Example:* The following creates an empty ArrayList object called fruits, with String elements and an initial capacity of 100:

ArrayList<String> fruits = **new** ArrayList<String> (100);

*Note:* There is also a default constructor. For example,

ArrayList<String> fruits = **new** ArrayList<String>( );

simply constructs an empty ArrayList object with a default initial capacity (namely, 10).

*Comparison to an array:* An array object can be constructed with a specified initial capacity. For example,

String [ ] vegetables = **new** String [10];

makes vegetables an array object with **null** references at indexes 0 through 9. Unlike an ArrayList object, an array object can consist of primitive elements. For example,

**double** [ ] salaries = **new double** [200];

constructs an array object whose elements will be of type **double** and whose initial capacity is 200. And, unlike an ArrayList object, an array object can be initialized when it is created, with an implicit initial capacity. For example,

String [ ] vegetables = {"corn", "peas", "potatoes"};

constructs a 3-element array object whose elements are "corn", "peas", and "potatoes" at indexes 0 through 2, respectively.

**3.**
```
/**
 * Constructs a list containing the elements of the specified collection, in the order
 * they are stored in the specified collection. This ArrayList object has an
 * initial capacity of 110% the size of the specified collection. The worstTime(n)
 * is O(n), where n is the number of elements in the specified collection.
 *
 * @param c – the specified collection whose elements this ArrayList object is
 *             initialized from.
 *
 */
public ArrayList (Collection<? extends E> c)
```

*Example:* Suppose that myList is an ArrayList object whose elements are the Strings "yes", "no", and "maybe". We can create another ArrayList object that initially contains a copy of myList as follows:

```
ArrayList<String> newList = new ArrayList<String> (myList);
```

*Note 1:* This constructor is called the *copy constructor.*

*Note 2:* The argument corresponding to the parameter c must be an instance of a class that implements the Collection interface, and the element type must be the same as the element type of the calling object or a subclass of that type. But that argument need not be an ArrayList object; the argument may be an ArrayCollection object or a LinkedList object, among others. For example, if salaryList is an ArrayList object whose elements are of type SalariedEmployee (a subclass of FullTimeEmployee), we can create an ArrayList object of type FullTimeEmployee as follows:

```
ArrayList<FullTimeEmployee> empList =
      new ArrayList<FullTimeEmployee> (salaryList);
```

All of the elements in empList are now of type SalariedEmployee and, therefore, of type FullTimeEmployee. We can add elements of type FullTime Employee to empList.

*Note 3:* Strictly speaking, the new ArrayList object contains a copy of the *references* to the elements in c; the elements themselves are not copied. For this reason, the copy constructor is said to produce a *shallow copy.*

*Note 4:* The clone( ) method is an alternative, but less desirable way to obtain a shallow copy of an ArrayList object. Here is the method specification:

```
/**
 * Returns a shallow copy of this ArrayList object.
 * The worstTime(n) is O(n).
 *
 * @return a shallow copy of this ArrayList object.
 */
public Object clone( )
```

For example, if myList is an ArrayList object, we can create a shallow copy of myList as follows:

ArrayList<String> newList = (ArrayList<String>)myList.clone( );

Unfortunately, there is no assurance of type safety, so the assignment will be made even if myList is an ArrayList object with Integer elements! See Programming Exercise 6.4 for details. For more discussion of clone drawbacks, see Bloch (2001, pp. 45–52).

***Comparison to an array:*** An array object can be copied with the **static** method arraycopy in the System of the package java.lang. For example,

System.arraycopy (vegetables, i, moreVeggies, 0, 3);

performs a shallow copy of the array object vegetables, starting at index i, to the array object moreVeggies, starting at index 0. A total of 3 elements are copied.

4.   /**
     * Appends the specified element to the end of this ArrayList object.
     * The worstTime(n) is O(n) and averageTime(n) is constant.
     *
     * @param element – the element to be appended to this ArrayList object.
     *
     * @return true (as per the general contract of the Collection.add method).
     *
     */
**public boolean** add (E element)

***Note:*** According to the general contract of the add method in the Collection interface, **true** is returned if the element is inserted. So this ArrayList method will *always* return **true**. Then why bother to have it return a value? Because if we replace the return type **boolean** with **void**, then the ArrayList class would no longer implement the Collection interface. Incidentally, there are some implementations—the TreeSet class, for example—of the Collection interface that do not allow duplicate elements, so **false** will sometimes be returned when a TreeSet object calls this version of the add method.

***Example:*** We can insert items at the end of an ArrayList object as follows:

ArrayList<String> fruits = **new** ArrayList<String> (100);
fruits.add ("kumquats");
fruits.add ("apples");
fruits.add ("durian");
fruits.add ("apples");

The ArrayList object fruits will now have "kumquats" at index 0, "apples" at index 1, "durian" at index 2, and "apples" at index 3.

***Comparison to an array:*** To insert into an array, an index must be specified:

```
String [ ] vegetables = new String [10];
vegetables [0] = "carrots";
vegetables [1] = "broccoli";
vegetables [2] = "spinach";
vegetables [3] = "corn";
```

**27.**
```
/**
  * Determines the number of elements in this ArrayList object.
  *
  * @return the number of elements in this ArrayList object.
  *
  */
public int size( )
```

*Example:* Suppose we create an ArrayList object as follows:

```
ArrayList<String> fruits = new ArrayList<String> (100);
fruits.add ("kumquats");
fruits.add ("apples");
fruits.add ("durian");
fruits.add ("apples");
```

Then

```
System.out.println (fruits.size( ));
```

will output 4.

*Comparison to an array:* Arrays have nothing that corresponds to a size( ) method. The length field contains the capacity of the array, that is, the *maximum* number of elements that can be inserted into the array, not the current number of elements in the array.

**14.**
```
/**
  * Returns the element at the specified index.
  *
  * @param index–the index of the element to be returned.
  *
  * @return the element at the specified index.
  *
  * @throws IndexOutOfBoundsException–if index is less than 0 or greater
  *          than size( ).
  */
public E get (int index)
```

*Note:* Since no time estimates are given, you may assume that worstTime(*n*) is constant.

*Example:* Suppose we start by constructing an ArrayList object:

```
ArrayList<String> fruits = new ArrayList<String> (100);
```

```
fruits.add ("kumquats");
fruits.add ("apples");
fruits.add ("durian");
fruits.add ("apples");
```

Then

```
System.out.println (fruits.get (2));
```

will output "durian".

***Comparison to an array:*** The get method is similar to, but weaker than, the index operator for arrays. For example, suppose we start by constructing an array object:

```
String [ ] vegetables = new String [10];
vegetables [0] = "carrots";
vegetables [1] = "broccoli";
vegetables [2] = "spinach";
vegetables [3] = "corn";
```

Then

```
System.out.println (vegetables [1]);
```

will output "broccoli". But we can also overwrite that element:

```
vegetables [1] = "potatoes";
```

In contrast, the following is illegal if fruits is an ArrayList object:

```
fruits.get (1) = "pears"; // illegal
```

26.
```
/**
 *
 * Replaces the element at the specified index in this ArrayList object with the
 * specified element.
 *
 * @param index – the index of the element to be replaced.
 * @param element – the element to be stored at the specified index.
 *
 * @return the element previously stored at the specified index.
 *
 * @throws IndexOutOfBoundsException – if index is less than 0 or greater
 *          than or equal to size( ).
 */
public E set (int index, E element)
```

***Note:*** The worstTime($n$) is constant.

***Example:*** Suppose we start by constructing an ArrayList object:

```
ArrayList<String> fruits = new ArrayList<String> (100);
fruits.add ("kumquats");
```

```
fruits.add ("apples");
fruits.add ("durian");
fruits.add ("apples");
```

Then

```
System.out.println (fruits.set (2, "bananas"));
```

will change the element at index 2 to "bananas" and output "durian", the element that had been at index 2 before the set method was invoked.

***Comparison to an array:*** As noted in the comparison for the get method, an array's index operator can be used on the left-hand side of an assignment statement. For example, if vegetables is an array object,

```
vegetables [1] = "potatoes";
```

will change the element at index 1 to "potatoes".

5.
```
/**
 * Inserts the specified element at the specified index in this ArrayList object.
 * All elements that were at positions greater than or equal to the specified
 * index have been moved to the next higher position. The worstTime(n) is
 * O(n).
 *
 * @param index – the index at which the specified element is to be inserted.
 * @param element – the element to be inserted at the specified index.
 *
 * @throws IndexOutOfBoundsException – if index is less than 0 or greater
 *         than size( ).
 */
public void add (int index, E element)
```

***Example:*** Suppose we start by constructing an ArrayList object:

```
ArrayList<String> fruits = new ArrayList<String> (100);
fruits.add ("kumquats");
fruits.add ("apples");
fruits.add ("durian");
fruits.add ("apples");
```

Then

```
fruits.add (1, "cherries");
for (int i = 0; i < fruits.size( ); i++)
        System.out.println (fruits.get (i));
```

will produce output of

```
kumquats
cherries
apples
durian
apples
```

*Comparison to an array:* For an insertion anywhere except at the end of the array object, the code must be written to open up the space. For example, suppose we start by constructing an array object:

```
String [ ] vegetables = new String [10];
vegetables [0] = "carrots";
vegetables [1] = "broccoli";
vegetables [2] = "spinach";
vegetables [3] = "corn";
```

We can insert "lettuce" at index 1 as follows:

```
for (int j = 4; j > 1; j–)
        vegetables [j] = vegetables [j − 1];
vegetables [1] = "lettuce";
```

The array **vegetables** now consists of "carrots", "lettuce", "broccoli", "spinach", "corn", **null, null, null, null, null**.

23. 
```
/**
 * Removes the element at the specified index in this ArrayList object.
 * All elements that were at positions greater than the specified index have
 * been moved to the next lower position. The worstTime(n) is O(n).
 *
 * @param index – the index of the element to be removed.
 *
 * @return the element removed the specified index.
 *
 * @throws IndexOutOfBoundsException – if index is less than 0 or greater
 *          than or equal to size( ).
 */
public E remove (int index)
```

*Example:* Suppose we start by constructing an ArrayList object:

```
ArrayList<String> fruits = new ArrayList<String> (100);
fruits.add ("kumquats");
fruits.add ("apples");
fruits.add ("durian");
fruits.add ("apples");
```

Then we can remove (and return) the element at index 2 as follows:

```
System.out.println (fruits.remove (2));
```

The output will be "durian", and **fruits** will now contain "kumquats", "apples", and "apples".

*Comparison to an array:* For removal anywhere except at the end of an array, the code must be written to close up the space. For example, suppose we start by creating an array object:

```
String [ ] vegetables = new String [10];
vegetables [0] = "carrots";
vegetables [1] = "broccoli";
vegetables [2] = "spinach";
vegetables [3] = "corn";
vegetables [4] = "potatoes";
vegetables [5] = "squash";
```

Then we can remove the element at index 2 as follows:

```
for (int j = 2; j < 5; j++)
        vegetables [j] = vegetables [j + 1];
vegetables [5] = null;
```

The array vegetables now consists of "carrots", "broccoli", "corn", "potatoes", "squash", **null**, **null**, **null**, **null**, and **null**.

16. 
```
/**
 * Searches for the first occurrence of a specified element, testing for equality with
 * the equals method. The worstTime(n) is O(n).
 *
 * @param element – the element to be searched for.
 *
 * @return the index of the first occurrence of element in this ArrayList object; if
 *          element is not in this ArrayList object, –1 is returned.
 *
 */
public int indexOf (Object element)
```

*Example:* Suppose we start by constructing an ArrayList object:

```
ArrayList<String> fruits = new ArrayList<String> (100);
fruits.add ("kumquats");
fruits.add ("apples");
fruits.add ("durian");
fruits.add ("apples");
```

Then

```
System.out.println (fruits.indexOf ("apples"));
```

will output 1, and

```
System.out.println (fruits.indexOf ("kiwi"));
```

will output −1.

*Note:* The type of the parameter element is Object, not E, so the following is legal:

```
System.out.println (fruits.indexOf (new Integer (8)));
```

Of course, the output will be −1, because all the elements in fruits are of type String.

*Comparison to an array:* An explicit search must be conducted to determine if an element occurs in an array. For example, suppose we start by creating an array object:

```
String [ ] vegetables = new String [10];
vegetables [0] = "carrots";
vegetables [1] = "broccoli";
vegetables [2] = "spinach";
vegetables [3] = "corn";
vegetables [4] = "potatoes";
vegetables [5] = "squash";
```

If myVeg is a String object, we can print the index of the first occurrence of myVeg in the vegetables array as follows:

```
boolean found = false;
for (int j = 0; j < 6 && !found; j++)
       if (vegetables [j].equals (myVeg))
       {
              System.out.println (j);
              found = true;
       } // if
if (!found)
       System.out.println (-1);
```

If myVeg does not occur in the array object vegetables, −1 will be output.

These represent just a sampling of the ArrayList class's methods, but even at this point you can see that an ArrayList object is superior, in most respects, to an array object.

## 6.2.2  A Simple Program with an ArrayList Object

Perhaps you need more convincing that ArrayList objects are more useful than array objects. Here is a simple program that creates an ArrayList object from a file of words (one word per line), and then searches for a word in the ArrayList object, removes all instances of a word, appends a word, and converts a word to uppercase. The resulting ArrayList object is then printed out. Because this is an illustrative program, not an application, all of the code is in the main method, and there are no constant identifiers.

```
public static void main (String[ ] args)
{
       List<String> aList = new ArrayList<String>( );

       BufferedReader keyboardReader = new BufferedReader
                                            (new InputStreamReader (System.in)),
                      fileReader;

       String inFilePath,
              line,
```

```
            word;
try
{
        System.out.print ("\nPlease enter the path for the input file: ");
        inFilePath = keyboardReader.readLine( );
        fileReader = new BufferedReader (new FileReader (inFilePath));
        while (true)
        {
                line = fileReader.readLine( );
                if (line == null)
                        break;
                aList.add (line);
        } // while not end of file

        System.out.print ("\n\nPlease enter the word you want to search for: ");
        word = keyboardReader.readLine( );
        if (aList.indexOf (word) >= 0)
                System.out.println (word + " was found.\n\n");
        else
                System.out.println (word + " was not found.\n\n");

        System.out.print ("Please enter the word you want to remove: ");
        word = keyboardReader.readLine( );
        int removalCount = 0;
        while (aList.remove (word))
                removalCount++;
        if (removalCount == 0)
                System.out.println (word + " was not found, so not removed.\n\n");
        else if (removalCount == 1)
                System.out.println ("The only instance of " + word +
                                " was removed.\n\n");
        else
                System.out.println ("All " + removalCount + " instances of " +
                                word + " were removed.\n\n");

        System.out.print ("Please enter the word you want to append: ");
        word = keyboardReader.readLine( );
        aList.add (word);
        System.out.println (word + " was appended.\n\n");

        System.out.print ("Please enter the word you want to upper case: ");
        word = keyboardReader.readLine( );
        int position = aList.indexOf (word);
        if (position >= 0)
        {
                aList.set (position, word.toUpperCase( ));
                System.out.println (word + " was converted to upper-case.\n\n");
```

```
                    } // if word is in aList
                    else
                            System.out.println (word +
                                            " was not found, so not upper-cased.\n\n");

                            System.out.println ("Here is the final version:\n" + aList);
            } // try
            catch (IOException e)
            {
                    System.out.println (e);
            } // catch
    } // method main
```

When this program was run, the file a.in1 contained the following words, one per line:

Don't get mad Don't get even Get over it and get on with

Here is a sample run, with input in boldface:

Please enter the path for the input file: **a.in1**

Please enter the word you want to search for: **even**
even was found.

Please enter the word you want to remove: **get**
All 3 instances of get were removed.

Please enter the word you want to append: **life**
life was appended.

Please enter the word you want to convert to upper case: **over**
over was converted to upper-case.

Here is the final version:
[Don't, mad, Don't, even, Get, OVER, it, and, on, with, life]

In the above program, each removal takes $O(n)$ time. Programming Exercise 6.8 suggests how to perform all removals in one loop iteration. And you are invited, in Programming Exercise 6.9, to endure the grind of converting the program from ArrayList-based to array-based.

In Sections 6.2.3 and 6.2.4, we briefly put on a developer's hat and look at the ArrayList class heading, fields, and a few method definitions. In Section 6.3, we return to a user's perspective with an application of the ArrayList class.

## 6.2.3 The ArrayList **Class's Heading and Fields**

Here is the heading of the ArrayList class:

**public class** ArrayList<E> **extends** AbstractList<E>
      **implements** List<E>, RandomAccess, Cloneable, java.io.Serializable

This says that the ArrayList class is a subclass of the class AbstractList, and implements four interfaces: List, RandomAccess, Cloneable, and Serializable. Figure 6.2 has a UML diagram to indicate where the ArrayList class fits in the Java Collections Framework, with a solid-line arrow from an extension (to a class or interface) and a dashed-line arrow from a class to an interface implemented by the class.

The AbstractCollection class provides a minimal implementation of the Collection interface, just as the AbstractList class provides a "bare bones" implementation of the List interface. As we saw in Section 6.1, the List interface extends the Collection interface by including some index-related methods, such as get (**int** index) and remove (**int** index).

Basically, a class that implements the Cloneable interface must have a clone( ) method that returns a shallow copy of the calling object. For a description of the clone( ) method, see Note 4 on the copy constructor (method 3) in Section 6.2.1. The RandomAccess interface ensures that if an implementation of the List interface satisfies the random-access property (with an underlying array), then any sublist of that list will also satisfy the random-access property. The Serializable interface, discussed in Appendix 3, has to do with saving objects to a stream (such as a disk file), which is called *serialization,* and restoring those objects from the stream, called *deserialization.*

It may come as no surprise to you that the ArrayList class has an array field:

**private transient** E[ ] elementData;

**Figure 6.2 I** The UML diagram to illustrate the relative position of the ArrayList<E> class in the Java Collections Framework.

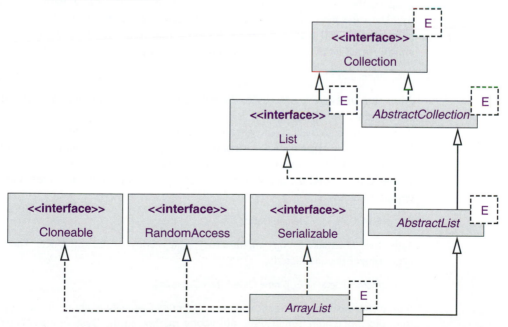

The reserved word **transient** indicates that this field is not saved during serialization (see Appendix 3). That is, each element would be saved, but not the entire array. The field is **private** instead of **protected** because the developers of the Java Collections Framework are opposed to giving users who subclass direct access to a superclass's fields. See Section 2.6 for a discussion of this choice.

The only other field defined in the ArrayList class is

    **private int** size;

So an ArrayList object has an array field to store the elements and an **int** field to keep track of the number of elements.

We will finish up our developer's view of the ArrayList class by studying the implementation of the add method that appends an element to the calling ArrayList object.

### 6.2.4 **Definition of the One-Parameter** add **Method**

To give you an idea of how expansion of an ArrayList object is accomplished, let's look at the definition of the one-parameter add method:

```
public boolean add (E element)
{
        ensureCapacity (size + 1);
        elementData [size++] = element;
        return true;
}
```

The call to the ensureCapacity method expands the underlying array, if necessary, to accommodate the new element; we'll get to the details of that method momentarily. Then the new element, element, is inserted at index size in the array, size is incremented, and **true** is returned. Suppose that fruits has been constructed as an empty ArrayList by a default-constructor call, and the next message is

    fruits.add ("kumquats");

After that message is processed, the elementData and size fields in fruits will have the contents shown in Figure 6.3.

Now let's get back to the ensureCapacity method. If the underlying array is not filled to capacity, then the call to ensureCapacity does nothing. But if size == element Data.length, then the argument size + 1 must be greater than elementData.length, so we need to expand the array. First, the array's current reference, elementData, is copied to oldData:

    E oldData [ ] = elementData;

This does not make a copy of the array, just a copy of the reference. Then a new array object is constructed:

    elementData = (E[ ]) **new** Object [newCapacity];

where (because the argument was size + 1) newCapacity is about 50 percent larger than oldData.length. Finally, the arraycopy method in the System class is called to

**Figure 6.3** | The contents of the **elementData** and size fields in the **ArrayList** object fruits after the message fruits.add ("kumquats") is sent. As usual, we pretend that the array contains objects instead of references.

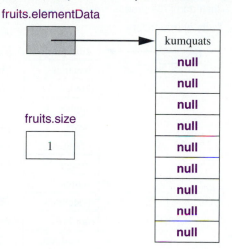

fruits.elementData

fruits.size

1

| kumquats |
| --- |
| **null** |
| **null** |
| **null** |
| **null** |
| **null** |
| **null** |
| **null** |
| **null** |
| **null** |

copy all the elements from oldData to elementData; the number of elements copied is the value of size.

Here is the complete definition:

```
public void ensureCapacity(int minCapacity)
{
        modCount++; // discussed in Appendix 3
        int oldCapacity = elementData.length;
        if (minCapacity > oldCapacity)
        {
                E oldData[ ] = elementData;
                int newCapacity = (oldCapacity * 3) / 2 + 1;
                if (newCapacity < minCapacity) // can't happen if argument is size + 1
                        newCapacity = minCapacity;
                elementData = (E) new Object [newCapacity];
                System.arraycopy(oldData, 0, elementData, 0, size);
        }
}
```

To see the effect of an expansion, suppose that the ArrayList object fruits already has 10 elements and the following message is sent:

```
fruits.add ("cantaloupes");
```

Figure 6.4 shows the effect of this message on the elementData and size fields of fruits.

What are the time estimates of the one-parameter add method? Let $n$ represent the number of elements in the calling ArrayList object. In the worst case, we will

**Figure 6.4** | The contents of the elementData and size fields in the ArrayList object
fruits if fruits already had 10 elements when the message fruits.add
("cantaloupes") was sent. As usual, we pretend that the array contains
objects instead of references.

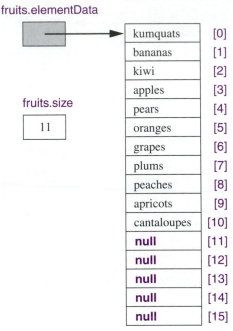

fruits.elementData

fruits.size

| | |
|---|---|
| kumquats | [0] |
| bananas | [1] |
| kiwi | [2] |
| apples | [3] |
| pears | [4] |
| oranges | [5] |
| grapes | [6] |
| plums | [7] |
| peaches | [8] |
| apricots | [9] |
| cantaloupes | [10] |
| **null** | [11] |
| **null** | [12] |
| **null** | [13] |
| **null** | [14] |
| **null** | [15] |

11

have $n$ = elementData.length, and so, in the ensureCapacity method, we will have
minCapacity > oldCapacity. Then the call to arrayCopy entails copying $n$ elements
from oldData to elementData. We conclude that worstTime($n$) is linear in $n$.

What about the average case? The only occasion for copying occurs when $n$ =
elementData.length. But then, by the details of the ensureCapacity method, no copying would have occurred in the previous $n / 3$ (approximately) calls to the one-
parameter add method. So in $n / 3 + 1$ calls to that add method, the total number of
elements copied would be $n$, and the average number of elements copied per call
would be about 3. We conclude, since the only non-constant-time code in the
ensureCapacity method is in the call to arrayCopy, that averageTime($n$) is constant
for the one-parameter add method.

Incidentally, the developers of the ArrayList class could have doubled old
Capacity instead of increasing it by about 50 percent. There is a trade-off: with doubling, additional space is allocated immediately, but then there will be a longer
period before the next resizing occurs. In fact, in the C++ analogue of the ArrayList
class, the old capacity *is* doubled when a resizing occurs.

The above examination of fields and implementation details is intended just to
give you the flavor of the developer's view of the ArrayList class. A few more
ArrayList method-definitions are covered in Lab 10. Of course, all of the ArrayList
definitions are available in the ArrayList (or AbstractList or AbstractCollection) class
of java.util.

**Lab 10: More Details on the** ArrayList **Class**

You are now prepared to do Lab 10.          All Labs Are Optional

Section 6.3 presents an application of the ArrayList class, so the emphasis once again is on the user's viewpoint.

# 6.3 | APPLICATION: HIGH-PRECISION ARITHMETIC

We now introduce high-precision arithmetic as an application of the ArrayList class. We will get to the details shortly, but it is worth recalling that the ***use*** of a class is independent (except for efficiency) of ***how*** the class is implemented. So we are not locked in to any particular implementation of the ArrayList class.

In public-key cryptography (see Simmons, 1992), information is encoded and decoded using integers more than 100 digits long. The essential facts about the role of these ***very long integers*** in public-key cryptography are:

1.  It takes relatively little time—$O(n^3)$—to generate a very long integer with $n$ digits that is prime.[1] For example, suppose we want to generate a prime number that has 500 digits. Then the number of loop iterations required is approximately $500^3 = 125,000,000$.

2.  It takes a very long time—currently, about $10^{n/2}$ loop iterations—to determine the prime factors of a very long integer with $n$ digits that is not prime. For example, suppose we want to factor a nonprime with 500 digits. Then the number of loop iterations required is approximately $(10^{500/2}) = 10^{250}$.

3.  Assume that you have generated $p$ and $q$, two very long integers that are prime. You then calculate another prime $e$ to be greater than $pq$. The product $pq$ can be calculated quickly, and you supply this product, and $e$, to anyone who wants to send you a message, $M$. First, the sender splits the message $M$ up into sequences of characters $M_1, M_2, \ldots$ . The sequence $M_i$ is then treated as a very long integer $V_i$ by concatenating the bits in each character in $M_i$. The encrypted integer corresponding to $V_i$ is $V_i^e \% pq$. That is, we raise $V_i$ to the power $e$ and then take the remainder when the result of that exponentiation is divided by $pq$. This seems complicated, but in fact, the calculation can be performed relatively quickly. See Simmons (1992) for details. The encoded message, as well as $pq$ and $e$, are ***public***, that is, transmitted over an insecure channel such as a telephone, postal service, or computer network.

4.  But decoding the message requires knowing the values of $p$ and $q$. Since determining the factors $p$ and $q$ takes prohibitively long, only you can decode the message.

Very long integers require far greater precision than is directly available in programming languages. We will now design and implement a simple version of the

---

[1] An integer $p > 1$ is **prime** if the only positive-integer factors of $p$ are 1 and $p$ itself.

VeryLongInt class. Programming Exercise 6.5 asks you to amplify this version, Lab 11 involves the development of a driver for the amplified version, and Programming Project 6.1 further expands the VeryLongInt class.

For an industrial-strength class that is applicable to public-key cryptography, see the BigInteger class in java.math. The BigInteger class includes efficient methods for primality testing, multiplication, and modular exponentiation.

### 6.3.1  **Method Specifications of the** VeryLongInt **Class**

There will be only three methods: A very long integer can be constructed from a string, converted to a string, or incremented by another very long integer. Here are the method specifications, with examples:

**1.**  /**
    * Initializes this VeryLongInt object from a given String object.
    * The worstTime(n) is O(n), where n represents the number of characters in s.
    *
    * @param s – the given String object.
    *
    * @throws NullPointerException – if s is null.
    *
    */
    **public** VeryLongInt (String s)

*Example*: Suppose we have

VeryLongInt veryLong = **new** VeryLongInt ("52?481");

Then veryLong will be initialized to the VeryLongInt object whose integer value is 52481. The "?" is ignored because it is not a digit character.

**2.**  /**
    * Returns a String representation of this VeryLongInt object. The worstTime(n) is
    * O(n), where n represents the number of digits in this VeryLongInt object.
    *
    * @return a String representation of this VeryLongInt object in the form '[' followed
    *      by the digits, separated by commas and single spaces, followed by ']'.
    *
    */
    **public** String toString( )

*Example:* Suppose we have

VeryLongInt veryLong = **new** VeryLongInt ("52?481");
System.out.println (veryLong); // same as
                        // System.out.println (veryLong.toString( ));

The output would be:

    [5, 2, 4, 8, 1]

**3.**
```
/**
 * Increments this VeryLongInt object by a specified VeryLongInt object.
 * The worstTime(n) is O(n), where n is the number of digits in the larger of this
 * VeryLongInt object (before the call) and the specified VeryLongInt object.
 *
 * @param otherVeryLong – the specified VeryLongInt object to be added to
 *        this VeryLongInt object.
 *
 * @throws NullPointerException – if otherVeryLong is null.
 *
 */
public void add (VeryLongInt otherVeryLong)
```

*Example:* Suppose that newInt and oldInt are VeryLongInt objects with values of 328 and 97, respectively, and the message sent is

```
newInt.add (oldInt);
```

Then the value of newInt has become 425.

*Note:* This method performs the arithmetic operation of addition. Contrast that to the ArrayList class's one-parameter add method, which appends the argument to the calling ArrayList object.

## 6.3.2 Fields in the VeryLongInt Class

As often happens in developing a class, the major decision involves the field(s) to represent the class. Should we store a very long integer in an array-based structure such as an ArrayList, or would a linked structure be better? (An array itself is not a good idea because then we would have to write the code—for example, to keep track of the number of elements in the array—instead of simply calling methods). In this chapter, we will use the ArrayList class and represent each very long integer as a sequence of digits. In Chapter 7, we will consider a linked structure.

Which is the appropriate relationship between VeryLongInt and ArrayList: **is-a** (inheritance) or **has-a** (aggregation)? That is, should VeryLongInt be a subclass of ArrayList, or should VeryLongInt have a field of type ArrayList? The primary purpose of the VeryLongInt class is to perform arithmetic; as such, it shares little functionality with the ArrayList class. So it makes more sense to say "a VeryLongInt object **has-an** ArrayList field" than "a VeryLongInt object **is-an** ArrayList object." The only field in the VeryLongInt class will be an ArrayList object whose elements are of type Integer:

```
protected ArrayList<Integer> digits;
```

Each element in the ArrayList object digits will be an Integer object whose value is a single digit (Concept Exercise 6.6 expands each value to a five-digit integer).

Figure 6.5 has the UML diagram for the VeryLongInt class.

**Figure 6.5 |** The class diagram for the VeryLongInt class.

### 6.3.3  **Method Definitions of the** VeryLongInt **Class**

The digits in the ArrayList field digits will be stored from left to right, that is, in their normal order. For example, if the value of a VeryLongInt object is 328, we would store the 3 at index 0 in digits, the 2 at index 1, and the 8 at index 2.

Notice that by having the insertions take place at the end of the ArrayList object, we take advantage of the average-case speed of the ArrayList class's one-parameter add method, which is not related to the VeryLongInt method named add. If, instead, we stored a number in reverse order, we would be repeatedly inserting at the front of the ArrayList object digits. Concept Exercise 6.7 explores the effect on efficiency if the digits are stored in reverse order.

We now define the String-parameter constructor, the toString( ) and add methods. While we do we will keep in mind the strengths (fast random access and fast end-insertions) and weakness (slow insertions at other-than-the-end positions) of the ArrayList class.

For the String-parameter constructor, we loop through the characters in s. For each character in s, if the character is a digit character, we convert that character to the corresponding digit by subtracting the Unicode representation of '0' from the character. For example,

$$\text{'7'} - \text{'0'} = 7$$

Finally, we append that digit (as an Integer) to digits. The ArrayList field digits never needs resizing during the execution of this constructor because that field is constructed with initial capacity of s.length( ). Here is the code:

```
public VeryLongInt (String s)
{
        final char LOWEST_DIGIT_CHAR = '0';

        digits = new ArrayList<Integer> (s.length( ));

        char c;

        int digit;
```

```
        for (int i = 0; i < s.length( ); i++)
        {
                c = s.charAt (i);
                if (Character.isDigit(c))
                {
                        digit = c - LOWEST_DIGIT_CHAR;
                        digits.add (digit); // digit is boxed to an Integer object
                } // if a digit
        } // for
  } // constructor with string parameter
```

How long will this method take? Assume that there are $n$ characters in the input. Then the loop will be executed $n$ times. For the ArrayList class's one-parameter add method, averageTime($n$) is constant, so for this constructor, averageTime($n$) is linear in $n$. As we saw in the analysis of that add method, if $n$ represents the number of elements in the ArrayList object, worstTime($n$) is $O(n)$—only because of the possibility of resizing. Since for this constructor, digits is never resized, worstTime($n$) is $O(n)$. In fact, because the worstTime($n$) cannot be less than averageTime($n$), worstTime($n$) must be linear in $n$.

For the toString( ) method, we simply invoke the ArrayList class's toString( ) method:

```
public String toString( )
{
        return digits.toString( );
} // method toString
```

For an example of a call to this method, if veryLong is a VeryLongInt object with a value of 6713, the output from the call to

```
System.out.println (veryLong); // same as System.out.println (veryLong.toString( ));
```

will be

    [6, 7, 1, 3]

For this method, worstTime($n$) is linear in $n$, the number of digits in the calling VeryLongInt object. To convince yourself of this estimate, you should look at the definition of the toString( ) method in the AbstractCollection class, a superclass of ArrayList.

Finally, we tackle the add (VeryLongInt otherVeryLong) method in the VeryLongInt class. We obtain partial sums by adding the value of otherVeryLong to the calling object digit by digit, starting with the least significant digit in each number. Each partial sum, modulo 10, is appended to the ArrayList object sumDigits, which is initially empty.

Because we will be using the ArrayList class's one-parameter add method on the partial sums, we must reverse sumDigits after adding so that the most significant digit will end up at index 0. For example, suppose newInt is a VeryLongInt object with the value 328 and oldInt is a VeryLongInt object with the value 47. If the message is

    newInt.add (oldInt);

then after adding and appending the partial sums to the ArrayList object sumDigits, sumDigits will have the value 573. When this is reversed—by the generic algorithm reverse in the Collections class of the package java.util—the sum will be correct. Note that the add method in the ArrayList class is used to append a digit to sumDigits; the ArrayList class's add method does not perform arithmetic!

Here is the definition of the add method in the VeryLongInt class:

```
public void add (VeryLongInt otherVeryLong)
{
        final int BASE = 10;

        int largerSize,
            partialSum,
            carry = 0;

        ArrayList<Integer> sumDigits = new ArrayList<Integer>( );

        if (digits.size( ) > otherVeryLong.digits.size( ))
                largerSize = digits.size( );
        else
                largerSize = otherVeryLong.digits.size( );

        for (int i = 0; i < largerSize; i++)
        {
                partialSum = least (i) + otherVeryLong.least (i) + carry;
                carry = partialSum / BASE;
                sumDigits.add (partialSum % BASE);
        } // for

        if (carry == 1)
                sumDigits.add (carry);
        Collections.reverse (sumDigits);
        digits = sumDigits;
} // method add
```

The call to the least method with an argument of i returns the ith least significant digit in the calling object's digits field. The unit's (rightmost) digit is considered the 0th least significant digit, the tens digit is considered the 1st least significant digit, and so on. For example, suppose that the calling VeryLongInt object has the value 3284971, and i has the value 2. Then the digit returned will be 9 because 9 is the 2nd least significant digit in the calling object's digits field; the 0th least significant digit is 1 and the 1st least significant digit is 7. The method definition is:

```
/**
 * Returns the ith least significant digit in digits if i is a nonnegative int less than
 * digits.size( ). Otherwise, returns 0.
```

```
          *
          * @param i – the number of positions from the right-most digit in digits to the
          *      digit sought.
          *
          * @return the ith least significant digit in digits, or 0 if there is no such digit.
          *
          * @throws IndexOutOfBoundsException – if i is negative.
          *
          */
         protected int least (int i)
         {
                if (i >= digits.size( ))
                        return 0;
                return digits.get (digits.size( ) - i - 1);
         } // least
```

We can now estimate the time requirements for the VeryLongInt class's add method. Assume, for simplicity, that the calling object and otherVeryLongInt are very long integers with $n$ digits. For the least method, worstTime($n$) is constant. There will be $n$ iterations of the **for** loop in the definition of the add method, and during each iteration, a digit is appended to sumDigits. For appending $n$ elements to an ArrayList, worstTime($n$) is linear in $n$; see Concept Exercise 6.2. The reverse generic algorithm also takes linear time, so for the add method in the VeryLongInt class, worstTime($n$) is linear in $n$.

## 6.3.4  A Driver for the VeryLongInt Class

To increase our confidence in the correctness of the VeryLongInt class, we now create a driver class, VeryLongDriver. The driver will read in, from the keyboard, the path for a file that holds the VeryLongInt method-calls information. For example, here are the contents of a sample input file (the comments are not part of the input file):

```
add 50            // throws NullPointerException; constructor should be called first
VeryLongInt 35    // initializes VeryLongInt object to have value of 35
VeryLongInt       // throws NullPointerException because no string supplied
VeryLongInt 56?7  // initializes VeryLongInt object to have value of 567
toString          // returns "[5, 6, 7]"
add 100           // VeryLongInt object now has value of 667
add               // throws NullPointerException because no string supplied
add 200           // VeryLongInt object now has value of 867
sub               // not a legal method
```

Also, the driver will read in the path for a file that will hold the results of making those calls; when those paths are read in, a file reader and file writer will be declared and opened. This openFiles( ) method returns (a reference to) the file writer so that file can be closed in the main method—after the output file has the results of processing the input file. The only other task for the driver is to test the VeryLongInt methods contained in the input file. Here are the method specifications:

```
/**
 * Reads in file paths and produces the output file by calling methods in the
 * input file.
 *
 * @return (a reference to) the file writer.
 *
 */
public PrintWriter openFiles( )

/**
 * Invokes methods specified in the input file.
 *
 */
public void testVeryLongIntMethods( )
```

The only fields in VeryLongDriver are the variables needed by both methods, namely the file reader and file writer:

```
protected BufferedReader fileReader;

protected PrintWriter fileWriter;
```

Figure 6.6 shows the combined class diagrams for VeryLongInt and VeryLongDriver. Note that there is an association, but not aggregation, between those two classes. The testVeryLongIntMethods method will certainly impact one or more VeryLongInt objects, but the VeryLongDriver class does not have a VeryLongInt object as a field.

## 6.3.5  **Implementation of the** VeryLongDriver **Class**

The openFiles( ) method reads in, from the keyboard, the input-file path and the output-file path, declares and opens the corresponding file reader and file writer, and

**Figure 6.6** I UML class diagrams for VeryLongDriver and VeryLongInt.

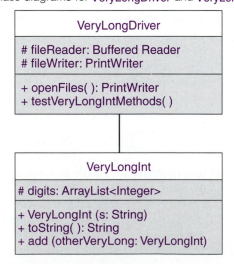

returns a reference to the file writer. A **while** loop is used to allow the end-user to recover from entering an incorrect path for either the input file or the output file. Here is the method definition:

```java
public PrintWriter openFiles( )
{
        final String IN_FILE_PROMPT =
                "\n\nPlease enter the path for the input file: ";

        final String OUT_FILE_PROMPT =
                "\n\nPlease enter the path for the output file: ";

        BufferedReader keyboardReader = new BufferedReader
                                (new InputStreamReader (System.in));

        String inFilePath,
                outFilePath;

        boolean pathsOK = false;

        while (!pathsOK)
        {
                try
                {
                        System.out.print (IN_FILE_PROMPT);
                        inFilePath = keyboardReader.readLine( );
                        fileReader = new BufferedReader (new FileReader (inFilePath));
                        System.out.print (OUT_FILE_PROMPT);
                        outFilePath = keyboardReader.readLine( );
                        fileWriter = new PrintWriter (new FileWriter (outFilePath));
                        pathsOK = true;
                } // try
                catch (IOException e)
                {
                        System.out.println (e);
                } // catch I/O exception
        } // while
        return fileWriter;
} // method openFiles
```

The testVeryLongIntMethods method loops through the input file, with a **try** block and a **catch** block (because we are reading from a file, Java requires that IOException be caught or propagated). During each loop iteration, one line is read from the input file, and the appropriate method—with an argument for the String-parameter constructor and the add method—is called. Here is the method definition:

```java
public void testVeryLongIntMethods( )
{
        final String LINE_MESSAGE = "The line is\n";
```

```java
        final String STRING_CONSTRUCTOR = "VeryLongInt";

        final String TO_STRING = "toString";

        final String ADD = "add";

        final String VERY_LONG_MESSAGE = "Here is the VeryLongInt: ";

        final String BAD_METHOD =
                "The line entered does not represent a legal method.";

        StringTokenizer tokens;

        String line,
               method,
               argument;

        VeryLongInt veryLong = null,
                    otherVeryLong;

        while (true)
        {
            try
            {
                line = fileReader.readLine( );
                if (line == null)
                    break;
                fileWriter.println (LINE_MESSAGE + line);
                tokens = new StringTokenizer (line);
                method = tokens.nextToken( );
                if (method.equals (STRING_CONSTRUCTOR))
                {
                    if (tokens.hasMoreTokens( ))
                    {
                        argument = tokens.nextToken( );
                        veryLong = new VeryLongInt (argument);
                    } // if more tokens
                    else
                        veryLong = new VeryLongInt (null);
                } // string-parameter constructor
                else if (method.equals (TO_STRING))
                {
                    // tested in last statement of this try block
                } // toString method
                else if (method.equals (ADD))
                {
                    if (tokens.hasMoreTokens( ))
                    {
```

```
                        argument = tokens.nextToken( );
                        otherVeryLong = new VeryLongInt (argument);
                        veryLong.add (otherVeryLong);
                } // if more tokens
                else
                        veryLong = new VeryLongInt (null);
            } // add method
            else
                    fileWriter.println (BAD_METHOD);
                    fileWriter.println (VERY_LONG_MESSAGE + veryLong + "\n\n");
        } // try
        catch (IOException e)
        {
                fileWriter.println (e + "\n\n");
        } // catch IOException
        catch (NullPointerException e)
        {
                fileWriter.println (e + "\n\n");
        } // catch NoSuchElementException
    } // while
} // method testVeryLongIntMethods
```

The main method invokes the driver methods inside a **try** block; the corresponding **finally** block simply closes the file writer.

```
public static void main (String[ ] args)
{
        PrintWriter writer = null;
        try
        {
                VeryLongDriver driver = new VeryLongDriver( );

                writer = driver.openFiles( );
                driver.testVeryLongIntMethods( );
        } // try
        finally
        {
                writer.close( );
        } // finally
} // method main
```

With this structure for a main method, the file writer will be closed, provided it was opened and the program terminated (no infinite loops).

Programming Exercise 6.5 expands on the VeryLongInt class. You should complete that exercise before you attempt to do Lab 11.

**Lab 11:** **Expanding the** VeryLongInt **Class**

You are now prepared to do Lab 11.                                  All Labs Are Optional

## SUMMARY

In this chapter we introduced the List interface, which extends the Collection interface by adding several index-based methods. We then studied the ArrayList class, an implementation of the List interface that allows random access—that is, constant-time access—of any element from its index. Using an ArrayList object is similar to using an array, but one important difference is that ArrayList objects are automatically resizable. When an ArrayList outgrows the current capacity of its underlying array, an array of 1.5 times that size is created, and the old array is copied to the larger array. This is similar to what hermit crabs do each time they outgrow their shell. A further advantage of ArrayList objects over arrays is that, for inserting and deleting, users are relieved of the burden of writing the code to make space for the new entry or to close up the space of the deleted entry.

The application of the ArrayList class was in high-precision arithmetic, an essential component of public-key cryptography.

## CONCEPT EXERCISES

**6.1**   State two advantages, and one disadvantage, of using an ArrayList object instead of an array object.

**6.2**   Show that, for the task of appending $n$ elements to an ArrayList object, worstTime($n$) is linear in $n$.

**6.3**   The one-parameter add method in the ArrayList class always returns **true**. Would it make sense to change the return type from **boolean** to **void**? Explain.

**6.4**   For the one-parameter add method in the ArrayList class, estimate worstSpace($n$) and averageSpace($n$).

**6.5**   In choosing fields for the VeryLongInt class, we decided to use, rather than inherit from, the ArrayList class. Why?

*Hint:* How much commonality is there between the methods in the ArrayList class and the methods in the VeryLongInt class?

**6.6**   Suppose you modified the VeryLongInt class as follows: each element in digits consists of a five-digit integer. What effect do you think this will have on Big-O time? What about run-time?

**6.7**   Suppose, in developing the VeryLongInt class, we decide that digits will contain the integer in reverse order. For example, if the constructor call is:

VeryLongInt veryLong = **new** VeryLongInt ("386");

we would have (Integer elements with values) 6, 8, 3 in positions 0 through 2, respectively, of digits. Redesign this constructor so that worstTime($n$) is still linear in $n$.

**6.8** Which parts of the VeryLongInt methods would have to be rewritten if digits were an array object of **int** elements instead of an ArrayList object of Integer elements?

**6.9** How can a user of the VeryLongInt class create a VeryLongInt object that is a copy of an already existing VeryLongInt object?

**6.10** In the callMethods( ) method of the VeryLongDriver class, suppose the input line has only one token (such as "VeryLongInt" or "add"). If tokens.next Token( ) were called after the first token is read in, NoSuchElementException would be thrown. Instead, the code is written so that the method is called with a **null** argument, and then NullPointerException is thrown. Explain why this is done.

# PROGRAMMING EXERCISES

**6.1** Hypothesize the output from the following code, and then test your hypothesis with a main method that includes the code:

```
ArrayList<Character> letters = new ArrayList<Character>( );

letters.add ('f');
letters.add (1, 'i');
letters.add ('e');
letters.add (1, 'r');
letters.add ('e');
letters.add (4, 'z');
System.out.println (letters);

letters.remove ('i');
int index = letters.indexOf ('e');
letters.remove (index);
letters.add (2, 'o');
System.out.println (letters);
```

**6.2** For each of the following program segments, hypothesize if the segment would generate a compile-time error, a run-time exception, or neither. Then test your hypotheses with a main method that includes each segment.

**a.**
```
ArrayList<String> myList = new ArrayList<String>( );
myList.add ("yes");
myList.add (7);
```

**b.**
```
ArrayList<Double> original = new ArrayList<Double>( );
original.add (7);
```

    **c.**   ArrayList<Integer> original = **new** ArrayList<Integer>( );
              **double** x = 7;
              original.add (x);

    **d.**   ArrayList<String> newList = **new** ArrayList<String>( );
              newList.add ("yes");
              Integer answer = (Integer)newList.get (0);

**6.3**    Suppose we have the following code:

```
ArrayList<String> myList = new ArrayList<String>( );

myList.add ("Karen");
myList.add ("Don");
myList.add ("Mark");

ArrayList<String> temp = new ArrayList<String> (myList);
ArrayList<String> sameList = myList;

myList.add (1, "Courtney");
```

Hypothesize what the contents of myList, temp, and sameList will be after this last insertion. Then test your hypothesis with a main method that includes the code.

**6.4**    Hypothesize what will happen when the following code fragment is run, and then test your hypothesis:

```
ArrayList<String> original = new ArrayList<String>( );
original.add ("yes");
ArrayList<Integer> copy = (ArrayList<Integer>)original.clone( );

System.out.println (copy.get (0));
```

*Hint:* This exercise illustrates why the copy constructor is superior to the clone( ) method.

**6.5**    Expand the VeryLongInt class by defining methods that have the following method specifications:

    **a.**   /**
```
 * Initializes this VeryLongInt object from a given int.
 *
 * @param n – the int from which this VeryLongInt is initialized.
 *
 * @throws IllegalArgumentException – if n is negative.
 *
 */
public VeryLongInt (int n)
```

    **b.**   /**
```
 * Returns the number of digits in this VeryLongInt object.
 *
 * @return the number of digits in this VeryLongInt object.
 *
```

```
        */
    public int size( )
```

c.
```
    /**
     * Returns true if this VeryLongInt object is less than another VeryLongInt
     * object. The worstTime(n) is O(n).
     *
     * @param otherVeryLong – the other VeryLongInt object.
     *
     * @return true – if this VeryLongInt is less than otherVeryLong.
     *
     * @throws NullPointerException – if otherVeryLong is null.
     *
     */
    public boolean less (VeryLongInt otherVeryLong)
```

d.
```
    /**
     * Returns true if this VeryLongInt object is greater than another VeryLongInt
     * object. The worstTime(n) is O(n).
     *
     * @param otherVeryLong – the other VeryLongInt object.
     *
     * @return true – if this VeryLongInt is greater than otherVeryLong.
     *
     * @throws NullPointerException – if otherVeryLong is null.
     *
     */
    public boolean greater (VeryLongInt otherVeryLong)
```

e.
```
    /**
     * Returns true if this VeryLongInt object is equal to a specified object.
     * The worstTime(n) is O(n).
     *
     * @param obj – the specified object that this VeryLongInt is compared to.
     *
     * @return true – if this VeryLongInt is equal to obj.
     *
     */
    public boolean equals (Object obj)
```

f.
```
    /**
     * Stores a Fibonacci number in this VeryLongInt object.
     *
     * @param n – the index in the Fibonacci sequence.
     *
     * @throws IllegalArgumentException – if n is not positive.
     *
     */
    public void fibonacci (int n)
```

*Example:* Suppose the following message is sent

tempInt.fibonacci (100);

Then tempInt's value will be 354224848179261915075—the 100th Fibonacci number.

*Hint:* Mimic the iterative design of the Fibonacci function from Lab 7. Both i and n will be ordinary **int** variables, but previous, current, and temp will be VeryLongInt objects. After the loop, instead of returning current, the calling object is modified by assigning current.digits to digits.

**6.6**   Assume that myList is (a reference to) an ArrayList<Double> object and that both i and j are **int** variables with values in the range from 0 to myList.size( ) − 1, inclusive. Hypothesize what the following accomplishes, and then test your hypothesis.

myList.set (i, myList.set (j, myList.get (i)));

**6.7**   Describe how to find the method definitions for the ArrayList class in your computing environment.

**6.8**   Modify the simple program in Section 6.2.2 so that all removals are performed in a single loop.

*Hint:* Create a temporary ArrayList object to hold the unremoved elements. What is a drawback to this approach?

**6.9**   Convert the simple program in Section 6.2.2 into one that uses an array object instead of an ArrayList object.

**6.10**  Modify the simple program in Section 6.2.2 to use a binary search instead of the sequential search used in the call to the indexOf method. The Collections class in java.util has a binarySearch method and a sort method.

**6.11**  Suppose scoreList is an ArrayList object of Integer elements, and the following message is sent:

scoreList.remove (3);

Does this message remove the element at index 3, or remove the first occurrence of **new** Integer (3)? Test your hypothesis.

**6.12**  Suppose we create the following ArrayList instance:

ArrayList<String> words = **new** ArrayList<String>( );

And then we insert several words into words. Write the code to print out each element of words that has exactly four letters. You should have three different versions of the code:

**a.**  Using an index.

**b.**  Using an iterator.

**c.**  Using an enhanced **for** statement.

## Programming Project 6.1

### Expanding the VeryLongInt Class

In the VeryLongInt class, develop a multiply method and a factorial method. Here is the method specification for multiply:

```
/**
 *   Stores in this VeryLongInt object the product of its pre-call value and the value
 *   of a specified VeryLongInt object. The worstTime(n) is O(n * n), where n is
 *   the maximum of the number of digits in the pre-call value of this
 *   VeryLongInt object and the number of digits in the specified VeryLongInt object.
 *
 *   @param otherVeryLong – the specified VeryLongInt object to be multiplied by
 *          this VeryLongInt object.
 *
 */
public void multiply (VeryLongInt otherVeryLong)
```

For factorial:

```
/**
 *   Stores, in this VeryLongInt object, the product of all integers between 1 and
 *   specified integer n. The worstTime(n) is O(n log (n!)): n multiplications, and
 *   each product has fewer digits than log (n!), the number of digits in n!
 *
 *   @param n – the number whose factorial will be stored in this VeryLongInt
 *          object.
 *
 *   @throws IllegalArgumentException – if n is negative.
 *
 */
public void factorial (int n)
```

Validate your methods by modifying the driver program from Lab 11.

## Programming Project 6.2

### The Deque Class

Implement the Deque class. A *deque*—pronounced "deck"—is a list such that:

1. Any element in the deque can be accessed in constant time.

2. An insertion at the *front* or back of the deque takes only constant time, on average.

3. A deletion at the front or back of the deque takes only constant time, even in the worst case.

Conceptually, the only difference between an ArrayList object and a Deque object is this: a Deque object can quickly add or remove at the front or back of itself, whereas an ArrayList object is fast only for adding or removing at the back of itself.

The Deque class has all of the methods that the ArrayList has, except that insertion or removal at the front is very fast. There are two Deque methods to take advantage of this speed (assume that E is the type parameter):

```
/**
 * Inserts a copy of a specified element at the front of this Deque object. The
 * averageTime(n) is constant. The worstTime(n) is O(n).
 *
 * @param element – the specified element to be inserted.
 *
 */
public void addFirst (E element)

/**
 * Removes and returns the element that had been at the front of this Deque
 * object before this call. The worstTime(n) is constant.
 *
 * @throws NoSuchElementException – if this Deque object is empty.
 *
 */
public E removeFirst( )
```

For the sake of simplicity, focus on only six methods: the default constructor, the two-parameter add method, the addFirst, removeFirst, size, and get methods. The last two methods will allow you to print out the entire Deque object.

*Hint:* There will be three fields:

```
protected int front,
               back;
protected E[ ] elementData;
```

(Making the Deque class a subclass of ArrayList is not an option because the elementData and size fields in the ArrayList class are **private**.)

There is a complication if, prior to an insertion in the front half of a Deque object, front has the value 0—or if, prior to an insertion in the back half of a Deque object, back has the value elementData.length − 1. In either case, we create a new array of size 2 * element Data.length. The original contents of elementData are stored in this new array—not at the beginning but in the middle—so there is room for growth both at the front and at the back. This new array reference is then assigned to elementData, and the values of the front and back fields are modified. The insertion can now be made as described above.

For example, suppose we make the following insertions to the Deque object from Example 3:

**4.**    addFirst ("can");

**5.**    addFirst ("do");

**6.**    addFirst ("if");

**7.**    addFirst ("on");

We now have front = 0, so if we call

**8.**    addFirst ("and");

then elementData will be resized and the elements recentered before the insertion is made. The result is

elementData

| null | null | null | null | null | null | and | on | if | do | can | no | yes | but | null | null | null | null | null | null |
|------|------|------|------|------|------|-----|----|----|----|-----|----|-----|-----|------|------|------|------|------|------|
| 0 | 1 | 2 | 3 | 4 | 5 | 6 | 7 | 8 | 9 | 10 | 11 | 12 | 13 | 14 | 15 | 16 | 17 | 18 | 19 |

front

6

back

13

Include a file-oriented driver to test the six methods (the default constructor, the two-parameter add method, and the methods addFirst, removeFirst, size, and get).

Assume the file deque.in1 contains the following:

    Deque
    add 0 but
    add 0 yes
    add 0 no
    addFirst can
    addFirst do
    addFirst if
    addFirst on

*(continued on next page)*

*(continued from previous page)*

addFirst and
size
get 0
get 7
removeFirst
size
get 0
get 7
addFirst wonder

System Test 1 (input in boldface):
Please enter the path for the input file: **Deque.1**
File not found exception.

Please enter the path for the input file: **Deque.in1**
File not found exception.

Please enter the path for the input file: **deque.in1**
Please enter the path for the output file: **deque.ou1**

The program has ended.

When the program has ended, the contents of deque.ou1 will be

Method: default constructor.

The deque now contains

Method: add
Index: 0
Element: but
The deque now contains
but

Method: add
Index: 0
Element: yes
The deque now contains
yes
but

Method: add
Index: 0
Element: no
The deque now contains
no
yes
but

Method: addFirst
Element: can
The deque now contains
can
no
yes
but

Method: addFirst
Element: do
The deque now contains
do
can
no
yes
but

Method: addFirst
Element: if
The deque now contains
if
do
can
no
yes
but

Method: addFirst
Element: on
The deque now contains
on
if
do
can
no
yes
but

Method: addFirst
Element: and
The deque now contains
and
on
if
do
can

*(continued on next page)*

*(continued from previous page)*

```
        no
        yes
        but

        Method: size
        Size: 8

        Method: get
        Index: 0
        Element: and

        Method: get
        Index: 7
        Element: but

        Method: removeFirst
        Element: and
        The deque now contains
        on
        if
        do
        can
        no
        yes
        but

        Method: size
        Size: 7

        Method: get
        Index: 0
        Element: on

        Method: get
        Index: 7
        IndexOutOfBoundsException

        Method: addFirst
        Element: wonder
        The deque now contains
        wonder
        on
        if
        do
        can
        no
        yes
        but
```

## Programming Project 6.3

### An Integrated Web Browser and Search Engine, Part 1

This is the first part of a sequence of related projects to create an integrated Web browser and search engine. The remaining parts are in Chapters 7 and 12 to 15. The overall project is based on a paper by Newhall and Meeden (2002).

#### Problem

Create a Scanner class with a getNextToken( ) method that returns a String. The Scanner class also includes a hasNextToken( ) method and a constructor that takes a Buffered Reader parameter. Each time the getNextToken( ) method is called, the next token in the file (corresponding to the constructor's BufferedReader parameter) is returned.

#### Analysis

1. The getNextToken( ) method should return the lowercase version of the word. For example, if the next word is "Sunless", the next token returned is "sunless".

2. The getNextToken( ) method should skip over common words such as "a", "and", and "in". The file common.in1 will contain the common words, one per line. Here are the (sample) contents of common.in1:

   ```
   a
   an
   and
   are
   did
   down
   in
   the
   where
   to
   ```

   You should assume that the file common.in1 is large enough so that it should be read in only once, and stored without a lot of unused space (the title of this chapter is a hint for the storage structure). Each search of the common words should take $O(\log n)$ time in the worst case. The file common.in1 may not be in alphabetical order, but the stored common words should be in alphabetical order (see Collections.java in java.util).

3. The getNextToken( ) method should skip over all characters in a tag, that is, all characters between < and >. You may assume that each < will be followed on the same line by a matching >. You may assume that the text between two link tags consists of a single word. That is, you might have <a href=...> singleword</a>.

   For example, suppose a line in the input file consists of

   Caverns are <a href =browser.in2>browser2</a> measureless to man

*(continued on next page)*

*(continued from previous page)*

Then the tokens returned would be

> caverns
> browser2
> measureless
> man

You may want to filter out the tags from a line before doing anything else to the line.

**4.**   The getNextToken( ) method should ignore punctuation—there is a StringTokenizer constructor that enables you to include commas, question marks, and so on as delimiters. For this project, the delimiters are the characters in the string "\n\r\t ,.;:?!".

**5.**   The input to the project consists of two lines: an input file that contains the original text, and an output file that contains the tokens, one per line. The Buffered Reader is constructed from the first input string. The tokens are printed to the file given in the second input string. Include appropriate messages and reprompts for incorrect input.

Incidentally, a scanner is essential for a search engine because the relevance of a document is based on the words the document contains.

### System Test 1 (prompts not included)

> kubla.in1
> kubla.ou1

If the file kubla.in1 consists of

> Caverns are <a href=browser.in2>browser2</a> measureless to man.

then the contents of kubla.ou1 will be

> caverns
> browser2
> measureless
> man

### System Test 2 (assume there is no file kubla.in2)

> kubla.in2
> Error: file kubla.in2 not found.
> kubla.in3
> kubla.ou3

If the file kubla.in3 consists of:

> In Xanadu did Kubla Khan
> A stately pleasure-dome decree:
> Where Alph, the sacred <a href=browser.in4>browser4</a> river, ran

Through caverns <a href=browser.in2>browser2</a> measureless to man
Down to a sunless sea.

then the contents of kubla.ou3 will be

xanadu

kubla

khan

stately

pleasure-dome

decree

alph

sacred

browser4

river

ran

through

caverns

browser2

measureless

man

sunless

sea

# Linked Lists

In this chapter we continue our study of collection classes by introducing the LinkedList class, part of the Java Collections Framework. Like the ArrayList class, the LinkedList class implements the List interface, so you are already familiar with most of the LinkedList method headings! There are some significant performance differences between the two classes. For example, LinkedList objects lack the random-access feature of ArrayList objects: to access a LinkedList's element from an *index* requires a loop that starts at the beginning or end of the list, whichever is closer to *index*. But LinkedList objects allow constant-time insertions and deletions, once the insertion point or deletion point has been accessed.

We will start with a general discussion of linked lists, and then introduce a simple linked structure, the SinglyLinkedList class. This toy class serves mainly to prepare you for the more powerful, and more complicated, LinkedList class. The application of the LinkedList class, a line editor, takes advantage of a LinkedList iterator's ability to insert or remove in constant time. ■

## CHAPTER OBJECTIVES

1. Be able to develop new methods for the SinglyLinkedList class.

2. Understand the LinkedList class from a user's perspective.

3. Given an application that requires a list, be able to decide whether an ArrayList or a LinkedList would be more appropriate.

4. Compare several choices of fields for the LinkedList class and, for each choice, be able to create a LinkedList object.

## 7.1 | WHAT IS A LINKED LIST?

Before we start investigating the LinkedList class, let's spend a little time on the general concept of a linked list. A ***linked list*** is a List object (that is, an object in a class that implements the List interface) in which the following property is satisfied:

> Each element is contained in an object, called an Entry object, that also includes a reference, called a ***link,*** to the Entry object that contains the next element in the list.

For the Entry object that holds the last element, there is no "next" element. For example, Figure 7.1 shows part of a linked list. We use an arrow to indicate that the field at the base of the arrow contains a reference to the Entry object pointed to by the tip of the arrow. And, for the sake of simplicity, we pretend that the type of element is String rather than reference-to-String.

Some linked lists also satisfy the following property:

> Each Entry object includes a link to the Entry object that contains the previous element in the list.

A linked list that satisfies the second property is called a ***doubly linked list.*** Otherwise, it is called a ***singly linked list.*** For example, Figure 7.2 shows part of a doubly linked list with three elements, and they happen to be in alphabetical order.

We have intentionally omitted any indication of how the first and last elements are identified, and what is stored in their previous and next links, respectively. In Section 7.3, we'll see that there are several options.

Most of this chapter is devoted to doubly linked lists, but we will start by studying singly linked lists because, as you might imagine, they are easier to develop (they are also less powerful).

## 7.2 | THE SinglyLinkedList CLASS—A SINGLY LINKED, TOY CLASS!

We now create a class, SinglyLinkedList, that partially implements the Collection interface of the Java Collections Framework. As suggested by Figure 7.1, the basic idea is to link the elements together in a chain: with each element we will include a reference to the next element in the collection. You will have the opportunity to

**Figure 7.1** I Part of a linked list.

**Figure 7.2** I Part of a doubly linked list.

expand on this SinglyLinkedList class in Lab 12 and in one of the programming projects at the end of this chapter.

The SinglyLinkedList class has very little functionality, and is not part of the
Java Collections Framework. You will never use it for application programs. Why
bother to learn it in the first place? You should view the SinglyLinkedList class as a
"toy" class that highlights the concepts of links and iterators, two essential features
of the Java Collections Framework. And, like any other toy, you will have the opportunity to play with the SinglyLinkedList class: to add new fields and methods, and to
alter the definitions of existing methods. You will study the SinglyLinkedList class
mainly to make it easier for you to understand the LinkedList class, which *is* in the
Java Collections Framework. The LinkedList class, doubly linked, is quite powerful
but also somewhat complex.

The elements in a SinglyLinkedList object are not stored contiguously, so with
each element we must provide information on how to get to the next element in the
collection. First, we create a class to hold a reference to an element and a "next" reference. In this Entry class, there are no methods (of course, there is always a default
constructor) and two fields, with E the type parameter:

```
protected class Entry<E>
{
        protected E element;
        protected Entry<E> next;
} // class Entry
```

The next field in an Entry holds a reference to another Entry object. A reference
to an Entry object is called a *link.* For example, Figure 7.3 depicts a sequence of
linked entries; each element is a String object. In the last Entry object, the next field
has the value **null**, which indicates that there is no subsequent Entry object.

The Entry class will be embedded in the SinglyLinkedList class. A class that is
embedded in another class is called a *nested class.* This embedding allows the
SinglyLinkedList class to access the two fields in an Entry object directly (a good
thing, too, because the Entry class has no methods). The Entry class has **protected**
visibility for the sake of future subclasses of SinglyLinkedList.

As with all other Collection classes, the SinglyLinkedList class is parameterized,
with E as the type parameter:

```
public class SinglyLinkedList<E> implements List<E>
```

We need not provide genuine implementations for each of the abstract methods in
the List interface. For methods we are not interested in, their definitions will simply

**Figure 7.3 |** Part of a singly linked list of three String elements.

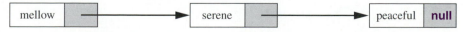

throw an exception. To start with, we will implement only five methods: a default constructor, isEmpty, add, size, and contains. Here are the method specifications:

1.  /**
    * Initializes this SinglyLinkedList object to be empty, with elements to be of
    * type E.
    *
    */
    **public** SinglyLinkedList( )

*Note:* Saying that a SinglyLinkedList object is empty means that the collection has no elements in it.

2.  /**
    * Determines if this SinglyLinkedList object has no elements.
    *
    * @return true – if this SinglyLinkedList object has no elements; otherwise,
    *          false.
    *
    */
    **public boolean** isEmpty ( )

*Example:* If we start with

SinglyLinkedList<Double> myLinked = **new** SinglyLinkedList<Double>( );

System.out.println (myLinked.isEmpty ( ));

The output would be

true

because the object referenced by myLinked has no elements.

3.  /**
    * Adds a specified element to the front of this SinglyLinkedList object.
    *
    * @param element – the element to be inserted (at the front).
    *
    * @return true.
    *
    */
    **public boolean** add (E element)

*Note 1:* Elements are inserted only ***at the front*** of a SinglyLinkedList object (this allows for a simpler implementation). For example, suppose the SinglyLinkedList object referenced by myLinked consists of "yes", "no", and "maybe", in that order, and the message is

myLinked.add ("simple");

Then the SinglyLinkedList object referenced by myLinked will consist of "simple", "yes", "no", and "maybe", in that order.

*Note 2:* The note associated with the specification of the add method for the ArrayList class in Section 6.2.1 explains why the return value is always **true**.

4.
```
/**
 * Determines the number of elements in this SinglyLinkedList object.
 * The worstTime(n) is O(n).
 *
 * @return the number of elements.
 *
 */
public int size ( )
```

*Example:* Suppose the SinglyLinkedList object referenced by myLinked consists of the elements "simple", "yes", "no", and "maybe", in that order. If the message is

```
System.out.println (myLinked.size ( ));
```

then the output will be

4

5.
```
/**
 * Determines if this SinglyLinkedList object contains a specified element.
 * The worstTime(n) is O(n).
 *
 * @param obj – the specified element being sought.
 *
 * @return true – if this SinglyLinkedList object contains obj; otherwise,
 *           false.
 *
 */
public boolean contains (Object obj)
```

*Note:* The user of this method is responsible for ensuring that the equals method is explicitly defined for the class that includes obj and the elements in the SinglyLinkedList. Otherwise, as noted in Section 2.7, the Object class's version of equals will be applied:

```
public boolean equals (Object element)
{
        return (this == element);
}
```

This method tests whether the reference to the calling object contains the same address as the reference obj. Because equality of references is tested instead of equality of elements, **false** will be returned if the calling-object reference and obj are references to distinct but identical objects!

These few methods do not provide much in the way of functionality: we cannot remove an element or even retrieve an element. And we haven't specified any index-based methods, a shortcoming for any class with "List" in its name. For now, this will be just a partial implementation of the List interface. But we have enough information to consider fields and method definitions.

### 7.2.1 Fields and Method Definitions in the SinglyLinkedList Class

Something is missing from Figure 7.3: a reference to the first Entry object. This missing "link" will be a field in the SinglyLinkedList class, in fact, the only field:

```
protected Entry<E> head;
```

Suppose a SinglyLinkedList object is constructed as follows:

```
SinglyLinkedList<Integer> scoreList = new SinglyLinkedList<Integer>( );
```

To make scoreList a reference to an empty SinglyLinkedList object, all the default constructor has to do is to initialize the head field to **null**. Since a reference field is automatically initialized to **null**, we need not define the default constructor, but we will do so for the sake of being explicit:

```
public SinglyLinkedList( )
{
        head = null;
} // default constructor
```

Now we can move on to the definitions of the isEmpty, add, size, and contains methods. How can the isEmpty( ) method determine if the list has no elements? By testing the head field:

```
public boolean isEmpty ( )
{
        return head == null;
} // method isEmpty
```

The definition of the add (E element) method is not as easy to develop. For inspiration, suppose we add a fourth element to the front of a singly linked list consisting of the three elements from Figure 7.3. Figure 7.4 shows the picture before the fourth element is added.

According to the method specification for the add method, each new element is inserted at the front of a SinglyLinkedList object. So if we now add "calm" to *the front of* this list, we will get the list shown in Figure 7.5.

In general, how should we proceed if we want to insert the element at the front of the calling SinglyLinkedList object? We start by constructing a new Entry object and assigning (a reference to) the new element to that Entry object's element field.

**Figure 7.4** I A SinglyLinkedList object of three String elements.

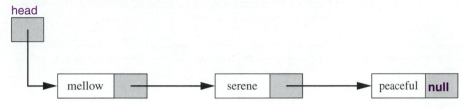

**Figure 7.5** I The SinglyLinkedList object from Figure 7.4 after inserting "calm" at the front of the list.

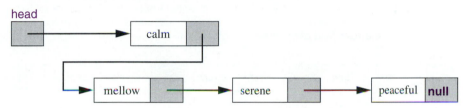

What about the Entry object's next field? The reference we assign to the next field should be a reference to what had been the first Entry before this call to add. In other words, we should assign head to the next field of the new Entry object. Finally, we adjust head to reference the new Entry object and return **true**. The complete definition is:

```
public boolean add (E element)
{
        Entry<E> newEntry = new Entry<E>( );
        newEntry.element = element;
        newEntry.next = head;
        head = newEntry;
        return true;
} // method add
```

Figures 7.6a through d show the effect of executing the first four statements in this method when "calm" is inserted at the front of the SinglyLinkedList object shown in Figure 7.4.

For the definition of the size method, we initialize a local **int** variable, count, to 0 and a local Entry reference, current, to head. We then loop until current is **null**, and increment count and current during each loop iteration. Incrementing count is a familiar operation, but what does it mean to "increment current?" That means to change current so that current will reference the next Entry after the one current is now referencing. That is, we set

```
current = current.next;
```

**Figure 7.6a** ❘ The first step in inserting "calm" at the front of the SinglyLinkedList object of Figure 7.4: constructing a new Entry object (whose two fields are automatically preinitialized to **null**).

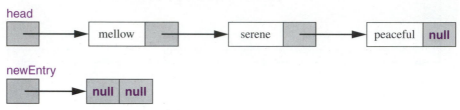

**Figure 7.6b** ❘ The second step in inserting "calm" at the front of the SinglyLinkedList object of Figure 7.4: assigning the object-reference element to the element field of the newEntry object.

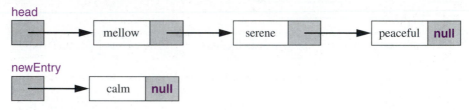

**Figure 7.6c** ❘ The third step in inserting "calm" at the front of the SinglyLinkedList object of Figure 7.4: assigning head to the next field of the newEntry object.

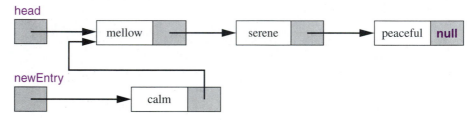

**Figure 7.6d** ❘ The fourth step in inserting "calm" at the front of the SinglyLinkedList object of Figure 7.4. The SinglyLinkedList object is now as shown in Figure 7.5.

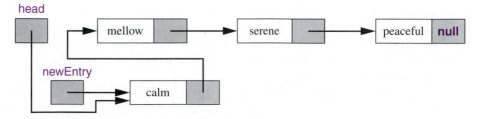

Here is the definition of the size method:

```
public int size ( )
{
        int count = 0;

        for (Entry<E> current = head; current != null; current = current.next)
                count++;
        return count;
} // method size
```

The loop goes through the entire SinglyLinkedList object, and so worstTime($n$) is linear in $n$ (as is averageTime($n$)). Note that if we add a size field to the Singly LinkedList class, the definition of the size( ) method becomes a one-liner, namely,

```
return size;
```

But then the definition of the add method would have to be modified to maintain the value of the size field.

Finally, for now, we develop the contains method. The loop structure is similar to the one in the definition of the size method, except that we need to compare element to current.element. And because **null** elements are allowed in a SinglyLinkedList object, we need a separate loop for the case where element is **null**. Here is the code:

```
public boolean contains (Object obj)
{
        if (obj == null)
        {
                for (Entry<E> current = head; current != null; current = current.next)
                        if (current.element == null)
                                return true;
        } // if obj == null
        else if (obj instanceof E)
                for (Entry<E> current = head; current != null; current = current.next)
                        if (obj.equals (current.element))
                                return true;
        return false;
} // method contains
```

As we discussed in Section 7.2, in the note following the method specification for contains (Object obj), make sure that the definition of the equals method in the element's class compares elements for equality. We needed a special case for obj == **null** because the message obj.equals (current.element) will throw NullPointer Exception if obj is **null**. And of course, if obj is not an instance of type E, **false** will be returned. We had to put the **instanceof** test after the obj == **null** test because **null instanceof** E returns **false**.

One important point of the SinglyLinkedList class is that a linked structure for storing a collection of elements is different from an array or ArrayList object in two key respects:

1. The size of the collection need not be known in advance. We simply add elements at will. So we do not have to worry, as we would with an array, about allocating too much space or too little space. But it should be noted that in each Entry object, the next field consumes extra space: it contains program information rather than problem information.

2. Random access is not available. To access some element, we would have to start by accessing the head element, and then accessing the next element after the head element, and so on.

### 7.2.2 **Iterating through a** SinglyLinkedList **Object**

We have not yet established a way for a user to loop through the elements in a SinglyLinkedList object. The solution, as we saw in Section 4.2.3, is to develop an Iterator class for SinglyLinkedList objects, that is, a class that implements the Iterator interface, and of which each instance will iterate over a SinglyLinkedList object.

The SinglyLinkedListIterator class will be a **protected** class embedded within the SinglyLinkedList class. We want our Iterator object to be positioned at an Entry so we can easily get the next element and determine if there are any more elements beyond where the Iterator object is positioned. For now,[1] the SinglyLinkedListIterator class will have only one field:

    **protected** Entry<E> next;

We will fully implement only three methods: a default constructor, next( ), and hasNext( ). The remove( ) method will simply throw an exception. Here is an outline of the class:

```
protected class SinglyLinkedListIterator implements Iterator<E>
{
        protected Entry<E> next;

        public SinglyLinkedListIterator( )
        {
             ...
        } // default constructor

        public boolean hasNext( )
        {
             ...
        } // method hasNext

        public E next( )
        {
             ...
        } // method next
```

---

[1] In Programming Project 7.1, two additional fields are added to the SinglyLinkedListIterator class.

```
        public void remove( )
        {
                throw new UnsupportedOperationException( );
        } // method remove
    } // class SinglyLinkedListIterator
```

Note that the SinglyLinkedIterator class has E as its type parameter because SinglyLinkedListIterator implements Iterator<E>.

In defining the three methods, there are three "nexts" we will be dealing with:

A next field in the SinglyLinkedListIterator class

A next( ) method in the SinglyLinkedListIterator class

A next field in the Entry class

You will be able to determine the correct choice by the context—and the presence or absence of parentheses.

An interface does not have any constructors because an interface cannot be instantiated, so the Iterator interface had no constructors. But we will need a constructor for the SinglyLinkedListIterator class. Otherwise, the compiler would generate a default constructor and the Java Virtual Machine would simply, but worthlessly, initialize the next field to **null**. What should the constructor initialize the next field to? To where we want to start iterating, at the head of the SinglyLinkedList:

```
    SinglyLinkedListIterator( )
    {
          next = head;
    } // default constructor
```

This method can access head because the SinglyLinkedListIterator class is embedded in the SinglyLinkedList class, where head is a field.

The hasNext( ) method should return true if the next field (in the SinglyLinked ListIterator class, not in the Entry class) is referencing an Entry object:

```
        public boolean hasNext ( )
        {
                return next != null;
        } // method hasNext
```

The definition of the remove( ) method will simply throw an exception, so all that remains is the definition of the next( ) method. Suppose we have a SinglyLinkedList of two String elements and the default constructor for the SinglyLinkedListIterator has just been called. Figure 7.7 shows the current situation (as usual, we pretend that a String object itself, not a reference, is stored in the element field of an Entry object):

Since we are just starting out, what element should the next( ) method return? The element returned should be "Karen", that is, next.element. And then the next field should be advanced to point to the next Entry object. That is, the SinglyLinked ListIterator's next field should get the reference stored in the next field of the Entry object that the SinglyLinkedListIterator's next field is currently pointing to. We can't

**Figure 7.7 |** The contents of the **next** field in the SinglyLinkedListIterator class just after the SinglyLinkedListIterator's constructor is called.

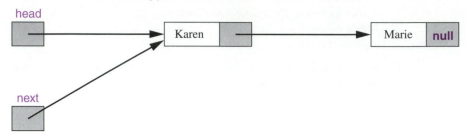

do anything after a return, so we save next.element before advancing next, and then we return (a reference to) the saved element. Here is the definition:

```
public E next( )
{
        E theElement = next.element;
        next = next.next;    // rightmost next is field in Entry class
        return theElement;
} // method next
```

Now that we have a SinglyLinkedListIterator class, we can work on the problem of iterating through a SinglyLinkedList object. First, we have to associate a SinglyLinked ListIterator object with a SinglyLinkedList object. The iterator( ) method in the Singly LinkedList class creates the necessary connection:

```
/**
 * Returns a SinglyLinkedListIterator object to iterate over this
 * SinglyLinkedList object.
 *
 */
public Iterator<E> iterator( )
{
        return new SinglyLinkedListIterator( );
} // method iterator
```

The value returned is a (reference to a) SinglyLinkedListIterator. The specified return type has to be Iterator<E> because that is what the iterator( ) method in the Iterator interface calls for. Any class that implements the Iterator interface—such as Singly LinkedListIterator—can be the actual return type.

With the help of this method, a user can create the appropriate iterator. For example, if myLinked is a SinglyLinkedList object of Boolean elements, we can do the following:

```
Iterator<Boolean> itr = myLinked.iterator( );
```

The variable itr is a polymorphic reference: it can be assigned a reference to an object in any class (for example, SinglyLinkedListIterator) that implements the Iterator <Boolean> interface. And myLinked.iterator( ) returns a reference to an object in the SinglyLinkedListIterator class, specifically, to an object that is positioned at the beginning of the myLinked object.

The actual iteration is straightforward. For example, to print out each element:

```
while (itr.hasNext ( ))
        System.out.println (itr.next ( ));
```

Or, even simpler, with the enhanced **for** statement:

```
for (Boolean b : myList)
        System.out.println (b);
```

For a complete example, the following main method reads in a nonempty list of grade-point averages from the input, stores each one in a SinglyLinkedList object, and then iterates through the collection to calculate the sum. Finally, the average grade-point average is printed.

```
public static void main (String [ ] args)
{
        final String SENTINEL = "***";

        final String PROMPT = "Please enter a GPA (or " + SENTINEL +
                " to quit): ";

        final String AVERAGE_MESSAGE = "\n\nThe average GPA is ";

        SinglyLinkedList<Double> gpaList = new SinglyLinkedList<Double>( );

        BufferedReader reader = new BufferedReader
                                (new InputStreamReader (System.in));

        String line;

        while (true)
        {
                try
                {
                        System.out.println (PROMPT);
                        line = reader.readLine ( );
                        if (line.equals (SENTINEL))
                                break;
                        gpaList.add (new Double (line));
                } // try
                catch (IOException e)
                        System.out.println (e);
                } // catch
        } // while
```

```
        double sum = 0.0;

    for (Double d : gpaList)
        sum += d;
    System.out.println (AVERAGE_MESSAGE + (sum / gpaList.size ( )));
} // method main
```

The SinglyLinkedList class, including its embedded Entry and SinglyLinkedList Iterator classes, is available from the book's website.

In Lab 12, you have the opportunity to define several other methods in the SinglyLinkedList class. Also, there are several programming exercises and a programming project related to the SinglyLinkedList class. But now that you have some familiarity with links, we turn to the focal point of this chapter: doubly linked lists.

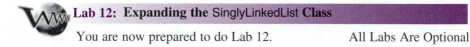

**Lab 12:  Expanding the** SinglyLinkedList **Class**

You are now prepared to do Lab 12.                 All Labs Are Optional

## 7.3 I DOUBLY LINKED LISTS

Suppose we want to insert "placid" in front of "serene" in the doubly linked list partially shown in Figure 7.2 and repeated here:

First we need to get a reference to the Entry object that holds "serene"; that will take linear-in-*n* time, on average, where *n* is the size of the linked list. After that, as shown in Figure 7.8, the insertion entails constructing a new Entry object, storing "placid" as its element, and adjusting four links (the previous and next links for "placid", the next link for the predecessor of "serene", and the previous link for "serene"). In other words, once we have a reference to an Entry object, we can insert a new element in front of that Entry object in constant time.

The process for removal of an element in a doubly linked list is similar. For example, suppose we want to remove "mellow" from the partially shown linked list in Figure 7.8. First, we get a reference to the Entry object that houses "mellow", and this takes linear-in-*n* time, on average. Then, as shown in Figure 7.9, we adjust the

**Figure 7.8** I The partially shown doubly linked list from Figure 7.2 after "placid" is inserted in front of "serene".

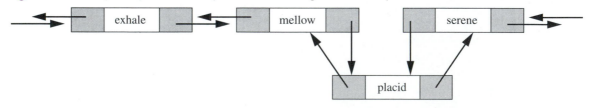

**Figure 7.9 |** The partially shown linked list from Figure 7.8 after "mellow" has been removed.

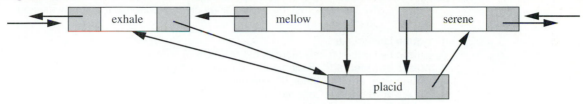

next link of the predecessor of "mellow" and the previous link of the successor of "mellow". Notice that there is no need to adjust either of the links in the Entry object that houses "mellow" because that object is not pointed to by any other Entry object's links.

The bottom line in the previous discussion is that it takes linear-in-$n$ time to get a reference to an Entry object that houses an element, but once the reference is available, any number of insertions, removals, or retrievals can be accomplished in constant time for each one.

Now that you have a rough idea of what a doubly linked list looks like and can be manipulated, we are ready to study the LinkedList class, the Java Collections Framework's design and implementation of doubly linked lists. First as always, we start with a user's perspective, that is, with the method specifications.

### 7.3.1  A User's View of the LinkedList Class

Because the LinkedList class implements the List interface, LinkedList objects support a variety of index-based methods such as get and indexOf. *The indexes always start at 0*, so a LinkedList object with three elements has its first element at index 0, its second element at index 1, and its third element at index 2.

As we did with the ArrayList class, let's start with the big picture from the user's point of view. Figure 7.10 has the method headings for all of the public methods in the LinkedList class. The LinkedList class is a parameterized type, with E as the type parameter representing the type of an element.

Section 7.3.2 has more details (still from the user's view): those LinkedList methods that are in some way different from those of the ArrayList class.

### 7.3.2  The LinkedList Class versus the ArrayList Class

Let's compare the LinkedList and ArrayList classes from a user's perspective. The LinkedList class does not have a constructor with an initial-capacity parameter because LinkedList objects grow and shrink as needed. And the related methods ensureCapacity and trimToSize are also missing from the LinkedList class.

The LinkedList class has six methods that are not in the ArrayList class. Their names are fairly descriptive: addFirst (E element), addLast (E element), getFirst( ), getLast( ), removeFirst( ), and removeLast( ). For each of these methods, worstTime($n$) is constant, where $n$ represents the number of elements in the calling object. These six methods are provided only for the convenience of users. They do not represent

**Figure 7.10** | Method headings for the public methods in the LinkedList class. Except for the constructors, the headings are in alphabetical order by method identifier.

1. **public** LinkedList( )
2. **public** LinkedList (Collection <? **extends** E> c)
3. **public boolean** add (E element)    // worstTime (n) is constant
4. **public void** add (**int** index, E element)
5. **public void** addAll (Collection <? **extends** E> c)
6. **public boolean** addAll (**int** index, Collection <? **extends** E> c)
7. **public boolean** addFirst (E element)
8. **public boolean** addLast (E element)
9. **public void** clear( )    // worstTime (n) is constant
10. **public** Object clone( )
11. **public boolean** contains (Object obj)
12. **public boolean** containsAll (Collection<?> c)
13. **public boolean** equals (Object obj)
14. **public** E get (**int** index)    // worstTime (n) is O (n)
15. **public** E getFirst ( )
16. **public** E getLast ( )
17. **public int** hashCode( )
18. **public int** indexOf (Object obj)
19. **public boolean** isEmpty( )
20. **public** Iterator<E> iterator( )
21. **public int** lastIndexOf (Object obj)
22. **public** ListIterator<E> listIterator( )// iterate backward or forward
23. **public** ListIterator<E> listIterator (**final int** index)
24. **public boolean** remove (Object obj)
25. **public** E remove (**int** index)
26. **public boolean** removeAll (Collection<?> c)
27. **public** E removeFirst( )    // worstTime (n) is constant
28. **public** E removeLast( )    // worstTime (n) is constant
29. **public boolean** retainAll (Collection<?> c)
30. **public** E set (**int** index, E element)
31. **public int** size( )
32. **public** List<E> subList (**int** fromIndex, **int** toIndex)
33. **public** Object[ ] toArray( )
34. **public** <T> T[ ] toArray (T[ ] a)
35. **public** String toString( )

an increase in the functionality of LinkedList objects. For example, if myList is a non-empty LinkedList object, the message

    myList.removeFirst( )

can be replaced with

    myList.remove (0)

and this last message takes only constant time. But if myList were a nonempty ArrayList object, the same message,

    myList.remove (0)

requires linear-in-$n$ time.

There are some other performance differences between LinkedList objects and ArrayList objects. Here are method specifications of some other LinkedList methods that have different worst times than their ArrayList counterparts. The numbering of the method specifications is from the numbering in Figure 7.10.

**2.**
```
/**
 * Appends a specified element to (the back of) this LinkedList object.
 *
 * @param element – the element to be appended.
 *
 * @return true – according to the general contract of the Collection interface's
 *            one-parameter add method.
 *
 */
public boolean add (E element)
```

*Note:* The worstTime($n$) is constant. With an ArrayList object, the worstTime($n$) is linear in $n$ for the one-parameter add method. This represents a significant difference for a single insertion. For multiple back-end insertions, the time estimates for the ArrayList and LinkedList classes are similar. Specifically, for $n$ back-end insertions, worstTime($n$) is linear in $n$ for both the ArrayList class and the LinkedList class. And averageTime($n$) is constant for both classes.

*Example:* Suppose we have the following:

```
LinkedList<String> fruits = new LinkedList<String>( );
fruits.add ("apples");
fruits.add ("kumquats");
fruits.add ("durian");
fruits.add ("limes");
```

The LinkedList object fruits now contains, in order, "apples", "kumquats", "durian", and "limes".

**14.**
```
/**
 * Finds the element at a specified position in this LinkedList object.
 * The worstTime(n) is O(n).
 *
 * @param index – the position of the element to be returned.
 *
 * @return the element at position index.
 *
 * @throws IndexOutOfBoundsException – if index is less than 0 or greater than
 *            or equal to size( ).
 */
public E get (int index)
```

*Note:* This method represents a major disadvantage of the LinkedList class compared to the ArrayList class. As noted in the method specification, the LinkedList version of this method has worstTime($n$) in $O(n)$—in fact, worstTime($n$) is linear in $n$ in the current implementation. But for the ArrayList version, worstTime($n$) is constant. So if your application has a preponderance of list accesses, an ArrayList object is preferable to a LinkedList object.

*Example:* Suppose the LinkedList object fruits consists of "apples", "kumquats", "durian", and "limes", in that order. Then the message

fruits.get (1)

would return "kumquats"; recall that list indexes start at zero.

**29.** /**
   * Replaces the element at a specified index with a specified element.
   * The worstTime(n) is O(n).
   *
   * @param index – the specified index where the replacement will occur.
   * @param element – the element that replaces the previous occupant at
   *          position index.
   *
   * @return the previous occupant (the element replaced) at position index.
   *
   * @throws IndexOutOfBoundsException – if index is either less than 0 or
   *          greater than or equal to size( ).
   *
   */
**public** E set (**int** index, E element)

*Note:* For the ArrayList version of this method, worstTime($n$) is constant.

*Example:* Suppose the LinkedList object fruits consists of "apples", "kumquats", "durian", and "limes", in that order. We can change (and print) the element at index 2 with the following:

System.out.println (fruits.set (2, "kiwi"));

The elements in the LinkedList object fruits are now "apples", "kumquats", "kiwi", and "limes", and the output will be "durian".

When we looked at the ArrayList class, iterators were ignored. That neglect was due to the fact that the random-access property of ArrayList objects allowed us to loop through an ArrayList object in linear time by using indexes. LinkedList objects do not support random access (in constant time), so iterators are an essential component of the LinkedList class.

### 7.3.3  LinkedList **Iterators**

In the LinkedList class, the iterators are bidirectional: they can move either forward (to the next element) or backward (to the previous element). The name of the class that defines the iterators is ListItr. The ListItr class—which implements the ListIterator interface—is nested as a **private** class in the LinkedList class. So a ListItr cannot be directly constructed by a user; instead there are LinkedList methods to create a ListItr object, just as there was a SinglyLinkedList method (namely, iterator( )), to create a SinglyLinkedListIterator object.

There are two LinkedList methods that return a (reference to a) ListIterator object, that is, an object in a class that implements the ListIterator interface. Their method specifications are as follows:

22. /**
    * Returns a ListIterator object positioned at the beginning of this LinkedList
    * object.
    *
    * @return a ListIterator object positioned at the beginning of this LinkedList
    *          object.
    *
    */
**public** ListIterator<E> listIterator( )

*Example:* Suppose that the fruits is a LinkedList object. Then we can create a ListItr object to iterate through fruits as follows:

ListIterator<String> itr1 = fruits.listIterator( );

23. /**
    * Returns a ListIterator object positioned at a specified index in this LinkedList
    * object. The worstTime(n) is O(n).
    *
    * @param index – the specified index where the returned iterator is positioned.
    *
    * @return a ListIterator object positioned at index.
    *
    * @throws IndexOutOfBoundsException – if index is either less than zero or
    *          greater than size( ).
    *
    */
**public** ListIterator<E> listIterator (**final int** index)

*Example:* Suppose the LinkedList object fruits consists of "apples", "kumquats", "durian", and "limes", in that order. The following statement creates a ListIterator object positioned at "durian":

ListIterator<String> itr2 = fruits.listIterator (2);

Figure 7.11 has the method headings for all of the methods in the ListItr class. We will look at some of the details—from a user's viewpoint—of these methods shortly.

We can iterate forwardly with an enhanced **for** statement (or the pair hasNext( ) and next( )), just as we did with the SinglyLinkedList class in Section 7.3.1. For example,

**Figure 7.11** I Method headings for all of the **public** methods in the ListItr class. *For each method, worstTime(n) is constant!*

IT1.  **public void** add (E element)
IT2.  **public boolean** hasNext( )
IT3.  **public boolean** hasPrevious( )
IT4.  **public** E next( )
IT5.  **public int** nextIndex( )
IT6.  **public** E previous( )
IT7.  **public int** previousIndex( )
IT8.  **public void** remove( )
IT9.  **public void** set (E element)

suppose the LinkedList object fruits consists of "kumquats", "bananas", "kiwi", and "apples", in that order. We can iterate through fruits from the first element to the last element as follows:

**for** (String s : fruits)
        System.out.println (s);

The output will be:

kumquats

bananas

kiwi

apples

For backward iterating, there is a hasPrevious( ) and previous( ) pair. Here are their method specifications, with method numbers from Figure 7.11:

**IT3.** /**
    * Determines whether this ListIterator object has more elements when traversing
    * in the reverse direction.
    *
    * @return true – if this ListIterator object has more elements when traversing
    *         in the reverse direction; otherwise, false.
    *
    */
**public boolean** hasPrevious( )

*Example:* Suppose the LinkedList object fruits consists of the elements "kumquats", "bananas", "kiwi", and "apples", in that order. The output from

ListIterator<String> itr = listIterator (2);
System.out.println (itr.hasPrevious( ));

would be

true

But the output from

```
ListIterator<String> itr = listIterator( ); // itr is positioned at index 0
System.out.println (itr.hasPrevious( ));
```

would be

```
false
```

**IT6.** /**
  * Retreats this ListIterator object to the previous element, and returns that
  * element.
  *
  * @return the element retreated to in this ListIterator object.
  *
  * @throws NoSuchElementException – if this ListIterator object has no
  *          previous element.
  *
  */
**public** E previous( )

*Example:* Suppose the LinkedList object fruits consists of "kumquats",
"bananas", "kiwi", and "apples", in that order. If we have

```
ListIterator<String> itr = fruits.listIterator( );
System.out.println (itr.next( ) + " " + itr.next( ) + " " + itr.previous( ));
```

the output will be

```
kumquats bananas bananas
```

Think of the "current" position in a LinkedList object as the index where the List
Iterator is positioned. Here is how the next( ) and previous( ) methods are related to
the current position:

- The next( ) method *advances* to the next position in the LinkedList object, but
  returns the element that had been at the current position before the call to next( ).
- The previous( ) method *first retreats to the position before the current position,
  and then returns* the element at that retreated-to position.

The next( ) method is similar to the postincrement operator ++, and the previous( )
method is similar to the predecrement operator−−. Suppose, for example, we have

```
int j = 4,
    k = 9;

System.out.println (j++);  // now j = 5
System.out.println (−−k); // now k = 8
```

The output will be

```
4
8
```

Because the previous( ) method returns the previous element, we must start "beyond" the end of a LinkedList object to iterate in reverse order. For example, suppose the LinkedList object fruits consists of "kumquats", "bananas", "kiwi", and "apples", in that order, and we have

```
ListIterator itr = fruits.listIterator (fruits.size( ));
while (itr.hasPrevious( ))
        System.out.println (itr.previous( ));
```

The output will be:

apples

kiwi

bananas

kumquats

Of course, the LinkedList object fruits has not changed. It still consists of "kumquats", "bananas", "kiwi", and "apples", in that order.

We can do even more! The ListItr class also has add, remove, and set methods. Here are the method specifications and examples (as usual, E is the type parameter representing the class of the elements in the LinkedList object):

**IT1.** /**
```
 * Inserts a specified element into the LinkedList object in front of the element that
 * would be returned by next( ), if any, and in back of the element that would be
 * returned by previous( ), if any. If the LinkedList object was empty before this
 * call, then the specified element is the only element in the LinkedList object.
 *
 * @param element – the element to be inserted.
 *
 */
public void add (E element)
```

*Example:* Suppose the LinkedList object fruits consists of "kumquats", "bananas", "kiwi", and "apples", in that order. We can repeatedly insert "pears" *after* each element in fruits as follows:

```
ListIterator<String> itr = fruits.listIterator( );
while (itr.hasNext( ))
{
     itr.next( );
     itr.add ("pears");
} // while
```

During the first iteration of the above **while** loop, the call to next( ) returns "kumquats" and (before returning) advances to "bananas". The first call to add ("pears") inserts "pears" in front of "bananas". During the second iteration, the call to next( ) returns "bananas" and advances to "kiwi". The second call to add ("pears") inserts "pears" in front of "kiwi". And so on. At the completion of the **while** statement, the LinkedList object fruits consists of "kumquats", "pears", "bananas", "pears", "kiwi", "pears", "apples", "pears"

*Note:* If the ListItr is not positioned at any element (for example, if the LinkedList object is empty), each call to the ListIterator class's add method will insert an element at the end of the LinkedList object.

IT8. ```
/**
 * Removes the element returned by the most recent call to next( ) or previous( ).
 * This method can be called only once per call to next( ) or previous( ), and
 * can be called only if this ListIterator's add method has not been called since
 * the most recent call to next( ) or previous( ).
 *
 * @throws IllegalStateException – if neither next( ) nor previous( ) has been
 *          called, or if either this ListIterator's add or remove method has
 *          been called since the most recent call to next( ) or previous( ).
 *
 */
public void remove( )
```

*Example:* Suppose the LinkedList object fruits consists of "kumquats", "pears", "bananas", "pears", "kiwi", "pears", "apples", and "pears", in that order. We can remove every other element from fruits as follows:

```
ListIterator<String> itr = fruits.listIterator (1); // NOTE: starting index is 1
while (itr.hasNext( ))
{
      itr.next( );
      itr.remove( );
      if (itr.hasNext( ))
             itr.next( );
} // while
```

Now fruits consists of "kumquats", "bananas", "kiwi", and "apples", in that order. If we eliminate the **if** statement from the above loop, every element except the first element will be removed.

IT9. ```
/**
 * Replaces the element returned by the most recent call to next( ) or previous( ) with
 * the specified element. This call can be made only if neither this ListIterator's add
 * nor remove method have been called since the most recent call to next( ) or
 * previous( ).
 *
 * @param element – the element to replace the element returned by the most
 *          recent call to next( ) or previous( ).
 *
 * @throws IllegalStateException – if neither next( ) nor previous( ) has been
 *          called, or if either this ListIterator's add or remove method has been
 *          called since the most recent call to next( ) or previous( ).
 *
```

```
    */
public void set (E element)
```

*Example:* Suppose the LinkedList object fruits consists of "kumquats", "bananas", "kiwi", and "apples", in that order. We can iterate through fruits and capitalize the first letter of each fruit as follows:

```
String aFruit;

char first;

ListIterator<String> itr = fruits.listIterator( );
while (itr.hasNext( ))
{
        aFruit = itr.next( );
        first = Character.toUpperCase (aFruit.charAt (0));
        aFruit = first + aFruit.substring (1); // substring from index 1 to end
        itr.set (aFruit);
} // while
```

The LinkedList object fruits now consists of "Kumquats", "Bananas", "Kiwi", and "Apples".

Programming Exercise 7.6 considers all possible sequences of calls to the add, next, and remove methods in the ListItr class.

As noted in Figure 7.11, all of the ListItr methods take only constant time. So if you iterate through a LinkedList object, for each call to the ListItr object's add or remove method, worstTime($n$) is constant. With an ArrayList object, for each call to add (**int** index, E element) or remove (**int** index), worstTime($n$) is linear in $n$. And the same linear worst time would apply for adding and removing if you decided to iterate through an ArrayList. The bottom line here is that a LinkedList object is faster than an ArrayList object when you have a lot of insertions or removals during an iteration.

What if you need to access or modify elements at different indexes in a list? With an ArrayList object, for each call to get (**int** index) or set (**int** index, E element), worstTime($n$) is constant. With a LinkedList object, for each call to get (**int** index) or set (**int** index, E element), worstTime($n$) is linear in $n$. If instead you iterate through a LinkedList object, and use the ListItr methods next( ) and set (E element) for accessing and modifying elements, each iteration takes linear-in-$n$ time. So if the elements to be accessed or modified are at indexes that are far apart, an ArrayList object will be faster than a LinkedList object.

To summarize the above discussion:

> If a large part of the application consists of iterating through a list and making insertions and/or removals during the iterations, a **LinkedList** can be much faster than an **ArrayList**.
>
> If the application entails a lot of accessing and/or modifying elements at widely varying indexes, an **ArrayList** will be much faster than a **LinkedList**.

### 7.3.4  A Simple Program that uses a LinkedList Object

The following program accomplishes the same tasks as the simple ArrayList program in Section 6.2.2. But the code has been modified to take advantage of the LinkedList class's ability to perform constant-time insertions or removals during an iteration.

```java
public static void main (String[ ] args)
{
        List<String> aList = new LinkedList<String>( );

        BufferedReader keyboardReader = new BufferedReader
                                        (new InputStreamReader (System.in)),
                   fileReader;

    String inFilePath,
           line,
           word;

    try
    {
            System.out.print ("\n\nPlease enter the path for the input file: ");
            inFilePath = keyboardReader.readLine( );
            fileReader = new BufferedReader (new FileReader (inFilePath));
            while (true)
            {
                line = fileReader.readLine( );
                if (line == null)
                        break;
                aList.add (line);
            } // while not end of file
            fileReader.close( );

            System.out.print ("\nPlease enter the word you want to search for: ");
            word = keyboardReader.readLine( );
            if (aList.indexOf (word) >= 0)
                    System.out.println (word + " was found.\n\n");
            else
                    System.out.println (word + " was not found.\n\n");

            System.out.print ("Please enter the word you want to remove: ");
            word = keyboardReader.readLine( );
            int removalCount = 0;
            ListIterator<String> itr = aList.listIterator( );
            while (itr.hasNext( ))
                    if (itr.next( ).equals (word))
                    {
                            itr.remove( );
                            removalCount++;
```

```
                             } // if another instance of word has been discovered
            if (removalCount == 0)
                    System.out.println (word + " was not found, so not removed.\n\n");
            else if (removalCount == 1)
                    System.out.println ("The only instance of " + word + " was
                            removed.\n\n");
            else
                    System.out.println ("All " + removalCount + " instances of " +
                                    word + " were removed.\n\n");

            System.out.print ("Please enter the word you want to append: ");
            word = keyboardReader.readLine( );
            aList.add (word);
            System.out.println (word + " was appended.\n\n");

            System.out.print("Please enter the word you want to convert to upper case: ");
            word = keyboardReader.readLine( );

            String currentWord;
            boolean found = false;
            itr = aList.listIterator( );
            while (itr.hasNext( ) && !found)
            {
                    currentWord = itr.next( );
                    if (word.equals (currentWord))
                    {
                            itr.set (word.toUpperCase( ));
                            System.out.println (word + " was converted to upper
                                    case.\n\n");
                            found = true;
                    } // found word to convert to upper case
            }
            if (!found)
                    System.out.println (word + " was not found, so not
                            upper-cased.\n\n");
            System.out.println ("Here is the final version:\n" + aList);
        } // try
        catch (IOException e)
        {
                System.out.println (e);
        } // catch
    } // method main
```

For removing all instances of a word, the iterator-based version above is clearly faster than repeatedly invoking aList.remove (word).

Lab 13 has an experiment on LinkedList iterators.

**Lab 13: Working with** LinkedList **Iterators**

You are now prepared to do Lab 13.          All Labs Are Optional

Now that you have seen both the ArrayList and LinkedList classes, you can run a timing experiment on them.

**Lab 14: Timing the** ArrayList **and** LinkedList **Classes**

You are now prepared to do Lab 14.          All Labs Are Optional

In Section 7.3.5, we briefly look at a developer's view of the LinkedList class. Specifically, we compare various alternatives for the fields in the LinkedList class. For the choice made in the Java Collections Framework, we develop a LinkedList object, and then, to give you the flavor of that implementation, we investigate the definition of the two-parameter add method.

### 7.3.5 Fields and Heading of the LinkedList Class

For the implementation of the LinkedList class, the primary decision is what the fields will be. For the sake of code reuse (beneficial laziness), we first consider the SinglyLinkedList class. Can we expand that class to satisfy all of the method specifications for the LinkedList class? The problem comes with the upper bounds of worstTime($n$) for some of the LinkedList methods.

For example, the addLast method's postcondition states that any implementation of that method should take constant time. Recall that the SinglyLinkedList class had one field only:

    **protected** Entry<E> head; // reference to first entry

The embedded Entry class had two fields, an element and a reference to the next entry:

    **protected** E element;

    **protected** Entry<E> next;

Clearly, it will take linear-in-$n$ time to add an element to the back of a SinglyLinkedList object. We can get around this difficulty by adding to the SinglyLinkedList class a tail field that holds a reference to the last entry in a SinglyLinkedList object. Figure 7.12 shows an example of a SinglyLinkedList object with these fields.

**Figure 7.12 I** A singly linked list with head and tail fields.

We can now define the addLast method without much difficulty (see Concept Exercise 7.5a). Implementing the removeLast presents a much more serious problem. We would need to change the next field of the Entry object *before* the Entry object referenced by tail. And for that task, a loop is needed, so worstTime($n$) would be linear in $n$. That would violate the performance requirement of the removeLast method that specifies worstTime($n$) must be constant.

So we must abandon a singly linked implementation of the LinkedList class because of the given performance specifications. But the above idea—having head and tail fields—suggests a viable alternative. The nested Entry class will support a doubly linked list by having three fields:

```
protected E element;

protected Entry<E> previous,    // reference to previous entry
                   next;        // reference to next entry
```

Figure 7.13 shows this doubly linked version of the three-element list from Figure 7.12.

With this version, we can implement the LinkedList class with method definitions that satisfy the given performance specifications. You will get to flesh out the details of the doubly linked, head and tail implementation if you undertake Programming Project 7.4.

The Java Collections Framework's implementation of the LinkedList class is doubly linked, but does not have head and tail fields. The class starts as follows:

```
public class LinkedList<E> extends AbstractSequentialList<E>,
                           implements List<E>,
                                      java.lang.Cloneable,
                                      java.io.Serializable
{
        private transient int size = 0;
        private transient Entry<E> header = new Entry<E> (null, null, null);
```

There are only two fields explicitly[2] declared: a size field to keep track of the number of elements in the calling LinkedList object, and a reference to an Entry object. As noted in Chapter 6, the **transient** modifier merely indicates that this field is not saved if the elements in a LinkedList object are serialized, that is, saved to an output stream. (Appendix 3 discusses serialization.)

**Figure 7.13 |** A doubly linked list with head and tail fields.

head                                                                          tail

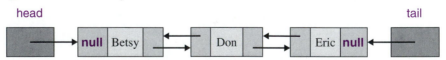

---

[2] The modCount field, inherited from AbstractCollection, is related to the fact that all of the Java Collections Framework's classes have "fail-fast iterators." Appendix 3 discusses this topic.

The Entry class has three fields, one for an element, and two for links. The only method in the Entry class is a constructor that initializes the three fields. Here is the complete Entry class

```
private static class Entry<E>
{
        E element;
        Entry<E> next;
        Entry<E> previous;

        Entry(E element, Entry<E> next, Entry<E> previous)
        {
                this.element = element;
                this.next = next;
                this.previous = previous;
        } // constructor
} // class Entry<E>
```

The element field will hold (a reference to) the Entry object's element; next will contain a reference to the Entry one position further in the LinkedList object, and previous will contain a reference to the Entry one position earlier in the LinkedList object.

Under normal circumstances, an object in a nested class has implicit access back to the enclosing object. For example, the nested ListItr class accesses the header field of the enclosing LinkedList object. But if the nested class is declared to be **static**, no such access is provided. The Entry class is a stand-alone class, so it would have been a waste of time and space to provide such access.

We can now make sense of the definition of the header field in the LinkedList class. That field initially references an Entry in which all three fields are **null**; see Figure 7.14.

The header field will always point to the same Entry object, called a *dummy entry* because its element field always contains **null**. The next field will point to the Entry object that houses the first element in the LinkedList object, and the previous field will point to the Entry object that houses the last element in the LinkedList object.

## 7.3.6 Creating and Maintaining a LinkedList Object

To get a better idea of how the fields in the LinkedList class and Entry class work in concert, let's create and maintain a LinkedList object. We start with a call to the default constructor:

```
LinkedList<String> names = new LinkedList<String>( );
```

**Figure 7.14 |** The header field in the LinkedList class.

As shown in Figure 7.15, the default constructor makes the previous and next fields in the dummy entry point to the dummy entry itself. It turns out that this simplifies the definitions of the methods that insert or delete elements.

Next, we append an element to that empty LinkedList object:

    names.add ("Betsy");

At this point, "Betsy" is both the first element in names and the last element in names. So the dummy entry both precedes and follows the Entry object that houses "Betsy". Figure 7.16 shows the effect of the insertion.

In general, adding an element at the end of a LinkedList object entails inserting the corresponding Entry object just before the dummy entry. For example, suppose the following message is now sent to the LinkedList object in Figure 7.16:

    names.add ("Eric");

What is the effect of appending "Eric" to the end of the LinkedList object names? Eric's Entry object will come before the dummy entry and after Betsy's Entry object. See Figure 7.17.

**Figure 7.15 |** An empty LinkedList object, names

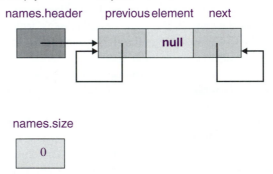

names.header     previous element     next

names.size

0

**Figure 7.16 |** The effect of inserting "Betsy" at the back of the empty LinkedList object in Figure 7.15.

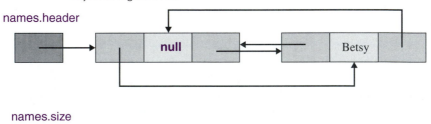

names.header

names.size

1

**Figure 7.17 I** A two-element LinkedList object. The first element is "Betsy" and the second element is "Eric".

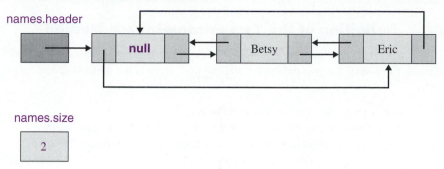

As you can see from Figure 7.17, a LinkedList object is stored circularly. The dummy entry precedes the first entry and follows the last entry. So we can iterate through a LinkedList object in the forward direction by starting at the first entry and repeatedly calling the next( ) method until we get to the dummy entry. Or we can iterate through a LinkedList object in the reverse direction by starting at the dummy entry and repeatedly calling the previous( ) method until we get to the first entry.

Finally, let's see what happens when the two-parameter add method is invoked. Here is a sample call:

    names.add (1, "Don");

To insert "Don" at index 1, we need to insert "Don" in front of "Eric". To accomplish this, we need to create an Entry object that houses "Don", and adjust the links so that Entry object follows the Entry object that houses "Betsy" and precedes the Entry object that houses "Eric". Figure 7.18 shows the result.

From the above examples, you should note that when an element is inserted in a LinkedList object, *no other elements in the list are moved.* In fact, when an element is appended with the LinkedList class's one-parameter add method, there are no

**Figure 7.18 I** The LinkedList object from Figure 7.17 after the insertion of "Don" in front of "Eric" by the call **names.add (1, "Don")**.

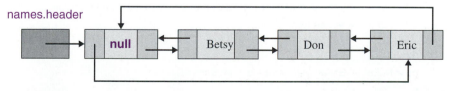

loops or recursive calls, so worstTime(*n*) is constant. What about an insertion at an index? Section 7.3.7 investigates the definition of the two-parameter add method.

## 7.3.7  **Definition of the Two-Parameter** add **Method**

To finish up this foray into the developer's view of the LinkedList class, we will look at the definition of the two-parameter add method. Here is the method specification:

```
/**
 * Inserts a specified element at a specified index.
 * All elements that were at positions greater than or equal to the specified index
 * before this call are now at the next higher position. The worstTime(n) is O(n).
 *
 * @param index – the specified index at which the element is to be inserted.
 * @param element – the specified element to be inserted.
 *
 * @throws IndexOutOfBoundsException – if index is less than zero or greater
 *        than size( ).
 *
 */
public void add (int index, E element)
```

For inserting an element at position index, the hard work is getting a reference to the Entry object that is currently at position index. This is accomplished—in the **private** method entry—in a loop that starts at header and moves forward or backward, depending on whether index < size / 2.

Once a reference, e, to the appropriate Entry has been obtained, element is stored in a new entry that is put in front of e by adjusting a few previous and next references. These adjustments are accomplished in the **private** addBefore method:

```
/**
 * Inserts an Entry object with a specified element in front of a specified Entry object.
 *
 * @param element – the element to be in the inserted Entry object.
 * @param e – the Entry object in front of which the new Entry object is to be
 *        inserted.
 *
 * @return – the Entry object that houses the specified element and is in front
 *        of the specified Entry object.
 *
 */
private Entry<E> addBefore (E element, Entry<E> e)
{
        Entry<E> newEntry = new Entry<E>(element, e, e.previous); // insert newEntry in
                                                                  // front of e
        newEntry.previous.next = newEntry;      // make newEntry follow its predecessor
        newEntry.next.previous = newEntry;      // make newEntry precede its successor, e
```

```
            size++;
            modCount++; // discussed in Appendix 3
            return newEntry;
    }
```

Here, basically, is the definition of the two-parameter add method

```
    public void add (int index, E element)
    {
            if (index == size)
                    addBefore (element, header);
            else
                    addBefore (element, entry (index));
    }
```

The bottom line in all of this is that to insert an Entry object in front of another Entry object, worstTime($n$) is constant, but to get (a reference to) the Entry object at a given index, worstTime($n$) is linear in $n$ (because of the loop in the entry method). The insertion is accomplished by adjusting references, not by moving elements.

The actual definition of the two-parameter add method is a one-liner:

```
    public void add (int index, A element)
    {
            addBefore(element, (index==size ? header : entry(index)));
    }
```

The ? and : are part of the *conditional operator*: a shorthand for the usual **if / else** statement.[3] The advantage of having a dummy entry is that every entry, even the first or last entry, has a predecessor and a successor, so there is no need for a special case to insert at the front or back of a LinkedList object.

---

[3] For example, instead of writing

```
    if (first > second)
            big = first;
    else
            big = second;
```

we can simply write:

```
    big = (first > second) ? first : second;
```

This can be read as "If first is greater than second, assign to big the value of first. Otherwise, assign to big the value of second."

The syntax for a conditional expression is:

```
    condition ? expression_t : expression_f
```

The semantics is this: if the condition has the value **true**, then the value of the conditional expression is the value of *expression*_t. Otherwise, the value of the conditional expression is the value of *expression*_f. If you like to write cryptic code, you'll love the conditional operator, one of the legacies that Java got from C. Note that it is the only *ternary* operator in Java. That means it has three operands.

The flow of the remove (**int** index) method is similar to that of add (**int** index, E element). We first get a reference, e, to the Entry object at position index, and then adjust the predecessor and successor of e's Entry.

As an application of the LinkedList class, we develop a line editor in Section 7.4.

## 7.4 | APPLICATION: A LINE EDITOR

A *line editor* is a program that manipulates text, line by line. At one time, line editors were state-of-the-art, but with the advent of full-screen editors (you move the cursor to the line you want to edit), line editors are seldom used. Linux/Unix and Windows still have a line editor, but they are used only when full-screen editors are unavailable.

We assume that each line is at most 75 characters long. The first line of the text is thought of as line 0 (just as Java programmers refer to their "zeroth" child), and one of the lines is designated as the *current line*. Each editing command begins with a dollar sign, and only editing commands begin with a dollar sign. There are seven editing commands. Here are four of the commands; the remaining three, and two system tests, are specified in Programming Project 7.5.

1.  **$Insert.** Each subsequent line, up to the next editing command, will be inserted in the text. If there is a designated current line, each line is inserted before that current line. Otherwise, each line is inserted at the end of the text; that is, the current line is then considered to be a dummy line beyond the last line of text. For example, suppose the text is empty and we have the following:

    $Insert
    Water, water every where,
    And all the boards did shrink;
    Water, water every where,
    Nor any drop to drink.

    Then after the insertions, the text would be as follows, with a caret, ">", indicating the current line:

    >    Water, water every where,
         And all the boards did shrink;
         Water, water every where,
         Nor any drop to drink.
    >

    For another example, suppose the text is:

         Now is the
         time for
    >    citizens to come to
         the
         aid of their country.

The sequence

$Insert
all
good

will cause the text to become

> Now is the
> time for
> all
> good
> \>citizens to come to
> the
> aid of their country.

2. **$Delete m n.** Each line in the text between lines *m* and *n*, inclusive, will be deleted. The current line becomes the first line after the last line deleted. So if the last line of text is deleted, the current line is beyond any line in the text.
   For example, suppose the text is

> Now is the
> time for
> all
> \>good
> citizens to come to
> the
> aid of their country.

Then the command

$Delete 2 4

will cause the text to become

> Now is the
> time for
> \>the
> aid of their country.

If the next command is

$Delete 3 3

then the text becomes:

> Now is the
> time for
> the
> \>

The following error messages should be printed when appropriate:

**Error: The first line number is greater than the second.**
**Error: The first line number is less than 0.**
**Error: The 2nd line number is greater than the last line number.**
**Error: The command should be followed by two integers.**

3. **$Line m.** Line *m* becomes the current line. For example, if the text is

> Mairzy doats
> an dozy doats
> &gt;an liddle lamsy divy.

then the command

$Line 0

will make line 0 the current line:

> &gt;Mairzy doats
> an dozy doats
> an liddle lamsy divy.

An error message should be printed if *m* is either less than 0 or greater than the number of lines in the text or if no integer is entered. See command 2 above.

4. **$Done.** This terminates the execution of the text editor. The entire text is printed.

An error message should be printed for any illegal command, such as "$End", "$insert", or "Insert".

### System Test 1 (Input is Boldfaced):

Please enter a line; a command must start with a $.
**$Insert**

Please enter a line; a command must start with a $.
**Yesterday, upon the stair,**

Please enter a line; a command must start with a $.
**I shot an arrow into the air.**

Please enter a line; a command must start with a $.
**It fell to earth, I know not where.**

Please enter a line; a command must start with a $.
**I met a man who wasn't there.**

Please enter a line; a command must start with a $.
**$Delete 1 2**

Please enter a line; a command must start with a $.
**$Line 2**

Please enter a line; a command must start with a $.
**$Insert**

Please enter a line; a command must start with a $.
**He wasn't there again today.**

Please enter a line; a command must start with a $.
**Oh how I wish he'd go away.**

Please enter a line; a command must start with a $.
**$Done**

Here is the final text:

   Yesterday, upon the stair,

   I met a man who wasn't there.

   He wasn't there again today.

   Oh how I wish he'd go away.

>

The editing has been completed.

### System Test 2 (Input is Boldfaced):

Please enter a line; a command must start with a $.
**Insert**
Error: not one of the given commands.

Please enter a line; a command must start with a $.
**$Insert**

Please enter a line; a command must start with a $.
**There is no patch for stupidity.**

Please enter a line; a command must start with a $.
**$Line**
Error: the command must be followed by a blank, followed by an integer.

Please enter a line; a command must start with a $.
**$Line 2**
Error: the number is greater than the number of lines in the text.

Please enter a line; a command must start with a $.
**$Line 0**

Please enter a line; a command must start with a $.
**$Insert**

Please enter a line; a command must start with a $.
**As Kevin Mittnick said,**

Please enter a line; a command must start with a $.
**$Delete 0**

Error: the command must be followed by a space, followed by an integer, followed by a space, followed by an integer.

Please enter a line; a command must start with a $.
**$Done**

Here is the final text:
   As Kevin Mittnick said,
> There is no patch for stupidity.

The editing has been completed.

### 7.4.1  **Design of the** Editor **Class**

We will create an Editor class to solve this problem. To separate the editing aspects from the input/output aspects, there will be an explicit driver that reads from an input file and prints to an output file. Then the same Editor class could later be used in a ***conversational program,*** that is, a program in which the input is entered in response to prompts. That later program could have a graphical user interface or use console input/output. The design and implementation of the EditorDriver class will be developed after we complete work on the Editor class.

Before we decide what fields and methods the Editor class should contain, we ask "What does an editor have to do?" From the commands given above, some responsibilities can be determined:

- To interpret whether the line contains a legal command, an illegal command, or a line of text
- To carry out each of the four commands

When one of the errors described above occurs, the offending method cannot print an error message because we want to separate editing from input/output. We could have the method return the error message as a String, but what if a method that is supposed to return a String has an error? You will encounter such a method in Programming Project 7.5. For the sake of consistency, each error will throw a Run TimeException; the argument will have the specific error message. For example, in the Editor class we might have

**throw new** RunTimeException ("Error: not one of the given commands.\n");

Each error message can then be printed in the driver when the exception is caught. RunTimeException is the superclass of most of the exceptions thrown during execution: NullPointerException, NumberFormatException, NoSuchElementException, and so on. Basically, RunTimeException includes all exceptions that are not related to input or output.

Here are the method specifications for a default constructor and the five methods outlined above. To ensure that each command method is properly invoked, a user has access only to the interpret method, which in turn invokes the appropriate command method.

```
/**
 * Initializes this Editor object.
 *
 */
public Editor( )

/**
 * Interprets whether a specified line is a legal command, an illegal command,
 * or a line of text.
 *
 * @param s – the specified line to be interpreted.
 *
 * @return the result of carrying out the command, if s is a legal command, and
 *       return null, if s is a line of text.
 *
 * @throws RunTimeException – if s is an illegal command; the argument
 *       indicates the specific error.
 *
 */
public String interpret (String s)

/**
 * Inserts a specified line in front of the current line.
 *
 * @param s – the line to be inserted.
 *
 * @throws RunTimeException – if s has more than MAX_LINE_LENGTH
 *       characters.
 *
 */
protected void insert (String s)

/**
 * Deletes a specified range of lines from the text, and sets the current line
 * to be the line after the last line deleted.
 *
 * @param m – the beginning index of the range of lines to be deleted.
 * @param n – the ending index of the range of lines to be deleted.
 *
 * @throws RunTimeException – if m is less than 0 or if n is less than m or if
 *       n is greater than or equal to the number of lines of text.
 *
 */
protected void delete (int m, int n)

/**
 * Makes a specified index the index of the current line in the text.
```

```
     *
     * @param m – the specified index of the current line.
     *
     * @throws RunTimeException – if m is less than 0 or greater than or equal to
     *         the number of lines of text.
     *
     */
    protected void line (int m)

    /**
     * Returns the final version of the text.
     *
     * @return the final version of the text.
     *
     */
    protected String done( )
```

In order to define these five methods, we have to decide what fields we will have. One of the fields will hold the text, so we'll call it text. The text will be a sequence of strings, and we will often need to make insertions/deletions in the interior of the text, so text should be (a reference to) an instance of the LinkedList class (surprise!). To keep track of the current line, we will have a ListIterator field, current. A **boolean** field, inserting, will determine whether the most recent command was $Insert.

Here are the constant identifiers and fields:

```
    public final static char COMMAND_START = '$';

    public final static String INSERT_COMMAND = "$Insert";

    public final static String DELETE_COMMAND = "$Delete";

    public final static String LINE_COMMAND = "$Line";

    public final static String DONE_COMMAND = "$Done";

    public final static String BAD_LINE_MESSAGE =
            "Error: a command should start with " + COMMAND_START + ".\n";

    public final static String BAD_COMMAND_MESSAGE =
            "Error: not one of the given commands.\n";

    public final static String INTEGER_NEEDED =
            "Error: The command should be followed by a blank space, " +
            "\nfollowed by an integer.\n";

    public final static String TWO_INTEGERS_NEEDED =
            "Error: The command should be followed by a blank space, " +
            "\nfollowed by an integer, followed by a blank space, " +
            "followed by an integer.\n";
```

**public final static** String FIRST_GREATER =
    "Error: the first line number given is greater than the second.\n";

**public final static** String FIRST_LESS_THAN_ZERO =
    "Error: the first line number given is less than 0.\n";

**public final static** String SECOND_TOO_LARGE =
    "Error: the second line number given is greater than the " +
    "\nnumber of the last line in the text.\n";

**public final static** String M_LESS_THAN_ZERO =
    "Error: the number is less than 0.\n";

**public final static** String M_TOO_LARGE =
    "Error: the number is larger than the number of lines in the text.\n";

**public final static** String LINE_TOO_LONG =
    "Error: the line exceeds the maximum number of characters allowed, ";

**public final static** int MAX_LINE_LENGTH = 75;

**protected** LinkedList<String> text;

**protected** ListIterator<String> current;

**protected boolean** inserting;

The delete method can be invoked only if the command line has two tokens. So we will have an auxiliary method, tryToDelete (StringTokenizer tokens), which calls delete provided there are two integer tokens in the tokenized command line. There is a similar auxiliary method for the line method. Figure 7.19 has the UML diagram for the Editor class.

**Figure 7.19** I The class diagram for the Editor class.

| Editor |
| --- |
| # text: LinkedList<String><br># current: ListIterator<String><br># inserting: **boolean** |
| + Editor( )<br>+ interpret (s: String): String<br># insert (s: String)<br># tryToDelete (tokens: StringTokenizer)<br># delete (m: **int**; n: **int**)<br># tryToSetLine (tokens: StringTokenizer)<br># line (m: **int**)<br># done( ): String |

### 7.4.2 **Method Definitions for the** Editor **Class**

As usual, the default constructor initializes the fields:

```java
public Editor( )
{
        text = new LinkedList<String>( );
        current = text.listIterator( );
        inserting = false;
} // default constructor
```

We can estimate the time requirements for this method because it does not call any other methods in the Editor class. In general, the time requirements for a given method depend on the time for the methods called by the given method. The worstTime($n$), where $n$ is the number of lines of text, is constant. For the remainder of the Editor class's methods, we postpone an estimate of worstTime($n$) until all of the methods have been defined.

The interpret method proceeds as follows. There are special cases if the first character in the line is not '$': the insert method is invoked if inserting is true; otherwise, a bad-line exception is thrown. If the first character in the line is '$', the line is tokenized and action appropriate to the command is taken. For the $Delete and $Line commands, the remaining tokens must first be checked—to make sure they are integers—before the delete and line methods can be called. That allows the delete and line methods to have **int** parameters.

Here is the definition of the interpret method:

```java
public String interpret (String s)
{
        StringTokenizer tokens = new StringTokenizer (s);

        String command;

        if (s.charAt (0) != COMMAND_START)
                if (inserting)
                        insert (s);
                else
                        throw new RuntimeException (BAD_LINE_MESSAGE);
        else
        {
                command = tokens.nextToken( );
                if (command.equals (INSERT_COMMAND))
                        inserting = true;
                else
                {
                        inserting = false;
                        if (command.equals (DELETE_COMMAND))
                                tryToDelete (tokens);
```

```
                else if (command.equals (LINE_COMMAND))
                        tryToSetLine (tokens);
                else if (command.equals (DONE_COMMAND))
                        return done( );
                else
                        throw new RuntimeException (BAD_COMMAND_MESSAGE);
            } // command other than insert
        } // a command
        return null;
    } // method interpret
```

The definition of the insert method is straightforward. The only error checking is for a too-long line; otherwise, the parameter s is inserted into the text in front of the current line. The method definition is:

```
protected void insert (String s)
{
        if (s.length( ) > MAX_LINE_LENGTH)
                throw new RuntimeException (LINE_TOO_LONG +
                                            MAX_LINE_LENGTH + "\n");
        current.add (s);
} // insert
```

The $Delete command can fail syntactically, if the line does not have two integers, or semantically, if the first line number is either greater than the second or less than zero, or if the second line number is greater than the last line in the text. The tryToDelete method checks for syntax errors:

```
protected void tryToDelete (StringTokenizer tokens)
{
        try
        {
                int m = Integer.parseInt (tokens.nextToken( ));
                int n = Integer.parseInt (tokens.nextToken( ));
                delete (m, n);
        }// try
        catch (RuntimeException e)
        {
                throw new RuntimeException (TWO_INTEGERS_NEEDED);
        } // not enough integer tokens
} // method tryToDelete
```

The delete method checks for semantic errors. If there are no errors, the List Iterator object current is positioned at line m, and a loop removes lines m through n. Then current will automatically be positioned beyond the last line removed. Here is the definition of the delete method:

```
protected void delete (int m, int n)
{
      if (m > n)
            throw new RuntimeException (FIRST_GREATER);
      if (m < 0)
            throw new RuntimeException (FIRST_LESS_THAN_ZERO);
      if (n >= text.size( ))
            throw new RuntimeException (SECOND_TOO_LARGE);
      current = text.listIterator (m);
      for (int i = m; i <= n; i++)
      {
            current.next( );
            current.remove( );
      } // for
} // method delete
```

The tryToSetLine method is similar to tryToDelete, except there is only one integer expected on the command line:

```
protected void tryToSetLine (StringTokenizer tokens)
{
      try
      {
            int m = Integer.parseInt (tokens.nextToken( ));
            line (m);
      } // try
      catch (RuntimeException e)
      {
            throw new RuntimeException (INTEGER_NEEDED);
      } // no next token or token not an integer
} // method tryToSetLine
```

The line method, called if there are no syntactic errors, checks for semantic errors, and if none is found, repositions current to the line whose line number is m. Here is the definition of the line method:

```
protected void line (int m)
{
      if (m < 0)
            throw new RuntimeException (M_LESS_THAN_ZERO);
      if (m > text.size( ))
            throw new RuntimeException (M_TOO_LARGE);
      current = text.listIterator (m);
} // method line
```

Finally, the done method returns a String representation of the text: suitable for printing. We create itr, a ListIterator object (specifically, a ListItr object) to iterate through the LinkedList object text. The current line should have a $>$ in front of it. But how can we determine when the line that itr is positioned at is the same as the line that current is positioned at? Here is one possibility:

> itr.equals (current)

The ListItr class does not define an equals method, so the Object class's version of equals is invoked. But that method compares references, not objects. The references will never be the same since they were, ultimately, allocated by different calls to the ListItr constructor. So that approach will not work.

Alternatively, we could compare elements:

> itr.next( ).equals (current.next( ))

But this could give incorrect information if the text had duplicate lines. The safe way to compare is by the nextIndex( ) method, which returns the index of the element that the iterator is positioned at. This is one of those rare occasions when we are not modifying a collection during an iteration, but an enhanced **for** statement will not work. Here is the method definition:

```
protected String done( )
{
        final String FINAL_TEXT_MESSAGE =
                "\n\nHere is the final text:\n";

        String s = FINAL_TEXT_MESSAGE;

        ListIterator itr = text.listIterator( );
        while (itr.hasNext( ))
                if (itr.nextIndex( ) == current.nextIndex( ))
                        s = s + "> " + itr.next( ) + '\n';
                else
                        s = s + " " + itr.next( ) + '\n';
        if (!current.hasNext( ))
                s = s + "> " + '\n';
        return s;
} // method done
```

**Big-O Analysis of the Editor Class Methods**  To estimate the time requirements for the methods in the Editor class's methods, let $n$ represent the size of the text—this is not necessarily the same as the n used as a parameter in several methods. The delete method calls the one-parameter listIterator (**int** index) method, for which worstTime($n$) is linear in $n$. There is then a loop in which some elements in the text are removed; each removal takes constant time. This number of elements is certainly less than or equal to $n$, the total number of elements in the text. So for the delete method, worstTime($n$) is linear in $n$.

The line method also calls the listIterator (**int** index) method, and that makes the worstTime($n$) linear in $n$ for the line method. The done method loops through the text, so its worstTime($n$) is also linear in $n$. All other methods take constant time, except those whose worstTime($n$) is linear in $n$ owing to their calling the delete, line, or done methods.

### 7.4.3  Design of the EditorDriver Class

The EditorDriver class is similar to the VeryLongDriver in Chapter 6. The paths for the input and output files are read in from the keyboard, and a file reader and file writer for those two files are declared and opened. The only other responsibility of the EditorDriver class is to edit the input file. Here are the method specifications:

```
/**
 * Initializes this EditorDriver object.
 */
public EditorDriver( )

/**
 * Reads in the file paths, creates and opens the input and output files, and
 * returns a reference to the file writer.
 *
 * @return a reference to the file writer
 */
public PrintWriter openFiles( )

/**
 * Edits the text by performing the input-file commands
 *
 */
public void editText( )
```

The only fields needed are an Editor object, a file reader, and a file writer:

```
protected Editor editor;

protected BufferedReader fileReader;

protected PrintWriter fileWriter;
```

Figure 7.20 has all the UML class diagrams for this project.

### 7.4.4  Implementation of the EditorDriver Class

The default constructor simply initializes the editor field. The definition of the open Files( ) method is identical to that of the openFiles( ) method from the VeryLongDriver class in Section 6.3.4, except that editText( ) is called instead of testVeryLongInt Methods( ).

The editText( ) method loops through the input file, with a **try** block and a **catch** block to handle all of the editing errors that may occur (and, because we are reading from a file, Java requires that IOException also be caught). During each loop iteration, the interpret method is called. The return value from this call will be **null** unless

**Figure 7.20 |** Class diagrams for the Editor project.

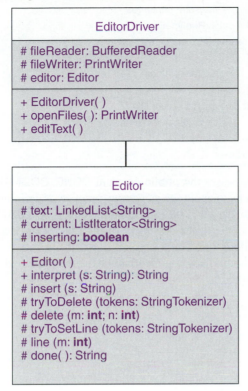

the command is "$Done", in which case the final text is printed.
   Here is the definition:

```
public void editText( )
{
    String line = new String( ),
          result = new String( );

    while (true)
    {
        try
        {
            line = fileReader.readLine( );
            if (line == null)
                break;
            fileWriter.println (line);
            result = editor.interpret (line);
        } // try
        catch (RuntimeException e)
```

```
                    {
                            fileWriter.println (e);
                    } // catch RuntimeException
                    catch (IOException e)
                    {
                            System.out.println (e);
                    } // catch IOException
                    if (line.equals (Editor.DONE_COMMAND))
                            fileWriter.println (result);
            } // while
      } // method editText
```

This method accesses the **public** constant DONE_COMMAND from the Editor class. That enables us to avoid the dangerous practice of defining the same constant identifier twice. The danger is that this identifier might be redefined in a subsequent application, for example, if the developer of the Editor class decided to change the command-start symbol from $ to #.

The main method is virtually identical to the main method from the VeryLong Driver class of Chapter 6.

```
      public static void main (String[ ] args)
      {
            PrintWriter writer = null;

            try
            {
                    EditorDriver driver = new EditorDriver( );

                    writer = driver.openFiles( );
                    driver.editText( );
            } // try
            finally
            {
                    writer.close( );
            } // finally
      } // method main
```

## SUMMARY

A *linked list* is a List object (that is, an object in a class that implements the List inter-face) in which the following property is satisfied:

Each element is contained in an object, called an Entry object, that also includes a refer-ence, called a *link,* to another Entry object. For each Entry object except the one that holds the last element in the collection, the link is to the Entry object that contains the next element in the collection.

A linked list that also satisfies the following property:

> Each Entry object except the first also includes a link to the Entry object that contains the previous element.

is called a ***doubly linked list.*** Otherwise, it is called a ***singly linked list.***

The SinglyLinkedList class (partially) implements a singly linked list. The purpose of developing the SinglyLinkedList class is to introduce you to the topics of links and iterators, and thus to prepare you for the focal point of the chapter: the LinkedList class, part of the Java Collections Framework. LinkedList objects lack the random-access ability of ArrayList objects. But, by using an iterator, an element can be added to or removed from a LinkedList in only constant time; for adding to or removing from an ArrayList object, worstTime(n) is linear in n. This advantage of LinkedList objects is best suited for consecutive insertions and deletions because, for the task of getting to the index of the first insertion or deletion, worstTime(n) is linear in n.

The Java Collections Framework's implementation of the LinkedList class stores the elements in a circular, doubly linked structure with a dummy entry. Another possible implementation is a noncircular, doubly linked structure with head and tail fields.

The application, a simple line editor, took advantage of the LinkedList class's ability to quickly make consecutive insertions and deletions anywhere in a Linked List object.

## CONCEPT EXERCISES

**7.1**  In the SinglyLinkedList class, define the following method without using an iterator.

```
/**
 * Finds the element at a specified position in this LinkedList object.
 * The worstTime(n) is O(n).
 *
 * @param index – the position of the element to be returned.
 *
 * @return the element at position index.
 *
 * @throws IndexOutOfBoundsException – if index is less than 0 or greater than
 *      or equal to size( ).
 */
public E get (int index)
```

**7.2**  Redo Concept Exercise 7.1 by using an iterator. Re-redo that exercise using an enhanced **for** statement.

**7.3**  Suppose we added each of the following methods to the ArrayList class:

```
public boolean addFirst (E element)
public boolean addLast (E element)
```

```
public E getFirst( )
public E getLast( )
public E removeFirst( )
public E removeLast( )
```

Determine worstTime(*n*) for each method.

**7.4** The listIterator( ) method can be called by a LinkedList object, but is not explicitly defined within the LinkedList class. In what class is that listIterator( ) method defined? What is that definition?

**7.5** One of the possibilities for fields in the LinkedList class was to have head and tail fields, both of type Entry, where the Entry class had element and next fields, but no previous field. Then we would have a singly linked list.

    **a.** Define the addLast method for this design. Here is the method specification:

```
/**
 * Appends a specified element to (the back of) this LinkedList object.
 *
 * @param element – the element to be appended.
 *
 * @return true.
 *
 */
public boolean addLast (E element)
```

    **b.** The definition of the removeLast( ) method would need to make **null** the next field in the Entry object before the Entry object tail. Could we avoid a loop in the definition of removeLast( ) if, in the LinkedList class, we added a beforeTail field that pointed to the Entry object before the Entry object tail? Explain.

**7.6** How can you distinguish between a call to the add (E element) method in the LinkedList class and a call to the add (E element) method in the ListItr class?

**7.7** Explain how to remove "Don" from the LinkedList object in Figure 7.18. Explain why, for the definition of the method remove (E element), worstTime(*n*) is linear in *n*?

**7.8** In the Java Collections Framework, the LinkedList class is designed as a circular, doubly linked list with a dummy entry (pointed to by the header field). What is the main advantage of this approach over a circular, doubly linked list with head and tail fields?

**7.9** For the three methods in the EditorDriver class, estimate worstTime(*n*), where *n* represents the number of lines of text.

## PROGRAMMING EXERCISES

**7.1** Use the SinglyLinkedList class three times. First, create a SinglyLinkedList object, team1, with elements of type String. Add three elements to team1.

Second, create team2, another SinglyLinkedList object with elements of type String. Add four elements to team2. Finally, create a SinglyLinkedList object, league, whose elements are SinglyLinkedList objects of teams. Add team1 and team2 to league.

**7.2**  Hypothesize the output from the following method segment:

```
LinkedList<Character> letters = new LinkedList<Character>( );

ListIterator<Character> itr = letters.listIterator( );

itr.add ('f');
itr.add ('t');
itr.previous( );
itr.previous( );
itr.add ('e');
itr.add ('r');
itr.next( );
itr.add ('e');
itr.add ('c');
itr = letters.listIterator( );
itr.add ('p');
System.out.println (letters);
```

Test your hypothesis with a project that includes the above code in a main method.

**7.3**  Rewrite the code in Programming Exercise 7.2 without using an iterator. For example, you would start with:

```
LinkedList<Character> letters = new LinkedList<Character>( );

letters.add (0, 'f');
```

Test your revision with a project that includes the above code in a main method.

**7.4**  Rewrite the code in Programming Exercise 7.2 with a native array. For example, you would start with:

```
char [ ] letters = new char [10];

letters [0] = 'f';
```

Test your revision with a project that includes the above code in a main method.

**7.5**  Hypothesize the error in the following code:

```
LinkedList<Double> duesList = new LinkedList<Double>( );

ListItr<Double> itr = duesList.listIterator( );
```

Test your hypothesis with a project that includes the above code in the main method.

**7.6**    Suppose we have the following:

LinkedList<Double> weights = **new** LinkedList<Double>( );

ListIterator<Double> itr;

weights.add (5.3);
weights.add (2.8);
itr = weights.listIterator( );

Hypothesize which of the following sequences of messages would now be legal:

**a.**    itr.add (8.8); itr.next( ); itr.remove( );

**b.**    itr.add (8.8); itr.remove( ); itr.next( );

**c.**    itr.next( ); itr.add (8.8); itr.remove( );

**d.**    itr.next( ); itr.remove( ); itr.add (8.8);

**e.**    itr.remove( ); itr.add (8.8); itr.next( );

**f.**    itr.remove( ); itr.next( ); itr.add (8.8);

Test your hypotheses with a project that includes the above code in the main method.

**7.7**    Suppose you decided to rewrite the VeryLongInt class, from Chapter 6, with a LinkedList instead of an ArrayList. The main change is to replace each occurrence of the identifier ArrayList with LinkedList. Another change, in the String-parameter constructor, is to replace

digits = **new** ArrayList<Integer> (s.length( ));

with

digits = **new** LinkedList<Integer>( );

But the add method will now take quadratic time because the least method will now take linear time. Modify the least method—including its heading—so that its worstTime($n$) will be constant. Make the corresponding changes to the add method so that method will take only linear time.

Test your revisions by using the driver.

**7.8**    Rewrite the insert method in the Editor class to insert the given line *after* the current line. For example, if the text is

>I was
  older then

and the command is

$Insert
so much

then the text becomes

I was
>so much
older then

The newly added line becomes the current line.

Test your change by using the driver.

**7.9** Modify the EditorDriver class to work with commands entered from the keyboard instead of a file. The output should go to the console window.

## Programming Project 7.1

### Expanding the SinglyLinkedList Class

Expand the SinglyLinkedList class from Lab 12 by providing genuine definitions—not just thrown exceptions—for each of the following methods:

```
/**
 * Inserts the elements of this SinglyLinkedList object into an array in the same
 * order as in this SinglyLinkedList object. The worstTime(n) is O(n).
 *
 * @return a reference to the array that holds the same elements, in the same
 *              order, as this SinglyLinkedList object.
 *
 */
public Object [ ] toArray ( )

/**
 * Determines if this SinglyLinkedList object contains all of the elements from a
 * specified collection.
 *
 * @param c – the specified collection.
 *
 * @return true – if this SinglyLinkedList object contains each element of c;
 *              otherwise, return false.
 *
 */
public boolean containsAll (Collection<?> c)

/**
 * Determines if this SinglyLinkedList object is equal to obj.
 *
 * @param obj – an object whose equality to this SinglyLinkedList object is
 *              being tested.
 *
 * @return true – if obj is a SinglyLinkedList object of the same size as this
 *              SinglyLinkedList object, and at each index, the element in this
 *              SinglyLinkedList object is equal to the element at the same
 *              index in obj.
 *
 */
public boolean equals (Object obj)
```

To test your method definitions, modify the SinglyLinkedDriver class from Lab 12. For the toArray method, print out the contents of the array returned.

Here are two system tests your program must pass:

**System Test 1:**

e1 SinglyLinkedList
e1 add yes
e1 add no
e2 SinglyLinkedList
e2 add yes
e2 add maybe
e2 add no
e1 containsAll e2
e2 containsAll e1
e2 containsAll e2
e1 equals e1
e1 equals e2
e1 add maybe
e1 containsAll e2
e1 toArray
e1 equals e2
e1 add no
e1 equals e2
e1 toArray
e2 containsAll e1

For the first call to the method toArray, the output should be "maybe", "no", "yes". For the second call to the method toArray, the output should be "no", "maybe", "no", "yes". For the five calls to the method containsAll, the output should be "false", "true", "true", "true", and "false", respectively. For the four calls to the method equals, the output should be "true", "false", "false", and "false", respectively.

**System Test 2:**

e1 SinglyLinkedList
e2 SinglyLinkedList
e1 containsAll e2
e1 equals e2
e1 toArray
e1 add 0
e1 add 1
e1 add 2
e1 add 3
e1 add 4
e1 add 5
e1 add 6
e1 add 7
e1 add 8
e1 add 9
e1 add 10
e1 toArray

Both e1 and e2 should be declared as SinglyLinkedList<String> for both system tests.

## Programming Project 7.2

### Implementing the remove( ) Method in the SinglyLinkedListIterator Class

1. Modify the **SinglyLinkedListIterator** class by implementing the remove( ) method. Here are revised fields in that class and a revised definition of the next( ) method:

```
protected Entry previous,      // reference to Entry before lastReturned Entry
                lastReturned,  // reference to Entry with element returned
                               // by most recent call to next( ) method.
                next;          // reference to Entry with element that will be
                               // returned by subsequent call to next( ) method

public E next ( )
{
      if (lastReturned != null)
          previous = lastReturned;
      lastReturned = next;
      next = next.next;
      return lastReturned.element;
} // method next
```

2. Create a SinglyLinkedDriver class to validate the newly implemented remove( ) method. Create two files from the following for the system tests—the comments should not be part of the files:

**Input for System Test 1:**
el SinglyLinkedList
el add yes
el add no
el remove yes
el add yes
el add maybe
el add serene
el iterator
next
remove // removes "serene"
next
next
remove // removes "yes"

**Input for System Test 2:**
el SinglyLinkedList
el add Maui
el add peaceful
el add serene

e1 add relaxed
e1 iterator
remove // throws IllegalStateException
next
e1 remove relaxed
remove // may throw NullPointerException
next
next
next
remove // removes "Maui"

Note the curious comment, "may throw NullPointerException". Whether that exception is thrown depends on how you define the remove( ) method in the SinglyLinkedListIterator class. For some definitions of remove( ), no exception will be thrown. In general, if an iterator is looping through a collection, it is risky to allow both the iterator and the collection to structurally modify (by inserting into or removing from) the collection. As described in Appendix 3, the Java Collections Framework has a technique to eliminate this risk: the iterator throws an exception as soon as it is discovered that the iterator and another object (either the collection itself or another iterator) are structurally modifying the collection.

## Programming Project 7.3

### Making a Circular SinglyLinkedList Class

Modify the SinglyLinkedList class to be circular. That is, the entry after the last entry should be the entry referenced by head. Here is an example, with three elements:

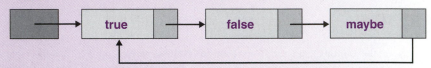

    The only methods you need to implement are the five methods listed in Section 7.2 and the iterator( ) method from Section 7.2.2. You will also need a driver to validate those methods.

## Programming Project 7.4

### Alternative Implementation of the LinkedList Class

Implement the LinkedList class with head and tail fields instead of a header field that points to a dummy entry. Your implementation should be doubly linked, that is, each Entry object should have a reference to the previous Entry object and a reference to the next Entry object. You get to choose whether your implementation will be circular. The Entry class will be unchanged from the header implementation, but the ListItr class will need to be modified.

    Validate your LinkedList and ListItr classes with a driver.

# Programming Project 7.5

## Expanding the Line Editor

Expand the Line Editor project by implementing the following additional commands:

**5.**   $Change %X%Y%

*Effect:* In the current line, each occurrence of the string given by X will be replaced by the string given by Y.

*Example:* Suppose the current line is

bear ruin'd choirs, wear late the sweet birds sang

Then the command

$Change %ear%are%

will cause the current line to become

bare ruin'd choirs, ware late the sweet birds sang

If we then issue the command

$Change %wa%whe%

the current line will be

bare ruin'd choirs, where late the sweet birds sang

*Notes:*

**a.** If either X or Y contains a percent sign, it is the end-user's responsibility to choose another delimiter. For example,

$Change #0.16#16%#

**b.** The string given by Y may be the null string. For example, if current line is

aid of their country.

then the command

$Change %of %%

will change the current line to

aid their country.

**c.** If the delimiter occurs fewer than three times, the error message to be generated is

**\*\*\* Error: Delimiter must occur three times. Please try again.**

*(continued on next page)*

*(continued from previous page)*

6.  $Last

    *Effect:* The line number of the last line in the text has been printed.

    *Example:* Suppose the text is

    >     I heard a bird sing
    > \> in the dark of December.
    >     A magical thing
    >     and a joy to remember.

    The command

    $Last

    will cause 3 to be printed. The text and the designation of the current line are unchanged.

7.  $Print m n

    *Effect:* Each line number and line in the text, from lines *m* through *n*, inclusive, will be printed.

    *Example:* Suppose the text is

    >     Winston Churchill once said that
    > \> democracy is the worst
    >     form of government
    >     except for all the others.

    The command

    $Print 0 2

    will cause the following to be printed:

    0 Winston Churchill once said that
    1 democracy is the worst
    2 form of government

    The text and the designation of the current line are unchanged.

    *Note:* If no line numbers are entered, the entire text should be printed. For example,

    $Print

    is the command to print the entire text, with line numbers.

    As with the delete command, an error message should be generated if (1) *m* is greater than *n* or if (2) *m* is less than 0 or if (3) *n* is greater than the last line number in the text.

*Note:* For the implementation of the $Last and $Print commands, the printing should not be done in the Editor class. The corresponding methods should return the information to be printed.

**Instead of having the input come from a file and the output go to a file, the input should come from the keyboard and the output should go to the screen.**

**System Test 1:**

For simplicity, prompts are omitted. Sample output is boldfaced.

```
$Insert
You can fool
some of the people
some of the times,
but you cannot foul
all of the peeple
all of the time.
$Line 2
$Print 2 1
```
**Error: The first line number is greater than the second.**

```
$Print 2 2
```
**2 some of the times,**
```
$Change %s%%
$Print 2 2
```
**2 ome of the time,**
```
$Change %o%so
```
**Error: Delimiter must occur three times. Please try again.**

```
$Change %o%so%
$Print 2 2
```
**2 some sof the time,**
```
Change
```
**Error: Not one of the given commands**

```
$Change %sof%of%
$Print 2 2
```
**2 some of the time,**
```
$Line 0
$Insert
Lincoln once said that
you can fool
some of the people
all the time and
```

*(continued on next page)*

*(continued from previous page)*

all of the time and
$Last
**10**
$Print 0 10
**0 Lincoln once said that**
**1 you can fool**
**2 some of the people**
**3 all the time and**
**4 all of the time and**
**5 You can fool**
**6 some of the people**
**7 some of the time,**
**8 but you cannot foul**
**9 all of the peeple**
**10 all of the time.**
$Line 5
$Change %Y%y%
$Print 5 5
**5 you can fool**
$Line 6
$Change %some%all%
$Print 6 6
**6 all of the people**
$Line 8
$Change %ul%ol%
$Print 8 8
**8 but you cannot fool**
$Line 9
$Change %ee%eo%
$Print 9 9
**9 all of the people**
$Delete 3 3
$Print 0 10
**Error: The second line number is greater than the number of the last line in**
**the text.**

$Last
**9**
$Print 0 9
**0 Lincoln once said that**
**1 you can fool**
**2 some of the people**
**3 all of the time and**

**4 you can fool**
**5 all of the people**
**6 some of the time,**
**7 but you cannot fool**
**8 all of the people**
**9 all of the time.**
$Done
**Here is the final text:**
      **Lincoln once said that**
      **you can fool**
      **some of the people**
      **all of the time and**
      **you can fool**
      **all of the people**
      **some of the time,**
      **but you cannot fool**
   > **all of the people**
      **all of the time.**

**System Test 2:**

$Insert
Life is full of
successes and lessons.
$Delete 1 1
$Insert
wondrous oppurtunities disguised as
hopeless situations.
$Last
2
$Print
**0 Life is full of**
**1 wondrous oppurtunities disguised as**
**2 hopeless situations.**
$Line 1
$Change %ur%or%
$Print 0 2
**0 Life is full of**
**1 wondrous opportunities disguised as**
**2 hopeless situations.**
$Done
**Here is the final text:**
      **Life is full of**
   > **wondrous opportunities disguised as**
      **hopeless situations.**

## Programming Project 7.6

### An Integrated Web Browser and Search Engine, Part 2

In this part of the project, you will add functionality to the forward button in a very simple browser. The partially completed browser already has a back button, a home button, and a line in which the end user can enter a uniform resource locator (URL). Basically, all the project does is to display pages. Initially the output area of the graphical user interface (GUI) window displays the home page. That page has a link to another page, and if the end-user clicks on the link, that page will be displayed in the output area. At any time, the end-user can type a URL in the input line, can click on the home button, can click on a link (if there is one) in the currently displayed page, and can go back to the previously displayed page (if there was a previously displayed page).

For simplicity, you may assume that each html reference tag will have the file name immediately after the $=$ and immediately before the $>$.

According to standard Web-browser protocol, you cannot go where you already are. So, for example, if you are on the home page, nothing happens if you click on the Home button. Also, whenever a new page is printed, all forward links are removed. For example, if you click on browser2, then browser4, then back, then home, the forward button would now be disabled (and colored red), so you could not click Forward to get to browser4.

The files you will need, from the book's website, are as follows:

Browser.java
GUI.java
GUIListener.java
GUIBrowser.java // contains a subclass of GUI
GUIBrowserListener.java
Process.java

The only class you will be altering is GUIBrowserListener.

Here are Web pages you can use to test your project:

browser1
browser2
browser4
browser5
home
network.in1

To learn more about GUIs, there is a tutorial from Sun Microsystems: http://java.sun.com/docs/books/tutorial/uiswing/.

When a button is enabled, its color should be green.

When a button is disabled, its color should be red.

**System Test 1:**

Click on browser2, browser4, back (browser2 appears), enter browser.in5, click on back (browser2 appears), forward (browser5 appears).

At this point, the Forward button is disabled.

**System Test 2:**

Click on browser2, browser4, back (browser2 appears), home, back (browser2 appears), back (home appears), forward (browser2 appears), forward (home appears).

At this point, the Forward button is disabled.

# Stacks and Queues

In this chapter we introduce two more abstract data types: stacks and queues. Stacks and queues can be modified in only a very limited way, so there are (several) straightforward implementations, that is, data structures, of the corresponding interfaces. Best of all, stacks and queues have a wide variety of applications. We'll start with stacks because a stack is somewhat easier to implement than a queue. ■

## CHAPTER OBJECTIVES

1. Understand the defining properties of stacks and queues.

2. Compare various implementations of both the PureStack and PureQueue interfaces, and be able to develop a linked implementation of the PureQueue class from scratch.

3. Explain the major flaw in the Java Collections Framework's Stack class and Queue interface.

4. Explore the use of stacks in the implementation of recursion and in converting from infix notation to postfix notation.

5. Examine the role of queues in computer simulation.

## 8.1 | STACKS

A *stack* is a finite sequence of elements in which the only element that can be removed is the element that was most recently inserted. That element is referred to as the *top* element on the stack.

For example, a tray-holder in a cafeteria holds a stack of trays. Insertions and deletions are made only at the top. To put it another way, the tray that was most recently put on the holder will be the next one to be removed. This defining property of stacks is sometimes abbreviated "last in, first out", or LIFO. In keeping with this view, an insertion is referred to as a *push,* and a removal as a *pop.* For the sake of alliteration, a retrieval of the top element is referred to as a *peek.*

Figure 8.1a shows a stack with three elements and Figures 8.1b, c, and d show the effect of two pops and then a push.

In Section 8.1.1, we define the PureStack interface, which corresponds to the abstract data type stack.

### 8.1.1  The PureStack Interface

In Chapter 6, we defined the List interface, which was implemented by the ArrayList class (in Chapter 6) and the LinkedList class (in Chapter 7). To describe the abstract data type stack, we will supply a PureStack interface.[1] There are only a few methods that the PureStack interface must have: size, isEmpty, push, pop, and peek. The isEmpty method is included only for convenience: we could define isEmpty from size. For the sake of simplicity, we allow only these five methods.

Here is the PureStack interface, parameterized with type parameter E. The phrase "this PureStack object" means "this calling object in the class that implements the PureStack interface."

```
public interface PureStack<E>          // Note: does not extend Collection
{
    /**
     * Determines the number of elements in this PureStack object.
     *
     * @return the number of elements in this PureStack object.
     *
```

**Figure 8.1** | A stack through several stages of pops and pushes: 17 and 13 are popped and then 21 is pushed. In each figure, the highest element is the top element.

```
17
13      13                      21
28      28          28          28
(a)     (b) pop     (c) pop     (d) push 21
```

---

[1] The reason the interface is named PureStack instead of Stack is to avoid confusion with the Java Collections Framework's Stack class, discussed in Section 8.1.2.

```
        */
       int size( );

       /**
        * Determines if this PureStack object has no elements.
        *
        * @return true – if this PureStack object has no elements; otherwise,
        *        return false.
        *
        */
       boolean isEmpty( );

       /**
        * Inserts a specified element on the top of this PureStack object.
        * The averageTime(n) is constant and worstTime(n) is O(n).
        *
        * @param element – the element to be pushed.
        *
        */
       void push (E element);

       /**
        * Removes the top element from this PureStack object.
        *
        * @return – the element removed.
        *
        * @throws NoSuchElementException – if this PureStack object is empty.
        *
        */
       E pop( );

       /**
        * Returns the top element on this PureStack object.
        *
        * @return – the element returned.
        *
        * @throws NoSuchElementException – if this PureStack object is empty.
        *
        */
       E peek( );

   } // interface PureStack
```

Note that the specified worst time for the push method estimates only an upper bound, namely, $O(n)$, where $n$ refers to the number of elements in the stack. It would be inappropriately restrictive to specify that worstTime($n$) is linear in $n$, because then a developer would not be allowed to improve on a lower bound of $\Omega(n)$. Note also that, since the specifications for the pop and peek (and size and isEmpty) methods do not explicitly estimate times, averageTime($n$) and worstTime($n$) are constant for those methods.

An interface cannot be used by itself, because interfaces are not instantiable. That is, we cannot construct an instance of an interface. To achieve instantiability, we now turn to implementations of the PureStack class. Each such implementation should have seven methods: a default constructor, a copy constructor, and the five methods in the PureStack interface.

### 8.1.2 Implementations of the PureStack Interface

In the next few sections, we will consider several implementations of the PureStack interface. We'll start with two "from scratch" implementations, that is, implementations that do not use any existing collection classes. The first of these implementations is contiguous (array-based), and the second is linked—like the SinglyLinkedList class in Chapter 7. Both of these implementations are not difficult to develop and are efficient. We then develop implementations that utilize the ArrayList and LinkedList classes, and these implementations are very easy to develop and are also efficient. Finally we look at the Java Collections Framework's implementation of the PureStack interface, and why this implementation is unsuitable.

**An Array-Based Implementation of the PureStack Interface**   We will store the elements of the stack in an array, but what index will correspond to the top of the stack? The "obvious" answer is to store the top element at index 0. But if the top element is at index 0, then each push and each pop will require linear time—because every element will have to be moved to the next higher index.

Instead, the index of the top element will correspond to the *size* of the stack. For example, initially, the size of the stack is 0, and so the first element is stored at index 0. After that insertion, the size of the stack is 1, and so the second element is stored at index 1.

When a call to the push method forces an expansion of the underlying array, a new array of twice the underlying array's capacity is created. In order to create this new array, we write

```
E[ ] newData = (E[ ]) new Object [data.length * 2];
```

instead of

```
E[ ] newData = new E [data.length * 2];        // illegal
```

because the **new** operator must be applied to a real type, not to a type parameter, which is a dummy type. This pattern also appears in the two constructors, and in similar method definitions in the ArrayList class.

With these details out of the way, the definition of the ArrayPureStack class is straightforward:

```
public class ArrayPureStack<E> implements PureStack<E>
{

        protected E[ ] data;
```

```
protected int size;

/**
 * Initializes this ArrayPureStack object to be empty, with an initial
 * capacity of 10.
 *
 */
public ArrayPureStack( )
{
        final int DEFAULT_INITIAL_CAPACITY = 10;

        data = (E[ ])new Object [DEFAULT_INITIAL_CAPACITY];
        size = 0;
} // default constructor

/**
 * Initializes this ArrayPureStack object to contain a shallow copy of
 * another ArrayPureStack object.
 * The worstTime(n) is O(n), where n is the size of the other ArrayPureStack
 * object.
 *
 * @param otherStack − the ArrayPureStack object to be copied to
 *        this ArrayPureStack object.
 *
 */
public ArrayPureStack (ArrayPureStack<E> otherStack)
{
        final int CAPACITY = (int)(otherStack.size * 1.10);// allows room for growth

        data = (E[ ])new Object [CAPACITY];
        size = otherStack.size;
        System.arraycopy (otherStack.data, 0, data, 0, otherStack.size);
} // copy constructor

/**
 * Determines the number of elements in this ArrayPureStack object.
 *
 * @return the number of elements in this ArrayPureStack object.
 *
 */
public int size( )
{
        return size;
} // method size

/**
 * Determines if this ArrayPureStack object has no elements.
 *
```

```
    * @return true – if this ArrayPureStack object has no elements.
    *
    */
   public boolean isEmpty( )
   {
          return size == 0;
   } // method isEmpty

   /**
    * Inserts a specified element on the top of this ArrayPureStack object.
    * The averageTime(n) is constant and worstTime(n) is O(n).
    *
    * @param element – the element to be pushed.
    *
    */
   public void push (E element)
   {
          if (size == data.length)
          {
                 E[ ] newData = (E[ ]) new Object [data.length * 2];
                 System.arraycopy (data, 0, newData, 0, size);
                 data = newData;
          } // if
          data [size++] = element;
   } // method push

   /**
    * Removes the top element from this ArrayPureStack object.
    *
    * @return – the element removed.
    * @throws NoSuchElementException – if this ArrayPureStack
    *       object is empty.
    */
   public E pop( )
   {
          return data [−−size];
   } // method pop

   /**
    * Returns the top element on this ArrayPureStack object.
    *
    * @return – the element returned.
    * @throws NoSuchElementException – if this ArrayPureStack object
    *       is empty.
    *
    */
```

```
        public E peek( )
        {
                return data [size − 1];
        } // method peek

} // class ArrayPureStack
```

For the push method, worstTime(*n*) is linear in *n* because resizing may occur.

Here is the ArrayPureStack code to create and maintain the stack in Figure 8.1.

```
ArrayPureStack<Integer> stack = new ArrayPureStack<Integer>( );

stack.push (28);
stack.push (13);
stack.push (17);
stack.pop( );
stack.pop( );
stack.push (21);
```

In the next section, we develop a linked implementation of the PureStack interface.

**A Linked Implementation of the** PureStack **Interface** In order for you to see another "from scratch" implementation of the PureStack interface, we will now develop a LinkedPureStack class. We will use a singly linked list, and so each element will be stored in an entry that also contains a reference to the entry that holds the next lowest element in the stack. The top field will hold a reference to the entry whose element is at the top of the stack. The LinkedPureStack class will have some similarities with the SinglyLinkedList class in Chapter 7, but neither inheritance nor aggregation is inappropriate because of the following differences:

1. The LinkedPureStack class has a size field to directly keep track of the number of elements in the stack.

2. The LinkedPureStack class has a copy constructor.

3. The only methods the two classes have in common are size( ) and isEmpty( ).

4. There are no iterators over a LinkedPureStack object.

Figure 8.2 shows the structure of a LinkedPureStack object with three elements.

The definition of the copy constructor deserves some comment. First, we call the default constructor to explicitly initialize the fields (the Java Virtual Machine will preinitialize those fields just before the execution of any constructor). Then, if otherStack is not empty, we copy the top element from otherStack to the calling (that is, just constructed) object. Finally, we loop through the remaining elements in other Stack and append each one to the calling object.

Here is the LinkedPureStack class, including the inner Entry class (the javadoc comments are omitted because they are essentially unchanged from the ArrayPure Stack class):

```
public class LinkedPureStack<E> implements PureStack<E>
{
```

**Figure 8.2** | A LinkedPureStack object with three elements, shown as **int** values even though they are actually references to Integer objects.

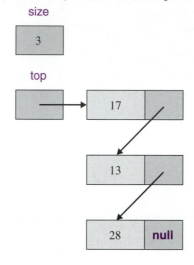

```
protected Entry<E> top;

protected int size;

public LinkedPureStack( )
{
        top = null;
        size = 0;
} // default constructor

public LinkedPureStack (LinkedPureStack<E> otherStack)
{
        this( );
        if (!otherStack.isEmpty( ))
        {
                // Copy first element from otherStack:
                top = new Entry<E>( );
                top.element = otherStack.top.element;
                top.next = null;
                size = 1;

                // Copy remaining elements from otherStack:
                Entry<E> current = top;
                for (Entry<E> otherCurrent = otherStack.top.next; otherCurrent
                                != null; otherCurrent = otherCurrent.next)
                {
```

```
                        current.next = new Entry<E>( );
                        current = current.next;
                        current.element = otherCurrent.element;
                        size++;
                } // for
                current.next = null;
        } // if
} // copy constructor

public int size( )
{
        return size;
}

public boolean isEmpty( )
{
        return size == 0;
}

public void push (E element)
{
        Entry<E> newEntry = new Entry<E>( );

        newEntry.element = element;
        newEntry.next = top;
        top = newEntry;
        size++;
}

public E pop( )
{
        E element = top.element;
        top = top.next;
        size--;
        return element;
}

public E peek( )
{
        return top.element;
}

protected static class Entry<E>
{
        protected E element;
        protected Entry<E> next;
} // inner class Entry<E>

} // class LinkedPureStack
```

In terms of performance, the only noteworthy difference between the Array PureStack and LinkedPureStack implementations is that, for the push method, worstTime($n$) is linear in $n$ for an ArrayPureStack object but constant for a Linked PureStack object. For both implementations, averageTime($n$) for the push method is constant.

**Other Implementations of the** PureStack **Interface** There is an implementation of the PureStack interface in the package java.util. The implementation starts with

```
public class Stack<E> extends Vector<E>
        . . .
```

For purposes of this discussion, the Vector class is equivalent to the ArrayList class.

For the sake of efficiency, the top element of a Stack object is at index size( ) − 1 of the underlying array, and the bottom of the stack is at index 0. Then the pop method takes only constant time because no other items need be moved. For push, averageTime($n$) is constant. Resizing will occasionally occur, so worstTime($n$) is linear in $n$.

A fatal drawback is that this implementation of the PureStack interface does not prohibit any methods from the Vector class, so it is legal to insert or remove anywhere in a Stack. Think about it: in the Stack class, it is legal to invoke methods that violate the definition of a stack! You could say that this implementation is "over the top."

We can overcome the glaring deficiency of the above implementation of the PureStack interface by defining a class that has a field whose type is ArrayList or Linked List. For example, the definition of the pop method—in either implementation—is as follows:

```
public E pop( )
{
        return list.remove (list.size( ) − 1);
} // method pop
```

In fact, all the definitions—in either implementation—are one-liners.

See Programming Exercise 8.2 for an opportunity to develop the LinkedListPure Stack implementation, and Programming Exercise 8.3 for the ArrayListPureStack implementation.

Now let's look at a couple of important applications.

## 8.1.3 Stack Application 1: How Compilers Implement Recursion

We saw several examples of recursive methods in Chapter 5. For the sake of abstraction, we focused on what recursion did and ignored the question of how recursion is implemented by a compiler or interpreter. It turns out that the visual aids—execution frames—are closely related to this implementation. We now outline how a stack is utilized in implementing recursion and the time-space implications for methods, especially recursive methods.

Each time a method call occurs, whether it is a recursive method or not, the return address in the calling method is saved. This information is saved so the computer will know where to resume execution in the calling method after the execution of the called method has been completed. Also, the values of the called method's local variables must be saved. This is done to prevent the destruction of that information in the event that the method is—directly or indirectly—recursive. As we noted in Chapter 5, the compiler saves this method information for all methods, not just the recursive ones. This information is collectively referred to as an ***activation record*** or ***stack frame.***

Each activation record includes:

1.  The return address, that is, the address of the statement that will be executed when the call has been completed;
2.  The value of each argument: a copy of the corresponding argument is made (if the type of the argument is reference-to-object, the reference is copied);
3.  The values of the called method's other local variables;

Part of main memory—the ***stack***—is allocated for a run-time stack onto which an activation record is pushed when a method is called and from which an activation record is popped when the execution of the method has been completed. During the execution of that method, the top activation record contains the current state of the method. For methods that return a value, that value—either a primitive value or a reference—is pushed onto the top of the stack just before there is a return to the calling method.

How does an activation record compare to an execution frame? Both contain values, but an activation record has no code. Of course, the entire method, in byte-code, is available at run-time. So there is no need for a checkmark to indicate the method that is currently executing.

For a simple example of activation records and the run-time stack, let's trace the execution of a main method that invokes the getBinary method from Chapter 5. The return addresses have been commented as RA1 and RA2.

```
public static void main (String[ ] args)
{
      try
      {
            final String PROMPT = "Please enter a base-10, nonnegative integer: ";

            final String RESULT = "The binary equivalent is ";

            BufferedReader reader = new BufferedReader
                                    (new InputStreamReader (System.in));

            System.out.print (PROMPT);
            int n = Integer.parseInt (reader.readLine( ));
            System.out.print (RESULT + getBinary (n)); // RA1
      } // try
      catch (IOException e)
```

```
                {
                        System.out.println (e);
                } // catch
                catch (IllegalArgumentException e)
                {
                        System.out.println (e);
                } // catch

        } // method main

        /**
         *
         * Determines the binary equivalent of a nonnegative integer. The worstTime(n)
         * is O(log n).
         *
         * @param n the nonnegative integer, in decimal notation.
         *
         * @return a String representation of the binary equivalent of n.
         *
         * @throws IllegalArgumentException if n is negative.
         */
        public static String getBinary (int n)
        {
             if (n < 0)
                     throw new IllegalArgumentException( );
             if (n <= 1)
                     return Integer.toString (n);
             return getBinary (n / 2) + Integer.toString (n % 2); // RA2
        } // method getBinary
```

The getBinary method has the formal parameter n as its only local variable, and so each activation record will have two components:

1.  The return address
2.  The value of the formal parameter $n$

Also, because the getBinary method returns a String reference, a copy of that String reference is pushed onto the stack just before a return is made. For simplicity, we will pretend that the String object itself is pushed.

Assume that the value read in is 6. When getBinary is called from the main method, an activation record is created and pushed onto the stack, as shown in Figure 8.3.

Since $n > 1$, getBinary is called recursively with 3 (that is, 6/2) as the value of the argument. A second activation record is created and pushed onto the stack. See Figure 8.4.

Since $n$ is still greater than 1, getBinary is called again, this time with 1 (that is, 3/2) as the value of the argument. A third activation record is created and pushed. See Figure 8.5.

**Figure 8.3 |** The activation stack just prior to getBinary's first activation. RA1 is the return address.

Activation stack

**Figure 8.4 |** The activation stack just prior to the second activation of getBinary.

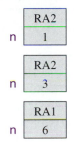

Activation stack

(two records)

**Figure 8.5 |** The activation stack just prior to the third activation of getBinary.

RA2
n   1

RA2
n   3

RA1
n   6

Activation stack

(three records)

Since $n \leq 1$, the top activation record is popped, the String "1" is pushed onto the top of the stack and a return is made to the address RA2. The resulting stack is shown in Figure 8.6.

The concatenation at RA2 in getBinary is executed, yielding the String "1" + Integer.toString (3 % 2), namely, "11". The top activation record on the stack is popped, the String "11" is pushed, and another return to RA2 is made, as shown in Figure 8.7.

The concatenation at RA2 is "11" + Integer.toString (6 % 2), and the value of that String object is "110". The stack is popped once more, leaving it empty, and then "110" is pushed. Then a return to RA1—at the end of the main method—is made. The output is

110

which is the binary equivalent of 6, the value input.

**Figure 8.6** | The activation stack just after the completion of the third activation of getBinary.

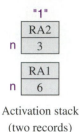

Activation stack
(two records)

**Figure 8.7** | The activation stack just after the completion of the second activation of getBinary.

"11"

| RA1 |
|---|
| n | 6 |

Activation stack

The above discussion should give you a general idea of how recursion is implemented by the compiler. The same stack is used for all method calls. And so the size of each activation record must be saved with each method call. Then the correct number of bytes can be popped. For the sake of simplicity, we have ignored the size of each activation record in the above discussion.

The compiler must generate code for the creation and maintenance, at run time, of the activation stack. Each time a call is made, the entire local environment must be saved. In most cases, this overhead pales to insignificance relative to the cost in programmer time of converting to an iterative version, but this conversion is always feasible.

On those rare occasions when you must convert a recursive method to an iterative method, one option is to simulate the recursive method with an iterative method that creates and maintains its own stack of information to be saved. For example, Programming Project 8.3 requires an iterative version of the (recursive) tryToReach Goal method in the backtracking application from Chapter 5. When you create your own stack, you get to decide what is saved. For example, if the recursive version of the method contains just one place where the recursive call is made, you need not save the return address. Here is an iterative, stack-based version of the getBinary method (see Programming Exercise 5.1 for an iterative version that is not stack-based, and see Programming Exercise 8.5 for related exercises.

```
/**
 *
 * Determines the binary equivalent of a nonnegative integer. The worstTime(n)
 * is O(log n).
 *
 * @param n the nonnegative integer, in decimal notation.
```

```
    *
    * @return a String representation of the binary equivalent of n.
    *
    * @throws IllegalArgumentException if n is negative.
    */
    public static String getBinary (int n)
    {
            ArrayPureStack<Integer> myStack = new ArrayPureStack<Integer>( );

            String binary = new String( );

            if (n < 0)
                    throw new IllegalArgumentException( );
            myStack.push (n % 2);
            while (n > 1)
            {
                    n /= 2;
                    myStack.push (n % 2);
            } // pushing
            while (!myStack.isEmpty( ))
                    binary += (myStack.pop( )).toString( );
            return binary + "\n\n";
    } // method getBinary
```

What is most important is that you not overlook the cost, in terms of programmer time, of making the conversion from a recursive method to an iterative method. Some recursive methods, such as the factorial method, can easily be converted to iterative methods. Sometimes the conversion is nontrivial, such as for the move and tryToReachGoal methods of Chapter 5 and the permute method of Lab 9. Furthermore, the iterative version may well lack the simple elegance of the recursive version, and this may complicate maintenance.

You certainly should continue to design recursive methods when circumstances warrant. That is, whenever the problem is such that complex instances of the problem can be reduced to simpler instances of the same form, and the simplest instance(s) can be solved directly. The above discussion on the activation stack enables you to make better-informed trade-off decisions.

## 8.1.4  Stack Application 2: Converting from Infix to Postfix

In Section 8.1.3, we saw how a compiler or interpreter could implement recursion. In this section we present another "internal" application: the translation of arithmetic expressions from infix notation into postfix notation. This can be one of the key tasks performed by a compiler as it creates machine-level code, or by an interpreter as it evaluates an arithmetic expression.

In infix notation, a binary operator is placed between its operands. For example, Figure 8.8 shows several arithmetic expressions in infix notation.

**Figure 8.8** | Several arithmetic expressions in infix notation.

$$a + b$$
$$b - c * d$$
$$(b - c) * d$$
$$a - c - h / b * c$$
$$a - (c - h) / (b * c)$$

For the sake of simplicity, we initially restrict our attention to expressions with single-letter identifiers, parentheses, and the binary operators +, −, *, and /. The usual rules of arithmetic apply:

1. Operations are normally carried out from left to right. For example, if we have

$$a + b - c$$

then the addition will be performed first.

2. If the current operator is + or − and the next operator is * or /, then the next operator is applied before the current operator. For example, if we have

$$b + c * d$$

then the multiplication will be carried out before the addition. For

$$a - b + c * d$$

the subtraction is performed first, then the multiplication and, finally, the addition.

We can interpret this rule as saying that multiplication and division have "higher precedence" than addition and subtraction.

3. Parentheses may be used to alter the order indicated by rules 1 and 2. For example, if we have

$$a - (b + c)$$

then the addition is performed first. Similarly, with

$$(a - b) * c$$

the subtraction is performed first.

Figure 8.9 shows the order of evaluation for the last two expressions in Figure 8.8.

The first widely used programming language was FORTRAN (from FORmula TRANslator), so named because its compiler could translate arithmetic formulas into machine-level code. In early (pre-1960) compilers, the translation was performed directly. But direct translation is awkward because the machine-level code for an operator cannot be generated until both of its operands are known. This requirement leads to difficulties when either operand is a parenthesized subexpression.

**Postfix Notation** Modern compilers do not translate arithmetic expressions directly into machine-level code. Instead, they can utilize an intermediate form known as *postfix notation.* In postfix notation, an operator is placed immediately after its operands. For example, given the infix expression a + b, the postfix form is

**Figure 8.9 |** The order of evaluation for the last two expressions in Figure 8.8.

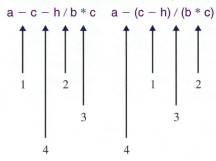

a b +. For a + b * c, the postfix form is a b c * + because the operands for + are a and the product of b and c. For (a + b) * c, the postfix form is a b + c *. Since an operator immediately follows its operands in postfix notation, parentheses are unnecessary and therefore not used. Figure 8.10 shows several arithmetic expressions in both infix and postfix notation.

How can we convert an arithmetic expression from infix notation into postfix notation? Let's view the infix notation as a string of characters and try to produce the corresponding postfix string. The identifiers in the postfix string will be in the same order as they are in the infix string, so each identifier can be appended to the postfix string as soon as it is encountered. But in postfix notation, operators must be placed after their operands. So when an operator is encountered in the infix string, it must be saved somewhere temporarily.

For example, suppose we want to translate the infix string

   a − b + c * d

into postfix notation. (The blanks are for readability only—they are not, for now, considered part of the infix expression.) We would go through the following steps:

   a is appended to postfix, which is now the string "a"

   − is stored temporarily

   b is appended to postfix, which is now the string "ab"

**Figure 8.10 |** Several arithmetic expressions in both infix and postfix notation.

| Infix | Postfix |
|---|---|
| a − b + c * d | ab − cd *+ |
| a + c − h / b * r | ac + hb / r * − |
| a + (c − h) / (b * r) | ach − br */+ |

When + is encountered, we note that since it has the same precedence as −, the subtraction should be performed first by the left-to-right rule (rule 1, above). So the − is appended to the postfix string, which is now "ab−" and + is saved temporarily. Then c is appended to postfix, which now is "ab−c".

The next operator, *, must also be saved somewhere temporarily because one of its operands (namely d) has not yet been appended to postfix. But * should be retrieved and appended to postfix *before* + since multiplication has higher precedence than addition.

When d is appended to postfix, the postfix string is "ab−cd". Then * is appended, making the postfix string "ab−cd*". Finally, + is appended to postfix, and the final postfix representation is

"ab−cd*+"

The temporary storage facility referred to in the previous paragraph is handled conveniently with a stack to hold operators. The rules governing this operatorStack are:

**1.**    Initially, operatorStack is empty.

**2.**    For each operator in the infix string,

   Loop until the operator has been pushed onto operatorStack:

   If operatorStack is empty or the operator has higher precedence than the operator on the top of operatorStack then

   Push the operator onto operatorStack.

   else

   Pop operatorStack and append that popped operator to the postfix string.

**3.**    Once the end of the input string is encountered,

   Loop until operatorStack is empty:

   Pop operatorStack and append that popped operator to the postfix string.

For example, Figure 8.11 shows the history of the operator stack during the conversion of

a + c − h / b * r

to its postfix equivalent.

How are parentheses handled? When a left parenthesis is encountered in the infix string, it is immediately pushed onto operatorStack, but its precedence is defined to be *lower* than the precedence of any binary operator. When a right parenthesis is encountered in the infix string, operatorStack is repeatedly popped, and the popped element appended to the postfix string, until the operator on the top of the stack is a left parenthesis. Then that left parenthesis is popped but not appended to postfix, and the scan of the infix string is resumed. This process ensures that parentheses will never appear in postfix notation.

For example, when we translate a * (b + c) into postfix, the operators *, (, and + would be pushed and then all would be popped (last in, first out) when the right parenthesis is encountered. The postfix form is

**Figure 8.11 |** The conversion of a + c − h / b * r to postfix notation. At each stage, the top of **operatorStack** is shown as the *rightmost* element.

| Infix expression: a + c − h * b * r | | |
|---|---|---|
| Infix | *operatorStack* | Postfix |
| a | (empty) | a |
| + | + | a |
| c | + | ac |
| − | − | ac+ |
| h | − | ac+h |
| / | −/ | ac+h |
| b | −/ | ac+hb |
| * | −* | ac+hb/ |
| r | −* | ac+hb/r |
| | − | ac+hb/r* |
| | (empty) | ac+hb/r* |

a b c + *

For a more complex example, Figure 8.12 illustrates the conversion of

x − (y * a / b − (z + d * e) + c) / f

into postfix notation.

**Transition Matrix** At each step in the conversion process, we know what action to take as long as we know the current character in the infix string and the top character on the operator stack. We can therefore create a matrix to summarize the conversion. The row indexes represent the possible values of the current infix character. The column indexes represent the possible values of the top character on the operator stack. The matrix entries represent the action to be taken. Such a matrix is called a *transition matrix* because it directs the transition of information from one form to another. Figure 8.13 shows the transition matrix for converting a simple expression from infix notation to postfix notation.

The graphical nature of the transition matrix in Figure 8.13 enables us to see at a glance how to convert simple expressions from infix to postfix. We could now design and implement a program to do just that. The program may well incorporate the transition matrix in Figure 8.13 for the sake of extensibility; more complex

**Figure 8.12** | The conversion of x − (y * a / b − (z + d * e) + c) / f from infix to postfix. At each stage, the top of **operatorStack** is shown as the *rightmost* element.

| Infix expression: x − (y * a / b − (z + d * e) + c) / f | | |
|---|---|---|
| Infix | *operatorStack* | Postfix |
| x | (empty) | x |
| − | − | x |
| ( | −( | x |
| y | −( | xy |
| * | −(* | xy |
| a | −(* | xya |
| / | −(/ | xya* |
| b | −(/ | xya*b |
| − | −(− | xya*b/ |
| ( | −(−( | xya*b/ |
| z | −(−( | xya*b/z |
| + | −(−(+ | xya*b/z |
| d | −(−(+ | xya*b/zd |
| * | −(−(+* | xya*b/zd |
| e | −(−(+* | xya*b/zde |
| ) | −(−(+ | xya*b/zde* |
|  | −(−( | xya*b/zde*+ |
|  | −(− | xya*b/zde*+ |
| + | −(+ | xya*b/zde*+− |
| c | −(+ | xya*b/zde*+−c |
| ) | −( | xya*b/zde*+−c+ |
|  | − | xya*b/zde*+−c+ |
| / | −/ | xya*b/zde*+−c+ |
| f | −/ | xya*b/zde*+−c+f |
|  | − | xya*b/zde*+−c+f/ |
|  | (empty) | xya*b/zde*+−c+f/− |

| Postfix expression:  x y a * b / z d e * + − c + f / − |
|---|

expressions can be accommodated by expanding the matrix. For the conversion, there would be a **switch** statement with one case for each matrix entry.

**Tokens**  A program that utilized a transition matrix would probably not work with the characters themselves because there are too many possible (legal) values for each character. For example, a transition matrix that used a row for each legal infix character would need 52 rows just for an identifier. And if we changed the specifications to allow multicharacter identifiers, we would need millions of rows!

Instead, the legal characters would usually be grouped together into "tokens." A *token* is the smallest meaningful unit in a program. Each token has two parts: a generic part that holds its category and a specific part that enables us to recapture the character(s) tokenized. For converting simple infix expressions to postfix the token categories would be: identifier, rightPar, leftPar, addOp (for + and −), multOp (for *

**Figure 8.13 I** The transition matrix for converting simple expressions from infix notation to postfix notation.

| Action taken | | Top character on operator stack | | | |
|---|---|---|---|---|---|
| | | ( | +, − | *, / | empty |
| Infix character | identifier | Append to postfix | Append to postfix | Append to postfix | Append to postfix |
| | ) | Pop; pitch '(' | Pop to postfix | Pop to postfix | Error |
| | ( | Push | Push | Push | Push |
| | +, − | Push | Pop to postfix | Pop to postfix | Push |
| | *, / | Push | Push | Pop to postfix | Push |
| | empty | Error | Pop to postfix | Pop to postfix | Done |

and /) and empty (for a dummy value). The specific part could contain the position, in the infix string, of the character tokenized. For example, given the infix string

(first + last) / sum

to tokenize last, we would set its category to identifier and its position to 9.

The structure of tokens varies widely among compilers. Typically, the specific part of a variable identifier's token contains an address into a table, called a ***symbol table.*** At that address would be stored the identifier, an indication that it is a variable identifier, its type, initial value, the block it is declared in, and other information helpful to the compiler. There is a symbol table in the project of Lab 15, and the creation of a symbol table is the subject of an application in Chapter 14.

In Lab 15, a complete infix-to-postfix project is developed, with tokens and massive input editing.

**Lab 15: Converting from Infix to Postfix**

You are now prepared to do Lab 15.          All Labs Are Optional

## 8.1.5  Prefix Notation

In Section 8.1.4 we described how to convert an infix expression into postfix notation. Another possibility is to convert from infix into ***prefix notation,*** in which each operator immediately precedes its operands.[2] Figure 8.14 shows several expressions in both infix and prefix notation.

How can we convert an arithmetic expression from infix to prefix? As in infix-to-postfix, we will need to save each operator until both of its operands have been obtained. But we cannot simply append each identifier to the prefix string as soon as it is encountered. Instead, we will need to save each identifier, in fact, each operand, until its operator has been obtained.

The saving of operands and operators is easily accomplished with the help of two stacks, operandStack and operatorStack. The precedence rules for operator Stack are exactly the same as we saw in converting from infix to postfix. Initially, both stacks are empty. When an identifier is encountered in the infix string, that identifier is pushed onto operandStack. When an operator is encountered, it is pushed onto operatorStack if that stack is empty. Otherwise, one of the following cases applies:

1.  If the operator is a left parenthesis, push it onto operatorStack (but left parenthesis has lowest precedence).

2.  If the operator has higher precedence than the top operator on operatorStack, push the operator onto operatorStack.

3.  If the operator's precedence is equal to or lower than the precedence of the top operator on operatorStack, pop the top operator, opt1, from operatorStack and pop the top two operands, opnd1 and opnd2, from operandStack. Concatenate (join together) opt1, opnd2, and opnd1 and push the result string onto operandStack. Note that opnd2 is in front of opnd1 in the result string because opnd2 was encountered in the infix string—and pushed onto operandStack—before opnd1.

4.  If the operator is a right parenthesis, treat it as having lower priority than +, −, *, and /. Then case 3 will apply until a left parenthesis is the top operator on operatorStack. Pop that left parenthesis.

**Figure 8.14** | Several arithmetic expressions in both infix and prefix notation.

| Infix | Prefix |
|-------|--------|
| a − b | − a b |
| a − b * c | − a * b c |
| (a − b) * c | * − a b c |
| a − b + c * d | + − a b * c d |
| a + c − h / b * d | − + a c * / h b d |
| a + (c − h) / (b * d) | + a / − c h * b d |

---

[2] Prefix notation was invented by Jan Lukasiewicz, a Polish logician. It is sometimes referred to as *Polish notation*. Postfix notation is then called *reverse Polish notation*.

The above process continues until we reach the end of the infix expression. We then repeat the following actions from case 3 (above) until *operatorStack* is empty:

Pop opt1 from operatorStack.

Pop opnd1 and opnd2, from operandStack.

Concatenate opt1, opnd2, and opnd1 together and push the result onto operandStack.

When operatorStack is finally empty, the top (and only) operand on operand Stack will be the prefix string corresponding to the original infix expression.

For example, if we start with

a + b * c

then the history of the two stacks would be as follows:

**1.**

|     | a   | a           |               |
| --- | --- | ----------- | ------------- |
|     | infix | operandStack | operatorStack |

**2.**

|     | +   | a           | +             |
| --- | --- | ----------- | ------------- |
|     | infix | operandStack | operatorStack |

**3.**

|     |     | b           |               |
| --- | --- | ----------- | ------------- |
|     | b   | a           | +             |
|     | infix | operandStack | operatorStack |

**4.**

|     |     | b           | *             |
| --- | --- | ----------- | ------------- |
|     | *   | a           | +             |
|     | infix | operandStack | operatorStack |

**5.**

|     |     | c           |               |
| --- | --- | ----------- | ------------- |
|     |     | b           | *             |
|     | c   | a           | +             |
|     | infix | operandStack | operatorStack |

**6.**

|     |     | *bc         |               |
| --- | --- | ----------- | ------------- |
|     |     | a           | +             |
|     | infix | operandStack | operatorStack |

**7.**

|     |     | +a*bc       |               |
| --- | --- | ----------- | ------------- |
|     | infix | operandStack | operatorStack |

The prefix string corresponding to the original string is

+ a * b c

For a more complex example, suppose the infix string is

a + (c − h) / (b * d)

Then the elements on the two stacks during the processing of the first right parenthesis would be as follows:

**1.**

|  |  |  |
|:---:|:---:|:---:|
|  | h | − |
|  | c | ( |
| ) | a | + |
| ---------------------------- | ---------------------------- | ---------------------------- |
| infix | operandStack | operatorStack |

**2.**

|  |  |
|:---:|:---:|
| −ch | ( |
| a | + |
| ---------------------------- | ---------------------------- |
| operandStack | operatorStack |

**3.**

|  |  |
|:---:|:---:|
| −ch |  |
| a | + |
| ---------------------------- | ---------------------------- |
| operandStack | operatorStack |

During the processing of the second right parenthesis in the infix string, we would have

**1.**

|  |  |  |
|:---:|:---:|:---:|
|  | d | * |
|  | b | ( |
|  | −ch | / |
| ) | a | + |
| ---------------------------- | ---------------------------- | ---------------------------- |
| infix | operandStack | operatorStack |

**2.**

|  |  |
|:---:|:---:|
| *bd | ( |
| −ch | / |
| a | + |
| ---------------------------- | ---------------------------- |
| operandStack | operatorStack |

The end of the infix expression has been reached, so operatorStack is repeatedly popped.

**3.**

|  |  |
|:---:|:---:|
| *bd |  |
| −ch | / |
| a | + |
| ---------------------------- | ---------------------------- |
| operandStack | operatorStack |

**4.**

```
                    /-ch*bd
                       a                              +
             --------------------------    --------------------------
                  operandStack                   operatorStack
```

**5.**

```
                   +a/-ch*bd
             --------------------------    --------------------------
                  operandStack                   operatorStack
```

The prefix string is

```
+ a / − c h * b d
```

# 8.2 | QUEUES

A *queue* is a finite sequence of elements in which:

1. Insertion is allowed only at the back of the sequence.
2. Removal is allowed only at the front of the sequence.

The term *enqueue* is used for inserting an element at the back of a queue, *dequeue* for removing the first element from a queue, and *front* to access the first element in a queue. A queue imposes a chronological order on its elements: the first element enqueued, at the back, will eventually be the first element to be dequeued, from the front. The second element enqueued will be the second element to be dequeued, and so on. This defining property of queues is sometimes referred to as "first come, first served", "first in, first out", or simply FIFO.

Figure 8.15 shows a queue through several stages of insertions and deletions. The examples of queues are widespread:

Cars in line at a drive-up window.

Fans waiting to buy tickets to a ballgame.

Customers in a check-out line at a supermarket.

Airplanes waiting to take off from an airport.

We could continue giving queue examples almost indefinitely. Later in this chapter we will develop an application of queues in the field of computer simulation.

Section 8.2.1 presents the PureQueue interface, which corresponds to the queue abstract data type.

## 8.2.1  The PureQueue Interface

In Chapter 6, we defined the List interface, which was implemented by the ArrayList class (in Chapter 6) and the LinkedList class (in Chapter 7). To describe the abstract data type queue, we will supply a PureQueue interface.[3] There are only a few

---

[3] The reason the interface is named PureQueue instead of Queue is to avoid confusion with the Java Collections Framework's Queue interface, discussed in Section 8.2.2.

**Figure 8.15** I A queue through several stages of insertions and deletions.

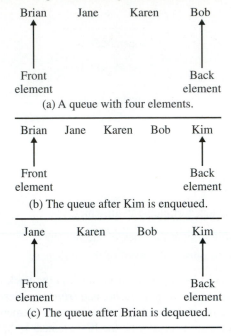

(a) A queue with four elements.

(b) The queue after Kim is enqueued.

(c) The queue after Brian is dequeued.

methods that the PureQueue interface will have: enqueue, dequeue, front, size, and isEmpty. As with the PureStack interface, the isEmpty method is included only for convenience: we could define isEmpty from size. For the sake of simplicity, we allow only these five methods.

Here is the PureQueue interface, parameterized with type parameter E. The phrase "this PureQueue object" means "this calling object in the class that implements the PureQueue interface."

```java
public interface PureQueue< E > // Note: does not extend Collection<E>
{
    /**
     * Determines the number of elements in this PureQueue object.
     *
     * @return the number of elements in this PureQueue object.
     *
     */
    int size( );

    /**
     * Determines if this PureQueue object has no elements.
     *
     * @return true – if this PureQueue object has no elements; otherwise,
```

```
 *      return false.
 *
 */
boolean isEmpty( );

/**
 * Inserts a specified element at the back of this PureQueue object.
 * The averageTime(n) is constant and worstTime(n) is O(n).
 *
 * @param element – the element to be appended.
 *
 */
void enqueue (E element);

/**
 * Removes the front element from this PureQueue object.
 *
 * @return – the element removed.
 *
 * @throws NoSuchElementException – if this PureQueue object is empty.
 *
 */
E dequeue( );

/**
 * Returns the front element in this PureQueue object.
 *
 * @return – the element returned.
 *
 * @throws NoSuchElementException – if this PureQueue object is empty.
 *
 */
E front( );

} // interface PureQueue
```

Note that the specified worst time for the enqueue method estimates only an upper bound, namely, $O(n)$. It would be inappropriately restrictive to specify that worstTime($n$) is linear in $n$, because then a developer would not be allowed to improve on the lower bound of $\Omega(n)$. Note also that, since the specifications for the dequeue and front (and size and isEmpty) methods do not explicitly estimate times, it is assumed that averageTime($n$) and worstTime($n$) are constant for those methods.

## 8.2.2 Implementations of the PureQueue Interface

In implementing the PureQueue interface, we have almost as much flexibility as we had for implementations of the PureStack interface. Here, we present (1) an easy-to-develop and efficient implementation that utilizes the LinkedList class, (2) the Java

Collections Framework's implementation, (3) a somewhat difficult-to-develop and somewhat inefficient contiguous implementation, and (4) the creation of a singly linked implementation (not too difficult to develop and efficient) as Programming Project 8.4.

**The** LinkedListPureQueue **Implementation of the** PureQueue **Interface** For the sake of code reuse, we will start with implementations that employ inheritance (is-a) or aggregation (has-a) of previously developed classes. Specifically, we will consider classes that are subclasses of either ArrayList or LinkedList, or classes with an ArrayList or LinkedList field. In light of the fact that the critical PureQueue methods are back insertions and front removals, which do you think would be the better superclass/field: ArrayList or LinkedList? The correct answer is the LinkedList class, which requires only constant time for inserting at the back or removing from the front—recall that the ArrayList class requires linear-in-$n$ time for removing the front element.

Our remaining choice is whether to define the implementation of the PureQueue interface as a subclass of LinkedList or with a LinkedList field. That is, we can define the implementation so that a PureQueue object *is-a* LinkedList object; we can also define the implementation so that a PureQueue object *has-a* LinkedList field. There is a problem with implementing the PureQueue interface as a subclass of the Linked List class (the *is-a* approach). Except for the size( ) and isEmpty( ) methods, *every* LinkedList class method would have to be overridden. For example, we would have

```
public boolean remove (E element)
{
        throw new UnsupportedOperationException( );
} // method remove
```

This requirement of wholesale overriding suggests that the *is-a* approach has a deeper problem: any class that implements the PureQueue interface has very little overlap with the LinkedList class. The *has-a* approach is a better alternative: we will implement the PureQueue interface with a LinkedList field. There will be a total of seven methods in the LinkedListPureQueue class: a default constructor, a copy constructor, and the five methods from the PureQueue interface. All the definitions are one-liners:

```
import java.util.*;

public class LinkedListPureQueue<E> implements PureQueue<E>
{
        protected LinkedList<E> list;

        /**
         * Initializes this LinkedListPureQueue object to be empty.
         *
         */
        public LinkedListPureQueue( )
        {
```

```
            list = new LinkedList<E>( );
    } // default constructor

    /**
     * Initializes this LinkedListPureQueue object to a shallow copy of a specified
     * LinkedListPureQueue object. The worstTime(n) is O(n), where n is the
     * number of elements in the specified LinkedListPureQueue object.
     *
     * @param otherQueue – the specified LinkedListPureQueue object that this
     *        LinkedListPureQueue object is initialized to a shallow copy of.
     *
     */
    public LinkedListPureQueue (LinkedListPureQueue<E> otherQueue)
    {
            list = new LinkedList<E> (otherQueue.list);
    } // copy constructor
```

*Note:* The access of the list field in otherQueue does not violate the Principle of Data Abstraction because it is legitimate to access a LinkedListPureQueue field within a LinkedListPureQueue method.

```
    /**
     * Determines the number of elements in this LinkedListPureQueue object.
     *
     * @return the number of elements in this LinkedListPureQueue object.
     *
     */
    public int size( )
    {
            return list.size( );
    } // method size

    /**
     * Determines if this LinkedListPureQueue object has no elements.
     *
     * @return true – if this LinkedListPureQueue object has no elements;
     *         otherwise, return false.
     *
     */
    public boolean isEmpty( )
    {
            return list.isEmpty( );
    } // method isEmpty

    /**
     * Inserts a specified element at the back of this LinkedListPureQueue
     * object. The averageTime(n) is constant and worstTime(n) is O(n).
```

```
         *
         * @param element – the element to be appended.
         *
         */
        public void enqueue (E element)
        {
                list.addLast (element);
        } // method enqueue

        /**
         * Removes the front element from this LinkedListPureQueue object.
         *
         * @return – the element removed.
         *
         * @throws NoSuchElementException – if this LinkedListPureQueue object is
         *         empty.
         *
         */
        public E dequeue( )
        {
                return list.removeFirst( );
        } // method dequeue

        /**
         * Returns the front element from this LinkedPureQueue object.
         *
         * @return – the element returned.
         *
         * @throws NoSuchElementException – if this LinkedListPureQueue object is
         *         empty.
         *
         */
        public E front( )
        {
                return list.getFirst( );
        } // method front

    } // LinkedListPureQueue class
```

The dequeue and front methods satisfy the (implicit) estimate of constant worst time. And the enqueue method takes only constant worst time, which clearly satisfies the estimate of $O(n)$ for worstTime($n$) given in the PureQueue interface.

Here is the code to create the queue in Figure 8.15:

```
PureQueue<String> queue = new LinkedListPureQueue<String>( );

// Figure 8.15.a.
queue.enqueue ("Brian");
```

```
queue.enqueue ("Jane");
queue.enqueue ("Karen");
queue.enqueue ("Bob");

// Figure 8.15.b.
queue.enqueue ("Kim");

// Figure 8.15.c.
queue.dequeue( );
```

**The Java Collections Framework's** Queue **Interface**    The Java Collections Framework does have a Queue interface that corresponds to the queue abstract data type. But that Queue interface extends the Collection interface, and so any class that fully implements the Queue interface would define methods that violate the definition of a queue! For example, the LinkedBlockingQueue class, also in the Java Collections Framework, implements the Queue interface. A user of that class could invoke the remove (Object obj) method to remove *any* element in the queue.

The rationale behind having the Queue interface extend the Collection interface is that, for some applications, it may be convenient to be able to remove an arbitrary element from a queue. For example, if a waiting list is implemented as a queue, a customer who decides to stop waiting could be removed. But convenience should not override correctness. If an application entails queue operations along with operations that violate the definition of a queue, then a LinkedList object or ArrayList object can be used. Names such as Queue can easily mislead users and readers into thinking that the only methods allowed will be those that are valid for a queue.

We noted above that the ArrayList class was unsuitable as the basis for an implementation of the PureQueue interface. Next, we explore a contiguous implementation of that interface.

**A Contiguous Implementation of the** PureQueue **Interface**    According to the discussion of the LinkedListPureQueue implementation earlier in this section, we can say either that an implementation of the PureQueue has-a LinkedList or, with a lot of overrides, that an implementation of the PureQueue interface is-a LinkedList. But defining a PureQueue implementation from the ArrayList class posed problems because removal from the front of an ArrayList object takes linear time.

Another option, also array-based, directly manipulates an array field to achieve constant time, on average, for enqueuing and dequeuing. There are four fields in this implementation:

```
protected E [ ] data;

protected int size,
              head,
              tail;
```

The data array holds the queue's elements, and size holds the number of elements in the queue. The front element of the queue is always at index head, but head does not always have the value 0. Basically, the queue "slides down" the array as enqueues and dequeues occur. The head field contains the index, in data, of the queue's front element, and the tail field contains the index of the queue's back element. We initialize tail to $-1$ to indicate an empty queue. Figure 8.16 shows the effect on these fields of two enqueues and a dequeue.

Figure 8.16 has several interesting features. First, notice that tail is incremented during each enqueue. During a dequeue, elements are not physically removed; all that happens is that head is incremented to indicate that the front element of the queue is at the next higher index. But if we increment tail during each enqueue and increment head during each dequeue, we could eventually arrive at the four-element queue shown in Figure 8.17.

What happens if we now enqueue "Jason"? The size of the queue is only 4, so there is no need to increase the length of the array data. Or we could move the four elements to indexes 0 through 3 and then insert "Jason" at index 4. But we should avoid moving the entire queue if we can avoid it. Do you see an alternative?

The slot at index 0 is available—"Kay" is no longer in the queue—so let's put "Jason" there. Figure 8.18 shows the resulting queue.

The queue in Figure 8.18 is *circular:* the element at index 0 follows the element at index 99. This arrangement takes some getting used to because tail < head. But the beauty of it is that such an enqueue takes constant time. And with the same idea—allowing head to advance to 0 after 99—dequeues also take constant time.

**Figure 8.16** I A queue; (a) initially; (b) after enqueue ("Kay"); (c) after enqueue ("Bob"); (d) after dequeue( ).

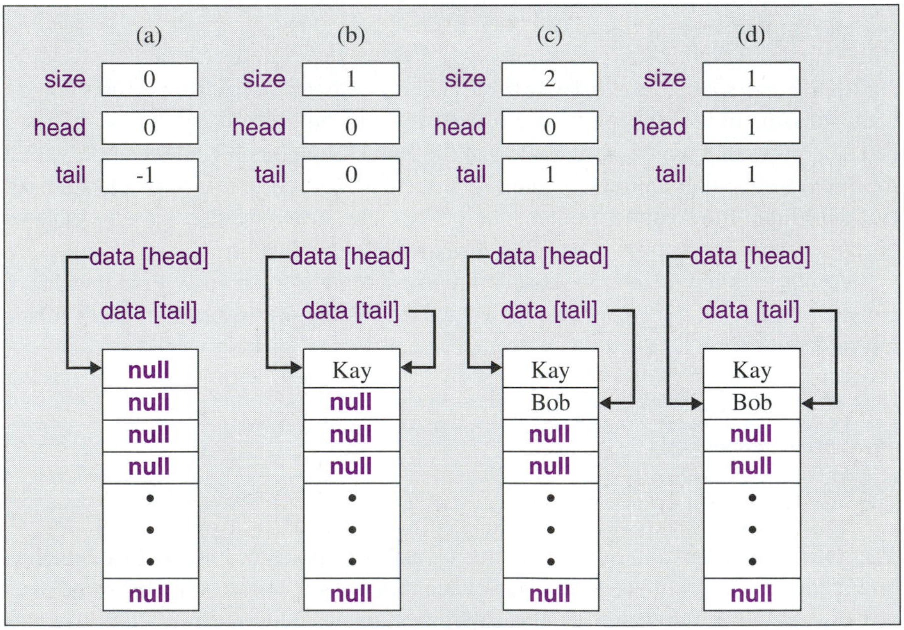

**Figure 8.17** | A four-element queue at indexes 96 through 99.

data[0]
Kay
data[1]
Bob
data[2]
Rashada
data[96]
Xenia
data[97]
Eric
data[98]
Mike
data[99]
Amanda
size
4
head
96
tail
99

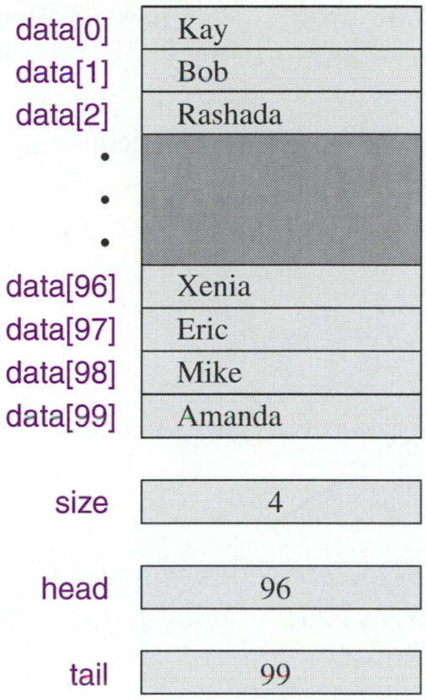

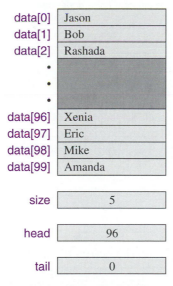

**Figure 8.18** | A five-element queue: the first four elements are at indexes 96 through 99, and the last element is at index 0.

data[0]
Jason
data[1]
Bob
data[2]
Rashada
data[96]
Xenia
data[97]
Eric
data[98]
Mike
data[99]
Amanda
size
5
head
96
tail
0

The only complication arises if the enqueue method is called and the queue occupies the entire data array, that is, if size = data.length, or equivalently, if (tail + 1) % data.length = head. We then create an array twice as large as data is, and copy the old array to this new array. The copying starts by calling the System class's **static** method arraycopy to copy the elements between index head and the end of the old array to the new array, starting at index 0. If head = 0, there is nothing more to be copied. Otherwise, we arraycopy the remaining elements in the old array (at indexes 0 . . . tail) to the new array, starting just after where the previous call to arraycopy finished.

For nonexpansion enqueuing, and for all dequeuing, we utilize modular arithmetic. For example, instead of

```
if (head == data.length)
        head = 0;
else
        head++;
```

we write, equivalently,

```
head = (head + 1) % data.length;
```

Here is the definition of the enqueue method. The declaration of the complete ArrayPureQueue class is left as Programming Exercise 8.1.

```
/**
 * Inserts a specified element at the back of this ArrayPureQueue object.
 * The averageTime(n) is constant and worstTime(n) is O(n).
 *
 * @param element – the element to be appended.
 *
 */
public void enqueue (E element)
        {
                if (size == data.length)
                {
                        // double the length of data
                        E [ ] oldData = data;
                        data = (E [ ]) new Object [data.length * 2];

                        // copy oldData [head. . .oldData.length−1] to data
                        //      [0. . .oldData.length-1 − head]
                        System.arraycopy (oldData, head, data, 0, oldData.length − head);

                        if (head > 0)

                                // copy oldData [0. . .tail] to data [oldData.length −
                                //      head. . .oldData.length−1]
                                System.arraycopy (oldData, 0, data, oldData.length − head,
                                        tail+1);

                        head = 0;
                        tail = oldData.length − 1;
                } // if this ArrayPureQueue object occupies all of data
                tail = (tail + 1) % data.length;
```

```
                size++;
                data [tail] = element;
    } // method enqueue
```

The analysis of the enqueue method is similar to that of the ArrayList class's one-parameter add method. Whether the length of the array is doubled (as with enqueue) or increased by only 50 percent (as with add) has no effect on the time estimates. When the array data is full, a new array of double the length of data is created and all the elements are copied to the new array. So worstTime($n$) is linear in $n$. But this full copy occurs only once in every $n$ enqueues, so averageTime($n$) is constant.

The bottom line is that the ArrayPureQueue implementation of the PureQueue interface is inferior to the LinkedListPureQueue implementation in terms of difficulty of development and estimated worst time. That should not surprise you: every method definition (except for the copy constructor) in the LinkedListPureQueue implementation is a simple one-liner whose worstTime($n$) is constant!

Occasionally, the array-based implementation may provide a space advantage. For example, suppose the size of the queue is very large, with a known maximum. Then the array-based implementation may occupy only one-third as much space as the LinkedListPureQueue implementation. That's because each Entry object in a LinkedListPureQueue object takes up a total of 12 bytes (4 for previous, 4 for the element-reference, and 4 for next), while each array entry takes up only 4 bytes (for the element-reference). And there is always the possibility that you will need to develop a queue class in a language that lacks a linked-list class.

Now that we have seen several possible implementations of the PureQueue interface, we turn our attention to applications.

## 8.2.3 Computer Simulation

A *system* is a collection of interacting parts. We are often interested in studying the behavior of a system, for example, an economic system, a political system, an ecological system, or even a computer system. Because systems are usually complicated, we may utilize a model to make our task manageable. A *model,* that is, a simplification of a system, is designed so that we may study the behavior of the system.

A *physical model* is similar to the system it represents, except in scale or intensity. For example, we might create a physical model of tidal movements in the Chesapeake Bay or of a proposed shopping center. War games, spring training, and scrimmages are also examples of physical models. Unfortunately, some systems cannot be modeled physically with currently available technology—there is, as yet, no physical substance that could be expected to behave like the weather. Often, as with pilot training, a physical model may be too expensive, too dangerous, or simply inconvenient.

Sometimes we may be able to represent the system with a *mathematical model:* a set of assumptions, variables, constants, and equations. Often, a mathematical model is easier to develop than a physical model. For example, such equations as distance = rate * time and the formula for the Pythagorean Theorem can be solved analytically in a short amount of time. But sometimes, this is not the case. For example, most differential equations cannot be solved analytically, and an economic model with thousands of equations cannot be solved by hand with any hope of correctness.

In such cases, the mathematical model is usually represented by a computer program. Computer models are essential in complex systems such as weather forecasting, space flight, and urban planning. The use of computer models is called ***computer simulation.*** There are several advantages to working with a computer model rather than the original system:

1. *Safety.* Flight simulators can assail pilot trainees with a welter of dangerous situations such as hurricanes and hijackings, but no one gets hurt.[4]

2. *Economy.* Simulation games in business-policy courses enable students to run a hypothetical company in competition with other students. If the company goes "belly up," the only recrimination is a lower grade for the students.

3. *Speed.* The computer usually makes predictions soon enough for you to act on them. This feature is essential in almost every simulation, from the stock market to national defense.

4. *Flexibility.* If the results you get do not conform to the system you are studying, you can change your model. This is an example of ***feedback:*** a process in which the factors that produce a result are themselves affected by that result. After the computer model is developed and run, the output is interpreted to see what it says about the original system. If the results are invalid—that is, if the results do not correspond to the known behavior of the original system— the computer model is changed. See Figure 8.19.

The above benefits are so compelling that computer simulation has become a standard tool in the study of complex systems. This is not to say that computer sim-

**Figure 8.19 |** Feedback in computer simulation.

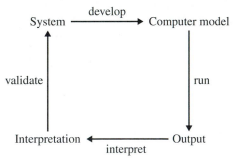

---

[4] According to legend, a trainee once panicked because one of his simulated engines failed during a simulated blizzard. He "bailed out" of his simulated cockpit and broke his ankle when he hit the unsimulated floor.

ulation is a panacea for all systems problems. The simplification required to model a system necessarily introduces a disparity between the model and the system. For example, suppose you had developed a computer simulation of the earth's ecosystem 30 years ago. You probably would have disregarded the effects of aerosol sprays and refrigerants that released chlorofluorocarbons. Many scientists now suspect that chlorofluorocarbons may have a significant impact on the ozone layer and thus on all land organisms.

Another disadvantage of computer simulation is that its results are often interpreted as predictions, and prediction is always a risky business. For this reason, a disclaimer such as the following usually precedes the results of a computer simulation: "If the relationships among the variables are as described and if the initial conditions are as described, then the consequences will probably be as follows . . . ."

### 8.2.4  Queue Application: A Simulated Car Wash

Queues are employed in many simulations. For example, we now illustrate the use of a queue in simulating traffic flow at Speedo's Car Wash.

**Problem**  Given the arrival times at the car wash, calculate the average waiting time per car.

**Analysis**  We assume that there is one station in the car wash, that is, there is one "server". Each car takes exactly 10 minutes to get washed. At any time there will be at most five cars waiting—in a queue—to be washed. If an arrival occurs when there is a car being washed and there are five cars in the queue, that arrival is turned away as an "overflow" and not counted. Error messages should be printed for an arrival time that is not an integer, less than zero, greater than the sentinel, or less than the previous arrival time.

The average waiting time is determined by adding up the waiting times for each car and dividing by the number of cars. Here are the details regarding arrivals and departures:

1.  If an arrival and departure occur during the same minute, the departure is processed first.
2.  If a car arrives when the queue is empty and no cars are being washed, the car starts getting washed immediately; it is not put on the queue.
3.  A car leaves the queue, and stops waiting, once the car starts through the 10-minute wash cycle.

The following is a sample list of arrival times; each will be on a separate line:

5 5 7 12 12 13 14 18 19 25 999 (a sentinel)

To calculate the waiting time for each car that is washed, we subtract its arrival time from the time when it entered the car wash. The first arrival, at time 5, entered the wash station right away, so its waiting time was 0. For the second arrival, also at time 5, it was enqueued at time 5, and then dequeued and entered the wash station when the first car left the wash station—at time 15. So the waiting time for the second arrival was 10 minutes. Here is the complete simulation:

| Arrival Time | Time Dequeued | Waiting Time |
|---|---|---|
| 5 | | 0 |
| 5 | 15 | 10 |
| 7 | 25 | 18 |
| 12 | 35 | 23 |
| 12 | 45 | 33 |
| 13 | 55 | 42 |
| 14—overflow | | |
| 18 | 65 | 47 |
| 19—overflow | | |
| 25 | 75 | 50 |

The sum of the waiting times is 223. The number of cars is 8 (the two overflows at 14 and 19 are not counted), so the average waiting time is 27.875 minutes.

Formally, we supply system tests to specify the expected behavior (that is, in terms of input and output) of the program. The system tests are created before the program is written and provide an indication of the program's correctness. But as we noted in Section 2.4, testing can establish the incorrectness—but not the correctness—of a program.

### System Test 1 (Input in Boldface):

Please enter the next arrival time. The sentinel is 999: **5**
Please enter the next arrival time. The sentinel is 999: **5**
Please enter the next arrival time. The sentinel is 999: **7**
Please enter the next arrival time. The sentinel is 999: **12**
Please enter the next arrival time. The sentinel is 999: **12**
Please enter the next arrival time. The sentinel is 999: **13**
Please enter the next arrival time. The sentinel is 999: **14**
Please enter the next arrival time. The sentinel is 999: **18**
Please enter the next arrival time. The sentinel is 999: **19**
Please enter the next arrival time. The sentinel is 999: **25**
Please enter the next arrival time. The sentinel is 999: **999**

Here are the results of the simulation:

| Time | Event | Waiting Time |
|---|---|---|
| 5 | Arrival | |
| 5 | Arrival | |
| 7 | Arrival | |
| 12 | Arrival | |

| | | |
|---|---|---|
| 12 | Arrival | |
| 13 | Arrival | |
| 14 | Arrival (overflow) | |
| 15 | Departure | 0 |
| 18 | Arrival | |
| 19 | Arrival (overflow) | |
| 25 | Departure | 10 |
| 25 | Arrival | |
| 35 | Departure | 18 |
| 45 | Departure | 23 |
| 55 | Departure | 33 |
| 65 | Departure | 42 |
| 75 | Departure | 47 |
| 85 | Departure | 50 |

The average waiting time, in minutes, was 27.875.

### System Test 2 (Input in Boldface):

Please enter the next arrival time. The sentinel is 999: **−3**

java.lang.NumberFormatException  The input must consist of a nonnegative integer less than the sentinel.

Please enter the next arrival time. The sentinel is 999: **5**

Please enter the next arrival time. The sentinel is 999: **m**

java.lang.NumberFormatException: m  The input must consist of a nonnegative integer less than the sentinel.

Please enter the next arrival time. The sentinel is 999: **3**

java.lang.IllegalArgumentException  The next arrival time must not be less than the current time.

Please enter the next arrival time. The sentinel is 999: **1000**

java.lang.NumberFormatException  The input must consist of a nonnegative integer less than the sentinel.

Please enter the next arrival time. The sentinel is 999: **10**

Please enter the next arrival time. The sentinel is 999: **999**

Here are the results of the simulation:

| Time | Event | Waiting Time |
|---|---|---|
| 5 | Arrival | |
| 10 | Arrival | |
| 15 | Departure | 0 |
| 25 | Departure | 5 |

The average waiting time, in minutes, was 2.5.

**Program Design** As usual, we will separate the processing concerns from the input/output concerns, so we will have two major classes: CarWash and CarWash Tester. The simulation will be *event driven,* that is, the pivotal decision in processing is whether the next event will be an arrival or a departure. After each of the next-arrival times has been processed, we need to wash any remaining cars and return the results of the simulation.

For now, four methods can be identified. Here are their specifications

```
/**
 * Initializes this CarWash object.
 *
 */
public CarWash( )

/**
 * The next arrival at the specified time has been processed.
 *
 * @param nextArrivalTime – the time when the next arrival will occur.
 *
 * @throws IllegalArgumentException – if nextArrivalTime is less than the
 *       current time.
 *
 */
public void process (int nextArrivalTime)

/**
 * Washes all cars that are still unwashed after the final arrival.
 *
 */
public void finishUp( )

/**
 * Returns the history of this CarWash object's arrivals and departures, and the
 * average waiting time.
 *
 * @return the history of the simulation, including the average waiting time.
 *
 */
public LinkedList<String> getResults( )
```

**Fields in the CarWash Class** The next step in the development of the CarWash class is to choose its fields. We'll start with a list of variables needed to solve the problem and then select the fields from this list.

As noted at the beginning of the design stage, the essential feature of processing is the determination of whether the next event is an arrival or a departure. We can make this decision based on the values of nextArrivalTime (which is read in) and nextDepartureTime. The variable nextArrivalTime holds the time when the next arrival will occur, and nextDepartureTime contains the time when the washing of the car now being washed will be finished. For example, suppose at some point in the simulation, nextArrivalTime contains 28 and nextDepartureTime contains 24. Then the next event in the simulation will be a departure at time 24. If the two times are the same, the next event will be an arrival (see note 1 of Analysis). What if there is no car being washed? Then the next event will be an arrival. When there is no car being washed, we will set nextDepartureTime to a large number—say 10000—to make sure the next event is an arrival no matter what nextArrivalTime holds.

The cars waiting to be washed should be saved in chronological order, so one of the variables needed will be the queue carQueue. Each element in carQueue is a Car object, so we temporarily suspend development of the CarWash class in order to determine the methods the Car class should have.

When a car leaves the queue to enter the wash station, we can calculate that car's waiting time by subtracting the car's arrival time from the current time. So the Car class will provide, at least, a getArrivalTime( ) method that returns the arrival time of the car that was just dequeued. Beyond that, all the Car class needs is a constructor to initialize a Car object from nextArrivalTime when a Car object is enqueued. The method specifications for the Car class are:

```
/**
 * Initializes this Car object from the specified time of the next arrival.
 *
 */
public Car (int nextArrivalTime)

/**
 * Determines the arrival time of this Car object.
 *
 * @return the arrival time of this Car object.
 *
 */
public int getArrivalTime( )
```

We now resume the determination of variables in CarWash. As indicated in the previous paragraph, we should have waitingTime and currentTime variables. To calculate the average waiting time, we need numberOfCarsWashed and sumOfWaiting Times. Finally, we need a variable, results, to hold each line of output of the simulation. We could simply make results a String variable, but then the concatenation operations would become increasingly expensive. Instead, each line will be appended to a linked list:

```
LinkedList<String> results;
```

At this point, we have amassed eight variables. Which of these should be fields? A simple heuristic (rule of thumb) is that most of a class's public, nonconstructor methods should access most of the class's fields; see Riel (1996) for more details. Clearly, the process method will need all of the variables. The finishUp method will handle the remaining departures, so that method must have access to carQueue, results, sumOfWaitingTimes, waitingTime, currentTime, and nextDepartureTime; these will be fields. The only other field is numberOfCars, needed by the getResults method. There is no need to make nextArrivalTime a field (it is needed only in the process method). Here are the constant identifiers and fields in the CarWash class:

```
protected final String HEADING =
        "\n\nTime\tEvent\t\tWaiting Time\n";

protected final int INFINITY = 10000;  // indicates no car being washed

protected final int MAX_SIZE = 5;      // maximum cars allowed in carQueue

protected final int WASH_TIME = 10; // minutes to wash one car

protected PureQueue<Car> carQueue;         // polymorphic reference

protected LinkedList<String> results;  // the sequence of events in the simulation

protected int currentTime,
             nextDepartureTime,        // when car being washed will finish
             numberOfCars,
             waitingTime,
             sumOfWaitingTimes;
```

Figure 8.20 has the UML diagrams for the CarWash, Car, and LinkedListPureQueue classes and the PureQueue interface. The aggregation relationship between CarWash and PureQueue is due to CarWash's polymorphic reference field, carQueue. For the sake of brevity, the LinkedListPureQueue methods are not shown.

**Method Definitions of the** CarWash **Class** We now start on the method definitions of the CarWash class. The constructor is straightforward:

```
public CarWash( )
{
        carQueue<Car> = new LinkedListPureQueue<Car>( );
        results = new LinkedList<String>( );
        results.add (HEADING);
        currentTime = 0;
        numberOfCars = 0;
        waitingTime = 0;
        sumOfWaitingTimes = 0;
        nextDepartureTime = INFINITY; // no car being washed
} // constructor
```

The process method takes the nextArrivalTime read in from the calling method. Then the decision is made, by comparing nextArrivalTime to nextDepartureTime, whether the next event is an arrival or departure. According to the specifications of the problem, we keep processing departures until the next event is an arrival, that is, until nextArrivalTime < nextDepartureTime. Then the arrival at nextArrivalTime is processed. By creating processArrival and processDeparture methods, we avoid getting bogged down in details, at least for now.

**Figure 8.20 |** The class diagrams for CarWash and associated classes and interfaces.

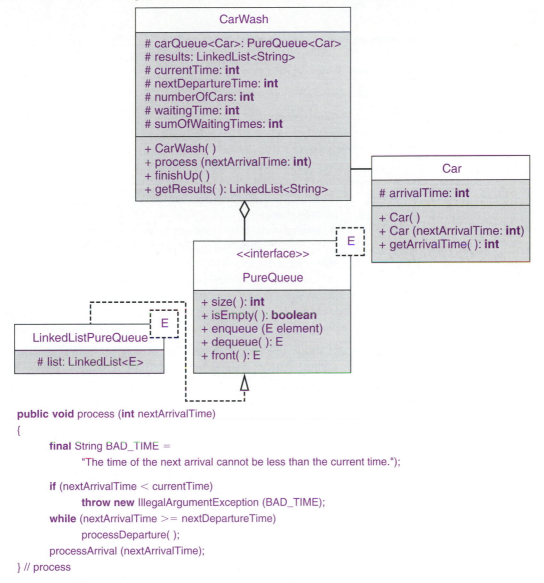

```
public void process (int nextArrivalTime)
{
        final String BAD_TIME =
                "The time of the next arrival cannot be less than the current time.");

        if (nextArrivalTime < currentTime)
                throw new IllegalArgumentException (BAD_TIME);
        while (nextArrivalTime >= nextDepartureTime)
                processDeparture( );
        processArrival (nextArrivalTime);
} // process
```

To process the arrival given by nextArrivalTime, we first update currentTime and check for an overflow. If this arrival is not an overflow, numberOfCars is incremented and the car either starts getting washed (if the wash station is empty) or is enqueued on carQueue. Here is the code:

```
/**
 * Moves the just-arrived car into the car wash (if there is room on the car queue),
 * or turns the car away (if there is no room on the car queue).
 *
```

```
 * @param nextArrivalTime – the arrival time of the just-arrived car.
 *
 */
protected void processArrival (int nextArrivalTime)
{
        final String OVERFLOW = " (Overflow)\n";

        final String ARRIVAL = "\tArrival";

        currentTime = nextArrivalTime;
        results.add (Integer.toString (currentTime) + ARRIVAL);
        if (carQueue.size( ) == MAX_SIZE)
                results.add (OVERFLOW);
        else
        {
                numberOfCars++;
                if (nextDepartureTime == INFINITY) // if no car is being washed
                        nextDepartureTime = currentTime + WASH_TIME;
                else
                        carQueue.enqueue (new Car (nextArrivalTime));
                results.add ("\n");
        } // not an overflow
} // method processArrival
```

This method reveals how the Car class gets involved: the constructor with next
ArrivalTime as its argument. Here is the complete definition of the Car class:

```
public class Car
{
        protected int arrivalTime;

        /**
         * Initializes this Car object.
         *
         */
        public Car( ) { } // for the sake of subclasses of Car

        /**
         * Initializes this Car object from the specified time of the next arrival.
         *
         *
         * @param nextArrivalTime – the time of the next arrival.
         *
         */
        public Car (int nextArrivalTime)
        {
                arrivalTime = nextArrivalTime;
        } // constructor with int parameter

        /**
         * Determines the arrival time of this Car object.
```

```
      *
      * @return the arrival time of this Car object.
      *
      */
     public int getArrivalTime( )
     {
             return arrivalTime;
     } // method getArrivalTime


  } // class Car
```

For this project, we could easily have avoided the Car class, but a subsequent extension of the project might want to know more about a car—its perimeter, whether it is a convertible, the number of axles, and so on.

To process a departure, we first update currentTime and results. Note that the waiting time for the departing car was calculated when that car entered the wash station—during the previous call to the processDeparture method. We then check to see if there are any cars on carQueue. If so, we dequeue the front car, calculate its waiting time, add that to sumOfWaitingTimes, and begin washing that car. Otherwise, we set waitingTime to 0 and nextDepartureTime to a large number to indicate that no car is now being washed. Here is the definition:

```
   /**
    * Updates the simulation to reflect the fact that a car has finished getting washed.
    *
    */
   protected void processDeparture( )
   {
           final String DEPARTURE = "\tDeparture\t\t";

           int arrivalTime;

           currentTime = nextDepartureTime;
           results.add (Integer.toString (currentTime) + DEPARTURE +
                       Integer.toString (waitingTime) + "\n");
           if (!carQueue.isEmpty( ))
           {
                   Car car = carQueue.dequeue( );
                   arrivalTime = car.getArrivalTime( );
                   waitingTime = currentTime − arrivalTime;
                   sumOfWaitingTimes += waitingTime;
                   nextDepartureTime = currentTime + WASH_TIME;
           } // carQueue was not empty
           else
           {
                   waitingTime = 0;
                   nextDepartureTime = INFINITY; // no car is being washed
           } // carQueue was empty
   } // method processDeparture
```

The finishUp and **getResults** methods are straightforward:

```
public void finishUp( )
{
        while (nextDepartureTime < INFINITY) // while there are unwashed cars
                processDeparture( );
} // finishUp

public LinkedList<String> getResults( )
{
        final String NO_CARS_MESSAGE = "There were no cars in the car wash.\n";

        final String AVERAGE_WAITING_TIME_MESSAGE =
                "\n\nThe average waiting time, in minutes, was ";

        if (numberOfCars == 0)
                results.add (NO_CARS_MESSAGE);
        else
                results.add (AVERAGE_WAITING_TIME_MESSAGE + Double.toString
                        ((double) sumOfWaitingTimes / numberOfCars));
        return results;
} // method getResults
```

**The** CarWashTester **Class**   The design of the CarWashTester class is simpler than
the drivers for the VeryLongInt and Editor classes because the four public CarWash
methods must be executed in the order they were developed. Also, the need for an
input file is removed later in this section.

The CarWashTester class has a default constructor, a readAndProcessArrival
Times method, and a printResults method. Here are the method specifications:

```
/**
 * Initializes this CarWashTester object.
 *
 */
public CarWashTester ( )

/**
 * Reads in all of the arrival times, runs the simulation, and calculates the average
 * waiting time.
 *
 */
public void readAndProcessArrivalTimes( )

/**
 * Prints the results of the simulation.
 *
 */
public void printResults( )
```

The only field is

> **protected** CarWash carWash;

Figure 8.21 has the UML class diagrams for this project. Some of the class diagrams presented in Figure 8.20 are abbreviated in Figure 8.21.

The definitions of the CarWashTester default constructor and printResults method need no explanation:

```
public CarWashTester( )
{
        carWash = new CarWash( );
} // default constructor
public void printResults( )
{
        final String RESULTS_HEADING =
                "\nHere are the results of the simulation:\n";
```

**Figure 8.21 |** UML class diagrams for the CarWash project.

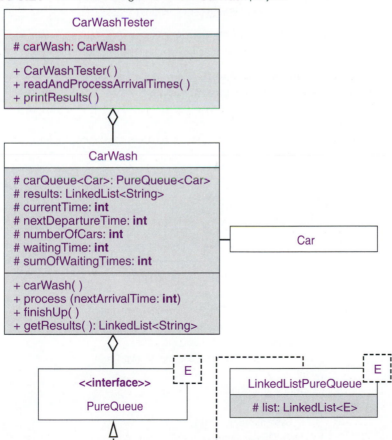

```
        LinkedList<String> results = carWash.getResults( );
        System.out.println (RESULTS_HEADING);
        for (String s : results)
                System.out.print (s);
    } // method printResults
```

The definition of readAndProcessArrivalTimes repeatedly—until the sentinel is reached—reads in a value for nextArrivalTime. Unless an exception is thrown, for example, if the value is not an **int**, the message

    carWash.process (nextArrivalTime)

is sent. When the sentinel is read in, the loop is exited and carWash.finishUp( ) is called. Here is the code:

```
public void readAndProcessArrivalTimes( )
{
        final int SENTINEL = 999;

        final String PROMPT = "\nPlease enter the next arrival time. The sentinel is "
                        + Integer.toString (SENTINEL) + ": ";

        final String OUT_OF_RANGE = " The input must consist of a non-" +
                "negative integer less than the sentinel.";

        BufferedReader keyboardReader = new BufferedReader
                (new InputStreamReader (System.in));

        String line;

        int nextArrivalTime;

        while (true)
        {
            System.out.print (PROMPT);
            try
            {
                    line = keyboardReader.readLine( );
                    nextArrivalTime = Integer.parseInt (line);
                    if (nextArrivalTime == SENTINEL)
                            break;
                    if (nextArrivalTime < 0 || nextArrivalTime > SENTINEL)
                            System.out.println (OUT_OF_RANGE);
                    else
                            carWash.process (nextArrivalTime);
            } // try
            catch (IOException e)
            {
                    System.out.println(e);
            } // catch IOException
            catch (IllegalArgumentException e)
```

```
            {
                    System.out.println (e);
            } // catch IllegalArgumentException
        } // while
        carWash.finishUp( );
    } // readAndProcessArrivalTimes
```

For the readAndProcessArrivalTimes method, worstTime($n$) is linear in $n$, where $n$ is the number of lines of input. There are loops in the definitions of the CarWash methods process and finishUp, but those loops are independent of $n$; in fact, the number of iterations of either loop is at most 5, the maximum size of the car queue.

Finally, the CarWashMain class consists of a main method that invokes each of the CarWashTester methods. The complete project is available from the book's website.

**Randomizing the Arrival Times**  It is not necessary that the arrival times be read in. They can be generated by your simulation program provided the input includes the *mean arrival time,* that is, the average time between arrivals for the population. In order to generate the list of arrival times from the mean arrival time, we need to know the distribution of arrival times. We now define a function that calculates the distribution, known as the *Poisson distribution,* of times between arrivals. The mathematical justification for the following discussion is beyond the scope of this book—the interested reader may consult a text on mathematical statistics.

Let $x$ be any time between arrivals. Then $F(x)$, the probability that the time until the next arrival will be at least $x$ minutes from now, is given by

$$F(x) = \exp(-x/\text{meanArrivalTime})$$

For example, $F(0) = \exp(0) = 1$; that is, it is certain that the next arrival will occur at least 0 minutes from now. Similarly, $F(\text{meanArrivalTime}) = \exp(-1) \approx 0.4$. $F(10000 * \text{meanArrivalTime})$ is approximately 0. The graph of the function $F$ is shown in Figure 8.22.

**Figure 8.22 |** Graph of the Poisson distribution of interarrival times.

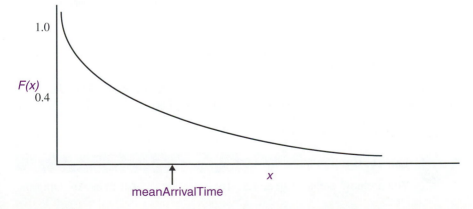

To generate the arrival times randomly, we introduce an integer variable called timeTillNext, which will contain the number of minutes from the current time until the next arrival. We determine the value for timeTillNext as follows. According to the distribution function $F$ given above, the probability that the next arrival will take at least timeTillNext minutes is given by

$$\exp(-\text{timeTillNext} / \text{meanArrivalTime})$$

This expression represents a probability, specifically, a floating point number that is greater than 0.0 and less than or equal to 1.0. To randomize this probability, we associate the expression with the value of a random variable, randomDouble, in the same range. So we set

randomDouble = random.nextDouble( );

Then randomDouble contains a **double** value that is greater than or equal to 0.0 and less than 1.0. So 1 − randomDouble will contain a value that is greater than 0.0 and less than or equal to 1.0. This is what we want, so we equate 1 − randomDouble with exp(−timeTillNext/meanArrivalTime):

$$1 - \text{randomDouble} = \exp(-\text{timeTillNext} / \text{meanArrivalTime})$$

To solve this equation for timeTillNext, we take logs of both sides:

$$\log(1 - \text{randomDouble}) = -\text{timeTillNext} / \text{meanArrivalTime}$$

Now each side is multiplied by − meanArrivalTime, to yield

$$\text{timeTillNext} = -\text{meanArrivalTime} * \log(1 - \text{randomDouble})$$

In Java code, we get:

timeTillNext = (**int**)Math.round (−meanArrivalTime * Math.log
(1 − randomDouble));

We round the result so that timeTillNext will be an integer.

To illustrate how the values would be calculated, suppose that the mean arrival time is 3 minutes and the list of values of 1 − randomDouble starts with 0.715842, 0.28016, and 0.409589. Then the first three, randomized values of timeTillNext will be

1, that is, (**int**)Math.round (−3 * log (0.715842))

4, that is, (**int**)Math.round (−3 * log (0.28016))

3, that is, (**int**)Math.round (−3 * log (0.409589))

The first car will arrive one minute after the car wash opens and the second car will arrive four minutes later, at minute 5. The third car will arrive three minutes later, at minute 8.

**Lab 16: Randomizing the Arrival Times**

You are now prepared to do Lab 16.                    All Labs Are Optional

# SUMMARY

A *stack* is a finite sequence of elements in which insertions and deletions can take place at only one end of the sequence, called the *top* of the stack. Because the most recently inserted element is the next element to be removed, a stack is a last in, first out (LIFO) structure. Compilers implement recursion by generating code for pushing and popping activation records onto the run-time stack whose top record holds the state of the method currently being executed. Another stack application occurs in the translation of infix expressions into machine code. With the help of an operator stack, an infix expression can be converted into a postfix expression, which is an intermediate form between infix and machine language. For this conversion, worstTime($n$) is linear in $n$, the size of the infix expression.

A *queue* is a finite sequence of elements in which insertions can take place only at the back, and removals can take place only at the front. Because the first element inserted will be the first element to be removed, a queue is a first in, first out (FIFO) structure. The inherent fairness of this *first come, first served* restriction has made queues important components of many systems. Specifically, queues play a key role in the development of computer models to study the behavior of those systems.

# CONCEPT EXERCISES

**8.1**   What advantage was obtained by implementing the List interface before implementing the PureQueue and PureStack interfaces?

**8.2**   Suppose we define:

LinkedListPureQueue<Integer> queue = **new** LinkedListPureQueue<Integer>( );

Show what queue will look like after each of the following messages is sent:

**a.**   queue.enqueue (2000);

**b.**   queue.enqueue (1215);

**c.**   queue.enqueue (1035);

**d.**   queue.enqueue (2117);

**e.**   queue.dequeue( );

**f.**   queue.enqueue (1999);

**g.**   queue.dequeue( );

**8.3**   Redo Exercise 8.2, parts a through g, for a stack instead of a queue, and show the effect on that stack when each of the messages is sent.

**8.4**   Suppose that elements 'a', 'b', 'c', 'd', and 'e' are pushed, in that order, onto an initially empty stack, which is then popped four times, and as each element is popped, it is enqueued into an initially empty queue. If one element is then dequeued from the queue, what is the *next* element to be dequeued?

**8.5**   The array-based implementation of the PureQueue interface had data, size, head, and tail fields. Show that the size field is redundant. Specifically, show that the size( ) method can be implemented using only the data, head, and tail fields.

**8.6**    Use a stack of activation records to trace the execution of the recursive factorial method after an initial call of factorial (4). Here is the method definition:

```
/**
 * Calculates the factorial of a nonnegative integer, that is, the product of all
 * integers between 1 and the given integer, inclusive. The worstTime(n) is O(n).
 *
 * @param n the nonnegative integer whose factorial is calculated.
 *
 * @return the factorial of n
 *
 * @throws IllegalArgumentException if n is less than 0.
 *
 */
public static long factorial (int n)
{
        if (n < 0)
                throw new IllegalArgumentException( );
        if (n <= 1)
                return 1;
        return n * factorial (n − 1);
} // method factorial
```

**8.7**    Translate the following expressions into postfix notation:

**a.**   x + y * z

**b.**   (x + y) * z

**c.**   x − y − z * (a + b)

**d.**   (a + b) * c − (d + e * f / ((g / h + i − j) * k)) / r

Test your answers by running the InfixToPostfixMain project in Lab 15.

**8.8**    Translate each of the expressions in Concept Exercise 8.7 into prefix notation.

**8.9**    An expression in postfix notation can be evaluated at run-time by means of a stack. For simplicity, assume that the postfix expression consists of integer values and binary operators only. For example, we might have the following postfix expression:

8 5 4 + * 7 -

The evaluation proceeds as follows: When a value is encountered, it is pushed onto the stack. When an operator is encountered, the first and second elements on the stack are retrieved and popped, the operator is applied (the second element is the left operand, the first element is the right operand) and the result is pushed onto the stack. When the postfix expression has been processed, the value of that expression is the top (and only) element on the stack.

For example, for the above expression, the contents of the stack would be as follows:

```
                              4
                      5       5
              8       8       8
    ------    ------  ------  ------

    9                 7
    8       72        72      65
    ------  ------    ------  ------
```

Convert the following expression into postfix notation and then use a stack to evaluate the expression:

$5 + 2 * (30 - 10 / 5)$

# PROGRAMMING EXERCISES

**8.1**  Complete the implementation of ArrayPureQueue class from Section 8.2.2.

*Hint:* Only one line is needed for the definition of the default constructor, isEmpty, size, front, and dequeue (using modular arithmetic for dequeue). For the copy constructor, each field in the parameter is copied to the calling object, and then System.arraycopy is invoked. Test your implementation with a driver.

**8.2**  Define the LinkedListPureStack class implementation of the PureStack interface. Test your implementation with a driver.

*Hint:* Each of the definitions is a one-liner.

**8.3**  Define an implementation of the PureStack class based on an ArrayList.

*Hint:* In the ArrayListPureStack class, the top of the stack is at index size( ) − 1.

**8.4**  Perform a run-time experiment to compare the five implementations of the PureStack interface: ArrayPureStack, LinkedPureStack, Stack (in java.util), ArrayListPureStack, and LinkedListPureStack. What is the one overwhelming conclusion you drew from the experiment?

**8.5**  Develop iterative, stack-based versions of the gcd, isPalindrome, power, and ways methods in Programming Exercises 5.3, 5.4, 5.6, and 5.7. Test your methods with a main method that calls your version.

# Programming Project 8.1

## Making the Speedo's Car Wash Simulation More Realistic

### Analysis:

The arrival times—with a Poisson distribution—should be generated randomly from the mean arrival time. Speedo has added a new feature: The service time is not necessarily 10 minutes, but depends on what the customer wants done, such as wash only, wash and wax, wash and vacuum, and so on. The service time for a car should be calculated just before the car enters the wash station—that's when the customer knows how much time will be taken until the customer leaves the car wash. The service times, also with a Poisson distribution, should be generated randomly from the mean service time; use the same random-number generator as for the arrival times.

The input consists of three positive integers: the mean arrival time, the mean service time, and the maximum arrival time. Repeatedly reprompt until each value is a positive integer.

Calculate the average waiting time and the average queue length, both to one fractional digit.[5] The average waiting time is the sum of the waiting times divided by the number of customers.

The average queue length is the sum of the queue lengths for each minute of the simulation divided by the number of minutes until the last customer departs. To calculate the sum of the queue lengths, we add, for each minute of the simulation, the total number of customers on the queue during that minute. We can calculate this sum another way: we add, for each customer, the total number of minutes that customer was on the queue. But this is the sum of the waiting times! So we can calculate the average queue length as the sum of the waiting times divided by the number of minutes of the simulation until the last customer departs. And we already calculated the sum of the waiting times for the average waiting time.

Also calculate the number of overflows. Use a seed of 100 for the random-number generator, so the output you get should have the same values as the output below.

### System Test 1 (Input in Boldface):

Please enter the mean arrival time: **3**

Please enter the mean service time: **5**

Please enter the maximum arrival time: **25**

| Time | Event | Waiting Time |
| --- | --- | --- |
| 4 | Arrival | |
| 5 | Departure | 0 |
| 7 | Arrival | |
| 10 | Arrival | |

---

[5] Given a **double** d, you can print d rounded to one fractional digit as follows:

```
System.out.println (Math.round (d * 10) / 10.0);
```

| | | |
|---|---|---|
| 13 | Arrival | |
| 14 | Arrival | |
| 15 | Departure | 0 |
| 16 | Arrival | |
| 18 | Arrival | |
| 20 | Arrival | |
| 21 | Departure | 5 |
| 32 | Departure | 8 |
| 34 | Departure | 18 |
| 37 | Departure | 18 |
| 41 | Departure | 19 |
| 46 | Departure | 21 |

The average waiting time was 11.1 minutes per car.

The average queue length was 1.9 cars per minute.

The number of overflows was 0.

**System Test 2 (Input in Boldface):**

Please enter the mean arrival time: **1**

Please enter the mean service time: **1**

Please enter the maximum arrival time: **23**

Here are the results of the simulation:

| Time | Event | Waiting Time |
|---|---|---|
| 1 | Arrival | |
| 1 | Departure | 0 |
| 2 | Arrival | |
| 3 | Arrival | |
| 4 | Departure | 0 |
| 4 | Departure | 1 |
| 4 | Arrival | |
| 5 | Departure | 0 |
| 5 | Arrival | |
| 6 | Departure | 0 |
| 6 | Arrival | |
| 8 | Arrival | |
| 8 | Arrival | |
| 9 | Arrival | |
| 10 | Arrival | |
| 11 | Departure | 0 |
| 11 | Arrival | |
| 11 | Arrival | |
| 11 | Arrival (Overflow) | |

*(continued on next page)*

*(continued from previous page)*

| | | |
|---|---|---|
| 12 | Arrival (Overflow) | |
| 12 | Arrival (Overflow) | |
| 13 | Departure | 3 |
| 13 | Arrival | |
| 14 | Departure | 5 |
| 14 | Departure | 5 |
| 14 | Departure | 4 |
| 14 | Arrival | |
| 15 | Departure | 3 |
| 15 | Departure | 4 |
| 15 | Arrival | |
| 16 | Departure | 2 |
| 16 | Departure | 2 |
| 18 | Arrival | |
| 19 | Departure | 1 |
| 20 | Departure | 1 |
| 22 | Arrival | |
| 22 | Departure | 0 |
| 22 | Arrival | |
| 23 | Arrival | |
| 23 | Arrival | |
| 24 | Departure | 0 |
| 24 | Departure | 1 |
| 24 | Departure | 1 |

The average waiting time was 1.7 minutes per car.

The average queue length was 1.4 cars per minute.

The number of overflows was 3.

# Programming Project 8.2

## Develop a Program to Evaluate a Condition

**Analysis:**

The input will consist of a condition (that is, a Boolean expression) followed by the values—one per line—of the variables as they are first encountered in the condition. For example:

```
b * a > a + c
6
2
7
```

The variable b gets the value 6, a gets the value 2, and c gets 7. The operator * has precedence over >, and + has precedence over >, so the value of the above expression is true (12 is greater than 9).

Each variable will be given as an identifier, consisting of lowercase letters only. All variables will be integer-valued. There will be no constant literals. The legal operators and precedence levels—high to low—are:

*, /, %

+, − (that is, integer addition and subtraction)

>, >=, <=, <

==, !=

&&

||

Parenthesized subexpressions are legal. *You need not do any input editing.*

**System Test 1 (Input in Boldface):**

Please enter a condition, or $ to quit: **b * a > a + c**

Please enter a value: **6**

Please enter a value: **2**

Please enter a value: **7**
The value of the condition is true.

Please enter a condition, or $ to quit: **b * a < a + c**

Please enter a value: **6**

Please enter a value: **2**

Please enter a value: **7**
The value of the condition is false.

*(continued on next page)*

*(continued from previous page)*

Please enter a condition, or $ to quit: **m + j * next == current * (next − previous)**

Please enter a value: **6**

Please enter a value: **2**

Please enter a value: **7**

Please enter a value: **5**

Please enter a value: **3**
The value of the condition is true.

Please enter a condition, or $ to quit: **m + j * next != current * (next − previous)**

Please enter a value: **6**

Please enter a value: **2**

Please enter a value: **7**

Please enter a value: **5**

Please enter a value: 3
The value of the condition is false.

Please enter a condition, or $ to quit: **a * (b + c / (d − b) * e) >= a + b + c + d + e**

Please enter a value: **6**

Please enter a value: **2**

Please enter a value: **7**

Please enter a value: **5**

Please enter a value: **3**
The value of the condition is true.

Please enter a condition, or $ to quit: **a * (b + c / (d − b) * e) <= a + b + c + d + e**

Please enter a value: **6**

Please enter a value: **2**

Please enter a value: **7**

Please enter a value: **5**

Please enter a value: **3**
The value of the condition is false.

Please enter a condition, or $ to quit: **$**

**System Test 2 (Input in Boldface):**

Please enter a condition, or $ to quit: **b < c && c < a**

Please enter a value: **10**

Please enter a value: **20**

Please enter a value: **30**
The value of the condition is true.

Please enter a condition, or $ to quit: **b < c && a < c**

Please enter a value: **10**

Please enter a value: **20**

Please enter a value: **30**
The value of the condition is false.

Please enter a condition, or $ to quit: **b < c || a < c**

Please enter a value: **10**

Please enter a value: **20**

Please enter a value: **30**
The value of the condition is true.

Please enter a condition, or $ to quit: **c < b || c > a**

Please enter a value: **10**

Please enter a value: **20**

Please enter a value: **30**
The value of the condition is true.

Please enter a condition, or $ to quit: **b != a || b <= c && a >= c**

Please enter a value: **10**

Please enter a value: **20**

Please enter a value: **30**
The value of the condition is true.

Please enter a condition, or $ to quit: **(b != a || b <= c) && a >= c**

Please enter a value: **10**

Please enter a value: **20**

Please enter a value: **30**
The value of the condition is false.

Please enter a condition, or $ to quit: **a / b * b + a % b == a**

Please enter a value: **17**

Please enter a value: **5**
The value of the condition is true.

Please enter a condition, or $ to quit: **$**

*Hint:* See Lab 15 on converting infix to postfix, and Concept Exercise 8.9. After constructing the postfix queue, create values, an ArrayList object with Integer elements. The values object corresponds to symbolTable, the ArrayList of identifiers. Use a stack, run TimeStack, for pushing and popping Integer and Boolean elements. Because runTimeStack contains both Integer and Boolean elements, it should have a type argument of Object.

## Programming Project 8.3

### Maze-Searching, Revisited

Redo the maze-search project in Chapter 5 by replacing tryToReachGoal with an iterative method. *Hint:* Use a stack to simulate the recursive calls to tryToReachGoal.

The original version of the project is available from the book's website.

## Programming Project 8.4

### A Linked Implementation of the PureQueue Interface

Develop a singly linked implementation of the PureQueue interface. Create a driver to test your implementation.

*Hint:* Use the LinkedPureStack implementation in Section 8.1.2 as a guide. To simplify the code to insert at the back of a queue, include a tail field:

```
protected Entry<E> head,
                      tail;

protected int size;
```

# Binary Trees

In this chapter we "branch" out from the linear structures of earlier chapters to introduce what is essentially a nonlinear construct: the binary tree. This brief chapter focuses on the definition and properties of binary trees, and that will provide the necessary background for the next four chapters. Chapters 10 through 13 will consider various specializations of binary trees: binary search trees, AVL trees, decision trees, red-black trees, heaps, and Huffman trees. There is no question that the binary tree is one of the most important concepts in computer science! Finally, to round out the picture, Chapter 15 presents the topic of trees in general. ■

## CHAPTER OBJECTIVES

1. Understand binary-tree concepts and important properties, such as the Binary Tree Theorem and the External Path Length Theorem.

2. Be able to perform various traversals of a binary tree.

## 9.1 | DEFINITION OF BINARY TREE

The following definition sets the tone for the whole chapter:

> A **binary tree** *t* is either empty or consists of an element, called the **root element,** and two distinct binary trees, called the **left subtree** and **right subtree** of *t*.

We denote those subtrees as leftTree(*t*) and rightTree(*t*), respectively. Functional notation, such as leftTree(*t*), is utilized instead of object notation, such as t.leftTree( ), because there is no binary-tree data structure. Why not? Different types of binary trees have widely differing methods—even different parameters lists—for such operations as inserting and removing. Note that the above definition of a binary tree is recursive, and many of the definitions associated with binary trees are naturally recursive.

In depicting a binary tree, the root element is shown at the top, by convention. To suggest the association between the root element and the left and right subtrees, we draw a southwesterly line from the root element to the left subtree and a southeasterly line from the root element to the right subtree. Figure 9.1 shows several binary trees.

**Figure 9.1 |** Several binary trees.

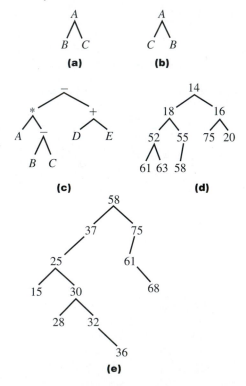

The binary tree in Figure 9.1a is different from the binary tree in Figure 9.1b because *B* is in the left subtree of Figure 9.1a but *B* is not in the left subtree of Figure 9.1b. As we will see in Chapter 15, those two binary trees *are* equivalent when viewed as general trees.

A subtree of a binary tree is itself a binary tree, and so Figure 9.1a has seven binary trees: the whole binary tree, the binary tree whose root element is *B*, the binary tree whose root element is *C*, and four empty binary trees. Try to calculate the total number of subtrees for the tree in Figures 9.1c, d, and e, and see if you discover the relationship between the number of elements and the number of subtrees.

The next section develops several properties of binary trees, and most of the properties are relevant to the material in later chapters.

## 9.2 | PROPERTIES OF BINARY TREES

In addition to "tree" and "root", botanical terms are used for several binary-tree concepts. The line from a root element to a subtree is called a **branch.** An element whose associated left and right subtrees are both empty is called a **leaf.** A leaf has no branches going down from it. In the binary tree shown in Figure 9.1e, there are four leaves: 15, 28, 36, and 68. We can determine the number of leaves in a binary tree recursively. Let *t* be a binary tree. The number of leaves in *t*, written **leaves(t),** can be defined recursively as follows:

> if *t* is empty
> > leaves(*t*) = 0
> else if *t* consists of a root element only
> > leaves(*t*) = 1
> else
> > leaves(*t*) = leaves(leftTree(*t*)) + leaves(rightTree(*t*))

This is a mathematical definition, not a Java method. The last line in the above definition states that the number of leaves in *t* is equal to the number of leaves in *t*'s left subtree plus the number of leaves in *t*'s right subtree. Just for practice, try to use this definition to calculate the number of leaves in Figure 9.1a. Of course, you can simply look at the whole tree and count the number of leaves, but the above definition of leaves(*t*) is atomic rather than holistic.

Each element in a binary tree is uniquely determined by its location in the tree. For example, let *t* be the binary tree shown in Figure 9.1c. There are two elements in *t* with value "−". We can distinguish between them by referring to one of them as "the element whose value is '−' and whose location is at the root of *t*" and the other one as "the element whose value is '−' and whose location is at the root of the right subtree of the left subtree of *t*." We loosely refer to "an element" in a binary tree when, strictly speaking, we should say "the element at such and such a location."

Some binary-tree concepts use familial terminology. Let *t* be the binary tree shown in Figure 9.2. We say that *x* is the **parent** of *y* and that *y* is the **left child** of *x*. Similarly, we say that *x* is the **parent** of *z* and that *z* is the **right child** of *x*.

**Figure 9.2** A binary tree with one parent and two children.

In a binary tree, each element has zero, one, or two children. For example, in Figure 9.1d, 14 has two children, 16 and 18; 55 has 58 as its only child; 61 is child-less, that is, it is a leaf. For any element $w$ in a tree, we write parent($w$) for the parent of $w$, left($w$) for the left child of $w$ and right($w$) for the right child of $w$.

In a binary tree, the root element does not have a parent, and every other element has exactly one parent. Continuing with the terminology of a family tree, we could define sibling, grandparent, grandchild, first cousin, ancestor, and descendant. For example, an element $A$ is an ***ancestor*** of an element $B$ if $B$ is in the subtree whose root element is $A$. To put it recursively, $A$ is an ***ancestor*** of $B$ if $A$ is the parent of $B$ or if $A$ is an ancestor of parent($B$). Try to define "descendant" recursively.

If $A$ is an ancestor of $B$, the ***path*** from $A$ to $B$ is the sequence of elements, starting with $A$ and ending with $B$, in which each element in the sequence (except the last) is the parent of the next element. For example, in Figure 9.1e, the sequence 37, 25, 30, 32 is the path from 37 to 32.

Informally, the height of a binary tree is the number of branches between the root and the farthest leaf, that is, the leaf with the most ancestors. For example, Figure 9.3 has a binary tree of height 3.

The height of the tree in Figure 9.3 is 3 because the path from $E$ to $S$ has three branches. Suppose for some binary tree, the left subtree has a height of 12 and the right subtree has a height of 20. What is the height of the whole tree? The answer is 21.

In general, the height of a tree is one more than the maximum of the heights of the left and right subtrees. This leads us to a recursive definition of the height of a binary tree. But first, we need to know what the base case is, namely, the height of an empty tree. We want the height of a single-element tree to be 0: there are no

**Figure 9.3** A binary tree of height 3.

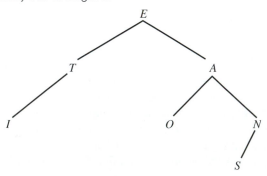

branches from the root element to itself. But that means that 0 is one more than the maximum heights of the left and right subtrees, which are both empty. So we need to define the height of an empty subtree to be, strangely enough, $-1$.

Let $t$ be a binary tree. We define *height(t),* the ***height*** of $t$, recursively as follows:

if $t$ is empty,
  height($t$) $= -1$
else
  height($t$) $= 1 + $ max[height(leftTree($t$)), height(rightTree($t$))]

It follows from this definition that a binary tree with a single element has height 0 because each of its empty subtrees has a height of $-1$. Also, the height of the binary tree in Figure 9.1a is 1. And, if you want to try some recursive gymnastics, you can verify that the height of the binary tree in Figure 9.1e is 5.

Height is a property of an entire binary tree. For each element in a binary tree, we can define a similar concept: the level of the element. Speaking nonrecursively, if $x$ is an element in a binary tree, we define *level(x),* the ***level*** of element $x$, to be the number of branches between the root element and element $x$. Figure 9.4 shows a binary tree, with levels.

In Figure 9.4, *level'N'* is 2. Notice that the level of the root element is 0, and the height of a tree is equal to the highest level in the tree. Here is a recursive definition of the level of an element. For any element $x$ in a binary tree, we define *level(x),* the ***level*** of element $x$, as follows:

if $x$ is the root element,
  level($x$) $= 0$
else
  level($x$) $= 1 + $ level(parent($x$))

An element's level is also referred to as that element's ***depth.*** Curiously, the *height* of a nonempty binary tree is the *depth* of the farthest leaf!

**Figure 9.4** A binary tree, with the levels of elements shown.

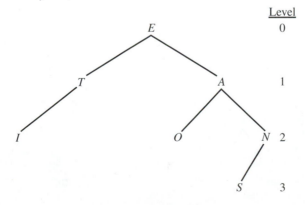

A **two-tree** is a binary tree that either is empty or in which each nonleaf has 2 branches going down from it. For example, Figure 9.5a is a two-tree and Figure 9.5b is not a two-tree.

Recursively speaking, a binary tree *t* is a **two-tree** if:

*t* is empty

or

both subtrees of *t* are empty or both subtrees of *t* are nonempty two-trees

A binary tree *t* is **full** if *t* is a two-tree with all of its leaves on the same level. For example, Figure 9.6a is full and Figure 9.6b is not full.

Recursively speaking, a binary tree *t* is **full** if:

*t* is empty

or

*t*'s left and right subtrees have the same height and both are full

**Figure 9.5** I (a) A two-tree; (b) a binary tree that is not a two-tree.

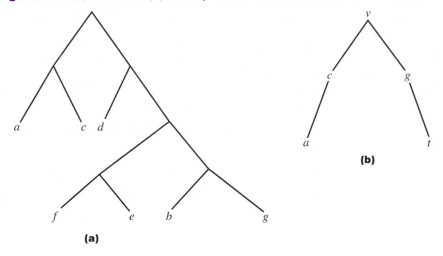

(a)

(b)

**Figure 9.6** I (a) A full binary tree; (b) a binary tree that is not full.

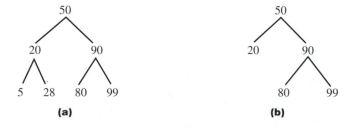

(a)

(b)

Of course, every full binary tree is a two-tree but the converse is not necessarily true. For example, the tree in Figure 9.6b is a two-tree but is not full. For full binary trees, there is a relationship between the height and number of elements in the tree. For example, the full binary tree in Figure 9.7 has a height of 2, so the tree must have exactly 7 elements.

How many elements must there be in a full binary tree of height 3? Of height 4? For a full binary tree $t$, can you conjecture the formula for the number of elements in $t$ as a function of $height(t)$? The answer can be found in Section 9.3.

A binary tree $t$ is **complete** if $t$ is full through the next-to-lowest level and all of the leaves at the lowest level are as far to the left as possible. By "lowest level," we mean the level farthest from the root.

Any full binary tree is complete, but the converse is not necessarily true. For example, Figure 9.8a has a complete binary tree that is not full. The tree in Figure 9.8b is not complete because it is not full at the next-to-lowest level: $C$ has only one child. The tree in Figure 9.8c is not complete because leaves $I$ and $J$ are not as far to the left as they could be.

In a complete binary tree, we can associate a "position" with each element. The root element is assigned a position of 0. For any positive integer $i$, if the element at position $i$ has children, the position of its left child is $2i + 1$ and the position of its right child is $2i + 2$. For example, if a complete binary tree has 10 elements, the positions of those elements are as indicated in Figure 9.9.

**Figure 9.7** I A full binary tree of height 2; such a tree must have exactly 7 elements.

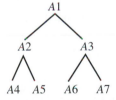

**Figure 9.8** I Three binary trees, of which only (a) is complete.

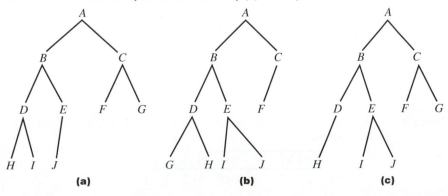

**Figure 9.9 |** The association of consecutive integers to elements in a complete binary tree.

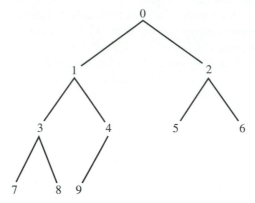

In Figure 9.9, the parent of the element at position 8 is in position 3, and the parent of the element in position 5 is in position 2. In general, if $i$ is a positive integer, the position of the parent of the element in position $i$ is in position $(i - 1)/2$, using integer division.

The position of an element is important because we can implement a complete binary tree with an array or an ArrayList. Specifically, we will store the element that is at position $i$ in the tree at index $i$ in the array. For example, Figure 9.10 shows an array with the elements from Figure 9.8a.

If a complete binary tree is implemented with an ArrayList object or array object, the random-access property of arrays allows us to access the children of a parent (or parent of a child) in constant time. That is exactly what we will do in Chapter 13.

We have shown how we can recursively calculate *leaves(t),* the number of leaves in a binary tree *t,* and *height(t),* the height of a binary tree *t.* We can also recursively calculate the number of elements, *n(t),* in *t:*

> if $t$ is empty
>   $n(t) = 0$
> else
>   $n(t) = 1 + n(\text{leftTree}(t)) + n(\text{rightTree}(t))$

**Figure 9.10 |** An array that holds the elements from the complete binary tree in Figure 9.8a.

| A | B | C | D | E | F | G | H | I | J |
|---|---|---|---|---|---|---|---|---|---|
| 0 | 1 | 2 | 3 | 4 | 5 | 6 | 7 | 8 | 9 |

# 9.3 | THE BINARY TREE THEOREM

For any binary tree $t$, leaves$(t) \leq n(t)$, and leaves$(t) = n(t)$ if and only if $t$ is empty or $t$ consists of one element only. The phrase "if and only if" indicates that each of the individual statements follows from the other. Namely, if $t$ is empty or $t$ consists of a single element only, then leaves$(t) = n(t)$; and if leaves$(t) = n(t)$, then $t$ is empty or $t$ consists of a single element only.

The following theorem characterizes the relationships among leaves$(t)$, height$(t)$, and $n(t)$.

---

**Binary Tree Theorem**  For any nonempty binary tree $t$,

1.  $\text{leaves}(t) \leq \dfrac{n(t) + 1}{2.0}$

2.  $\dfrac{n(t) + 1}{2.0} \leq 2^{\text{height}(t)}$

3.  Equality holds in part 1 if and only if $t$ is a two-tree.

4.  Equality holds in part 2 if and only if $t$ is full.

---

*Note:* Because 2.0 is the denominator of the division in part 1, the quotient is a floating point value. For example, $7/2.0 = 3.5$. We cannot use integer division because of part 3: let $t$ be the binary tree in Figure 9.11. For the tree in Figure 9.11, leaves$(t)$ $= 2 = (n(t) + 1)/2$ if we use integer division. But $t$ is not a two-tree. Note that $(n(t) + 1)/2.0 = 2.5$.

Parts 3 and 4 each entails two subparts. For example, for part 3, we must show that if $t$ is a nonempty two-tree, then

$$\text{leaves}(t) = \frac{n(t) + 1}{2.0}$$

And if

$$\text{leaves}(t) = \frac{n(t) + 1}{2.0}$$

then $t$ must be a nonempty two-tree.

**Figure 9.11** | A binary tree $t$ with floor $((n(t) + 1)/2)$ leaves that is not a two-tree.

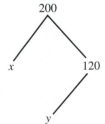

All four parts of this theorem can be proved by induction on the height of *t*. As it turns out, most theorems about binary trees can be proved by induction on the *height* of the tree. The reason for this is that if *t* is a binary tree, then both leftTree(*t*) and rightTree(*t*) have height less than height(*t*), and so the strong form of the Principle of Mathematical Induction (see Section A2.5 of Appendix 2) often applies. For example, Example A2.5 of Section A2.5 of Appendix 2 has a proof of part 1. The proofs of the remaining parts are left as Concept Exercises 9.13 and 9.14, with a hint for each exercise.

Suppose *t* is a full binary tree, then from part 4 of the Binary Tree Theorem, and the fact that any empty tree has height of $-1$, we have the equation

$$\frac{n(t) + 1}{2.0} = 2^{\text{height}(t)}$$

If we solve this equation for height(*t*), we get

$$\begin{aligned} \text{height}(t) &= \log_2((n(t) + 1)/2.0) \\ &= \log_2(n(t) + 1) - 1 \end{aligned}$$

So we can say that the height of a full tree is logarithmic in *n*, where *n* is the number of elements in the tree; we often use *n* instead of *n(t)* when it is clear which tree we are referring to. Even if *t* is merely complete, its height is still logarithmic in *n*. See Concept Exercise 9.7. On the other hand, *t* could be a chain. A ***chain*** is a binary tree in which each non-leaf has exactly one child. For example, Figure 9.12 has an example of a binary tree that is a chain.

If *t* is a chain, then height(*t*) $= n(t) - 1$, so for chains the height is linear in *n*. Much of our work with trees in subsequent chapters will be concerned with maintaining logarithmic height and avoiding linear height. Basically, for inserting into or removing from a binary tree whose height is logarithmic in *n*, worstTime(*n*) is logarithmic in *n*. That is why, in many applications, binary trees are preferable to lists.

**Figure 9.12 |** A binary tree that is a chain: each nonleaf has exactly one child.

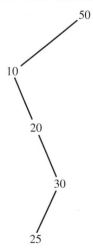

Recall that with both ArrayList objects and LinkedList objects, for inserting or removing at a specific index, worstTime($n$) is linear in $n$.

## 9.4 | EXTERNAL PATH LENGTH

You may wonder why we would be interested in adding up all the root-to-leaf path lengths, but the following definition does have some practical value. Let $t$ be a nonempty binary tree. $E(t)$, the ***external path length*** of $t$, is the sum of the depths of all the leaves in $t$. For example, in Figure 9.13, the sum of the depths of the leaves is $2 + 4 + 4 + 4 + 5 + 5 + 1 = 25$.

The following lower bound on external path lengths yields an important result in the study of sorting algorithms (see Chapter 11).

---

**External Path Length Theorem** Let $t$ be a binary tree with $k > 0$ leaves. Then

$$E(t) \geq (k / 2) \text{ floor } (\log_2 k)$$

***Proof:*** It follows from the Binary Tree Theorem that if a nonempty binary tree is full and has height $h$, then the tree has $2^h$ leaves. And we can obtain any binary tree by "pruning" a full binary tree of the same height; in so doing we reduce the number of leaves in the tree. So any nonempty binary tree of height $h$ has, at most, $2^h$ leaves. To put that in a slightly different way, if $k$ is any positive integer, any nonempty binary tree of height floor($\log_2 k$) has at most $k$ leaves. (We have to use the floor function because the height must be an integer, but $\log_2 k$ might not be an integer.)

Now suppose $t$ is a nonempty binary tree whose height is floor($\log_2 k$) for some positive integer $k$. By the previous paragraph, $t$ has at most $k$ leaves. How many of those leaves will be at level floor($\log_2 k$), the level farthest from the root? To answer that question, we ask how many leaves must be at a level less than floor($\log_2 k$). That is, how many leaves must there be in the subtree $t'$ of $t$ formed by removing all leaves at level floor($\log_2 k$)? The height of $t'$ is floor($\log_2 k$) $-1$. Note that

$$\text{floor}(\log_2 k) - 1 = \text{floor}(\log_2 k - 1)$$
$$= \text{floor}(\log_2 k - \log_2 2)$$
$$= \text{floor}(\log_2(k/2))$$

By the previous analysis, the total number of leaves in $t'$ is, at most, $k/2$. But every leaf in $t$ that is at a level less than floor($\log_2 k$) is also a leaf in $t'$. And so, in $t$, there must be, at least, $k/2$ leaves at level floor($\log_2 k$).

Each of those $k/2$ leaves contributes floor($\log_2 k$) to the external path length of $t$, so we must have

$$E(t) \geq (k / 2) \text{floor}(\log_2 k)$$

***Note:*** This result is all we will need in Chapter 11, but at a cost of a somewhat more complicated proof, we could show that $E(t) \geq k \log_2 k$ for any nonempty two-tree with $k$ leaves. See Kruse (1987, pp. 177–178) for details.

**Figure 9.13**  I A binary tree whose external path length is 25.

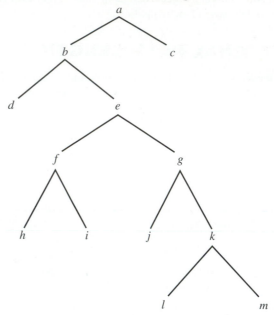

## 9.5  ITRAVERSALS OF A BINARY TREE

A *traversal* of a binary tree *t* is an algorithm that processes each element in *t* exactly once. In this section, we restrict our attention to algorithms only; there are no methods here. We make no attempt to declare a BinaryTree class or interface: it would not be flexible enough to support the variety of insertion and removal methods already in the Java Collections Framework. But the traversals we discuss in this section are related to code: specifically, to iterators. One of the iterators will turn up in Section 10.1.2, and two other iterators will appear in Chapter 15.

We identify four different kinds of traversal.

**Traversal 1. inOrder Traversal: Left-Root-Right**   The basic idea of this recursive algorithm is that we first perform an inOrder traversal of the left subtree, then we process the root element, and finally, we perform an inOrder traversal of the right subtree. Here is the algorithm—assume that *t* is a binary tree:

```
inOrder (t)
{
        if (t is not empty)
        {
                inOrder (leftTree (t));
                process the root element of t;
                inOrder (rightTree (t));
        } // if
} // inOrder traversal
```

Let $n$ represent the number of elements in the tree. Corresponding to each element there are 2 subtrees, so there will be $2n$ recursive calls to inOrder($t$). We conclude that worstTime($n$) is linear in $n$. Ditto for averageTime($n$).

We can use this recursive algorithm to list the elements in an inOrder traversal of the binary tree in Figure 9.14.

The tree $t$ in Figure 9.14 is not empty, so we start by performing an inOrder traversal of leftTree($t$), namely,

47

This one-element tree becomes the current version of $t$. Since its left subtree is empty, we process the root element of this $t$, namely 47. That completes the traversal of this version of $t$ since rightTree($t$) is empty. So now $t$ again refers to the original tree. We next process $t$'s root element, namely,

31

After that, we perform an inOrder traversal of rightTree($t$), namely,

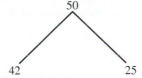

This becomes the current version of $t$. We start by performing an inOrder traversal of leftTree($t$), namely,

42

Now this tree with one element becomes the current version of $t$. Since its left subtree is empty, we process $t$'s root element, 42. The right subtree of this $t$ is empty. So we have completed the inOrder traversal of the tree with the single element 42, and now, once again, $t$ refers to the binary tree with 3 elements:

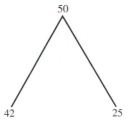

**Figure 9.14**  I A binary tree.

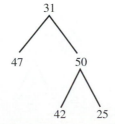

We next process the root element of this version of *t,* namely,

50

Finally, we perform an inOrder traversal of rightTree(*t*), namely,

25

Since the left subtree of this single-element tree *t* is empty, we process the root element of *t,* namely 25. We are now done since *t*'s right subtree is also empty.

The complete listing is

47  31  42  50  25

Figure 9.15 shows the original tree, with arrows to indicate the order in which elements are processed.

The inOrder traversal gets its name from the fact that, for a special kind of binary tree—a binary search tree—an inOrder traversal will process the elements in order. For example, Figure 9.16 has a binary search tree.

An inOrder traversal processes the elements of the tree in Figure 9.16 as follows:

25, 31, 42, 47, 50

In a binary search tree, all of the elements in the left subtree are less than the root element, which is less than all of the elements in the right subtree. What other property do you think a binary search tree must have so that an inOrder traversal processes the elements in order? ***Hint:*** The binary tree in Figure 9.17 is *not* a binary search tree.

We will devote Chapters 10 and 12 to the study of binary search trees.

**Figure 9.15 |** An inOrder traversal of a binary tree.

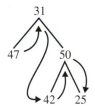

**Figure 9.16 |** A binary search tree.

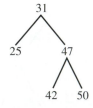

**Figure 9.17 |** A binary tree that is not a binary search tree.

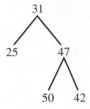

**Traversal 2. postOrder Traversal: Left-Right-Root** The idea behind this recursive algorithm is that we perform postOrder traversals of the left and right sub-trees before processing the root element. The algorithm, with *t* a binary tree, is:

```
postOrder (t)
{
        if (t is not empty)
        {
                postOrder (leftTree (t));
                postOrder (rightTree (t));
                process the root element of t;
        } // if
} // postOrder traversal
```

Just as with an inOrder traversal, the worstTime($n$) for a postOrder traversal is linear in $n$ because there are $2n$ recursive calls to postOrder($t$).

Suppose we conduct a postOrder traversal of the binary tree in Figure 9.18. A postOrder traversal of the binary tree in Figure 9.18 will process the elements in the path shown in Figure 9.19.

In a linear form, the postOrder traversal shown in Figure 9.19 is

A B C + *

We can view the binary tree in Figure 9.18 as an *expression tree:* each nonleaf is a binary operator whose operands are the associated left and right subtrees. With this interpretation, a postOrder traversal produces postfix notation!

**Figure 9.18 |** A binary tree.

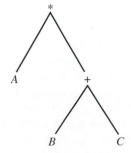

**Figure 9.19 |** The path followed by a postOrder traversal of the binary tree in Figure 9.18.

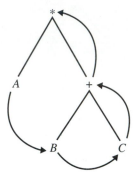

**Traversal 3. preOrder Traversal: Root-Left-Right**  Here we process the root element and then perform preOrder traversals of the left and right subtrees. The algorithm, with *t* a binary tree, is:

```
preOrder (t)
{
        if (t is not empty)
        {
                process the root element of t;
                preOrder (leftTree (t));
                preOrder (rightTree (t));
        } // if
} // preOrder traversal
```

As with the inOrder and postOrder algorithms, worstTime($n$) is linear in $n$. For example, a preOrder traversal of the binary tree in Figure 9.20 will process the elements in the order indicated in Figure 9.21.

If we linearize the path in Figure 9.21, we get

* A + B C

For an expression tree, a preOrder traversal produces prefix notation.

A search of a binary tree that employs a preOrder traversal is called a ***depth-first search*** because the search goes to the left as deeply as possible before searching to the right. The search stops when (if) the element sought is found, so the traversal may not be completed. For an example of a depth-first search, Figure 9.22 shows a binary tree and the path followed by a depth-first search for H.

The *backtracking* strategy from Chapter 5 includes a depth-first search, but at each stage there may be more than two choices. For example, in the maze-search, the choices are to move north, east, south, or west. Because moving north is the first option, that option will be repeatedly applied until either the goal is reached or moving north is not possible. Then a move east will be taken, if possible, and then as many moves north as possible or necessary. And so on. In Chapter 15, we will revisit backtracking for a generalization of binary trees.

**Figure 9.20 |** An expression tree.

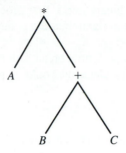

**Figure 9.21 |** The order in which the elements in the expression tree of Figure 9.20 are processed.

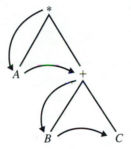

**Figure 9.22 |** A depth-first search for H.

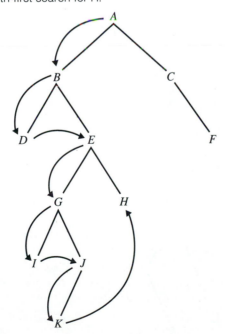

**Traversal 4. breadthFirst Traversal: Level-by-Level** To perform a breadth-first traversal of a nonempty binary tree *t,* first process the root element, then the children of the root, from left to right, then the grandchildren of the root, from left to right, and so on.

For example, suppose we perform a breadth-first traversal of the binary tree in Figure 9.23. The order in which elements would be processed in a breadthFirst traversal of the tree in Figure 9.23 is

A B C D E F G H I J K

One way to accomplish this traversal is to generate, level-by-level, a list of (references to) nonempty subtrees. We need to retrieve these subtrees in the same order they were generated so the elements can be processed level-by-level. What kind of collection allows retrievals in the same order as insertions? A queue! Here is the algorithm, with *t* a binary tree:

```
breadthFirst (t)
{
        // queue is a queue of (references to) binary trees
        // tree is a (reference to a) binary tree
        if (t is not empty)
        {
                queue.enqueue (t);
                while (queue is not empty)
```

**Figure 9.23 I** A binary tree.

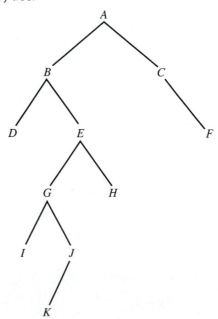

```
            {
                tree = queue.dequeue( );
                process tree's root;
                if (leftTree (tree) is not empty)
                        queue.enqueue (leftTree (tree));
                if (rightTree (tree) is not empty)
                        queue.enqueue (rightTree (tree));
            } // while
        } // if t not empty
    } // breadthFirst traversal
```

During each loop iteration, one element is processed, so worstTime($n$) is linear in $n$.

We used a queue for a breadth-first traversal because we wanted the subtrees retrieved in the same order they were saved (first in, first out). With inOrder, post Order, and preOrder traversals, the subtrees are retrieved in the reverse of the order they were saved in (last in, first out). For each of those three traversals, we utilized recursion, which, as we saw in Chapter 8, can be replaced with an iterative, stack-based algorithm.

We will encounter this type of traversal again in Chapter 15 when we study breadth-first traversals of structures less restrictive than binary trees. Incidentally, if we are willing to be more restrictive, specifically, if we require a complete binary tree, then the tree can be implemented with an array, and a breadth-first traversal is simply an iteration through the array. The root is at index 0, the root's left child at index 1, the root's right child at index 2, the root's leftmost grandchild at index 3, and so on.

## SUMMARY

A *binary tree* $t$ is either empty or consists of an element, called the *root element,* and two distinct binary trees, called the *left subtree* and *right subtree* of $t$. This is a recursive definition, and there are recursive definitions for many of the related terms: height, number of leaves, number of elements, two-tree, full tree, and so on. The interrelationships among some of these terms is given by the binary tree theorem.

---

**Binary Tree Theorem**   For any nonempty binary tree $t$,

$$\text{leaves}(t) \leq \frac{n(t) + 1}{2.0} \leq 2^{\text{height}(t)}$$

Equality holds for the first relation if and only if $t$ is a two-tree. Equality holds for the second relation if and only if $t$ is a full tree.

---

For a binary tree $t$, the *external path length* of $t$, written $E(t)$, is the sum of the distances from the root to the leaves of $t$. A lower bound for comparison-based sorting algorithms can be obtained from the external path length theorem.

> **External Path Length Theorem**   Let $t$ be a binary tree with $k > 0$ leaves. Then
>
> $$E(t) \geq (k \, / \, 2) \, \text{floor}(\log_2 k)$$

There are four commonly used traversals of a binary tree: inOrder (recursively: left subtree, root item, right subtree), postOrder (recursively: left subtree, right subtree, root item), preOrder (recursively: root item, left subtree, right subtree), and breadth-first (that is, starting at the root, level-by-level, and left-to-right at each level).

## CONCEPT EXERCISES

**9.1**   Answer the questions below about the following binary tree:

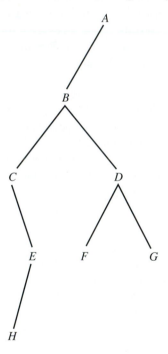

 **a.**   What is the root element?
 **b.**   How many elements are in the tree?
 **c.**   How many leaves are in the tree?
 **d.**   What is the height of the tree?
 **e.**   What is the height of the left subtree?
 **f.**   What is the height of the right subtree?
 **g.**   What is the level of $F$?
 **h.**   What is the depth of $C$?

    **i.**   How many children does *C* have?

    **j.**   What is the parent of *F*?

    **k.**   What are the descendants of *B*?

    **l.**   What are the ancestors of *F*?

    **m.**  What would the output be if the elements were written out during an inOrder traversal?

    **n.**  What would the output be if the elements were written out during a postOrder traversal?

    **o.**  What would the output be if the elements were written out during a preOrder traversal?

    **p.**  What would the output be if the elements were written out during a breadth-first traversal?

**9.2**  **a.**   Construct a binary tree of height 3 that has 8 elements.

    **b.**   Can you construct a binary tree of height 2 that has 8 elements?

    **c.**   For *n* going from 1 to 20, determine the minimum height possible for a binary tree with *n* elements.

    **d.**   On the basis of your calculations in part c, try to develop a formula for the minimum height possible for a binary tree with *n* elements, where *n* can be any positive integer.

    **e.**   Use the Principle of Mathematical Induction (strong form) to prove the correctness of your formula in part d.

**9.3**  **a.**   What is the maximum number of leaves possible in a binary tree with 10 elements? Construct such a tree.

    **b.**   What is the minimum number of leaves possible in a binary tree with 10 elements? Construct such a tree.

**9.4**  **a.**   Construct a two-tree that is not complete.

    **b.**   Construct a complete tree that is not a two-tree.

    **c.**   Construct a complete two-tree that is not full.

    **d.**   How many leaves are there in a two-tree with 17 elements?

    **e.**   How many leaves are there in a two-tree with 731 elements?

    **f.**   A two-tree must always have an odd number of elements. Why? *Hint:* Use the Binary Tree Theorem and the fact that the number of leaves must be an integer.

    **g.**   How many elements are there in a full binary tree of height 4?

    **h.**   How many elements are there in a full binary tree of height 12?

    **i.**   Use the Binary Tree Theorem to determine the number of leaves in a full binary tree with 63 elements.

    **j.**   Construct a complete two-tree that is not full, but in which the heights of the left and right subtrees are equal.

**9.5**   For the following binary tree, show the order in which elements would be processed for an inOrder, postOrder, preOrder, and breadthFirst traversal.

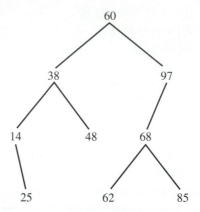

**9.6**   Show that a binary tree with $n$ elements has $2n + 1$ subtrees (including the entire tree). How many of these subtrees are empty?

**9.7**   Show that if $t$ is a complete binary tree, then

$$\text{height}(t) = \text{ceil}[\log_2(n(t) + 1)] - 1$$

The ceil function returns the smallest integer greater than or equal to its argument. For example, $\text{ceil}(35.3) = 36$.

*Hint:* Let $t$ be a complete binary tree and let $t1$ be a full binary tree whose height is one less than $t$'s. Let $t2$ be a full binary tree whose height is the same as $t$'s. So $n(t1) < n(t) \leq n(t2)$. Because the $\log_2$ function is strictly increasing:

$$\log_2(n(t1) + 1) - 1 < \log_2(n(t) + 1) - 1 \leq \log_2(n(t2) + 1) - 1$$

The value of the left-hand side of the first inequality is an integer (why?) that is exactly one less than the value of the integer on the right-hand side of the second inequality (why?). So

$$\text{ceil}(\log_2(n(t) + 1)) - 1 = \log_2(n(t2) + 1) - 1$$

Also,

$$\text{height}(t) = \text{height}(t2) \quad (\text{why?})$$

**9.8**   The Binary Tree Theorem is stated for nonempty binary trees. Show that parts 1, 2, and 4 hold even for an empty binary tree.

**9.9**   Give an example of a nonempty binary tree that is *not* a two-tree but $\text{leaves}(t) = (n(t) + 1)/2$

*Hint:* The denominator is 2, not 2.0, so integer division is performed.

**9.10**   Let $t$ be a nonempty tree. Show that if

$$\text{leaves}(t) = \frac{n(t) + 1}{2.0}$$

then either both subtrees of $t$ are empty or both subtrees of $t$ are nonempty.

**9.11** Show that in any complete binary tree $t$, at least half of the elements are leaves. *Hint:* If $t$ is empty, there are no elements, so the claim is vacuously true. If the leaf at the highest index is a right child, then $t$ is a two-tree, and the claim follows from part 3 of the Binary Tree Theorem. Otherwise, $t$ was formed by adding a left child to the complete two-tree with $n(t) - 1$ elements.

**9.12** Compare the inOrder traversal algorithm in Section 9.5 with the move method from the Towers of Hanoi application in Section 5.4 of Chapter 5. They have the same structure, but worstTime($n$) is linear in $n$ for the inOrder algorithm and exponential in $n$ for the move method. Explain.

**9.13** Let $t$ be a nonempty binary tree. Use the strong form of the Principle of Mathematical Induction to show each of the following:

**a.** $\dfrac{n(t) + 1}{2.0} \le 2^{\text{height}(t)}$

**b.** If $t$ is a two-tree, then $\text{leaves}(t) = \dfrac{n(t) + 1}{2.0}$

**c.** If $t$ is a full tree, then $\dfrac{n(t) + 1}{2.0} = 2^{\text{height}(t)}$

*Hint:* The outline of the proof is the same as in Example 5 of Appendix 2.

**9.14** Let $t$ be a nonempty binary tree. Use the strong form of the Principle of Mathematical Induction to show each of the following:

**a.** If $\text{leaves}(t) = \dfrac{n(t) + 1}{2.0}$ then $t$ is a two-tree.

**b.** If $\dfrac{n(t) + 1}{2.0} = 2^{\text{height}(t)}$ then $t$ is a full tree.

*Hint:* The proof for both parts has the same outline. For example, here is the outline for part a:

For $h = 0, 1, 2, \ldots$, let $S_h$ be the statement.

If $t$ is a binary tree of height $h$ and

$$\text{leaves}(t) = \frac{n(t) + 1}{2.0}$$

then $t$ is a two-tree.

In the inductive case, let $h$ be any nonnegative integer and assume that $S_0, S_1, \ldots, S_h$ are all true. To show that $S_{h+1}$ is true, let $t$ be a binary tree of height $h + 1$ such that

$$\text{leaves}(t) = \frac{n(t) + 1}{2.0}$$

First, show that

leaves(leftTree($t$)) + leaves(rightTree($t$))

$$= \frac{n(\text{leftTree}(t)) + 1}{2.0} + \frac{n(\text{rightTree}(t)) + 1}{2.0}$$

For any nonnegative integers $a$, $b$, $c$, and $d$, if $a + b = c + d$ and $a \le c$ and $b \le d$, then $a = c$ and $b = d$.

**9.15**   Find the flaw in the following proof.

***Claim:*** All dogs have the same hair color.

***Proof:*** For $n = 1, 2, \ldots$, let $S_n$ be the statement:

    In any set of $n$ dogs, all dogs in the set have the same hair color.

***Base case:*** If $n = 1$, there is only one dog in the set, so all dogs in that set have the same hair color. Thus, $S_1$ is true.

***Inductive case:*** Let $n$ be any positive integer and assume that $S_n$ is true; that is, in any set of $n$ dogs, all the dogs in the group have the same hair color. We need to show that $S_{n+1}$ is true. Suppose we have a set of $n + 1$ dogs:

$d_1, d_2, d_3, \ldots, d_n, d_{n+1}$

The set $d_1, d_2, d_3, \ldots, d_n$ has size $n$, so by the induction hypothesis, all the dogs in that set have the same hair color.

    The set $d_2, d_3, \ldots, d_n, d_{n+1}$ also has size $n$, so by the induction hypothesis, all the dogs in that set have the same hair color.

    But the two sets have at least one dog, $d_n$, in common. So whatever color that dog's hair is must be the color of all dogs in both sets, that is, of all $n + 1$ dogs. In other words, $S_{n+1}$ is true.

Therefore, by the Principle of Mathematical Induction, $S_n$ is true for any nonnegative integer $n$.

# Binary Search Trees

In Chapter 9, you studied an important conceptual tool: the binary tree. This chapter presents the binary search tree data type and a corresponding data structure, the BinarySearchTree class. BinarySearchTree objects are valuable collections because they require only logarithmic time, on average, for inserting, removing, and searching (but linear time in the worst case). This performance is far better than the linear average-case time for insertions, removals, and searches in an array, ArrayList, or LinkedList object. For example, if $n = 1,000,000,000$, $\log_2 n < 30$.

The BinarySearchTree class is not part of the Java Collections Framework. The reason for this omission is that the framework includes the TreeMap class, which boasts logarithmic time for inserting, removing, and searching even in the worst case. The BinarySearchTree class should be viewed as a "toy" class that is simple enough for you to play with and will help you to better understand the TreeMap class. The implementation of the TreeMap class is based on a kind of "balanced" binary search tree, namely, the red-black tree.

To further prepare you for the study of red-black trees and the TreeMap class, this chapter also explains what it means to say that a binary search tree is balanced. To add some substance to that discussion, we introduce the AVL tree data type, which is somewhat simpler to understand than the red-black tree data type. ■

## CHAPTER OBJECTIVES

1. Compare the time efficiency of the BinarySearchTree class's insertion, removal, and search methods to that of the corresponding methods in the ArrayList and LinkedList classes.

2. Discuss the similarities and differences of the BinarySearchTree class's contains method and the binarySearch methods in the Arrays and Collections classes.

3. Explain why the BinarySearchTree class's remove method and the TreeIterator class's next method are somewhat difficult to define.

4. Be able to perform each of the four possible rotations.

5. Understand why the height of an AVL tree is always logarithmic in $n$.

## 10.1 | BINARY SEARCH TREES

We start with a recursive definition of a binary search tree:

A **binary search tree** *t* is a binary tree such that either *t* is empty or

1.   Each element in leftTree(*t*) is less than the root element of *t*.

2.   Each element in rightTree(*t*) is greater than the root element of *t*.

3.   Both leftTree(*t*) and rightTree(*t*) are binary search trees.

Figure 10.1 shows a binary search tree.

An inOrder traversal of a binary search tree accesses the items in increasing order. For example, with the binary search tree in Figure 10.1, an inOrder traversal accesses the following sequence:

15 25 28 30 32 36 37 50 55 59 61 68 75

As we have defined a binary search tree, duplicate elements are not permitted. Some authors have "less than or equal to" and "greater than or equal to" in the above definition. For the sake of consistency with some classes in the Java Collections Framework that are based on binary search trees, we opt for strictly less than and strictly greater than.

Section 10.1.1 describes the BinarySearchTree class. As we noted at the beginning of this chapter, this is a "toy" class that provides a gentle introduction to related

**Figure 10.1** | A binary search tree.

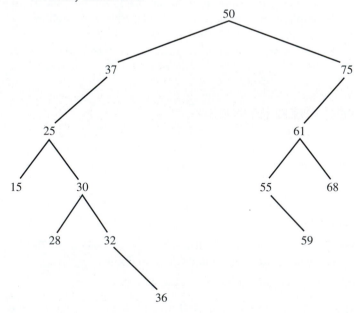

classes in the Java Collections Framework. Much of the code for the Binary SearchTree class is either identical to or a simplification of code in the TreeMap class of the Java Collections Framework. Overall, the BinarySearchTree class's performance is not good enough for applications—because its worst-case height is linear in *n*—but you will be asked to add new methods and to modify existing methods.

### 10.1.1 The BinarySearchTree Implementation of the Set Interface

We will study the binary-search-tree data type through the method specifications of the BinarySearchTree class. The BinarySearchTree class is not part of the Java Collections Framework, but it implements the Collection interface. In fact, the Binary SearchTree class implements a slight extension of the Collection interface: the Set interface. The Set interface does not provide any new methods. The only difference between the Collection and Set interfaces is that duplicate elements are not allowed in a Set, and this affects the specifications of the default constructor and the add method in the BinarySearchTree class. We will see these differences shortly.

Another feature that distinguishes the BinarySearchTree class from previous Collection classes we have seen is that the elements in a BinarySearchTree must be maintained in order. For simplicity, we assume that the elements are instances of a class that implements the Comparable interface, which was introduced in Section 5.5. Here is that interface:

```
public interface Comparable
{
     /**
      * Returns an int less than, equal to, or greater than 0, depending on
      * whether the calling object is less than, equal to, or greater than a
      * specified object.
      *
      * @param obj – the specified object that the calling object is compared to.
      *
      * @return an int value less than, equal to, or greater than 0, depending on
      *         whether the calling object is less than, equal to, or greater than
      *         obj, respectively.
      *
      * @throws ClassCastException – if the calling object and obj are not in the
      *         same class.
      *
      */
     public int compareTo(Object obj)
} // interface Comparable
```

From now on, when we refer to the "natural" order of elements, we assume that the element's class implements the Comparable interface; then the natural order is the order imposed by the compareTo method in the element's class. For example, the Integer class implements the Comparable interface, and the "natural" order of Integer objects is based on the numeric comparison of the underlying **int** values. For example, suppose we have the following:

```
Integer myInt = new Integer (25);

System.out.println (myInt.compareTo (107));
```

The output will be less than 0 because 25 is less than 107. Specifically, the output will be −1 because when the compareTo method is used for numeric comparisons, the result is either −1, 0, or 1, depending on whether the calling object is less than, equal to, or greater than the argument.

For a more involved example, the following Student class has name and gpa fields. The compareTo method uses the alphabetical ordering of names; for equal names, the ordering is by *decreasing* grade point averages. For example,

```
new Student ("Lodato", 3.8).compareTo (new Student ("Zsoldos", 3.5))
```

returns −1 because "Lodato" is, alphabetically, less than "Zsoldos". But

```
new Student ("Dufresne", 3.4).compareTo (new Student ("Dufresne", 3.6))
```

returns 1 because 3.4 is less than 3.6, and the return value reflects decreasing order.
Here is the Student class:

```java
public class Student implements Comparable
{
        protected String name;

        protected double gpa;

        public Student( ) { }

        /**
         * Initializes this Student object from a specified name and gpa.
         *
         * @param name – the specified name.
         * @param gpa – the specified gpa.
         *
         */
        public Student (String name, double gpa)
        {
                this.name = name;
                this.gpa = gpa;
        } // constructor

        /**
         * Compares this Student object with a specified object.
         * The comparison is alphabetical; for two objects with the same name,
         * the comparison is by grade point averages.
         *
```

```
* @param obj – the specified object that this Student
*       object is being compared to.
*
* @return −1, if this Student object's name is alphabetically less than obj's
*                name, or if the names are equal and this Student object's grade
*                point average is greater than obj's grade point average;
*            0, if this Student object's name and grade point average
*                are the same as obj's name and grade point average;
*            1, if this Student object's name is alphabetically greater
*                than obj's name, or if the names are equal and
*                this Student object's grade point average is less than
*                obj's grade point average.
*
* @throws ClassCastException – if the run-time type of obj is not Student.
*
*/
public int compareTo (Object obj)
{
        Student otherStudent = (Student)obj;
        if (name.compareTo (otherStudent.name) < 0)
                return −1;
        if (name.compareTo (otherStudent.name) > 0)
                return 1;
        if (gpa > otherStudent.gpa)
                return −1;
        if (gpa < otherStudent.gpa)
                return 1;
        return 0;
} // method compareTo

/**
 * Determines if this Student object's name and grade point average are
 * the same as some specified object.
 *
 * @param obj – the specified object that this Student object is being
 *       compared to.
 *
 * @return true – if obj is a Student object and this Student object has the
 *       same name and grade point average as obj.
 *
 */
public boolean equals (Object obj)
{
        return (obj instanceof Student) &&
                name.equals (((Student)obj).name) &&
                gpa == ((Student)obj).gpa;
```

```
        } // method equals

        /**
         * Returns a String representation of this Student object.
         *
         * @return a String representation of this Student object: name, blank,
         *         grade point average.
         *
         */
        public String toString( )
        {
                return name + " " + gpa;
        } // method toString

} // class Student
```

Rather than start from scratch, we will let the BinarySearchTree class extend some class already in the Framework. Then we need implement only those methods whose definitions are specific to the BinarySearchTree class. The AbstractSet class is a good place to start. That class has garden-variety implementations for many of the Set methods: isEmpty, toArray, clear, and the bulk operations (addAll, contains All, removeAll, and retainAll). So the class heading is

```
public class BinarySearchTree<E> extends AbstractSet<E>
```

Figure 10.2 shows the relationships among the classes and interfaces we have discussed so far.

Here are the method specifications for the methods we will explicitly implement:

```
/**
 * Initializes this BinarySearchTree object to be empty, to contain only elements
 * of type E, to be ordered by the Comparable interface, and to contain no
 * duplicate elements.
 *
 */
public BinarySearchTree( )

/**
 * Initializes this BinarySearchTree object to contain a shallow copy of
 * a specified BinarySearchTree object.
 * The worstTime(n) is O(n), where n is the number of elements in the
 * specified BinarySearchTree object.
 *
 * @param otherTree − the specified BinarySearchTree object that this
 *        BinarySearchTree object will be assigned a shallow copy of.
 *
 */
public BinarySearchTree (BinarySearchTree<E> otherTree)

/**
```

**Figure 10.2 |** A UML diagram that includes part of the BinarySearchTree class.

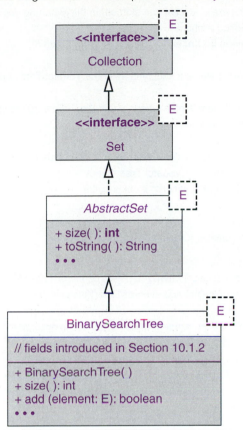

```
 * Returns the size of this BinarySearchTree object.
 *
 * @return the size of this BinarySearchTree object.
 *
 */
public int size( )

/**
 * Returns an iterator positioned at the smallest element in this
 * BinarySearchTree object.
 *
 * @return an iterator positioned at the smallest element in this
 *         BinarySearchTree object.
 *
 */
public Iterator<E> iterator( )
```

```
/**
 * Determines if there is at least one element in this BinarySearchTree object that
 * equals a specified element.
 * The worstTime(n) is O(n) and averageTime(n) is O(log n).
 *
 * @param obj – the element sought in this BinarySearchTree object.
 *
 * @return true – if there is an element in this BinarySearchTree object that
 *         equals obj; otherwise, return false.
 *
 * @throws ClassCastException – if obj cannot be compared to the
 *         elements in this BinarySearchTree object.
 * @throws NullPointerException – if obj is null.
 *
 */
public boolean contains (Object obj)

/**
 * Ensures that this BinarySearchTree object contains a specified element.
 * The worstTime(n) is O(n) and averageTime(n) is O(log n).
 *
 * @param element – the element whose presence is ensured in this
 *         BinarySearchTree object.
 *
 * @return true – if this BinarySearchTree object changed as a result of this
 *         method call (that is, if element was actually inserted); otherwise,
 *         return false.
 *
 * @throws ClassCastException – if element cannot be compared to the
 *         elements already in this BinarySearchTree object.
 * @throws NullPointerException – if element is null.
 *
 */
public boolean add (E element)

/**
 * Ensures that this BinarySearchTree object does not contain a specified
 * element.
 * The worstTime(n) is O(n) and averageTime(n) is O(log n).
 *
 * @param obj – the object whose absence is ensured in this
 *         BinarySearchTree object.
 *
 * @return true – if this BinarySearchTree object changed as a result of this
 *         method call (that is, if obj was actually removed); otherwise,
 *         return false.
 *
```

```
* @throws ClassCastException – if obj cannot be compared to the
*       elements in this BinarySearchTree object.
* @throws NullPointerException – if obj is null.
*
*/
public boolean remove (Object obj)
```

These method specifications, together with the method specifications of methods not overridden from the AbstractSet class, constitute the abstract data type Binary Search Tree: all that is needed for *using* the BinarySearchTree class. For example, here is a main method that creates and manipulates three BinarySearchTree objects: two of String elements and one of Student elements:

```
public static void main (String[ ] args)
{
        BinarySearchTree<String> tree1 = new BinarySearchTree<String>( );
        tree1.add ("yes");
        tree1.add ("no");
        tree1.add ("maybe");
        tree1.add ("always");
        tree1.add ("no"); // not added: duplicate element
        if (tree1.remove ("often"))
                System.out.println ("How did that happen?");
        else
                System.out.println (tree1.remove ("maybe"));
        System.out.println (tree1);

        BinarySearchTree<String> tree2 = new BinarySearchTree<String> (tree1);

        System.out.println (tree2);

        BinarySearchTree<Student> tree3 = new BinarySearchTree<Student>( );

        tree3.add (new Student ("Jones", 3.17));
        tree3.add (new Student ("Smith", 3.82));
        tree3.add (new Student ("Jones", 3.5));
        if (tree3.contains (new Student ("Smith", 3.82)))
                System.out.println ("The number of elements in tree3 is " +
                                        tree3.size( ));
        System.out.println (tree3);
} // method main
```

The output is

```
true

[always, no, yes]
[always, no, yes]

The number of elements in tree3 is 3

[Jones 3.5, Jones 3.17, Smith 3.82]
```

### 10.1.2 **Implementation of the** BinarySearchTree **Class**

In this section, we will develop an implementation of the BinarySearchTree class. To confirm that Binary Search Tree is an abstract data type that has several possible implementations, you will have the opportunity in Programming Project 10.1 to develop an array-based implementation.

The only methods we need to implement are the seven methods described in Section 10.1.1. But to implement the iterator( ) method, we will need to develop a class that implements the Iterator interface, with hasNext( ), next( ), and remove( ) methods. So we will create a TreeIterator class embedded within the BinarySearch Tree class.

The definitions of the default constructor, size( ), iterator( ), and hasNext( ) are one-liners. Also, the definition of the copy constructor is straightforward, and the TreeIterator class's remove method is almost identical to the BinarySearchTree class's remove method. But the remaining four methods—contains, add, and remove in BinarySearchTree, and next in TreeIterator—get to the heart of how the implementation of the BinarySearchTree class differs from that of, say, the LinkedList class.

**Fields and Nested Classes in the** BinarySearchTree **Class**   What fields and embedded classes should we have in the BinarySearchTree class? We have already noted the need for a TreeIterator class. From the fact that a binary search tree is a binary tree—with a root item and two subtrees—and from our earlier investigation of the LinkedList class, we can see the value of having an embedded Entry class. The only fields in the BinarySearchTree class are:

> **protected** Entry<E> root;

> **protected int** size;

The Entry class, as you may have expected, has an element field, of type (reference to) E, and left and right fields, of type (reference to) Entry. To facilitate going back up the tree during an iteration, the Entry class will also have a parent field, of type (reference to) Entry. Figure 10.3 shows the representation of a BinarySearch Tree object with elements of type (reference to) String. To simplify the figure, we pretend that the elements are of type String instead of reference to String.

Here is the nested Entry class:

```
protected static class Entry<E>
{
    protected E element;

    protected Entry<E> left = null,
                       right = null,
                       parent;

    /**
     * Initializes this Entry object from element and parent.
     *
     */
```

**Figure 10.3 |** A BinarySearchTree object with four elements.

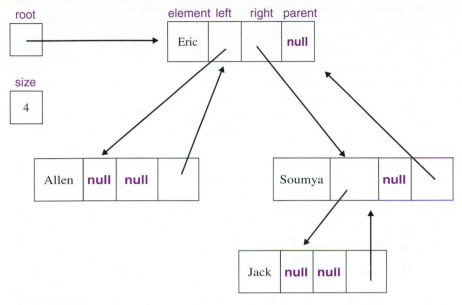

```
        protected Entry <E> (E element, Entry<E> parent)
        {
               this.element = element;
               this.parent = parent;
        } // constructor

   } // class Entry
```

   Recall, from Section 7.3.5, that the Entry class nested in the Java Collections Framework's LinkedList class was given the **static** modifier. The BinarySearchTree's nested Entry class is made static for the same reason: to avoid the time and space needed to maintain a reference back to the enclosing object.

   Now that we have declared the fields and nested classes, we are ready to tackle the BinarySearchTree method definitions.

**Implementation of Simple Methods in the** BinarySearchTree **Class** We can immediately develop a few method definitions:

```
   public BinarySearchTree( )
   {
          root = null;
          size = 0;
   } // default constructor
```

   We could have omitted the assignments to the root and size fields because each field is given a default initial value (**null** for a reference, 0 for an **int**, **false** for a

**boolean**, and so on) just prior to the invocation of the constructor. But explicit assignments facilitate understanding; default initializations do not.

```java
public int size( )
{
        return size;
} // method size( )

public Iterator<E> iterator( )
{
        return new TreeIterator( );
} // method iterator

public BinarySearchTree (BinarySearchTree<E> otherTree)
{
        root = null;
        size = 0;
        for (E element : otherTree)
                add (element);
} // copy constructor
```

**Definition of the** contains **Method**   The elements in a binary search tree are stored in the "natural" order, that is, the order imposed by the compareTo method in the element class. The definition of the contains (Object obj) method takes advantage of that fact by moving down the tree in the direction of where obj is or belongs. Specifically, an Entry object temp is initialized to root and then obj is compared to temp.element in a loop. If they are equal, **true** is returned. If obj is less than temp.element, temp is replaced with temp.left. Otherwise, temp is replaced with temp.right. The loop continues until temp is **null**. Here is the complete definition:

```java
public boolean contains (Object obj)
{
        Entry<E> temp = root;

        int comp;

        while (temp != null)
        {
                comp = ((Comparable)obj).compareTo (temp.element);
                if (comp == 0)
                        return true;
                else if (comp < 0)
                        temp = temp.left;
                else
                        temp = temp.right;
        } // while
        return false;
} // method contains
```

The cast of obj to a Comparable object is necessary for the compiler because the Object class does not have a compareTo method.

How long does this method take? For this method, indeed, for all of the non-easy methods in the BinarySearchTree class, the essential feature for estimating worstTime($n$) or averageTime($n$) is the *height* of the tree. Suppose the search is successful; a similar analysis can be used for the unsuccessful case. In the worst case, we will have a chain, and will be seeking the leaf. For example, suppose we are seeking 25 in the binary search tree in Figure 10.4. In such a case, the number of loop iterations is equal to the height of the tree. In general, if $n$ is the number of elements in the tree, and the tree is a chain, the height of the tree is $n - 1$, so worstTime($n$) is linear in $n$.

We now determine averageTime($n$) for a successful search. Again, the crucial factor is the height of the tree. For binary search trees constructed through random insertions and removals, the average height H is logarithmic in $n$—see Cormen (2002). The contains method starts searching at level 0, and each loop iteration descends to the next lower level in the tree. Since averageTime($n$) requires no more than $H$ iterations, we immediately conclude that averageTime($n$) is $O(\log n)$. That is, averageTime($n$) is less than or equal to some function of $\log n$.

To establish that averageTime($n$) is logarithmic in $n$, we must also show that averageTime($n$) is greater than or equal to some function of $\log n$. The average—over all binary search trees—number of iterations is greater than or equal to the average number of iterations for a complete binary search tree with $n$ elements. In a complete binary tree $t$, at least half of the elements are leaves (see Concept Exercise 9.11), so the average number of iterations by the contains method must be at least (height($t$) − 1)/2, which, by Concept Exercise 9.7, is (ceil ($\log_2(n(t) + 1)$) − 2)/2. That is, the average number of iterations for the contains method is greater than or

**Figure 10.4 |** A binary search tree.

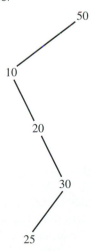

equal to a function of log $n$. So averageTime($n$) is greater than or equal to some function of log $n$.

We conclude from the two previous paragraphs that averageTime($n$) is logarithmic in $n$. Incidentally, that is why we defined the contains method above instead of inheriting the one in the AbstractCollection class (the superclass of AbstractSet). For that version, an iterator loops through the elements in the tree, starting with the smallest, so its averageTime($n$) is linear in $n$.

The binary search tree gets its name from the situation that arises when the contains method is invoked on a full tree. For then the contains method accesses the same elements, in the same order, as a binary search of an array with the same elements. For example, the root element in a full binary search tree corresponds to the middle element in the array.

You may have been surprised (and even disappointed!) that the definition of the contains method was not recursive. Up to this point in our study of binary trees, most of the concepts—including binary search tree itself—were defined recursively. But when it comes to method definitions, looping is the rule rather than the exception. Why is that? The glib answer is that left and right are of type Entry, not of type Binary SearchTree, so we cannot call

```
left.contains(obj) // illegal
```

But we can make contains a wrapper method for a protected, recursive contains Element method:

```
public boolean contains (Object obj)
{
        return containsElement (root, obj);
} // method contains

protected boolean containsElement (Entry<E> p, Object obj)
{
      if (p == null)
            return false;
      int comp = ((Comparable)obj).compareTo (p.element);

      if (comp == 0)
            return true;
      if (comp < 0)
            return containsElement (p.left, obj);
      return containsElement (p.right, obj);
} // method contains
```

This recursive version would be nominally less efficient—in both time and space—than the iterative version above. And it is this slight difference that sinks the recursive version. For the iterative version is virtually identical to one in the TreeMap class, part of the Java Collections Framework, where efficiency is prized above elegance. Besides, some of the luster of recursion is diminished by the necessity of having a wrapper method.

**Definition of the add Method**  The definition of the add (E element) method is only slightly more complicated than the definition of contains (Object obj). Basically, the add method starts at the root and branches down the tree searching for the element; if the search fails, the element is inserted as a leaf.

Specifically, if the tree is empty, we construct a new Entry object and initialize that object with the given element and a **null** parent, then increment the size field and return **true**. Otherwise, as we did in the definition of the contains method, we initialize an Entry object, temp, to root and compare element to temp.element in a loop. If element equals temp.element, we have an attempt to add a duplicate, so we return **false**. If element is less than temp.element, replace temp with temp.left unless temp.left is **null**, in which case we insert element in an Entry object whose parent is temp. The steps are similar when element is greater than temp.element.

For example, suppose we are trying to insert 45 into the binary search tree in Figure 10.5. The insertion is made in a loop that starts by comparing 45 to 31, the root element. Since 45 > 31, we advance to 47, the right child of 31. See Figure 10.6.

Because 45 < 47, we advance to 42, the left child of 47, as indicated in Figure 10.7. At this point, 45 > 42, so we would advance to the right child of 42 if 42 had a right child. It does not, so 45 is inserted as the right child of 42. See Figure 10.8.

**Figure 10.5 |** A binary search tree into which 45 will be inserted.

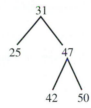

**Figure 10.6 |** The effect of comparing 45 to 31 in the binary search tree of Figure 10.5.

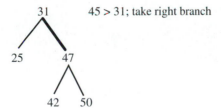

**Figure 10.7 |** The effect of comparing 45 to 47 in the binary search tree of Figure 10.6.

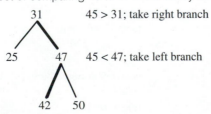

**Figure 10.8 |** The effect of inserting 45 into the binary search tree in Figure 10.7.

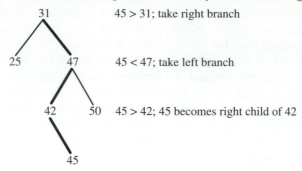

In general, the search fails if the element to be inserted belongs in an empty subtree of temp. Then the element is inserted as the only element in that subtree. That is, the inserted element *always becomes a leaf in the tree*. This has the advantage that the tree is not reorganized after an insertion.

An unusual feature of the following loop is that it continues indefinitely until, during some iteration, **true** (or **false**) is returned. Here is the complete definition:

```
public boolean add (E element)
{
      if (root == null)
      {
            root = new Entry<E> (element, null);
            size++;
            return true;
      } // empty tree
      else
      {
            Entry temp = root;

            int comp;

            while (true)
            {
                  comp = ((Comparable)element).compareTo (temp.element);
                  if (comp == 0)
                        return false;
                  if (comp < 0)
                        if (temp.left != null)
                              temp = temp.left;
                        else
                        {
                              temp.left = new Entry<E> (element, temp);
                              size++;
                              return true;
```

```
                            } // temp.left == null
                  else if (temp.right != null)
                          temp = temp.right;
                  else
                  {
                          temp.right = new Entry<E> (element, temp);
                          size++;
                          return true;
                  } // temp.right == null
          } // while
      } // root not null
  } // method add
```

The timing estimates for the add method are identical to those for the contains method, and depend on the height of the tree. To insert at the end of a binary search tree that forms a chain, the number of iterations is one more than the height of the tree. The height of a chain is linear in $n$, so worstTime($n$) is linear in $n$. And, with the same argument we used for the contains method, we conclude that averageTime($n$) is logarithmic in $n$.

In Programming Exercise 10.4, you will get the opportunity to define the add method recursively.

**The Definition of the remove Method**   The only other BinarySearchTree method to be defined is

```
          public boolean remove (Object obj)
```

The definition of the remove method in the BinarySearchTree class is more complicated than the definition of the add method above. The reason for the extra complexity is that the remove method requires a restructuring of the tree—unless the element to be removed is a leaf. With the add method, the inserted element always becomes a leaf, and no restructuring is needed.

The basic strategy is this: we first get (a reference to) the Entry object that holds the element to be removed, and then we delete that Entry object. Here is the definition:

```
  public boolean remove (Object obj)
  {
          Entry<E> e = getEntry (obj);
          if (e == null)
                  return false;
          deleteEntry (e);
          return true;
  } // method remove
```

Of course, we need to postpone the analysis of the remove method until we have developed both the getEntry and deleteEntry methods. The **protected** method get Entry searches the tree—in the same way as the contains method was defined in "Definition of the contains Method," above—for an Entry object whose element is obj. For example, Figure 10.9 shows what happens if the getEntry method is called to get a reference to the Entry whose element is 50.

Here is the definition of the getEntry method:

```
/**
 * Finds the Entry object that houses a specified element, if there is such an Entry.
 * The worstTime(n) is O(n), and averageTime(n) is O(log n).
 *
 * @param obj – the element whose Entry is sought.
 *
 * @return the Entry object that houses obj – if there is such an Entry;
 *         otherwise, return null.
 *
 * @throws ClassCastException – if obj is not comparable to the elements
 *         already in this BinarySearchTree object.
 * @throws NullPointerException – if obj is null.
 *
 */
protected Entry<E> getEntry (Object obj)
{
    int comp;

    Entry<E> e = root;
    while (e != null)
    {
        comp = ((Comparable)obj).compareTo (e.element);
        if (comp == 0)
            return e;
        else if (comp < 0)
```

**Figure 10.9 |** The effect of calling the getEntry method to get a reference to the Entry whose element is 50. A copy of the reference e is returned.

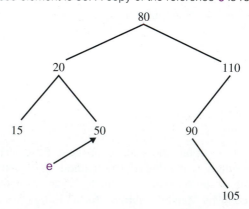

```
                        e = e.left;
                else
                        e = e.right;
        } // while
        return null;
    } // method getEntry
```

The analysis of the getEntry method is the same as for the contains method in "Definition of the contains Method": worstTime($n$) is linear in $n$ and averageTime($n$) is logarithmic in $n$.

The structure of the **while** loop in the getEntry method is identical to that in the contains method. In fact, we can redefine the contains method to call getEntry. Here is the new definition, now a one-liner:

```
    public boolean contains (Object obj)
    {
            return getEntry (obj) != null;
    } // method contains
```

For the deleteEntry method, let's start with a few simple examples of how a binary search tree is affected by a deletion; then we'll get into the details of defining the deleteEntry method. As noted above, removal of a leaf requires no restructuring. For example, suppose we remove 50 from the binary search tree in Figure 10.10. To delete 50 from the tree in that figure, all we need to do is change to **null** the right field of 50's parent Entry—the Entry object whose element is 20. We end up with the binary search tree in Figure 10.11.

In general, if p is (a reference to) the Entry object that contains the leaf element to be deleted, we first decide what to do if p is the root. In that case, we set

```
    root = null;
```

**Figure 10.10** | A binary search tree from which 50 is to be removed.

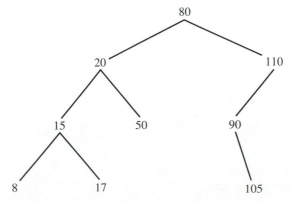

**Figure 10.11 |** The binary search tree from Figure 10.10 after the removal of 50.

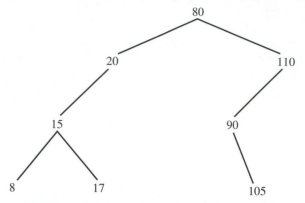

Otherwise, the determination of which child of p.parent gets the value **null** depends on whether p is a left child or a right child:

```
if (p == p.parent.left)
        p.parent.left = null;
else
        p.parent.right = null;
```

Notice how we check to see if p is a (reference to) a left child: if p equals p's parent's left child.

It is almost as easy to remove an element that has only one child. For example, suppose we want to remove 20 from the binary search tree in Figure 10.11. We cannot leave a hole in a binary search tree, so we must replace 20 with some element. Which one? The logical choice is 15, the child of the element to be removed. So we need to link 15 to 20's parent. When we do, we get the binary search tree shown in Figure 10.12.

In general, let replacement be the Entry that replaces p, which has exactly one child. Then replacement should get the value of either p.left or p.right, whichever is not empty—they cannot both be empty because p has one child. We can combine this case, where p has one child, with the previous case, where p has no children:

```
Entry replacement;
if (p.left != null)
        replacement = p.left;
else
        replacement = p.right;

// If p has at least one child, link replacement to p.parent.
if (replacement != null)
{
        replacement.parent = p.parent;
        if (p.parent == null)
```

**Figure 10.12 |** The binary search tree from Figure 10.11 after 20 was removed by replacing 20's entry with 15's entry.

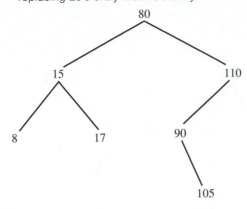

```
            root = replacement;
    else if (p == p.parent.left)
            p.parent.left = replacement;
    else
            p.parent.right = replacement;
} // p has at least one child
else if (p.parent == null) // p is the root and has no children
    root = null;
else    // p has a parent and has no children
{
    if (p == p.parent.left)
            p.parent.left = null;
    else
            p.parent.right = null;
} // p has a parent but no children
```

Finally, we come to the interesting case: when the element to be removed has two children. For example, suppose we want to remove 80 from the binary search tree in Figure 10.12.

As in the previous case, 80 must be replaced with some other element in the tree. But which one? To preserve the ordering, a removed element should be replaced with either its immediate predecessor (in this case, 17) or its immediate successor (in this case, 90). We will, in fact, need a successor method for an inOrder iterator. So assume we already have a successor method that returns an Entry object's immediate successor. In general, the immediate successor, s, of a given Entry object p is the leftmost Entry object in the subtree p.right. **Important:** the left child of this leftmost Entry object will be **null**. (Why?)

The removal of 80 from the tree in Figure 10.12 is accomplished as follows: first, we copy the successor's element to p.element, as shown in Figure 10.13. Next, we assign to p the value of (the reference) s. See Figure 10.14. Then we delete p's

**Figure 10.13 I** The first step in the removal of 80 from the binary search tree in Figure 10.12: 90, the immediate successor of 80, replaces 80.

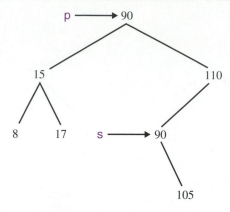

**Figure 10.14 I** The second step in the removal of 80 in the binary search tree of Figure 10.12: p points to the successor entry.

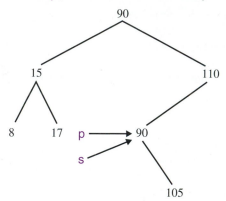

Entry object from the tree. As noted above, the left child of p must now be **null**, so the removal follows the replacement strategy of removing an element with no children or one child. In this case, p has a right child (105), so 105 replaces p's element, as shown in Figure 10.15.

Because the 2-children case reduces to the 0-or-1-child case developed earlier, the code for removal of any Entry object starts by handling the 2-children case, followed by the code for the 0-or-1-child case.

As we will see in Section 10.2.3, it is beneficial for subclasses of BinarySearch Tree if the deleteEntry method returns the Entry object that is actually deleted. For example, if the deleteEntry method is called to delete an entry that has two children, the successor of that entry is actually removed from the tree.

Here is the complete definition:

```
/**
 * Deletes the element in a specified Entry object from this BinarySearchTree.
```

**Figure 10.15 |** The final step in the removal of 80 from the binary search tree in Figure 10.12: p's element (90) is replaced with that element's right child (105).

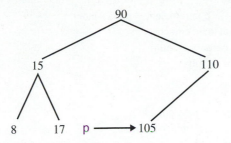

```
 *
 * @param p – the Entry object whose element is to be deleted from this
 *      BinarySearchTree object.
 *
 * @return the Entry object that was actually deleted from this BinarySearchTree
 *      object.
 *
 */
protected Entry<E> deleteEntry (Entry<E> p)
{
        size--;

        // If p has two children, replace p's element with p's successor's
        // element, then make p reference that successor.
        if (p.left != null && p.right != null)
        {
                Entry<E> s = successor (p);
                p.element = s.element;
                p = s;
        } // p had two children

        // At this point, p has either no children or one child.

        Entry<E> replacement;

        if (p.left != null)
                replacement = p.left;
        else
                replacement = p.right;

        // If p has at least one child, link replacement to p.parent.
        if (replacement != null)
        {
                replacement.parent = p.parent;
                if (p.parent == null)
                        root = replacement;
```

```
                    else if (p == p.parent.left)
                            p.parent.left = replacement;
                    else
                            p.parent.right = replacement;
                } // p has at least one child
                else if (p.parent == null)
                        root = null;
                else
                {
                        if (p == p.parent.left)
                                p.parent.left = null;
                        else
                                p.parent.right = null;
                } // p has a parent but no children

                return p;
        } // method deleteEntry
```

We still have the **successor** method to develop. Here is the method specification:

```
/**
 * Finds the successor of a specified Entry object in this BinarySearchTree.
 * The worstTime(n) is O(n) and averageTime(n) is constant.
 *
 * @param e – the Entry object whose successor is to be found.
 *
 * @return the successor of e, if e has a successor; otherwise, return null.
 *
 */
protected Entry<E> successor (Entry<E> e)
```

This method has **protected** visibility to reflect the fact that Entry—the return type and parameter type—has **protected** visibility.

How can we find the successor of an Entry object? For inspiration, look at the binary search tree in Figure 10.16.

In the tree in Figure 10.16, the successor of 50 is 55. To get to this successor from 50, we move right (to 75) and then move left as far as possible. Will this always work? Only for those entries that have a non-null right child. What if an Entry object—for example, the one whose element is 36—has a null right child? If the right child of an Entry object e is **null**, we get to e's successor by going back up the tree to the left as far as possible; the successor of e is the parent of that leftmost ancestor of e. For example, the successor of 36 is 37. Similarly, the successor of 68 is 75. Also, the successor of 28 is 30; since 28 is a left child, we go up the tree to the left zero times—remaining at 28—and then return that Entry object's parent, whose element is 30. Finally, the successor of 75 is **null** because its leftmost ancestor is 50, whose parent is **null**.

**Figure 10.16** | A binary search tree.

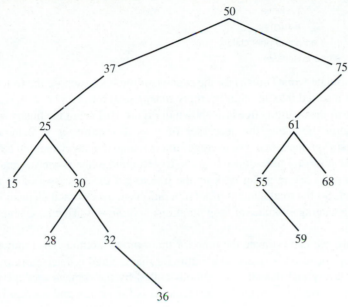

Here is the method definition:

```
protected Entry<E> successor (Entry<E> e)
{
     if (e == null)
            return null;
     else if (e.right != null)
     {
            // successor is leftmost Entry in right subtree of e
            Entry<E> p = e.right;
            while (p.left != null)
                   p = p.left;
            return p;
     } // e has a right child
     else
     {
            // go up the tree to the left as far as possible, then go up
            // to the right.
            Entry<E> p = e.parent;
            Entry<E> child = e;
            while (p != null && child == p.right)
            {
                   child = p;
```

```
                p = p.parent;
          } // while
          return p;
      } // e has no right child
  } // method successor
```

To estimate worstTime($n$) for the successor method, suppose the following elements are inserted into an initially empty binary search tree: $n, 1, 2, 3, \ldots, n - 1$. The shape of the resulting tree is as shown in Figure 10.17. For the binary search tree in the figure, obtaining the successor of $n - 1$ requires $n - 2$ iterations, so worstTime($n$) is linear in $n$. For averageTime($n$), note that an element in the tree will be reached at most 3 times: once to get to its left child, once as the successor of that left child, and once in going back up the tree to get the successor of its rightmost descendant. So the total number of loop iterations to access each element is at most $3n$, and the average number of loop iterations is $3n/n = 3$. That is, averageTime($n$) is constant.

Finally, we can estimate the time for the remove method. The remove method has no loops or recursive calls, so the time for that method is determined by the time for the getEntry and deleteEntry methods called by the remove method. As noted above, for the getEntry method, worstTime($n$) is linear in $n$ and averageTime($n$) is logarithmic in $n$. The deleteEntry method has no loops or recursive calls, but calls the successor method, whose worstTime($n$) is linear in $n$ and whose averageTime($n$) is constant. We conclude that for the remove method, worstTime($n$) is linear in $n$ and averageTime($n$) is logarithmic in $n$.

To complete the development of the BinarySearchTree class, we develop the nested TreeIterator class below.

**The** TreeIterator **Class** All we have left to implement is the TreeIterator class, nested in the BinarySearchTree class. The method specifications for hasNext( ), next( ), and remove( ) were given in the Iterator interface back in Chapter 4. The only fields are a reference to the element returned by the most recent call to the next( )

**Figure 10.17** I A binary search tree in which finding the successor of $n - 1$ requires $n - 2$ iterations.

method, and a reference to the element to be returned by the next call to the next( ) method. The declaration of the TreeIterator class starts out with

```
protected class TreeIterator implements Iterator<E>
{
        protected Entry<E> lastReturned = null,
                        next;
```

Before we get to defining the three methods mentioned above, we should define a default constructor. Where do we want to start? That depends on how we want to iterate. For a preOrder or breadth-first iteration, we would start at the root Entry object. For an inOrder or postOrder iteration, we would start at the leftmost Entry object. We will want to iterate over the elements in a BinarySearchTree in ascending order, so we want to initialize the next field to the leftmost (that is, smallest) Entry object in the BinarySearchTree. To obtain that first Entry object, we start at the root and go left as far as possible:

```
/**
 * Positions this TreeIterator to the smallest element, according to the Comparable
 * interface, in the BinarySearchTree object.
 * The worstTime(n) is O(n) and averageTime(n) is O(log n).
 *
 */
protected TreeIterator( )
{
        next = root;
        if (next != null)
                while (next.left != null)
                        next = next.left;
} // default constructor
```

To estimate the time for this default constructor, the situation is the same as for the contains and add methods in the BinarySearchTree class: worstTime($n$) is linear in $n$ (when the tree consists of a chain of left children), and averageTime($n$) is logarithmic in $n$.

The hasNext( ) method simply checks to see if the next field has the value null:

```
/**
 * Determines if there are still some elements, in the BinarySearchTree object this
 * TreeIterator object is iterating over, that have not been accessed by this
 * TreeIterator object.
 *
 * @return true – if there are still some elements that have not been accessed by
 *      this TreeIterator object; otherwise, return false.
 *
 */
public boolean hasNext( )
```

```
        {
                return next != null;
        } // method hasNext
```

The definition of the next( ) method is quite simple because we have already defined the successor method:

```
    /**
     * Returns the element in the Entry this TreeIterator object was positioned at
     * before this call, and advances this TreeIterator object.
     * The worstTime(n) is O(n) and averageTime(n) is constant.
     *
     * @return the element this TreeIterator object was positioned at before this call.
     *
     * @throws NoSuchElementException – if this TreeIterator object was not
     *         positioned at an Entry before this call.
     *
     */
    public E next( )
    {
            if (next == null)
                    throw new NoSuchElementException( );
            lastReturned = next;
            next = successor (next);
            return lastReturned.element;
    } // method next
```

Finally, the TreeIterator class's remove method deletes the Entry that was last returned. Basically, we call deleteEntry (lastReturned). A slight complication arises if lastReturned has two children. For example, assume lastReturned references the Entry object whose element is (the Integer whose value is) 40 in the BinarySearch Tree object of Figure 10.18.

For the BinarySearchTree object of Figure 10.18, suppose we simply call

```
    deleteEntry (lastReturned);
```

Then next will reference an Entry object that is no longer in the tree. To avoid this problem, we set

```
    next = lastReturned;
```

before calling

```
    deleteEntry (lastReturned);
```

Then the tree from Figure 10.18 would be changed to the tree in Figure 10.19. After deleteEntry (lastReturned) is called for the tree in Figure 10.19, we get the tree in Figure 10.20. For the tree in Figure 10.20, next is positioned where it should be positioned. We then set lastReturned to **null** to preclude a subsequent call to remove( ) before a call to next( ).

**Figure 10.18 |** A binary search tree from which 40 is to be removed.

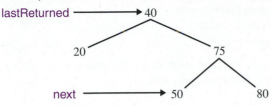

**Figure 10.19 |** A binary search tree in which the element referenced by lastReturned is to be removed. Before deleteEntry (lastReturned) is called, next is assigned the value of lastReturned.

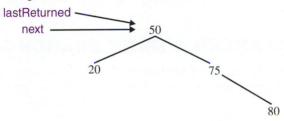

Here is the method definition:

```
/**
 * Removes the element returned by the most recent call to this TreeIterator
 * object's next( ) method.
 * The worstTime(n) is O(n) and averageTime(n) is constant.
 *
 * @throws IllegalStateException – if this TreeIterator's next( ) method was not
 *        called before this call, or if this TreeIterator's remove( ) method was
 *        called between the call to the next( ) method and this call.
 *
 */
public void remove( )
{
        if (lastReturned == null)
                throw new IllegalStateException( );
        if (lastReturned.left != null && lastReturned.right != null)
```

**Figure 10.20** The tree from Figure 10.19 after deleteEntry (lastReturned) is called.

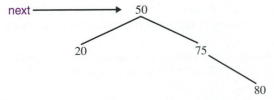

```
                    next = lastReturned;
               deleteEntry(lastReturned);
               lastReturned = null;
          } // method remove
```

Lab 17 provides run-time support for the claim made above that the average height of a BinarySearchTree is logarithmic in *n*.

 **Lab 17:  A Run-Time Estimate of the Average Height of a**
**BinarySearchTree Object**

You are now prepared to do Lab 17.          All Labs Are Optional

## 10.2 | BALANCED BINARY SEARCH TREES

Keep in mind that the height of a BinarySearchTree is the determining factor in estimating the time to insert, remove, or search. In the average case, the height of a Binary SearchTree object is logarithmic in *n*, so inserting, removing, and searching take only logarithmic time. This implies that BinarySearchTree objects represent an improvement, on average, over ArrayList objects and LinkedList objects, for which inserting, removing, and searching take linear time.[1] But in the worst case, a Binary SearchTree object's height can be linear in *n*, which leads to linear-in-*n* worstTime(*n*) for inserting, removing, or searching.

We do not include any applications of the BinarySearchTree class because any application would be superseded by redefining the tree instance from one of the classes in Chapter 12: TreeMap or TreeSet. For either of those classes, the height of the tree is *always* logarithmic in *n*, so insertions, removals, and searches take logarithmic time, even in the worst case. As we noted at the beginning of this chapter, the TreeMap class is based on a somewhat complicated concept: the red-black tree. This section and the following two sections will help prepare you to understand red-black trees.

A binary search tree is ***balanced*** if its height is logarithmic in *n*, the number of elements in the tree. Three widely known data structures in this category of balanced binary search trees are AVL trees, red-black trees, and splay trees. AVL trees are introduced in Section 10.2.1. Red-black trees are investigated in Chapter 12. For information on splay trees, the interested reader may consult Bailey (1999).

For all of these balanced binary search trees, the basic mechanism that keeps a tree balanced is the rotation. A ***rotation*** is an adjustment to the tree around an element that maintains the required ordering of elements. The ultimate goal of rotating is to restore some balance property that has temporarily been violated by an insertion or removal. For example, one such balance property is that the heights of the

---

[1] The corresponding methods in the ArrayList and LinkedList classes are add (**int** index, E element), remove (Object obj), and contains (Object obj). Note that ArrayList objects and LinkedList objects are not necessarily in order.

left and right subtrees of any element should differ by at most 1. Let's start with a simple classification of rotations: left and right.

In a ***left rotation,*** some adjustments are made to the element's parent, left subtree, and right subtree. The effect of these adjustments is the same as if the element were moved to where its left child is, and the element's right child were moved to where the element was. For example, Figure 10.21 shows a left rotation around the element 50. Note that before and after the rotation, the tree is a binary search tree.

Figure 10.22 has another example of a left rotation, around the element 80, that reduces the height of the tree from 3 to 2. The noteworthy feature of Figure 10.22 is that 85, which was in the right subtree of the before-rotation tree, ends up in the left subtree of the after-rotation tree. This phenomenon is common to all left rotations around an element $x$ whose right child is $y$. The left subtree of $y$ becomes the right subtree of $x$. This adjustment is necessary to preserve the ordering of the binary search tree: any element that was in $y$'s left subtree is greater than $x$ and less than $y$. So any such element should be in the right subtree of $x$ (and in the left subtree of $y$). Technically, the same phenomenon also occurred in Figure 10.21, but the left subtree of 50's right child was empty.

Figure 10.23 shows the rotation of Figure 10.22 in a broader context: the element rotated around is not the root of the tree. Before and after the rotation, the tree is a binary search tree. Figure 10.23 illustrates another aspect of all rotations: all the elements above the rotated element are unaffected by the rotation. That is, in both trees, we still have:

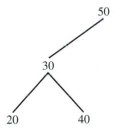

**Figure 10.21** I A left rotation around 50.

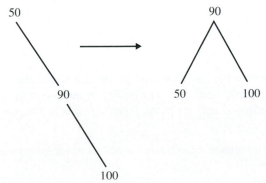

**Figure 10.22** I A left rotation around 80.

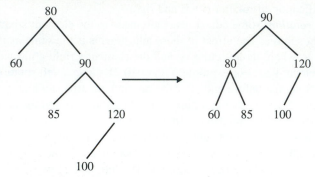

**Figure 10.23** I The left rotation around 80 from Figure 10.22, but here 80 is not the root element.

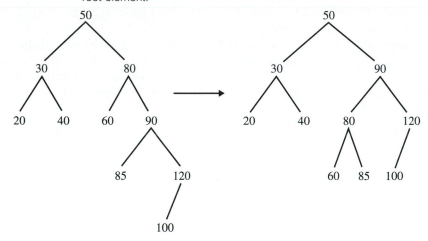

   If we implement a rotation in the BinarySearchTree class, no elements are actually moved; only the references are manipulated. Suppose that p (for "parent") is a reference to an Entry object and r (for "right child") is a reference to p's right child. Basically, a left rotation around p can be accomplished in just two steps:

```
p.right = r.left; // for example, look at 85 in Figure 10.22
r.left = p;
```

Unfortunately, we also have to adjust the parent fields, and that adds quite a bit of code. Here is the complete definition of a leftRotate method in the BinarySearchTree class (the same definition appears in the TreeMap class in Chapter 12):

```
/**
 * Performs a left rotation in this BinarySearchTree object around a specified
 * Entry object.
```

```
        *
        * @param p – the Entry object around which the left rotation is performed.
        *
        * @throws NullPointerException – if p is null or p.right is null.
        *
        * @see Cormen, 2002.
protected void rotateLeft (Entry p)
{
        Entry r = p.right;
        p.right = r.left;
        if (r.left != null)
                r.left.parent = p;
        r.parent = p.parent;
        if (p.parent == null)
                root = r;
        else if (p.parent.left == p)
                p.parent.left = r;
        else
                p.parent.right = r;
        r.left = p;
        p.parent = r;
} // method rotateLeft
```

This indicates how much of a bother parents can be! But on the bright side, no elements get moved, and the time is constant.

What about a right rotation? Figure 10.24 shows a simple example: a right rotation around 50. Does this look familiar? Figure 10.24 is just Figure 10.21 with the direction of the arrow reversed. In general, if you perform a left rotation around an element and then perform a right rotation around the new parent of that element, you will get back the tree you started with.

Figure 10.25 shows a right rotation around an element, 80, in which the right child of 80's left child becomes the left child of 80. This is analogous to the left rotation in Figure 10.22.

Here are details on implementing right rotations in the BinarySearchTree class. Let p be a reference to an Entry object and let l (for "left child") be a reference to the

**Figure 10.24 |** A right rotation around 50.

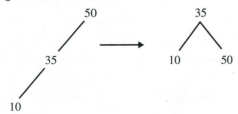

**Figure 10.25** I A right rotation around 80.

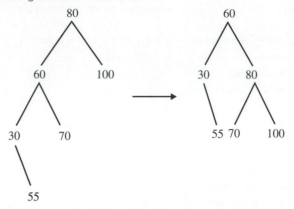

left child of p. Basically, a right rotation around p can be accomplished in just two steps:

    p.left = l.right; // for example, look at 70 in the rotation of Figure 10.8
    l.right = p;

Of course, once we include the parent adjustments, we get a considerably longer—but still constant-time—method. In fact, if you interchange "left" and "right" in the definition of the leftRotate method, you get the definition of rightRotate!

In all of the rotations shown so far, the height of the tree was reduced by 1. That is not surprising; in fact, reducing height is the motivation for rotating. But it is not necessary that every rotation reduce the height of the tree. For example, Figure 10.26 shows a left rotation—around 50—that does not affect the height of the tree.

It is true that the left rotation in Figure 10.26 did not reduce the height of the tree. But a few minutes of checking should convince you that no single rotation can reduce

**Figure 10.26** I A left rotation around 50. The height of the tree is still 3 after the rotation.

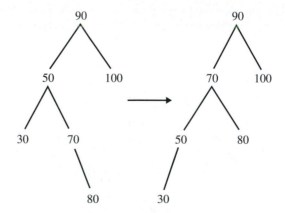

the height of the tree on the left side of Figure 10.26. Now look at the tree on the right side of Figure 10.26. Can you figure out a rotation that will reduce the height of *that* tree? Not a right rotation around 70; that would just get us back where we started. How about a right rotation around 90? Bingo! Figure 10.27 shows the effect.

The rotations in Figures 10.26 and 10.27 should be viewed as a package: a left rotation around 90's left child, followed by a right rotation around 90. This is referred to as a ***double rotation.*** In general, if p is a reference to an Entry object, then a double rotation around p can be accomplished as follows:

```
leftRotate (p.left);
rightRotate (p);
```

Figure 10.28 shows another kind of double rotation: a right rotation around the right child of 50, followed by a left rotation around 50.

**Figure 10.27 |** A right rotation around 90. The height of the tree has been reduced from 3 to 2.

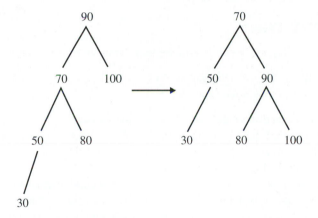

**Figure 10.28 |** Another kind of double rotation: a right rotation around 50's right child, followed by a left rotation around 50.

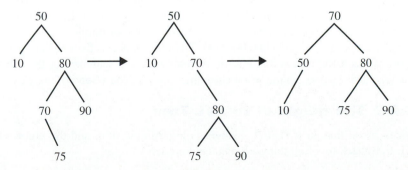

Before we move on to Section 10.2.1 with a specific kind of balanced binary search tree, let's list the major features of rotations:

1. There are four kinds of rotation:
   a. Left rotation
   b. Right rotation
   c. A left rotation around the left child of an element, followed by a right rotation around the element itself
   d. A right rotation around the right child of an element, followed by a left rotation around the element itself
2. Elements not in the subtree of the element rotated about are unaffected by the rotation.
3. A rotation takes constant time.
4. Before and after a rotation, the tree is still a binary search tree.
5. The code for a left rotation is symmetric to the code for a right rotation (and vice versa): simply swap the words "left" and "right".

Section 10.2.1 introduces the AVL tree, a kind of binary search tree that employs rotations to maintain balance.

## 10.2.1 AVL Trees

An *AVL tree* is a binary search tree that either is empty or in which:

1. The heights of the left and right subtrees differ by at most 1, and
2. The left and right subtrees are AVL trees.

AVL trees are named after the two Russian mathematicians, Adelson-Velski and Landis, who invented them in 1962. Figure 10.29 shows three AVL trees, and Figure 10.30 shows three binary search trees that are not AVL trees.

The first tree in Figure 10.30 is not an AVL tree because its left subtree has height 1 and its right subtree has height $-1$. The second tree is not an AVL tree because its left subtree is not an AVL tree; neither is its right subtree. The third tree is not an AVL tree because its left subtree has height 1 and its right subtree has height 3.

In Section 10.2.2, we show that an AVL tree is a balanced binary search tree, that is, that the height of an AVL tree is always logarithmic in $n$. This compares favorably to a binary search tree, whose height is linear in $n$ in the worst case (for example, a chain). The difference between linear and logarithmic can be huge. For example, suppose $n = 1,000,000,000,000$. Then $\log_2 n$ is less than 40. The practical import of this difference is that insertions, removals, and searches for the AVLTree class take far less time, in the worst case, than for the BinarySearchTree class.

## 10.2.2 The Height of an AVL Tree

We can prove that an AVL tree's height is logarithmic in $n$, and the proof relates AVL trees back to, of all things, Fibonacci numbers!

**Figure 10.29 |** Three AVL trees.

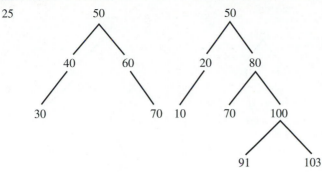

**Figure 10.30 |** Three binary search trees that are not AVL trees.

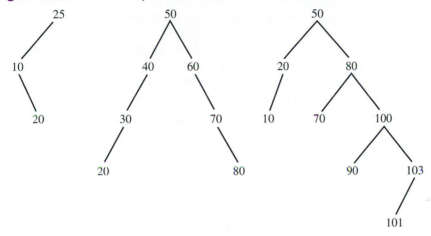

**Claim** If $t$ is a nonempty AVL tree, height($t$) is logarithmic in $n$, where $n$ is the number of elements in $t$.

**Proof** We will show that, even if an AVL tree $t$ has the maximum height possible for its $n$ elements, its height will still be logarithmic in $n$. How can we determine the maximum height possible for an AVL tree with $n$ elements? As Kruse (1987) suggests, rephrasing the question can help us get the answer. Given a height $h$, what is the minimum number of elements in any AVL tree of that height?

For $h = 0, 1, 2, \ldots$, let $\min_h$ be the minimum number of elements in an AVL tree of height $h$. Clearly, $\min_0 = 1$ and $\min_1 = 2$. The values of $\min_2$ and $\min_3$ can be seen from the AVL trees in Figure 10.31.

In general, if $h1 > h2$, then $\min_{h1}$ is greater than the number of elements needed to construct an AVL tree of height $h2$. That is, if $h1 > h2$, then $\min_{h1} > \min_{h2}$. In other words, $\min_h$ is an increasing function.

Suppose that $t$ is an AVL tree with $h$ height and $\min_h$ elements, for some value of $h > 1$. What can we say about the heights of the left and right subtrees of $t$? By

**Figure 10.31** I AVL trees of heights 2 and 3 in which the number of elements is minimal.

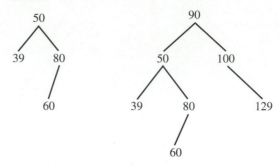

the definition of height, one of those subtrees must have height $h - 1$. And by the definition of an AVL tree, the other subtree must have height of $h - 1$ or $h - 2$. In fact, because $t$ has the minimum number of elements for its height, one of its subtrees must have height $h - 1$ and $\min_{h-1}$ elements, and the other subtree must have height $h - 2$ and $\min_{h-2}$ elements.

A tree always has one more element than the number of elements in its left and right subtrees. So we have the following equation, called a ***recurrence relation:***

$$\min_h = \min_{h-1} + \min_{h-2} + 1 \quad \text{for any integer } h > 1$$

Now that we can calculate $\min_h$ for any positive integer $h$, we can see how the function $\min_h$ is related to the maximum height of an AVL tree. For example, because $\min_6 = 33$ and $\min_7 = 54$, the maximum height of an AVL tree with 50 elements is 6.

The above recurrence relation looks a lot like the formula for generating Fibonacci numbers (see Lab 7). The term ***Fibonacci tree*** refers to an AVL tree with the minimum number of elements for its height. From the above recurrence relation and the values of $\min_0$ and $\min_1$, we can show, by induction on $h$, that

$$\min_h = \text{fib}(h + 3) - 1 \quad \text{for any nonnegative integer } h$$

We can further show, by induction on $h$ (see Concept Exercise 10.8),

$$\text{fib}(h + 3) - 1 \geq (3/2)^h \quad \text{for any nonnegative integer } h$$

Combining these results,

$$\min_h \geq (3/2)^h \quad \text{for any nonnegative integer } h$$

Taking logs in base 2 (but any base will do), we get

$$\log_2(\min_h) \geq h \cdot \log_2(3/2) \quad \text{for any nonnegative integer } h$$

Rewriting this in a form suitable for a Big-O claim, with $1/\log_2(1.5) < 1.75$, gives

$$h \leq 1.75 \log_2(\min_h) \quad \text{for any nonnegative integer } h$$

If $t$ is an AVL tree with $h$ height and $n$ elements, we must have $\min_h \leq n$, so for any such AVL tree,

$$h \leq 1.75 \log_2(n)$$

This implies that the height of any AVL tree is $O(\log n)$. Is $O(\log n)$ a tight upper bound? That is, is the height of any AVL tree logarithmic in $n$? Yes, and here's why. For any binary tree of height $h$ with $n$ elements,

$$h \geq \log_2(n + 1) - 1$$

by the Binary Tree Theorem. We conclude that any AVL tree with $n$ elements has height that is logarithmic in $n$, even in the worst case.

This completes the proof.

To give you a better idea of how AVL trees relate to binary search trees, we sketch the design and implementation of the AVLTree class in Section 10.2.3. To complete the implementation, you will need to tackle Programming Projects 10.3 and 10.4. Those projects deal with some of the details of the add and remove methods, respectively.

### 10.2.3 The AVLTree Class

The AVLTree class will be developed as a subclass of the BinarySearchTree class. There will not be any additional fields, but each entry object has an additional field:

**char** balanceFactor = '=';

The purpose of this additional field in the Entry class is to make it easier to maintain the balance of an AVLTree object. If an Entry object has a balanceFactor value of '=', the Entry object's left subtree has the same height as the Entry object's right subtree. If the balanceFactor value is 'L', the left subtree's height is one greater than the right subtree's height. And a balanceFactor value of 'R' means that the right subtree's height is one greater than the left subtree's height. Figure 10.32 shows an AVL tree with each element's balance factor shown below the element.

**Figure 10.32 |** An AVL tree with the balance factor under each element.

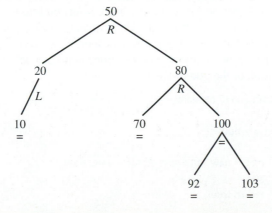

Here is the new entry class, nested in the AVLTree class:

```
protected static class AVLEntry<E> extends BinarySearchTree.Entry<E>
{
       protected char balanceFactor = '=';

       /**
        * Initializes this AVLEntry object from a specified element and a
        * specified parent AVLEntry.
        *
        * @param element – the specified element to be housed in this
        *        AVLEntry object.
        * @param parent – the specified parent of this AVLEntry object.
        *
        */
       protected AVLEntry (E element, AVLEntry<E> parent)
       {
              this.element = element;
              this.parent = parent;
       } // constructor
} // class AVLEntry
```

The only methods that the AVLTree class overrides from the BinarySearchTree class are those that involve the AVLEntry class's balanceFactor field. Specifically, the AVLTree class will override the add and deleteEntry methods from the Binary SearchTree class. The balancing mechanism discussed below is from Sahni; see Sahni (2000).

One intriguing feature of the AVLTree class is that the contains method is not overridden from the BinarySearchTree class, but worstTime($n$) is different: logarithmic in $n$, versus linear in $n$ for the BinarySearchTree class! This speed reflects the fact that the height of an AVL tree is always logarithmic in $n$.

The definition of the add method in the AVLTree class resembles the definition of the add method in the BinarySearchTree class. But as we work our way down the tree from the root to the insertion point, we keep track of the inserted AVLEntry object's closest ancestor whose balanceFactor is 'L' or 'R'. We refer to this Entry object as imbalanceAncestor. For example, if we insert 60 into the AVLTree object in Figure 10.33, imbalanceAncestor is the Entry object whose element is 80.

After the element has been inserted, BinarySearchTree-style, into the AVLTree object, we call a fix-up method to handle rotations and balanceFactor adjustments. Here is the definition of the add method:

```
public boolean add (E element)
{
       if (root == null)
       {
              root = new AVLEntry<E> (element, null);
              size++;
              return true;
```

**Figure 10.33** | An AVLTree object.

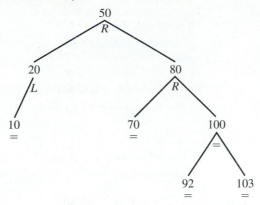

```
      } // empty tree
      else
      {
            AVLEntry<E> temp = (AVLEntry<E>)root,
                        imbalanceAncestor = null; // nearest ancestor of
                                                  // element with
                                                  // balanceFactor not '='
            int comp;

            while (true)
            {
                  comp = ((Comparable)element).compareTo (temp.element);
                  if (comp == 0)
                        return false;
                  if (comp < 0)
                  {
                        if (temp.balanceFactor != '=')
                              imbalanceAncestor = temp;
                        if (temp.left != null)
                              temp = (AVLEntry<E>)temp.left;
                        else
                        {
                              temp.left = new AVLEntry<E> (element, temp);
                              fixAfterInsertion ((AVLEntry<E>)temp.left,
                                          imbalanceAncestor);
                              size++;
                              return true;
                        } // temp.left == null
                  } // comp < 0
                  else
                  {
```

```
                    if (temp.balanceFactor != '=')
                            imbalanceAncestor = temp;
                    if (temp.right != null)
                            temp = (AVLEntry<E>)temp.right;
                    else
                    {
                            temp.right = new AVLEntry<E>(element, temp);
                            fixAfterInsertion ((AVLEntry<E>)temp.right,
                                            imbalanceAncestor)
                            size++;
                            return true;
                    } // temp.right == null
            } // comp > 0
        } // while
    } // root not null
} // method add
```

This code differs from that of the BinarySearchTree class's add method in three respects:

1.  The new entry is an instance of AVLEntry<E>.
2.  The imbalanceFactor variable is maintained.
3.  The fixAfterInsertion method is called to rebalance the tree, if necessary.

The definition of the fixAfterInsertion method is left as Programming Project 10.3. The bottom line is that, for the add method, worstTime($n$) is $O(\log n)$. In fact, because the **while** loop in the add method can require as many iterations as the height of the AVL tree, worstTime($n$) is logarithmic in $n$.

The definition of the deleteEntry (called by the inherited remove method) method starts by performing a BinarySearchTree-style deletion, and then invokes a fixAfterDeletion method. Fortunately, for the sake of code reuse, we can explicitly call the BinarySearchTree class's deleteEntry method, so the complete definition of the AVLTree class's deleteEntry method is simply:

```
protected Entry<E> deleteEntry (Entry<E> p)
{
        AVLEntry<E> deleted = (AVLEntry<E>)super.deleteEntry (p);
        fixAfterDeletion (deleted.element, (AVLEntry<E>)deleted.parent);
        return deleted;
} // method deleteEntry
```

Of course, we are not done yet; we are not even close: the definition of the fixAfter Deletion method is left as Programming Project 10.4. For the remove method, worstTime($n$) is $O(\log n)$. In fact, because we start with a BinarySearchTree-style deletion, worstTime($n$) is logarithmic in $n$.

The book's website includes an applet that will help you to visualize insertions in and removals from an AVLTree object.

## 10.2.4 Run-Time Estimates

We close out this chapter with a brief look at some run-time issues. For the AVLTree class's add method, worstTime($n$) is logarithmic in $n$, whereas for the BinarySearch Tree class's add method, worstTime($n$) is linear in $n$. And so, as you would expect, the worst-case run-time behavior of the AVLTree class's add method is much faster than that of the BinarySearchTree class's add method.

What about averageTime($n$)? The averageTime($n$) is logarithmic in $n$ for the add method in those two classes. Which do you think will be faster in run-time experiments? Because quite a bit of effort goes into maintaining the balance of an AVLTree object, the average height of a BinarySearchTree object is about 50 percent larger than the average height of an AVLTree object: $2.1 \log_2 n$ versus $1.44 \log_2 n$. But the extra maintenance makes AVLTree insertions slightly slower, in spite of the height advantage, than BinarySearchTree insertions.

In Chapter 12, we present another kind of balanced binary search tree: the red-black tree. Insertions in red-black trees are slightly faster, on average, than for AVL trees, and that is why the red-black tree was selected as the underlying structure for the Java Collections Framework's TreeMap and TreeSet classes. Both of these classes are extremely useful; you will get some idea of this from the applications and programming projects in Chapter 12.

## SUMMARY

A *binary search tree* $t$ is a binary tree such that either $t$ is empty or

1. Each element in leftTree($t$) is less than the root element of $t$
2. Each element in rightTree($t$) is greater than the root element of $t$
3. Both leftTree($t$) and rightTree($t$) are binary search trees

The BinarySearchTree class maintains a sorted collection of Comparable elements. The time estimates for searching, inserting, and deleting depend on the height of the tree. In the worst case—for example, if the tree is a chain—the height is linear in $n$, the number of elements in the tree. The average height of a binary search tree is logarithmic in $n$. So for the contains, add, and remove methods, worstTime($n$) is linear in $n$ and averageTime($n$) is logarithmic in $n$.

A binary search tree is *balanced* if its height is logarithmic in $n$, the number of elements in the tree. Often, the balancing is maintained with rotations. A *rotation* is an adjustment to the tree around an element that maintains the required ordering of elements. This chapter introduced one kind of balanced binary search tree: the AVL tree. An *AVL tree* is a binary search tree that either is empty or in which:

1. The heights of the left and right subtrees differ by at most 1, and
2. The left and right subtrees are AVL trees.

The AVLTree class is a subclass of the BinarySearchTree class. The only overridden methods are those related to maintaining balance: add and deleteEntry.

# CONCEPT EXERCISES

**10.1  a.**   Show the effect of making the following insertions into an initially empty binary search tree:

30, 40, 20, 90, 10, 50, 70, 60, 80

   **b.**   Find a different ordering of the above elements whose insertions would generate the same binary search tree as in part a.

**10.2**   Describe in English how to remove each of the following from a binary search tree:

   **a.**   An element with no children

   **b.**   An element with one child

   **c.**   An element with two children

**10.3  a.**   For any positive integer *n*, describe how to arrange the integers 1, 2, . . . , *n* so that when they are inserted into a BinarySearchTree object, the height of the tree will be linear in *n*.

   **b.**   For any positive integer *n*, describe how to arrange the integers 1, 2, . . . , *n* so that when they are inserted into a BinarySearchTree object, the height of the tree will be logarithmic in *n*.

   **c.**   For any positive integer *n*, describe how to arrange the integers 1, 2, . . . , *n* so that when they are inserted into an AVLTree object, the height of the tree will be logarithmic in *n*.

   **d.**   For any positive integer *n*, is it possible to arrange the integers 1, 2, . . . , *n* so that when they are inserted into an AVLTree object, the height of the tree will be linear in *n*? Explain.

**10.4**   In each of the following binary search trees, perform a left rotation around 50.

   **a.**

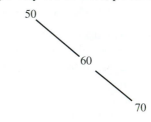

   **b.**

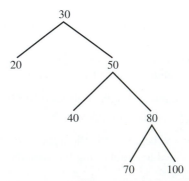

c.

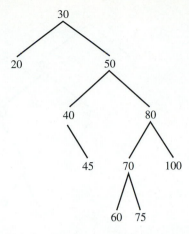

**10.5** In each of the following binary search trees, perform a right rotation around 50.

a.

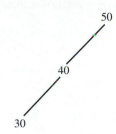

b.

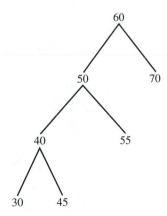

**c.**

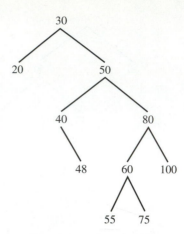

**10.6** In the following binary search tree, perform a double rotation (a left rotation around 20 and then a right rotation around 50) to reduce the height to 2.

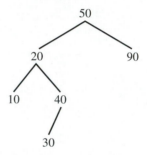

**10.7** In the following binary search tree, perform a double rotation to reduce the height to 2:

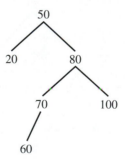

**10.8** Show that for any nonnegative integer $h$,

$$\text{fib}(h + 3) - 1 \geq (3/2)^h$$

*Hint:* Use the strong form of the Principle of Mathematical Induction and note that, for $h > 1$,

$$(3/2)^{h-1} + (3/2)^{h-2} = (3/2)^{h-2} \cdot (3/2 + 1) > (3/2)^{h-2} \cdot 9/4$$

**10.9** Suppose we define $\max_h$ to be the maximum number of elements in an AVL tree of height $h$.

    **a.** Calculate $\max_3$.

    **b.** Determine the formula for $\max_h$ for any $h \geq 0$. **Hint:** Use the Binary Tree Theorem from Chapter 9.

    **c.** What is the maximum height of an AVL tree with 100 elements?

**10.10** Show that the height of an AVL tree with 32 elements must be exactly 5.

    *Hint:* Calculate $\max_4$ and $\min_6$.

**10.11** For the contains method in the BinarySearchTree class, worstTime($n$) is linear in $n$. The AVLTree class does not override that method, but for the contains method in the AVLTree class, worstTime($n$) is logarithmic in $n$. Explain.

## PROGRAMMING EXERCISES

**10.1** In the BinarySearchTree class, develop a leaves method. Here is the method specification:

```
/**
 * Returns the number of leaves in this BinarySearchTree object.
 * The worstTime(n) is O(n).
 *
 * @return – the number of leaves in this BinarySearchTree object.
 *
 */
public int leaves( )
```

Test your method after you modify the BinarySearchTreeDriver class from the book's website.

*Hint:* A recursive version, invoked by a wrapper method, can mimic the definition of leaves($t$) from Section 9.1. Or, you can also develop an iterative version by creating a new iterator class in which the next method increments a count for each Entry object whose left and right fields are **null**.

**10.2** Modify the BinarySearchTree class so that the iterators are fail-fast (see Appendix 3 for details on fail-fast iterators). Test your class with a main method.

**10.3** Modify the BinarySearchTree class so that BinarySearchTree objects are serializable (see Appendix 3 for details on serializability). Test your class with a project that serializes a BinarySearchTree object, and another project that deserializes and prints that object.

**10.4** Create a recursive version of the add method. *Hint:* Make the add method a wrapper for a recursive method. Test your version with the BinarySearch TreeDriver class.

**10.5**  In the BinarySearchTree class, modify the getEntry method so that it is a wrapper for a recursive method. Test your version with the BinarySearch TreeDriver class, which calls the remove method.

**10.6**  Create a driver for the AVLTree class. *Hint:* Make very minor modifications to the BinarySearchTree driver.

**10.7**  In the AVLTree class, define the following method:

```
// Postcondition: The height of this AVLTree object has been returned. The
//                worstTime(n) is O(log n).
public int height( )
```

*Hint:* Use the balanceFactor field in the AVLEntry class to guide you down the tree.

## Programming Project 10.1

### An Alternative Implementation of the Binary-Search-Tree Data Type

This project illustrates that the binary-search-tree data type has more than one implementation. You can also use the technique described below to save a binary search tree (in fact, any binary tree) to disk so that it can be subsequently retrieved with its original structure. This gives you an alternative to the effect of Programming Exercise 10.3.

Develop an array-based implementation of the binary-search-tree data type. Your class, BinarySearchTreeArray, will have the same method specifications as the Binary SearchTree class but will use indexes to simulate the parent, left, and right links. For example, the fields in your embedded Entry class might have:

        E element;
        **int** parent,
            left,
            right;

Similarly, the BinarySearchTreeArray class might have the following three fields:

        Entry<E>[ ] tree;

        **int** root,
            size;

The root Entry object is stored in tree [0], and a **null** reference is indicated by the index −1. For example, suppose we create a binary search tree by entering the String objects "dog", "turtle", "cat", "ferret". The tree would be as follows:

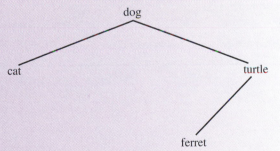

The array representation, with the elements stored in the order in which they are entered, is

| 0 | dog | −1 | 2 | 1 |
|---|-----|----|----|----|
| 1 | turtle | 0 | 3 | −1 |
| 2 | cat | 0 | −1 | −1 |
| 3 | ferret | 1 | −1 | −1 |
| . . . | | | | |

*(continued on next page)*

*(continued from previous page)*

The method definitions are very similar to those in the BinarySearchTree class, except that an expression such as

    root.left

is replaced with

    tree [root].left

For example, here is a possible definition of the getEntry method:

```
protected Entry<E> getEntry (E element)
{
        int temp = root,
            comp;

        while (temp != −1)
        {
            comp = ((Comparable)element).compareTo (tree [temp].element);
            if (comp == 0)
                    return temp;
            else if (comp < 0)
                    temp = tree [temp].left;
            else
                    temp = tree [temp].right;
        } // while
        return −1;
} // method getEntry
```

You will also need to modify the TreeIterator class.

## Programming Project 10.2

### Printing a BinarySearchTree Object

In the BinarySearchTree class, implement the following method:

```
/**
 * Returns a String representation of this BinarySearchTree object.
 * The worstTime(n) is linear in n.
 *
 * @return a String representation of this BinarySearchTree object.
 *
 */
public String toTreeString( )
```

*Note:* The String returned should incorporate the structure of the tree. For example, suppose we have the following:

```
BinarySearchTree<Integer> tree = new BinarySearchTree<Integer>( );

tree.add (55);
tree.add (12);
tree.add (30);
tree.add (97);
System.out.println (tree.toTreeString( ));
```

The output would be:

```
                              55
              12                          97
                    30
```

In what sense is the above approach better than developing a printTree method in the BinarySearchTree class?

## Programming Project 10.3

### The fixAfterInsertion **Method**

Define the fixAfterInsertion method in the AVLTree class. Here is the method specification:

```
/**
 * Restores the AVLTree properties, if necessary, by rotations and balance-
 * factor adjustments between a specified inserted entry and the specified nearest
 * ancestor of inserted that has a balanceFactor of 'L' or 'R'.
 * The worstTime(n) is O(log n).
 *
 * @param inserted – the specified inserted AVLEntry object.
 * @param imbalanceAncestor – the specified AVLEntry object that is the
 *        nearest ancestor of inserted.
 *
 */
    protected void fixAfterInsertion (AVLEntry<E> inserted, AVLEntry<E> imbalance
        Ancestor)
```

*Hint:* If imbalanceAncestor is **null**, then each ancestor of the inserted AVLEntry object has a balanceFactor value of '='. For example, Figure 10.34 shows the before-and-after for this case.

There are three remaining cases when the balanceFactor value of imbalanceAncestor is 'L'. The three cases when that value is 'R' can be obtained by symmetry.

**Figure 10.34** | On the left-hand side, an AVLTree object just before the call to fixAfterInsertion; the element inserted was 55, and all of its ancestors have a balance factor of '='. On the right-hand side, the AVLTree object with adjusted balance factors.

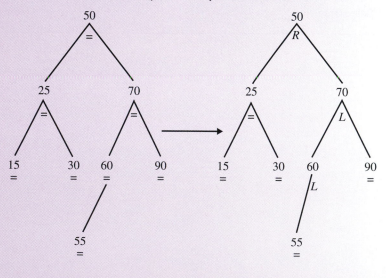

**Case 1**  imbalanceAncestor.balanceFactor is 'L' and the insertion is made in the right sub-tree of imbalanceAncestor. Figure 10.35 shows the before-and-after for this case.

**Figure 10.35** I On the left-hand side, an AVL tree into which 55 has just been inserted. The balance factors of the other entries are *preinsertion*. On the right-hand side, the same AVL tree after the balance factors have been adjusted. The only balance factors adjusted are those in the path between 55 and 50, exclusive.

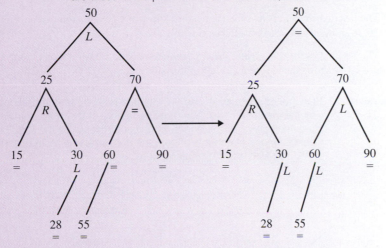

**Case 2**  imbalanceAncestor.balanceFactor is 'L' and the insertion is made in the left sub-tree of the left subtree of imbalanceAncestor. The restructuring can be accomplished with a rotation. Figure 10.36 shows the before-and-after in this case.

**Figure 10.36** I On the left side, what was an AVL tree has become imbalanced by the insertion of 13. The balance factors of the other entries are *preinsertion*. In this case, imbalanceAncestor is the AVLEntry object whose element is 50. On the right side, the restructured AVL tree with adjusted balanced factors.

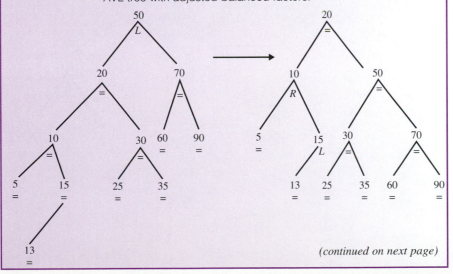

*(continued on next page)*

*(continued from previous page)*

**Case 3** imbalanceAncestor.balanceFactor is 'L' and the inserted entry is in the right subtree of the left subtree of *imbalanceAncestor*. The restructuring can be accomplished with a rotation. There are three subcases:

3a.   imbalanceAncestor's postrotation parent is the inserted entry. Figure 10.37 shows the before-and-after in this subcase.

3b.   The inserted element is less than imbalanceAncestor's postrotation parent. Figure 10.38 shows the before-and-after in this subcase.

3c.   The inserted element is greater than imbalanceAncestor's postrotation parent. Figure 10.39 shows the before-and-after in this subcase.

**Figure 10.37 |** On the left side, what was an AVL tree has become imbalanced by the insertion of 40. The balance factors of the other entries are *preinsertion*. In this subcase, imbalanceAncestor is the AVLEntry object whose element is 50. On the right side, the restructured AVL tree with adjusted balanced factors.

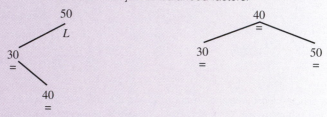

**Figure 10.38 |** On the left side, what was an AVL tree has become imbalanced by the insertion of 35. The balance factors of the other entries are *preinsertion*. In this case, imbalanceAncestor is the AVLEntry object whose element is 50. On the right side, the restructured AVL tree with adjusted balanced factors.

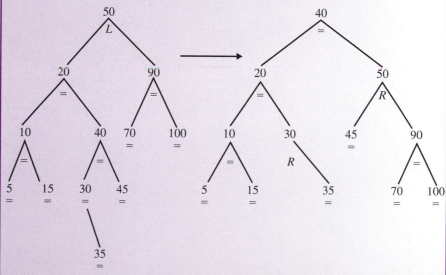

**Figure 10.39** I On the left side, what was an AVL tree has become imbalanced by the insertion of 42. The balance factors of the other entries are *preinsertion*. In this case, imbalanceAncestor is the AVLEntry object whose element is 50. On the right side, the restructured AVL tree with adjusted balanced factors.

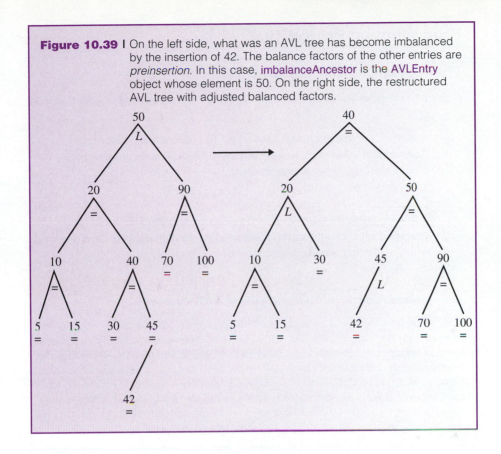

## Programming Project 10.4

### The fixAfterDeletion Method

Define the fixAfterDeletion method in the AVLTree class. Here is the method specification:

```
/**
 * Restores the AVL properties, if necessary, by rotations and balance-factor
 * adjustments between the element actually deleted and a specified ancestor
 * of the AVLEntry object actually deleted.
 * The worstTime(n) is O(log n).
 *
 * @param element – the element actually deleted from this AVLTree object.
 * @param ancestor – the specified ancestor (initially, the parent) of the
 *            element actually deleted.
 *
 */
    protected void fixAfterDeletion (E element, AVLEntry ancestor)
```

*Hint:* Loop until the tree is an AVL tree with appropriate balance factors. Within the loop, suppose the element removed was in the right subtree of ancestor (a symmetric analysis handles the left-subtree case). Then there are three subcases, depending on whether ancestor.balanceFactor is '=', 'R', or 'L', In all three subcases, ancestor.balance Factor must be changed. For the '=' subcase, the loop then terminates. For the 'R' subcase, ancestor is replaced with ancestor.parent and the loop continues. For the 'L' subcase, there are three sub-subcases, depending on whether ancestor.left.balanceFactor is '=', 'R', or 'L'. And the 'R' sub-subcase has three sub-sub-subcases!

# Sorting

One of the most common computer operations is ***sorting,*** that is, putting a collection of elements in order. From simple, one-time sorts for small collections to highly efficient sorts for frequently used mailing lists and dictionaries, the ability to choose among various sort methods is an important skill in every programmer's repertoire. ■

## CHAPTER OBJECTIVES

1. Compare the Comparable interface to the Comparator interface, and know when to use each one.

2. Be able to decide which sort algorithm is appropriate for a given application.

3. Understand the limitations of each sort algorithm.

4. Explain the criteria for a divide-and-conquer algorithm.

## 11.1 | INTRODUCTION

Our focus will be on comparison-based sorts; that is, the sorting entails comparing elements to other elements. Comparisons are not necessary if we know, in advance, the final position of each element. For example, if we start with an unsorted list of 100 distinct integers in the range 0 to 99, we know without any comparisons that the integer 0 must end up in position 0, and so on. The best-known sort algorithm that is not comparison-based is Radix Sort; see Section 11.5.

All of the sort algorithms presented in this chapter are generic algorithms, that is, **static** methods: they have no calling object, and operate on the parameter that specifies the collection to be sorted. Two of the sort methods, Merge Sort and Quick Sort, are included in the Java Collections Framework, and can be found in the Collections or Arrays classes in the package java.util.

The parameter list may include an array of primitive values (**int**s or **double**s, for example), an array of objects, or a List object—that is, an instance of a class that implements the List interface. In illustrating a sort algorithm, we gloss over the distinction between an array of **int**s, an array of Integer objects, and a List object whose elements are of type Integer. In Section 11.3, we'll see how to sort objects by a different ordering than that provided by the compareTo method in the Comparable interface.

In estimating the efficiency of a sorting method, our primary concerns will be averageTime($n$) and worstTime($n$). In some applications, such as national defense and life-support systems, the worst-case performance of a sort method can be critical. For example, we will see a sort algorithm that is quite fast, both on average and in the worst case. And we will also look at a sort algorithm that is extremely fast, on average, but whose worst-case performance is achingly slow.

The space requirements will also be noted, because some sort algorithms make a copy of the collection that is to be sorted, while other sort algorithms have only negligible space requirements. An **in-place sort** is one that requires space for only a constant number of elements. For the collection to be sorted, the sort algorithm is sent a reference to the entire collection, so in-place sorts are possible.

The other criterion we'll use for measuring a sort method is stability. A **stable** sort method preserves the relative order of equal elements. For example, suppose we have an array of students in which each student consists of a last name and the total quality points for that student, and we want to sort by total quality points. If the sort method is stable and before sorting, ("Balan", 28) appears at an earlier index than ("Wang", 28), then after sorting ("Balan" 28) will still appear at an earlier index than ("Wang" 28). Stability can simplify project development. For example, assume that the above array is already in order by name, and the application calls for sorting by quality points; for students with the same quality points the ordering should be alphabetical. A stable sort will accomplish this without any additional work to make sure students with the same quality points are ordered alphabetically.

Each sort method will be illustrated on the following collection of 20 **int**s:

59 46 32 80 46 55 50 43 44 81 12 95 17 80 75 33 40 61 16 87

# 11.2 | SIMPLE SORTS

We'll start with a few sort algorithms that are fairly easy to develop, but provide slow execution times when $n$ is large. In each case, we will sort an array of **int** values into ascending order, and duplicates will be allowed. These algorithms could easily be modified to sort an array of **double**s, for example, into ascending order or into descending order. We could also sort objects in some class that implements the Comparable interface. The ordering, provided by the compareTo method, would be "natural": for example, String objects would be ordered lexicographically. In Section 11.3, we'll see how to achieve a different ordering of objects than the one provided by the compareTo method.

## 11.2.1  Insertion Sort

Insertion Sort repeatedly sifts out-of-place elements down into their proper positions in an array. Given an array x of **int** values, x [1] is inserted where it belongs relative to x [0], so x [0] and x [1] will be swapped if x [0] > x [1]. At this point, we have x [0] ≤ x [1]. Then x [2] will be inserted where it belongs relative to x [0] and x [1]; there will be 0, 1, or 2 swaps. At that point, we have x [0] ≤ x [1] ≤ x [2]. Then x [3] will be inserted where it belongs relative to x [0] . . . x [2]. And so on.

*Example*  Suppose the array x initially has the following values:

59 46 32 80 46 55 50 43 44 81 12 95 17 80 75 33 40 61 16 87

We first insert x [1], 46, where it belongs relative to x [0], 59. One swap is needed, and this gives us:

<u>46 59</u> 32 80 46 55 50 43 44 81 12 95 17 80 75 33 40 61 16 87

The underlined values are in their correct order. We then insert x [2], 32, where it belongs relative to the sorted subarray x [0] . . . x [1], and two swaps are required. We now have

<u>32 46 59</u> 80 46 55 50 43 44 81 12 95 17 80 75 33 40 61 16 87

Next, we insert x [3], 80, where it belongs relative to the sorted subarray x [0] . . . x [2]; this step does not require any swaps, and the array is now

<u>32 46 59 80</u> 46 55 50 43 44 81 12 95 17 80 75 33 40 61 16 87

We then insert x [4], 46, where it belongs relative to the sorted subarray x [0] . . . x [3]. Two swaps are required, and we get

<u>32 46 46 59 80</u> 55 50 43 44 81 12 95 17 80 75 33 40 61 16 87

This process continues until, finally, we insert x [19], 87, where it belongs relative to the sorted subarray x [0] . . . x [18]. The array is now sorted:

<u>12 16 17 32 33 40 43 44 46 46 50 55 59 61 75 80 80 81 87 95</u>

At each stage in the above process, we have an **int** variable i in the range 1 through 19, and we insert x [i] into its proper position relative to the sorted subarray x [0], x [1], . . . , x [i−1]. During each iteration, there is another loop in which an **int** variable j starts at i and works downward until either j = 0 or x [j−1] ≤ x[j]. During each inner-loop iteration, x [j] and x [j−1] are swapped.

Here is the method definition:

```
/**
 * Sorts a specified array of int values into ascending order.
 * The worstTime(n) is O(n * n).
 *
 * @param x – the array to be sorted.
 *
 */
public static void insertionSort (int[ ] x)
{
      for (int i = 1; i < x.length; i++)
            for (int j = i; j > 0 && x [j − 1] > x [j]; j−−)
                  swap (x, j, j − 1);
} // method insertionSort
```

The definition of the swap method is:

```
/**
 * Swaps two specified elements in a specified array.
 *
 * @param x – the array in which the two elements are to be swapped.
 * @param a – the index of one of the elements to be swapped.
 * @param b – the index of the other element to be swapped.
 *
 */
public static void swap (int [ ] x, int a, int b)
{
      int t = x[a];
      x[a] = x[b];
      x[b] = t;
} // method swap
```

For example, if scores is an array of **int** values, we could sort the array with the following call:

insertionSort (scores);

*Analysis*   Let *n* be the number of elements to be sorted. The outer **for** loop will be executed exactly *n* − 1 times. For each value of i, the number of iterations of the inner loop is the number of swaps required to sift x [i] into its proper position in x [0], x [1], . . . , x [i−1]. In the worst case, the collection starts out in decreasing order, so i swaps are required to sift x [i] into its proper position. That is, the number of iterations of the inner **for** loop will be

$$0 + 1 + 2 + 3 + \cdots + n - 2 + n - 1 = \sum_{i=1}^{n-1} i = n(n-1)/2$$

The total number of outer-loop and inner-loop iterations is $n−1 + n(n−1)/2$, so worstTime($n$) is quadratic in $n$. In practice, what really slows down insertionSort in the worst case is that the number of *swaps* is quadratic in $n$. But these can be replaced with single assignments (see Concept Exercise 11.9).

To simplify the average-time analysis, assume that there are no duplicates in the array to be sorted. When x [1] is sifted into its proper place, half of the time there will be a swap and half of the time there will be no swap.[1] The expected number of inner-loop iterations is (0 + 1)/2.0, which is 1/2.0. When x [2] is sifted into its proper place, the expected number of inner-loop iterations is (0 + 1 + 2)/3.0 = 1.0 = 2/2.0. In general, in sifting x [i] to its proper position, the expected number of loop iterations is

$$(0 + 1 + 2 + \cdots + i) / (i + 1.0) = i/2.0$$

The total number of inner-loop iterations, on average, is

$$1/2.0 + 2/2.0 + 3/2.0 + \cdots + (n - 1)/2.0 = \sum_{i=1}^{n-1} i/2.0 = n(n-1)/4$$

We conclude that averageTime($n$) is quadratic in $n$. In the Java Collections Framework, Insertion Sort is used for sorting subarrays of fewer than 7 elements. Instead of a method call, there is in-line code (off contains the first index of the subarray to be sorted, and len contains the number of elements to be sorted):

```
// Insertion sort on smallest arrays
if (len < 7)
{
        for (int i=off; i<len+off; i++)
                for (int j=i; j>off && x[j−1]>x[j]; j−−)
                        swap(x, j, j−1);
        return;
}
```

For small subarrays, other sort methods—usually faster than Insertion Sort—are actually slower because their powerful machinery is designed for large-sized arrays. The

---

[1] As always in averaging, we assume that each event is equally likely.

choice of 7 for the cutoff is based on empirical studies described in Bentley (1993). The best choice for a cutoff will depend on machine-dependent characteristics.

An interesting aspect of Insertion Sort is its best-case behavior. If the original array happens to be in ascending order—of course the sort method does not "know" this—then the inner loop will not be executed at all, and the total number of iterations is linear in $n$. In general, if the array is already in order or nearly so, Insertion Sort is very quick. So it is sometimes used at the tail end of a sort method that takes an arbitrary array of elements and produces an "almost" sorted array. For example, this is exactly what happens with the sort method in C++'s Standard Template Library.

The space requirements for Insertion Sort are modest: a couple of loop-control variables, a temporary for swapping, and an activation record for the call to swap (which we lump together as a single variable). So worstSpace($n$) is constant, which implies that Insertion Sort is an in-place sort.

Because the inner loop of Insertion Sort swaps x [j−1] and x [j] only if x [j−1] > x [j], equal elements will not be swapped, so Insertion Sort is stable.

## 11.2.2 Selection Sort

Perhaps the simplest of all sort algorithms is Selection Sort: given an array x of **int** values, swap the smallest element with the element at index 0, swap the second smallest element with the element at index 1, and so on.

> *Example* Suppose the array x initially has the usual values, with an arrow pointing to the element at the current index, and the smallest value from that index on in boldface:
>
> 59 46 32 80 46 55 50 43 44 81 **12** 95 17 80 75 33 40 61 16 87
> ↑
>
> The smallest value in the array, 12, is swapped with the value 59 at index 0, and we now have (with the sorted subarray underlined)
>
> <u>12</u> 46 32 80 46 55 50 43 44 81 59 95 17 80 75 33 40 61 **16** 87
>    ↑
>
> Now 16, the smallest of the values from index 1 on, is swapped with the value 46 at index 1:
>
> <u>12 16</u> 32 80 46 55 50 43 44 81 59 95 **17** 80 75 33 40 61 46 87
>       ↑
>
> Then 17, the smallest of the values from index 2 on, is swapped with the value 32 at index 2:
>
> <u>12 16 17</u> 80 46 55 50 43 44 81 59 95 **32** 80 75 33 40 61 46 87
>         ↑
>
> Finally, during the nineteenth loop iteration, 87 will be swapped with the value 95 at index 18, and the whole array will be sorted:

12 16 17 32 33 40 43 44 46 46 50 55 59 61 75 80 80 81 87 95

In other words, for each value of i between 0 and x.length − 1, the smallest value in the subarray from x [i] to x [x.length − 1] is swapped with x [i]. Here is the method definition:

```
/**
 * Sorts a specified array of int values into ascending order.
 * The worstTime(n) is O(n * n).
 *
 * @param x – the array to be sorted.
 *
 */
public static void selectionSort (int [ ] x)
{
       // Make x [0 . . . i] sorted and <= x [i + 1] . . . x [x.length − 1]:
       for (int i = 0; i < x.length − 1; i++)
       {
              int pos = i;
              for (int j = i + 1; j < x.length; j++)
                     if (x [j] < x [pos])
                            pos = j;
              swap (x, i, pos);
       } // for i
} // method selectionSort
```

***Analysis*** First, note that the number of loop iterations is independent of the initial arrangement of elements, so worstTime($n$) and averageTime($n$) will be identical. There are $n − 1$ iterations of the outer loop; when the smallest values are at indexes $x [0]$, $x [1]$, . . . , $x [n − 2]$, the largest value will automatically be at index $x [n − 1]$. During the first iteration, with i = 0, there are $n − 1$ iterations of the inner loop. During the second iteration of the outer loop, with i = 1, there are $n − 2$ iterations of the inner loop. The total number of inner-loop iterations is

$$(n − 1) + (n − 2) + \cdots + 1 = \sum_{i=1}^{n-1} i = n(n − 1)/2$$

We conclude that worstTime($n$) is quadratic in $n$. For future reference, note that only $n − 1$ swaps are made.

The worstSpace($n$) is constant: only a few variables are needed, and so Selection Sort is an in-place sort. But Selection Sort is *not* stable; see Concept Exercise 11.14.

As we noted in Section 11.2.1, Insertion Sort requires only linear-in-$n$ time if the array is already sorted, or nearly so. That is a clear advantage over Selection Sort, which always takes quadratic-in-$n$ time. In the average case or worst case, Insertion Sort takes quadratic-in-$n$ time, and so a run-time experiment is needed to distinguish between Insertion Sort and Selection Sort. You will get the opportunity to do this in Lab 18.

## 11.2.3 Bubble Sort

*Warning:* Do not use this method. Information on Bubble Sort is provided to illustrate a very inefficient algorithm with an appealing name. In this section, you will learn why Bubble Sort should be avoided, so you can illuminate any unfortunate person who has written, used, or even mentioned Bubble Sort.

Given an array x of **int** values, compare each element to the next element in the array, swapping where necessary. At this point, the largest value will be at index x.length − 1. Then start back at the beginning, and compare and swap elements. To avoid needless comparisons, go only as far as the last interchange from the previous iteration. Continue until no more swaps can be made: the array will then be sorted.

> *Example*  Suppose the array x initially has the following values:
>
> 59 46 32 80 46 55 50 43 44 81 12 95 17 80 75 33 40 61 16 87
>
> Because 59 is greater than 46, those two elements are swapped, and we have
>
> 46 59 32 80 46 55 50 43 44 81 12 95 17 80 75 33 40 61 16 87
>
> Then 59 and 32 are swapped, 59 and 80 are not swapped, 80 and 46 (at index 4) are swapped, and so on. After the first iteration, x contains
>
> 46 32 59 46 55 50 43 44 80 12 81 17 80 75 33 40 61 16 87 95
>
> The last swap during the first iteration was of the elements 95 and 87 at indexes 18 and 19, so in the second iteration, the final comparison will be between the elements at indexes 17 and 18. After the second iteration, the array contains
>
> 32 46 46 55 50 43 44 59 12 80 17 80 75 33 40 61 16 81 87 95
>
> The last swap during the second iteration was of the elements 81 and 16 at indexes 16 and 17, so in the third iteration, the final comparison will be between the elements at indexes 15 and 16.
>
> Finally, after 18 iterations, and many swaps, we end up with
>
> 12 16 17 32 33 40 43 44 46 46 50 55 59 61 75 80 80 81 87 95
>
> Here is the method definition:

```
/**
 * Sorts a specified array of int values into ascending order.
 * The worstTime(n) is O(n * n).
 *
 * @param x – the array to be sorted.
 *
 */
```

```
public static void bubbleSort (int[ ] x)
{
        int finalSwapPos = x.length − 1,
          swapPos;

        while (finalSwapPos > 0)
        {
              swapPos = 0;
              for (i = 0; i < finalSwapPos; i++)
                    if (x [i] > x [i + 1])
                    {
                          swap (x, i, i + 1);
                          swapPos = i;
                    } // if
              finalSwapPos = swapPos;
        } // while
} // method bubbleSort
```

***Analysis*** If the array starts out in reverse order, then there will be $n − 1$ swaps during the first outer-loop iteration, $n − 2$ swaps during the second outer-loop iteration, and so on. The total number of swaps, and inner-loop iterations, is

$$(n − 1) + (n − 2) + \cdots + 1 = \sum_{i=1}^{n-1} i = n(n − 1)/2$$

We conclude that worstTime($n$) is quadratic in $n$.

What about averageTime($n$)? The average number of inner-loop iterations, as you probably would have guessed, is

$$(n^2 − n)/2 − (n + 1) \ln (n + 1)/2$$
$$+ (n + 1)/2 \cdot \left\{ \ln 2 + \lim_{k \to \infty} \left[ \sum_{i=1}^{k} (1/i) − \ln k \right] \right.$$
$$\left. + (2/3)\sqrt{(2\pi(n + 1))} \right\} + 31/36 + \text{some terms in } O(n^{-1/2})$$

What is clear from the first term in this formula is that averageTime($n$) is quadratic in $n$.

It is not a big deal, but Bubble Sort is very efficient if the array happens to be in order. Then, only $n$ inner-loop iterations (and no swaps) take place. What if the entire array is in order, except that the smallest element happens to be at index x.length − 1? Then $n(n − 1)/2$ inner-loop iterations still occur!

Swaps take place only when, for some index i, the element at index i is greater than the element at index i + 1. This implies that Bubble Sort is stable. And with just a few additional variables needed, Bubble Sort is an in-place sort.

What drags Bubble Sort down, with respect to run-time performance, is the large number of swaps that occur, even in the average case. You will get first-hand experience with Bubble Sort's run-time sluggishness if you complete Lab 18. As Knuth (1973) says, "In short, the bubble sort seems to have nothing going for it, except a catchy name and the fact that it leads to some interesting theoretical problems."

## 11.3 | THE Comparator INTERFACE

Insertion Sort, Selection Sort, and Bubble Sort produce an array of **int** values in ascending order. We could easily modify those methods to sort into descending order. Similarly straightforward changes would allow us to sort arrays of values from other primitive types, such as **long** or **double**. What about sorting objects? For objects in a class that implements the Comparable interface, we can sort by the "natural" ordering, as described in Section 10.1.1. For example, here is the heading for a Selection Sort that sorts an array of objects:

```
/**
 * Sorts a specified array of objects into ascending order.
 * The worstTime(n) is O(n * n).
 *
 * @param x – the array to be sorted.
 *
 */
public static void selectionSort (Object [ ] x)
```

For the definition of this version, we replace the line

```
if (x [j] < x [pos])
```

in the original version with

```
if (((Comparable)x [j]).compareTo (x [pos]) < 0)
```

and change heading of the swap method and the type of temp in that method.

As we saw in Section 10.1.1, the String class implements the Comparable interface with a compareTo method that reflects a lexicographic ordering. If names is an array of String objects, we can sort names into lexicographical order with the call

```
selectionSort (names);
```

This raises an interesting question: What if we did not want the "natural" ordering? For example, what if we wanted String objects ordered by the length of the string?

For applications in which the "natural" ordering—through the Comparable interface—is inappropriate, elements can be compared with the Comparator interface. The Comparator interface, with type parameter T (for "type") has a method to compare two elements of type T:

```
/**
 * Compares two specified elements.
 *
 * @param element1 – one of the specified elements.
 * @param element2 – the other specified element.
 *
 * @return a negative integer, 0, or a positive integer, depending on
```

```
    *       whether element1 is less than, equal to, or greater than
    *       element2.
    *
    */
    int compare (T element1, T element2);
```

We can implement the Comparator interface to override the natural ordering. For example, we can implement the Comparator interface with a ByLength class that uses the natural ordering for String objects of the same length, and otherwise returns the difference in lengths. Then the 3-character string "yes" is considered greater than the 3-character string "and", but less than the 5-character string "maybe". Here is the declaration of ByLength:

```
public class ByLength implements Comparator<String>
{
    /**
     * Compares two specified String objects lexicographically if they have the same
     * length, and otherwise returns the difference in their lengths.
     *
     * @param s1 – one of the specified String objects.
     * @param s2 – the other specified String object.
     *
     * @return s1.compareTo(s2), if s1 and s2 have the same length;
     *         otherwise, return s1.length( ) – s2.length( ).
     *
     */
    public int compare (String s1, String s2)
    {
        int len1 = s1.length( ),
            len2 = s2.length( );
        if (len1 == len2)
                return s1.compareTo(s2);
        return len1 – len2;
    } // method compare

} // class ByLength
```

One advantage to using a Comparator object is that no changes need be made to the element class: the compare method's parameters are the two elements to be ordered. Leaving the element class unchanged is especially valuable when, as with the String class, users are prohibited from modifying the class.

Here is a definition of Selection Sort, which sorts an array of objects according to a comparator that compares any two objects:

```
/**
 * Sorts a specified array into the order specified by a specified Comparator
 * object.
 * The worstTime(n) is O(n * n).
 *
 * @param x – the array to be sorted.
```

```
    * @param comp – the Comparator object used for ordering.
    *
    */
   public static void selectionSort (Object [ ] x, Comparator<Object> comp)
   {
        // Make x [0 . . . i] sorted and <= x [i + 1] . . . x [x.length − 1]:
        for (int i = 0; i < x.length − 1; i++)
        {
             int pos = i;
             for (int j = i + 1; j < x.length; j++)
                  if (comp.compare (x [j], x [pos]) < 0)
                       pos = j;
             swap (x, i, pos);
        } // for i
   } // method selectionSort
```

The corresponding swap method is:

```
   public static void swap (Object[ ] x, int a, int b)
   {
        Object temp = x [a];
        x [a] = x [b];
        x [b] = temp;
   } // swap
```

To complete the picture, here is a main method that applies this version of selection Sort (note that the enhanced **for** statement also works for arrays):

```
   public static void main(String[ ] args)
   {
        String[ ] words = {"yes", "true", "maybe", "relax", "heavenly", "good", "halcyon"};

        selectionSort (s, new ByLength( ));
        for (String s : words)
             System.out.print (s + " ");
   } // method main
```

The output will be

yes good true maybe relax halcyon heavenly

The material in this section will be helpful in Section 11.4.1, where we will encounter one of the sort methods in the Java Collections Framework. For this method, called Merge Sort, the element type cannot be primitive; it must be Object, or subclass of Object. The method comes in four flavors: the collection to be sorted can be either an array object or a List object, and the ordering may be according to the Comparable interface or the Comparator interface. And Chapters 12 and 13 have sort methods with similar flexibility.

In Section 11.4, we consider two important questions: For comparison-based sorts, is there a lower bound for worstTime($n$)? Is there a lower bound for averageTime($n$)?

# 11.4 I HOW FAST CAN WE SORT?

If we apply Insertion Sort, Selection Sort, or (perish the thought) Bubble Sort, worstTime($n$) is quadratic in $n$. Before we look at some faster sorts, let's see how much of an improvement is possible. The tool we will use for this analysis is the decision tree. A ***decision tree*** is a binary tree in which each nonleaf represents a comparison between two elements and each leaf represents a sorted sequence of those elements. For example, Figure 11.1 shows a decision tree for applying Insertion Sort in which the elements to be sorted are stored in the variables $a_1$, $a_2$ and $a_3$.

A decision tree must have one leaf for each permutation of the elements to be sorted.[2] The total number of permutations of $n$ elements is $n!$, so if we are sorting $n$ elements, the corresponding decision tree must have $n!$ leaves. According to the Binary Tree Theorem, the number of leaves in any nonempty binary tree $t$ is $\leq 2^{\text{height }(t)}$. Thus, for a decision tree $t$ that sorts $n$ elements,

$$n! \leq 2^{\text{height }(t)}$$

Taking logs, we get

$$\text{height}(t) \geq \log_2(n!)$$

In other words, for any comparison-based sort, there must be a leaf whose depth is at least $\log_2(n!)$. In the context of decision trees, that means that there must be an arrangement of elements whose sorting requires at least $\log_2(n!)$ comparisons. That is, worstTime($n$) $\geq \log_2(n!)$. According to Concept Exercise 11.7, $\log_2(n!) \geq n/2 \log_2(n/2)$, which makes $n/2 \log_2(n/2)$ a lower bound of worstTime($n$) for any comparison-based sort. According to the material on lower bounds from Chapter 3, $n/2 \log_2(n/2)$ is $\Omega(n \log n)$. So we can say, crudely, that $n \log n$ is a lower bound for worstTime($n$). Formally, we have

> **Sorting Fact 1**   For comparison-based sorts, worstTime($n$) is $\Omega(n \log n)$.

What does Sorting Fact 1 say about upper bounds? We can say, for example, that for any comparison-based sort, worstTime($n$) is not $O(n)$. But can we say that for any comparison-based sort, worstTime($n$) is $O(n \log n)$? No, because for each of the sorts in Sections 11.2.1 to 11.2.3, worstTime($n$) is $O(n^2)$. We cannot even be sure, at this point, that there are any comparison-based sorts whose worstTime($n$) is $O(n \log n)$. Fortunately, this is not some lofty, unattainable goal. For the comparison-based sort algorithms in Sections 11.4.1, 12.5, and 13.3.3, worstTime($n$) is $O(n \log n)$. When we combine that upper bound with the lower bound from Sorting Fact 1, we will have several sort methods whose worstTime($n$) is linear-logarithmic in $n$.

What about averageTime($n$)? For any comparison-based sort, $n \log n$ is a lower bound of averageTime($n$) as well. To obtain this result, suppose $t$ is a decision tree for sorting $n$ elements. Then $t$ has $n!$ leaves. The average, over all $n!$ permutations,

---

[2] For the sake of simplicity, we assume the sort method does not make any redundant comparisons. Otherwise, the number of leaves in the decision tree would be greater than $n!$.

**Figure 11.1** | A decision tree for sorting 3 elements by Insertion Sort.

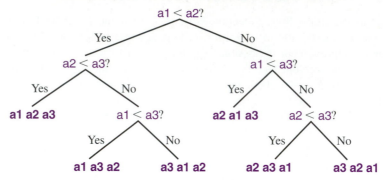

number of comparisons to sort the $n$ elements is the total number of comparisons divided by $n!$. In a decision tree, the total number of comparisons is the sum of the lengths of all paths from the root to the leaves. This sum is the external path length of the decision tree. By the External Path Length Theorem in Chapter 9, $E(t) \geq (n!/2)$ floor $(\log_2(n!))$. So we get

$$\begin{aligned}
\text{averageTime}(n) &\geq \text{average number of comparisons} \\
&= E(t)/n! \\
&\geq (n!/2) \text{ floor } (\log_2(n!))/n! \\
&= (1/2) \text{ floor } (\log_2(n!)) \\
&\geq (1/4) \log_2(n!) \\
&\geq (n/8) \log_2(n/8) \quad \text{[by Concept Exercise 11.7]}
\end{aligned}$$

We conclude that $n \log n$ is a lower bound of averageTime($n$). That is,

**Sorting Fact 2** For comparison-based sorts, averageTime($n$) is $\Omega(n \log n)$.

We noted above that there are several sort methods whose worstTime($n$) is linear-logarithmic in $n$. We can use that fact to show that their averageTime($n$) must also be linear-logarithmic in $n$. Why? Suppose we have a sort algorithm for which worstTime($n$) is linear-logarithmic in $n$. That is, crudely, $n \log n$ is both an upper bound and a lower bound of worstTime($n$). But if $n \log n$ is an upper bound of worstTime($n$), $n \log n$ must also be an upper bound of averageTime($n$). According to Sorting Fact 2, $n \log n$ is a lower bound on averageTime($n$). Since $n \log n$ is both an upper bound and a lower bound of averageTime($n$), we conclude that averageTime($n$) must be linear-logarithmic in $n$. That is,

**Sorting Fact 3** For comparison-based sorts, if worstTime($n$) is linear-logarithmic in $n$, then averageTime($n$) must be linear-logarithmic in $n$.

In Sections 11.4.1 and 11.4.3, we will study two sort algorithms, Merge Sort and Quick Sort, whose averageTime($n$) is linear-logarithmic in $n$. For Merge Sort, worstTime($n$) is also linear-logarithmic in $n$, while for Quick Sort, worstTime($n$) is quadratic in $n$. Strangely enough, Quick Sort is generally considered the most efficient all-around sort! Quick Sort's worst-case performance is bad, but for average-case run-time speed, Quick Sort is the best of the lot.

## 11.4.1 Merge Sort

The Merge Sort algorithm, in the Java Collections Framework, sorts a collection of objects. We start with two simplifying assumptions, which we will then dispose of. First, we assume the objects to be sorted are in an array. Second, we assume the ordering is to be accomplished through the Comparable interface.

The basic idea is to keep splitting the array in two until, at some step, each of the subarrays has size less than 7 (the choice of 7 is based on run-time experiments; see Bentley (1993)). Insertion Sort is then applied to each of two small-sized subarrays, and the two sorted subarrays are merged together into a sorted double-sized subarray. Eventually, that subarray is merged with another sorted double-sized subarray to produce a sorted quadruple-sized subarray. This process continues until, finally, two sorted subarrays of size $n/2$ are merged back into the original array, now sorted, of size $n$.

Here is the method specification for Merge Sort:

```
/**
 * Sorts a specified array of objects according to the compareTo method
 * in the specified class of elements.
 * The worstTime(n) is linear-logarithmic in n.
 *
 * @param a – the array of objects to be sorted.
 *
 */
public static void sort (Object[ ] a)
```

Up until now, the time estimates in a method specification have used upper bounds only, which for this method would be $O(n \log n)$. But the method specification for Merge Sort has "linear-logarithmic in $n$" instead of $O(n \log n)$. Why? By Sorting Fact 1 in Section 11.3, worstTime($n$) must be $\Omega(n \log n)$. If worstTime($n$) is also $O(n \log n)$, then $n \log n$ is both a lower bound and an upper bound. That is, worstTime($n$) is linear-logarithmic in $n$. By Sorting Fact 3, averageTime($n$) must also be linear-logarithmic in $n$.

This method has the identifier sort because it is the only method in the Java Collections Framework for sorting an array of objects according to the Comparable interface. Later in this chapter we will encounter a different sort method—also with the identifier sort—for sorting an array of values from a primitive type. The distinction is easy to make from the context, namely, whether the argument is an array of objects or an array from a primitive type such as **int** or **double**.

*Example* To start with a small example, here are the **int** values in an array of Integer objects:

59 46 32 80 46 55 87 43 44 81

To simplify the sorting process, we use a temporary array. We first clone the parameter a into aux (an abbreviation for "auxiliary"). We now have two arrays with (separate references to) identical elements. The recursive method mergeSort is then called to sort the elements in aux back into a. Here is the definition of the sort method:

```
public static void sort (Object[ ] a)
{
        Object aux[ ] = (Object [ ])a.clone( );
        mergeSort (aux, a, 0, a.length);
} // method sort
```

The method specification for mergeSort is

```
/**
 * Sorts, by the Comparable interface, a specified range of a specified array
 * into the same range of another specified array.
 * The worstTime(k) is linear-logarithmic in k, where k is the size of the subarray.
 *
 * @param src – the specified array whose elements are to be sorted into another
 *         specified array.
 * @param dest – the specified array whose subarray is to be sorted.
 * @param low – the smallest index in the range to be sorted.
 * @param high: 1 + the largest index in the range to be sorted.
 *
 */
private static void mergeSort (Object src[ ], Object dest[ ], int low, int high)
```

The reason we have two arrays is to make it easier to merge two sorted subarrays into a larger subarray. The reason for the **int** parameters low and high is that their values will change when the recursive calls are made. Note that *high's value is one greater than the largest index* of the subarray being mergeSorted.[3]

When the initial call to mergeSort is made with the example data, Insertion Sort is not performed because high − low ≥ 7. Instead, two recursive calls are made:

```
mergeSort (a, aux, 0, 5);
mergeSort (a, aux, 5, 10);
```

When the first of these calls is executed, high − low = 5 − 0 < 7, so Insertion Sort is performed on the first five elements of aux:

---

[3] Technically, there is a fifth parameter. But since we assume that the entire array is being sorted, we can ignore that parameter.

a [0 . . . 4] = {59, 46, 32, 80, 46}
aux [0 . . . 4] = {32, 46, 46, 59, 80}

In general, the two arrays will be identical until an Insertion Sort is performed. When the second recursive call is made, high − low = 10 − 5, so Insertion Sort is performed on the second five elements of aux:

a [5 . . . 9] = {55, 87, 43, 44, 81}
aux [5 . . . 9] = {43, 44, 55, 81, 87}

Upon the completion of these two calls to mergeSort, the 10 elements of aux, in two sorted subarrays of size 5, are merged back into a, and we are done. The merging is accomplished with the aid of two indexes, p and q. In this example, p starts out as 0 (the low index of the left subarray of aux) and q starts out as 5 (the low index of the right subarray of aux). In the following figure, arrows point from p and q to the elements at aux [p] and aux [q]:

```
aux    32 46 46 59 80   43 44 55 81 87
        ↑                ↑
        p                q
```

The smaller of aux [p] and aux [q] is copied to a [p] and then the index, either p or q, of that smaller element is incremented:

```
aux    32 46 46 59 80   43 44 55 81 87
           ↑             ↑
           p             q
a      32
```

The process is repeated: the smaller of aux [p] and aux [q] is copied to the next location in the array a, and then the index, either p or q, of that smaller element is incremented:

```
aux    32 46 46 59 80   43 44 55 81 87
           ↑                ↑
           p                q
a      32 43
```

The next three iterations will copy 44, 46, and 46 into a. The process continues until all of the elements from both subarrays have been copied into a. Since each iteration copies one element to a, merging two subarrays of size $c$ requires exactly $2c$ iterations. In general, to merge $n/k$ subarrays, each of size $k$, requires exactly $n$ iterations.

Figure 11.2 summarizes the sorting of the above array of 10 elements. Figure 11.3 incorporates the example in merge sorting an array of 20 elements. Two pairs of recursive calls are required to merge sort 20 elements.

**Figure 11.2** I The effect of a call to mergeSort on an array of 10 elements.

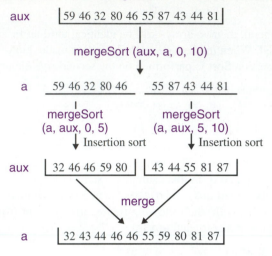

**Figure 11.3** I The effect of a call to mergeSort on an array of 20 elements.

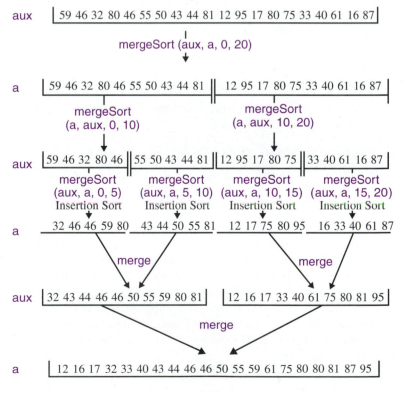

The successive calls to mergeSort resemble a ping-pong match:

aux→a→aux→a→aux→a

The original call, from within the sort method, is always of the form

mergeSort (aux, a, ...);

So after all of the recursive calls have been executed, the sorted result ends up in a. After the Insertion Sorting has been completed for the two successive subarrays in the recursive call to mergeSort, a merge of those sorted subarrays is performed, and that completes a recursive call to mergeSort.

Here is the complete mergeSort method, including an optimization (starting with // If left subarray ...) that you can safely ignore.

```
/**
 * Sorts, by the Comparable interface, a specified range of a specified array
 * into the same range of another specified array.
 * The worstTime(k) is linear-logarithmic in k, where k is the size of the subarray.
 *
 * @param src – the specified array whose range is to be sorted into another
 *        specified array.
 * @param dest – the specified array whose subarray is to be sorted.
 * @param low – the smallest index in the range to be sorted.
 * @param high – 1 + the largest index in the range to be sorted.
 *
 */
private static void mergeSort (Object src[ ], Object dest[ ], int low, int high)
{
        int length = high − low;

        // Use Insertion Sort for small subarrays.
        if (length < INSERTIONSORT_THRESHOLD /* = 7*/)
        {
                for (int i = low; i < high; i++)
                        for (int j = i; j >low && ((Comparable)dest[j − 1])
                                        .compareTo(dest[j]) > 0; j−−)
                                swap (dest, j, j−1);
                return;
        } // if length < 7

        // Sort left and right halves of src into dest.
        int mid = (low + high) >> 1; // >> 1 has same effect as / 2, but is faster
        mergeSort (dest, src, low, mid);
        mergeSort (dest, src, mid, high);

        // If left subarray less than right subarray, copy src to dest.
        if (((Comparable)src [mid-1]).compareTo (src [mid]) <= 0)
```

```
        {
                System.arraycopy (src, low, dest, low, length);
                return;
        }

        // Merge sorted subarrays in src into dest.
        for (int i = low, p = low, q = mid; i < high; i++)
        if (q>=high || (p<mid && ((Comparable)src[p]).compareTo (src[q])<= 0))
                dest [i] = src [p++];
        else
                dest[i] = src[q++];
} // method mergeSort
```

***Analysis*** We want to get an upper bound on worstTime($n$), where $n$ is the number of elements to be sorted. There are four phases: cloning, calls to mergeSort, Insertion Sorting, and merging.

The cloning requires $n$ iterations.

Let $L$ (for "levels") be the number of pairs of recursive calls to mergeSort. The initial splitting into subarrays requires approximately $L$ statements (that is, $L$ pairs of recursive calls). $L$ is equal to the number of times that $n$ is divided by 2. By the Splitting Rule from Chapter 3, the number of times that $n$ can be divided by 2 until $n$ equals 1 is, approximately, $\log_2 n$. But when the size of a subarray is less than 7, we stop dividing by 2. So $L$ is approximately $\log_2(n/7)$.

For the Insertion Sort phase, we have fewer than $n$ subarrays, each of size less than 7. The maximum number of iterations executed when Insertion Sort is applied to each one of these subarrays is less than 49 because Insertion Sort's worst time is quadratic in the number of elements. So the total number of iterations for this phase is less than $49n$.

Finally, the merging back into double-sized subarrays takes, approximately, $L$ times the number of iterations per level, that is, $\log_2(n/7)$ times the number of iterations executed at any level. At any level, *exactly* $n$ elements are copied from a to aux (or from aux to a). So the total number of iterations is, approximately, $n \log_2 (n/7)$.

The total number of iterations is approximately

$$n + \log_2(n/7) + 49n + \log_2(n/7) \cdot n$$

From this we conclude that worstTime($n$) is approximately

$$n + \log_2(n/7) + 49n + n \log_2(n/7)$$

That is, worstTime($n$) is $O(n \log n)$. By Sorting Fact 1 in Section 11.4, for any comparison-based sort, worstTime($n$) is $\Omega(n \log n)$. Since $n \log n$ is both an upper bound and a lower bound of worstTime($n$), worstTime($n$) must be linear-logarithmic in $n$ (that is, $\Theta(n \log n)$: Big Theta of $n \log n$). That implies, by Sorting Fact 3, that averageTime($n$) is also linear-logarithmic in $n$.

Not only is mergeSort as good as you can get in terms of estimates of worstTime($n$) and averageTime($n$), but the actual number of comparisons made is close to the theoretical minimum; see Kruse (1987, pp. 251–254).

What is worstSpace($n$)? The temporary array aux, of size $n$, is created before mergeSort is called, and this implies that Merge Sort is *not* an in-place sort. During the execution of mergeSort, activation records are created at each level. At the first level, two activation records are created; at the second level, four activation records are created; and so on. The total number of activation records created is

$$2 + 4 + 8 + 16 + \cdots + 2L = 2\left( \sum_{i=1}^{L} 2^i \right) = 2(2^{L+1} - 1) = 2^{L+2} - 2$$

(The result on the sum of powers of 2 is from Exercise A2.6 in Appendix 2.) Since $L \approx \log_2 (n/7)$, and $2^{\log_2 n} = n$, we conclude that the total number of activation records created is linear in $n$. When we add up the linear-in-$n$ space for aux and the linear-in-$n$ space for activation records, we conclude that worstSpace($n$) is linear in $n$.

Both the Insertion Sorting phase and the merging phase preserve the relative order of elements. That is, mergeSort is a stable sort.

**Other Merge Sort Methods**　The Arrays class also has a version of Merge Sort that takes a Comparator parameter:

**public static** <T> **void** sort (T [ ], Comparator<? **super** T> c)

The essential difference between this version and the Comparable version is that an expression such as

(Comparable)dest[j-1]).compareTo(dest[j])>0

is replaced with

c.compare(dest[j-1], dest[j])>0

For example, suppose words is an array of String objects. To perform Merge Sort on words by the lengths of the strings (but lexicographically for equal-length strings), we utilize the ByLength class from Section 11.3:

Arrays.sort (words, **new** ByLength( ));

The Collections class, also in the package java.util, has two versions—depending on whether or not a comparator is supplied—of a Merge Sort method. Each version starts by copying the list to an array. Then the appropriate version of sort from the Arrays class is called. Finally, during an iteration of the list, each element is assigned the value of the corresponding element in the array. Here, for example, is the Comparator version:

```
/**
 * Sorts a specified List object of elements from class T according to a
```

```
       * specified Comparator object.
       * The worstTime(n) is linear-logarithmic in n.
       *
       * @param list – the List object to be sorted.
       * @param c – the Comparator object that determines the ordering of elements.
       *
       */
      public static <T> void sort (List<T> list, Comparator<? super T> c)
      {
            Object a[ ] = list.toArray( );
            Arrays.sort(a, c);
            ListIterator<T> i = list.listIterator( );
            for (int j=0; j<a.length; j++)
            {
                  i.next( );
                  i.set(a[j]);
            } // for
      } // method sort
```

Both versions of Merge Sort in the Collections class work for any class that implements the List interface, such as ArrayList and LinkedList. The run-time will be somewhat slower than for the Arrays-class versions because of the copying from the list to the array before sorting and the copying from the array to the list after sorting.

One limitation to the current versions of Merge Sort is that they do not allow an array of primitives to be merge-sorted. The effect of this restriction can be overcome by merge sorting the corresponding array of objects. For example, to Merge Sort an array of **int** values, create an array of Integer objects, convert each **int** value to the corresponding Integer object, apply Merge Sort to the array of Integer objects, then convert the Integer array back to an array of **int** values. But this roundabout approach will increase the run-time for merge sorting.

## 11.4.2 The Divide-and-Conquer Design Pattern

The mergeSort method is an example of the divide-and-conquer design pattern. Every *divide-and-conquer* algorithm has the following characteristics:

■ The method consists of at least two recursive calls to the method itself.

■ The recursive calls are independent and can be executed in parallel.

■ The original task is accomplished by combining the effects of the recursive calls.

In the case of mergeSort, the sorting of the left and right subarrays can be done separately, and then the left and right subarrays are merged, so the requirements of a divide-and-conquer algorithm are met.

How does a divide-and-conquer algorithm differ from an arbitrary recursive algorithm that includes two recursive calls? The difference is that, for an arbitrary recursive algorithm, the recursive calls need not be independent. For example, in the

Towers of Hanoi problem, $n - 1$ disks had to be moved from the source to the temporary pole *before* the same $n - 1$ disks could be moved from the temporary pole to the destination. Note that the original Fibonacci method from Lab 7 was a divide-and-conquer algorithm, but the fact that the two method calls were independent was an indication of the method's gross inefficiency.

Section 11.4.3 has another example of the divide-and-conquer design pattern.

## 11.4.3 Quick Sort

One of the most efficient and therefore widely used sorting algorithms is Quick Sort, developed by C. A. R. Hoare (1962). The generic algorithm, sort, is a Quick Sort algorithm based on "Engineering a Sort Function" [see Bentley (1993)]. In the Arrays class, Quick Sort refers to any method named sort whose parameter is an array of primitive values, and Merge Sort refers to any method named sort whose parameter is an array of objects.

There are seven versions[4] of Quick Sort in the Arrays class: one for each primitive type (**int**, **byte**, **short**, **long**, **char**, **double**, and **float**) except **boolean**. The seven versions are identical, except for the specific type information; there is no code reuse. We will illustrate Quick Sort on the **int** version and, for simplicity, assume that the entire array is to be sorted. The actual code, somewhat harder to follow, allows a specified subarray to be sorted. Here is the (simplified) method specification:

```
/**
 * Sorts a specified array of int values into ascending order.
 * The worstTime(n) is O(n * n), and averageTime(n) is linear-logarithmic in n.
 *
 * @param a – the array to be sorted.
 *
 */
public static void sort (int[ ] a)
{
        sort1(a, 0, a.length);
} // method sort
```

The **private** sort1 method has the following method specification:

```
/**
 * Sorts into ascending order the subarray of a specified array, given
 * an initial index and subarray length.
 * The worstTime(n) is O(n * n) and averageTime(n) is linear-logarithmic in
 * n, where n is the length of the subarray to be sorted.
 *
 * @param x – the array whose subarray is to be sorted.
 * @param off – the start index in x of the subarray to be sorted.
```

---

[4] Actually, there are 14 versions, because for each primitive type, there is a version that allows Quick Sort to be applied to an entire array, and another version for a specified subarray.

```
    * @param len – the length of the subarray to be sorted.
    *
    */
   private static void sort1(int x[ ], int off, int len)
```

The basic idea behind the sort1 method is this: we first partition the array x into a left subarray and a right subarray so that each element in the left subarray is less than or equal to each element in the right subarray. The sizes of the subarrays need not be the same. We then Quick Sort the left and right subarrays, and we are done. Since this last statement is easily accomplished with two recursive calls to sort1, we will concentrate on the partitioning phase.

Let's start with the essentials; later, in "Optimizations to the Quick Sort Algorithm," we'll look at some of the finer points. The first task in partitioning is to choose an element, called the *pivot,* that each element in x will be compared to. Elements less than the pivot will end up in the left subarray, and elements greater than the pivot will end up in the right subarray. Elements equal to the pivot may end up in either subarray.

What makes Quick Sort fast? With other sorts, it may take many comparisons to put an element in the general area where it belongs. But with Quick Sort, a partition can move many elements close to where they will finally end up. This assumes that the value of the pivot is close to the median[5] of the elements to be partitioned. We could, of course, sort the elements to be partitioned and then select the median as the pivot. But that begs the question of how we are going to sort the elements in the first place.

How about choosing x [off] as the pivot? If the elements happen to be in order (a common occurrence), that would be a bad choice. Why? Because the left subarray would be empty after partitioning, so the partitioning would reduce the size of the array to be sorted by only one. Another option is to choose x [off + len / 2] as the pivot, that is, the element in the middle position. If the range happens to be in order, that is the perfect choice; otherwise, it is as good a blind choice as any other.

With a little extra work, we can substantially increase the likelihood that the pivot will split the range into two subarrays of approximately equal size. The pivot is chosen as the median of the elements at indexes off, off + len/2, and off + len −1. The median of those three elements is taken as a simply calculated estimate of the median of the whole range.

---

[5] The *median* of a collection of values is the value that would be in the middle position if the collection were sorted. For example, the median of

100 32 77 85 95

is 85. If the collection contains an even number of values, the median is the average of the two values that would be in the two middle positions if the collection were sorted. For example, the median of

100 32 77 85 95 80

is 82.5.

Before looking at any more details, let's go through an example.

*Example* We start with the usual sample of 20 values given earlier:

59 46 32 80 46 55 50 43 44 81 12 95 17 80 75 33 40 61 16 87

In this case, we choose the median of the three **int** values at indexes 0, 10, and 19. The median of 59, 12, and 87 is 59, so that is the original pivot.

We now move to the left subarray all the elements that are less than 59 and move to the right subarray all the elements that are greater than 59. Elements with a value of 59 may end up in either subarray, and the two subarrays need not have the same size.

To accomplish this partitioning, we create two counters: b, which starts at off and moves upward, and c, which starts at off + len − 1 and moves downward. There is an outer loop that contains two inner loops. The first of these inner loops increments b until x [b] >= pivot. Then the second inner loop decrements c until x [c] <= pivot. If b is still less than or equal to c when this second inner loop terminates, x [b] and x [c] are swapped, b is incremented, c is decremented and the outer loop is executed again. Otherwise, the outer loop terminates.

The reason we loop until x [b] >= pivot instead of x [b] > pivot is that there might not be any element whose value is greater than the pivot. In "Optimizations to the Quick Sort Algorithm," below, we'll see a slightly different loop condition to avoid stopping at, and therefore swapping, the pivot.

For the usual sample of values, pivot has the value 59, b starts at 0, and c starts at 19. In Figure 11.4, arrows point from an index to the corresponding element in the array. The first inner loop terminates immediately because x [b] = 59 and 59 is the pivot. The second inner loop terminates when c is decremented to 18 because at that point, x [c] = 16 < 59. When 59 and 16 are swapped and b and c are bumped, we get the situation shown in Figure 11.5.

Now b is incremented twice more, and at that point we have x [b] = 80 > 59. Then c is decremented once more, to where x [c] = 40 < 59. After swapping x [b] with x [c] and bumping b and c, we have the state shown in Figure 11.6.

**Figure 11.4 I** The start of partitioning.

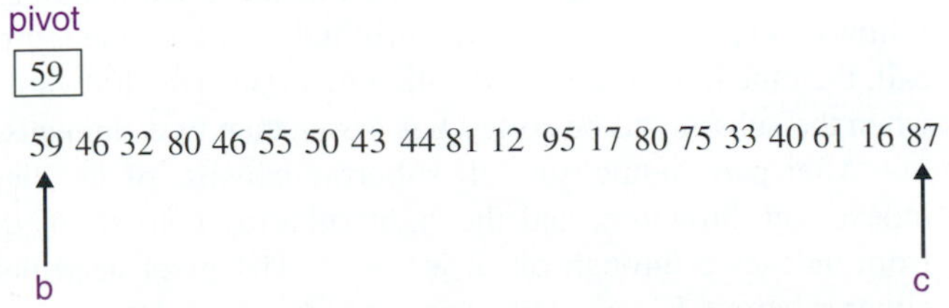

pivot

| 59 |

59 46 32 80 46 55 50 43 44 81 12 95 17 80 75 33 40 61 16 87

b                                                                           c

**Figure 11.5 |** The state of partitioning after the first iteration of the outer loop.

**Figure 11.6 |** The state of partitioning after the second iteration of the outer loop.

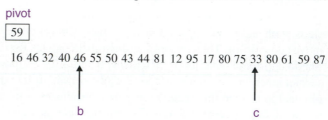

During the next iteration of the outer loop, b is incremented five more times, c is not decremented, 81 and 33 are swapped, then the two counters are bumped, and we have the state shown in Figure 11.7.

During the next iteration of the outer loop, b is incremented once (x [b] = 95), and c is decremented twice (x [c] = 17). Then 95 and 17 are swapped, and b and c are bumped. See Figure 11.8. The outer loop terminates because b > c. All of the elements in the subarray at indexes 0 through c are less than or equal to the pivot, and all the elements in the subarray at indexes b through 19 are greater than or equal to the pivot.

We finish up by making two recursive calls to sort1:

```
sort1 (x, off, c + 1 − off);  // for this example, sort1 (x, 0, 12);
sort1 (x, b, off + len − b); // for this example, sort1 (x, 12, 8);
```

In this example, the call to sort1 (x, off, c + 1 − off) will choose a new pivot, partition the subarray of 12 elements starting at index 0, and make two calls to sort1. After those two calls (and *their* recursive calls) are completed, the call to sort1 (x, b, off + len − b) will choose a new pivot, and so on. If we view each pair of recursive calls as the left and right child of the parent call, the execution of the corresponding binary tree follows a preOrder traversal: the original call, then the left child of that call, then the left child of *that* call, and so on. This leftward chain stops when the subarray to be sorted has fewer than two elements.

After partitioning, the left subarray consists of the elements from indexes off through c, and the right subarray consists of the elements from indexes b through off + len − 1. The pivot need not end up in either subarray. For example, suppose at some point in sorting, the sub-

**Figure 11.7|** The state of partitioning after the third iteration of the outer loop.

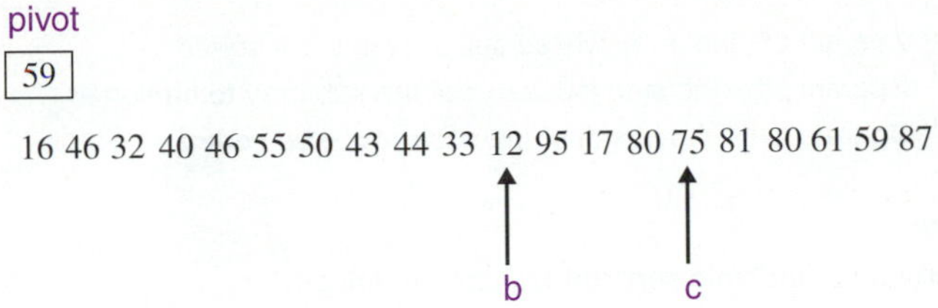

pivot

59

16 46 32 40 46 55 50 43 44 33 12 95 17 80 75 81 80 61 59 87

b                                                                 c

**Figure 11.8|** The state of partitioning after the outer loop is exited.

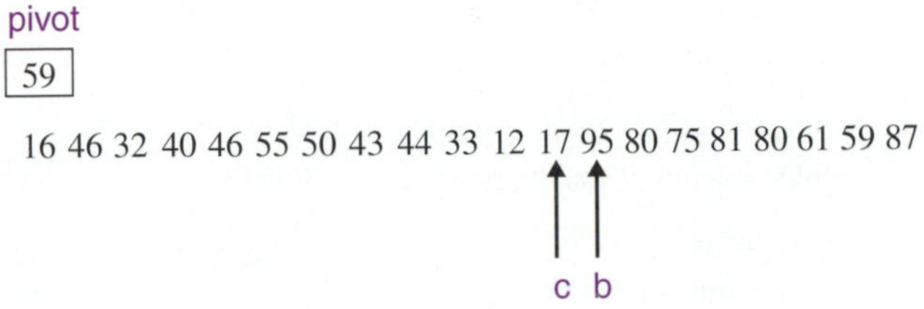

pivot

59

16 46 32 40 46 55 50 43 44 33 12 17 95 80 75 81 80 61 59 87

c b

array to be partitioned contains

15 45 81

The pivot, at index 1, is 45, and both b and c move to that index in searching for an element greater than or equal to the pivot and less than or equal to the pivot, respectively. Then (wastefully) x [b] is swapped with x [c], b is incremented to 2, and c is decremented to 0. The outer loop terminates, and no further recursive calls are made because the left subarray consists of 15 alone, and the right subarray consists of 81 alone. The pivot is, and remains, where it belongs.

Similarly, one of the subarrays may be empty after a partitioning. For example, if the subarray to be partitioned is

15 45

The pivot is 45, both b and c move to that index, 45 is swapped with itself, b is incremented to 2, and c is decremented to 0. The left subarray consists of 15 alone, the pivot is in neither subarray, and the right subarray is empty.

Here is the method definition for the above-described version of sort1 (the version in the Arrays class has a few optimizations, discussed in "Optimizations to the Quick Sort Algorithm"):

```
/**
 * Sorts into ascending order the subarray of a specified array, given
 * an initial index and subarray length.
 * The worstTime(n) is O(n * n) and averageTime(n) is linear-logarithmic in
```

```
 * n, where n is the length of the subarray to be sorted.
 *
 * @param x – the array whose subarray is to be sorted.
 * @param off – the start index in x of the subarray to be sorted.
 * @param len – the length of the subarray to be sorted.
 *
 */
private static void sort1(int x[ ], int off, int len)
{
        // Choose a pivot element, v
        int m = off + len/2,
            l = off,
            n = off + len − 1;

        m = med3 (x, l, m, n); // median of 3
        int v = x [m]; // v is the pivot

        int b = off,
            c = off + len − 1;
        while(true)
        {
              while (x [b] < v)
                    b++;
              while (x [c] > v)
                    c−−;
              if (b > c)
                    break;
              swap (x, b++, c−−);
        } // while true

        if (c + 1 − off > 1)
              sort1 (x, off, c + 1 − off);
        if (off + len − b > 1)
              sort1 (x, b, off + len − b);
} // method sort1

/**
 * Finds the median of three specified elements in a given array.
 *
 * @param x – the given array.
 * @param a – the index of the first element.
 * @param b – the index of the second element.
 * @param c – the index of the third element.
 *
 * @return the median of x [a], x [b], and x [c].
 *
 */
private static int med3(int x[ ], int a, int b, int c) {
```

```
        return (x[a] < x[b] ?
               (x[b] < x[c] ? b : x[a] < x[c] ? c : a) :
               (x[b] > x[c] ? b : x[a] > x[c] ? c : a));
   } // method med3

   /**
    * Swaps two specified elements in a specified array.
    *
    * @param x – the array in which the two elements are to be swapped.
    * @param a – the index of one of the elements to be swapped.
    * @param b – the index of the other element to be swapped.
    *
    */
   private static void swap(int x[ ], int a, int b) {
        int t = x[a];
        x[a] = x[b];
        x[b] = t;
   } // method swap
```

*Analysis* We can view the effect of sort1 as creating an imaginary binary search tree, whose root element is the pivot and whose left and right subtrees are the left and right subarrays. For example, suppose we call Quick Sort for the following array of 15 integers

68 63 59 77 98 87 84 51 17 12 8 25 42 35 31

The first pivot chosen is 51; after the first partitioning, the pivot of the left subarray is 25 and the pivot of the right subarray is 77. Figure 11.9 shows the full binary search tree induced during the sorting of the given array. In general, we get a full binary search tree when each partition splits its subarray into two subarrays that have the same size. We would also get such a tree if, for example, the elements were originally in order or in reverse order, because then the pivot would always be the element at index off + len/2, and that element would always be the actual median of the whole sequence.

**Figure 11.9 |** The imaginary binary search tree created by repeated partitions, into equal sized subarrays, of the array [68 63 59 77 98 87 84 51 17 12 8 25 42 35 31].

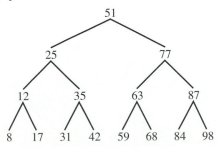

Contrast the tree shown in Figure 11.9 with the tree shown in Figure 11.10. The tree in Figure 11.10 represents the partitioning generated, for example, by the following sequence of 38 elements (the pivot is the median of 1, 37, and 36):

1, 2, 3, . . . , 17, 18, 0, 37, 19, 20, 21, . . . , 35, 36

The worst case will occur when, during each partition, the pivot is either the next-to-smallest or next-to-largest element. That is what happens for the sequence that generated the tree in Figure 11.10.

For any array to be sorted, the induced binary search tree can help to determine how many comparisons are made in sorting the tree. At level 0, each element is compared to the original pivot, for a total of approximately $n$ loop iterations (there will be an extra iteration just before the counters cross). At level 1, there are two subarrays, and each element in each subarray is compared to its pivot, for a total of about $n$ iterations. In general, there will be about $n$ iterations at each level, and so the total number of iterations will be, approximately, $n$ times the number of levels in the tree.

We can now estimate the average time for the method sort1. The average is taken over all n! initial arrangements of elements in the array. At each level in the binary search tree that represents the partitioning, about $n$ iterations are required. The number of levels is the average height of that binary search tree. Since the average height of a binary search tree is logarithmic in $n$, we conclude that the total number of iterations is linear-logarithmic in $n$. That is, averageTime($n$) is linear-logarithmic in $n$. By Sorting Fact 2 in Section 11.4, the averageTime($n$) for Quick Sort is optimal.

**Figure 11.10** | Worst-case partitioning: each partition reduces by only 2 the size of the subarray to be Quick Sorted. The corresponding binary search tree has a leaf at every non-root level. The subtrees below 32 are not shown.

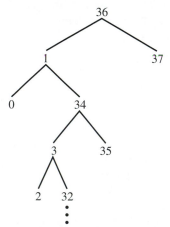

In the worst case, the first partition requires about $n$ iterations and produces a subarray of size $n - 2$ (and another subarray of size 1). When this subarray of size $n - 2$ is partitioned, about $n - 2$ iterations are required, and a subarray of size $n - 4$ is produced. This process continues until the last subarray, of size 2, is partitioned. The total number of iterations is approximately $n + (n - 2) + (n - 4) + \cdots + 4 + 2$, which is, approximately, $n^2/4$. We conclude that worstTime($n$) is quadratic in $n$.

Quick Sort's space needs are due to the recursive calls, so the space estimates depend on the longest chain of recursive calls, because that determines the maximum number of activation records in the run-time stack. In turn, the longest chain of recursive calls corresponds to the height of the induced binary search tree. In the average case, that height is logarithmic in $n$, and we conclude that averageSpace($n$) is logarithmic in $n$. In the worst case, that height is linear in $n$, so worstSpace($n$) is linear in $n$. But Quick Sort *is* an in-place sort because only a few elements (such as the pivot and a temporary) are needed beyond the elements in the array itself.

Quick Sort is not a stable sort. For example, in the example given at the beginning of this section, there are two copies of 80. The one at index 3 is swapped into index 16, and the one at index 13 remains where it starts.

Quick Sort is another example of the divide-and-conquer design pattern. Each of the recursive calls to sort1 can be done in parallel, and the combined effect of those calls is a sorted array.

**Optimizations to the Quick Sort Algorithm** The Java Collections Framework's sort1 method has several modifications to the definition given in Section 11.4.3. The modifications deal with handling small subarrays, handling large subarrays, and excluding the pivot (and elements equal to the pivot) from either subarray.

The partitioning and Quick Sorting continues only for subarrays whose size is at least 7. For subarrays of size less than 7, Insertion Sort is applied. This avoids using the partitioning and recursive-call machinery for a task that can be handled efficiently by Insertion Sort. The choice of 7 for the pivot is based on empirical tests described in Bentley (1993). For arrays of size 7, the pivot is chosen as x [off + len/2]. For arrays of size 8 through 40, the pivot is chosen—as we did in Section 11.4.3—as the median of the three elements at the first, middle, and last indexes of the subarray to be partitioned.

For subarrays of size greater than 40, an extra step is made to increase the likelihood that the pivot will partition the array into subarrays of about the same size. The region to be sorted is divided into three parts, the median-of-three technique is applied to each part, and then the median of those three medians becomes the pivot. For example, if off = 0 and len = 81, Figure 11.11 shows how the pivot would be calculated for a sample arrangement of the array x. These extra comparisons have a price, but they increase the likelihood of an even split during partitioning.

**Figure 11.11** | The calculation of the pivot as the median of three medians. The
median of (139, 287, 275) is 275; the median of (407, 258, 191) is
258; the median of (260, 126, 305) is 260. The median of (275, 258,
260) is 260, and that is chosen as the pivot.

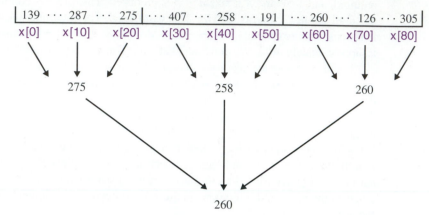

There are two additional refinements, both related to the pivot. Instead of incrementing b until an element greater than or equal to the pivot is found, the search is given by

**while** (b <= c && x[b] <= v)

A similar modification is made in the second inner loop. This appears to be an optimization because the pivot won't be swapped, but the inner-loop conditions also test b <= c. That extra test may impede the speed of the loop more than avoiding needless swaps would enhance speed.

That refinement enables another pivot-related refinement. For the sort1 method defined above, the pivot may end up in one of the subarrays and be included in subsequent comparisons. These comparisons can be avoided if, after partitioning, the pivot is always stored where it belongs. Then the left subarray will consist of elements strictly less than the pivot, and the right subarray will consist of elements strictly greater than the pivot. It may be more efficient for the pivot—indeed, all elements equal to the pivot—to be ignored in the rest of the Quick Sorting. So after the execution of the outer loop, the relation of segments of the subarray to the pivot v will be as shown in Figure 11.12.

At this point, equal-to-pivot elements are swapped back into the middle of the subarray. The left and right subarrays in the recursive calls do not include the equal-to-pivot elements.

As the partitioning of a subarray proceeds, the equal-to-pivot elements are moved to the beginning and end of the subarray with the help of a couple of additional variables:

**int** a = off,
    d = off + len − 1;

**Figure 11.12 |** The relationship of the pivot, **v**, to the elements in the subarray to be partitioned. The leftmost segment and rightmost segment consist of copies of the pivot.

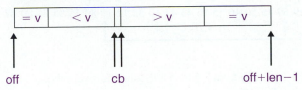

The index a will be one more than the highest index of an equal-to-pivot element in the left subarray, and d will be one less than the lowest index of an equal-to-pivot element in the right subarray. In the first inner loop, if x [b] = v, we call

```
swap (x, a++, b);
```

Similarly, in the second inner loop, if x [c] = v, we call

```
swap (x, c, d--);
```

Figure 11.13 indicates where indexes a and d would occur in Figure 11.12.

For an example that has several copies of the pivot, suppose we started with the following array of 20 **ints**:

59 46 59 80 46 55 87 43 44 81 95 12 17 80 75 33 40 59 16 50

During partitioning, copies of 59 are moved to the leftmost and rightmost part of the array. After b and c have crossed, we have the arrangement shown in Figure 11.14. Now all the duplicates of 59 are swapped into the middle, as shown in Figure 11.15. We now have the array shown in Figure 11.16.

The next pair of recursive calls is:

```
sort1 (x, 0, 11);
sort1 (x, 14, 6);
```

**Figure 11.13 |** A refinement of Figure 11.12 to include indexes a and d.

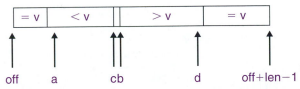

**Figure 11.14 |** The status of the indexes a, b, c, and d after partitioning.

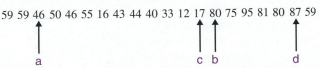

**Figure 11.15** | The swapping of equal-to-pivot elements to the middle of the array.

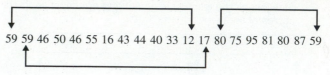

59 59 46 50 46 55 16 43 44 40 33 12 17 80 75 95 81 80 87 59

**Figure 11.16** | The array from Figure 11.15 after the swapping.

12 17 46 50 46 55 16 43 44 40 33 59 59 59 75 95 81 80 87 80

The duplicates of 59, at indexes 11, 12, and 13, are in their final resting place.

Here, from the Arrays class, is the complete definition (the swap and med3 method definitions were given in Section 11.4.3):

```
/**
 * Sorts into ascending order the subarray of a specified array, given
 * an initial index and subarray length.
 * The worstTime(n) is O(n * n) and averageTime(n) is linear-logarithmic in
 * n, where n is the length of the subarray to be sorted.
 *
 * @param x – the array whose subarray is to be sorted.
 * @param off – the start index in x of the subarray to be sorted.
 * @param len – the length of the subarray to be sorted.
 *
 */
private static void sort1(int x[ ], int off, int len) {
        // Insertion sort on smallest arrays
        if (len < 7) {
                for (int i=off; i<len+off; i++)
                        for (int j=i; j>off && x[j-1]>x[j]; j−−)
                                swap(x, j, j-1);
                return;
        }

        // Choose a partition element, v
        int m = off + len/2;        // Small arrays, middle element
        if (len > 7) {
                int l = off;
                int n = off + len - 1;
                if (len > 40) { // Big arrays, pseudomedian of 9
                        int s = len/8;
                        l = med3(x, l, l+s, l+2*s);
                        m = med3(x, m-s, m, m+s);
                        n = med3(x, n-2*s, n-s, n);
                }
```

```
                m = med3(x, l, m, n); // Mid-size, med of 3
        }
        int v = x[m]; // v is the pivot

        // Establish Invariant: = v; < v; > v; = v
        int a = off, b = a, c = off + len - 1, d = c;
        while(true) {
                while (b <= c && x[b] <= v) {
                        if (x[b] == v)
                                swap(x, a++, b);
                        b++;
                }
                while (c >= b && x[c] >= v) {
                        if (x[c] == v)
                                swap(x, c, d--);
                        c--;
                }
                if (b > c)
                        break;
                swap(x, b++, c--);
        }

        // Swap partition elements back to middle
        int s, n = off + len;
        s = Math.min(a-off, b-a); vecswap(x, off, b-s, s);
        s = Math.min(d-c, n-d-1); vecswap(x, b, n-s, s);

        // Recursively sort nonpartition-elements
        if ((s = b-a) > 1)
                sort1(x, off, s);
        if ((s = d-c) > 1)
                sort1(x, n-s, s);
}

/**
 * Swaps the elements in two specified subarrays of a given array.
 * The worstTime(n) is O(n), where n is the number of pairs to be swapped.
 *
 * @param x – the array whose subarrays are to be swapped.
 * @param a – the start index of the first subarray to be swapped.
 * @param b – the start index of the second subarray to be swapped.
 * @param n – the number of elements to be swapped from each subarray.
 *
 */
private static void vecswap(int x[ ], int a, int b, int n) {
        for (int i=0; i<n; i++, a++, b++)
                swap(x, a, b);
} // method vecswap
```

With these optimizations, the results of the analysis in Section 11.4.3 still hold. For example, we now show that if Quick Sort is applied to a large array, worstTime($n$) will still be quadratic in $n$. For $n > 40$, the worst case occurs when the 9 elements involved in the calculation of the median of medians are the five smallest and four largest elements. Then the fifth-smallest element is the best pivot possible, and the partitioning will reduce the size of the subarray by 5. In partitioning the subarray of size $n - 5$, we may have the four smallest and five largest tested for median of medians, and the size will again be reduced by only 5. Since the number of iterations at each level is, approximately, the size of the subarray to be partitioned, the total number of iterations is, approximately,

$$n + (n - 5) + (n - 10) + (n - 15) + \cdots + 45$$

which is, approximately, $n^2/10$. That is, worstTime($n$) is quadratic in $n$.

For a discussion of how, for any positive integer $n$, to create an array of **int** values for which Quick Sort takes quadratic time, see McIlroy (1999).

One debatable issue with the above Quick Sort algorithm is its approach to duplicates of the chosen pivot. The overall algorithm is significantly slowed by the test for equality in the inner loops of sort1. Whether this approach enhances or diminishes efficiency depends on the number of multiple pivot copies in the array. This issue is further explored in Lab 18, which conducts a run-time experiment on the sort methods in this chapter.

We finish up this chapter with a sort method that is not comparison-based, and therefore is essentially different from the other sort methods we have seen.

## 11.5 | RADIX SORT

Radix Sort is different from the other sorts presented in this chapter. The sorting is based on the internal representation of the elements to be sorted, not on comparisons between elements. For this reason, the restriction that worstTime($n$) can be no better than linear-logarithmic in $n$ no longer applies.

Radix Sort was widely used on electromechanical punched-card sorters that appear in old FBI movies. The interested reader may consult Shaffer (1998).

For the sake of simplicity, suppose we want to sort an array of nonnegative integers of at most two decimal digits. The representation is in base 10, also referred to as radix 10—this is how Radix Sort gets its name. In addition to the array to be sorted, we also have an array, lists, of 10 linked lists, with one linked list for each of the 10 possible digit values.

During the first outer-loop iteration, each element in the array is appended to the linked list corresponding to the units digit (the least-significant digit) of that element. Then, starting at the beginning of each list, the elements in lists [0], lists [1], and so on are stored back in the original array. This overwrites the original array. In the second outer-loop iteration, each element in the array is appended to the linked list corresponding to the element's tens digit. Then, starting at the beginning of each list, the elements in lists [0], lists [1], and so on are stored back in the original array.

Here is the method specification:

```
/**
 * Sorts a specified array into ascending order.
 * The worstTime(n) is O(n log N), where n is the length of the array, and N is the largest
 * number (in absolute value) of the numbers in the array.
 *
 * @param a – the array to be sorted.
 *
 */
public static void radixSort (int[ ] a)
```

*Example* Suppose we start with the following array of 12 **int** values:

85 3 19 43 20 55 42 21 91 85 73 29

After each of these is appended to the linked list corresponding to its units (that is, rightmost) digit, the array of linked lists will be as shown in Figure 11.17. Then, starting at the beginning of each list, elements in lists [0], lists [1], and so on are stored back in a. See Figure 11.18. The elements in the array a have now been ordered by their units digits.

In the next outer-loop iteration, each element in a is appended to the list corresponding to the element's tens digit, as shown in Figure 11.19.

Finally (because the integers had at most two digits), starting at the beginning of each list, the integers in lists [0], lists [1], and so on are stored back in a:

3 19 20 21 29 42 43 55 73 85 85 91

**Figure 11.17 I** An array of linked lists after each element in the original array is appended to the linked list that corresponds to the element's units digit.

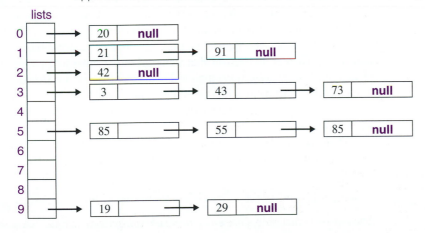

**Figure 11.18 I** The contents of the array a, with the elements ordered by their units digits.

20 21 91 42  3  43 73 85 55 85 19 29

**Figure 11.19** | The array of linked lists after each element in the array a has been appended to the linked list corresponding to its tens digit.

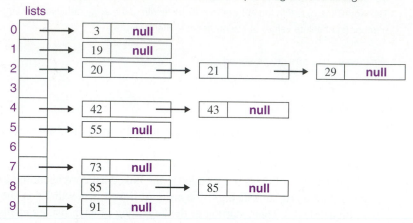

The elements in a have been ordered by their tens digits, and for numbers with the same tens digits, they have been ordered by their units digits. In other words, the array a is sorted.

What happens in general? Suppose we have two integers $x$ and $y$, with $x < y$. We'll see how Radix Sort ensures that $x$ ends up at a smaller index in the array. If $x$ has fewer digits than $y$, then in the final iteration of the outer loop, $x$ will be placed in lists [0] and $y$ will be placed in a higher-indexed list because $y$'s leftmost digit is not zero. Then when the lists are stored back in the array, $x$ will be at a smaller index than $y$.

If $x$ and $y$ have the same number of digits, start at the leftmost digit in each number and, moving to the right, find the first digit in $x$ that is smaller than the corresponding digit in $y$. (For example, if $x = 28734426$ and $y = 28736843$, the thousands digit in $x$ is less than the thousands digit in $y$.) Then at the start of that iteration of the outer loop, $x$ will be placed in a lower-indexed list than $y$. Then when the lists are stored back in the array, $x$ will be at a smaller index than $y$. And from that point on, the relative positions of $x$ and $y$ in the array will not change because they agree in all remaining digits.

There is a slight difficulty in converting the outline in the previous paragraphs into a Java method definition. The following statement is illegal:

```
LinkedList<Integer>[ ] lists = new LinkedList<Integer> [10];
```

The reason is that arrays use *covariant subtyping* (for example, the array Double[ ] is a subtype of Object[ ]), but parameterized types use *invariant subtyping* (for example, LinkedList<Double> is *not* a subtype of LinkedList<Object>). So we will create the array with the raw type LinkedList, and then construct the individual linked lists with a parameterized type.

Here is the method definition:

```
/**
 * Sorts a specified array into ascending order.
 * The worstTime(n) is O(n log N), where n is the length of the array, and N is
 * the largest number (in absolute value) of the numbers in the array.
 *
 * @param a – the array to be sorted.
 *
 */
public static void radixSort (int [ ] a)
{
        final int RADIX = 10;

        int biggest = a [0],
            i;

        for (i = 1; i < a.length; i++)
               if (a [i] > biggest)
                       biggest = a [i];

        int maxDigits = (int)Math.floor (Math.log (biggest) / Math.log (10)) + 1;

        long quotient = 1; // the type is long because the largest number may have
                           // 10 digits; the successive quotients are 1, 10, 100, 1000,
                           // and so on. 10 to the 10th is too large for an int value.

        LinkedList[ ] lists = new LinkedList [RADIX];

        for (int m = 0; m < RADIX; m++)
               lists [m] = new LinkedList<Integer>( );

        // Loop once for each digit in the largest number:
        for (int k = 0; k < maxDigits; k++)
        {
               // Store each int in a as an Integer in lists at the index of a [i]'s
               // kth-smallest digit:
               for (i = 0; i < a.length; i++)
                       ((LinkedList<Integer>)lists [(int)(a [i] / quotient) %
                               RADIX]).add (a [i]);

               i = 0;
               // Store each Integer in list [0], list [1], . . ., as an int in a:
               for (int j = 0; j < RADIX; j++)
               {
                       for (Integer anInt : (LinkedList<Integer>)lists [j])
                               a [i++] = anInt; // unboxing
                       lists [j].clear( );
               } // for j
               quotient *= RADIX;
        } // for k
} // method radixSort
```

*Analysis*  Suppose $N$ is the largest integer in the array. The number of outer-loop iterations must be at least ceil ($\log_{10} N$), and each inner loop is executed $n$ times, so worstTime($n$, $N$) is $O(n \log N)$. If the array also includes negative integers, $N$ is chosen as the largest number in absolute value. Each array element is also stored in a linked list, and so worstSpace($n$) is linear in $n$: Radix Sort is not an in-place sort.

The elements are stored first in, first out in each list, and that makes Radix Sort stable.

*Note:* The elements in this example of Radix Sort are of type **int**, but with a slight change, the element type could also be String, for example. There would be one list for each possible character in the String class. Because each Unicode character occupies 16 bits, the number of distinct characters is $2^{16} = 65,536$ characters. That would require 65,536 linked lists! Instead, the allowable character set would probably be reduced to ASCII, an 8-bit code, so there would be only $2^8 = 256$ characters, and therefore 256 lists.

Lab 18 includes Radix Sort in a run-time experiment on sort methods.

 **Lab 18: Run-Times for Sort Methods**

You are now prepared to do Lab 18.                    All Labs Are Optional

## SUMMARY

Table 11.1 provides a thumbnail sketch of the sort algorithms presented in this chapter.

**Table 11.1** | Important Features of Sort Algorithms from Chapter 11

| Sort algorithm | Element type restriction | Stable? | worstTime($n$) | averageTime($n$); run-time rank | In-place? | worstSpace($n$) |
|---|---|---|---|---|---|---|
| **Insertion Sort** | | Yes | Quadratic | Quadratic; **5** | Yes | Constant |
| **Selection Sort** | | No | Quadratic | Quadratic; **4** | Yes | Constant |
| **Bubble Sort** | | Yes | Quadratic | Quadratic; **6** | Yes | Constant |
| **Merge Sort** | Reference (in JCF) | Yes | Linear-logarithmic | Linear-logarithmic; **2** | No | Linear |
| **Quick Sort** | Primitive (in JCF) | No | Quadratic | Linear-logarithmic; **1** | Yes | Linear |
| **Radix Sort** | | Yes | $n \log N$ | $n \log N$; **3** | No | Linear |

Run-time rank is based on the time to sort $n$ randomly-generated integers. The restrictions on element type are for the versions of Merge Sort and Quick Sort in the Java Collections Framework (JCF). For Radix Sort, $N$ refers to the largest number in the collection.

# CONCEPT EXERCISES

**11.1** Trace the execution of each of the six sort methods—Insertion Sort, Selection Sort, Bubble Sort, Merge Sort, Quick Sort, and Radix Sort—with the following array of values:

10 90 45 82 71 96 82 50 33 43 67

**11.2 a.** For each sort method, rearrange the list of values in Concept Exercise 11.1 so that the minimum number of element-comparisons would be required to sort the array.

**b.** For each sort method, rearrange the list of values in Concept Exercise 11.1 so that the maximum number of element-comparisons would be required to sort the sequence.

**11.3** Suppose you want a sort method whose worstTime($n$) is linear-logarithmic in $n$, but requires only linear-in-$n$ time for an already sorted collection. None of the sorts in this chapter have those properties. Create a sort method that does have those properties. *Hint:* Add a front end to Merge Sort to see if the collection is already sorted.

**11.4** For the optimized Quick Sort in Section 11.4.3, under "Optimizations to the Quick Sort Algorithm," find an arrangement of the integers $0 \cdots 49$ for which the first partition will produce a subarray of size 4 and a subarray of size 44. Recall that because the number of values is greater than 40, the pivot is the "supermedian," that is, the median of the three medians-of-three.

**11.5 a.** Suppose we have a sort algorithm whose averageTime($n$) is linear-logarithmic in $n$. For example, either Merge Sort or Quick Sort would qualify as such an algorithm. Let runTime($n$) represent the time, in seconds, for the implementation of the algorithm to sort $n$ random integers. Then we can write:

runTime($n$) $\approx k\,(c) \cdot n \cdot \log_c n$ seconds,

where $c$ is a an integer variable and $k$ is a function whose value depends on $c$. Show that runTime($cn$) $\approx$ runTime($n$) $\cdot (c + c/\log_c n)$.

**b.** Use the technique in Concept Exercise 11.5a to estimate runTime (200000) if runTime(100000) $==$ 10.0 seconds.

**11.6** Show that seven comparisons are sufficient to sort any collection of five elements.

*Hint:* Compare the first and second elements. Compare the third and fourth elements. Compare the two larger elements from the earlier comparisons. With three comparisons, we have an ordered chain of three elements, with the fourth element less than (or equal to) one of the elements in the chain. Now compare the fifth element to the middle element in the chain. Complete the sorting in three more comparisons. Note that ceil($\log_2 5!$) = 7, so some collections of five elements cannot be sorted with 6 comparisons.

**11.7** Show that $\log_2 n! \geq n/2 \log_2(n/2)$

*Hint:* For any positive integer $n$,

$$n! = \prod_{i=1}^{n} i \geq \prod_{i=1}^{n/2} (n/2) = (n/2)^{n/2}$$

**11.8** Show how Quick Sort's partitioning can be used to develop a method, median, that finds the median of an array of **int** values. For the method median, averageTime($n$) must be linear in $n$.

*Hint:* Suppose we want to find the median of $x$ [0 · · · 10000]. Of course, if we Quick Sort the array, the median would be in $x$ [5000], but then average Time($n$) would be linear-logarithmic in $n$. To get an idea of how to proceed, let's say that the first partition yields a left subarray $x$ [0 · · · 3039] and a right subarray $x$ [3055 · · · 10000], with copies of the pivot in $x$ [3040 · · · 3054]. Since every **int** value in the left subarray is less than every **int** value in the right subarray, which subarray *must* contain the median? The other subarray can be ignored from then on, so the array is not completely sorted.

**11.9** Consider the following consecutive improvements to Insertion Sort:

**a.** Replace the call to the method swap with in-line code:

```java
public static void insertionSort (int[ ] x)
{
    int temp;

    for (int i = 1; i < x.length; i++)
        for (int j = i; j > 0 && x [j−1] > x [j]; j−−)
        {
            temp = x [j];
            x [j] = x [j−1];
            x [j−1] = temp;
        } // inner for
} // method insertionSort
```

**b.** Notice that in the inner loop in part a, temp is repeatedly assigned the *original* value of x [i]. For example, suppose the array x has

32 46 59 80 35

and j starts at 4. Then 35 hops its way down the array, from index 4 to index 1. The only relevant assignment from temp is that last one. Instead, we can move the assignments to and from temp out of the inner loop:

```java
int temp;

for (int i = 1; i < x.length; i++)
{
    int temp = x [i];
```

```
        for (int j = i; j > 0 && x [j − 1] > temp; j−−)
                x [j] = x [j − 1];
            x [i] = temp;
    } // outer for
```

Will these changes affect the estimates for worstTime(*n*) and averageTime(*n*)?

**11.10** If x is an array, Arrays.sort(x) can be called. Will x be Merge Sorted or Quick Sorted? How is the determination made?

**11.11** Show how Merge Sort can be used to sort an array of primitives with the help of the wrapper classes.

**11.12** The Java Collections Framework's version of Quick Sort can be applied only to an array of a primitive type, such as **int** or **double**. Exactly what would have to be changed to create a Quick Sort method that could be applied to an array of objects?

**11.13** If Merge Sort is applied to a collection with 25 elements, what are the values of the index arguments for the first two recursive calls?

**11.14** Give an example to show that Selection Sort is not a stable sort. *Hint:* You need only three elements.

## PROGRAMMING EXERCISES

**11.1** For Concept Exercise 11.9, conduct a timing experiment to estimate the run-time effect of the changes made.

**11.2** In the Java Collections Framework version of Quick Sort, special care is taken during partitioning to make sure that the pivot, and elements equal to the pivot, are not in either of the subarrays created. Estimate—in percentage terms—how much faster Quick Sort would run, on average, if this special care were not taken. Conduct a timing experiment to test your hypothesis.

**11.3** In the med3 method, replace the two applications of the conditional operator with **if** statements.

**11.4** For the original version of Quick Sort in Section 11.4.3, replace the inner-loop conditions from

**while** (x [b] < v)   and   **while** (x [c] > v)

to

**while** ( b <= c && x [b] <= v)   and   **while** (c >= b && x [c] >= v)

Create a main method to apply this version of Quick Sort to the following array of **int** values:

46 59

Explain the results.

**11.5** Develop a version of Radix Sort to sort an array of String objects. You may assume that each String object contains only ASCII characters, and that the maximum size of any String object is 30. Create a main method to test your radixSort method. *Hint:* Instead of the quotient variable, use the charAt method in the String class.

**11.6** Modify the radixSort method in Section 11.5 to use an ArrayList instead of an array of linked lists. *Hint:* Start with

ArrayList<LinkedList<Integer>> lists = **new** ArrayList<LinkedList<Integer>>(RADIX);

Then append 10 empty linked lists to lists.

# Programming Project 11.1

## Sorting a File into Ascending Order

**Analysis:**

The input line will contain the path to the file to be sorted. Each element in the file will consist of a name—last name followed by a blank followed by first name followed by a blank followed by middle name—and social security number. The file is to be sorted by name; equal names should be ordered by social security number. For example, after sorting, part of the file might be as follows:

Jones Jennifer Mary 222222222

Jones Jennifer Mary 644644644

For convenience, you may assume that each name will have a middle name.

    Suppose the file persons.dat consists of the following:

Kiriyeva Marina Alice 333333333

Johnson Kevin Michael 555555555

Misino John Michael 444444444

Panchenko Eric Sam 888888888

Taoubina Xenia Barbara 111111111

Johnson Kevin Michael 222222222

Deusenbery Amanda May 777777777

Dunn Michael Holmes 999999999

Reiley Timothy Patrick 666666666

**System Test 1:**

In the Input line, please enter the path for the file to be sorted.

**persons.dat**

The file persons.dat has been sorted. Please close this output window when you are ready.

    The file persons.dat will now consist of

Deusenbery Amanda May 777777777

Dunn Michael Holmes 999999999

Johnson Kevin Michael 222222222

Johnson Kevin Michael 555555555

Kiriyeva Marina Alice 333333333

Misino John Michael 444444444

Panchenko Eric Sam 888888888

Reiley Timothy Patrick 666666666

Taoubina Xenia Barbara 111111111

*(continued on next page)*

*(continued from previous page)*

For a larger system test, randomly generated, use the same name for each person. The social security numbers will be randomly generated **int**s in the range 0 · · · 999999999. For example, part of the file might have

a a a 238749736

a a a 701338476

a a a 408955917

*Hint:* This would be a fairly simple problem if we could be certain that the entire file would fit in main memory. Unfortunately, this is not the case. Suppose we want to sort a large file of objects from the class **Person**. For specificity, we assume that an object in the **Person** class occupies 50 bytes and that the maximum storage for an array is 500,000 bytes. So the maximum size of an array of **Person** objects is 10,000.

We start by reading in the file of persons, in blocks of 10,000 persons each. Each block is Merge Sorted and stored, in an alternating fashion, on one of two temporary files: leftTop and leftBottom. Figure 11.20 illustrates the effect of this first stage in file sorting.

We then go through an alternating process that continues until all of the elements are sorted and in a single file. The temporary files used are leftTop, leftBottom, and rightBottom; personsFile itself plays the role of rightTop. At each stage, we merge a top and bottom pair of files, with the resulting double-sized blocks stored alternately on the other top and bottom pair. The code for merging sorted blocks in two files into sorted, double-sized blocks in another file is essentially what was followed—using subarrays instead of file blocks—at the end of Merge Sort. Here is that code:

```
// Merge sorted subarrays in src into dest.
for (int i = low, p = low, q = mid; i < high; i++) {
    if (q>=high || (p<mid && ((Comparable)src[p]).compareTo (src[q])<= 0))
        dest [i] = src [p++];
    else
        dest[i] = src[q++];
```

Figure 11.21 illustrates the first merge pass.

**Figure 11.20** I The first stage in file sorting: each of the unsorted blocks in personsFile is Merge Sorted and stored in leftTop or leftBottom.

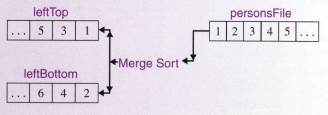

**Figure 11.21** | The first merge pass in file sorting. The files leftTop and leftBottom contain sorted blocks, and personsFile and rightBottom contain double-sized sorted blocks.

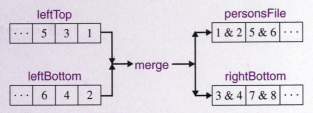

If rightBottom is still empty after a left-to-right merge, then the sort is complete and personsFile holds the sorted file. Otherwise a right-to-left merge is performed, after which we check to see if leftBottom is still empty. If so, leftTop is copied onto persons-File and the sort is complete.

How much time will this take? Suppose that we have $n$ elements in $n/k$ blocks, each of size $k$. In the Merge Sort phase, creating each of the $n/k$ sorted blocks takes, roughly, $k \log_2 k$ time, on average. Each Merge phase takes about $n$ iterations, and there are about $\log_2 (n/k)$ Merge phases. The total time is the sum of the times for all phases: roughly,

$$(n/k) \cdot k \log_2 k + n \cdot \log_2 (n/k) = n \log_2 k + n \log_2 (n/k)$$
$$= n \log_2 k + n \log_2 n - n \log_2 k$$
$$= n \log_2 n$$

Because the averageTime($n$) is optimal, namely linear-logarithmic in $n$, a sorting method such as this is often used for a system sort utility.

# Tree Maps and Tree Sets

We begin this chapter by introducing another kind of balanced binary tree: the red-black tree. Red-black trees provide the underpinning for two extremely valuable classes: the TreeMap class and the TreeSet class, both of which are in the Java Collections Framework. Each element in a TreeMap object has two parts: a *key* part—by which the element is compared to other elements—and a *value* part consisting of the rest of the element. No two elements in a TreeMap object can have the same key. A TreeSet object is a TreeMap object in which all the elements have the same value part. There are applications of both the TreeMap class (a simple thesaurus) and the TreeSet class (a spell-checker). TreeMap objects and TreeSet objects are close to ideal: For inserting, removing, and searching, worstTime($n$) is logarithmic in $n$. ∎

## CHAPTER OBJECTIVES

1. Be able to define what a red-black tree is, and be able to distinguish between a red-black tree and an AVL tree.

2. Understand the Map interface and the overall idea of how the TreeMap implementation of the Map interface is based on red-black trees.

3. Compare TreeMap and TreeSet objects.

4. Explain how Tree Sort works.

## 12.1 | RED-BLACK TREES

Basically, a red-black tree is a binary search tree in which we adopt a coloring convention for each element in the tree. Specifically, with each element we associate a color of either red or black, according to rules we will give shortly. One of the rules involves paths. Recall, from Chapter 9, that if element *A* is an ancestor of element *B,* the ***path*** from *A* to *B* is the sequence of elements, starting with *A* and ending with *B,* in which each element in the sequence (except the last) is the parent of the next element. Specifically, we will be interested in paths from the root to elements with no children *or with one child.*[1] For example, in the following tree, there are five paths from the root to elements (boxed) with no children or one child. Note that one of the paths is to the element 40, which has one child. So the paths described are not necessarily to a leaf.

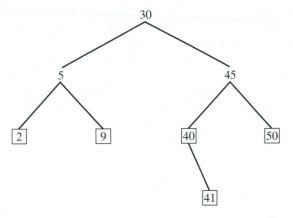

A ***red-black tree*** is a binary search tree that is empty or in which the root element is colored black, every other element is colored red or black, and the following properties are satisfied:

*Red Rule:* If an element is red, none of its children can be red.

*Path Rule:* The number of black elements must be the same in all paths from the root element to elements with no children **or with one child.**

For example, Figure 12.1 shows a red-black tree in which the elements are values of Integer objects and colored ("blue" for red, and "black" for black). Observe that this is a binary search tree with a black root. Since no red element has any red children, the Red Rule is satisfied. Also, there are two black elements in each of the five paths (one path ends at 40) from the root to elements with no children or one child, so the Path Rule is satisfied. In other words, the tree is a red-black tree.

---

[1] Equivalently, we could define the rule in terms of paths from the root element to an empty subtree, because an element with one child also has an empty subtree, and a leaf has two empty subtrees. When this approach is taken, the binary search tree is expanded to include a special kind of element, a stub leaf, for each such empty subtree.

**Figure 12.1** I A red-black tree with eight elements.

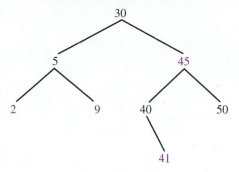

The tree in Figure 12.2 is *not* a red-black tree even though the Red Rule is sat-isfied and every path from the root to a leaf has the same number of black elements. The Path Rule is violated because, for example, the path from 70 to 40 (an element with one child) has three black elements, but the path from 70 to 110 has four black elements. That tree is badly unbalanced: most of its elements have only one child. The Red and Path Rules preclude most single children in red-black trees. In fact, if a red element has any children, it must have two children and they must be black. And if a black element has only one child, that child must be a red leaf.

**Figure 12.2** I A binary search tree that is not a red-black tree.

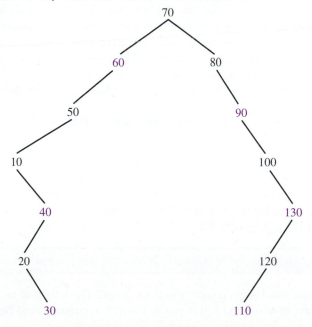

**Figure 12.3** | A red-black tree that is not "evenly" balanced.

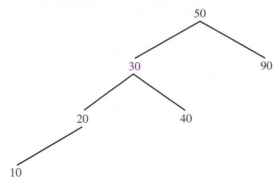

The red-black tree in Figure 12.1 is fairly evenly balanced, but not every red-black tree has that characteristic. For example, Figure 12.3 shows one that droops to the left. You can easily verify that this is a black-rooted binary search tree and that the Red Rule is satisfied. For the Path Rule, there are exactly two black elements in any path from the root to an element with no children or with one child. That is, the tree is a red-black tree. But there are limits to how unbalanced a red-black tree can be. For example, we could not hang another element under element 10 without rebalancing the tree. For if we tried to add a red element, the Red Rule would no longer be satisfied. And if we tried to add a black element, the Path Rule would fail.

If a red-black tree is complete, with all black elements except for red leaves at the lowest level, the height of that tree will be minimal, approximately $\log_2 n$. To get the maximum height for a given $n$, we would have as many red elements as possible on one path, and all other elements black. For example, Figure 12.3 contains one such tree, and Figure 12.4 contains another. The path with all of the red elements will be about twice as long as the path(s) with no red elements. These trees lead us to hypothesize that the maximum height of a red-black tree is less than $2 \log_2 n$.

## 12.1.1  The Height of a Red-Black Tree

Red-black trees are fairly bushy in the sense that almost all nonleaves have two children. In fact, if an element has only one child, that element must be black and the child must be a red leaf. This bushiness leads us to believe that a red-black tree is balanced, that is, has height that is logarithmic in $n$, even in the worst case. Compare that with the worst-case height that is linear in $n$ for a binary search tree! As shown in Example A2.6 of Appendix 2,

> The height of a red-black tree is always logarithmic in $n$, the size of the tree.

How do red-black trees compare to AVL trees? The height of an AVL tree is also logarithmic in $n$. Any AVL tree can be colored to become a red-black tree, and

**Figure 12.4 |** A red-black tree of 14 elements with maximum height, 5.

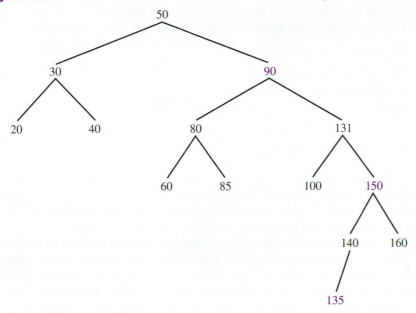

the converse is not true (see Concept Exercises 12.6 and 12.7). That is, red-black trees can have larger heights than AVL trees with the same number of elements.

In Section 12.2, we introduce the Map interface, and in Section 12.3, a class that implements the Map interface. That class, the TreeMap class, is based on a red-black tree, and is part of the Java Collections Framework. The developers of the framework found that using a red-black tree for the underlying structure of the TreeMap class provided slightly faster insertions and removals than using an AVL tree.

## 12.2 | THE Map INTERFACE

A *map* is a collection[2] in which each element has two parts: a unique *key* part and a *value* part. The idea behind this definition is that there is a "mapping" from each key to the corresponding value. For example, we could have a map of social security numbers and names. The keys will be social security numbers and the values will be names. The social security numbers are unique: no two elements in the collection are

---

[2] Recall, from Chapter 4, that a *collection* is an object that is composed of elements. A collection is not necessarily a Collection object, that is, a collection need not implement the Collection interface. For example, an array is a collection but not a Collection object.

allowed to have the same social security number. But two elements may have the same name. For example, we could have the following map, in which all of the social security numbers are unique, but two elements have the same name:

123-45-6789   Builder, Jay

222-22-2222   Johnson, Alan

555-55-5555   Nguyen, Viet

666-66-6666   Chandramouli, Soumya

888-88-8888   Kalsi, Navdeep

999-99-9999   Johnson, Alan

A dictionary is another example of a map. The key is the word being defined and the value consists of the definition, punctuation, and etymology. The term *dictionary* is sometimes used as a synonym for map. In this sense, a dictionary is simply a collection of key-value pairs in which there are no duplicate keys.

The Java Collections Framework has a Map interface that provides method headings for the abstract-data-type map. The Map interface does not extend the Collection interface because many Map methods are oriented toward the key-value relationship. In fact, the type parameters are K (for the key class) and V (for the value class). But the Map interface has some standard methods such as size, equals, and clear. Here are specifications for several of the other methods in the Map interface—no time estimates are given because different implementations have substantially different estimates:

**1.**   /**
      * Associates a specified key with a specified value in this Map object.
      *
      * @param key – the key with which the specified value is to be associated.
      * @param value – the value to be associated with the specified key.
      *
      * @return previous value associated with specified key, or null if there was
      *       no mapping for specified key (note that null could also be the
      *       previous value associated with the specified key).
      *
      * @throws NullPointerException – if key is null and this Map object uses
      *       the natural order, or the comparator does not allow null keys.
      *
      */
   **public** V put (K key, V value)

*Note 1:* The phrase "Map object" denotes an object in a class that implements the Map interface.

*Note 2:* The put method is somewhat more versatile than an add method because the put method handles replacement—of the value associated with a given key—as well as insertion of a new key-value pair.

**2.** /**
\* Determines if this Map object contains a mapping for a specified key.
\*
\* @param key – the specified key.
\*
\* @return true – if there is at least one mapping for the specified key in
\*      this Map object.
\*
*/
**public boolean** containsKey (Object key)

**3.** /**
\* Determines if there is at least one mapping with a specified value in this
\* Map object.
\*
\* @param value – the specified value for which a mapping is sought.
\*
\* @return true – if there is at least one mapping with the specified value
\*      in this Map object.
\*
*/
**public boolean** containsValue (Object value)

**4.** /**
\* Returns the value to which a specified key is mapped in this Map
\* object.
\*
\* @param key – the specified key.
\*
\* @return the value to which the specified key is mapped, if the specified
\*      key is mapped to a value; otherwise, return null.
\*
*/
**public** V get (Object key)

*Note:* The value **null** might also be returned if the given key maps to **null**. To distinguish between this situation and the no-matching-key situation, the containsKey method can be used. For example, if persons is an object in a class that implements the Map interface and key is an object in the key class (which implements a toString( ) method), we can do the following:

```
if (!persons.containsKey(key))
            System.out.println (key + " does not match any key in this map.");
else if (persons.get(key) == null)
            System.out.println (key + " maps to null");
```

**5.** /**
 * Removes the mapping with a specified key from this Map object, if there
 * was such a mapping.
 *
 * @param key – the specified key whose mapping, if present, is to be
 *        removed from this Map object.
 *
 * @return the value to which the specified key is mapped, if there is such
 *         a mapping; otherwise, return null (note that null could also be the
 *         previous value associated with the specified key).
 *
 */
**public** V remove (Object key)

**6.** /**
 * Returns a Set view of the key-value pairs in this Map object.
 *
 * @return a Set view of the key-value pairs in this Map object.
 *
 */
**public** Set entrySet( )

*Note:* Recall, from Chapter 10, that a *set* is a collection of elements in which duplicates are not allowed. We can pretend—*view* is the technical term—that a Map object is just a set of key-value pairs. The advantage to this view is that we can then iterate over the Map object, and the elements returned will be the key-value pairs of the Map object. Why is this important? The Map interface does not have an iterator( ) method, so you cannot iterate over a Map object except through a view. And the Map interface has a **public**, nested Entry interface that has getKey( ) and getValue( ) methods.

For example, suppose that persons is an instance of a class that implements the Map interface, and that the element class has a social security number as the (Integer) key and a name as the (String) value. Then we can print out the name of each person whose social security number begins with 555 as follows:

**for** (Map.Entry<Integer, String> entry : persons.entrySet( ))
   **if** (entry.getKey( ) / 1000000 == 555)
      System.out.println (entry.getValue( ));

There are also keySet( ) and values( ) methods that allow iterating over a Map viewed as a set of keys and as a collection of values, respectively. The term "collection of values" is appropriate instead of "set of values" because there may be duplicate values.

Section 12.3 has an implementation of the Map interface, namely, the TreeMap class. Chapter 14 has another implementation, the HashMap class. The TreeMap class, since it is based on a red-black tree, boasts logarithmic time, even in the worst case, for insertions, removals, and searches. The HashMap class's claim to fame is that, on average, it takes only *constant* time for insertions, removals, and searches! But its worst-case performance is poor: linear in *n*.

The TreeMap class actually implements a slight extension of the Map interface, namely, the SortedMap interface. The SortedMap interface mandates that for any instance of any implementing class, the elements will be in ascending order of keys (for example, when iterating over an entry-set view). The ordering is either the natural ordering—that is, the key class implements the Comparable interface—or an ordering supplied by a comparator. Here are several new methods:

```
/**
 * Returns the comparator for this sorted map, or null, if it uses the
 * keys' natural ordering.
 *
 * @return the comparator for this sorted map, or null, if this sorted
 *         map uses the keys' natural ordering.
 *
 */
Comparator<? super K> comparator( );

/**
 * Returns the first (that is, smallest) key currently in this sorted map.
 *
 * @return the first (that is, smallest) key currently in this sorted map.
 *
 * @throws NoSuchElementException, if this sorted map is empty.
 *
 */
K firstKey( );

/**
 * Returns the last (that is, largest) key currently in this sorted map.
 *
 * @return the last (that is, largest) key currently in this sorted map.
 *
 * @throws NoSuchElementException, if this sorted map is empty.
 *
 */
K lastKey( );
```

# 12.3 | THE TreeMap IMPLEMENTATION OF THE SortedMap INTERFACE

Here is the heading of the TreeMap class:

```
pubilc class TreeMap<K, V> extends AbstractMap<K, V>
           implements SortedMap<K, V>, Cloneable, java.io.serializable
```

For the put, containsKey, get, and remove methods, worstTime($n$) is logarithmic in $n$. Why? In a TreeMap object, the key-value pairs are stored in a red-black tree ordered by the keys. Can you hypothesize why, for the containsValue method, worstTime($n$) is linear in $n$ instead of logarithmic in $n$?

We will look at the fields and method definitions in Section 12.3.2. But our main emphasis is on the *use* of data structures, so let's start with a simple example. The following main method creates a TreeMap object of students. Each student has a name and a grade point average; the ordering is alphabetical by student names. The method prints each student, each student whose grade point average is greater than 3.9, and the results of several removals and searches.

```
public static void main (String[ ] args)
{
        TreeMap<String,Double> students = new TreeMap<String,Double>( );

        students.put ("Bogan, James", 3.85);
        students.put ("Zawada, Matt", 3.95);
        students.put ("Balan, Tavi", 4.00);
        students.put ("Nikolic, Lazar", 3.85);

        System.out.println (students);

        for (Map.Entry<String, Double> entry : students.entrySet( ))
            if (entry.getValue( ) > 3.9)
                System.out.println (entry.getKey( ) + " " + entry.getValue( ));

        System.out.println (students.remove ("Brown, Robert"));
        System.out.println (students.remove ("Zawada, Matt"));
        System.out.println (students.containsKey ("Tavi Balan"));
        System.out.println (students.containsKey ("Balan, Tavi"));
        System.out.println (students.containsValue (3.85));
} // method main
```

The output will be

```
{Balan, Tavi=4.0, Bogan, James=3.85, Nikolic, Lazar=3.85, Zawada, Matt=3.95}
Balan, Tavi 4.0
Zawada, Matt 3.95
null
3.95
false
true
true
```

The reason that the students object is alphabetically ordered by student names is that the key class is String. As we saw in Section 10.1.1, the String class implements the Comparable interface with a compareTo method that reflects the Unicode collating sequence. For applications in which the "natural" ordering—through the Comparable interface—is inappropriate, elements can be compared with the

Comparator interface, discussed in Section 11.3. In the TreeMap class, there is a special constructor:

```
/**
 * Initializes this TreeMap object to be empty, with keys to be compared
 * according to a specified Comparator object.
 *
 * @param c – the Comparator object by which the keys in this TreeMap
 *     object are to be compared.
 *
 */
public TreeMap (Comparator<? super K> c)
```

We can implement the Comparator interface to override the natural ordering. For example, suppose we want to create a TreeMap of Integer keys (and Double values) in *decreasing* order. We cannot rely on the Integer class because that class implements the Comparable interface with a compareTo method that reflects increasing order. Instead, we create a class that implements the Comparator interface by reversing the meaning of the compareTo method in the Integer class:

```
public class Decreasing implements Comparator<Integer>
{
        /**
         * Compares two specified Integer objects.
         *
         * @param i1 – one of the Integer objects to be compared.
         * @param i2 – the other Integer object.
         *
         * @return the value of i2's int – the value of i1's int.
         *
         */
        public int compare (Integer i1, Integer i2)
        {
                return i2.compareTo (i1);
        } // method compare

} // class Decreasing
```

Notice that the Decreasing class need not specify a type parameter since that class is implementing the Comparator interface parameterized with Integer.

A TreeMap object can then be constructed as follows:

```
TreeMap<Integer, Double> inventory =
        new TreeMap<Integer, Double>(new Decreasing( ));
```

For another example, here is the ByLength class from Section 11.3:

```
public lass ByLength implements Comparator<String>
{
```

```
/**
 * Compares two specified String objects lexicographically if they have
 *      the same length, and otherwise returns the difference in their lengths.
 *
 * @param s1 – one of the specified String objects.
 * @param s2 – the other specified String object.
 *
 * @return s1.compareTo(s2) if s1 and s2 have the same length;
 *      otherwise, return s1.length( ) – s2.length ( ).
 *
 */
public int compare (String s1, String s2)
{
        int len1 = s1.length( ),
            len2 = s2.length ( );
        if (len1 == len2)
                return s1.compareTo(s2);
        return len1 – len2;
} // method compare

} // class ByLength
```

The following main method utilizes the ByLength class with a TreeMap object in which the keys are words—stored in order of increasing word lengths—and the values are the number of letters in the words.

```
public static void main (String[ ] args)
{
    TreeMap<String, Integer> wordLengths =
            new TreeMap<String, Integer>(new ByLength( ));

    wordLengths.put ("serendipity", new Integer(11));
    wordLengths.put ("always", new Integer(6));
    wordLengths.put ("serenity", new Integer(8));
    wordLengths.put ("utopia", new Integer(6));

    System.out.println (wordLengths);
} // method main
```

The output will be

```
{always=6, utopia = 6, serenity=8, serendipity=11}
```

Now that we have seen a little of a user's view of the TreeMap class, Sections 12.3.1 and 12.3.2 will spend a little time looking "under the hood" at the fields, the embedded Entry class, and the method definitions. Then Section 12.4 will present an application of the TreeMap class: creating a thesaurus.

## 12.3.1 The TreeMap Class's Fields and Nested Entry Class

Whenever you want to design a class, the critical decision is the choice of fields. Two of the field identifiers are the same as in the BinarySearchTree class of Chapter 10:

```
private transient Entry<K, V> root = null;
```

```
private transient int size = 0;
```

To flag illegal modifications (see Appendix 3) to the structure of the tree during an iteration:

```
private transient int modCount = 0;
```

The only other field in the TreeMap class is used for comparing elements:

```
private Comparator<? super K> comparator = null;
```

This gives a user of the TreeMap class a choice. If the user wants the "natural" ordering, such as alphabetical order for String keys or increasing order for Integer keys, the user creates a TreeMap instance with the default constructor. Then the keys' class must implement the Comparable interface, so comparisons are based on the compareTo method. Alternatively, as we saw in Section 12.3.1, a user can override the "natural" ordering by supplying a Comparator object in the constructor call.

The designers of the Java Collections Framework's TreeMap class chose a red-black tree as the underlying structure because it had a slight speed advantage over an AVL tree for insertions, removals, and searches. We will now start to get into the red-black aspects of the TreeMap class. There are two constant identifiers that supply the colors:

```
private static final boolean RED = false;
```

```
private static final boolean BLACK = true;
```

These constant identifiers apply, not to the tree as a whole, but to the Entry objects in the tree. The Entry class, embedded in the TreeMap class, is similar to the Entry class that is embedded in the BinarySearchTree class, except that the TreeMap class's Entry class has key and value fields (instead of just an element field), and a color field:

```
static class Entry<K, V> implements Map.Entry<K, V>
    K key;
    V value;
    Entry left = null;
    Entry right = null;
    Entry parent;
    boolean color = BLACK; // ensures that root's color will start out BLACK

    . . .
```

Every Entry object's color field is initialized to BLACK. But during an insertion, the inserted Entry object is colored RED; this simplifies the maintenance of the Path Rule. The Entry class also has a default-visibility constructor to initialize the key, value, and parent fields. And there are a few **public** methods, such as getKey and getValue, which are useful in iterating over the entries in a TreeMap object after a call to the entrySet method.

To finish up our overview of the TreeMap implementation of the Map interface, we consider a few method definitions in Section 12.3.2.

## 12.3.2 Method Definitions in the TreeMap Class

We will focus on the definitions of the put and remove methods. As you might expect, the definitions of those methods are quite similar to the definitions of the add and remove methods in the AVLTree class. But one obvious difference is that, for the sake of simplicity, we restricted AVLTree elements to the "natural" ordering with an implementation of the Comparable interface. Users of the TreeMap class can guarantee the elements in a TreeMap instance will be ordered "naturally" by invoking the default constructor. Or, as we saw in Section 12.3.1, a user can override the natural ordering by invoking the constructor that takes a Comparator argument.

To reconcile the two kinds of ordering, the TreeMap class has a compare method[3] that invokes the appropriate key-comparison method:

```
/**
 * Compares two specified elements according to Comparable or a
 * Comparator object.
 *
 * @param k1 – one of the specified elements.
 * @param k2 – the other specified element.
 *
 * @return a negative integer, 0, or a positive integer, depending on
 *         whether k1 is less than, equal to or greater than k2.
 *
 */
private int compare (K k1, K k2)
{
        return (comparator==null
                ? ((Comparable)k1).compareTo (k2)
                : comparator.compare (k1, k2));
}
```

The somewhat inscrutable conditional operator, introduced in Section 7.3.7, obscures the basic idea behind this definition: if the comparator is **null**, the "natural" ordering applies; otherwise, the ordering is supplied by the comparator's compare method.

The definition of the put (K key, V value) method starts by initializing an Entry:

```
Entry t = root;
```

Then, just as we did in the add method of the AVLTree class, we work our way down the tree until we find where key is or belongs, except that the put method:

- Compares key to t.key with the compare method (of the TreeMap class) defined at the beginning of this section.
- Returns t.setValue (value) if the call to the compare method returns 0 (if key and t.key are the same, value replaces t.value, and the old value is returned).

---

[3] Not to be confused with the compare method in the Comparator interface.

■ After an insertion, calls a special method, fixAfterInsertion, to recolor and rotate the tree if the Red Rule is no longer satisfied (the Path Rule will still be satisfied because the newly inserted entry is colored RED at the start of fixAfterInsertion).

Here is the complete definition:

```java
public V put (K key, V value)
{
        Entry t = root;

        if (t == null)
        {
                incrementSize( ); // increments size and modCount
                root = new Entry (key, value, null);
                return null;
        } // if empty tree
        while (true)
        {
                int cmp = compare(key, t.key);
                if (cmp == 0)
                {
                        return t.setValue (value);
                }
                else if (cmp < 0)
                {
                        if (t.left != null)
                                t = t.left;
                        else
                        {
                                incrementSize( );
                                t.left = new Entry(key, value, t);
                                fixAfterInsertion(t.left);
                                return null;
                        } // if left link is null
                }
                else
                { // cmp > 0
                        if (t.right != null)
                                t = t.right;
                        else
                        {
                                incrementSize( );
                                t.right = new Entry(key, value, t);
                                fixAfterInsertion(t.right);
                                return null;
                        } // if right link is null
                } // key > t.key
```

```
        } // while
    } // method put
```

Notice that the fixAfterInsertion method is not called when an insertion is made at the root. So root remains BLACK in that case.

The definition of the fixAfterInsertion method is not intuitively obvious. In fact, even if you study the code, it makes no sense! Red-black trees were originally developed in Bayer (1972). The algorithms for inserting and removing in these trees, called "2-3-4 trees," were lengthy but the overall strategy was easy to understand. Shorter but harder-to-follow methods were supplied when the red-black coloring was imposed on these structures in Guibas (1978).

Lab 19 investigates the fixAfterInsertion method in some detail.

 **Lab 19: The** fixAfterInsertion **Method**

You are now ready for Lab 19.        All Labs Are Optional

In Section 12.1.1, we stated that the height of any red-black tree is logarithmic in $n$, the number of elements in the tree. So for the part of the put method that finds where the element is to be inserted, worstTime($n$) is logarithmic in $n$. Then a call to fixAfterInsertion is made, for which worstTime($n$) is also logarithmic in $n$. We conclude that, for the entire put method, worstTime($n$) is logarithmic in $n$.

The remove method, only slightly changed from that of the BinarySearchTree class, gets the Entry object corresponding to the given key and then deletes that Entry object from the tree:

```
public V remove (K key)
{
        Entry p = getEntry (key);
        if (p == null)
                return p;
        V oldValue = p.value;
        deleteEntry (p);
        return oldValue;
} // method remove
```

The getEntry method is identical to the BinarySearchTree class's getEntry method except that the compare method (from the beginning of this section) replaces the compareTo method.

The deleteEntry method mimics the BinarySearchTree class's (and AVLTree class's) deleteEntry method, except now we must ensure that the Path Rule is still satisfied after the deletion. To see how we might have a problem, suppose we want to delete the entry with key 50 from the TreeMap object in Figure 12.5. The value parts are omitted because they are irrelevant to this discussion, and we pretend that the keys are of type **int**; they are actually of type reference-to-Integer.

Just as we did with the BinarySearchTree class's deleteEntry method, the successor's key (namely, 70) replaces 50 and then p references that successor. See Figure 12.6.

**Figure 12.5 I** A TreeMap (with value parts not shown) from which 50 is to be deleted.

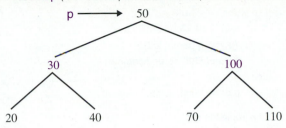

**Figure 12.6 I** An intermediate stage in the deletion of 50 from the TreeMap object of Figure 12.5.

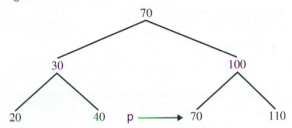

If we were performing a BinarySearchTree-style deletion, we would simply unlink p's Entry object and be done. But if we unlink that Entry object from the TreeMap object of Figure 12.6, the Path Rule would be violated. To perform any necessary recoloring and restructuring, there is a fixAfterDeletion method.

Here is the definition of the deleteEntry method, which is very similar to the definition of the deleteEntry method in both the BinarySearchTree and AVLTree classes:

```
private void deleteEntry (Entry p)
{
        decrementSize( );

        // If strictly internal, replace p's element with its successor's element
        // and then make p reference that successor.
        if (p.left != null && p.right != null)
        {
                Entry s = successor (p);
                p.key = s.key;
                p.value = s.value;
                p = s;
        } // p has two children

        // Start fixup at replacement node, if it exists.
        Entry replacement = (p.left != null ? p.left : p.right);
        if (replacement != null)
        {
                // Link replacement to parent
```

```
                    replacement.parent = p.parent;
                    if (p.parent == null)
                            root = replacement;
                    else if (p == p.parent.left)
                            p.parent.left = replacement;
                    else
                            p.parent.right = replacement;

                    // Fix replacement
                    if (p.color == BLACK)
                            fixAfterDeletion(replacement);
            }
            else if (p.parent == null)
            { // return if we are the only node.
                    root = null;
            }
            else
            { // No children. Use self as phantom replacement and unlink.
                    if (p.color == BLACK)
                            fixAfterDeletion(p);
                    if (p.parent != null)
                    {
                            if (p == p.parent.left)
                                    p.parent.left = null;
                            else if (p == p.parent.right)
                                    p.parent.right = null;
                    } // non-null parent
            } // p has no children
    } // method deleteEntry
```

The fixAfterDeletion method, the subject of Lab 20, has even more cases than the fixAfterDeletion method.

 **Lab 20:** **The** fixAfterDeletion **Method**

You are now ready for Lab 20.                    All Labs Are Optional

The book's website includes an applet that will help you to visualize insertions in and removals from a red-black tree.

In Section 12.4, we develop an application of the TreeMap class to print out the synonyms of given words.

## 12.4 | APPLICATION OF THE TreeMap CLASS: A SIMPLE THESAURUS

A *thesaurus* is a dictionary of synonyms. For example, here is a small thesaurus, with each word followed by its synonyms:

close near confined
confined cramped
correct true
cramped confined
near close
one singular unique
singular one unique
true correct
unique singular one

The problem we want to solve is this: given a thesaurus file and words entered from the keyboard, print the synonym of each word entered.

## Analysis

If there is no file with the path input, a file-not-found message should be printed, followed by a reprompt. The thesaurus file will be in alphabetical order. For each word entered from the keyboard, the synonyms of that word should be printed (to the screen) if the word's synonyms are in the thesaurus file. Otherwise, a synonyms-not-found message should be printed. The sentinel is "***". In the following system test, assume that the thesaurus shown above is in the file "thesaurus.dat".

### System Test (Input Is Boldfaced)

Please enter the path for the thesaurus file: **thesaraus.dat**
java.io.FileNotFoundException: thesaraus.dat (The system cannot find the file specified)

Please enter the path for the thesaurus file: **thesaurus.dat**

Please enter the sentinel (***) or a word: **one**
The synonyms of that word are [singular, unique]

Please enter the sentinel (***) or a word: **two**
The word is not in the thesaurus.

Please enter the sentinel (***) or a word: **close**
The synonyms of that word are [near, confined]

Please enter the sentinel (***) or a word: ***

We will create two classes to solve this problem: a Thesaurus class to store the synonym information, and a ThesaurusTester class to handle the input/output. The term "tester" is more appropriate than "driver" because the Thesaurus-class methods must be entered in the same fixed order, and there will be no output file.

## 12.4.1 Design and Implementation of the Thesaurus Class

The Thesaurus class will have three responsibilities: to initialize a thesaurus object, to add a line of synonyms to a thesaurus, and to return the synonyms of a given word. The synonyms will be returned in a LinkedList object. In the specifications, $n$ refers to the number of lines in the thesaurus file.

Here are the method specifications:

```
/**
 * Initializes this Thesaurus object.
 *
 */
public Thesaurus( )

/**
 * Adds a specified line of synonyms to this Thesaurus object.
 * The worstTime(n) is O(log n), where n is the number of lines in the thesaurus.
 *
 * @param line – the specified line of synonyms to be added to this
 *        Thesaurus object.
 *
 */
public void add (String line)

/**
 * Finds the LinkedList of synonyms of a specified word in this Thesaurus.
 * The worstTime(n) is O(log n).
 *
 * @param word – the specified word, whose synonyms are to be
 *        returned.
 *
 * @return the LinkedList of synonyms of word.
 *
 */
public LinkedList<String> getSynonyms (String word)
```

As usual, the key (hint!) decision is to select the fields. The only field is a TreeMap object in which the key is a word and the value is the linked list of synonyms of the word:

```
protected TreeMap<String, LinkedList<String>> thesaurusMap;
```

The implementation of the Thesaurus class is fairly straightforward; most of the work is done in the put and get methods of the TreeMap class. The Thesaurus class's add method tokenizes the line, saves the first token as the key and saves the remaining tokens in a LinkedList object as the value.

Here are the method definitions and time estimates:

```
public Thesaurus( )
{
        thesaurusMap = new TreeMap<String, LinkedList<String>>( );
} // default constructor

public void add (String line)
{
```

```
            LinkedList<String> synonymList = new LinkedList<String>( );

            StringTokenizer st = new StringTokenizer (line);

            String word = st.nextToken( );

            while (st.hasMoreTokens( ))
                    synonymList.add (st.nextToken( ));
            thesaurusMap.put (word, synonymList);
      } // method add
```

For the put method in the TreeMap class, worstTime($n$) is logarithmic in $n$, and so that is also the time estimate for the add method. Note that the **while** loop takes constant time because it is independent of $n$, the number of lines in the thesaurus.

```
      public LinkedList<String> getSynonyms (String word)
      {
            return thesaurusMap.get (word);
      } // method getSynonyms
```

For the getSynonyms method, worstTime($n$) is logarithmic in $n$ because that is the time estimate for the TreeMap class's get method.

## 12.4.2  Design of the ThesaurusTester **Class**

The ThesaurusTester class is what you would probably expect. It will have three responsibilities: to initialize a calling ThesaurusTester object, to create a thesaurus from a file-path read in from the keyboard, and to print the synonyms of each subsequent word read in from the keyboard. Here are the corresponding method specifications:

```
/**
  * Initializes this ThesaurusTester object.
  *
  */
public ThesaurusTester( )

/**
  * Constructs this ThesaurusTester from a path read in from the keyboard.
  * The worstTime(n) is O(n log n).
  *
  */
public void constructThesaurus( )

/**
  * Prints the synonyms of each word entered from the keyboard, or a
  * no-synonyms-found message.
  * The worstTime(n, m) is O(m log n), where n is the number of lines in
  * the thesaurus file, and m is the number of words entered from the
  * keyboard.
```

```
            *
            */
        public void printSynonyms( )
```

The only fields are thesaurus and keyboardReader (because it is read from, both in the constructThesaurus method and in the printSynonyms method):

```
        protected Thesaurus thesaurus;

        protected BufferedReader keyboardReader;
```

Figure 12.7 has the UML class diagrams for this project. The hollow diamond just below the diagram for ThesaurusTester signifies that the ThesaurusTester class has-a Thesaurus-class field (namely, thesaurus).

## 12.4.3  Implementation of the ThesaurusTester Class

The ThesaurusTester's default constructor initializes the two fields:

```
        public ThesaurusTester( )
        {
            thesaurus = new Thesaurus( );
            keyboardReader = new BufferedReader
                            (new InputStreamReader (System.in));
        } // default constructor
```

The constructThesaurus method reads a file path (and keeps reading until a legal file path is read in) and then adds each line in the file to the thesaurus:

**Figure 12.7** | Class diagrams for the Thesaurus project.

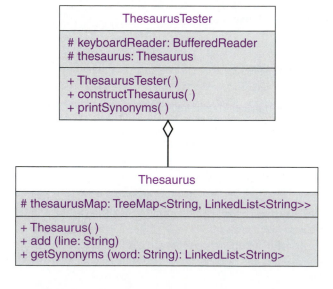

```java
public void constructThesaurus( )
{
    final String FILE_PROMPT =
        "\nPlease enter the path for the thesaurus file: ";

    final String NO_INPUT_FILE_FOUND_MESSAGE =
        "Error: there is no file with that path.\n\n";

    BufferedReader fileReader;

    String inFilePath,
           line;

    boolean pathOK = false;

    while (!pathOK)
    {
        try
        {
            System.out.print (FILE_PROMPT);
            inFilePath = keyboardReader.readLine( );
            fileReader = new BufferedReader (new FileReader (inFilePath));
            pathOK = true;
            while (true)
            {
                line = fileReader.readLine( );
                if (line == null)
                    break;
                thesaurus.add (line);
            } // while not at end of file
        } // try
        catch (IOException e)
        {
            System.out.println (e);
        } // catch
    } // while !pathOK
} // method constructThesaurus
```

Intuitively, since it takes logarithmic-in-$n$ time for each insertion, it should take linear-logarithmic-in-$n$ time for $n$ insertions. But the first insertion is into an empty tree, the second insertion is into a tree with one element, and so on. Specifically, for $i = 1, 2, \ldots, n$, it takes approximately $\log_2 i$ loop iterations to insert the $i$th element into a red-black tree. To insert $n$ elements, the total number of iterations is, approximately,

$$\sum_{i=1}^{n} \log_2 i = \log_2 n! \qquad \text{// sum of logs = log of product}$$

$$\approx n \log_2 n \qquad \text{// by the logarithmic form of Stirling's}$$
$$\text{// approximation of factorials } [\text{see Zwillinger, 2002}]$$

In other words, our intuition is correct, and worstTime($n$) is linear-logarithmic in $n$.

The printSynonyms method consists of a read-loop that continues until the sentinel is entered. For each word read, the synonyms of that word are fetched from the thesaurus and printed; an error message is printed if the word is not in the thesaurus. Here is the method definition:

```
public void printSynonyms( )
{
      final String SENTINEL = "****";

      final String WORD_PROMPT = "\n\nPlease enter the sentinel (" +
            SENTINEL + ") or a word: ";

      final String WORD_NOT_FOUND_MESSAGE =
            "That word does not appear in the thesaurus.";

      final String SYNONYM_MESSAGE =
            "The synonyms of that word are ";

      String word;

      LinkedList<String> synonymList;

      while (true)
      {
            try
            {
                  System.out.print (WORD_PROMPT);
                  word = keyboardReader.readLine( );
                  if (word.equals (SENTINEL))
                        break;
                  synonymList = thesaurus.getSynonyms (word);
                  if (synonymList == null)
                        System.out.println (WORD_NOT_FOUND_MESSAGE);
                  else
                        System.out.println (SYNONYM_MESSAGE + synonymList);
            } // try
            catch (IOException e)
            {
                  System.out.println (e);
            } // catch
      } // while
} // printSynonyms
```

To estimate how long the printSynonyms method takes, we must take into account the number of words entered from the keyboard as well as the size of thesaurusMap. Assume there are $m$ words entered from the keyboard. (We cannot use $n$ here because that represents the size of thesaurusMap.) Then the **while** loop in printSynonyms is executed $O(m)$ times. During each iteration of the **while** loop, there is a call to the get method in the TreeMap class, and that call takes $O(\log n)$ time. So worstTime($n$, $m$) is $O(m \log n)$; in fact, to utilize the notation from Chapter 4, worstTime($n$, $m$) is $\Theta(m \log n)$ because $m \log n$ provides a lower bound as well as an upper bound on worstTime($n$, $m$). The worstTime function has two arguments because the total number of statements executed depends on both $n$ and $m$.

The main method simply invokes the three thesaurusTester methods:

```java
public static void main (String[ ] args)
{
        ThesaurusTester tester = new ThesaurusTester( );

        tester.constructThesaurus( );
        tester.printSynonyms( );
} // method main
```

TreeMap objects cannot have duplicate keys, but we can still achieve a sort method (including duplicates) whose worstTime($n$) is linear-logarithmic in $n$. Section 12.5 explains how this is done, and compares treeSort, as this method is called, to the other fast sorts from Chapter 11.

## 12.5 | Tree Sort

If we iterate over a TreeMap object, the elements will be returned in order by keys. This gives us another static sort method. For now, we'll assume the ordering is "natural," with the Comparable interface. The only parameter is

aList, a List object (that is, an object in a class that implements the List interface), and whose elements are Comparable objects (that is, objects in a class that implements the Comparable interface).

Basically, each element from aList is inserted into a TreeMap object as a key. What if the element in the List object occurs more than once? Then the value field in the TreeMap element will contain the number of occurrences. For example, suppose the List object consists of String elements, and "nevermore" appears three times. Then one of the elements in the TreeMap object will have a key of "nevermore" and a value of 3 (as an Integer object).

To store the TreeMap object back into the List object, we iterate over the entries, and for each key, we store number-of-occurrences copies of the key into the List object. Here is the definition:

```java
/**
 * Sorts a specified List object, according to the ordering given by
 * the compareTo method of the elements' class.
 * The worstTime(n) is O(n log n).
 *
 * @param aList – the List object to be sorted.
 *
 */
```

```
public static <E> void treeSort (List<E> aList)
{
        TreeMap<E, Integer> aMap = new TreeMap<E, Integer>( );

        E element;

        Integer value;

        for (E element : aList)
        {
                value = aMap.get (element);
                if (value == null)
                        aMap.put (element, 1);
                else
                        aMap.put (element, value + 1);   //unboxing and boxing
        } // for each element in aList
        aList.clear( );

        for (Map.Entry<E, Integer> entry : aMap.entrySet( ))
                for (int i = 0; i < entry.getValue( ); i++)
                        aList.add (entry.getKey( ));
} // method treeSort
```

### 12.5.1 **Example of** Tree Sort

For example, suppose we start with an ArrayList object, scores, of Integer elements with the following values:

> 59 46 32 80 46 55 87 43 44 81 95 12 17 80 75 33 40 61 16 50

The following call to treeSort will put scores into increasing order:

> treeSort (scores);

When these elements are stored in aMap, we get the following red-black tree (the counts are shown only for 80 and 46, both of which occur twice; all other counts have the value 1):

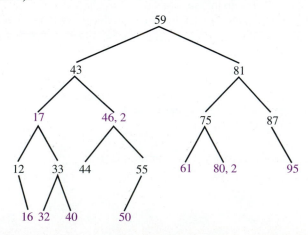

The iteration over aMap appends each element to scores, which ends up with

12 16 17 32 33 40 43 44 46 46 50 55 59 61 75 80 80 81 87 95

## 12.5.2 **Analysis of** Tree Sort

By the same analysis we used for the constructThesaurus method in Section 12.4.3, we find that for the insertions into the TreeMap object, worstTime($n$) is linear-logarithmic in $n$. For iterating through the entries, worstTime($n$) is only linear in $n$. So for the entire treeSort method, worstTime($n$) is linear-logarithmic in $n$, and this earns Tree Sort a place on the honor roll of fast sort methods.

The space requirements for Tree Sort are substantial. Each mapping in the TreeMap object has, in addition to a key reference, a value reference and left, right, and parent references. As a result, worstSpace($n$) is linear in $n$.

Is Tree Sort stable; that is, does Tree Sort preserve the relative order of equal elements? Tree Sort is not stable; in fact, Tree Sort may destroy equal elements! For example, suppose the list to be sorted includes two elements that are equal but not identical, such as

. . . , Balan 28, . . . , Wang 28, . . .

Each element has two components: a student's name and the total quality points for that student. Equality is defined according to total quality points, so the two elements shown are equal but not identical. After Tree Sort is applied, part of the list will have

. . . , Balan 28, Balan 28, . . .

This shows that Tree Sort can actually alter the elements to be sorted. In general, do not use Tree Sort if the list to be sorted may include elements that are equal but not identical.

There is also a version of the treeSort method that takes a Comparator parameter:

```
/**
 * Sorts a specified List object, according to the ordering given by
 * the specified Comparator object.
 * The worstTime(n) is O(n log n).
 *
 * @param aList – the List object to be sorted.
 * @comp – the Comparator object used for ordering the elements.
 *
 */
public static <E> void treeSort (List<E> aList, Comparator<E> comp)
```

The definition of this version differs from the earlier version only in the declaration of the TreeMap object:

```
TreeMap<E, Integer> aMap = new TreeMap<E, Integer>(comp);
```

Rather than having two versions with virtually identical code, the Comparator version would be coded completely, and the Comparable version would be a one-liner:

```
public static <E> void treeSort (List<E> aList)
{
```

```
        treeSort (aList, null);
    } // method treeSort
```

Recall, from Section 12.3.1, that for the TreeMap constructor with a Comparator parameter, if the parameter has the value **null**, the Comparable interface is used instead.

The final topic in this chapter is the TreeSet class, which is implemented as a TreeMap in which each Entry object has the same dummy value-part.

## 12.6 | **THE** TreeSet **CLASS**

We need to go through a little bit of background before we can discuss the TreeSet class. Recall, from Chapter 10, that the Set interface extends the Collection interface by stipulating that duplicate elements are not allowed. The SortedSet interface extends the Set interface in two ways. First, by stipulating that its iterator must traverse the Set in order of ascending elements. Second, by including a few new methods relating to the ordering, such as first( ), which returns the smallest element in the instance, and last( ), which returns the largest element in the instance. The TreeSet class implements the SortedSet interface, and extends the AbstractSet class, which has a bare-bones implementation of the Set class.

The bottom line is that a TreeSet object is a Collection object in which the elements are ordered from smallest to largest, and there are no duplicates. Most importantly, for the TreeSet class's contains, add, and remove methods, worstTime($n$) is logarithmic in $n$. So if these criteria suit your application, use a TreeSet instead of an ArrayList, LinkedList, BinarySearchTree, or array. For those four collections, if the elements are to be maintained in order from smallest to largest, worstTime($n$) is linear in $n$ for insertions and removals.

How does the TreeSet class compare with the AVLTree class? The TreeSet class is superior because it is part of the Java Collections Framework. As a result, the class is available to you on any Java compiler. Also, the methods have been thoroughly tested. Finally, you are not restricted to the "natural" ordering of elements: You can override that ordering with a comparator.

We already saw most of the TreeSet methods when we studied the Binary SearchTree and AVLTree classes in Chapter 10.

The following main method illustrates both the default constructor and the constructor with a comparator parameter (and the Decreasing class from Section 12.3), as well as a few other methods:

```
public static void main (String[ ] args)
{
        final String START = "Here is the TreeSet:\n";

        final String ADD =
            "After adding \"tranquil\", here is the TreeSet:\n";

        final String REMOVE =
            "After removing \"serene\", here is the TreeSet:\n";

        final String REVERSE =
```

```
                    "\nHere are the scores in decreasing order:\n";

            final String SUM = "The sum of the scores is ";

            TreeSet<String> mySet = new TreeSet<String>( );

            TreeSet<Integer> scores = new TreeSet<Integer> (new Decreasing ( ));

            mySet.add ("happy");
            mySet.add ("always");
            mySet.add ("yes");
            mySet.add ("serene");
            System.out.println (START + mySet);

            if (mySet.add ("happy"))
                    System.out.println ("ooops");
            else
                    System.out.println
                            ("\"happy\" was not added because it was already there");
            mySet.add ("tranquil");
            System.out.println (ADD + mySet);
            System.out.println ("size = " + mySet.size( ));
            if (mySet.contains ("no"))
                    System.out.println ("How did \"no\" get in there?");
            else
                    System.out.println
                            ("\"no\" is not in the TreeSet");
            if (mySet.remove ("serene"))
                    System.out.println (REMOVE + mySet);

            for (int i = 0; i < 5; i++)
                    scores.add (i);
            System.out.println (REVERSE + scores);
            int sum = 0;
            for (Integer i : scores)
                    sum += i;
            System.out.println (SUM + sum);
    } // method main
```

Here is the output:

```
Here is the TreeSet:
[always, happy, serene, yes]

"happy" was not added because it was already there

After adding "tranquil", here is the TreeSet:
[always, happy, serene, tranquil, yes]

size = 5

"no" is not in the TreeSet
```

After removing "serene", here is the TreeSet:
[always, happy, tranquil, yes]

Here are the scores in decreasing order:
[4, 3, 2, 1, 0]

The sum of the scores is 10

After we take a brief look at the implementation of the TreeSet class, we will return to a user's view by developing an application on spell checking.

### 12.6.1  **Implementation of the** TreeSet **Class**

The TreeSet class is based on the TreeMap class, which implements a red-black tree. Basically, a TreeSet object is a TreeMap object in which each element has the same dummy value. Recall that it is legal for different TreeMap elements to have the same values; it would be illegal for different TreeMap elements to have the same keys. Here is the start of the TreeSet class:

```
public class TreeSet<E> extends AbstractSet<E>
        implements SortedSet<E>, Cloneable, java.io.serializable
{
        private transient SortedMap<E, Object> m;  // The backing Map

        private transient Set<E> keySet; // The keySet view of the backing Map

        // Dummy value to associate with an Object in the backing Map
        private static final Object PRESENT = new Object( );
```

To explicitly construct a TreeSet object from a given SortedMap object, usually a TreeMap object, there is a private constructor:

```
/**
 * Initializes this TreeSet object from a specified SortedMap object.
 *
 * @param m – the SortedMap that this TreeSet object is initialized from.
 *
 */
private TreeSet<E> (SortedMap<E, Object> m)
{
        this.m = m;
        keySet = m.keySet( );
} // constructor with map parameter
```

Given the TreeSet fields and this constructor, we can straightforwardly implement the rest of the TreeSet methods. In fact, most of the definitions are one-liners. For example, here are the definitions of the default constructor, the constructor with a comparator parameter, and the contains, add, and remove methods:

```
/**
 * Initializes this TreeSet object to be empty, with the elements to be
 * ordered by the Comparable interface.
 *
```

```
     */
public TreeSet( )
{
        this (new TreeMap<E, Object>( ));
} // default constructor

/**
 * Initializes this TreeSet object to be empty, with elements to be ordered
 * by a specified Comparator object.
 *
 * @param c – the specified Comparator object by which the elements in
 *        this TreeSet object are to be ordered.
 *
 */
public TreeSet (Comparator<? super E> c)
{
        this (new TreeMap<E, Object>(c));
}

/**
 * Determines if this TreeSet object contains a specified element.
 * The worstTime(n) is O(log n).
 *
 * @param obj – the specified element sought in this TreeSet object.
 *
 * @return true – if obj is equal to at least one of the elements in this
 *        TreeSet object; otherwise, return false.
 *
 * @throws ClassCastException – if obj cannot be compared to the
 *        elements in this TreeSet object.
 *
 */
public boolean contains (Object obj)
{
        return m.containsKey (obj);
} // method contains

/**
 * Inserts a specified element where it belongs in this TreeSet object,
 * the element is already in this TreeSet object.
 *
 * @param element – the element to be inserted, unless already there, into
 *        this TreeSet object.
 *
 * @return true – if this element was inserted; return false – if this element
 *        was already in this TreeSet object.
 *
 */
```

```
    public boolean add (E element)
    {
            return m.put (element, PRESENT) == null;
    } // method add

    /**
     * Removes a specified element from this TreeSet object, unless the
     * element was not in this TreeSet object just before this call.
     * The worstTime(n) is O (log n).
     *
     * @param element – the element to be removed, unless it is not there,
     *        from this TreeSet object.
     *
     * @return true – if element was removed from this TreeSet object;
     *         otherwise, return false.
     *
    public boolean remove (Object element)
    {
            return m.remove (element) == PRESENT;
    } // method remove
```

Section 12.2 has an application of the TreeSet class: developing a spell checker.

## 12.6.2  Application: A Simple Spell Checker

One of the most helpful features of modern word processors is spell checking: scanning a document for possible misspellings. We say "possible" misspellings because the document may contain words that are legal but not found in a dictionary. For example, "iterator" and "postorder" were cited as *not found* by the word processor used in typing this chapter.

The overall problem is this: given a dictionary and a document, in files whose names are provided by the end user, print out all words in the document that are not found in the dictionary.

**Analysis**  We make some simplifying assumptions:

1.  The dictionary consists of lowercase words only, one per line (with no definitions).

2.  Each word in the document consists of letters only—some or all may be in uppercase.

3.  Each word in the document is followed by zero or more punctuation symbols followed by any number of blanks and end-of-line markers.

4.  The dictionary file is in alphabetical order. The document file, not necessarily in alphabetical order, will fit in memory (along with the dictionary file) if duplicates are excluded.

Here are the contents of a small dictionary file called "dictionary.dat", a small document file called "document.dat", and the words in the latter that are not in the former.

```
// the dictionary file:
a
algorithms
asterisk
coat
equal
he
pied
pile
plus
programs
separate
she
structures
wore
```

```
// the document file:
Alogrithms plus Data Structures equal Programs.
She woar a pide coat.
```

```
// the possibly misspelled words:
alogrithms, data, pide, woar
```

To isolate the spell-checking details from the input/output aspects, we create two classes: SpellChecker and SpellCheckerTester.

**Design and Implementation of the** SpellChecker **Class** The SpellChecker class will have four responsibilities:

- To initialize a SpellChecker object
- To add a word to the set of dictionary words
- To add the words in a line to the set of document words
- To return a LinkedList of words from the document that are not in the dictionary

The use of the term "set" in the second and third responsibilities implies that there will be no duplicates in either collection; there may have been duplicates in the dictionary or document files. Here are the method specifications for the methods in the SpellChecker class:

```
/**
 * Initializes this SpellChecker object.
 *
 */
public SpellChecker( )

/**
 * Inserts a specified word into the dictionary set of words.
 * The worstTime(n) is O(log n), where n is the number of words in the
```

```
     * dictionary set of words.
     *
     * @param word – the word to be inserted into the dictionary set of words.
     *
     */
    public void addToDictionarySet (String word)

/**
     * Inserts all of the words in a specified line into the document set of words.
     * The worstTime(m) is O(log m), where m is the number of (unique) words
     * in the document set of words.
     *
     * @param line – the line whose words are added to the document set of
     *        words.
     *
     */
    public void addToDocumentSet (String line)

/**
     * Determines all words that are in the document set but not in the
     * dictionary set.
     * The worstTime(m, n) is O(m log n), where m is the number of words
     * in the document set, and n is the number of words in the dictionary set.
     *
     * @return a LinkedList consisting of all the words in the document set that
     *        are not in the dictionary set.
     *
     */
    public LinkedList<String> compare( )
```

The SpellChecker class has only two fields:

```
    protected TreeSet<String> dictionarySet,
                              documentSet;
```

The dictionarySet field holds the (unique) words in the dictionary file. The documentSet field holds each unique word in the document file—there is no purpose in storing multiple copies of any word.

The definitions of the default constructor and addToDictionarySet methods hold no surprises:

```
    public SpellChecker( )
    {
          dictionarySet = new TreeSet<String>( );
          documentSet = new TreeSet<String>( );
    } // default constructor

    public void addToDictionarySet (String word)
    {
```

```
            dictionarySet.add (word);
    } // method addToDictionary
```

The definition of addToDocumentSet (String line) is slightly more complicated. The line is tokenized, with delimiters that include punctuation symbols. Each word, as a token, is converted to lowercase and inserted into documentSet unless the word is already in documentSet. Here is the definition:

```
public void addToDocumentSet (String line)
{
        final String DELIMITERS = " \\\"\n\r\t;:.,!?( )";

        StringTokenizer tokens = new StringTokenizer (line, DELIMITERS);

        String word;

        while (tokens.hasMoreTokens( ))
        {
                word = tokens.nextToken( ).toLowerCase( );
                documentSet.add (word);
        } // while line has more tokens
} // method addToDocumentSet
```

Let $m$ represent the number of words in documentSet. Each call to the TreeSet class's add method takes logarithmic-in-$m$ time. The number of words on a line is independent of $m$, so for the addToDocumentSet method, worstTime(m) is logarithmic in $m$.

The compare method iterates through documentSet; each word that is not in dictionarySet is appended to a LinkedList object of (possibly) misspelled words. Here is the definition:

```
public LinkedList<String> compare( )
{
        LinkedList<String> misspelled = new LinkedList<String>( );

        for (String word : documentSet)
                if (!dictionarySet.contains (word))
                        misspelled.add (word);
        } // while
        return misspelled;
} // method compare
```

For iterating through documentSet, worstTime(m) is linear in $m$, and for each call to the TreeSet class's contains method, worstTime(n) is logarithmic in $n$. So for the compare method in the SpellChecker class, worstTime(n, m) is $O(m \log n)$. In fact, worstTime(n, m) is $\Theta(m \log n)$.

In Chapter 14, we will encounter another class that implements the Set interface: the HashSet class. In this class, the average time for insertions, removals, and searches is constant! So we can redo the above problem with HashSet object for dictionarySet and documentSet. No other changes need be made! For that version of the spell-check project, averageTime($n$) would be constant for the addToDictionary Set method, and averageTime($m$) would be constant for the addToDocumentSet method. For the compare method, averageTime($m, n$) would be linear in $m$. But don't sell your stock in TreeSets-R-Us. For the HashSet version of the SpellChecker class, the worstTime($m, n$) for compare, for example, would be $\Theta(mn)$.

**Design of the** SpellCheckerTester **Class** The SpellCheckerTester class has a default constructor, a readFile method with a parameter to indicate whether the file to be read is a dictionary file or a document file, and a printResults method that prints the possibly misspelled words.

Here are the method specifications:

```
/**
 * Initializes this SpellCheckerTester object.
 *
 */
public SpellCheckerTester ( )

/**
 * Reads in and save a file of a specified type ("dictionary" or "document").
 * The worstTime(t) is O(t log t), where t is the number of lines in the file.
 *
 * @param fileType – a String object representing the type of file,
 *       "dictionary" or "document", to be read in.
 *
 */
public void readFile (String fileType)

/**
 * Prints the misspelled words – those that are in the document set but not
 * in the dictionary set.
 * The worstTime(m, n) is O(m log n), where m is the number of words in
 * the document set and n is the number of words in the dictionary set.
 *
 */
public void printResults( )
```

The only field is:

```
protected SpellChecker spellChecker;
```

Figure 12.8 shows the class diagrams for this project.

**Implementation of the** SpellCheckerTester **Class** The SpellCheckerTester's default constructor initializes the only field:

```
public SpellCheckerTester ( )
{
        spellChecker = new SpellChecker( );
```

**Figure 12.8 |** Class diagrams for the Spell Checker project.

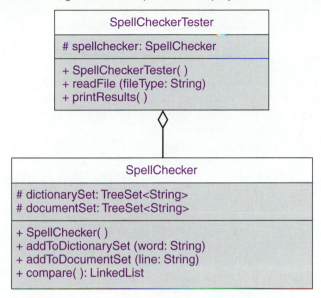

} // default constructor

The readFile method reads a file path from the keyboard and constructs a file reader for that file. Then, depending on whether fileType is "dictionary" or "document", each line from the file is read and added to the dictionary set or the document set, respectively. Here is the method definition:

```
public void readFile (String fileType)
{
        final String FILE_PROMPT =
                "\nPlease enter the path for the " + fileType + " file: ";

        final String DICTIONARY = "dictionary";

        BufferedReader keyboardReader = new BufferedReader
                                        (new InputStreamReader (System.in)),
                        fileReader;

        String filePath,
                line;

        boolean pathOK = false;

        while (!pathOK)
        {
                try
```

```
          {
                System.out.print (FILE_PROMPT);
                filePath = keyboardReader.readLine( );
                fileReader = new BufferedReader (new FileReader (filePath));
                pathOK = true;

                while (true)
                {
                      line = fileReader.readLine( );
                      if (line == null)
                            break;
                      if (fileType.equals (DICTIONARY))
                            spellChecker.addToDictionarySet (line);
                      else
                            spellChecker.addToDocumentSet (line);
                } // while not at end of file
          } // try
          catch (IOException e)
          {
                System.out.println (e);
          } // catch IOException
     } // while
} // method readFile
```

Since both dictionarySet and documentSet are TreeSet objects, the worst-time estimate for the readFile method is linear-logarithmic in the size of the set written to.

The printResults method prints out the LinkedList of possible misspellings. Here is the definition:

```
public void printResults( )
{
     final String ALL_CORRECT =
           "\n\nAll the words are spelled correctly.";

     final String MISSPELLED =
           "\n\nThe following words are misspelled:";

     LinkedList<String> misspelled = spellChecker.compare( );
     if (misspelled == null)
           System.out.println (ALL_CORRECT);
     else
           System.out.println (MISSPELLED + misspelled);
} // method printResults
```

The time estimate for this method derives wholly from the call to the SpellChecker class's compare method, whose worstTime($n$, $m$) is $\Theta(m \log n)$, where $n$ is the number of words in the dictionary set and $m$ is the number of words in the document set.

# SUMMARY

A *red-black tree* is a binary search tree in which the root element is colored black, every other element is colored either red or black, and for which the following two rules hold:

1. **Red Rule:** if an element is colored red, none of its children can be colored red.
2. **Path Rule:** the number of black elements is the same in all paths from the root to elements with one child or with no children.

The height of a red-black tree is always logarithmic in $n$, the number of elements in the tree.

The Java Collections Framework implements red-black trees in the TreeMap class. In a TreeMap object each element has a unique *key* part—by which the element is identified—and a *value* part, which contains the rest of the element. The elements are stored in a red-black tree in key-ascending order, according to their "natural" order (implementing the Comparable interface) or by the order specified by a user-supplied Comparator object (there is a constructor in which the Comparator object is supplied). For the containsKey, get, put, and remove methods, worstTime($n$) is logarithmic in $n$.

The treeSort method is a fast sort based on a TreeMap object.

A TreeSet is a Collection in which duplicate elements are not allowed and in which the elements are stored in order (according to the Comparable ordering or a user-supplied Comparator). The TreeSet class is implemented in the Java Collections Framework as a TreeMap in which each element has the same dummy value-part. For the contains, add, and remove methods, worstTime($n$) is logarithmic in $n$.

# CONCEPT EXERCISES

**12.1** Construct a red-black tree of height 2 with six elements. Construct a red-black tree of height 3 with six elements.

**12.2** Construct two different red-black trees with the same three elements.

**12.3** What is the maximum number of black elements in a red-black tree of height 4? What is the minimum number of black elements in a red-black tree of height 4?

**12.4** It is impossible to construct a red-black tree of size 20 with no red elements. Explain.

**12.5** Suppose $v$ is an element with one child in a red-black tree. Explain why $v$ must be black and $v$'s child must be a red leaf.

**12.6** Construct a red-black tree that (when the colors are ignored) is not an AVL tree.

**12.7** Guibas and Sedgewick (1978) provide a simple algorithm for coloring any AVL tree into a red-black tree:

For each element in the AVL tree, if the height of the subtree rooted at that element is an even integer and the height of its parent's subtree is odd, color the element red; otherwise, color the element black.

For example, here is an AVL tree from Chapter 10:

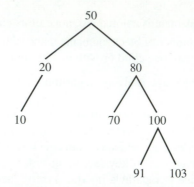

In this tree, 20's subtree has a height of 1, 80's subtree has a height of 2, 10's subtree has a height of 0, and 70's subtree has a height of 0. Note that since the root of the entire tree has no parent, this algorithm guarantees that the root will be colored black. Here is that AVL tree, colorized to a red-black tree:

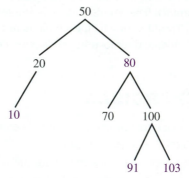

Create an AVL tree of height 4 with $min_4$ elements (that is, the minimum number of elements for an AVL tree of height 4), and then colorize that tree to a red-black tree.

**12.8** Suppose, in the definition of red-black tree, we replace the Path Rule with the following:

**Pathetic Rule: The number of black elements must be the same in all paths from the root element to a leaf.**

**a.** With this new definition, describe how to construct a red-black tree of 101 elements whose height is 50.

**b.** Give an example of a binary search tree that cannot be colored to make it a red-black tree (even with this new definition).

**12.9**  Show the effect of making the following insertions into an initially empty TreeSet object:

30, 40, 20, 90, 10, 50, 70, 60, 80

**12.10** Delete 20 and 40 from the TreeSet object in Exercise 12.9. Show the complete tree after each deletion.

**12.11** Pick any integer $h \geq 1$, and create a TreeSet object as follows:

Let $k = 2^{h+1} + 2^h - 2$.

Insert 1, 2, 3, . . . , $k$. Remove $k, k - 1, k - 2, \ldots, 2^h$. Try this with $h = 1$, 2, and 3. What is unusual about the red-black trees that you end up with? Alexandru Balan developed this formula.

**12.12** From a user's point of view, what is the difference between the TreeMap class and the TreeSet class?

**12.13** From a developer's point of view, what is the relationship between the TreeMap class and the TreeSet class?

## PROGRAMMING EXERCISES

**12.1**  Suppose we are given the name and division number for each employee in a company. There are no duplicate names. We would like to store this information alphabetically, by name. For example, part of the input might be the following:

| | |
|---|---|
| Misino,John | 8 |
| Nguyen,Viet | 14 |
| Panchenko,Eric | 6 |
| Dunn,Michael | 6 |
| Deusenbery,Amanda | 14 |
| Taoubina,Xenia | 6 |

We want these elements stored in the following order:

| | |
|---|---|
| Deusenbery,Amanda | 14 |
| Dunn,Michael | 6 |
| Misino,John | 8 |
| Nguyen,Viet | 14 |
| Panchenko,Eric | 6 |
| Taoubina,Xenia | 6 |

How should this be done? TreeMap? TreeSet? Comparable? Comparator? Develop a small project to test your hypotheses.

**12.2**  Redo Programming Exercise 12.1, but now the ordering should be by increasing division numbers, and within each division number, by alphabetical order of names. For example, part of the input might be the following:

|                    |    |
|--------------------|----|
| Misino,John        | 8  |
| Nguyen,Viet        | 14 |
| Panchenko,Eric     | 6  |
| Dunn,Michael       | 6  |
| Deusenbery,Amanda  | 14 |
| Taoubina,Xenia     | 6  |

We want these elements stored in the following order:

|                    |    |
|--------------------|----|
| Dunn,Michael       | 6  |
| Panchenko,Eric     | 6  |
| Taoubina,Xenia     | 6  |
| Misino,John        | 8  |
| Deusenbery,Amanda  | 14 |
| Nguyen,Viet        | 14 |

How should this be done? TreeMap? TreeSet? Comparable? Comparator? Develop a small project to test your hypotheses.

**12.3**   Declare two TreeSet objects, set1 and set2, whose elements come from the same Student class. Each student has a name and grade point average. In set1, the students are in alphabetical order. In set2, the elements are in decreasing order of grade point averages. Insert a few students into each set and then print out the set. Include everything needed for this to work, including the two declarations of TreeSet objects, the insertion messages, the declaration of the Student class, and any other necessary class(es).

**12.4**   Develop a program that creates an ArrayList object of 10,000 random Doubles and determine how long it takes to sort the ArrayList with treeSort. Hypothesize how long it will take to sort 20,000 random Doubles with treeSort. Rerun the program to confirm your hypothesis.

**12.5**   Give an example to show that the put method in the TreeMap class does not necessarily throw NullPointerException if the first argument is **null**, even if the natural order (that is, the Comparable interface) is used.

# Programming Project 12.1

## Spell Check, Revisited

Modify the spell-check project. If document word $x$ is not in the dictionary but word $y$ is in the dictionary and $x$ differs from $y$ either by an adjacent transposition or by a single letter, then $y$ should be proposed as an alternative for $x$. For example, suppose the document word is "asteriks" and the dictionary contains "asterisk". By transposing the adjacent letters 's' and 'k' in "asteriks", we get "asterisk". So "asterisk" should be proposed as an alternative. Similarly, if the document word is "seperate" or "seprate" and the dictionary word is "separate", then "separate" should be offered as an alternative in either case.

Here are the dictionary words for both system tests:

a
algorithms
asterisk
coat
equals
he
pied
pile
plus
programs
separate
structures
wore

Here is document file doc1.dat:

She woar a pide coat.

And here is document file doc2.dat:

Alogrithms plus Data Structures equal Pograms

**System Test 1 (with Input in Boldface):**

In the Input line, please enter the name of the document file.
**doc1.dat**

| Possible Misspellings | Possible Alternatives |
|---|---|
| pide | pied, pile |
| she | he |
| woar | |

**System Test 2:**

In the Input line, please enter the name of the document file.
**doc2.dat**

| Possible Misspellings | Possible Alternatives |
|---|---|
| alogrithms | algorithms |
| data | |
| pograms | programs |

## Programming Project 12.2

### Word Frequencies

Given a text, determine the frequency of each word, that is, the number of times each word occurs in the text. Include Big-O time estimates of all methods.

**Analysis:**

1. The first line of input will contain the path to the text file. The second line of input will contain the path to the output file.

2. Each word in the text consists of letters only—some or all may be in uppercase.

3. Each word in the text is followed by zero or more punctuation symbols followed by any number of blanks and end-of-line markers.

4. The output should consist of the words, lowercased and in alphabetical order; each word is followed by its frequency.

5. For the entire program, worstTime($n$) is $O(n \log n)$, where $n$ is the number of distinct words in the text.

Assume that doc1.in contains the following file:

This program counts the
number of words in a text.
The text may have many words
in it, including big words.

Also, assume that doc2.in contains the following file:

Fuzzy Wuzzy was a bear.
Fuzzy Wuzzy had no hair.
Fuzzy Wuzzy was not fuzzy.
Was he?

**System Test 1:**

In the Input line, please enter the path to the text file.
**doc1.in**
In the Input line, please enter the path to the output file.
**doc1.out**

(Here are the contents of doc1.out after the completion of the program.)

Here are the words and their frequencies:

a: 1
big: 1
counts: 1
have: 1
in: 2
including: 1
it: 1
many: 1

may: 1
number: 1
of: 1
program: 1
text: 2
the: 2
this: 1
words: 3

**System Test 2:**

In the Input line, please enter the path to the text file.
**doc2.in**
In the Input line, please enter the path to the output file.
**doc2.out**

(Here are the contents of doc2.out after the completion of the program.)

Here are the words and their frequencies:

a: 1
bear: 1
fuzzy: 4
had: 1
hair: 1
he: 1
no: 1
not: 1
was: 3
wuzzy: 3

## Programming Project 12.3

### Building a Concordance

Given a text, develop a concordance for the words in the text. A **concordance** consists of each word in the text and, for each word, each line number that the word occurs in. Include Big-O time estimates of all methods.

#### Analysis

1. The first line of input will contain the path to the text file. The second line of input will contain the path to the output file.

2. Each word in the text consists of letters only—some or all may be in uppercase.

3. Each word in the text is followed by zero or more punctuation symbols followed by any number of blanks and end-of-line markers.

4. The output should consist of the words, lowercased and in alphabetical order; each word is followed by each line number that the word occurs in. The line numbers should be separated by commas.

5. The line numbers in the text start at 1.

6. For the entire program, worstTime($n$) is $O(n \log n)$, where $n$ is the number of distinct words in the text.

Assume that doc1.in contains the following file:

This program counts the
number of words in a text.
The text may have many words
in it, including big words.

Also, assume that doc2.in contains the following file:

Fuzzy Wuzzy was a bear.
Fuzzy Wuzzy had no hair.
Fuzzy Wuzzy was not fuzzy.
Was he?

#### System Test 1:

In the Input line, please enter the path to the text file.
**doc1.in**
In the Input line, please enter the path to the output file.
**doc1.out**

(Here are the contents of doc1.out after the completion of the program.)

Here is the concordance:

a: 2
big: 4
counts: 1
have: 3

in: 2, 4
including: 4
it: 4
many: 3
may: 3
number: 2
of: 2
program: 1
text: 2, 3
the: 1, 3
this: 1
words: 2, 3, 4

### System Test 2:

In the Input line, please enter the path to the text file.
**doc2.in**
In the Input line, please enter the path to the output file.
**doc2.out**

(Here are the contents of doc2.out after the completion of the program.)

Here is the concordance:

a: 1
bear: 1
fuzzy: 1, 2, 3
had: 2
hair: 2
he: 4
no: 2
not: 3
was: 1, 3, 4
wuzzy: 1, 2, 3

## Programming Project 12.4

### An Integrated Web Browser and Search Engine, Part 3

In this part of the project, you will add functionality to the Search button. Assume the file search.in1 consists of file names (for web pages), one per line. When the end-user clicks on the Search button, the output window is cleared and then a prompt is printed in the Output window to request that a search string be entered in the Input window.

For each file name in search.in1, the web page corresponding to that file is then searched for the individual words in the search string. Then the link is printed in the Output window, along with the relevance count: the sum of the word frequencies of each word in the search string. For example, suppose the search string is "neural network", the file name is "browser.in6", and that web page has

> A network is a network, neural or not. If every neural network were
> combined, that would be a large neural network for networking.

The output corresponding to that web page would be

browser.in6 7

because "neural" appears 3 times on the web page, and "network" appears 4 times ("networking" does not count).

Use your Scanner class from Part 2 of this project to get each word in the Web page (excluding an expanded file of common words, and so on) and determine the frequency of each such word on that web page. Then, for each word in the search string, add up the frequencies.

You will need to modify the GUIBrowserListener class, but you should not modify Browse, Process, GUIBrowser, GUI, or GUIListener. All of the necessary source and data files are available from the book's website.

For each of the $n$ words in the web page, the worstTime($n$) for incrementing that word's frequency must be logarithmic in $n$. Also, for each word in the search string, calculating its frequency in the web page must also take logarithmic-in-$n$ time, even in the worst case.

For testing, assume search.in1 contains just a few files, for example,

browser.in6
browser.in7
browser.in8

Click to get the contents of those files:

browser.in6
browser.in7
browser.in8

**System Test 1: Neural Network**

Here are the files and relevance frequencies
browser.in6 7

browser.in7 0
browser.in8 2

neural

Here are the files and relevance frequencies
browser.in6 3
browser.in7 0
browser.in8 1

If the end-user now clicks on the Back button, the search page for "neural network" should reappear.

### System Test 2: Network

Here are the files and relevance frequencies:
browser.in6 4
browser.in7 0
browser.in8 1

*Note:* The Search button should be green as soon as the GUI window is opened.

# Priority Queues

In this chapter, we examine the priority queue data type. A ***priority queue*** is a collection in which only the element with highest priority can be removed, according to some method for comparing elements. This restriction allows an implementation with an add method whose average time is constant. This implementation uses a specialized binary tree known as a ***heap.*** The Java Collections Framework's Priority Queue class allows arbitrary removals, so we will define our own PurePriorityQueue interface and implement that interface with a Heap class. The chapter concludes by using a priority queue to generate a Huffman Tree—a necessary component of a popular data-compression technique called Huffman compression. ∎

## CHAPTER OBJECTIVES

1. Define what a priority queue is.

2. Understand the heap operations of percolateUp and percolateDown.

3. Examine the Huffman algorithm for data compression.

4. Determine the characteristic of a greedy algorithm.

## 13.1 | INTRODUCTION

A variation of the queue, the priority queue is a commonplace structure. The basic idea is that we have elements waiting in line for service, as with a queue. But removals are not strictly on a first in, first out basis. For example, patients in an emergency room are treated according to the severity of their injuries, not on when they arrived. Similarly, in air-traffic control, there is a queue of planes waiting to land, but the controller can move a plane to the front of the queue if the plane is low on fuel or has a sick passenger.

A shared printer in a network is another example of a resource suited for a priority queue. Normally, jobs are printed on the basis of arrival time, but while one job is printing, several others may enter the service queue. Highest priority could be given to the job with the fewest pages to print. This would optimize the average time for job completion. The same idea of prioritized service can be applied to any shared resource: a central processing unit, a family car, the courses offered next semester, and so on.

Here is the definition:

A **_priority queue_** is collection in which removal is of the highest-priority element in the collection, according to some method for assigning priorities.

For example, if the elements are of type Integer and comparisons use the "natural" ordering, then the highest-priority element is the one whose corresponding **int** has the *smallest* value in the priority queue. But if elements are of type Integer and the comparisons use the reverse of the natural ordering, then the highest-priority element is the one whose corresponding **int** has the largest value in the priority queue. The abstract data type priority queue corresponds to the PurePriorityQueue interface. The programmer who implements the PurePriorityQueue interface determines the comparison method. We encountered a similar situation with the sort methods in Chapter 11 and with the TreeMap and TreeSet classes in Chapter 12.

By default, the smallest-valued element has highest priority. For this reason, a removal is referred to as removeMin and a retrieval is referred to as getMin.

The above definition says nothing about insertions. An implementer of the PurePriorityQueue interface is free to determine *how* insertions will be handled. But the average-time and worst-time specifications for inserting an element and for removing the highest-priority element may indirectly restrict that freedom.

You might wonder what happens if two or more elements are tied for highest priority. In the interest of fairness, the tie should be broken in favor of the element that has been in the priority queue for the longest time. This appeal to fairness is not part of the definition, and is not part of the PurePriorityQueue interface. In fact, as will be seen later in this chapter, ties are not handled fairly in the standard implementation of the PurePriorityQueue interface. Lab 21 provides a solution to this problem.

Most of this chapter is devoted to the premier application of priority queues: Huffman encoding. Also, Chapter 15 has two priority-queue applications: Prim's minimum-spanning-tree algorithm and Dijkstra's shortest-path algorithm. For a lively discussion of the versatility of priority queues, see Dale (1990).

## 13.2 | THE PurePriorityQueue INTERFACE

As we did in Chapter 8 with the PureQueue and PureStack interfaces, we take an austere approach to the PurePriorityQueue interface. The only methods in the interface are size, isEmpty, add, getMin, and removeMin. The type parameter is E. The term "PurePriorityQueue object" means "object in a class that implements the Pure PriorityQueue interface."

Here are the method specifications:

1. 
```
/**
 * Returns the number of elements in this PurePriorityQueue object.
 *
 * @return the number of elements in this PurePriorityQueue object.
 *
 */
int size( )
```

2. 
```
/**
 * Determines if this PurePriorityQueue object has no elements.
 *
 * @return true – if this PurePriorityQueue object has no elements;
 *         otherwise, return false;
 *
 */
boolean isEmpty( )
```

3. 
```
/**
 * Inserts a specified element into this PurePriorityQueue object.
 * The worstTime(n) is O(n).
 *
 * @param element – the element to be inserted into this PurePriorityQueue
 *        object.
 *
 */
void add (E element)
```

4. 
```
/**
 * Returns the highest-priority element in this PurePriorityQueue object.
 * The worstTime(n) is O(log n).
 *
 * @return the highest-priority element in this PurePriorityQueue object.
 *
 * @throws NoSuchElementException – if this PurePriorityQueue object is empty.
```

```
      *
      */
    E getMin( )

5.   /**

      * Removes the highest-priority element from this PurePriorityQueue object.
      * The worstTime(n) is O(log n).
      *
      * @return the element removed.
      *
      * @throws NoSuchElementException – if this PurePriorityQueue object is empty.
      *
      */
    E removeMin( )
```

## 13.3 | IMPLEMENTATIONS OF THE
## PurePriorityQueue INTERFACE

Let's look at several options for implementing the PurePriorityQueue interface:

*Option A.* Store the elements in a class that implements the PureQueue interface. Then the add method in the implementation of the PurePriorityQueue interface would have to invoke the enqueue method—there is no other way to insert in a PureQueue object. But this would not guarantee that the highest-priority element would be at the front of the queue, as is required for getMin and removeMin (implemented with calls to the methods front and dequeue). So this option is not viable.

*Option B.* Store the elements in an array of queues, with one array entry for each priority. But what if the elements are of type String, and the ordering is lexicographical? Then we would need one array entry for each possible String value. Even if we restrict the String elements to 10 lower-case letters, we would need $10^{26}$ entries. This option is not feasible.

*Option C.* Store the elements in an array (or ArrayList) object, ordered by highest priority. For example, if the smallest value has highest priority we could store 10 Integer values in the following array:

| 26 | 30 | 32 | 36 | 48 | 50 | 55 | 80 | 85 | 107 | … |
|----|----|----|----|----|----|----|----|----|-----|---|

The getMin method would take constant time, but both the add and removeMin methods would require $O(n)$ time in the worst case. (Why?) This option is not viable because removeMin takes too long, violating the method specification. But if you make the array circular, the removeMin method takes only constant time in the worst case. You can fill in the details if you complete Programming Exercise 13.5.

***Option D.*** Store the elements in a LinkedList object ordered by highest priority. Then the getMin and removeMin methods would take constant time, and the add method would take $O(n)$ time. This option is also worth pursuing. The class declaration starts with:

```
public class LinkedListPurePriorityQueue<E> implements PurePriorityQueue<E>
{
      LinkedList<E> list;

      Comparator<E> comparator;
```

As was done with the TreeMap class, we initialize comparator to **null** in the default constructor to signify that the elements are Comparable. And there will be a constructor with a Comparator parameter for applications in which the "natural" ordering is inappropriate. The nonpublic compare method is the same as we saw in Section 12.3.2 for the TreeMap class.

Except for the add method, all the method definitions are one-liners. For example, here is removeMin:

```
public E removeMin( )
{
     return list.removeFirst( );
} // method removeMin
```

The add method appends element to list if that list is empty or if element is greater than or equal to the element at the back of list. Otherwise, we iterate from the front of list until we find an element greater than element; we then insert element *in front of* that element. The ListItr class's add method inserts in back of the element where the iterator is positioned, so we need to call the previous method before the ListItr's add method. Note that the following **while** loop has an empty body:

```
public void add (E element)
{
     if (list.isEmpty( ) || compare (element, list.get (list.size( ) −1)) >= 0)
          list.add (element);
     else
     {
          ListIterator<E> itr = list.listIterator( );
          while (itr.hasNext( ) && compare (element, itr.next( )) >= 0)
               ;
          itr.previous( ); // back up one position
          itr.add (element);
     } // else
} // method add
```

The insertion takes place in back of any element already in the priority queue with equal or higher priority. In other words, this is a *fair* implementation of the PurePriorityQueue interface.

This option is quite efficient. For the getMin and removeMin methods, worstTime($n$) is constant, and for the add method, worstTime($n$) is linear in $n$.

Concept Exercise 13.1 explores the details and drawback of a TreeSet implementation. Section 13.3.1 describes an implementation of the PurePriorityQueue interface that is so efficient it is the standard implementation. With this implementation, worstTime($n$) for getMin is constant, worstTime($n$) for removeMin is logarithmic in $n$, and worstTime($n$) for add is linear in $n$—but averageTime($n$) is constant.

### 13.3.1  The Heap Class

In this implementation of the PurePriorityQueue interface, the elements are stored in a heap. A *heap* $t$ is a complete binary tree such that either $t$ is empty or

1.  The root element is the smallest element in $t$, according to some method for comparing elements.

2.  The left and right subtrees of $t$ are heaps.

The heap we have defined is called a "minHeap". In a "maxHeap", the root element is the largest element.

Recall from Chapter 9 that a complete binary tree is full except, possibly, at the level farthest from the root, and at that farthest level, the leaves are as far to the left as possible. Figure 13.1 shows a heap of 10 Integer elements with the "natural" ordering. Notice that duplicates are allowed, in contrast to the prohibition against duplicates for binary search trees.

The ordering in a heap is top-down, but not left-to-right: the root element of each subtree is less than or equal to each of its children, but some left siblings may be less than their right siblings and some may be greater than or equal to their right siblings. In Figure 13.1, for example, 48 is less than its right sibling, 50, but 107 is greater than its right sibling, 80.

**Figure 13.1** I A heap with 10 Integer elements; the **int** values of the Integer elements are shown.

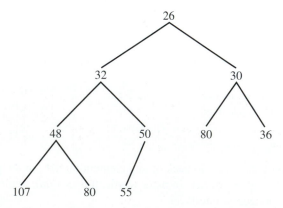

A heap is a complete binary tree. As we saw in Chapter 9, with each of the $n$ elements in a complete binary tree $t$, we can associate a position in the range $0 \cdots n - 1$. If we think of these positions as indexes, we see that a heap can be implemented in an array. Figure 13.2 shows the array version of Figure 13.1, with each index under its element.

The random-access feature of arrays is convenient for heap processing: given the index of an element, we can quickly retrieve that element's children. For example, the children of the element at index $i$ are at indexes $2i + 1$ and $2i + 2$. And the parent of the element at index $j$ is at index $(j - 1)/2$, where / represents integer division. As we will see shortly, the ability to quickly swap the values of a parent and its smaller-valued child makes an array an efficient storage structure for a heap-based implementation of the PurePriorityQueue interface.

The Heap class has four constructors, one with an initial capacity, one for default, one to provide a new Comparator, and a copy constructor:

1.  ```
    /**
     * Initializes this Heap object to be empty, with a given initial capacity, and elements
     * in a class that implements the Comparable interface.
     *
     * @param initialCapacity – the initial capacity of this Heap object.
     *
     */
    public Heap (int initialCapacity)
    ```

    For example, we can create a Heap object with an initial capacity of 1000 Double objects as follows:

    ```
    Heap<Double> salaries = new Heap<Double> (1000);
    ```

2.  ```
    /**
     * Initializes this Heap object to be empty, with a default initial capacity and with
     * elements in a class that implements the Comparable interface.
     *
     */
    public Heap( )
    ```

    For example, we can create a Heap object with String elements as follows:

    ```
    Heap<String> employees = new Heap<String>( );
    ```

**Figure 13.2 |** The array representation of the heap from Figure 13.1.

| 26 | 32 | 30 | 48 | 50 | 80 | 36 | 107 | 80 | 55 | ... |

3.   /**
     * Initializes this Heap object to be empty, with elements compared according
     * to the Comparator object comp.
     *
     * @param comp – the Comparator object used for comparing elements in
     *        this Heap object.
     *
     */
     **public** Heap<E> (Comparator<E> comp)

For example, suppose we want the Heap object to consist of Integer elements, and the highest-priority element will be the one with the highest **int**. We can utilize the Decreasing class from Section 12.3:

```
class Decreasing implements Comparator<Integer>
{
        /**
         * Compares two specified Integer objects.
         *
         * @param i1 – one of the specified Integer objects.
         * @param i2 – the other specified Integer object.
         *
         * @return a negative integer, 0, or a positive integer, depending on
         *         whether i2 is less than, equal to, or greater than i1.
         *
         */
        public int compare (Integer i1, Integer i2)
        {
                return i2.compareTo (i1);
        } // method compare

} // class Decreasing
```

We can then declare

```
Heap<Integer> myHeap = new Heap<Integer> (new Decreasing( ));
```

Similarly, if the elements in the priority queue are of type String, and we want the highest-priority element to be the one whose length is least, we can utilize the ByLength class from Section 12.3:

```
class ByLength implements Comparator<String>
{
        public int compare (String s1, String s2)
        {
                int len1 = s1.length( ),
                    len2 = s2.length( );
```

```
        if (len1 == len2)
                return s1.compareTo(s2);
        return len1 – len2;
    } // method compare
} // class ByLength
```

A Heap instance can then be declared as follows:

```
Heap<String> heap2 = new Heap<String>(new ByLength( ));
```

4.  ```
    /**
     * Initializes this Heap object to a shallow copy of a specified Heap object.
     * The elements in this Heap object will be compared as in the specified
     * Heap object.
     * The worstTime(n) is O(n), where n is the number of elements in the
     * specified Heap object.
     *
     * @param otherHeap – the specified Heap object to be copied to this
     *        Heap object.
     *
     */
    public Heap (Heap<E> otherHeap)
    ```

Here is a main method that creates and maintains a Heap of students. Each line of input—except for the sentinel—consists of a name and the corresponding grade point average (GPA). The highest-priority student is the one whose GPA is lowest. In the Student class, the Comparable interface is implemented; in Programming Exercise 13.1, you are asked to modify the code to use a Comparator parameter instead.

```
public static void main (String[ ] args)
{

        final String PROMPT1 = "Please enter student's name and GPA, or " ;

        final String PROMPT2 = " to quit: ";

        final String SENTINEL = "****";

        final String RESULTS = "\nHere are the student names and GPAs:";

        Heap<Student> heap = new Heap<Student>( );

        BufferedReader keyboardReader = new BufferedReader
                (new InputStreamReader (System.in));

        String line;

        try
        {
                while (true)
```
```

```
                    {
                            System.out.print (PROMPT1 + SENTINEL + PROMPT2);
                            line = keyboardReader.readLine( );
                            if (line.equals (SENTINEL))
                                    break;
                            heap.add (new Student (line));
                    } // while
                    System.out.println (RESULTS);
                    while (!heap.isEmpty( ))
                            System.out.println (heap.removeMin( ));
            } // try
            catch (Exception e)
            {
                    System.out.println (e);
            } // catch
    } // method main

    import java.util.*;

    public class Student implements Comparable
    {
            protected String name;
            protected double gpa;

            /**
             * Initializes this Student object from a specified String object.
             *
             * @param s – the String object used to initialize this Student object.
             *
             * @throws NullPointerException, NoSuchElementException,
             *         NumberFormatException
             *
             */
            public Student (String s)
            {
                    StringTokenizer tokens = new StringTokenizer (s);

                    name = tokens.nextToken( );
                    gpa = Double.parseDouble (tokens.nextToken( ));
            } // constructor

            /**
             * Compares this Student object to a specified object by grade point
             * average.
             *
             * @param obj – the specified object.
             *
             * @return a negative integer, 0, or a positive integer, depending
```

```
    *       on whether this Student object's grade point average is less than,
    *       equal to, or greater than obj's grade point average.
    *
    * @throws ClassCastException – if the run-time type
    *       of obj is not Student.
    *
    */
    public int compareTo (Object obj)
    {
            Student otherStudent = (Student)obj;
            if (gpa < otherStudent.gpa)
                    return −1;
            if (gpa == otherStudent.gpa)
                    return 0;
            return 1;
    } // method compareTo

    /**
     * Returns a String representation of this Student object.
     *
     * @return a String representation of this Student object: name " " gpa
     *
     */
    public String toString( )
    {
            return name + " " + gpa;
    } // method toString

} // class Student
```

The Student class implements the Comparable interface with a compareTo method that returns −1, 0, or 1, depending on whether the calling Student object's grade point average is less than, equal to, or greater than the another student's grade point average. So, as you would expect, the Student with the lowest grade point average is the highest-priority element. Suppose the input is as follows:

Soumya 3.4
Navdeep 3.5
Viet 3.5

Here is the output of the students as they are removed from heap:

Soumya 3.4
Viet 3.5
Navdeep 3.5

Notice that Viet is printed before Navdeep even though they have the same grade point average, and Navdeep was input earlier than Viet. As mentioned earlier, the Heap implementation of the PurePriorityQueue interface—like life—is unfair. In Section 13.3.2, we look at the implementation of the Heap class, which will help to explain how this unfairness comes about. Lab 21 will show you how to remedy the problem.

### 13.3.2 The Heap Implementation of the PurePriorityQueue Interface

The critical field in the Heap class will hold the elements. To enable fast access of a parent from a child and vice versa, we want a collection that supports random access. The choices are an ArrayList field or an array field. With an ArrayList object, the size of the collection is automatically maintained, including resizing when needed. But the get and set methods access and modify the underlying array indirectly, whereas an array object can directly perform these operations. So an ArrayList object will require less work, but may be slightly slower. To emphasize design simplicity over run-time speed, we choose an ArrayList field.

Here is the start of the class declaration (recall that E is the type parameter):

```
public class Heap<E> implements PurePriorityQueue<E>
{
        protected static final int DEFAULT_INITIAL_CAPACITY = 11;

        protected ArrayList<E> list;
```

The only other field is

```
        protected Comparator<E> comparator;
```

It turns out that the implementation of most of the methods in the Heap class is fairly straightforward. Here are the constructor definitions:

```
/**
 * Initializes this Heap object to be empty, with a given initial capacity, and elements
 * ordered by the given Comparator object.
 *
 * @param initialCapacity – the initial capacity of this Heap object.
 * @param comp – the Comparator object.
 *
 */
public Heap (int initialCapacity, Comparator<E> comp)
{
        list = new ArrayList (initialCapacity);
        comparator = comp;
} // constructor with initial capacity

/**
 * Initializes this Heap object to be empty, with a default initial capacity and with
 * elements in a class that implements the Comparable interface.
 *
```

```
  */
public Heap( )
{
      this (DEFAULT_INITIAL_CAPACITY, null);
} // default constructor

/**
 * Initializes this Heap object to be empty, with a default initial capacity and
 * with elements compared according to the Comparator object comp.
 *
 * @param comp – the Comparator object used for comparing elements in
 *       this Heap object.
 *
 */
public Heap (Comparator comp)
{
      this (DEFAULT_INITIAL_CAPACITY, comp);
} // constructor with Comparator parameter

/**
 * Initializes this Heap object to a shallow copy of a specified Heap object.
 * The elements in this Heap object will be compared as in the specified
 * Heap object.
 * The worstTime(n) is O(n), where n is the number of elements in the
 * specified Heap object.
 *
 * @param otherHeap – the specified Heap object to be copied to this
 *       Heap object.
 *
 */
public Heap (Heap<E> otherHeap)
{
      list = new ArrayList (otherHeap.list);
      comparator = otherHeap.comparator;
} // copy constructor
```

Now let's define the add, getMin, and removeMin methods. The add method inserts the new element at the back of the ArrayList object list, and an auxiliary method, percolateUp, is called to restore the heap property. Here is the definition:

```
/**
 * Inserts a specified element into this Heap object.
 * The worstTime(n) is O(n) and averageTime(n) is constant.
 *
 * @param element – the element to be inserted into this PurePriorityQueue
 *       object.
```

```
 *
 */
public void add (E element)
{
        list.add (element);
        percolateUp( );
} // method add
```

For example, Figure 13.3 shows what the heap in Figure 13.1 will look like after an Integer with **int** value 28 is appended.

**The** percolateUp **Method**   The complete binary tree in Figure 13.3 is not a heap because 28 is less than its parent. The heap property is restored by the percolateUp method. Here is the method specification:

```
/**
 * Restores the heap properties to this Heap object, which was a heap, except,
 * possibly, at index size( ) – 1.
 * The worstTime(n) is O(log n), and averageTime(n) is constant.
 *
 */
protected void percolateUp( )
```

Before we get into the definition of this method, let's see what it accomplishes. Figure 13.4 shows the result of a call to percolateUp on the complete binary tree in Figure 13.3.

The percolateUp method starts at the back of the ArrayList object list, and swaps parent and child until the heap property of the whole tree has been restored. Note that each such swap restores the heap property *locally* for the subtree rooted at the parent. When there are no more localities that violate the heap property, the whole

**Figure 13.3** | The complete binary tree—*not a heap*—formed by inserting 28 as the right child of 50 in the heap of Figure 13.1.

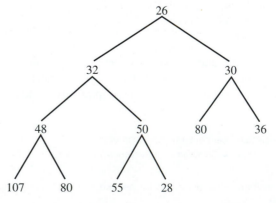

**Figure 13.4 I** The heap formed by invoking percolateUp on the complete binary tree in Figure 13.3.

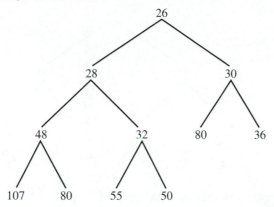

tree is a heap. For example, let's begin with the complete binary tree in Figure 13.3, with the element to be inserted in boldface:

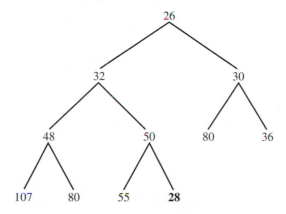

Now what? Because 28 is less than 50, we swap those two elements, and we have the tree (not yet a heap) in Figure 13.5. We now compare 28 with its parent's value, namely 32. Because 28 is less than 32, we swap those elements, and that gives us the heap shown in Figure 13.6.

The key to the efficiency of the percolateUp method is that a parent's index is readily computable from either of its children's indexes: if $k$ contains a child's index, then its parent's index must be

$$(k - 1)/2$$

(The / refers to integer division.) And because list is an ArrayList object, the element at that parent index can be accessed or modified in constant time.

**Figure 13.5** I The complete binary tree of Figure 13.3 after swapping the elements with values 28 and 50; the tree is not yet a heap.

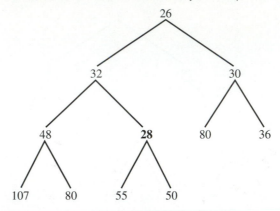

**Figure 13.6** I The heap formed when 28 is added to the heap in Figure 13.1.

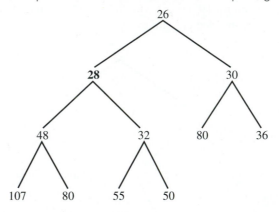

Here is the definition of percolateUp (for the sake of reusability, we factor out the swapping into a separate method):

```
/**
 * Restores the heap properties to this Heap object, which was a heap, except,
 * possibly, at index size( ) − 1.
 * The worstTime(n) is O(log n), and averageTime(n) is constant.
 *
 */
protected void percolateUp( )
{
      int child = list.size( ) − 1,
          parent;

      while (child > 0)
```

```
          {
                  parent = (child − 1) >> 1; // >>1 is slightly faster than / 2
                  if (compare (list.get (child), list.get (parent)) >= 0)
                          break;
                  swap (parent, child);
                  child = parent;
          } // while
  } // method percolateUp
```

The compare method is the same as we saw in the **TreeMap** class of Chapter 12:

```
  /**
   * Compares two specified elements according to Comparable or a Comparator
   * object.
   *
   * @param element1 − one of the specified elements.
   * @param element2 − the other specified element.
   *
   * @return a negative integer, 0, or a positive integer, depending on whether
   *         element1 is less than, equal to or greater than element2.
   *
   */
  private int compare (E element1, E element2)
  {
          return (comparator == null ? ((Comparable)element1).compareTo(element2)
                                     : comparator.compare (element1, element2));
  } // method compare
```

The swap method has a simple definition:

```
  /**
   * Swaps a specified parent and child in this Heap object.
   *
   * @param parent − the position of the parent element.
   * @param child − the position of the child element.
   *
   */
  protected void swap (int parent, int child)
  {
          E temp = list.get (parent);
          list.set (parent, list.get (child));
          list.set (child, temp);
  } // method swap
```

In the worst case for the percolateUp method, the element inserted will have a smaller value than any of its ancestors, so the number of loop iterations will be, approximately, the height of the heap. As we saw in Chapter 9, the height of a complete binary tree is logarithmic in $n$. So worstTime($n$) is logarithmic in $n$, which satisfies the worst-time estimate in the method specification.

In the average case, about half of the elements in the heap will have a smaller value than the element inserted, and about half will have a larger value. But heaps are very bushy: at least half of the elements are leaves. And because of the heap property, most of the larger-valued elements will be at or near the leaf level. In fact, the average number of loop iterations is less than 3 [see Schaffer (1993)], which satisfies the specification that averageTime($n$) be constant.

Now we can analyze the add method. The worst case occurs when underlying array of the ArrayList object list is full. Then—see the definition of the ensure Capacity method in Section 6.2.4—a new array that is 50% larger is constructed and the old array is copied over. So worstTime($n$) is linear in $n$. But this doubling occurs infrequently—once in every $n$ insertions—so averageTime($n$) is constant, just as for percolateUp.

The getMin method simply returns the element at index 0:

```
/**
 * Returns the smallest-valued element in this Heap object.
 *
 * @return the smallest-valued element in this Heap object.
 *
 * @throws NoSuchElementException – if this Heap object is empty.
 *
 */
public E getMin( )
{
        return list.get (0);
} // method getMin
```

The removeMin method's main task is to delete the root element. But simply doing this would leave a hole where the root used to be. So, just as we did when we removed a BinarySearchTree object's element that had two children, we replace the removed element with some other element in the tree. Which one? The obvious answer is the smaller of its children. And ultimately, that must happen in order to preserve the heap property. But if we start by replacing the root element with its smaller child, we could open up another hole, as is shown in the following picture:

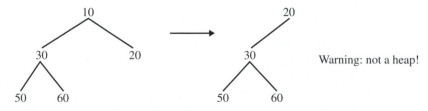

When 10 is replaced with 20, its smaller child, the resulting tree is not a heap because it is not a complete binary tree.

A few minutes' reflection should convince you that, to preserve the completeness of the binary tree, there is only one possible replacement for the root element: the last element in the heap—at index size( ) − 1. Of course, we will then have a lot of adjustments to make; after all, we have taken one of the largest elements and put it at the top of the heap. These adjustments are handled in a percolateDown method that starts at the new root and moves down to the leaf level. So the removeMin method saves the element at index 0, copies the last element (at index size( ) − 1) into index 0, removes that last element, calls percolateDown (0), and returns the saved element. (The percolateDown method has a parameter for the sake of Programming Exercise 13.6.)

Here is the method definition:

```
/**
 * Removes the smallest-valued element from this Heap object.
 * The worstTime(n) is O(log n).
 *
 * @return the element removed.
 *
 * @throws NoSuchElementException – if this Heap object is empty.
 *
 */
public E removeMin( )
{
        E minElem = list.get (0);
        list.set (0, list.get (list.size( ) − 1));
        list.remove (list.size( ) − 1);
        percolateDown (0);
        return minElem;
} // method removeMin
```

The definition of the percolateDown method is developed in the following section.

**The** percolateDown **Method**   To see how to define percolateDown, let's start with the heap from Figure 13.1, repeated below:

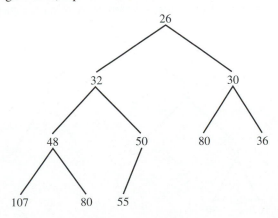

If we now call removeMin( ), then the contents of the not-quite-a-heap, just before the call to percolateDown, are as shown in Figure 13.7.

Notice that since we started with a heap, the heap property guarantees that the root's left and right subtrees are still heaps. So percolateDown's task is to restore the heap property to a complete binary tree whose left and right subtrees are heaps.

In contrast to percolateUp, the percolateDown method works its way down the tree, starting at the index supplied as the argument, in this case, 0 (in Programming Exercise 13.6, we'll see a situation in which we want to start at another index). Each parent is swapped with its smaller-valued child until, eventually, either the parent's value is less than or equal to those of its children or a leaf is swapped. For example, in the tree of Figure 13.7, 30 is smaller than 32, so 30's element is swapped with the root element, and we have the tree shown in Figure 13.8. We still need one more iteration because 55 is greater than the smaller of its children, namely, 80 and 36. We end up with the heap shown in Figure 13.9.

If $k$ contains the parent index, then $2k + 1$ is the index of the left child and $2k + 2$ is the index of the right child (if the parent has a right child). And because list is an ArrayList object, the elements at those indexes can be accessed or modified in constant time.

Here is the definition of percolateDown:

```
/**
 * Restores the heap properties to this Heap object, which is a heap except,
 * possibly, at a specified position.
 * The worstTime(n) is O(log n).
 *
 * @param start – the specified position where the restoration of the heap
 *        will begin.
 *
 */
```

**Figure 13.7 |** A complete binary tree that is not a heap, because the root element's value (in boldface) is not less than or equal to the values of its children.

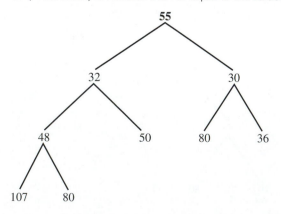

**Figure 13.8 I** The complete binary tree from Figure 13.4 after the smaller-valued of the root's children is swapped with the root. The element that keeps this tree from being a heap, 55, is boldfaced.

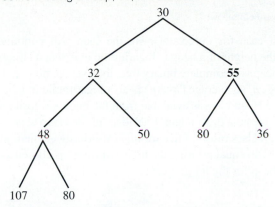

**Figure 13.9 I** The heap formed by swapping the elements with values 36 and 55 in the tree of Figure 13.8.

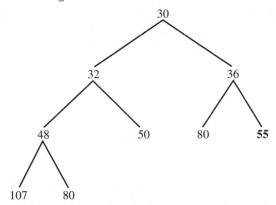

```
protected void percolateDown (int start)
{
        int parent = start,
            child = (parent << 1) + 1; // parent <<1 is slightly faster than 2 * parent

        while (child < list.size( ))
        {
                if (child < list.size( ) -1 &&
                        compare (list.get (child), list.get (child+1)) > 0)
                child++; // child indexes smallest child
                if (compare (list.get (child), list.get (parent)) >= 0)
                        break;
                swap (parent, child);
```

```
                    parent = child;
                    child = (parent << 1) + 1;
            } // while
        } // method percolateDown
```

In the worst case for percolateDown, the loop will continue until a leaf is swapped. Since the height of a heap is logarithmic in $n$, worstTime($n$) is logarithmic in $n$. Because a heap is a complete binary tree, the average number of loop iterations will be nearly $\log_2 n$, so averageTime($n$) is also logarithmic in $n$.

The complete Heap class is available from the book's website and in Lab 21. In that lab, you will create a descendant, FairHeap, of the Heap class. As its name suggests, the FairHeap class resolves ties for highest-priority element in favor of seniority. For elements with equal priority, the highest-priority is chosen as the element that has been on the heap for the longest time.

**Lab 21: Incorporating Fairness in Heaps**

You are now ready for Lab 21.                    All Labs Are Optional

Section 13.3.3 presents a simple application of the Heap class: the heapSort method. Actually, the Heap class was created many years after the invention of the heapSort method, which was originally based on the idea of using an array to store a heap.

### 13.3.3 The heapSort Method

The heapSort method was invented by J.W.J. Williams [see Williams (1964)]. Given a List object, aList, to be sorted, we first create a Heap object, aHeap, with an initial capacity of aList.size( ), and add each element in aList to aHeap. We then clear aList and repeatedly remove from aHeap the minimum element, appending it to aList.

As we did with the treeSort method from Chapter 12, we start with the simple, Comparable-based version. Here is the method definition:

```
/**
 * Sorts a specified List object into the order determined by the compareTo
 * method in the elements' class.
 * The worstTime(n) is O(n log n).
 *
 * @param aList – the List object to be sorted.
 *
 */
public static <E> void heapSort (List<E> aList)
{
        Heap<E> aHeap = new Heap<E> (aList.size( ));
```

```
        for (E element : aList)
            aHeap.add (element);

        aList.clear( );
        // Copy elements, smallest to largest, from heap to aList:
        while (aHeap.size( ) > 0)
            aList.add (aHeap.removeMin( ));
    } // method heapSort
```

For an example, let's start with aList consisting of the following values in the order given:

59 46 32 80 46 55 87 43 44 81 95 12 17 80 75 33 40 61 16 50

We insert each element in aList into aHeap. Figure 13.10 shows the result. We now call the removeMin method 20 times, and append each element returned to the List object. This completes the sorting of the List object.

For an example of a call to heapSort, we can proceed as follows:

```
List<Integer> scoreList = new ArrayList<Integer>( );
scoreList.add (88);
scoreList.add (55);
scoreList.add (77);
scoreList.add (55);
scoreList.add (91);

heapSort (scoreList);
System.out.println (scoreList);
```

**Figure 13.10 I** The effect of making a heap from the given List object aList.

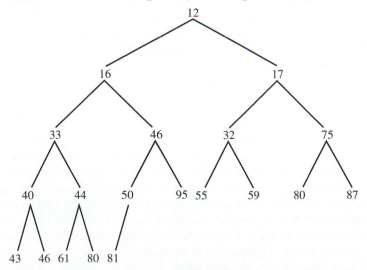

The output will be

[55, 55, 77, 88, 91]

There is also a version of heapSort with a second parameter of type Comparator:

```
/**
 * Sorts a specified List object into the order determined by a specified Comparator
 * object.
 * The worstTime(n) is O(n log n).
 *
 * @param aList – the List object to be sorted.
 * @param comp – the Comparator object that determines the ordering.
 *
 */
public static <E> void heapSort (List<E> aList, Comparator<E> comp)
```

To sort scoreList into decreasing order, we utilize the Decreasing class from Section 13.3.1. The above call to the heapSort method would be replaced with:

```
heapSort (scoreList, new Decreasing( ));
```

The new output, as expected, is

[91, 88, 77, 55, 55]

### 13.3.4  Analysis of heapSort

As with mergeSort and treeSort, we first estimate worstTime($n$) for heapSort. The worst case occurs when the List argument is in the reverse of its Comparable or Comparator order. We'll look at the two explicit loops in heapSort separately:

1. To iterate through aList requires $n$ iterations. During each iteration, the current element is added to aHeap, for which worstTime($n$) is logarithmic in $n$. (There is no resizing of the heap, so we avoid linear-in-$n$ worstTime($n$).) The total number of iterations in creating the heap is linear-logarithmic in $n$ in the worst case.

2. Each one of the $n$ calls to removeMin( ) entails a call to percolateDown(0), for which worstTime($n$) is logarithmic in $n$. So the total number of iterations for this loop is linear-logarithmic in $n$ in the worst case.

The total number of iterations in the worst case is linear-logarithmic in $n$. That is, worstTime($n$) is linear-logarithmic in $n$. And so, by Sorting Fact 3 in Section 11.4, averageTime($n$) is also linear-logarithmic in $n$. Because its averageTime($n$) is optimal, heapSort is one of the premier sort methods, along with mergeSort and treeSort. When heapSort is applied to a list of randomly generated integers, the elapsed time is somewhat slower than for quickSort, slightly slower than for mergeSort, slightly faster than for treeSort, and much, much faster than for insertionSort, selectionSort, and bubbleSort. Of course, these last three sorts take quadratic time on average, so they would be expected to bring up the rear.

The space requirements are substantial: The entire List object is copied to the Heap object, so worstSpace($n$) and averageSpace($n$) are linear in $n$. There is a version of Heap Sort for which worstSpace (*n*) is constant; see Programming Exercise 13.6.

That heapSort is *not* stable can be seen if we start with the following List object of quality-of-life scores and cities ordered by quality-of-life scores:

20 Portland

46 Easton

46 Bethlehem

Converting this List object to a heap requires no work at all because the heap property is already satisfied:

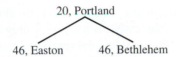

Then removeMin( ) is called three times. After the first call, we get

Notice that (46 Bethlehem) did not percolate down because its child (46 Easton) was not less than (46 Bethlehem). After two more calls to removeMin( ), with the return values appended to the List object, the contents of the List object are:

(20 Portland) (46 Bethlehem) (46 Easton)

The positions of (46 Bethlehem) and (46 Easton) have flipped from the original List object, so the heapSort method is not stable.

Another implementation of the PurePriorityQueue interface is with leftist trees, described in Sahni (2000). A leftist tree is useful in applications where several priority queues must be melded together.

## 13.4 | APPLICATION: HUFFMAN CODES

Suppose we have a large file of information. It would be advantageous if we could save space by compressing the file without losing any of the information. Even more valuable, the time to transmit the information might be significantly reduced if we could send the compressed version instead of the original.

Let's consider how we might encode a message file so that the encoded file has smaller size—that is, fewer bits—than the message file. For the sake of simplicity and specificity, assume the message file M contains 100,000 characters, and each character is either a, b, c, d, e, f, or g. Since there are seven characters, we can encode each character uniquely with ceil (log$_2$ 7) bits,[1] which is 3 bits. For example, we could use 000 for a, 001 for b, 010 for c, and so on. A word such as "cad" would be encoded as 010000011. Then the encoded file E need take up only 300,000 bits, plus an extra few bits for the encoding itself: a = 000, and so on.

---

[1] Recall that ceil(x) returns the smallest integer greater than or equal to x.

We can save space by reducing the number of bits for some characters. For example, we could use the following encoding:

$$a = 0$$
$$b = 1$$
$$c = 00$$
$$d = 01$$
$$e = 10$$
$$f = 11$$
$$g = 000$$

This would reduce the size of the encoded file E by about one-third (unless the character g occurred very frequently). But this encoding leads to ambiguities. For example, the bit sequence 001 could be interpreted as "ad" or as "cb" or as "aab", depending on whether we grouped the first two bits together or the last two bits together, or treated each bit individually.

The reason the above encoding scheme is ambiguous is that some of the encodings are prefixes of other encodings. For example, 0 is a prefix of 00, so it is impossible to determine whether 00 should be interpreted as "aa" or "c". We can avoid ambiguities by requiring that the encoding be **prefix-free,** that is, no encoding of a character can be a prefix of any other character's encoding.

One way to guarantee prefix-free bit encodings is to create a binary tree in which a left branch is interpreted as a 0 and a right branch is interpreted as a 1. If each encoded character is a *leaf* in the tree, then the encoding for that character could not be the prefix of any other character's encoding. In other words, the path to each character provides a prefix-free encoding. For example, Figure 13.11 has a binary tree that illustrates a prefix-free encoding of the characters a through g.

To get the encoding for a character, start with an empty encoding at the root of the binary tree, and continue until the leaf to be encoded is reached. Within the loop, append 0 to the encoding when turning left and append 1 to the encoding when turning right. For example, b is encoded as 01 and f is encoded as 1110. Because each encoded character is a leaf, the encoding is prefix-free and therefore unambiguous. But it is not certain that this will save space or transmission time. It all depends on the frequency of each character. Since three of the encodings take up 2 bits and 4

**Figure 13.11** | A binary tree that determines a prefix-free encoding of a · · · g.

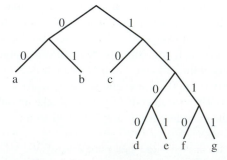

encodings take up 4 bits, this encoding scheme may actually take up more space than the simple, 3-bits-per-character encoding introduced earlier.

This suggests that if we start by determining the frequency of each character and then make up the encoding tree based on those frequencies, we may be able to save a considerable amount of space. The idea of using character frequencies to determine the encoding is the basis for **Huffman encoding** [Huffman (1952)]. Huffman encoding is a prefix-free encoding strategy that is guaranteed to be optimal—among prefix-free encodings. Huffman encoding is the basis for the Unix compress utility, and also part of the JPEG (Joint Photographic Experts Group) encoding process.

We begin by calculating the frequency of each character in a given message M. Note that the time for these calculations is linear in the length of M. For example, suppose that the characters in M are the letters a $\cdots$ g as above, and their frequencies are as given in Figure 13.12.

The size of M is 100,000 characters. If we ignored frequencies and encoded each character into a unique 3-bit sequence, we would need 300,000 bits to encode the message M. We'll soon see how far this is from an optimal encoding.

Once we have calculated the frequency of each character, we will insert each character-frequency pair into a priority queue ordered by increasing frequencies. That is, the top character-frequency pair in the priority queue will have the *least* frequently occurring character. These characters will end up being farthest from the root in the Huffman tree, so their encoding will have the most bits. Conversely, characters that occur most frequently will have the fewest bits in their encodings.

Initially we insert the following pairs into the priority queue:

(a:5000) (b:2000) (c:10000) (d:8000) (e:22000) (f:49000) (g:4000)

In observance of the Principle of Data Abstraction, we will not rely on any implementation details of the PurePriorityQueue interface. So all we know about this priority queue is that an access or removal would be of the pair (b: 2000). We do not assume any order for the remaining elements, but for the sake of simplicity, we will henceforth show them in increasing order of frequencies—as they would be returned by repeated calls to removeMin( ).[2] Note that there is no need to sort the priority queue.

**Figure 13.12 |** Sample character-frequencies for a message of 100,000 characters from a $\cdots$ g.

| | |
|---|---|
| a: | 5,000 |
| b: | 2,000 |
| c: | 10,000 |
| d: | 8,000 |
| e: | 22,000 |
| f: | 49,000 |
| g: | 4,000 |

---

[2] In fact, if we did store the elements in a heap implemented as an array, the contents of that array would be in the following order: (b:2000), (a:5000), (g:4000), (d:8000), (e:22000), (f:49000), (c:10000).

### 13.4.1 Huffman Trees

The binary tree constructed from the priority queue of character-frequency pairs is called a ***Huffman tree.*** We create the Huffman tree from the bottom up because the front of the priority queue has the least frequently occurring character. We start by calling removeMin method twice to get the two characters with lowest frequencies. The first character removed, b, becomes the left leaf in the binary tree, and g becomes the right leaf. The sum of their frequencies becomes the root of the tree and is added to the priority queue. We now have the following Huffman tree:

(6000)
0 ∧ 1
b       g

The priority queue contains

(a:5000) ( :6000) (d:8000) (c:10000) (e:22000) (f:49000)

Technically, the priority queue and the Huffman tree consist of character-frequency pairs. But the character can be ignored when two frequencies are summed, and the frequencies can be ignored in showing the leaves of the Huffman tree. And anyway, the algorithm works with references to the pairs rather than the pairs themselves. This allows references to represent the typical binary-tree constructs—left, right, root, parent—that are needed for navigating through the Huffman tree.

When the pairs (a:5000) and ( :6000) are removed from the priority queue, they become the left and right branches of the extended tree whose root is the sum of their frequencies. That sum is added to the priority queue. We now have the Huffman tree:

The priority queue contains

(d:8000) (c:10000) ( :11000) (e:22000) (f:49000)

When d and c are removed, they cannot yet be connected to the main tree, because neither of their frequencies is at the root of that tree. So they become the left and right branches of another tree, whose root—their sum—is added to the priority queue. We temporarily have two Huffman trees:

and

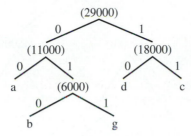

The priority queue now contains

( :11000) ( :18000) (e:22000) (f:49000)

When the pair ( :11000) is removed, it becomes the left branch of the binary tree whose right branch is the next pair removed, ( :18000). The sum becomes the root of this binary tree, and that sum is added the priority queue, so we have the following Huffman tree:

The priority queue contains

(e:22000) ( :29000) (f:49000)

When the next two pairs are removed, e becomes the left branch and (29000) the right branch of the Huffman tree whose root, ( :51000), is added to the priority queue. Finally the last two pairs, (f:49000) and ( :51000) are removed and become the left and right branches of the final Huffman tree. The sum of those two frequencies is the frequency of the root, ( :100000), which is added as the sole element into the priority queue. The final Huffman tree is shown in Figure 13.13.

To get the Huffman encoding for d, for example, we start at the leaf d and work our way back up the tree to the root. As we do, each bit encountered is prepended—placed at the front of—the bit string that represents the Huffman encoding. So the encoding, in stages, is

0
10
110
1110

That is, the encoding for d is 1110. Here are the encodings for all of the characters:

a: 1100
b: 11010
c: 1111
d: 1110
e: 10
f: 0
g: 11011

**Figure 13.13 |** The Huffman tree for the character-frequencies in Figure 13.11.

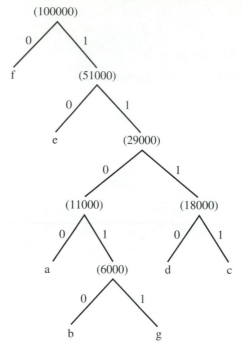

It is now an easy matter to translate the message M into an encoded message E. For example, if the message M starts out with

fad...

Then the encoded message E starts out with the encoding for f (namely, 0) followed by the encoding for a (namely, 1100) followed by the encoding for d (namely, 1110). So E has

011001110...

What happens on the receiving end? How easy is it to decode E to get the original message M? Start at the root of the tree and the beginning of E, take a left branch in the tree for a 0 in E, and take a right branch for a 1. Continue until a leaf is reached. That is the first character in M. Start back at the top of the tree and continue reading E. For example, if M starts with "cede", then E starts with 111110111010. Starting at the root of the tree, the four ones at the beginning of E lead us to the leaf c. Then we go back to the root, and continue reading E with the fifth 1. We take a right branch for that 1 and then a left branch for the 0, and we are at e. The next few bits produce d and e. In other words, we now have "cede", and that, as expected, is the start of M.

The size of the message E is equal to the sum, over all characters, of the number of bits in the encoding of the character times the frequency of that character in M. So to get the size of E in this example, we take the product of the 4 bits in the encoding of a and the 5000 occurrences of a, add to that the product of the 5 bits in the encoding of b and the 2000 occurrences of b, and so on. We get:

$$(4 \cdot 5000) + (5 \cdot 2000) + (4 \cdot 10000) + (4 \cdot 8000) + (2 \cdot 22000) + (1 \cdot 49000)$$
$$+ (5 \cdot 4000) = 215,000$$

This is about 30 percent less than the 300,000 bits required with the fixed-length, 3-bits-per-character encoding discussed earlier. So the savings in space required and transmission time is significant. But it should be noted that a fixed-length encoding can usually be decoded more quickly than a Huffman encoding; for example, the encoded bits can be interpreted as an array index—the entry at that index is the character encoded.

## 13.4.2 Greedy Algorithm Design Pattern

Huffman's algorithm for encoding a message is an example of the greedy-algorithm design pattern. In a *greedy algorithm,* locally optimal choices lead to a globally optimal solution. In the case of Huffman's algorithm, during each loop iteration the two smallest-valued elements are removed from the priority queue and made the left and right branches of a binary tree. Choosing the smallest-valued elements is locally optimal, that is, greedy. And the end result—globally optimal—is a minimal prefix-free encoding. We will encounter two more examples of greedy algorithms in Chapter 15; they also involve priority queues.

## 13.4.3 The Huffman Encoding Project

To add substance to the above discussion, let's develop a project that handles the encoding of a message. The decoding phase is covered in Programming Project 13.1. The input will consist of a file path for the original message, and a file path denoting where the character codes and encoded message should be saved. For example, suppose that the file huffman.in1 contains the following message:

    more money needed

**System Test 1** (input in boldface):
Please enter the path for the input file: **huffman.in1**
Please enter the path for the output file: **huffman.ou1**

After the execution of the program, the file huffman.ou1 will consist of two parts. The first part will have each character in the original message and that character's code. The second part, separated from the first by **, will have the encoded message. Here is the complete file:

    0110
    1011
    d 100
    e 11
    m 001
    n 000

o 010

r 0111

y 1010

**

0010100111111011001010000111010101100011111100111000110

In the encoding, the first character given is the carriage-return character, \r. When the output file is viewed, the first line is blank because a carriage return is carried out. The second line starts with a space, followed by the code for the carriage-return character. Subsequent lines start with the character encoded, a space, and the code for that character.

For System Test 2, assume that the file huffman.in2 contains the following message:

In Xanadu did Kubla Khan

A stately pleasure-dome decree:

Where Alph, the sacred river, ran

Through caverns measureless to man

Down to a sunless sea.

**System Test 2** (input in boldface):

Please enter the path for the input file: **huffman.in2**

Please enter the path for the output file: **huffman.ou2**

Here is the complete file huffman.ou2 after execution of the program (the encoded message has been split over several lines to fit on the page):

10001

 101

, 001000

- 0100000

. 0100001

: 0010100

A 001011

D 0100110

I 0100101

K 001110

T 0011011

W 0010101

X 0011000

a 000

b 0011001

c 110010

d 11110

e 011

g 0011010

h 11111

i 001111

l 11101

m 110011
n 0101
o 11000
p 001001
r 1001
s 1101
t 10000
u 11100
v 010001
w 0100111
y 0100100
**

0100101010110100110000000101000111101110010111110001111111101010011101
1100001100111101000101001110111110000101100010010111011101100000001000
0011111010100100101001001111010110001101111001001011010000011110110001
1001101110111110011110010100101101100101001000100101011111101110010111
0100101111101001001111110010001011000011111011101110100011001010010111
1110101100100111010000101110010010001011001000010110001001101111111100
1110001110000110101111110111001000001000101110010101110110111001101100
0110111100100101111101011110111011011000011000101110011000010110001010
0110110000100111010110110000110001010001011101111000101111010111101110
1101110101100001000011000  1

As always, we embrace modularity by separating the input-output details from the Huffman-encoding details, in a Huffman class. We start with the lower-level class, Huffman, in the following section.

**The** Huffman **Class**　The Huffman class has several responsibilities. First, it must initialize a Huffman object. Also, it must determine the frequency of each character. This must be done line-by-line so that the Huffman class can avoid entanglement in input-output issues. The other responsibilities are to create the priority queue and Huffman tree, to calculate the Huffman codes, and to return both the character codes and, line-by-line, the encoded message. Here are the method specifications:

```
/**
 * Initializes this Huffman object.
 *
 */
public Huffman( )

/**
 * Updates the frequencies of the characters in line.
 *
 */
public void updateFrequencies (String line)

/**
 * Creates the priority queue from the frequencies.
 *
```

```
                */
            public void createPQ( )

            /**
             * Creates the Huffman tree.
             *
             */
            public void createHuffmanTree( )

            /**
             * Calculates the Huffman codes.
             *
             */
            public void calculateHuffmanCodes( )

            /**
             * Returns, as a String object, the characters and their Huffman codes.
             *
             * @return the characters and their Huffman codes.
             *
             */
            public String getCodes( )

            /**
             * Returns a String representation of the encoding of a specified line.
             *
             * @param line – the line whose encoding is returned.
             *
             * @return a String representation of the encoding of line.
             *
             */
            public String getEncodedLine (String line)
```

By convention, since no time estimates are given, you may assume that for each method, worstTime($n$) is constant, where $n$ is the size of the original message.

As suggested by the outline in Section 13.4.1, the Huffman class will need to be able to access the entries, that is, the elements in the priority queue and Huffman tree. For this we will create an Entry class. In previous collections, the Entry class was nested. But here we give the Entry class default visibility so that the Entry fields can be accessed in a class that decodes a message (see Programming Project 13.1). Also, there is no type parameter for the Entry class: the elements will always be of type **char**. The Entry class has three fields related to the encoding, three fields related to binary-tree traversal, and a compareTo method based on frequencies:

```
            class Entry implements Comparable
            {
                  int freq;

                  String code;

                  char id;
```

```
Entry left,
        right,
        parent;

    public int compareTo (Object entry)
    {
            return freq – ((Entry)entry).freq;
    } // compareTo

} // class Entry
```

Now that we have decided on an Entry class, we can determine the fields in the Huffman class. Given a character in the input, it will be stored in a leaf in the Huffman tree, and we want to be able to access that leaf entry quickly. To allow random-access, we can choose an ArrayList field or an array field, just as we had a choice for the Heap class. But here the nod goes to an array field because of the speed of directly utilizing the index operator, [ ], versus indirect access with the ArrayList's get and set methods. Note that if the message file is very large, most of the processing time will be consumed in updating the frequencies of the characters and, later, in calculating the codes corresponding to the characters in the message file. Both of these tasks entail accessing or modifying entries.

Here is the declaration:

```
protected Entry [ ] leafEntries;
```

For the sake of simplicity, we restrict ourselves to the 256 characters in the extended ASCII character set, so we have one array slot for each ASCII character:

```
public final static int SIZE = 256;
```

For example, if the input character is B, the information for that character is stored at index (**int**)'B', which is 66. If the encoding for B is 0100 and the frequency of B in the input message is 2880, then the entry at leafEntries [66] would be

The left and right references are **null** because leaves have no children. The reason that we use references rather than indexes for parent, left, and right is that some of the entries represent sums, not leaf-characters, so those entries are not in leafEntries. Every leaf is an entry, but not every entry is a leaf.

The only other field is a priority queue:

```
protected PurePriorityQueue<Entry> pq;
```

We do not need an explicit class for a Huffman tree because we will create the tree by adjusting the parent, left, and right fields in the Entry objects.

Figure 13.14 has the UML diagram for the Huffman class. For the sake of brevity, the methods in the Heap class (which implement the methods in the PurePriority Queue interface) are omitted.

**Figure 13.14 |** UML diagram for the Huffman class.

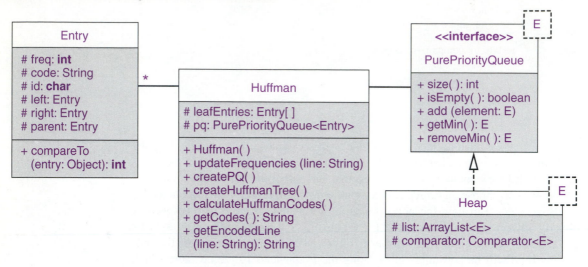

**Method Definitions in the** Huffman **Class** The constructor performs the expected initializations:

```
/**
 * Initializes this Huffman object.
 *
 */
public Huffman( )
{
        Entry entry;

        leafEntries = new Entry [SIZE];
        for (int i = 0; i < SIZE; i++)
        {
                leafEntries [i] = new Entry( );
                entry = leafEntries [i];
                entry.freq = 0;
                entry.left = null;
                entry.right = null;
                entry.parent = null;
        } // initializing leafEntries

        pq = new Heap<Entry>( );
} // default constructor
```

To run the project with a different implementation of the PurePriorityQueue interface, the only statement to be changed is the last one in this constructor.

The updateFrequencies method adds 1 to the frequency for each character in the parameter line. The carriage-return character is included in this updating to ensure that the line structure of the original message will be preserved in the encoding. Here is the method definition:

```
/**
 * Updates the frequencies of the characters in line.
 *
 */
public void updateFrequencies (String line)
{
      Entry entry;

      for (int j = 0; j < line.length( ); j++)
      {
            entry = leafEntries [(int)(line.charAt (j))];
            entry.freq++;
      } // for

      // Account for the end-of-line marker:
      entry = leafEntries [(int)'\r'];
      entry.freq++;
} // method updateFrequencies
```

As noted earlier, worstTime($n$) for this method (and for the other methods in the Huffman class) is constant because $n$ refers to the size of the entire message file, and this method works on a single line.

The priority queue is created from the entries with nonzero frequencies:

```
/**
 * Creates the priority queue from the frequencies.
 *
 */
public void createPQ( )
{
      Entry entry;

      for (int i = 0; i < SIZE; i++)
      {
            entry = leafEntries [i];
            if (entry.freq > 0)
                  pq.add (entry);
      } // for
} // createPQ
```

The Huffman tree is created "on the fly." Until the priority queue consists of a single entry, a pair of entries is removed from the priority queue and become the left and right children of an entry that contains the sum of the pair's frequencies; the sum entry is added to the priority queue. Here is the definition:

```
/**
 * Creates the Huffman tree.
 *
 */
public void createHuffmanTree( )
```

```
        {
                Entry left,
                      right,
                      sum;

                while (pq.size( ) > 1)
                {
                        left = pq.removeMin( );
                        left.code = "0";

                        right = pq.removeMin( );
                        right.code = "1";

                        sum = new Entry( );
                        sum.parent = null;
                        sum.freq = left.freq + right.freq;
                        sum.left = left;
                        sum.right = right;
                        left.parent = sum;
                        right.parent = sum;
                        pq.add (sum);
                } // while
        } // method createHuffmanTree
```

The Huffman codes are determined for each leaf entry whose frequency is nonzero. We create the code for that entry as follows: starting with an empty string variable code, we prepend the entry's code field (either 0 or 1) to code, and then replace the entry with the entry's parent. The loop stops when the entry is the root. The final value of code is then inserted as the code field for that entry in leafEntries. For example, suppose part of the Huffman tree is as follows:

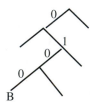

Then the code for B would be 0100, and this value would be stored in the code field of the Entry at index 66 of leafEntries—recall that (**int**)'B' = 66 in the ASCII (and Unicode) collating sequence.

Here is the method definition:

```
        /**
         * Calculates the Huffman codes.
         *
         */
        public void calculateHuffmanCodes( )
        {
```

```
String code;

Entry entry;

for (int i = 0; i < SIZE; i++)
{
        code = "";
        entry = leafEntries [i];
        if (entry.freq > 0)
        {
                while (entry.parent != null)
                {
                        code = entry.code + code;    // current bit prepended to
                        entry = entry.parent;        // code as we go up the tree
                } // while
                leafEntries [i].code = code;
        } // if
} // for
} // calculateHuffmanCodes
```

In the getCodes method, a String object is constructed from each character and its code, and that String object is then returned:

```
/**
 * Returns, as a String object, the characters and their Huffman codes.
 *
 * @return the characters and their Huffman codes.
 *
 */
public String getCodes( )
{
        Entry entry;

        String codes = new String( );

        for (int i = 0; i < SIZE; i++)
        {
                entry = leafEntries [i];
                if (entry.freq > 0)
                        codes += (char)i + " " + entry.code + "\n";
        } // for
        return codes;
} // method getCodes
```

Finally, in the getEncodedLine method, a String object is constructed from the code for each character (including the carriage-return character) in line, and that String object is returned:

```
/**
 * Returns a String representation of the encoding of a specified line.
```

```
        *
        * @param line – the line whose encoding is returned.
        *
        * @return a String representation of line.
        *
        */
        public String getEncodedLine (String line)
        {
              Entry entry;

              String encodedLine = new String( );

              for (int j = 0; j < line.length( ); j++)
              {
                    entry = leafEntries [(int)(line.charAt (j))];
                    encodedLine += entry.code;
              } // for
              entry = leafEntries [(int)'\r'];
              encodedLine += entry.code;
              return encodedLine;
        } // method getEncodedLine
```

The following section finishes up the project by developing the HuffmanTester class (not a driver because the Huffman class methods must be invoked in a fixed order) and, for the sake of completeness, the HuffmanMain class.

### 13.4.4 The HuffmanTester Class

The HuffmanTester class must initialize any of its instances, open the input and output files from paths read in from the keyboard, create the Huffman encoding, and save the encoded message to the output file. Here are the method specifications:

```
        /**
         * Initializes this HuffmanTester object.
         *
         */
        public HuffmanTester( )

        /**
         * Reads in file paths and opens the input and output files.
         *
         * @return (a reference to) the file writer.
         *
         */
        public PrintWriter openFiles( )

        /**
         * Creates the Huffman encoding.
         * The worstTime(n) is O(n).
```

```
    *
    */
public void createEncoding( )

/**
 * Saves the Huffman codes and the encoded message to a file.
 * The worstTime(n) is O(n).
 *
 */
public void saveEncodedMessage( )
```

Beyond a Huffman field, the other three fields are related to input and output:

```
protected BufferedReader fileReader;

protected PrintWriter fileWriter;

protected Huffman huffman;

protected String inFilePath;
```

Figure 13.15 has all of the UML class diagrams for this project.

**Implementation of the** HuffmanTester **Class** The default constructor simply initializes the huffman field:

```
/**
 * Initializes this HuffmanTester object.
 *
 */
public HuffmanTester( )
{
        huffman = new Huffman( );
} // default constructor
```

The openFiles( ) method has a loop that continues until a correct input-file path has been read in:

```
/**
 * Reads in file paths
 *
 * @return (a reference to) the file writer
 *
 */
public PrintWriter openFiles( )
{
        final String IN_FILE_PROMPT =
                "\nPlease enter the path for the input file: ";

        final String OUT_FILE_PROMPT =
                "\nPlease enter the path for the output file: ";
```

**Figure 13.15 |** Class diagrams for the Huffman Encoding project. For the sake of simplicity, the Heap class's methods are not listed.

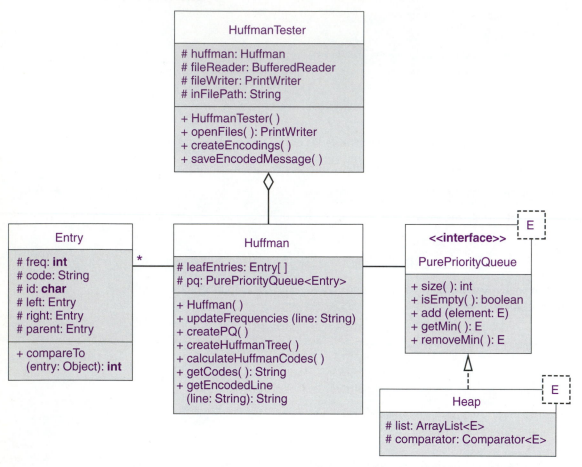

```
BufferedReader keyboardReader = new BufferedReader
                                      (new InputStreamReader (System.in));

String outFilePath,
       line;

boolean pathsOK = false;

while (!pathsOK)
{
       try
       {
              System.out.print (IN_FILE_PROMPT);
              inFilePath = keyboardReader.readLine( );
```

```
                    fileReader= new BufferedReader(new FileReader (inFilePath));
                    System.out.print (OUT_FILE_PROMPT);
                    outFilePath = keyboardReader.readLine( );
                    fileWriter = new PrintWriter (new FileWriter (outFilePath));
                    pathsOK = true;
             } // try
             catch (IOException e)
             {
                    System.out.println (e);
             } // catch
        } // while !pathOK
        return fileWriter;
    } // method openFiles
```

Most of the Huffman-related work is done in the createEncoding method: the message file is read and the frequencies of each character are updated. Then the priority queue and Huffman tree are created, and the Huffman codes are calculated. Here is the method definition:

```
/**
 * Creates the Huffman encoding.
 * The worstTime(n) is O(n).
 *
 */
public void createEncoding( )
{
      String line;

      try
      {
            while (true)
            {
                  line = fileReader.readLine( );
                  if (line == null)
                        break;
                  huffman.updateFrequencies (line);
            } // while
            fileReader.close( ); // re-opened in saveEncodedMessage
            huffman.createPQ( );
            huffman.createHuffmanTree( );
            huffman.calculateHuffmanCodes( );
      } // try
      catch (IOException e)
      {
            System.out.println (e);
      } // catch IOException
} // method createEncoding
```

The Huffman codes and encoded message (line-by-line) are retrieved with calls to getCodes and getEncodedLine, and saved to the output file. Here is the method definition:

```java
/**
 * Saves the Huffman codes and the encoded message to a file.
 * The worstTime(n) is O(n).
 *
 */
public void saveEncodedMessage( )
{
    String line;

    try
    {
        fileWriter.print (huffman.getCodes( ));
        fileWriter.println ("***"); // to separate codes from encoded message
        fileReader = new BufferedReader (new FileReader (inFilePath));

        while (true)
        {
            line = fileReader.readLine( );
            if (line == null)
                break;
            fileWriter.println (huffman.getEncodedLine (line));
        } // while
    } // try
    catch (IOException e)
    {
        System.out.println (e);
    } // catch IOException
} // method saveEncodedMessage
```

Finally, the HuffmanMain method invokes the methods in the HuffmanTester class and closes the output file:

```java
public static void main (String[ ] args)
{
    PrintWriter writer = null;

    try
    {
        HuffmanTester tester = new HuffmanTester( );

        writer = tester.openFiles( );
        tester.createEncoding( );
        tester.saveEncodedMessage( );
    } // try
    finally
```

```
        {
                writer.close( );
        } // finally
   } // method main
```

All of the files are available from the book's website.

Later, another user may want to decode the message. This is done in two steps. First, the encoding is read in and the Huffman tree is re-created. Second, the encoded message is read in, and the output is the decoded message, which should be identical to the original message. Decoding the encoded message is the subject of Programming Project 13.1.

## SUMMARY

This chapter introduced the *priority queue:* a collection in which removal is allowed only of the highest-priority element in the sequence, according to some method for comparing elements. The PurePriorityQueue interface may be implemented in a variety of ways. The most widely used implementation is the Heap class. A *heap* $t$ is a complete binary tree such that either $t$ is empty or

1.  The root element of $t$ is smallest element in $t$, according to some method for comparing elements.

2.  The left and right subtrees of $t$ are heaps.

Because array-based representations of complete binary trees allow rapid calculation of a parent's index from a child's index and vice versa, the heap can be implemented as an array or ArrayList. This utilizes an array's ability to randomly access the element at a given index.

The heapSort method is a fast sort that creates a heap from a list, clears the list, and then repeatedly removes the smallest element in the heap and appends it to the list.

The application of priority queues was in the area of data compression. Given a message, it is possible to encode each character, unambiguously, into a minimum number of bits. One way to achieve such a minimum encoding is with a Huffman tree. A *Huffman tree* is a two-tree in which each leaf represents a distinct character in the original message, each left branch is labeled with a 0, and each right branch is labeled with a 1. The Huffman code for each character is constructed by tracing the path from that leaf character back to root, and prepending each branch label in the path.

## CONCEPT EXERCISES

**13.1**  Suppose we decide to implement the PurePriorityQueue interface with a TreeSet object:

**public class** TreeSetPriorityQueue<E> **implements** PurePriorityQueue<E>
{
    TreeSet<E> set;

    ...

Then the definitions of the getMin, removeMin, and add methods are one-liners. For example, here is the definition of the getMin method:

```
public E getMin( )
{
       return set.first( );
} // method getMin
```

Estimate worstTime($n$) for those three methods. What is the major drawback to implementing the PurePriorityQueue class with a class that implements the Set interface? Explain how to overcome this drawback—in effectiveness, but not in efficiency—by implementing the PurePriorityQueue interface with the TreeMap class instead.

**13.2** Define a Heap in which the highest-priority element is the String object of greatest length in the priority queue. For example, if the elements are "yes", "maybe", and "no", the highest-priority element would be "maybe".

**13.3** In practical terms, what is the difference between the Comparable interface and the Comparator interface? Give an example in which the Comparator interface must be used.

**13.4** Show the resulting heap after each of the following alterations is made, consecutively, to the following heap:

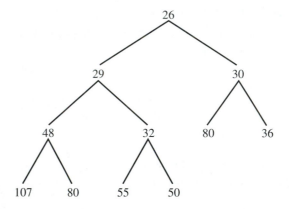

   **a.**   add (29);

   **b.**   add (30);

   **c.**   removeMin( );

   **d.**   removeMin( );

**13.5** For the following character frequencies, create the heap of character-frequency pairs (highest priority = lowest frequency):

a: 5,000

b: 2,000

c: 10,000

d: 8,000

e: 22,000

f: 49,000

g: 4,000

**13.6** Use the following Huffman code to translate "faced" into a bit sequence:

a: 1100

b: 11010

c: 1111

d: 1110

e: 10

f: 0

**13.7** Use the following Huffman tree to translate the bit sequence
11101011111100111010 back into letters a · · · g:

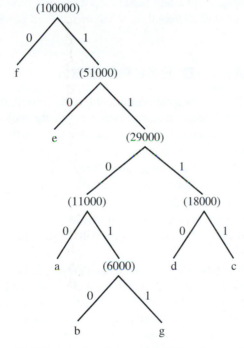

**13.8** For the following Huffman code, give an example of a sequence of 5 bits
that could not be the start of any encoded message:

a: 1100

b: 11010

c: 1111

d: 1110

e: 10

f: 0

Can you find another such 5-bit sequence? Explain.

**13.9** Must a Huffman tree be a two-tree? Explain.

**13.10** Provide a message with the alphabet a $\cdots$ e in which two of the letters have a Huffman code of 4 bits. Explain why it is impossible to create a message with the alphabet a $\cdots$ e in which two of the letters have a Huffman code of 5 bits. Create a message with the alphabet a $\cdots$ h in which all of the letters have a Huffman code of 3 bits.

**13.11** In Figure 13.13, the sum of the frequencies of all the nonleaves is 215,000. This is also the size of the encoded message E. Explain why in any Huffman tree, the sum of the frequencies of all nonleaves is equal to the size of the encoded message.

**13.12** Give an example of a heap of 10 unique elements in which, during the call to removeMin, the call to percolateDown(0) would entail only one swap of parent and child.

**13.13** In heapSort, there are $n$ additional loop iterations if the List object is an ArrayList instead of a LinkedList. What method call generates those extra iterations?

## PROGRAMMING EXERCISES

**13.1** In Section 13.3.1, a heap of Student objects is created; the Student class implements the Comparable interface. Rewrite the project so that the Comparator interface is implemented instead. Rerun the project to confirm your revisions.

**13.2** Rewrite the Heap class with an array field instead of an ArrayList field. Rerun the Huffman Encoding project with System Tests 1 and 2 to test your revision.

**13.3** Rewrite the Huffman class with an ArrayList field instead of an array field. Rerun the Huffman Encoding project with System Tests 1 and 2 to test your revision.

**13.4** Create an Employee class in which each employee has a name and a salary. Create a LinkedList object in which each element is an Employee object. Add several employees to the LinkedList object, and then apply heapSort: the list should be ordered alphabetically, by employee name. Print the LinkedList object before and after the sorting. Create an ArrayList object in which each element is an Employee object. Add several employees to the ArrayList object, and then apply heapSort: the list should be in decreasing order of salaries. Print the ArrayList object before and after the sorting.

**13.5** For the array-based (Option C) implementation of the PurePriorityQueue interface in Section 13.3, develop the add and removeMin methods. To keep the worstTime($n$) for removeMin( ) constant, use a circular array, similar to the one developed in Section 8.2.2.

**13.6** Develop an in-place version of Heap Sort in the Heap class. The method is *not* static, and the parameter is an ArrayList. Here is the method specification:

```
/**
 * Sorts a specified ArrayList object into the order determined by the
 * compareTo method in the elements' class.
 * The worstTime(n) is O(n log n).
 *
 * @param aList – the Array List object to be sorted.
 *
 */
public void heapSort (ArrayList<E> aList)
```

*Hint:* The definition starts by assigning

```
list = aList;
```

where list is the field in the Heap class.

The next step is to convert list into a heap. The percolateDown (**int** start) method converts into a heap the complete binary tree—rooted at start—that is a heap except, possibly, at index start. Because each leaf is a heap, the heapification of list loops as i goes from the last non-leaf index in list down to 0, and calls percolateDown (i) during each loop iteration.

Now that list is a heap, we repeatedly remove from that heap the element at index 0, and append that element to the back of list. This removing and appending might seem to be simply

```
list.add (removeMin( ));
```

But the element appended is no longer part of the heap. So, basically, the removeMin and percolateDown methods must be rewritten to operate only on that part of list that is a heap. This can be accomplished with the help of a heapSize variable:

```
int heapSize = list.size( );
while (heapSize > 0)
{
        E minElem = list.get (0);
        list.set (0, list.get (heapSize − 1));
        list.remove (−−heapSize);
        int parent = 0,
            child = (parent << 1) + 1;

        while (child < heapSize)
                ...
```

## Programming Project 13.1

### Decoding a Huffman-Encoded Message

Suppose a message has been encoded by a Huffman encoding. Develop a project to decode the encoded message and thus retrieve the original message.

**Analysis:**

For the entire project, worstTime ($n$) must be O($n$), where $n$ is the size of the original message. As shown in the output file in the Huffman project of this chapter, the input file will consist of two parts:

1. Each character and its encoding.

2. The encoded message.

A sample input file, huffman.ou1, is shown below. The first line contains the carriage-return character, followed by a space, followed by its encoding. The carriage-return character, when viewed, forces a line-feed. So the first line below is blank, and the second starts with a space, followed by the code for the carriage-return character. The encoded message has been split into more than one line to fit on this page:

```
 0010
  0111
a 000
b 1
c 0011
d 010
e 0110
**
100001001110011011001001100111001100010111010000100100100110000010011
0100000100111001100001000101111111111111111111111111111110010
```

**System Test 1 (Input in Boldface)**

Please enter the name of the input file: **huffman.ou1**

Please enter the name of the output file: **decode.ou1**

The file decode.ou1 will contain:

```
bad cede cab dab
dead dad cad
bbbbbbbbbbbbbbbbbbbbbbbbbbbbbb
```

Suppose the file huffman.ou2 contains the following (the message is from Coleridge's "Rubiyat of Omar Khayam"):

```
10001
 101
, 001000
```

```
- 0100000
. 0100001
: 0010100
A 001011
D 0100110
I 0100101
K 001110
T 0011011
W 0010101
X 0011000
a 000
b 0011001
c 110010
d 11110
e 011
g 0011010
h 11111
i 001111
l 11101
m 110011
n 0101
o 11000
p 001001
r 1001
s 1101
t 10000
u 11100
v 010001
w 0100111
y 0100100
**
0100101010110100110000000101000111101110010111110001111
1110101001110111000011001111010001010011011111000010110
0010010111011101100000001000001111101010010010100100111
0101100011011110010010110100000111101100011001101101111
1001111001010010110100101001000100101011111101110010111
0100101111101001001111110010001011000011110111011101000
1100101001011111101011001001110100010111001001000101100
1000010110001001101111111100110001110000110101111110111
0010000010001011001010110110111001101100011011111001001
0111110101111011101101100001100010111001100001010110001010
0110110000100111010110110000110001010001011101111000011
1101011110111011011110101100001000011001
```

*(continued)*

*(continued from previous page)*

**System Test 2:**

Please enter the name of the input file: **huffman.ou2**

Please enter the name of the output file: **decode.ou2**

The file decode.ou2 will contain

> In Xanadu did Kubla Khan
> A stately pleasure-dome decree:
> Where Alph, the sacred river, ran
> Through caverns measureless to man
> Down to a sunless sea.

# Programming Project 13.2

## Integrated Web Browser and Search Engine, Part 4

In Part 3, you printed the search-results as they were obtained. In this part of the project, you will save the results, and then print them in decreasing order of frequencies. For example, if you ran System Test 1 from Part 3, the output would now be:

Here are the files and relevance frequencies, in decreasing order:
browser.in6 7
browser.in8 2
browser.in7 0

In saving the results, the data structure must satisfy the following:

> To insert a result into the data structure, worstTime($n$) must be $O(n)$, and average-Time($n$) must be constant;

> To remove a result from the data structure, worstTime($n$) and averageTime($n$) must be $O(\log n)$.

**System Test 1 (Assume search.in1 Contains browser.in6, 7, 8):**
**neural network**

Here are the files and relevance frequencies, in decreasing order:
browser.in6 7
browser.in8 2
browser.in7 0

**System Test 2 (Assume search.in1 Contains browser.in10, 11, 12, 13):**
**neural network**

Here are the files and relevance frequencies, in decreasing order:
browser.in10 8
browser.in13 8
browser.in11 6
browser.in12 6

*Note 1:* In your code, do not use complete path names, such as "h:\\Project3\\home.in1". Instead, use "home.in1".

*Note 2:* The Search button should be green as soon as the GUI window is opened. A constructor in GUIBrowserListener can be modified to handle this.

# Hashing

We start this chapter by reviewing some search algorithms from earlier chapters as a prelude to the introduction of a new search technique: hashing. The basic idea with hashing is that we perform some simple operation on an element's key to obtain an index in an array. The element is stored at that index. With an appropriate implementation, hashing allows searches (as well as insertions and removals) to be performed in constant average time! Our primary focus will be on understanding and using the HashMap class in the Java Collections Framework, but we will also consider other approaches to hashing. The application will use hashing to insert identifiers into a symbol table. ■

## CHAPTER OBJECTIVES

1. Understand how hashing works, when it should be used, and when it should not be used.

2. Explain the significance of the Uniform Hashing Assumption.

3. Compare the various collision handlers: chaining, offset-of-1, quotient-offset.

# 14.1 | A FRAMEWORK TO ANALYZE SEARCHING

Before we begin looking at hashing, we need a systematic way to analyze search methods in general. Because the search may be successful or unsuccessful, the analysis of search methods should include both possibilities. For each search method we estimate $averageTime_S(n)$, the average time—over all $n$ elements in the collection—of a successful search. As always for average time, we make the simplifying assumption that each element in the collection is equally likely to be sought.

We will also be interested in $worstTime_S(n)$, the largest number of statements needed to successfully search for an element. That is, for a given value of $n$, we look at all permutations of the $n$ elements and all possible choices of the element to be successfully sought. For each permutation and element, we determine the number of iterations (or recursive calls) to find that element. Then $worstTime_S(n)$ corresponds to the largest number of iterations attained.

We also estimate $averageTime_U(n)$, the average time of an unsuccessful search, and $worstTime_U(n)$. For an unsuccessful search, we assume that on average, every possible failure is equally likely. For example, in an unsuccessful search of a sequence of $n$ elements, there are $n + 1$ possibilities for where the given element can occur:

Before the first element in the sequence;

Between the first and second elements;

Between the second and third elements;

. . .

Between the $(n - 1)$st and $n$th elements;

After the $n$th element.

The next section reviews the search methods employed so far.

# 14.2 | REVIEW OF SEARCHING

Up to this point, we have seen three different kinds of searches: sequential search, binary search, and red-black tree search. Let's look at each one in turn.

## 14.2.1 Sequential Search

A *sequential search*—also called a "linear search"—of a collection starts at the beginning of the collection and iterates until either the element sought is found or the end of the collection is reached. For example, the contains method in the Abstract Collection class uses a sequential search:

```
/**
 * Determines if this AbstractCollection object contains a specified element.
 * The worstTime(n) is O(n).
 *
 * @param obj – the element searched for in this AbstractCollection object.
 *
```

```
 * @return true – if this AbstractionCollection object contains obj; otherwise,
 *        return false.
 */
public boolean contains(Object obj)
{
        Iterator<E> e = iterator( ); // E is the type parameter for this class
        if (obj == null)
        {
                while (e.hasNext( ))
                        if (e.next( )==null)
                                return true;
        } // if obj == null
        else
        {
                while (e.hasNext( ))
                        if (obj.equals(e.next( )))
                                return true;
        } // obj != null
        return false;
} // method contains
```

The contains method in the ArrayList class and the containsValue method in the TreeMap class use sequential searches similar to the above.

For a successful sequential search of a collection, we assume that each of the $n$ elements in the collection is equally likely to be sought. So the average number of loop iterations is $(1 + 2 + \cdots + n)/n$, which is $(n + 1)/2$, and the largest possible number of loop iterations is $n$. We conclude that both $averageTime_S(n)$ and $worstTime_S(n)$ are linear in $n$.

For an unsuccessful sequential search, even if the collection happens to be ordered, we must access all $n$ elements before concluding that the given element is not in the collection, so $averageTime_U(n)$ and $worstTime_U(n)$ are both linear in $n$. As we will see in Sections 14.2.2 and 14.2.3, ordered collections can improve on these times by employing nonsequential searches.

## 14.2.2 Binary Search

Sometimes we know beforehand that the collection is sorted. For sorted collections, we can perform a *binary search,* so called because the size of the segment searched is repeatedly divided by two. Here, as investigated in Lab 8, is the binarySearch method from the Arrays class of the Java Collections Framework:

```
/**
 * Searches a specified array for a specified element.
 * The array must be sorted in ascending order according to the natural ordering
 * of its elements (that is, by the compareTo method); otherwise, the results are
 * undefined.
 * The worstTime(n) is O(log n).
 *
```

```
     * @param a – the array to be searched.
     * @param key – the element to be searched for in the array.
     *
     * @return the index of an element equal to key – if the array contains at least one
     *         such element; otherwise, – insertion point – 1, where insertion point is
     *         the index where key would be inserted. Note that the return value is
     *         less than zero only if the key is not found in the array.
     *
     */
    public static int binarySearch (Object[ ] a, Object key)
    {
          int low = 0;
          int high = a.length − 1;

          while (low <= high)
          {
                int mid =(low + high)/2;
                Comparable midVal = (Comparable)a [mid];
                int cmp = midVal.compareTo(key);

                if (cmp < 0)
                      low = mid + 1;
                else if (cmp > 0)
                      high = mid − 1;
                else
                      return mid; // key found
          } // while
          return − (low + 1); // key not found
    } // method binarySearch
```

A binary search is much faster than a sequential search. For either a successful or unsuccessful search, the number of elements to be searched is $n = $ high $+ 1 − $ low. The **while** loop will continue to divide $n$ by 2 until either key is found or high $+ 1 = $ low, that is, until $n = 0$. The number of loop iterations will be the number of times $n$ can be divided by 2 until $n = 0$. By the Splitting Rule in Chapter 3, that number is, approximately, $\log_2 n$ (also, see Example A2.2 of Appendix 2). So we get average $\text{Time}_S(n) \approx \text{worstTime}_S(n) \approx \text{averageTime}_U(n) \approx \text{worstTime}_U(n)$, which is logarithmic in $n$.

There is also a Comparator-based version of this method; the heading is

```
    public static <T> int binarySearch (T[ ] a, T key, Comparator<? super T> c)
```

For example, if words is an array of String objects ordered by the length of the string, we can utilize the ByLength class from Section 11.3 and call

```
    System.out.println (Arrays.binarySearch (words, "misspell", new ByLength( )));
```

## 14.2.3 Red-Black Tree Search

Red-black trees were introduced in Chapter 12. One of that class's **public** methods, containsKey, has a one-line definition: all it does is call the **private** getEntry method.

The getEntry method, which returns the Entry corresponding to a given key, has a definition that is similar to the definition of the binarySearch method. Here is the definition of getEntry:

```
private Entry<K, V> getEntry(Object key)
{
    Entry<K, V> p = root;
    K k = (K)key;
    while (p != null)
    {
        int cmp = compare (k,p.key);
        if (cmp == 0)
            return p;
        else if (cmp < 0)
            p = p.left;
        else
            p = p.right;
    } // while
    return null;
} // method getEntry
```

The height of a red-black tree $t$ is logarithmic in $n$, the number of elements (see Example A2.6 in Appendix 2). For an unsuccessful search, the getEntry method iterates from the root to an empty subtree. In the worst case, the empty subtree will be a distance of height($t$) branches from the root, and the number of iterations will be logarithmic in $n$. That is, worstTime$_U(n)$ is logarithmic in $n$.

The number of iterations in the average case depends on bh(root): the number of black elements in the path from the root to an element with no children or with one child. The path length from the root to such an element is certainly less than or equal to the height of the tree. As shown in Example A2.6 of Appendix 2, bh(root) $\geq$ height($t$)/2. So the number of iterations for an unsuccessful search is between height($t$)/2 and height($t$). That is, averageTime$_U(n)$ is also logarithmic in $n$.

For a successful search, the worst case occurs when the element sought is a leaf, and this requires only one less iteration than an unsuccessful search. That is, worstTime$_S(n)$ is logarithmic in $n$. It is somewhat more difficult to show that average Time$_S(n)$ is logarithmic in $n$. But the strategy and result are the same as in Concept Exercise 5.7, which showed that for the recursive version of the binarySearch method, averageTime$_S(n)$ is logarithmic in $n$.

Section 14.3 introduces a class that allows us to break the log $n$ barrier for insertions, removals, and searches.

## 14.3 I **THE** HashMap **IMPLEMENTATION OF THE** Map **INTERFACE**

The HashMap class implements the Map interface, so you saw most of the method headings when we studied the TreeMap class in Chapter 12. The main changes have to do with the timing estimates in some of the method specifications. Basically, for the put, remove, and containsKey methods, the average number of loop iterations is constant! There are also size( ), isEmpty( ), clear( ), toString( ), entrySet( ), keySet, and values( ) methods, whose specifications are the same as for their TreeMap counterparts.

The class heading, with K for key and V for value, is

```
public class HashMap<K,V>
        extends AbstractMap<K,V>
        implements Map<K,V>, Cloneable, Serializable
```

Here is an example of the creation of a simple HashMap object. The entire map, both keys and values, is printed. Then the keys alone are printed by iterating through the map viewed as a Set object with keys as elements. Finally, the values alone are printed by iterating through the map as if it were a Collection of values.

```
import java.util.*;

public static void main (String[ ] args)
{
        HashMap<String, Integer> ageMap = new HashMap<String, Integer>( );

        ageMap.put ("dog", 15);
        ageMap.put ("cat", 20);
        ageMap.put ("human", 75);
        ageMap.put ("turtle", 100);
        System.out.println (ageMap);

        for (String s : ageMap.keySet( ))
                System.out.println (s);

        for (Integer i : ageMap.values( ))
                System.out.println (i);
} // method main
```

The output will be as follows:

```
{dog=15, cat=20, turtle=100, human=75}
dog
cat
turtle
human
15
20
100
75
```

Notice that the output is not in order of increasing keys, nor in order of increasing values. (When we get to the details of the HashMap class, we'll see how the order of elements is determined.) This unsortedness is one of the few drawbacks to the HashMap class. The HashMap class is outstanding for insertions, removals, and searches, on average, but if you also need a sorted collection, you should probably use a TreeMap instead.

In trying to decide on fields for the HashMap class, you might at first be tempted to bring back a contiguous or linked design from a previous chapter. But if the elements are unordered, we will need sequential searches, and these take linear time. Even if the elements are ordered and we utilize that ordering, the best we can get is logarithmic time for searching.

The rest of this chapter is devoted to showing how, through the miracle of hashing, we can achieve searches—and insertions and removals—in constant time, on average. After we have defined what hashing is and how it works, we will spend a little time on the Java Collections Framework's implementation of the HashMap class. Then we will consider an application—hashing identifiers into a symbol table—before we consider alternative implementations.

## 14.3.1 Hashing

We have already ruled out a straightforward contiguous design, but just to ease into hashing, let's look at a contiguous design with the following two fields:

```
transient Entry table[ ];      // an array of entries;
transient int size:            // number of mappings in the HashMap object
```

Recall, from Chapter 6, that the **transient** modifier indicates that the field will not be saved during serialization. Appendix 3 includes a discussion of serialization.

We first present a hypersimple example and then move on to something more realistic. Suppose that the array is constructed to hold 1024 mappings, that is, 1024 key and value pairs. The key is an Integer object that contains a three-digit **int** for a person's ID. The value will be a String holding a person's name, but the values are irrelevant to this discussion, so they will be ignored. We start by calling a constructor that initializes the table length to 1024:

```
HashMap<String, Integer> persons = new HashMap<String, Integer>(1024);
```

At this point, we have the state shown in Figure 14.1.

**Figure 14.1 I** The design representation of an empty HashMap object (simplified design).

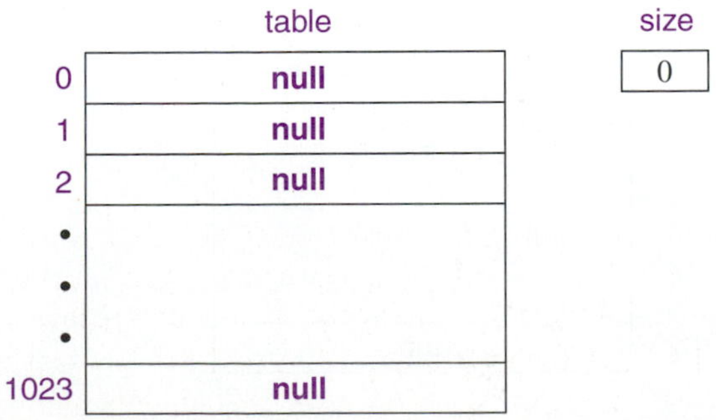

At what index should we store the element with key 251? An obvious choice is index 251. The advantages are several:

1. The element can be directly inserted into the array without accessing any other elements.
2. Subsequent searches for the element require accessing only location 251.
3. The element can be removed directly, without first accessing other elements.

We now add three elements to this HashMap object:

```
persons.put (251, "Smolenski");
persons.put (118, "Schwartz");
persons.put (335, "Beh-Forrest");
```

Figure 14.2 shows the contents of the HashMap object. We show the **int** values, rather than the Integer references, for the keys of inserted elements, and the names are omitted.

So far, this is no big deal. Now, for a slightly different application, suppose that table.length is still 1024, but each element has a social security number as the key. We need to transform the key into an index in the array, and we want this transfor-

**Figure 14.2 |** The HashMap object of Figure 14.1 after three elements have been inserted. For each non-null element, all that is shown is the **int** corresponding to the Integer key. The value parts are omitted.

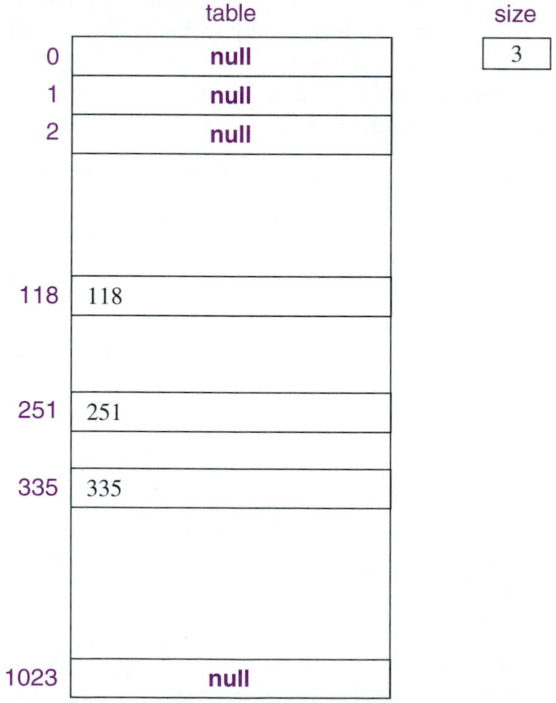

mation to be accomplished quickly, that is, with few loop iterations. To allow fast access, we can perform a logical "and" of the social security number and table.length − 1. For example, the element with a key value of 214-30-3261—the hyphens are for readability only—has a binary representation of

00001100110001100000001000011101

The binary representation of 1023 is

00000000000000000000001111111111

The result of applying the **&** operator to a pair of bits is 1 if both bits are 1, and otherwise 0. We get

$$
\begin{array}{r}
00001100110001100000001000011101 \\
\& \ \underline{00000000000000000000001111111111} \\
00000000000000000000001000011101
\end{array}
$$

The decimal value of the result is 541, and so the element whose key is 214-30-3261 is stored at index 541. Similarly, the element with a key value of 033-51-8000 would be stored at location 432.

Figure 14.3 shows the resulting HashMap object after the following two insertions:

```
persons.put (214303261, "Albert");
persons.put (033518000, "Schranz");
```

You might already have noticed a potential pitfall with this scheme: two distinct keys might produce the same index. For example, 214-30-3261 and 323-56-8157 both produce the index 541. Such a phenomenon is called a **collision,** and the colliding keys are called **synonyms.** We will deal with collisions shortly. For now we simply acknowledge that the possibility of collisions always exists when the size of the key space, that is, the number of legal key values, is larger than the size of the index space, the number of locations available.

**Hashing** is the process of transforming a key into an array index. One component of this transformation is the key class's hashCode( ) method. The purpose of this method is to perform some easily computable operation on the key object. The key class, which may be Integer, String, FullTimeEmployee, or whatever, usually defines its own hashCode( ) method. Alternatively, the key class can inherit a hashCode( ) method from one of its ancestors; ultimately, the Object class defines a hashCode( ) method.[1] Here is the definition of the String class's hashCode( ) method:

```
/**
 * Returns a hash code for this String object.
 *
```

---

[1] But the hashCode( ) method in the Object class will most likely return the reference itself, that is, the machine address, as an **int.** Then two different references to identical copies of an object would return different **int** values!

**Figure 14.3 I** A HashMap object with two elements. The key is a social security number. The value is a name, but that is irrelevant, so it is not shown.

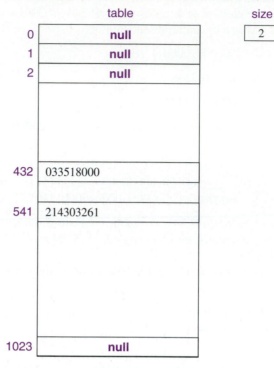

```
     * @return a hash code value for this String object.
     */
    public int hashCode( )
    {
        int h = 0;
        int off = offset;        // index of first character in array value
        char val[ ] = value; // value is the array of char that holds the String
        int len = count;         // count holds the number of characters in the String

        for (int i = 0; i < len; i++)
            h = 31*h + val[off++];

        return h;
    } // method hashCode
```

The multiplication of partial sums by 31 increases the likelihood that the **int** value returned will be greater than table.length, so the resulting indexes can span the entire table. For example, suppose we have

    System.out.println ("graduate".hashCode( ));

The output will be

    90004811

In the HashMap class, the hashCode( ) method is called from a static hash method whose only parameter is a key, x. The hash function calls x.hashCode( ), and then further scrambles the **int** returned by the hashCode( ) method. In fact, the basic idea of hashing is to "make hash" out of the key. The additional scrambling is accomplished with a few bitwise operations, such as a left shift. For example,

> hash ("graduate")

will return

> −186650269

The **int** value returned from this hash method is then logically "anded" with table.length − 1 to obtain an index in the range from 0 to table.length − 1. For example, if table.length = 1024, the output from

> System.out.println (hash ("graduate") & 1023);

will be

> 355

And that is the index "graduate" hashes to. As indicated in the previous three paragraphs, the overall strategy is

> hash (key) & (table.length − 1)
> key ⎯⎯⎯⎯⎯⎯⎯⎯⎯⎯⎯⎯⎯⟶ index

One of the requirements of the HashMap class is that table.length must be a power of 2. (This requirement is specific to the Java Collections Framework, and does not apply generally.) For example, if table.length = 1024 = $2^{10}$, then the index returned by

> hash (key) & (table.length − 1)

consists of the rightmost 10 bits of hash (key). Because a poor-quality hashCode( ) method may not adequately distinguish the rightmost bits in the keys, the additional scrambling from the bitwise operators in the hash method is usually enough to prevent a large number of collisions from occurring.

You may have noticed that, because the table size is a power of 2, the result of

> hash (key) & (table.length − 1)

is the same as the result of

> hash (key) **mod** table.length

The advantage of the former expression is that its calculation is quite a bit faster than for the latter expression. Modular arithmetic is computationally expensive but is commonly utilized in hashing (outside of the Java Collections Framework) because its effectiveness does not require that the table size be a power of 2.

How would you go about developing your own hashCode( ) method? To see how this might be done, let's develop a simple hashCode( ) method for the Full TimeEmployee class. The method should involve the two fields—name and gross

Pay—because these distinguish one FullTimeEmployee object from another. We have already seen the String class's hashCode( ) method. All of the wrapper classes, including Double, have their own hashCode( ) method, so we are led to the following method:

```
public int hashCode( )
{
        return name.hashCode( ) + new Double (grossPay).hashCode( );
} // method hashCode in class FullTimeEmployee
```

For example, if a FullTimeEmployee object has the name "Dominguez" and a gross pay of 4000.00, the value returned by the hashCode( ) method will be $-319687574$. When this hashCode( ) method is followed by the additional bit manipulation of the HashMap class's hash method, the result will probably appear to be random.

The final ingredient in hashing is the collision handler, which determines what happens when two keys hash to the same index. As you might expect, if a large number of keys hash to the same index, the performance of a hashing algorithm can be seriously degraded. Collision handling will be investigated in Section 14.3.3. But first, Section 14.3.2 reveals the major assumption of hashing: basically, that there will not be a lot of keys hashing to the same index.

### 14.3.2  The Uniform Hashing Assumption

For each value of key in an application, a table index is calculated as

```
int hash = hash (key),
    index = hash & (table.length − 1);        // table.length will be a power of 2
```

Hashing is most efficient when the values of index are spread throughout the table. This notion is referred to as the *Uniform Hashing Assumption.* Probabilistically speaking, the Uniform Hashing Assumption states that the set of all possible keys is uniformly distributed over the set of all table indexes. That is, each key is equally likely to hash to any one of the table indexes.

No class's hashCode method will satisfy the Uniform Hashing Assumption for all applications, although the supplemental scrambling in the hash function makes it extremely likely (but not guaranteed) that the assumption will hold.

Even if the Uniform Hashing Assumption holds, we must still deal with the possibility of collisions. That is, two distinct keys may hash to the same index. In the HashMap class, collisions are handled by a simple but quite effective technique called "chaining". Section 14.3.3 investigates chaining, and an alternative approach to collisions is introduced in Section 14.5.

### 14.3.3  Chaining

To resolve collisions, we store at each table location the singly linked list of all elements whose keys have hashed to that index in table. This design is called *chained hashing* because the elements in each list form a chain. We still have the table and size fields from Section 14.3.1:

```
/**
 * An array; at each index, store the singly linked list of entries whose keys hash
 * to that index.
 *
 */
transient Entry table[ ];

/**
 * The number of mappings in this HashMap object.
 */
transient int size;
```

Each element is stored in an Entry object, and the embedded Entry class has the following fields:

```
final K key;

V value;

final int hash;        // to avoid re-calculation

Entry<K,V> next;   // reference to next Entry in linked list
```

The **final** modifier mandates that the key and hash fields can be assigned to only once. A singly linked list, instead of the LinkedList class, is used to save space: There is no header, and no previous field. The Entry class also has a four-parameter constructor to initialize each of the fields.

To see how chained hashing works, consider the above problem of storing persons with social security numbers as keys. Since each key is an Integer object, the hashCode( ) method simply returns the corresponding **int**, but the rest of the hash function sufficiently garbles the key that the **int** returned seems random. Initially, each location contains an empty list, and insertions are made at the *front* of the linked list. Figure 14.4 shows what we would have after inserting elements with the following Integer keys (each is shown as an **int**, followed by the index the key hashed to) into a table of length 1024:

| key | index |
|-----|-------|
| 587771904 | 754 |
| 81903292 | 919 |
| 33520048 | 212 |
| 735668100 | 919 |
| 214303261 | 212 |
| 214303495 | 212 |
| 301336785 | 80 |
| 298719753 | 529 |

The keys in Figure 14.4 were "rigged" so that there would be some collisions. If the keys were chosen randomly, it is unlikely there would have been any collisions, so there would have been eight linked lists, each with a single entry. Of course, if the number of entries is large enough, there will be collisions and multientry lists. And

**Figure 14.4 |** A HashMap object into which eight elements have been inserted. For each Entry object, only the key and next fields are shown. At all indexes not shown there is a **null** Entry.

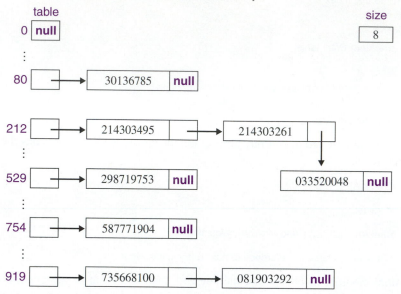

that raises an interesting question: Should the table be subject to resizing? Suppose the initial table length is 1024. If $n$ represents the number of entries and $n$ can continue to increase, the average size of each linked list will be $n/1024$, which is linear in $n$. But then, for searching, inserting, and removing, worstTime($n$) will be linear in $n$—a far cry from the constant time that was promised earlier!

Given that resizing must be done under certain circumstances, what are those circumstances? We will resize whenever the size of the map reaches a preset threshold. In the HashMap class, the default threshold is 75 percent of table.length. So when size $\geq$ (**int**)(table.length * 0.75), the table will be resized. That means that the average size of each linked list will be less than one, and that is how constant average time can be achieved for inserting, deleting, and searching. There are two additional fields relating to this discussion[2]:

```
/**
 * the maximum ratio of size / table.length before re-sizing will occur
 *
 */
final float loadFactor;
```

---

[2] The first definition is nonstandard. In hashing terminology, ***load factor*** is simply the ratio of the number of elements in the collection to its capacity. In the Framework's HashMap and HashSet classes, load factor is the upper bound of that ratio.

```
/**
 * (int)(table.length * loadFactor); when size++ ≥ threshold, re-size table
 *
 */
int threshold;
```

There are three constant identifiers related to table and loadFactor:

```
/**
 * The default initial capacity – MUST be a power of two.
 */
static final int DEFAULT_INITIAL_CAPACITY = 16;

/**
 * The maximum capacity, 2 to the 31st power, used if a higher value
 * is implicitly specified by either of the constructors with arguments.
 *
 */
static final int MAXIMUM_CAPACITY = 1 << 30;

/**
 * The load factor used when none specified in constructor.
 */
static final float DEFAULT_LOAD_FACTOR = 0.75f;
```

The value for loadFactor presents an interesting time-space tradeoff. With a low value (say, less than 1.0), searches and removals are fast, and insertions are fast unless the insertion triggers a resizing. That insertion will require linear-in-$n$ time and space. On the other hand, with a high value for loadFactor, searches, removals, and insertions will be slower than with a low loadFactor, but there will be fewer resizings. Similarly, if table.length is large, there will be fewer resizings, but more space consumed. Ultimately, the application will dictate the need for speed (how small a load factor) and the memory available (how large a table).

Now that we have decided on the fields in the HashMap and Entry classes, we can don our developer's hat to tackle the implementation of a couple of HashMap methods: a constructor and containsKey.

## 14.3.4 Implementation of the HashMap Class

All of the constructors deal with the load factor and the size of table. The fundamental constructor—the one called by the others—is the following:

```
/**
 * Constructs an empty <tt>HashMap</tt> with the specified initial
 * capacity and load factor.
 *
 * @param initialCapacity The initial capacity.
 * @param loadFactor The load factor.
 * @throws IllegalArgumentException if the initial capacity is negative
```

```
 *      or the load factor is nonpositive.
 */
public HashMap(int initialCapacity, float loadFactor)
{
    if (initialCapacity < 0)
        throw new IllegalArgumentException("Illegal initial capacity: " +
            initialCapacity);
    if (initialCapacity > MAXIMUM_CAPACITY)
        initialCapacity = MAXIMUM_CAPACITY;
    if (loadFactor <= 0 || Float.isNaN(loadFactor)) // Not a Number
        throw new IllegalArgumentException("Illegal load factor: " +
            loadFactor);
    // Find a power of 2 ≥ initialCapacity
    int capacity = 1;
    while (capacity < initialCapacity)
        capacity <<= 1; // same as capacity = capacity << 1;

    this.loadFactor = loadFactor;
    threshold = (int)(capacity * loadFactor);
    table = new Entry[capacity];
    init( ); // allows readObject to handle subclasses of HashMap (see Appendix 3)
}
```

This constructor is utilized, for example, in the definition of the default constructor:

```
/**
 * Constructs an empty <tt>HashMap</tt> with the default initial capacity
 * (16) and the default load factor (0.75).
 */
public HashMap( )
{
    this.loadFactor = DEFAULT_LOAD_FACTOR;
    threshold = (int)(DEFAULT_INITIAL_CAPACITY *
                    DEFAULT_LOAD_FACTOR);
    table = new Entry[DEFAULT_INITIAL_CAPACITY];
    init( );
}
```

We finish up this section by looking at the definition of the containsKey method. The other signature methods for a Map object—put, get, and remove—share the same basic strategy as containsKey: hash the key to an index in table, and then search the linked list at table [index] for a matching key. But first, there is a hang-up: the **null** key.

For the sake of completeness, it is legal to insert one **null** key into a HashMap object; internally, the **null** key is represented by

```
static final Object NULL_KEY = new Object( );
```

With this representation of a **null** key, all keys can invoke their hashCode method without throwing NullPointerException.

To compare keys, there is a **static** method within the HashMap class:

```
static boolean eq (Object x, Object y)
{
        return x == y || x.equals(y);
}
```

Offhand, a call to eq (key1, key2) would seem to be less efficient than key1. equals(key2). But in most applications, the keys in a HashMap object are String objects, and often, those String objects are "interned," that is, there is only one version of each String object. When that occurs, the test x == y returns **true** whenever x and y are referencing the same object. Then the call x.equals (y) is avoided. So the eq method may actually provide a speedup.

Here is the definition of the containsKey method:

```
/**
  * Determines if this HashMap object contains a mapping for the
  * specified key.
  * The worstTime(n) is O(n). If the Uniform Hashing Assumption holds,
  * averageTime(n) is constant.
  *
  * @param key The key whose presence in this HashMap object is to be tested.
  *
  * @return true – if this map contains a mapping for the specified key.
  *
  */
public boolean containsKey(Object key)
{
        Object k = maskNull (key); // use NULL_KEY if key is null
        int hash = hash (k);
        int i = indexFor (hash, table.length); // = hash & (table.length − 1)
        Entry e = table [i];
        while (e != null)
        {
                if (e.hash == hash && eq (k, e.key))
                        return true;
                e = e.next;
        } // while
        return false;
} // method containsKey
```

Notice that both the hash and key fields are compared. Concept Exercise 14.4 indicates why both fields are checked.

Before we leave this section on the implementation of the HashMap class, there is an important detail about insertions that deserves mention. When a resizing takes place; that is, when

```
size++ ≥ threshold
```

the table is doubled in size. But the old entries cannot simply be copied to the new table: They must be rehashed. Why? Because the index where an entry is stored is calculated as

```
hash & (table.length − 1)
```

When table.length changes, the index of the entry changes, so a rehashing is required. For example,

```
hash ("myList") & 1023     // 1023 = 2 to the 10th − 1
```

returns 231, but

```
hash ("myList") & 2047     // 2047 = 2 to the 11th − 1
```

returns 1255.

After the keys have been rehashed, subsequent calls to the containsKey method, for example, will search the linked list at the appropriate index.

In Section 14.3.5, we show that the containsKey method takes only constant time, on average.

## 14.3.5 Analysis of the containsKey Method

For the sake of brevity, we let $n = $ size and $m = $ table.length. We assume that the Uniform Hashing Assumption holds, that is, we expect the $n$ elements to be fairly evenly distributed over the $m$ lists. Then a successful search will examine a list that has about $n/m$ elements,[3] on average. A successful, sequential search of such a list requires, approximately, $n/2m$ loop iterations, so the average time depends on both $n$ and $m$. We get

$$\text{averageTime}_S\ (n, m) \approx n/2m \text{ iterations.}$$

For an unsuccessful search with chained hashing, an entire list must be searched. Since each list contains, on average, $n/m$ elements,

$$\text{averageTime}_U\ (n, m) \approx n/m \text{ iterations.}$$

The value of loadFactor is set in the HashMap object's constructor, and is fixed for the lifetime of the HashMap object. But the table will be resized (and table.length doubled) whenever size / table.length ≥ loadFactor. Therefore, we must always have

$$n/m < \text{loadFactor}$$

Since loadFactor is fixed, $n/m$ is less than a fixed value, and we conclude that averageTime$_S(n, m)$ and averageTime$_U(n, m)$ are both constant.

---

[3] In common hashing terminology, the load factor is simply the ratio of $n$ to $m$. In the Java Collections Framework, load factor is the maximum ratio of $n$ to $m$ before resizing takes place.

Figure 14.5 summarizes the average search time estimates for chained hashing. In each approximation, the time depends, not on $n$ alone, but on the ratio $n/m$. In the following two figures, we assume that the Uniform Hashing Assumption holds.

Figure 14.6 estimates the number of loop iterations for successful and unsuccessful searches with various values of the ratio $n/m$.

So far we have blithely ignored any discussion of worstTime. This is the Achilles' heel of hashing, just as worstTime was the vulnerable aspect of Quick Sort. The Uniform Hashing Assumption is more often a hope than a fact. If the hashCode method is inappropriate for the keys in the application, the additional scrambling in the hash function may not be enough to prevent an inordinate number of keys from hashing to just a few locations, leading to linear-in-$n$ searches. Even if the Uniform Hashing Assumption holds, we could have a worst-case scenario: the given key hashes to index, and the number of keys at table [index] is linear in $n$. So worstTime $(n, m)$, for both successful and unsuccessful searches, is linear in $n$.

The bottom line is this: unless you are confident that the Uniform Hashing Assumption is reasonable for the key space in the application or you are not worried about linear-in-$n$ worst time, use a TreeMap object, with its guarantee of logarithmic worst time.

The final topic in our introduction to the HashMap class is the HashIterator class.

## 14.3.6  The HashIterator **Class**

This section will clear up a mystery from when we first introduced the HashMap class: in what order are iterations performed? The answer is fairly straightforward. Starting at index table.length$-1$ and working down to index 0, the linked list at each index is traversed in sequential order. Starting at the back makes the continuation condition

**Figure 14.5 |** A summary of the average-time estimates for successful and unsuccessful searches with chained hashing. We make the Uniform Hashing Assumption. In the figure, $n = $ size; $m = $ table.length.

Chaining:

$$\text{averageTime}_S\ (n, m) \approx \frac{n}{2m} \text{ iterations}$$

$$\text{averageTime}_U\ (n, m) \approx \frac{n}{m} \text{ iterations}$$

**Figure 14.6 |** Search-time (approximately, the number of loop iterations) estimates for various ratios of $n$ to $m$, with chained hashing. The Uniform Hashing Assumption is made. In the figure, $n = $ size; $m = $ table.length.

| $\frac{n}{m}$ | 0.25 | 0.5 | 0.75 | 0.9 | 0.99 |
|---|---|---|---|---|---|
| Successful | 0.13 | 0.25 | 0.38 | 0.45 | 0.5 |
| Unsuccessful | 0.25 | 0.5 | 0.75 | 0.9 | 0.99 |

slightly more efficient: index > 0 (a constant) instead of index < table.length (a variable). In each singly linked list, the sequential order is *last in, first out*. For example, here is a repeat of the HashMap object from Figure 14.4:

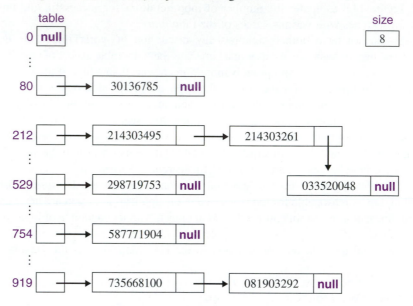

Here is the order in which the keys would appear in an iteration:

735668100
081903292
587771904
298719753
214303495
214303261
033520048
301336785

Just as with the TreeMap class, the iteration can be by keys, by values, or by entries. For example:

```
for (K key : myMap.keySet( ))
for (V value : myMap.values( ))
for (Map.Entry<K, V> entry : myMap.entrySet( ))
```

Or, if the iteration might entail removals:

```
Iterator<K> itr1 = myMap.keySet( ).iterator( );
Iterator<V> itr2 = myMap.values( ).iterator( );
Iterator<Map.Entry<K, V>> itr3 = myMap.entrySet( ).iterator( );
```

An iteration through a HashMap object must peruse the singly linked list at each index in the table. Even if most of those linked lists are empty, each one must be checked. The total number of loop iterations is size + table.length, and this indicates a drawback to having a very large table. If the Uniform Hashing Assumption holds, then the time estimates for the next( ) method are the same as for the containsKey method in the HashMap class. In the terminology of Section 14.3.5, for example,

$$\text{averageTime}(n, m) = (n + m)/n = 1 + m/n$$

The value of $n$ ranges from 0 to $m \cdot \text{loadFactor}$, with an average value of $m \cdot \text{load Factor}/2$. This implies that

$$\text{averageTime}(n, m) = 1 + m/n \approx 1 + 2/\text{loadFactor}$$

Since loadFactor is fixed, we conclude that averageTime($n$, $m$) is constant for the next( ) method.

In the worst case, a call to the next( ) method will start at the end of the linked list at table [table.length $-$ 1], with empty linked lists at indexes table.length $-$ 2, table.length $-$ 3, . . . , 2, 1, and a non-empty linked list at table [0]. We conclude that worstTime($n$, $m$) is linear in $m$.

If you would like to have control about the order in which elements in a hash map are iterated over, Programming Exercise 14.6 will show you the way.

In Section 14.3.7, we look at the premiere application of the HashMap class: the hashing of identifiers into a symbol table by a compiler.

### 14.3.7 Creating a Symbol Table by Hashing

Most compilers use hashing to create a *symbol table:* an array that contains information about word-symbols, mainly identifiers, in a program. This is a good environment for hashing: almost all of the activity consists of retrieving a symbol-table entry, given a key. And a reasonable upper bound on the number of identifiers is the size of the program, so we can initialize the size of the symbol table to preclude resizing.

To avoid getting bogged down in the myriad details of symbol-table creation and maintenance, we will solve the following restricted problem: given a program in a source file, print to a file all the unique identifiers in the program. The main issue is how to separate identifiers from reserved words. The list of legal reserved words[4] is fixed, so we will read in a file that contains the reserved words before we read in the source file.

For example, suppose the file "reserved.dat" contains the list, one per line, of reserved words in Java. And the file "HasherTemp.java" contains the following program:

```java
import java.io.*;

public class HasherTemp
{
        public static void main(String[ ] args)
        {
```

---

[4] Technically, **true**, **false**, and **null** are not reserved words. They are literals, that is, constant values for a type, just as "exhale" and 574 are literals. But we include them in with the reserved words because they cannot be used as identifiers.

```
                       int i = 75;

                       Integer top,
                                bottom;

                       /* all */ int z1 = 1;
                       /* int z2 = 2;
                       int z3 = 3;
                       int z4 = 4; */ int z5 = 5; /* int z6 = 6;*/
                       String ans = "All string literals, such as this, are ignored."; char x = 'x';
                       for (int j = 0; j < i; j++)
                                System.out.println (i + " " + j);
              } // method main

       } // class HasherTemp
```

**System Test 1 (the input is boldfaced):**

Please enter the path for the file that holds the reserved words: **reserved.dat**

Please enter the path for the file that holds the source code: **HasherTemp.java**

Please enter the path for the file that will hold the identifiers: **hasher.out**

At the end of the execution of the program, the file hasher.out will have:

```
Here are the identifiers:

ans
top
Integer
println
main
bottom
x
i
z1
String
System
z5
out
j
HasherTemp
args
```

We will filter out comments, string literals, and **import** directives. Then each line (what remains of it) will be tokenized. The delimiters will include punctuation, parentheses, and so on. For the sake of simplicity, both reserved words and identifiers will be saved in a symbol table, implemented as a HashMap object. Each key will be a word, either a reserved word or an identifier, and each value will be an indication of the word's type, either "reserved word" or "identifier".

We will create a Hasher class to solve this problem. The responsibilities of the Hasher class are as follows:

1. Read, from the keyboard, the paths for the files that hold the reserved words and source code, and the file that will hold the identifiers.

2. Read in the reserved words and hash each one (with "reserved word" as the value part) to the symbol table.

3. Read in the lines from the source file. For each identifier in each line, post the identifier (with "identifier" as the value part) to the symbol table.

4. For each mapping in the symbol table, print the key to the output file if the value is "identifier".

**Design of the** Hasher **Class** The method specifications are easily gleaned from the four responsibilities above:

```
/**
 * Initializes this Hasher object.
 */
public Hasher( )

/**
 * Reads from the keyboard, the paths for the files that hold the reserved words
 * and source code, and the file that will hold the identifiers; return a reference
 * to the output file writer.
 *
 */
public PrintWriter openFiles( )

/**
 * Reads in the reserved words and posts them to the symbol table.
 *
 */
public void readReservedWords( )

/**
 * Reads the source file and posts identifiers to the symbol table.
 * The averageTime(n, m) is O(n), and worstTime(n, m) is O(n * n), where
 * n is the number of identifiers and m is the size of the symbol table.
 */
public void readSourceCode( )

/**
 * Outputs to a file all identifiers in the symbol table.
 * The worstTime(n, m) is O(n + m), where n is the number of identifiers
 * and m is the size of the symbol table.
 */
public void printIdentifiers( )
```

Beyond the symbol table, the only other fields are for the input and output files. There are also two constant identifiers:

```
protected final String IDENTIFIER = "identifier";

protected final String RESERVED_WORD = "reserved word";

protected HashMap<String, String> symbolTable;

protected BufferedReader keyboardReader,
                         reservedFileReader,
                         sourceFileReader;

protected PrintWriter identifierFileWriter;
```

Here is the class diagram for the Hasher class:

| Hasher |
| --- |
| # symbolTable: HashMap<String, String><br># keyboardReader: BufferedReader<br># reservedFileReader: BufferedReader<br># sourceFileReader: Buffered Reader<br># identifierFileWriter: PrintWriter |
| + Hasher( )<br>+ openFiles( ): PrintWriter<br>+ readReservedWords( )<br>+ readSourceFile( )<br>+ printIdentifiers( ) |

**Implementation of the** Hasher **Class** The default constructor has an empty body because all of the fields are initialized in the openFiles( ) method. The definition of the openFiles( ) method is straightforward, except for the initialization of the symbol table. To avoid the need for resizing, the symbol table is created with an initial capacity of the size of the source file. This number is returned by the length( ) method of a File object, so we first create (a reference to) such an object from the input path.

```
/**
 * Reads from the keyboard, the paths for the files that hold the reserved words
 * and source code, and the file that will hold the identifiers; return a reference
 * to the output file writer.
 *
 */
public PrintWriter openFiles( )
{
        final String SOURCE_FILE_PROMPT =
                "\nPlease enter the path for the file that holds the source code: ";

        final String RESERVED_FILE_PROMPT =
                "\nPlease enter the path for the file that holds the reserved words: ";
```

```java
            final String IDENTIFIER_FILE_PROMPT =
                    "\nPlease enter the path for the output file that will hold the identifiers: ";

            boolean pathsOK = false;

            while (!pathsOK)
            {
                    try
                    {
                            BufferedReader keyboardReader =
                                    new BufferedReader (new InputStreamReader (System.in));

                            System.out.print (RESERVED_FILE_PROMPT);
                            String reservedFilePath = keyboardReader.readLine( );
                            reservedFileReader =
                                    new BufferedReader (new FileReader (reservedFilePath));

                            System.out.print (SOURCE_FILE_PROMPT);
                            String sourceFilePath = keyboardReader.readLine( );
                            sourceFileReader =
                                    new BufferedReader (new FileReader (sourceFilePath));
                            File sourceFile = new File (sourceFilePath);
                            symbolTable = new HashMap<String, String>
                                    ((int)sourceFile.length( ));

                            System.out.print (IDENTIFIER_FILE_PROMPT);
                            String identifierFilePath = keyboardReader.readLine( );
                            identifierFileWriter = new PrintWriter (new FileWriter
                                    (identifierFilePath));
                            pathsOK = true;
                    } // try
                    catch (IOException e)
                    {
                            System.out.println (e);
                    } // catch
            } // while !pathsOK
            return identifierFileWriter;
    } // method openFiles
```

The readReservedWords method loops through the file of reserved words and posts each one as a key in the symbol table; the value is the String "reserved word".

```java
    /**
     * Reads in the reserved words and posts them to the symbol table.
     *
     */
    public void readReservedWords( )
    {
            String reservedWord;
```

```
    try
    {
            while (true)
            {
                    reservedWord = reservedFileReader.readLine( );
                    if (reservedWord == null)
                            break;
                    symbolTable.put (reservedWord, RESERVED_WORD);
            } // while not end of file
    } // try
    catch (IOException e)
    {
            System.out.println (e);
    } // catch
} // method readReservedWords
```

It is easy enough to determine if a token is the first occurrence of an identifier:
it must start with a letter, and not already be in symbolTable (recall that the reserved
words were posted to symbolTable earlier). The hard part of the method is filtering
out comments, such as in the following:

```
/* all */ int z1 = 1;
/* int z2 = 2;
   int z3 = 3;
   int z4 = 4; */ int z5 = 5; /* int z6 = 6;*/
```

Here is the method definition:

```
/**
 * Reads the source file and posts identifiers to the symbol table.
 * The averageTime(n, m) is O(n), and worstTime(n, m) is O(n * n), where
 * n is the number of identifiers and m is the size of the symbol table.
 */
public void readSourceCode( )
{
        final String DELIMITERS = " \\n\r\t;:.,!?( )[ ]@/*+−/=><{}";

        String line,
               word;

        StringTokenizer tokens;

        int start,
            finish;

        boolean skip = false ;

        try
        {
                while (true)
```

```
{
        line = sourceFileReader.readLine( );
        if (line == null)
                break;
        line = line.trim( );

        // Ignore lines beginning with "import".
        if (line.indexOf("import ") == 0)
                continue; // start another iteration of this loop

        // Ignore string literals.
        while ((start = line.indexOf ("\"")) >= 0)
        {
                finish = line.indexOf("\"", 1 + start);
                while (line.charAt (finish − 1) == '\\')
                        finish = line.indexOf ("\"", finish + 1);
                line = line.substring(0, start) + line.substring(finish + 1);
        } // while line still has a string literal

        // Ignore // comments
        if ((start = line.indexOf("//")) >= 0)
                line = line.substring(0, start);

        // Ignore any line between /* and */.
        if ((line.indexOf ("*/") == −1) && skip)
                continue;

        // Remove substring up to */ if matching /* on earlier line.
        if ((start = line.indexOf("*/")) >= 0 && skip)
        {
                skip = false;
                line = line.substring (start + 2);
        } // first part of line a comment

        // Handle lines that have /*.
        while ((start = line.indexOf ("/*")) >= 0)
                if ((finish = line.indexOf("*/", start + 2)) >= 0)
                        line = line.substring(0, start) + line.substring(finish + 2);
                else
                {
                        line = line.substring(0, start);
                        skip = true;
                } // matching */ not on this line

        // Tokenize line to find identifiers.
        tokens = new StringTokenizer(line, DELIMITERS);
        while (tokens.hasMoreTokens( ))
        {
                word = tokens.nextToken( );
```

```
                    if (Character.isLetter(word.charAt(0)) &&
                            symbolTable.get(word) == null)
                        symbolTable.put(word, IDENTIFIER);
                } // while not at end of line
            } // while not end of file
        } // try
        catch (IOException e)
    {
            System.out.println (e);
    } // catch
} // method readSourceCode
```

Let *n* be the number of identifiers in the source file, and let *m* be the size of the symbol table. Because *m* is fixed in the openFiles method, only *n* is relevant for estimating. From the analysis of containsKey method in Section 14.3.5, we extrapolate that each call to the HashMap methods get and put will take constant time on average, and linear-in-*n* time in the worst case. We conclude that for processing all *n* identifiers in the readSourceCode method, averageTime(*n*) is linear in *n* and worstTime(*n*) is quadratic in *n*.

Finally, the printIdentifiers method iterates through the entries in symbolTable and prints to the output file each key whose value is "identifier":

```
/**
 * Prints all identifiers in the symbol table.
 * The worstTime(n, m) is O(n + m), where n is the number of identifiers and
 * m is the length of the symbol table.
 */
public void printIdentifiers( )
{
        final String HEADING = "Here are the identifiers:\n";

        identifierFileWriter.println (HEADING);
        for (Map.Entry<String, String> entry : symbolTable.entrySet( ))
            if (entry.getValue( ).equals (IDENTIFIER))
                    identifierFileWriter.println (entry.getKey( ));
} // method printIdentifiers
```

An iteration through a HashMap object requires $n + m$ iterations in all cases, so worstTime($n, m$) and averageTime($n, m$) are both $\Theta (n + m)$. We can say, crudely, that $n + m$ is both a lower bound and an upper bound of worstTime($n, m$) and averageTime($n, m$).

The main method, as usual, simply invokes the other class's methods and closes the output file:

```
public static void main (String[ ] args)
{
        PrintWriter writer = null;

        try
```

```
        {
               Hasher hasher = new Hasher( );

               writer = hasher.openFiles( );
               hasher.readReservedWords( );
               hasher.readSourceCode( );
               hasher.printIdentifiers( );
        } // try
        finally
        {
               writer.close( );
        } // finally
    } // method main
```

One interesting feature of the above program is that Hasher.java itself can be the input file! The output file will then contain the identifiers in the Hasher class.

The identifiers in the output file are not in order. To remedy this, instead of printing out each key, we could insert the key into a TreeSet object, and then print out the TreeSet object, which would be in order. This sorting would take linear-logarithmic in $n$ time: on average, that would be longer than the rest of the application!

To finish up the Java Collections Framework treatment of hashing, the next section takes a brief look at the HashSet class.

## 14.4 | **THE** HashSet **CLASS**

With hashing, all of the work involves the key-to-index relationship. It doesn't matter if the value associated with a key has meaning in the application or if each key is associated with the same dummy value. In the former case, we have a HashMap object and in the latter case, we have a HashSet object. The method definitions in the HashSet class are almost identical to those of the TreeSet class from Chapter 12. The major difference is that several of the constructor headings for the HashSet class involve the initial capacity and load factor.

Lab 22 covers the crucial aspect of HashMap objects and HashSet objects: their speed.

**Lab 22: Timing the Hash Classes**

You are now prepared to do Lab 22.          All Labs Are Optional

As indicated above, the Java Collections Framework's implementation of hashing uses chaining to handle collisions. Section 14.5 explores another important collision handler, one that avoids linked lists.

## 14.5 | OPEN-ADDRESS HASHING

To handle collisions with chaining, the basic idea is this: when a key hashes to a given index in table, that key's entry is inserted at the front of the linked list at table [index]. Each entry contains not only hash, key, and value fields, but a next field that points to another entry in the linked list. The total number of Entry references is equal to size + table.length. For some applications, this number may be too large.

Open addressing provides another approach to collision handling. With **open addressing,** each table location contains a single entry; there are no linked lists, and the total number of Entry references is equal to table.length. To insert an entry, if the entry's key hashes to an index whose entry contains a different key, the rest of the table is searched systematically until an empty, that is, "open" location is found.

The simplest open-addressing strategy is to use an offset of 1. That is, to insert an entry whose key hashes to index j, if table [j] is empty, the entry is inserted there. Otherwise, the entry at index j + 1 is investigated, then at index j + 2, and so on until an open slot is found. Figure 14.7 shows the table created when elements with the following Integer keys are inserted:

| | |
|---|---|
| 587771904 | 754 |
| 081903292 | 919 |
| 033520048 | 212 |
| 735668100 | 919 |
| 214303261 | 212 |
| 214303495 | 212 |
| 301336785 | 80 |
| 298719753 | 529 |

In this example, table.length is 1024, but in general, we will not require that the table length be a power of two. In fact, we will see in Section 14.5.2 that we want the table length to be a prime number.

There are a couple of minor details with open addressing:

1.   To ensure that an open location will be found if one is available, the table must wrap around: if the location at index table.length − 1 is not open, the next index tried is 0.

2.   The number of entries cannot exceed the table length, so the load factor cannot exceed 1.0. It will simplify the implementation and efficiency of the containsKey, put, and remove methods if the table always has at least one open (that is, empty) location. So we require that the load factor be strictly less than 1.0. Recall that with chaining, the load factor can exceed 1.0.

Let's see what is involved in the implementation of a HashMap class with open addressing and an offset of 1. We'll have many of the same fields as in the chained-hashing implementation: table, size, loadFactor, and threshold. The embedded Entry class will have hash, key, and value fields, but no next field. We will focus on the containsKey, put, and remove methods: they will have to be redefined because now there are no linked lists.

## 14.5.1  The remove **Method**

We need to consider the remove method before the containsKey and put methods because the details of removing elements have a subtle impact on searches and inser-tions. To see what this is all about, suppose we want to remove the entry with key

**Figure 14.7 I** A table to which 8 elements have been inserted. Open addressing, with an offset of 1, handles collisions.

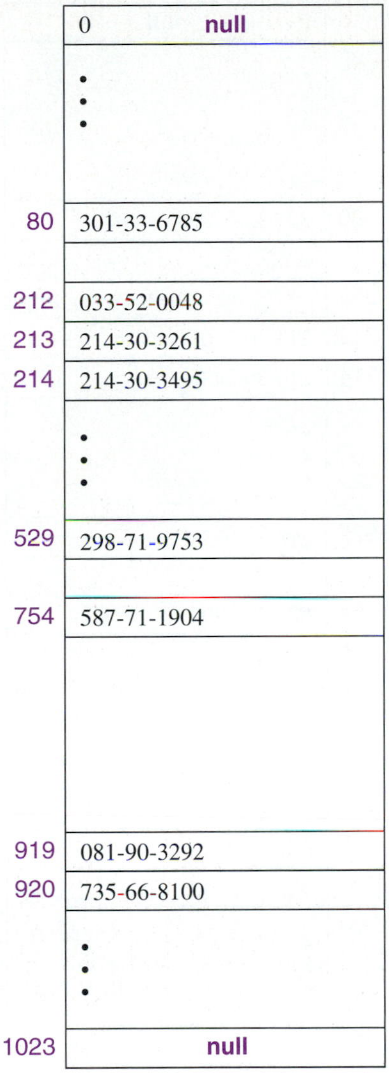

| | |
|---|---|
| 0 | **null** |
| | • |
| | • |
| | • |
| 80 | 301-33-6785 |
| | |
| 212 | 033-52-0048 |
| 213 | 214-30-3261 |
| 214 | 214-30-3495 |
| | • |
| | • |
| | • |
| 529 | 298-71-9753 |
| | |
| 754 | 587-71-1904 |
| | |
| 919 | 081-90-3292 |
| 920 | 735-66-8100 |
| | • |
| | • |
| | • |
| 1023 | **null** |

033-52-0048 from the table in Figure 14.7. If we simply make that entry **null**, we will get the table in Figure 14.8.

Do you see the pitfall with this removal strategy? The path taken by synonyms of 033-52-0048 has been blocked. A search for the entry with key 214-303495 would be unsuccessful, even though there is such an entry in the table.

Instead of nulling out a removed entry, we will add another field to the Entry class:

```
boolean markedForRemoval;
```

**Figure 14.8 |** The effect of removing the entry with key 033-52-0048 from the table in Figure 14.7 by nulling out the entry at index 212.

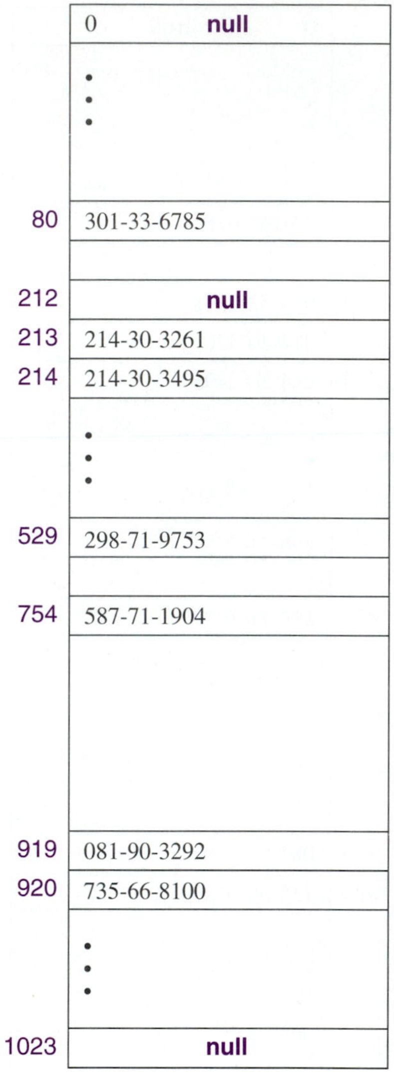

| | |
|---|---|
| 0 | **null** |
| | • • • |
| 80 | 301-33-6785 |
| | |
| 212 | **null** |
| 213 | 214-30-3261 |
| 214 | 214-30-3495 |
| | • • • |
| 529 | 298-71-9753 |
| 754 | 587-71-1904 |
| | |
| 919 | 081-90-3292 |
| 920 | 735-66-8100 |
| | • • • |
| 1023 | **null** |

This field is initialized to **false** when the table is created. The remove method sets this field to **true**. The markedForRemoval field, when **true**, indicates that its entry is no longer part of the hash map, but allows the offset-of-1 collision handler to continue along its path. Figure 14.9 shows a table after 8 insertions, and Figure 14.10 shows the subsequent effect of the message

remove (033520048)

**Figure 14.9 |** A table to which 8 elements have been inserted. Open addressing, with an offset of 1, handles collisions. In each entry, only the key and markedForRemoval fields are shown.

| | | |
|---|---|---|
| 0 | **null** | **false** |
| | •••  | |
| 80 | 301-33-6785 | **false** |
| | | |
| 212 | 033-52-0048 | **false** |
| 213 | 214-30-3261 | **false** |
| 214 | 214-30-3495 | **false** |
| | ••• | |
| 529 | 298-71-9753 | **false** |
| | | |
| 754 | 587-71-1904 | **false** |
| | ••• | |
| 919 | 081-90-3292 | **false** |
| 920 | 735-66-8100 | **false** |
| | ••• | |
| 1023 | **null** | **false** |

A search for the entry with the key 214303495 would now be successful. In the definition of the remove method, a loop is executed until a **null** or matching entry is found. Note that an entry's key is examined only if that entry is not marked for removal.

The containsKey method loops until an empty or matching entry is found. As with the remove method, an entry's key is checked only if that entry is not marked for removal. The definition of the containsKey method is only slightly revised from the chained-hashing version. For example, here we use modular arithmetic instead of the & operator because the table length need not be a power of 2.

**Figure 14.10** I The table from Figure 14.9 after the message remove (033520048) has been sent.

| | | |
|---|---|---|
| 0 | **null** | **false** |
| | • • • | |
| 80 | 301-33-6785 | **false** |
| | | |
| 212 | 033-52-0048 | **true** |
| 213 | 214-30-3261 | **false** |
| 214 | 214-30-3495 | **false** |
| | • • • | |
| 529 | 298-71-9753 | **false** |
| | | |
| 754 | 587-71-1904 | **false** |
| | • • • | |
| 919 | 081-90-3292 | **false** |
| 920 | 735-66-8100 | **false** |
| | • • • | |
| 1023 | **null** | **false** |

```
/**
 * Determines if this HashMap object contains a mapping for the
 * specified key.
 * The worstTime(n) is O(n). If the Uniform Hashing Assumption holds,
 * averageTime(n) is constant.
 *
```

```
 * @param key The key whose presence in this HashMap object is to be tested.
 *
 * @return true – if this map contains a mapping for the specified key.
 *
 */
public boolean containsKey(Object key)
{
        Object k = maskNull (key);              // use NULL_KEY if key is null
        int hash = hash (k);
        int i = indexFor (hash, table.length);  // hash % table.length
        Entry e = table [i];
        while (e != null)
        {
                if (!e.markedForRemoval && e.hash == hash && eq (k, e.key))
                        return true;
                e = table [(++i) % table.length]; // table.length may not be a power of 2
        } // while
        return false;
} // method containsKey
```

With the help of the markedForRemoval field, we solved the problem of removing an element without breaking the offset-of-1 path. The put method hashes a key to an index and stores the key and value at that index if that location is unoccupied: either a **null** key or marked for removal.

## 14.5.2 Primary Clustering

There is still a disturbing feature of the offset-of-1 collision handler: all the keys that hash to a given index will probe the same path: index, index + 1, index + 2, and so on. What's worse, all keys that hash to any index in that path will follow the same path from that index on. For example, Figure 14.11 shows part of the table from Figure 14.9.

In Figure 14.11, the path traced by keys that hash to 212 is 212, 213, 214, 215, . . . . And the path traced by keys that hash to 213 is 213, 214, 215, . . . . A *cluster* is

**Figure 14.11 I** The path traced by keys that hash to 212 overlaps the paths traced by keys that hash to 213 or 214.

| 211 | null | |
|-----|------|---|
| 212 | 214-30-3261 | false |
| 213 | 819-02-9261 | false |
| 214 | 033-30-8262 | false |
| | | |
| 215 | null | |

a sequence of nonempty locations (assume the elements at those locations are not marked for removal). With the offset-of-1 collision handler, clusters are formed by synonyms, including synonyms from different collisions. In Figure 14.11, the locations at indexes 212, 213, and 214 form a cluster. As each entry is added to a cluster, the cluster not only gets bigger, but also grows faster, because any keys that hash to that new index will follow the same path as keys already stored in the cluster. *Primary clustering* is the phenomenon that occurs when the collision handler allows the growth of clusters to accelerate.

Clearly, the offset-of-1 collision handler is susceptible to primary clustering. The problem with primary clustering is that we get ever-longer paths that are sequentially traversed during searches, insertions, and removals. Long sequential traversals are the bane of hashing, so we should try to solve this problem.

What if we choose an offset of, say, 32 instead of 1? We would still have primary clustering: keys that hashed to index would overlap the path traced by keys that hashed to index + 32, index + 64, and so on. In fact, this could create an even bigger problem than primary clustering! For example, suppose the table size is 128 and a key hashes to index 45. Then the only locations that would be allowed in that cluster have the following indexes:

45, 77, 109, 13

Once those locations fill up, there would be no way to insert any entry whose key hashed to any one of those indexes. The reason we have this additional problem is that the offset and table size have a common factor. We avoid this problem by making the table size a prime number, instead of a power of 2. But we still have primary clustering.

### 14.5.3 Double Hashing

We can avoid primary clustering if, instead of using the same offset for all keys, we make the offset dependent on the key. Basically, the offset will be hash / table.length. There is a problem here: hash may be negative. To remedy this, we perform a logical "and" with hash and the largest positive **int** value, written as 0x7FFFFFFF in hexadecimal (base 16) notation. The result is guaranteed to be nonnegative. The assignment for offset is

```
int offset = (hash & 0x7FFFFFFF) / table.length;
```

And then, whether searching, inserting, or removing, replace

```
e = table [(++i) % table.length];          // offset of 1
```

with

```
e = table [(i + offset) % table.length];
```

To see how this works in a simple setting, let's insert the following keys into a table of size 19:

33
72

71
55
112
109

These keys were created, not randomly, but to illustrate that keys from different collisions, even from the same collision, do not follow the same path. Here are the relevant moduli and quotients:

| key | key % 19 | key / 19 |
|-----|----------|----------|
| 33  | 14       | 1        |
| 72  | 15       | 3        |
| 71  | 14       | 3        |
| 112 | 17       | 5        |
| 55  | 17       | 2        |
| 109 | 14       | 5        |

The first key, 33, is stored at index 14, and the second key, 72, is stored at index 15. The third key, 71, hashes to 14, but that location is occupied, so the index 14 is incremented by the offset 3 to yield index 17; 71 is stored at that location. The fourth key, 112, hashes to 17 (occupied); the index 17 is incremented by the offset 5. Since 22 is beyond the range of the table, we try index 22 % 19, that is, 3, an unoccupied location. The key 112 is stored at index 3. The fifth key, 55, hashes to 17 (occupied) and then to (17 + 2) % 19, that is, 0, an empty location. The sixth key, 109, hashes to 14 (occupied) and then to (14 + 5) % 19, that is, 0 (occupied), and then to (0 + 5) % 19, that is, 5, an unoccupied location. Figure 14.12 shows the effect of the insertions.

This collision handler is known as *double hashing,* or the *quotient-offset* collision handler. There is one last problem we need to address before we get to the code and analysis: what happens if the offset is a multiple of the table size? For example, suppose we try to add the entry whose key is 736 to the table in Figure 14.12. We have

$$736 \% 19 = 14$$
$$736 / 19 = 38$$

Because location 14 is occupied, the next location tried is (14 + 38) % 19, which is 14 again! To avoid this impasse, we use 1 as the offset whenever key/table.length is a multiple of table.length. This is an infrequent occurrence: it happens, on average, once in every $m$ keys, where $m$ = table.length. Concept Exercise 14.5 shows that if this collision handler is used and the table size is a prime number, the sequence of offsets from any key covers the whole table.

Because the table size must be a prime number, the call to the resize method—inside the put method—must be changed from the offset-of-1 version:

```
resize (2 * table.length);
```

With the quotient-offset collision handler, we have

```
resize (nextPrime (2 * table.length));
```

**Figure 14.12** I The effect of inserting 6 entries into a table; the collision handler uses the hash value divided by the table size as the offset.

| | |
|---|---|
| 0 | 55 |
| 1 | |
| 2 | |
| 3 | 112 |
| 4 | |
| 5 | 109 |
| 6 | |
| 7 | |
| 8 | |
| 9 | |
| 10 | |
| 11 | |
| 12 | |
| 13 | |
| 14 | 33 |
| 15 | 72 |
| 16 | |
| 17 | 71 |
| 18 | |

The static method nextPrime returns the smallest prime larger than the argument.

If you undertake Programming Project 14.1, you will get to fill in the details of double hashing. If we make the Uniform Hashing Assumption, the average time for insertions, removals, and searches is constant [see Collins (2003, pp. 554–56)]. Figure 14.13 summarizes the time estimates for successful and unsuccessful searches (that is, invocations of the containsKey method). For purposes of comparison, the information in Figure 14.5 on chained hashing is included.

Figure 14.14 provides some specifics: the expected number of loop iterations for various ratios of $n$ to $m$. For purposes of comparison, the information in Figure 14.6 on chained hashing is included.

A cursory look at Figure 14.14 suggests that chained hashing is much faster than double hashing. But the figures given are mere estimates of the number of loop iterations. Run-time testing may, or may not, give a different picture. Run-time comparisons are included in Programming Project 14.1.

The main reason we looked at open-address hashing is that it is widely used; for example, some programming languages do not support linked lists. Also, open-address hashing can save space relative to chained hashing, which requires $n + m$ references versus only $m$ references for open-address hashing.

**Figure 14.13** I Estimates of average times for successful and unsuccessful calls to the containsKey method, under both chaining and double hashing. In the figure, $n$ = number of elements inserted; $m$ = table.length.

Chaining:

$$\text{averageTime}_S\,(n, m) \approx \frac{n}{2m} \text{ iterations}$$

$$\text{averageTime}_U\,(n, m) \approx \frac{n}{m} \text{ iterations}$$

Double hashing:

$$\text{averageTime}_S\,(n, m) \approx \frac{m}{n} \ln\left(\frac{1}{1 - \frac{n}{m}}\right) \text{ iterations}$$

$$\text{averageTime}_U\,(n, m) \approx \left(\frac{1}{1 - \frac{n}{m}}\right) \text{ iterations}$$

**Figure 14.14** I Estimated average number of loop iterations for successful and unsuccessful calls to the containsKey method, under both chained hashing and double hashing. In the figure, $n$ = number of elements inserted; $m$ = table.length.

| $\frac{n}{m}$ | 0.25 | 0.50 | 0.75 | 0.90 | 0.99 |
|---|---|---|---|---|---|
| **Chained hashing:** | | | | | |
| Successful | 0.13 | 0.25 | 0.38 | 0.45 | 0.50 |
| Unsuccessful | 0.25 | 0.50 | 0.75 | 0.90 | 0.99 |
| **Double hashing:** | | | | | |
| Successful | 1.14 | 1.39 | 1.85 | 2.56 | 4.65 |
| Unsuccessful | 1.33 | 2.00 | 4.00 | 10.00 | 100.00 |

Even if the Uniform Hashing Assumption applies, we could still, in the worst case, get every key to hash to the same index and yield the same offset. So for the containsKey method under double hashing, worstTime$_S(n, m)$ and worstTime$_U(n, m)$ are linear in $n$.

For open addressing, we eliminated the threat of primary clustering with double hashing. Another way to avoid primary clustering is through **quadratic probing:** the sequence of offsets is $1^2, 2^2, 3^2, \ldots$ For details, the interested reader may consult Weiss (2002).

# SUMMARY

In this chapter, we studied the Java Collections Framework of the HashMap class, for which key searches, insertions, and removals can be very fast, on average. This exceptional performance is due to ***hashing,*** the process of transforming a key into an array index. A hashing algorithm must include a collision handler for the possibility that two keys might hash to the same index. A widely used collision handler is chaining. With ***chaining,*** the HashMap object is represented as an array of singly linked lists. Each list contains the elements whose keys hashed to that index in the array.

Let $n$ represent the number of elements currently in the table, and let $m$ represent the capacity of the table. The ***load factor*** is the maximum ratio of $n$ to $m$ before rehashing will take place. The load factor is an estimate of the average size of each list, assuming that the hash method scatters the keys uniformly throughout the table. With that assumption—the **Uniform Hashing Assumption**—the average time for successful and unsuccessful searches depends only on the ratio of $n$ to $m$. The same is true for insertions and removals. If we double the table size whenever the ratio of $n$ to $m$ exceeds the load factor, then the size of each list, on average, will be less than or equal to the load factor. This shows that with chained hashing, the average time to insert, remove, or search is constant.

A HashSet object is simply a HashMap in which each key has the same dummy value. Almost all of the HashSet methods are one-liners that invoke the corresponding HashMap method.

An alternative to chaining is open addressing. When open addressing is used to handle collisions, each location in the table consists of entries only; there are no linked lists. If a key hashes to an index at which another key already resides, the table is searched systematically until an open address, that is, empty location is found. With an offset of 1, the sequence searched if the key hashes to index, is

index, index + 1, index + 2, . . ., table.length − 1, 0, 1, . . . , index − 1.

The offset-of-1 collision handler is susceptible to ***primary clustering:*** the phenomenon of having accelerating growth in the size of collision paths. Primary clustering is avoided with ***double hashing:*** the offset is the (positivized) hash value divided by table.length. If the Uniform Hashing Assumption holds and the table size is prime, the average time for both successful and unsuccessful searches with double hashing is constant.

## CONCEPT EXERCISES

**14.1**  Why does the HashMap class use singly linked lists instead of the LinkedList class?

**14.2**  Suppose you have a HashMap object, and you want to insert an element unless it is already there. How could you accomplish this?

*Hint:* The put method will insert the element even if it is already there (in which case, the new value will replace the old value).

**14.3**  For each of the following methods, estimate averageTime($n$) and worstTime($n$):

    **a.**  Making a successful call—that is, the element was found—to the contains method in the LinkedList class.

**b.** Making a successful call to the contains method in the ArrayList class;

**c.** Making a successful call to the generic algorithm binarySearch in the Arrays class; assume the elements in the array are in order.

**d.** Making a successful call to the contains method in the BinarySearch Tree class.

**e.** Making a successful call to the contains method in the TreeSet class.

**f.** Making a successful call to the contains method in the HashSet class— you should make the Uniform Hashing Assumption. Estimate average Time($n$, $m$) and worstTime($n$, $m$).

**14.4** This exercise helps to explain why both the hash and key fields are compared in the contains and put (and remove) methods of the HashMap class.

**a.** Suppose the keys in the HashMap are from a class that overrides the Object class's equals method but does not override the Object class's hashCode method. (This is in violation of the contract for the Object class's hashCode method, namely, equal objects should have the same hash code). The Object class's hashCode method converts the Object reference to an **int** value. So it would be possible for a key to be constructed with a given reference, and an identical key constructed with a different reference. For example, we could have:

Key key1 = **new** Key ("Webucation"),
    key2 = **new** Key ("Webucation");

HashMap <Key, String> myMap = **new** HashMap<Key, String>( );

myMap.put (key1, ""); // the value part is the empty String

If the hash fields were *not* compared in the containsKey and put methods, what would be returned by each of the following messages:

myMap.containsKey (key2)

myMap.put (key2, "")

**b.** In some classes, the hashCode method may return the same **int** value for two distinct keys. For example, in the String class, we can have two distinct String objects—even with the same characters—that have the same hash code:

String key1 = "! @"; // exclamation point, blank, at sign

String key2 = " @!"; // blank, at sign, exclamation point

HashMap <String, String> myMap = **new** HashMap <String, String>( );

myMap.put (key1, ""); // the value part is the empty String

System.out.println (key1.hashCode( ) + " " + key2.hashCode( ));

The output will be

32769 32769

If the key fields were *not* compared in the containsKey and put methods, what would be returned by each of the following messages:

myMap.containsKey (key2)

myMap.put (key2, "")

**14.5**  Assume that $p$ is a prime number. Use modular algebra to show that for any positive integers *index* and *offset* (with offset not a multiple of $p$), the following set has exactly $p$ elements:

$$\{ (index + k \cdot offset) \% p; k = 0, 1, 2, \ldots, p - 1\}$$

**14.6**  Compare the space requirements for chained hashing and open-address hashing with quotient offsets. Assume that a reference occupies 4 bytes and a **boolean** value occupies one byte. Under what circumstances (size, load Factor, table.length) will chained hashing require more space? Under what circumstances will double hashing require more space?

**14.7**  We noted in Chapter 12 that the term *dictionary,* viewed as an arbitrary collection of key-value pairs, is a synonym for *map.* If you were going to create a real dictionary, would you prefer to store the elements in a TreeMap object or in a HashMap object? Explain.

**14.8**  In open addressing, with the quotient-offset collision handler, insert the following keys into a table of size 13:

20
33
49
22
26
202
140
508
9

Here are the relevant remainders and quotients:

| key | key % 13 | key / 13 |
|----|----|----|
| 20 | 7 | 1 |
| 33 | 7 | 2 |
| 49 | 10 | 3 |
| 22 | 9 | 1 |
| 26 | 0 | 2 |
| 202 | 7 | 15 |
| 140 | 10 | 10 |
| 508 | 1 | 39 |
| 9 | 9 | 0 |

# PROGRAMMING EXERCISES

**14.1** Construct a HashMap object of the 25,000 students at Excel University. Each student's key will be that student's unique 6-digit ID. Each student's value will be that student's grade point average. Which constructor should you use and why?

**14.2** Construct a HashMap object of the 25,000 students at Excel University. Each student's key will be that student's unique 6-digit ID. Each student's value will be that student's grade point average and class rank. Insert a few elements into the HashMap object. Note that the value does not consist of a single component.

**14.3** Construct a HashSet object of identifiers. Insert a few elements into the HashSet object.

**14.4** As a programmer who *uses* the HashSet class, develop a toSortedString method:

```
/**
 * Returns a String representation of a specified HashSet object, with the natural
 * ordering,
 * The worstTime(n) is O(n log n).
 *
 * @param hashSet – the HashSet object whose String representation, sorted, is
 *         to be returned.
 *
 * @return a String representation of hashSet, with the natural ordering.
 *
 */
public static <E>String toSortedString (HashSet <E> hashSet)
```

*Note:* As a user, you cannot access any of the fields in the HashSet class.

**14.5** Given the following program fragment, add the code to print out all of the keys, and then add the code to print out all of the values:

```
HashMap<String, Integer> ageMap = new HashMap<String, Integer>( );

ageMap.put ("dog", 15);
ageMap.put ("cat", 20);
ageMap.put ("turtle", 100);
ageMap.put ("human", 75);
```

**14.6** The LinkedHashMap class superimposes a LinkedList object on a HashMap object, that is, there is a doubly linked list of all of the elements in the HashMap object. For example, suppose we have

```
LinkedHashMap<String, Integer> ageMap =
        new LinkedHashMap<String, Integer>( );

ageMap.put ("dog", 15);
ageMap.put ("cat", 20);
```

```
ageMap.put ("turtle", 100);
ageMap.put ("human", 75);

System.out.println (ageMap);
```

The output will reflect the order in which elements were inserted, namely,

```
{dog=15, cat=20, turtle=100, human=75}
```

Revise the above code segment so that only the pets are printed, and in alphabetical order.

## Programming Project 14.1

### The Double Hashing Implementation of the HashMap Class

Develop the implementation of the HashMap class that uses double hashing—see Section 14.5 and following. Define only a small number of methods: a default constructor, containsKey, put, and remove. Test your implementation with a driver; make sure to test resizing. The toString method is inherited from AbstractMap.

For system tests, run the Hasher program with input files Hasher.temp and Hasher.java itself. Then modify the Hasher program to print out, not each identifier, but merely the number of identifiers. Generate a large, random file of identifiers, and—for both chained hashing and double hashing—determine how long the Hasher program takes to create the symbol table.

## Programming Project 14.2

### Integrated Web Browser and Search Engine, Part 5

At this point, your search engine has created a TreeMap object for each Web page: the key was a word, and the value was the number of occurrences of the word. This approach worked well for a small number of Web pages, but would not scale up to the millions (even billions) of Web pages. In fact, the approach would be infeasible even if we used a HashMap object instead of a TreeMap object.

To enable searches to be completed quickly, a search engine must have a Web crawler that operates all the time. The Web crawler more or less randomly searches Web pages and saves ("caches") the results of the searches. For example, for each possible search word, each file in which the search word occurs (and the frequency of occurrences) are saved. When an end-user clicks on the Search button and then enters a search string, the cached results allow for quick searches.

Initially, you will be given a file, "search.ser", that contains a search-string HashMap in serialized form (see Appendix 3 for details on serializing and deserializing). Each key is a search word, and each value is a file-count HashMap in which the key is a file name and the value is the frequency of the search word in the file.

You will need to deserialize the search string HashMap. When the end-user enters a search string, there are two possibilities. If the search string already appears as a key in the search string HashMap, the file names and counts in the file-count HashMap are put into a priority queue and Part 4 of the project takes over. If the search string does not appear as a key in the search string HashMap, the individual words in the search string are used to search the search string HashMap, and the combined result becomes a new entry in the search string HashMap.

For example, suppose the universe of Web pages consists of the files browser.in10, in11, in12, and in13 from Part 4. The search string HashMap starts out with keys that include "neural", "decree", and "network". If the end-user clicks on the Search button and then enters "network", the output will be

Here are the results of the old search for network:

browser.in13 4
browser.in12 4
browser.in11 4
browser.in10 4

But if the end-user searches for "neural network", that string is not in the search string HashMap. So the results from the individual words "neural" and "network" are combined, and the output will be

Here are the results of the new search for neural network:

browser.in13 8
browser.in10 8
browser.in12 6
browser.in11 6

The search string "neural network" and the results will now be added to the search string HashMap. If, later in the same run, the end-user searches for "neural network", the output will be

Here are the results of the old search for neural network:

browser.in13 8
browser.in10 8
browser.in12 6
browser.in11 6

**System Test 1:**
(Assume the end-user searches for "neural network".)

Here are the results of the new search for neural network:

browser.in13 8
browser.in10 8
browser.in12 6
browser.in11 6

(Assume the end-user searches for "network".)

Here are the results of the old search for network:

browser.in13 4
browser.in12 4
browser.in11 4
browser.in10 4

(Assume the end-user searches for "neural network".)

Here are the results of the old search for neural network:

browser.in13 8
browser.in10 8
browser.in12 6
browser.in11 6

**System Test 2:**
(Assume the end-user searches for "network decree".)

Here are the results of the new search for network decree:

browser.in12 6
browser.in13 5
browser.in11 5
browser.in10 5

*Note 1:* By the end of each execution of the project, the file "search.ser" should contain the updated search string HashMap in serialized form. For example, by the end of System Test 1, "neural network" will be one of the search strings serialized in "search.ser". You may update "search.ser" after each search.

*Note 2:* The file search.ser is available from the ch14 directory of the book's website. And, in case you are curious, the Java program that creates search.ser is also available from that ch14 directory.

*Note 3:* If the search string does not occur in any of the files, the output should be "The search string does not occur in any of the files."

# 15

# Graphs, Trees, and Networks

There are many situations in which we want to study the relationship between objects. For example, in a curriculum, the objects are courses and the relationship is based on prerequisites. In airline travel, the objects are cities; two cities are related if there is a flight between them. It is visually appealing to describe such situations graphically, with points (called *vertices*) representing the objects and lines (called *edges*) representing the relationships. In this chapter, we will introduce several collections based on vertices and edges. Finally, we will design and implement one of those collections in a class from which the other structures can be defined as subclasses. Neither the class nor the subclasses are currently part of the Java Collections Framework. ■

## CHAPTER OBJECTIVES

1. Define the terms *graph* and *tree* for both directed/undirected and weighted/unweighted collections.

2. Compare breadth-first traversal and depth-first traversal.

3. Understand Prim's greedy algorithm for finding a minimum-cost spanning tree and Dijkstra's greedy algorithm for finding a minimum-cost path between vertices.

4. Compare the HashMap/LinkedList implementation and the adjacency-matrix implementation of the Network class.

5. Be able to solve problems that include backtracking through a graph.

## 15.1 | UNDIRECTED GRAPHS

An *undirected graph* consists of a collection of distinct elements called *vertices,* connected to other elements by distinct vertex-pairs called *edges.* Here is an example of an undirected graph:

Vertices: *A, B, C, D, E*

Edges: (*A, B*), (*A, C*), (*B, D*), (*C, D*), (*C, E*)

The vertex pair in an edge is enclosed in parentheses to indicate the pair of vertices is unordered. For example, to say there is an edge from *A* to *B* is the same as saying there is an edge from *B* to *A*. That's why "undirected" is used. Figure 15.1 depicts this undirected graph, with each edge represented as a line connecting its vertex pair.

From the illustration in Figure 15.1 we could obtain the original formulation of the undirected graph as a collection of vertices and edges. And furthermore, Figure 15.1 gives us a better grasp of the undirected graph than the original formulation. From now on we will often use illustrations such as Figure 15.1 instead of the formulations.

Figure 15.2 contains several additional undirected graphs. Notice that the number of edges can be fewer than the number of vertices (Figures 15.2a and b), equal to the number of vertices (Figure 15.1), or greater than the number of vertices (Figure 15.2c).

An undirected graph is *complete* if it has as many edges as possible. What is the number of edges in a complete undirected graph? Let $n$ represent the number of vertices. Figure 15.3 shows that when $n = 6$, the maximum number of edges is 15.

**Figure 15.1** | A visual representation of an undirected graph.

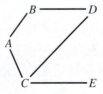

**Figure 15.2a** | An undirected graph with six vertices and five edges.

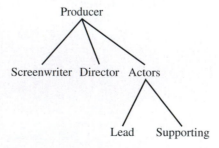

**Figure 15.2b |** An undirected graph with eight vertices and seven edges.

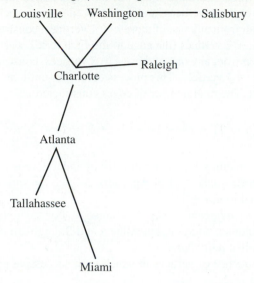

**Figure 15.2c |** An undirected graph with eight vertices and eleven edges.

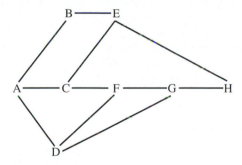

**Figure 15.3 |** An undirected graph with 6 vertices and the maximum number (15) of edges for any undirected graph with 6 vertices.

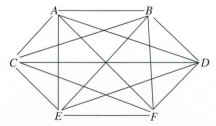

Can you determine a formula that holds for any positive integer $n$? In general, start with any one of the $n$ vertices, and construct an edge to each of the remaining $n - 1$ vertices. Then from any one of those $n - 1$ vertices, construct an edge to each of the remaining $n - 2$ vertices (the edge to the first vertex was constructed in the previous step). Then from any one of those $n - 2$ vertices, construct an edge to each of the remaining $n - 3$ vertices. This process continues until, at step $n - 1$, a final edge is constructed. The total number of edges constructed is:

$$(n - 1) + (n - 2) + (n - 3) + \cdots + 2 + 1 = \sum_{i=1}^{n-1} i = n(n - 1)/2$$

This last equality can either be proved directly by induction on $n$ or can be derived from the proof—in Example A2.1 of Appendix 2—that the sum of the first $n$ positive integers is equal to $n(n + 1)/2$.

Two vertices are **_adjacent_** if they form an edge. For example, in Figure 15.2b, Charlotte and Atlanta are adjacent, but Atlanta and Raleigh are not adjacent. Adjacent vertices are called **_neighbors._**

A **_path_** is a sequence of vertices in which each successive pair is an edge. For example, in Figure 15.2c,

> $A, B, E, H$

is a path from $A$ to $H$ because $(A, B)$, $(B, E)$, and $(E, H)$ are edges. Another path from $A$ to $H$ is

> $A, C, F, D, G, H$

For a path of $k$ vertices, the **_length_** of the path is $k - 1$. In other words, the path length is the number of *edges* in the path. For example, in Figure 15.2.c the following path from $C$ to $A$ has a length of 3:

> $C, F, D, A$

There is, in fact, a shorter path from $C$ to $A$, namely,

> $C, A$

In general, there may be several shortest paths between two vertices. For example, in Figure 15.2c,

> $A, B, E$

and

> $A, C, E$

are both shortest paths from $A$ to $E$.

A **_cycle_** is a path in which the first and last vertices are the same and there are no repeated *edges*. For example, in Figure 15.1,

> $A, B, D, C, A$

is a cycle. In Figure 15.2c,

*B, E, H, G, D, A, B*

is a cycle, as is

*E, C, A, B, E*

The undirected graph in Figures 15.2a and b are **acyclic;** that is, they do not contain any cycles. In Figure 15.2a,

Producer, Director, Producer

is *not* a cycle since the edge (Producer, Director) is repeated—recall that an edge in an undirected graph is an unordered pair.

An undirected graph is **connected** if, for any pair of vertices *x* and *y*, there is a path from *x* to *y*. Informally, an undirected graph is connected if it is "all one piece." For example, all of the graphs in the above figures are connected. The following undirected graph, with 6 vertices and 5 edges, is not connected:

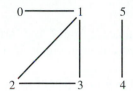

## 15.2 I **DIRECTED GRAPHS**

Up to now we have not concerned ourselves with the direction of edges. If we could go from vertex *V* to vertex *W*, we could also go from vertex *W* to vertex *V*. In many situations this assumption may be unrealistic. For example, suppose the edges represent streets and the vertices represent intersections. If the street connecting vertex *V* to vertex *W* is one-way going from *V* to *W*, there would be no edge connecting *W* to *V*.

A *directed graph*—sometimes called a *digraph*—is a collection of vertices and edges in which the edges are ordered pairs of vertices. For example, here is a directed graph, with edges in angle brackets to indicate an ordered pair:

Vertices: *A, T, V, W, Z*
Edges: $<A, T>, <A, V>, <T, A>, <V, A>, <V, W>, <W, Z>, <Z, W>,$
 $<Z, T>$

Pictorially, these edges are represented by arrows, with the arrow's direction going from the first vertex in the ordered pair to the second vertex. For example, Figure 15.4 contains the directed graph just defined.

A path in a directed graph must follow the direction of the arrows. Formally a *path* in a directed graph is a sequence of $k > 1$ vertices $V_0, V_1, \ldots, V_{k-1}$ such that $<V_0, V_1>, <V_1, V_2>, \ldots, <V_{k-2}, V_{k-1}>$ are edges in the directed graph. For example, in Figure 15.4,

*A, V, W, Z*

**Figure 15.4** | A directed graph.

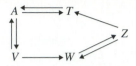

**Figure 15.5** | A digraph that is not connected.

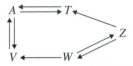

is a path from *A* to *Z* because <*A, V*>, <*V, W*>, and <*W, Z*> are edges in the directed graph. But

> *A, T, Z, W*

is not a path because there is no edge from *T* to *Z*. A few minutes' checking should convince you that for any two vertices in Figure 15.4, there is a path from the first vertex to the second.

A digraph *D* is **connected** if, for any pair of vertices *x* and *y*, there is a path from *x* to *y*. Figure 15.4 is a connected digraph, but the digraph in Figure 15.5 is not connected (try to figure out why).

From these examples, you can see that we actually could have defined the term "undirected graph" from "directed graph": an **undirected graph** is a directed graph in which, for any two vertices *V* and *W*, if there is an edge from *V* to *W*, there is also an edge from *W* to *V*. This observation will come in handy when we get to developing Java classes.

In the next two sections, we will look at specializations of graphs: trees and networks.

## 15.3 | TREES

An **undirected tree** is a connected, acyclic, undirected graph with one element designated as the **root element.** For example, here is the undirected tree from Figure 15.2a; producer is the root element.

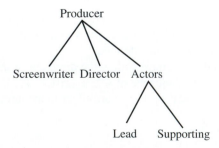

On most occasions, we are interested in directed trees, that is, trees that have arrows from a parent to its children. A *tree,* sometimes called a ***directed tree,*** is a directed graph that either is empty or has an element, called the ***root element*** such that:

1. There are no edges coming into the root element.
2. Every nonroot element has exactly one edge coming into it.
3. There is a path from the root to every other element.

For example, Figure 15.6 shows that we can easily redraw the above, undirected tree as a directed tree.

Many of the binary-tree terms from Chapter 9—such as "child", "leaf", "branch"—can be extended to apply to arbitrary trees. For example, the tree in Figure 15.6 has four leaves and height 2. But "full" does not apply to trees in general because there is no limit to the number of children a parent can have. In fact, we cannot simply define a binary tree to be a tree in which each element has at most two children. Why not? Figure 15.7 has two distinct binary trees that are equivalent as trees.

We can define a binary tree to be a (directed) tree in which each vertex has at most two children, labeled the "left" child and the "right" child of that vertex.

Trees allow us to study hierarchical relationships such as parent-child and supervisor-supervisee. With arbitrary trees, we are not subject to the at-most-two-children restriction of binary trees.

**Figure 15.6 |** A (directed) tree.

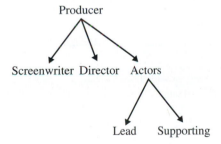

**Figure 15.7 |** Two distinct binary trees, one with an empty right subtree and one with an empty left subtree.

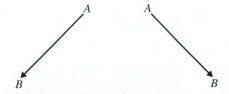

## 15.4 | NETWORKS

Sometimes we associate a nonnegative number with each edge in a graph (which can be directed or undirected). The nonnegative numbers are called *weights,* and the resulting structure is called a *weighted graph* or *network.* For example, Figure 15.8 has an undirected network in which each weight represents the distance between cities for the graph of Figure 15.2b.

Of what value is a directed network, that is, why might the direction of a weighted edge be significant? Even if one can travel in either direction on an edge, the weight for going in one direction may be different from the weight going in the other direction. For example, suppose the weights represent the time for a plane flight between two cities. Because of the prevailing westerly winds, the time to fly from New York to Los Angeles is usually longer than the time to fly from Los Angeles to New York.

Figure 15.9 shows a directed network in which the weight of the edge from vertex D to vertex F is different from the weight of the edge going in the other direction.

With each path between two vertices in a network, we can calculate the total weight of the path. For example, in Figure 15.9, the path *A, C, D, E* has a total weight of 10.0. Can you find a shorter path from *A* to *E,* that is, a path with smaller total weight?[1] The shortest path from *A* to *E* is *A, B, D, E* with total weight 8.0. Later in this chapter we will develop an algorithm to find a shortest path (there may be several of them) between two vertices in a network.

**Figure 15.8** | An undirected network in which vertices represent cities, and each edge's weight represents the distance between the two cities in the edge.

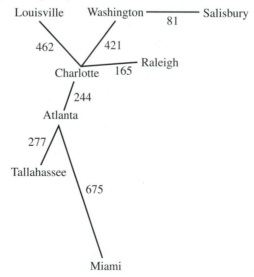

---

[1] This is different from the meaning of "shorter" in the graph sense, namely, having fewer edges in the path.

**Figure 15.9 |** A directed network with 8 vertices and 11 edges.

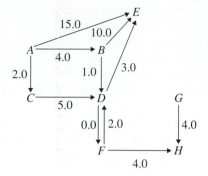

The directed network in Figure 15.9 is not connected because, for example, there is no path from *B* to *C*. Recall that a path in a directed graph must follow the direction of the arrows.

Now that we have seen how to define a graph or tree (directed or undirected, weighted or unweighted), we can outline some well-known algorithms. The implementation of those algorithms, and their analyses, will be handled in Section 15.6.3.

## 15.5 | GRAPH ALGORITHMS

A prerequisite to other graph algorithms is being able to iterate through a graph, so we start by looking at iterators in general. We focus on two kinds of iterators: breadth-first and depth-first. These terms may ring a bell; in Chapter 9, we studied breadth-first and depth-first (also known as preorder) traversals of a binary tree.

### 15.5.1 Iterators

There are several kinds of iterators associated with directed or undirected graphs, and these iterators can also be applied to trees and networks (directed or undirected). First, we can simply iterate over all of the vertices in the graph. The iteration need not be in any particular order. For example, here is an iteration over the vertices in the weighted digraph of Figure 15.9:

*A, B, D, F, G, C, E, H*

In addition to iterating over all of the vertices in a graph, we are sometimes interested in iterating over all vertices reachable from a given vertex. For example, in the weighted digraph of Figure 15.9, we might want to iterate over all vertices reachable from *A*, that is, over all vertices that are in some path that starts at *A*. Here is one such iteration:

*A, B, C, D, E, F, H*

The vertex *G* is not reachable from *A*, so *G* will not be in any such iteration from *A*.

**Breadth-First Iterators** A *breadth-first iterator,* similar to a breadth-first traversal in Chapter 9, visits vertices in order, beginning with some vertex identified as the "start vertex." What is the order? Roughly, it can be described as "neighbors first." As soon as a vertex has been visited, each neighbor of that vertex is considered to be "reached," and vertices are visited in the order in which they are reached. The first vertex reached and visited is the start vertex, then the neighbors of the start vertex are considered reached, so they are visited, then the neighbors of those neighbors, and so on.

No vertex is visited more than once, and any vertex that is not on some path from the start vertex will not be visited at all. For example, assume that the vertices in the following graph—from Figure 15.2.b—were entered in alphabetical order:

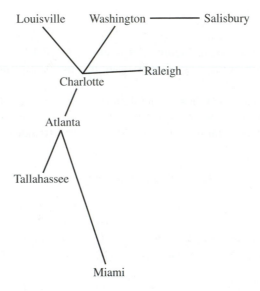

We will perform a breadth-first iteration starting at Atlanta and visit neighbors in alphabetical order. So we start with

$$r, v$$
Atlanta

The *r* and *v* above Atlanta indicate that Atlanta has been reached and visited. The neighbors of Atlanta are now considered to be reached:

$$r, v \quad\quad r \quad\quad r \quad\quad r$$
Atlanta, Charlotte, Miami, Tallahassee

Each of those neighbors of Atlanta is then visited, which makes *their* neighbors reached. When we visit Charlotte, we have

$$r, v \quad\quad r, v \quad\quad r \quad\quad r \quad\quad r \quad\quad r \quad\quad r$$
Atlanta, Charlotte, Miami, Tallahassee, Louisville, Raleigh, Washington

Notice that the first neighbor of Charlotte, Atlanta, is ignored because we have already reached (and visited) Atlanta. Then Miami is visited (it has no unreached neighbors), Tallahassee (no unreached neighbors), Louisville (no unreached neighbors), Raleigh (no unreached neighbors) and Washington, whose not-yet-reached neighbor is Salisbury. We now have

$r, v$     $r, v$     $r, v$     $r, v$     $r, v$     $r, v$     $r, v$     $r$

Atlanta, Charlotte, Miami, Tallahassee, Louisville, Raleigh, Washington, Salisbury

When we visit Salisbury we are done because Salisbury has no not-yet-reached neighbors. In other words, we have iterated through all cities reachable from Atlanta, starting at Atlanta:

Atlanta, Charlotte, Miami, Tallahassee, Louisville, Raleigh, Washington, Salisbury

The order of visiting cities would be different if we started a breadth-first iteration at Louisville:

Louisville, Charlotte, Atlanta, Raleigh, Washington, Miami, Tallahassee, Salisbury

Let's do some preliminary work on the design of the BreadthFirstIterator class. When a vertex has been reached, that vertex will be visited. To make sure that vertex is not revisited, we will keep track of which vertices have already been reached. To do this, we will store the reached vertices in some kind of collection. Specifically, we want to visit the neighbors of the current vertex in the order in which those neighbors were initially stored in the collection. Because we want the vertices removed from the collection in the order in which they were added to the collection, a *queue* is the appropriate collection. And we will also want to keep track of the current vertex.

We can now develop high-level algorithms for the BreadthFirstIterator methods—the details will have to be postponed until we create a class, such as Network, in which BreadthFirstIterator will be embedded. The constructor enqueues the start vertex and marks all other vertices as not-yet-reached:

```
public BreadthFirstIterator (Vertex start)
{
        for every vertex in the graph:
                mark that vertex as not reached.
        mark start as reached.
        queue.enqueue (start);
} // algorithm for constructor
```

The hasNext( ) method returns !queue.isEmpty( ). The next( ) method removes the front vertex from the queue, makes that vertex the current vertex, and enqueues each neighbor of the current vertex that has not yet been reached:

```
public Vertex next( )
{
        current = queue.dequeue( )
```

```
            for each vertex that is a neighbor of current:
                    if that vertex has not yet been reached
                    {
                            mark that vertex as reached;
                            enqueue that vertex;
                    } // if
            return current;
        } // algorithm for method next
```

The analysis of this algorithm is postponed until Section 15.6.3, when we will have all of the details associated with the BreadthFirstIterator class.

The remove( ) method deletes from the graph the current vertex, that is, the vertex most recently returned by a call to the next( ) method.

For an example of how the queue and the next( ) method work together in a breadth-first iteration, suppose we create a directed network by entering the sequence of edges and weights in Figure 15.10.

The directed network created is the same one shown in Figure 15.9:

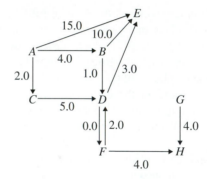

**Figure 15.10** | A sequence of edges and weights to generate the directed network in
Figure 15.9.

```
A B  4.0
A C  2.0
A E 15.0
B D  1.0
B E 10.0
C D  5.0
D E  3.0
D F  0.0
F D  2.0
F H  4.0
G H  4.0
```

To conduct a breadth-first iteration starting at *A,* for example, we first enqueue *A* in the constructor. The first call to next( ) dequeues *A,* enqueues *B, C,* and *E,* and returns *A.* The second call to next( ) dequeues *B,* enqueues *D,* and returns *B.* Figure 15.11 shows the queue generated by a breadth-first iteration starting at *A.*

Notice that vertex *G* is missing from Figure 15.11. The reason is that *G* is not reachable from *A;* that is, there is no path from *A* to *G.* If we performed a breadth-first iteration from any other vertex, there would be even fewer vertices visited than in Figure 15.11. For example, a breadth-first iteration starting at vertex B would visit

   *B, D, E, F, H*

in that order.

Breadth-first iterators are especially useful in iterating over a tree. The start vertex is the root and, as we saw in Chapter 9, the vertices are visited level-by-level: the root, the root's children, the root's grandchildren, and so on.

**Depth-First Iterators** The other specialized iterator is a ***depth-first iterator.*** A depth-first iterator is a generalization of the preorder traversal of Chapter 9. To refresh your memory, here is the algorithm for a preorder traversal of a binary tree *t:*

```
preOrder (t)
{
        if (t is not empty)
        {
                access the root element of t;
                preOrder (leftTree (t));
                preOrder (rightTree (t));
        } // if
} // preOrder traversal
```

To further help you recall how a preorder traversal works, Figure 15.12 shows a binary tree and a preorder traversal of its elements.

**Figure 15.11** | A breadth-first iteration of the vertices, from Figure 15.9, starting at *A.* The vertices are enqueued—and therefore dequeued—in the same order in which they were entered in Figure 15.10.

| Queue | Vertex returned by next( ) |
|---|---|
| A | |
| B, C, E | A |
| C, E, D | B |
| E, D | C |
| D | E |
| F | D |
| H | F |
| | H |

**Figure 15.12** ▍ A binary tree and the order in which its elements would be visited during a pre-order traversal.

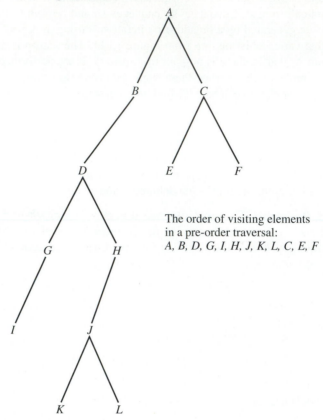

The order of visiting elements
in a pre-order traversal:
*A, B, D, G, I, H, J, K, L, C, E, F*

We can describe a preorder traversal of a binary tree as follows: Start with a leftward path from the root. Once the end of a path is reached, the algorithm *backtracks* to an element that has an as-yet-unreached right child. Another leftward path is begun, starting with that right child.

A depth-first iteration of a graph proceeds similarly, except "leftward" has no meaning in a graph. We first mark as not reached each vertex, then mark as reached, and visit, the start vertex. Then we mark as reached each not-yet-reached neighbor of the start vertex. Next, we visit the most recently reached vertex of those neighbors, and mark as reached each not-yet-reached neighbor of that vertex. Another path is begun starting with that unvisited vertex. This continues as long as there are vertices reachable from the start vertex that have not yet been reached.

For example, let's perform a depth-first iteration of the following graph, starting at Atlanta—we assume that the vertices were initially entered in alphabetical order:

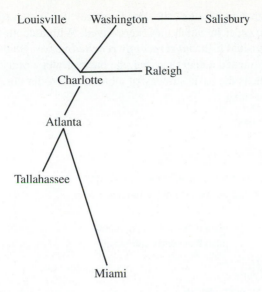

We first visit the start vertex:

*r, v*

Atlanta

Then we mark as reached the neighbors of Atlanta:

*r, v*     *r*     *r*     *r*

Atlanta, Charlotte, Miami, Tallahassee

We then visit the *most recently reached* vertex, namely Tallahassee, *not* Charlotte. Tallahassee has no unreached neighbors, so we visit the next-most-recently reached vertex: Miami. Miami also has no unreached neighbors, so we visit Charlotte, and mark as reached the following vertices. We now have

*r, v*   *r, v*   *r, v*   *r, v*    *r*    *r*    *r*

Atlanta, Charlotte, Miami, Tallahassee, Louisville, Raleigh, Washington

Washington, the most recently reached vertex, is visited, and its only unreached neighbor, Salisbury, is marked as reached. We now have

*r, v*   *r, v*   *r, v*   *r, v*    *r*    *r*   *r, v*    *r*

Atlanta, Charlotte, Miami, Tallahassee, Louisville, Raleigh, Washington, Salisbury

Now Salisbury is the most recently reached vertex, so Salisbury is visited. Finally, Raleigh and then Louisville are visited. The order in which vertices are visited is as follows:

Atlanta, Tallahassee, Miami, Charlotte, Washington, Salisbury, Raleigh, Louisville

For a depth-first iteration starting at Charlotte, the order in which vertices are visited is:

Charlotte, Washington, Salisbury, Raleigh, Louisville, Atlanta, Tallahassee, Miami

With a breadth-first iteration, we saved vertices in a queue so that the vertices were visited in the order in which they were saved. With a depth-first iteration, the next vertex to be visited is the *most recently reached* vertex. So the vertices will be *stacked* instead of queued. Other than that, the basic strategy of a depth-first iterator is exactly the same as the basic strategy of a breadth-first iterator. Here is the high-level algorithm for next( ):

```
public Vertex next( )
{
        current = stack.pop( );

        for each vertex that is a neighbor of current:
                if that vertex has not yet been reached
                {
                        mark that vertex as reached;
                        push that vertex onto stack;
                } // if
        return current;
} // algorithm for method next
```

The analysis of this algorithm is the same as that of the next( ) method in the BreadthFirstIterator class; see Section 15.6.3.

Suppose, as we did above, we create a directed network from the following input, in the order given:

A B 4.0
A C 2.0
A E 15.0
B D 1.0
B E 10.0
C D 5.0
D E 3.0
D F 0.0
F D 2.0
F H 4.0
G H 4.0

The directed network created is the same one shown in Figure 15.9:

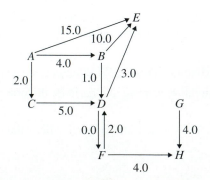

Figure 15.13 shows the sequence of stack states and the vertices returned by *next( )* for a depth-first iteration of the weighted digraph in Figure 15.9, as generated from the input in Figure 15.10. We could have developed a backtrack version of the next( ) method. The vertices would be visited in the same order, but recursion would be utilized instead of a stack.

When should you use a breadth-first iterator and when should you use a depth-first iterator? If you are looping through all vertices reachable from the start vertex, there's not much reason to pick. The only difference is the order in which the vertices will be visited. But if you are at some start vertex and you are searching for a specific vertex reachable from that start vertex, there can be a difference. If, somehow, you know that there is a short path from the start vertex to the vertex sought, a breadth-first iterator is preferable: the vertices on a path of length 1 from the start vertex are visited, then the vertices on a path of length 2, and so on. On the other hand, if you know that the vertex sought may be very far from the start vertex, a depth-first search will probably be quicker.

## 15.5.2 Connectedness

In Section 15.1, we defined an undirected graph to be **connected** if, for any pair of vertices *x* and *y*, there is a path from *x* to *y*. For example, the following is a connected, undirected graph:

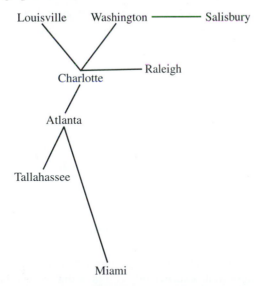

For a digraph, that is, a directed graph, connectedness means that for any two vertices, there is a path—that follows the directions of the arrows—between them. A breadth-first or depth-first iteration over all vertices in a graph can be performed only if the graph is connected. In fact, we can use the ability to iterate between any two vertices as a test for connectedness of a digraph.

Given a digraph, let itr be an iterator over the digraph. For each vertex v in the digraph, let bfitr be a breadth-first iterator starting at v. We check to make sure that the

**Figure 15.13 |** A depth-first iteration of the vertices reachable from *A*. We assume the vertices were entered as in Figure 15.10.

| Stack (top vertex is shown leftmost) | Vertex returned by next( ) |
|---|---|
| A | |
| E, C, B | A |
| C, B | E |
| D, B | C |
| F, B | D |
| H, B | F |
| B | H |
| | B |

number of vertices reachable from v (including v itself) is equal to the number of vertices in the digraph.

Here is a high-level algorithm to determine connectedness in a digraph:

```
public boolean isConnected( )
{
        for each Vertex v in this digraph
        {
                // Count the number of vertices reachable from v.
                 Construct a BreadthFirstIterator, bfltr, starting at v.
                int count = 0;
                while (bfltr.hasNext( ))
                {
                        bfltr.next( );
                        count ++;
                } // while
                if (count < number of vertices in this digraph)
                        return false;
        } // for
        return true;
} // algorithm for isConnected
```

For an undirected graph, the isConnected( ) algorithm is somewhat simpler: there is no need for an outer loop to iterate through the entire graph. See Concept Exercise 15.4.

In the next two sections, we outline the development of two important network algorithms. Each algorithm is sufficiently complex that it is named after the person (Prim, Dijkstra) who invented the algorithm.

## 15.5.3  Generating a Minimum Spanning Tree

Suppose a cable company has to connect a number of houses in a community. Given the costs, in hundreds of dollars, to lay cable between the houses, determine the minimum cost of connecting the houses to the cable system. This can be cast as a connected network problem; each weight represents the cost to lay cable between two neighbors. Figure 15.14 gives a sample layout. Some house-to-house distances are not given because they represent infeasible connections (over a mountain, for example).

In a connected network, a **spanning tree** is a weighted tree that consists of all of the vertices and some of the edges (and their weights) from the network. The network (that is, weighted graph) may be directed or undirected. Because a tree must be connected, a spanning tree connects all of the vertices of the original graph. For example, Figures 15.15 and 15.16 show two spanning trees for the network in Figure 15.14. For the sake of specificity, we designate vertex $A$ as the root of each tree, but any other vertex would serve equally well.

**Figure 15.14 |** A connected network in which the vertices represent houses and the weights represent the cost, in hundreds of dollars, to connect the two houses.

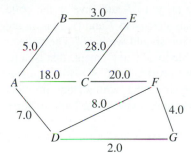

**Figure 15.15 |** A spanning tree for the network in Figure 15.14.

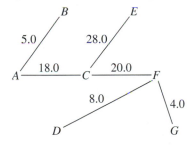

**Figure 15.16 |** Another spanning tree for the network in Figure 15.14.

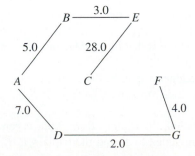

A *minimum spanning tree* is a spanning tree in which the sum of all the weights is no greater than the sum of all the weights in any other spanning tree. The original problem about laying cable can be restated in the form of constructing a minimum spanning tree for a connected network. To give you an idea of how difficult it is to solve this problem, try to construct a minimum spanning tree for the network in Figure 15.14. How difficult would it be to "scale up" your solution to a community with 1000 houses?

An algorithm to construct a minimum spanning tree is due to R. C. Prim (1957). Here is the basic strategy. Start with an empty tree $T$ and pick any vertex $v$ in the network. Add $v$ to $T$. For each vertex $w$ such that $(v, w)$ is an edge with weight *wweight*, save the ordered triple $<v, w, wweight>$ in a collection—we'll see what kind of collection shortly. Then loop until $T$ has as many vertices as the original network. During each loop iteration, remove from the collection the triple $<x, y, yweight>$ for which *yweight* is the smallest weight of all triples in the collection; if $y$ is not already in $T$, add $y$ and the edge $(x, y)$ to $T$ and save in the collection every triple $<y, z, zweight>$ such that $z$ is not already in $T$ and $(y, z)$ is an edge with weight *zweight*.

What kind of collection should we have? The collection should be ordered by weights; we need to be able to add an element, that is, a triple, to the collection and to remove the triple with lowest weight. A *priority queue* will perform these tasks quickly. Recall from Chapter 13 that with a Heap implementation, averageTime($n$) for the add method is constant, and averageTime($n$) for the removeMin method is logarithmic in $n$.

To see how Prim's algorithm works, let's start with the network in Figure 15.14, repeated here:

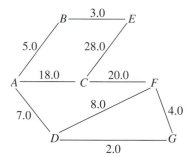

Initially, the tree $T$ and the priority queue pq are both empty. Add $A$ to $T$, and add to pq each triple of the form $<A, w, wweight>$ where $(A, w)$ is an edge with weight *wweight*. Figure 15.17 shows the contents of $T$ and pq at this point. For the sake of readability, the triples in pq are shown in increasing order of weights; strictly speaking, all we know for sure is that the getMin and removeMin methods return the triple with smallest weight.

When the lowest-weighted triple, $<A, B, 5.0>$ is removed from pq, the vertex $B$ and the edge $(A, B)$ are added to $T$, and the triple $<B, E, 3.0>$ is added to pq. See Figure 15.18.

During the next iteration, the triple $<B, E, 3.0>$ is removed from pq, the vertex $E$ and edge $(B, E)$ are added to $T$, and the triple $<E, C, 28.0>$ is added to pq. See Figure 15.19.

**Figure 15.17 |** The contents of T and pq at the start of Prim's algorithm as applied to the network in Figure 15.14.

| T | pq |
|---|---|
| A | <A, B, 5.0> |
|   | <A, D, 7.0> |
|   | <A, C, 18.0> |

**Figure 15.18 |** The contents of T and pq during the application of Prim's algorithm to the network in Figure 15.14.

**Figure 15.19 |** The contents of T and pq during the application of Prim's algorithm to the network in Figure 15.14.

During the next iteration, the triple <A, D, 7.0> is removed from pq, the vertex D and the edge (A, D) are added to T, and the triples <D, F, 8.0> and <D, G, 2.0> are added to pq. See Figure 15.20.

During the next iteration, the triple <D, G, 2.0> is removed from pq, the vertex G and the edge (D, G) are added to T, and the triple <G, F, 4.0> is added to pq. See Figure 15.21.

During the next iteration, the triple <G, F, 4.0> is removed from pq, the vertex F and the edge (G, F) are added to T, and the triple <F, C, 20.0> is added to pq. See Figure 15.22.

During the next iteration, the triple <D, F, 8.0> is removed from pq. But *nothing* is added to T or pq because F is already in T.

During the next iteration, the triple <A, C, 18.0> is removed from pq, the vertex C and the edge (A, C) are added to T, and nothing is added to pq. The reason nothing is added to pq is that, for all of C's edges, (C, A), (C, E), and (C, F), the second element in the pair is already in T. See Figure 15.23.

Even though pq is not empty, we are finished because every vertex in the original network is also in T.

From the way T is constructed, we know that T is a spanning tree. We can show, by contradiction, that T is a minimum spanning tree. In general, a proof by contradiction assumes some statement to be false, and shows that some other statement—

**Figure 15.20** I The contents of *T* and pq during the application of Prim's algorithm to the network in Figure 15.14.

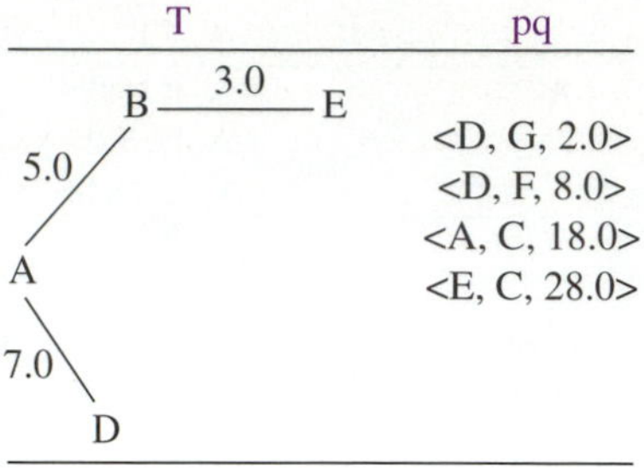

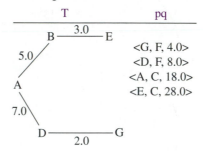

**Figure 15.21** I The contents of *T* and pq during the application of Prim's algorithm to the network in Figure 15.14.

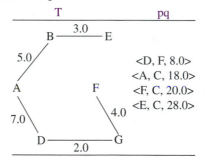

**Figure 15.22** I The contents of *T* and pq during the application of Prim's algorithm to the network in Figure 15.14.

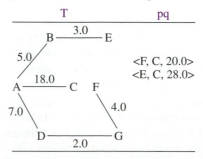

**Figure 15.23** I The contents of *T* and pq after the last iteration in the application of Prim's algorithm to the network in Figure 15.14.

known to be true—must also be false. We then conclude that the original statement must have been true.

Assume that $T$ is not a minimum spanning tree. Then during some iteration, a triple $<x, y, yweight>$ is removed from pq and the edge $(x, y)$ is added to $T$, but there is some vertex $v$, already in $T$, and $w$, not in $T$, such that edge $(v, w)$ has lower weight than edge $(x, y)$. Pictorially:

```
T          Not in T
─────────────────────
x───────y



v───────w
─────────────────────
```

Note that since $v$ is already in $T$, the triple starting with $<v, w, ?>$ must have been added to pq earlier. But the edge $(v, w)$ could not have a lower weight than the edge $(x, y)$ because the triple $<x, y, yweight>$ was removed from pq, not the triple starting with $<v, w, ?>$. This contradicts the claim that $(v, w)$ had lower edge weight than $(x, y)$. So $T$, with edge $(x, y)$ added, must still be minimum.

The definition of the getMinimumSpanningTree method is found in Section 15.6.3, and then we will estimate the time requirements for that method.

Prim's algorithm is another example of the greedy algorithm design pattern (the Huffman encoding algorithm in Chapter 13 is also a greedy algorithm). During each loop iteration, the locally optimal choice is made: the edge with lowest weight is added to $T$. This sequence of locally optimal—that is, greedy—choices leads to a globally optimal solution: $T$ is a minimum spanning tree.

Another greedy algorithm appears in Section 15.5.4. Concept Exercise 15.7 and Lab 23 show that greed does not always succeed.

## 15.5.4  Finding the Shortest Path through a Network

In Section 15.5.3, we developed a strategy for constructing a minimum spanning tree in a network. A similar strategy applies to finding a shortest path in a network (directed or undirected) from some vertex $v1$ to some other vertex $v2$. In this context, "shortest" means having the lowest total weight. Both algorithms are greedy, and both use a priority queue. The shortest-path algorithm, due to Edsgar Dijkstra (1959), is essentially a breadth-first iteration that starts at $v1$ and stops as soon as $v2$'s pair is removed from the priority queue pq. (Dijkstra's algorithm actually found a shortest path from $v1$ to every other vertex in the network.) Each pair consists of a vertex $w$ and the sum of the weights of all edges on the shortest path so far from $v1$ to $w$.

The priority queue is ordered by lowest *total* weights. To keep track of total weights, we have a map, weightSum, in which each key is a vertex $w$ and each value is the sum of the weights of all the edges on the shortest path so far from $v1$ to $w$. To enable us to reconstruct the shortest path when we are through, there is another map, predecessor, in which each key is a vertex $w$, and each value is the vertex that is the immediate predecessor of $w$ on the shortest path so far from $v1$ to $w$.

Basically, weightSum maps each given vertex to the minimum total weight, so far, of the path from $v1$ to the given vertex. Initially, pq consists of vertex $v1$ and its weight, 0.0. On each iteration we greedily choose the vertex-weight pair $<x$, total

**Figure 15.24** I The minimum-weight path from vertex $v1$ to vertex $y$ had been 15, but the path from vertex $v1$ through vertex $x$ to vertex $y$ has a lower total weight.

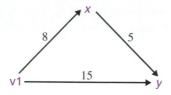

weight> in pq that has the minimum total weight among all vertex-weight pairs in pq. If there is a neighbor $y$ of $x$ whose total weight can be reduced by the path $<v1, \ldots, x, y>$, then $y$'s path and minimum weight are altered, and $y$ (and its new total weight) is added to pq. For example, we might have the partial network shown in Figure 15.24. Then the total weight between $v1$ and $y$ is reduced to 13, the pair $<y, 13>$ is added to pq, and $y$'s predecessor becomes $x$. Eventually, this yields the shortest path from $v1$ to $v2$, if there is a path between those vertices.

To start, weightSum associates with each vertex a very large total weight, and predecessor associates with each vertex an empty vertex. We then refine those initializations by mapping $v1$'s weightSum to 0.0, mapping $v1$'s predecessor to $v1$ itself, and adding $<v1, 0.0>$ to pq. This completes the initialization phase.

Suppose we want to find the shortest path from A to E in the network from Figure 15.9, repeated here:

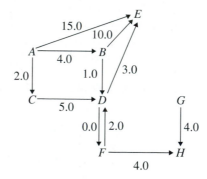

Initially, we have

| weightSum | predecessor | pq |
|---|---|---|
| A, 0.0 | A | <A, 0.0> |
| B, 10000.0 | **null** | |
| C, 10000.0 | **null** | |
| D, 10000.0 | **null** | |
| E, 10000.0 | **null** | |
| F, 10000.0 | **null** | |
| H, 10000.0 | **null** | |

After initializing, we keep looping until the shortest path is found or pq is empty. During the first iteration of this loop, the minimum (and only) pair, $<A, 0.0>$, is removed from pq. Since that pair's weight, 0.0, is less than or equal to A's weightSum value, we iterate, in an inner loop, over the neighbors of *A*. For each neighbor, weight Sum and predecessor are updated, and the neighbor and its total weight (so far) are added to pq. The effects are shown in Figure 15.25. Note that vertex *G* is ignored because *G* is not reachable from *A*.

After the processing shown in Figure 15.25, the outer loop is executed for a second time: the pair $<C, 2.0>$ is removed from pq and we iterate (the inner loop) over the neighbors of *C*. The only vertex on an edge from *C* is *D*, and the weight of that edge is 5.0. This weight plus 2.0 (*C*'s weight sum) is 7.0, which is less than *D*'s weight sum, 10000.0). So in weightSum, *D*'s weight sum is upgraded to 7.0. Figure 15.26 shows the effect on weightSum, predecessor, and pq.

Figure 15.26 indicates that at this point, the lowest-weight path from *A* to *D* has a total weight of 7.0. During the third iteration of the outer loop, $<B, 4.0>$ is removed from pq and we iterate over the neighbors of *B*, namely, *D* and *E*. The effects are shown in Figure 15.27.

**Figure 15.25** | Dijkstra's shortest-path algorithm, after the first iteration of the outer loop.

| weightSum | predecessor | pq |
|---|---|---|
| A, 0.0 | A | $<C, 2.0>$ |
| B, 4.0 | A | $<B, 4.0>$ |
| C, 2.0 | A | $<E, 15.0>$ |
| D, 10000.0 | **null** | |
| E, 15.0 | A | |
| F, 10000.0 | **null** | |
| H, 10000.0 | **null** | |

**Figure 15.26** | The state of the application of Dijkstra's shortest-path algorithm after the second iteration of the outer loop.

| weightSum | predecessor | pq |
|---|---|---|
| A, 0.0 | A | $<B, 4.0>$ |
| B, 4.0 | A | $<D, 7.0>$ |
| C, 2.0 | A | $<E, 15.0>$ |
| D, 7.0 | C | |
| E, 15.0 | A | |
| F, 10000.0 | **null** | |
| H, 10000.0 | **null** | |

**Figure 15.27** | The state of the application of Dijkstra's shortest-path algorithm after the third iteration of the outer loop.

| weightSum | predecessor | pq |
|---|---|---|
| A, 0.0 | A | $<D, 5.0>$ |
| B, 4.0 | A | $<D, 7.0>$ |
| C, 2.0 | A | $<E, 14.0>$ |
| D, 5.0 | B | $<E, 15.0>$ |
| E, 14.0 | B | |
| F, 10000.0 | **null** | |
| H, 10000.0 | **null** | |

At this point, the lowest-weight path to D has a total weight of 5.0 and the lowest-weight path to E has a total weight of 14.0. During the fourth iteration of the outer loop, <D, 5.0> is removed from pq, and we iterate over the neighbors of D, namely, F and E. Figure 15.28 shows the effects of this iteration.

During the fifth outer-loop iteration, <F, 5.0> is removed from pq, the neighbors of F, namely D and H, are examined, and the collections are updated. See Figure 15.29.

During the sixth iteration of the outer loop, <D, 7.0> is removed from pq. The minimum total weight, so far, from A to D is recorded in weightsum as 5.0. So there is no inner-loop iteration.

During the seventh iteration of the outer loop, <E, 8.0> is removed from pq. Because E is the vertex we want to find the shortest path to, we are done. How can we be sure there are no shorter paths to E? If there were another path to E with total weight $t$ less than 8.0, then the pair <E, $t$> would have been removed from pq before the pair <E, 8.0>.

We construct the shortest path, as a LinkedList of vertices, from predecessor: starting with an empty LinkedList object, we prepend E; then prepend D, the predecessor of E; then prepend B, the predecessor of D; finally, prepend A, the predecessor of B. The final contents of the LinkedList object are, in order,

A, B, D, E

**Figure 15.28** | The state of the application of Dijkstra's shortest-path algorithm after the fourth iteration of the outer loop.

| weightSum | predecessor | pq |
|---|---|---|
| A, 0.0 | A | <F, 5.0> |
| B, 4.0 | A | <D, 7.0> |
| C, 2.0 | A | <E, 8.0> |
| D, 5.0 | B | <E, 14.0> |
| E, 8.0 | D | <E, 15.0> |
| F, 5.0 | D | |
| H, 10000.0 | **null** | |

**Figure 15.29** | The state of the application of Dijkstra's shortest-path algorithm after the fifth iteration of the outer loop.

| weightSum | predecessor | pq |
|---|---|---|
| A, 0.0 | A | <D, 7.0> |
| B, 4.0 | A | <E, 8.0> |
| C, 2.0 | A | <H, 9.0> |
| D, 5.0 | B | <E, 14.0> |
| E, 8.0 | D | <E, 15.0> |
| F, 5.0 | D | |
| H, 9.0 | F | |

There are a few details that are missing in the above description of Dijkstra's algorithm. For example, how will the vertices, edges, and neighbors be stored? What are worstTime($n$) and averageTime($n$)? To answer these questions, we will develop a network class in Section 15.6.3, and fill in the missing details.

### 15.5.5 Finding the Longest Path through a Network?

Interestingly, it is often important to be able to find a longest path through a network. A *project network* is an acyclic, not; directed network with a single *source* (no arrows coming into it) and a single *sink* (no arrows going out from it). The source and sink are usually labeled $S$ (for start) and $T$ (for terminus), respectively. Figure 15.30 shows a project network.

We can interpret the edges in a project network as activities to be performed, the weights as the time in days (or cost in dollars) required for the activities, and the vertices as events that indicate the completion of all activities coming into the event. With that interpretation, the *project length,* that is, the length of a longest path, represents the number of days required to complete the project. For example, in Figure 15.30, there are two longest paths:

$S, A, B, E, T$

and

$S, C, F, T$

Each of those paths has a length of 42, so the project, as scheduled, will take 42 days. Dijkstra's algorithm can easily be modified to find a longest path.

In a project network, some activities can occur concurrently, and some activities can be delayed without affecting the project length. A project manager may want to know *which* activities can be delayed without delaying the entire project. First, we need to make some calculations.

For each event $w$, we can calculate ET($w$), the *earliest time* that event $w$ can be completed. For event $S$, ET($S$) is 0. For any other event $w$, ET($w$) is the maximum of $\{$ET($v$) + weight $(v, w)\}$ for any event $v$ such that $<v, w>$ forms an edge. For example, in Figure 15.30, ET($C$) = 6, ET ($B$) = max $\{12, 18, 11\}$ = 18, ET($E$) = 23, ET($D$) = max $\{21, 27\}$ = 27, and so on.

**Figure 15.30** | A project network.

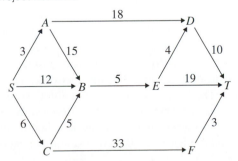

For each event $w$, we can also calculate LT($w$), the ***latest time*** by which $w$ must be completed to avoid delaying the entire project. For event $T$, LT($T$) is the project length; for any other event $w$, LT($w$) is the minimum of $\{$LT($x$) − weight($w$, $x$)$\}$ for any event $x$ such that $<w, x>$ forms an edge. For example, in Figure 15.30, LT($T$) = 42, LT($D$) = 32, LT($E$) = min $\{28, 23\}$ = 23, LT($B$) = 18, LT($C$) = min $\{6, 13\}$ = 6, and so on.

Finally, ST($y$, $z$), the ***slack time*** of activity $<y, z>$, is calculated as follows:

$$ST(y, z) = LT(z) − ET(y) − \text{weight}(y, z)$$

An activity's slack time is the amount of time by which that activity can be delayed or extended without increasing the project length. For example, in Figure 15.30,

$$ST(S, C) = LT(C) − ET(S) − \text{weight}(S, C) = 6 − 0 − 6 = 0$$
$$ST(A, B) = LT(B) − ET(A) − \text{weight}(A, B) = 18 − 3 − 15 = 0$$
$$ST(A, D) = LT(D) − ET(A) − \text{weight}(A, D) = 32 − 3 − 18 = 11$$

An activity with a slack time of zero is called a ***critical activity,*** and any path that consists only of critical activities is called a ***critical path.*** The idea is that special attention should be given to any critical activity because any delay in that activity will lengthen the project length.

Activities that are not on a critical path are less constrained: They may be delayed or take longer than scheduled without affecting the length of the entire project. For example, in Figure 15.30, the activity $<A, D>$ has a slack time of 11 days: That activity can be delayed or take longer than scheduled, as long as the activity is completed by day 32. The significance of this is that resources allocated to activity $<A, D>$ can be diverted to a critical task, and thereby speed up the completion of the entire project.

Programming Project 15.3 entails finding the slack time for each project in a project network. In order to calculate the earliest times for each event, the events must be ordered so that for example, when ET($w$) is to be calculated for some vertex $w$, the value of ET($v$) must already be available for each vertex $v$ such that $<v, w>$ forms an edge. The next section describes that kind of ordering.

**Topological Sorting**    The calculation of earliest times and latest times for the project network in Section 15.5.5 requires that the events be in order. Specifically, to calculate ET($w$) for some vertex $w$, we need to know ET($v$), for any vertex $v$ such that $<v, w>$ forms an edge. If the project network is small and the calculations are being done by hand, this ordering can be made implicitly. But for a large project, or for a program to perform the calculations, the ordering must be explicit. To calculate LT($w$) for any vertex $w$, the reverse of this ordering is needed.

The ordering is not, necessarily, the one provided by a breadth-first iterator, a depth-first iterator, or an iterator over the entire network. The ordering is called a "topological ordering." The vertices $v_1$, $v_2$, . . . of a digraph are in ***topological order*** if $v_i$ precedes $v_j$ in the ordering whenever $<v_i, v_j>$ forms an edge in the digraph. The arranging of vertices into a topological ordering is called ***topological sorting.*** For example, for the digraph in Figure 15.30, here is a topological order:

*S, A, C, B, E, F, D, T*

Notice that *D* had to come after both *A* and *E* because *<A, D>* and *<E, D>* are edges in the digraph. Another topological order is

*S, A, C, F, B, E, D, T*

Concept Exercise 15.17 has more information about topological order, and Programming Exercise 15.4 suggests how to perform a topological sort.

# 15.6 | A Network **CLASS**

In this chapter, we have introduced eight different data types: a graph and a tree, each of which can be directed or undirected, and weighted or unweighted. We would like to develop classes for these collections with a maximum amount of code sharing. The object-oriented solution is to utilize inheritance, but exactly how should this be done? If we make the Digraph class a subclass of UndirectedGraph, then virtually all of the code relating to edges will have to be overridden. That's because in an undirected graph, each edge *A, B* represents two links: from *A* to *B* and from *B* to *A*. Similarly, code written for graphs would have to be rewritten for networks.

A better approach is to define the (directed) Network class, and make the other classes subclasses of that class. For example, we can view an undirected network as a directed network in which all edges are two-way. So to add an edge *A, B* in an undirected network, the method is:

```
/**
 * Ensures that a given edge with a given weight is in this UndirectedNetwork
 * object.
 *
 * @param v1 – the first vertex of the edge.
 * @param v2 – the second vertex of the edge (the neighbor of v1).
 * @param weight – the weight of the edge (v1, v2).
 *
 * @return true – if this UndirectedNetwork object changed as a result of this call.
 *
 */
public boolean addEdge (Vertex v1, Vertex v2, double weight)
{
        return super.addEdge (v1, v2, weight) && super.addEdge (v2, v1, weight);
} // method addEdge in UndirectedNetwork class, a subclass of Network
```

Furthermore, we can view a digraph as a network in which all weights have the value of 1.0. The Digraph class will have the following method:

```
/**
 * Ensures that a given edge with a given weight is in this UndirectedNetwork
 * object.
 *
```

```
* @param v1 – the first vertex of the edge.
* @param v2 – the second vertex of the edge (the neighbor of v1).
* @param weight – the weight of the edge (v1, v2).
*
* @return true – if this UndirectedNetwork object changed as a result of this call.
*
*/
public boolean addEdge (Vertex v1, Vertex v2)
{
        return super.addEdge (v1, v2, 1.0);
} // method addEdge in DiGraph class, a subclass of Network
```

Figure 15.31 shows the inheritance hierarchy. Technically, the hierarchy is not a tree because in the Unified Modeling Language, the arrows go from the subclass to the superclass.

In the following section, we develop a (directed) Network class, that is, a weighted digraph class. The development of the subclasses—DirectedWeightedTree, DirectedTree, Digraph, UndirectedNetwork, UndirectedWeightedTree, Undirected Graph, and UndirectedTree—are left as programming exercises.

The class heading, with Vertex as the type parameter, is

```
public class Network<Vertex> implements Iterable<Vertex>
```

The Iterable interface has only one method, iterator( ), which returns an iterator that implements hasNext( ) and next( )—and may implement other methods (such as remove( ) and previous( )). By implementing the Iterable interface, we are able to utilize the enhanced **for** statement for Network objects. We have not mentioned the Iterable interface up to now because we have applied the enhanced **for** statement

**Figure 15.31** I The UML inheritance hierarchy for the collections in this chapter.

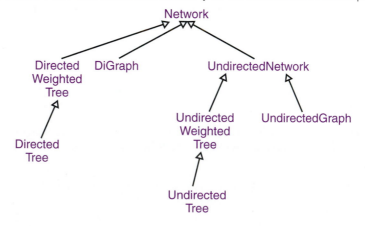

only to instances of classes that implement the Collection interface. The start of that interface is

> **public class** Collection $<$E$>$ **implements** Iterable$<$E$>$

An important issue in developing the Network class is to decide what public methods the class should have: these constitute the abstract data–type network, that is, the user's view of the Network class. For the Network class, we have vertex-related methods, edge-related methods, and network-as-a-whole methods. To simplify matters, we estimate average times only, with $V$ representing the number of vertices and $E$ representing the number of edges. If the specifications do not include time estimates, you may assume that averageTime($V, E$) is constant.

## 15.6.1 **Method Specifications of the** Network **Class**

Here are the vertex-related method specifications:

```
/**
 * Determines if this Network object contains a specified Vertex object.
 *
 * @param vertex – the Vertex object whose presence is sought.
 *
 * @return true – if vertex is an element of this Network object.
 *
 */
public boolean containsVertex (Vertex vertex)

/**
 * Ensures that a specified Vertex object is an element of this Network object.
 *
 * @param vertex – the Vertex object whose presence is ensured.
 *
 * @return true – if vertex was added to this Network object by this call; returns
 *         false if vertex was already an element of this Network object when
 *         this call was made.
 *
 */
public boolean addVertex (Vertex vertex)

/**
 * Ensures that a specified Vertex object is not an element of this Network object.
 * The averageTime (V, E) is O(E).
 *
 * @param vertex – the Vertex object whose absence is ensured.
 *
 * @return true – if vertex was removed from this Network object by this call;
 *         returns false if vertex was not an element of this Network object
 *         when this call was made.
```

```
        *
        */
    public boolean removeVertex (Vertex vertex)

    /**
        * Returns a LinkedList object of the neighbors of a specified Vertex object.
        *
        * @param v – the Vertex object whose neighbors are returned.
        *
        * @return a LinkedList of the vertices that are neighbors of v.
        *
        */
    public LinkedList<Vertex> neighbors (Vertex v)
```

Here are the edge-related method specifications:

```
    /**
        * Returns the number of edges in this Network object.
        * The averageTime (V, E) is O (V).
        *
        * @return the number of edges in this Network object.
        *
        */
    public int getEdgeCount( )

    /**
        * Determines the weight of an edge in this Network object.
        * The averageTime (V, E) is O (E / V).
        *
        * @param v1 – the beginning Vertex object of the edge whose weight is sought.
        * @param v2 – the ending Vertex object of the edge whose weight is sought.
        *
        * @return the weight of edge <v1, v2>, if <v1, v2> forms an edge; return –1.0 if
        *         <v1, v2> does not form an edge in this Network object.
        *
        */
    public double getEdgeWeight (Vertex v1, Vertex v2)

    /**
        * Determines if this Network object contains an edge specified by two vertices.
        * The averageTime (V, E) is O (E / V).
        *
        * @param v1 – the beginning Vertex object of the edge sought.
        * @param v2 – the ending Vertex object of the edge sought.
        *
        * @return true – if this Network object contains the edge <v1, v2>.
        *
        */
    public boolean containsEdge (Vertex v1, Vertex v2)
```

```
/**
 * Ensures that an edge is in this Network object.
 *
 * The averageTime(V, E) is O(E/V).
 *
 * @param v1 – the beginning Vertex object of the edge whose presence is ensured.
 * @param v2 – the ending Vertex object of the edge whose presence is ensured.
 * @param weight – the weight of the edge whose presence is ensured.
 *
 * @return true – if the given edge (and weight) were added to this Network
 *       object by this call; return false, if the given edge (and weight)
 *       were already in this Network object when this call was made.
 *
 */
public boolean addEdge (Vertex v1, Vertex v2, double weight)

/**
 * Ensures that an edge specified by two vertices is absent from this Network
 * object.
 * The averageTime (V, E) is O (E / V).
 *
 * @param v1 – the beginning Vertex object of the edge whose absence is ensured.
 * @param v2 – the ending Vertex object of the edge whose absence is ensured.
 *
 * @return true – if the edge <v1, v2> was removed from this Network object
 *       by this call; return false if the edge <v1, v2> was not in this
 *       Network object when this call was made.
 *
 */
public boolean removeEdge (Vertex v1, Vertex v2)
```

Finally, we have the method specifications for those methods that apply to the network as a whole, including three flavors of iterators:

```
/**
 * Initialized this Network object to be empty.
 *
 */
public Network( )

/**
 * Initializes this Network object to have a specified initial capacity.
 *
 * @param capacity – the initial capacity of this Network object.
 *
 * @throws IllegalArgumentException – if capacity is less than 0.
 *
 */
```

**public** Network (**int** capacity)

```
/**
 * Initializes this Network object to a shallow copy of a specified Network
 * object.
 * The averageTime(V, E) is O(E).
 *
 * @param network – the Network object that this Network object is
 *        initialized to a shallow copy of.
 *
 */
```

**public** Network (Network<Vertex> network)

```
/**
 * Determines if this Network object contains no vertices.
 *
 * @return true – if this Network object contains no vertices.
 *
 */
```

**public boolean** isEmpty( )

```
/**
 * Determines the number of vertices in this Network object.
 *
 * @return the number of vertices in this Network object.
 *
 */
```

**public int** size( )

```
/**
 * Returns an Iterator object over the vertices in this Network object.
 *
 * @return an Iterator object over the vertices in this Network object.
 *
 */
```

**public** Iterator<Vertex> iterator( )

```
/**
 * Returns a breadth-first Iterator object over all vertices reachable from
 * a specified Vertex object.
 * The averageTime(V, E) is O(V).
 *
 * @param v – the start Vertex object for the Iterator object returned.
 *
 * @return a breadth-first Iterator object over all vertices reachable from v.
 *
 * @throws IllegalArgumentException – if v is not an element of this Network object.
 *
 */
```

**public** Iterator<Vertex> breadthFirstIterator (Vertex v)

```
/**
 * Returns a depth-first Iterator object over all vertices reachable from
 * a specified Vertex object.
 * The averageTime(V, E) is O(V).
 *
 * @param v – the start Vertex object for the Iterator object returned.
 *
 * @return a depth-first Iterator object over all vertices reachable from v.
 *
 * @throws IllegalArgumentException – if v is not an element of this Network object.
 *
 */
```
**public** Iterator<Vertex> depthFirstIterator (Vertex v)

```
/**
 * Determines if this (directed) Network object is connected.
 * The averageTime(V, E) is O(VE).
 *
 * @return true – if this (directed) Network object is connected.
 *
 */
```
**public boolean** isConnected( )

```
/**
 * Returns a minimum spanning tree for this connected Network object.
 * The averageTime(V, E) is O(E log V).
 *
 * @return a minimum spanning tree for this connected Network object.
 *
 * @throws UnsupportedOperationException – if there is no path from the chosen
 *      root to every other vertex in this Network object.
 *
 */
```
**public** WeightedTree<Vertex> getMinimumSpanningTree( )

```
/**
 * Finds a shortest path between two specified vertices in this Network
 * object, and the total weight of that path.
 * The averageTime(V, E) is O(E log V).
 *
 * @param v1 – the beginning Vertex object.
 * @param v2 – the ending Vertex object.
 *
 * @return a LinkedList object containing the vertices in a shortest path
 *      from Vertex v1 to Vertex v2. The last element in the LinkedList object is
```

```
 *       the total weight of the path.
 *
 */
public LinkedList<Object> getShortestPath (Vertex v1, Vertex v2)

/**
 * Returns a String representation of this Network object.
 * The averageTime(V, E) is O(E).
 *
 * @return a String representation of this Network object.
 *
 */
public String toString( )
```

Before we turn to developer's issues in Section 15.6.2, we illustrate some of the Network class's methods in a **main** method that essentially consists of one method call after another. (There is no attempt at modularization.)

```
public static void main (String[] args)
{
        final String PROMPT1 =
                "\nPlease enter the vertices whose shortest path you want: ";

        final String SENTINEL = "***";

        final String PROMPT2 = "\nPlease enter " +
                "two vertices and a weight (the sentinel is " + SENTINEL + "): ";

        final String SHORTEST_PATH_MESSAGE1 =
                "\n\n\nThe shortest path from ";

        final String SHORTEST_PATH_MESSAGE2 = " and its total weight are ";

        Network<String> network = new Network<String>( );

        BufferedReader reader = new BufferedReader
                (new InputStreamReader (System.in));

        StringTokenizer tokens;

        String start,
               finish,
               vertex1,
               vertex2,
               line;

        double weight;

        try
        {
                // Get start and finish vertices.
                System.out.print (PROMPT1);
```

```
line = reader.readLine( );
tokens = new StringTokenizer (line);
start = tokens.nextToken( );
finish = tokens.nextToken( );

// Get edges and weights.
while (true)
{
        System.out.print (PROMPT2);
        line = reader.readLine( );
        if (line.equals(SENTINEL))
                break;
        tokens = new StringTokenizer (line);
        vertex1 = tokens.nextToken( );
        vertex2 = tokens.nextToken( );
        weight = Double.parseDouble (tokens.nextToken( ));
        network.addEdge (vertex1, vertex2, weight);
} // while

System.out.println ("\nnetwork = " + network);
LinkedList pathList = network.getShortestPath (start, finish);
System.out.println (SHORTEST_PATH_MESSAGE1 + start + " to " + finish
        + SHORTEST_PATH_MESSAGE2 + pathList);
System.out.println ("neighbors of start = " + network.neighbors (start));

boolean networkIsConnected = network.isConnected( );
System.out.println ("is connected is " + networkIsConnected);
if (networkIsConnected)
        System.out.println ("spanning tree = " +
                                network.getMinimumSpanningTree( ));

System.out.println ("empty is " + network.isEmpty( ));
System.out.println ("vertex count = " + network.size( ));
System.out.println ("edge count = " + network.getEdgeCount( ));
System.out.println ("contains f is " + network.containsVertex ("f"));
System.out.println ("contains edge a t is " + network.containsEdge ("a", "t"));
System.out.println("contains edge a d is " + network.containsEdge ("a", "d"));

System.out.println ("\n\nbreadth-first iterating from " + start + ": ");
Iterator itr = network.breadthFirstIterator (start);
while (itr.hasNext( ))
        System.out.print (itr.next( ) + " ");

System.out.println ("\n\ndepth-first iterating from " + start + ": ");
itr = network.depthFirstIterator (start);
while (itr.hasNext( ))
        System.out.print (itr.next( ) + " ");

System.out.println ("\n\niterating over network:");
```

```
                    for (String s : network)

                    System.out.print (s + " ");
                    network.removeEdge ("b", "c");
                    network.removeVertex ("d");
                    System.out.println ("\n\niterating over network after removing b-c and d:");
                    for (String s : network)
                            System.out.print (s + " ");

                    System.out.println ("\n\nedge weight of a b is " +
                            network.getEdgeWeight ("a", "b"));

                    pathList = network.getShortestPath (start, finish);
                    System.out.println (SHORTEST_PATH_MESSAGE1 + start + " to "
                                    + finish + SHORTEST_PATH_MESSAGE2
                                    + pathList);
            } // try
            catch (IOException e)
            {
                    System.out.println (e);
            } // catch
    } // method main
```

## 15.6.2  **Fields in the** Network **Class**

As usual, the fundamental decisions about designing a class involve selecting its
fields. In the (directed) Network class, we will associate with each vertex *v* the collection of all vertices that are adjacent to *v*. That is, a vertex *w* will be included in
this collection if $<v, w>$ forms an edge. Because this is a network, we will include
with each adjacent vertex the weight of the edge. In other words, we will associate
with each vertex *v* in the Network object the collection of all vertex-weight pairs of
the form

$<w, \text{weight}>$

where $<v, w>$ forms an edge with given weight.

Two questions still remain: What collection will be used to hold "all vertex-
weight pairs", and what collection will be used to hold the association of each vertex to its "all vertex-weight pairs" collection?

To answer the first question, we do not know beforehand how many vertex-
weight pairs there will be, and the order of the vertex-weight pairs is not important.
We will probably want to iterate over all of the vertex-weight pairs associated with a
given vertex, so we will choose a LinkedList object to hold the vertex-weight pairs.
The nested VertexWeightPair class will have methods VertexWeightPair (Vertex vertex,
**double** weight), getVertex( ), getWeight( ), equals (Object obj), compareTo (Object
obj), and toString( ). The compareTo method returns the result of comparing the two
weights.

To answer the second question, we need a collection to associate a given vertex
*v* with the LinkedList object whose elements are vertex-weight pairs $<w, \text{weight}>$,

where $<v, w>$ is an edge with weight weight. The crucial feature of this association is that, given a vertex $v$, we want to quickly access the associated LinkedList. As the term "association" suggests, we will "map" each vertex to its LinkedList. For speed, a HashMap object is indicated. Recall from Chapter 14 that the averageTime for inserting, removing, or searching a HashMap object is constant—provided the Uniform Hashing Assumption holds. For the remainder of this chapter, we assume that the Uniform Hashing Assumption does hold.

In summary, the only field in the Network class is

> **protected** HashMap<Vertex,
>      LinkedList<VertexWeightPair> adjacencyMap;

Each key in a HashMap object will be a vertex. Each value will be a LinkedList object whose elements are VertexWeightPair objects. Because each vertex is associated with a list of its adjacent vertices, this representation is referred to as an ***adjacency list*** representation.

Figure 15.32 shows a simple network, and Figure 15.33 shows its internal representation. Figure 15.33 has two kinds of linked lists. The HashMap class stores the two entries that hash to 6 in a singly linked list at that index. And for each entry in the HashMap, there is also a LinkedList object of vertex-weight pairs corresponding to an edge. In those LinkedList objects, the header field is not shown, and the previous field in each vertex-weight-pair entry is not shown.

The default constructor for the HashMap class creates a table whose length is 16. (The HashMap class in the Java Collections Framework uses chaining and requires that the table length be a power of 2; if, instead, we chose open-address hashing with quotient offsets, the table length should be prime.) The index in adjacencyMap for any vertex v is determined by

> hash (v) & 15

For example, for the vertex "Karen", the hashCode method in the String class returns 72266597, the static hash method in the HashMap class further jumbles this to $-713494077$; the index is calculated as $-713494077 \ \& \ 15 = 3$.

**Figure 15.32** | A network whose internal representation is shown in Figure 15.33.

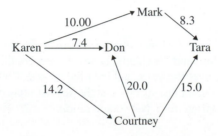

**Figure 15.33 |** The internal representation of the network in Figure 15.32. Each Entry in adjacencyMap object consists of four fields: hash, key, value, and next. Each value is a LinkedList. Each Entry in a LinkedList object consists of three fields: previous (not shown), element— a VertexWeightPair object—and next.

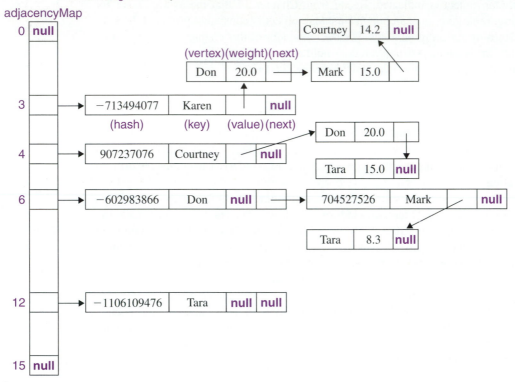

### 15.6.3 **Method Definitions in the** Network **Class**

Because the only field in the Network class is HashMap object, there are several one-line method definitions. For example, to iterate over all vertices in the Network object, we apply the iterator( ) method from the keySet view of a HashMap:

```
public Iterator<Vertex> iterator( )
{
        return adjacencyMap.keySet( ).iterator( );
} // method iterator
```

For the Network class, an iteration is performed over the vertices in the network, whereas for the HashMap (and TreeMap) classes, there were three choices for an iteration: over the entries, over the keys, and over the values. That is why the iterator( ) method in the Network class must specify that the key-set view of the HashMap object adjacencyMap is appropriate for a Network iteration.

Adding a vertex to a Network object is straightforward:

```
public boolean addVertex (Vertex vertex)
{
        if (adjacencyMap.containsKey (vertex))
                return false;
        adjacencyMap.put (vertex, new LinkedList<VertexWeightPair>( ));
        return true;
} // method addVertex
```

Because all of the action is centered on a HashMap object, the number of vertices and edges does not affect timing, at least on average. That is, averageTime($V, E$) is constant, where $V$ is the number of vertices and $E$ is the number of edges.

The definition of removeVertex requires some work. It is easy to remove a Vertex object vertex from adjacencyMap, and thus remove its associated LinkedList object of edges going out from vertex. But each edge going *into* vertex must also be removed. Since the edge information is stored in a vertex-weight pair in a LinkedList object, we will iterate over all vertices in the Network object. For each vertex in the network, we iterate over its linked list of vertex-weight pairs looking for vertex, the vertex to be removed. Whenever vertex is found in one of those vertex-weight pairs, the vertex-weight pair is removed from that linked list. Here is the definition:

```
/**
 * Ensures that a specified Vertex object is not an element of this Network object.
 * The averageTime (V, E) is O (E).
 *
 * @param vertex – the Vertex object whose absence is ensured.
 *
 * @return true – if vertex was removed from this Network object by this call;
 *         returns false if vertex was not an element of this Network object
 *         when this call was made.
 *
 */
public boolean removeVertex (Vertex vertex)
{
        if (!adjacencyMap.containsKey (vertex))
                return false;

        for (Vertex v : adjacencyMap.keySet( ))
        {
                LinkedList<VertexWeightPair>list = adjacencyMap.get(v);

                // If vertex is in a vertex-weight pair on list, remove that pair from list.
                Iterator<VertexWeightPair> listItr = list.iterator( );
                while (listItr.hasNext( ))
                        if ((listItr.next( )).getVertex( ).equals (vertex))
                        {
```

```
                            listItr.remove( );
                            break;
                    } // vertex-weight pair found and removed from list
            } // while iterating over all vertices
            adjacencyMap.remove (vertex);
            return true;
    } // removeVertex
```

How long does this take? The total number of iterations of the outer loop is *V,* and the total number of iterations of the inner loop varies from 0 to *E,* so averageTime(*V, E*) is linear in *V + E,* which is linear in *E.*

Next, we'll develop the definition of an edge-related method. To count the number of edges in a Network object, we use the fact that the size of any vertex's associated LinkedList object represents the number of edges going out from that vertex. So we iterate over all the vertices in the Network object, and accumulate the sizes of the associated linked lists. Here is the definition:

```
    /**
     * Returns the number of edges in this Network object.
     * The averageTime (V, E) is O (V).
     *
     * @return the number of edges in this Network object.
     *
     */
    public int getEdgeCount( )
    {
            int count = 0;

            for (Vertex vertex : adjacencyMap.keySet( ))
                    count += (adjacencyMap.get (vertex)).size( );
            return count;
    } // method getEdgeCount
```

The getEdgeCount method iterates over all vertices in the network, so average Time(*V, E*) is linear in *V.*

Before we get to the methods that deal with the Network object as a whole, we need to say a few words about the BreadthFirstIterator class (similar comments apply to the DepthFirstIterator class).

The main issue with regard to the BreadthFirstIterator class is how to ensure a quick determination of whether a given vertex has been reached. To this end, we make reached a HashMap object, with Vertex keys and Boolean values. The heading and fields of this embedded class are:

```
    protected class BreadthFirstIterator implements Iterator<Vertex>
    {

            protected PureQueue<Vertex> queue;
```

> **protected** HashMap<Vertex, Boolean> reached;
>
> **protected** Vertex current;

From this point, the method definitions in the BreadthFirstIterator class closely follow the algorithms in Section 15.5.1 For a time estimate of the next( ) method, assume, for the sake of simplicity, that the network is connected. Then an iteration over the whole network loops through $V$ vertices, and for each vertex, its associated linked list is iterated over. So for all $V$ calls to the next( ) method, the total number of iterations is approximately $V + E$. We conclude that, for the next( ) method, averageTime($V, E$) is linear in $(V + E)/V$, that is, linear in $E/V$.

Last, but by no means least, is the getShortestPath method to find a shortest path from vertex v1 to vertex v2. We start by filling in some of the details from the earlier outline. For the sake of speed, weightSum will be a HashMap object that associates each Vertex object w with the sum of the weights of all the edges on the shortest path so far from v1 to w. Similarly, predecessor will be a HashMap object that associates each vertex w with the vertex that is the immediate predecessor of w on the shortest path so far from v1 to w.

The heading and variables in the getShortestMap method are as follows:

```
/**
 * Finds a shortest path between two specified vertices in this Network object.
 * The averageTime(V, E) is O(E log V).
 *
 * @param v1 – the beginning Vertex object.
 * @param v2 – the ending Vertex object.
 *
 * @return a LinkedList object containing the vertices in a shortest path
 *         from Vertex v1 to Vertex v2.
 *
 */
public LinkedList<Object> getShortestPath (Vertex v1, Vertex v2)
{
        final double MAX_PATH_WEIGHT = Double.MAX_VALUE;

        HashMap<Vertex,Double> weightSum = new HashMap<Vertex,Double>( );

        HashMap<Vertex,Vertex> predecessor = new HashMap<Vertex,Vertex>( );

        PurePriorityQueue<VertexWeightPair> pq =
                                new Heap<VertexWeightPair>( );
        Iterator<VertexWeightPair> listItr;

        Vertex vertex,
               to = null,
               from;

        VertexWeightPair vertexWeightPair;

        double weight;
```

If either v1 or v2 is not in the Network, we return an empty LinkedList and we are done. Otherwise, we perform the initializations referred to in Section 15.5.4. Here is this initialization code:

```
if (! (adjacencyMap.containsKey (v1) && adjacencyMap.containsKey (v2)))
        return new LinkedList<Object>( );
Iterator<Vertex> netItr = breadthFirstIterator(v1);
while (netItr.hasNext( ))
{
        vertex = netItr.next( );
        weightSum.put (vertex, MAX_PATH_WEIGHT);
        predecessor.put (vertex, null);
} // initializing weightSum and predecessor
weightSum.put (v1, 0.0);
predecessor.put (v1, v1);
pq.add (new VertexWeightPair (v1, 0.0));
```

Now we find the shortest path, if there is one, from v1 to v2. As noted in Section 15.5.4, we have an outer loop that removes a vertex-weight pair <from, total Weight> from pq and then an inner loop that iterates over the neighbors of from. The purpose of this inner loop is to see if any of those neighbors to can have its weight Sum value reduced to from's weightSum value plus the weight of the edge <from, to>. Here are these nested loops:

```
boolean pathFound = false;
while (!pathFound && !pq.isEmpty( ))
{

        vertexWeightPair = pq.removeMin( );
        from = vertexWeightPair.getVertex( );
        if (from.equals (v2))
                pathFound = true;
        else if (vertexWeightPair.getWeight( ) <= weightSum.get(from))
        {
                for (VertexWeightPair pair : adjacencyMap.get (from))
                {
                        to = pair.getVertex( );
                        weight = pair.getWeight( );
                        if (weightSum.get (from) + weight < weightSum.get (to))
                        {
                                weightSum.put (to, weightSum.get (from) + weight);
                                predecessor.put (to, from);
                                pq.add (new VertexWeightPair (to,weightSum.get (to)));
                        } // if
                } // while from's neighbors have not been processed
        } // else path not yet found
} // while not done and priority queue not empty
```

All that remains is to create the path. We start by inserting v2 into an empty LinkedList object, and then, using the predecessor map, keep *prepending* predecessors until v1 is prepended. Finally, we add v2's total weight, as a Double object, to the end of this LinkedList object, and return the LinkedList object. Note that this LinkedList object has Object as the type parameter because the list contains both vertices and Double values. Here is the remaining code in the getShortestPath method:

```
LinkedList<Object> path = new LinkedList<Object>( );
if (pathFound)
{
        Vertex current = v2;
        while (!(current.equals (v1)))
        {
                path.addFirst (current);
                current = predecessor.get (current);
        } // while not back to v1
        path.addFirst (v1);
} // if path found
path.addLast (weightSum.get (v2));
return path;
```

We now estimate averageTime(*V, E*) for the getShortestPath method. We'll first establish upper bounds for averageTime(*V, E*). For each edge <x, y>, y will be added to pq provided

weightSum.get (x) + weight of <x, y> is less than weightSum.get (y)

Because the vertex at the end of each edge may be added to pq, the size of pq—and therefore the number of outer-loop iterations—is O(*E*). During each outer-loop iteration, one vertex-weight pair is removed from the pq, and this requires O(log *E*) iterations (in the removeMin method). Also, for each removal of a vertex y, there is an inner loop in which each edge <y, z> is examined to see if z should be added to pq. The total number of edges examined during all of these inner-loop iterations is O(*E*).

From the previous paragraph, we see that the total number of iterations, on average is O(*E* log *E* + *E*). We conclude that averageTime(*V, E*) is O(*E* log *E* + *E*). Also,

$$O(E \log E + E) = O(E \log E) = O(E \log V)$$

The last equality follows from the fact that $\log E \le \log V^2 = 2 \log V$. We have average Time(*V, E*) is O(*E* log *V*). If the (directed) network is connected, $V \le E$, and so log *E* $\ge$ log *V*. All of the upper bounds on iterations from above are also lower bounds, and we conclude that averageTime(*V, E*) is $\Theta$(*E* log *V*). Incidentally, worstTime(*V, E*) is also $\Theta$(*E* log *V*).

The complete Network class, the main method from Section 15.6.1, and a driver class are available from the book's website.

Lab 23 introduces the best-known network problem, further explores the greedy-algorithm design pattern, and touches on the topic of *very hard* problems.

 **Lab 23: The Traveling Salesperson Problem**

You are now ready for Lab 23.                    All Labs Are Optional

### 15.6.4 Alternative Implementation of the Network Class

In the above implementation of the Network class, vertices were stored as keys in a HashMap object. Each value field in the HashMap was an adjacency list of vertex-weight pairs, specifically, a linked list of the neighbors (and edge weights) of the vertex key. This adjacency-list implementation works well for *sparse* networks, that is, networks in which the number of edges is not much larger than the number of vertices. In any connected, directed network, we must have

$$V \leq E \leq V(V - 1)$$

There are $E$ edges in $V$ adjacency lists, so the average size of an adjacency list is $E/V$.

For the containsEdge method, one adjacency list is searched, so the average Time($V, E$) is linear in $E/V$. If the number of edges is linear in $V$, then the average size of each adjacency list will be constant, and we can quickly iterate through an adjacency list to determine if the network has a given edge. On the other hand, if the number of edges is quadratic in $V$, the average size of an adjacency list will be linear in $V$. This implies that for the iteration, necessarily sequential, through an adjacency list, averageTime($V, E$) is linear in $V$, and that is also averageTime($V, E$) for the entire containsEdge method if the number of edges is quadratic in $V$.

Another common representation of networks uses an adjacency matrix instead of adjacency lists. An *adjacency matrix* is a two-dimensional array with $V$ rows and $V$ columns. At adjacencyMatrix [i] [j] we store the weight of the edge from the ith vertex to the jth vertex. Also, we need to be able to quickly associate a vertex with an array index, and to quickly associate an index with its vertex. For this last task, we create an array of vertices; vertices [i] contains the vertex corresponding to adjacency Matrix [i]—the ith row in the matrix.

For the association of vertices to array indexes, we create vertexMap, a HashMap object in which each key is a vertex and each value is the index corresponding to its vertex key. Figure 15.34 shows the corresponding representation of the network in Figure 15.32, repeated here:

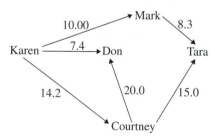

Figure 15.34 assumes the vertices were added to the network in the following order: "Karen", "Mark", "Don", "Courtney", "Tara". Each time a vertex is added to the network, the vertex is stored at the next unoccupied index in the array vertices, and that vertex/index pair is added to the vertexMap object. Note that the entry with "Don" appears in vertexMap before the entry with "Mark" because new entries are prepended to the linked list (of entries whose keys hash to the same index).

There are four fields in this representation:

**double** [ ] [ ] adjacencyMatrix;            // holds the weight of each edge

Vertex [ ] vertices;                          // holds the vertices

HashMap<Vertex, Integer> vertexMap; // associates each vertex with its index

**int** next;                                  // the index in vertices where the next vertex will go

In the constructor that has the initial capacity as its parameter, each slot in adjacencyMatrix is initialized to $-1.0$, the vertices and vertexMap fields are initialized

**Figure 15.34** I An adjacency-matrix representation of a network. An entry of $-1.0$ in the adjacency matrix indicates no edge. For the sake of visibility, the weights of the edges are in boldface.

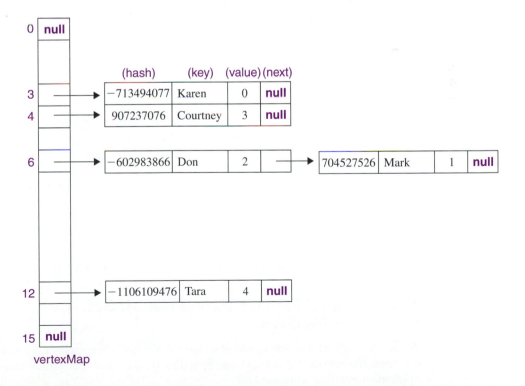

to an empty array and an empty HashMap object, respectively, and next is initialized to 0. Even though all weights are initialized to $-1.0$ in this constructor, average Time($V, E$) is constant because the initial capacity is a fixed value.

The addVertex method returns **false** if the argument vertex is already in the network. Otherwise, the four fields are adjusted and **true** is returned. The average Time($V, E$) is constant—we make the Uniform Hashing Assumption. But in the worst case, a resizing takes place. Because adjacencyMatrix has $V^2$ slots, worst Time($V, E$) is quadratic in $V$. Here is the definition:

```
/**
 * Ensures that a specified Vertex object is an element of this Network object.
 * The worstTime(V, E) is O(V * V).
 *
 * @param vertex – the Vertex object whose presence is ensured.
 *
 * @return true – if vertex was added to this Network object by this call; returns false if
 *        vertex was already an element of this Network object when this call was made.
 *
 */
public boolean addVertex (Vertex vertex)
{
        if (vertexMap.containsKey (vertex))
               return false;
        if (next == vertices.length – 1)
                resize( );
        vertices [next] = vertex;
        vertexMap.put (vertex, next);
        next++;
        return true;
} // method addVertex
```

Quite a few other methods also take constant time, on average: addEdge, contains Vertex, containsEdge, size, isEmpty, getEdgeWeight, removeEdge, and iterator. But for removeVertex, averageTime($V, E$) is quadratic in $V$ because an entire row (and an entire column) in adjacencyMatrix must be removed. Recall that for the adjacency-list version of the Network class in Section 15.6.3, the averageTime($V, E$) for the removeVertex method is linear in $E$. The rest of this implementation of the Network class is the subject of Programming Project 15.1.

The final topic in this chapter is backtracking. In Chapter 5, we saw how backtracking could be used to solve a variety of applications. Now we expand the application domain to include networks and therefore, graphs and trees.

## 15.7 | BACKTRACKING THROUGH A NETWORK

When backtracking was introduced in Chapter 5, we saw three applications in which the basic framework did not change. Specifically, the same BackTrack class and Application interface were used for

1. Searching a maze.
2. Placing eight queens—none under attack by another queen—on a chess board.
3. Illustrating that a knight could traverse every square in a chess board without landing on any square more than once.

A network (or graph or tree) is also suitable for backtracking. For example, suppose we have a network of cities. Each edge weight represents the distance, in miles, between its two cities. Given a start city and a finish city, find a path *in which each edge's distance is less than the previous edge's distance.* Figure 15.35 has sample data; the start and finish cities are given first, followed by each edge. Figure 15.36 depicts the network generated by the data in Figure 15.35.

**Figure 15.35** | A network: The first line contains the start and finish cities; each other line contains two cities and the distance from the first city to the second city.

| | | |
|---|---|---|
| Boston | Washington | |
| Albany | Washington | 371 |
| Boston | Albany | 166 |
| Boston | Hartford | 101 |
| Boston | New York | 214 |
| Boston | Trenton | 279 |
| Harrisburg | Philadelphia | 106 |
| Harrisburg | Washington | 123 |
| New York | Harrisburg | 168 |
| New York | Washington | 232 |
| Trenton | Washington | 178 |

**Figure 15.36** | A network of cities; each edge weight represents the distance between the cities in the edge.

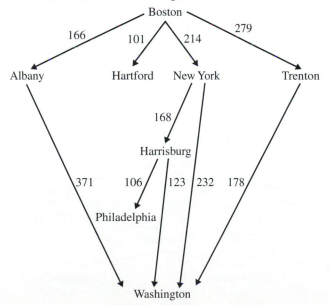

One solution to this problem is the following path:

$$214 \qquad 168 \qquad 123$$
$$\text{Boston} \rightarrow \text{New York} \rightarrow \text{Harrisburg} \rightarrow \text{Washington}$$

A lower-total-weight solution is:

$$279 \qquad 178$$
$$\text{Boston} \rightarrow \text{Trenton} \rightarrow \text{Washington}$$

The lowest-total-weight path is illegal for this problem because the distances increase (from 214 to 232):

$$214 \qquad 232$$
$$\text{Boston} \rightarrow \text{New York} \rightarrow \text{Washington}$$

When a dead end is reached, we can backtrack through the network. The basic strategy with backtracking is to utilize a depth-first search starting at the start position. At each position, we iterate through the neighbors of that position. The order in which neighboring positions are visited is the order in which the corresponding edges are initially inserted into the network. So we are guaranteed to find a solution path if one exists, but not necessarily the lowest-total-weight solution path.

Here is the sequence of steps in the solution generated by backtracking:

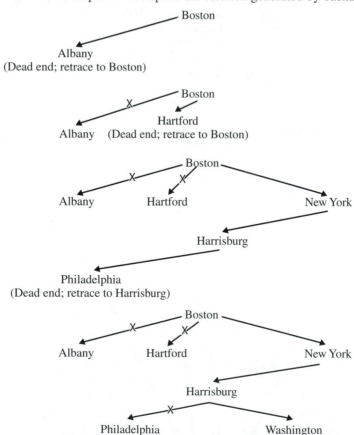

The framework introduced in Chapter 5 supplies the BackTrack class and Application interface. What about the Position class? That class must be modified: row and column have no meaning in a network. And the MazeMain, MazeDriver, and Maze classes must be revised as well. The details are left as Programming Project 15.2.

# SUMMARY

An **undirected graph** consists of a collection of distinct elements called **vertices,** connected to other elements by distinct vertex-pairs called **edges.** If the pairs are ordered, we have a **directed graph.** A **tree,** sometimes called a **directed tree,** is a directed graph that either is empty or has an element, called the **root element** such that:

1.  There are no edges coming into the root element.
2.  Every nonroot element has exactly one edge coming into it.
3.  There is a path from the root to every other element.

A **network** (or undirected network) is a directed graph (or undirected graph) in which each edge has an associated nonnegative number called the **weight** of the edge. Some of the important graph/network algorithms are:

1.  Breadth-first iteration of all vertices reachable from a given vertex.
2.  Depth-first iteration of all vertices reachable from a given vertex.
3.  Determining if a given graph is connected, that is, if for any two vertices, there is a path from the first vertex to the second.
4.  Finding a minimum spanning tree for a network.
5.  Finding a shortest path between two vertices in a network.

One possible implementation of the Network class is to associate, in a HashMap object, each vertex with its neighbors. Specifically, we declare

    HashMap<Vertex, LinkedList<VertexWeightPair>> adjacencyMap;

Here, adjacencyMap is a HashMap object in which each key is a Vertex object v and each value is a LinkedList object of vertex-weight pairs, <w, weight>, where weight is the weight of edge <v, w>. This is referred to as the **adjacency-list** implementation.

An alternative implementation, the **adjacency-matrix** implementation, stores the weights in a two-dimensional array with $V$ rows and $V$ columns, where $V$ is the number of vertices. Specifically, the weight of the edge connecting vertex i and vertex j is stored at adjacencyMatrix [i] [j]. The trade-off for this vertex restriction is that some methods—such as containsEdge—take only constant time, even if the number of edges is quadratic in $V$. With the adjacency-list implementation, the containsEdge method requires linear-in-$V$ time if the number of edges is quadratic in $V$.

Some network problems can be solved through backtracking. The iteration around a given position corresponds to an iteration through the linked list of vertex-weight pairs that comprise the neighbors of a given vertex.

## CONCEPT EXERCISES

**15.1  a.**   Draw a picture of the following undirected graph:

Vertices: *A, B, C, D, E*

Edges: {*A, B*}, {*C, D*}, {*D, A*}, {*B, D*}, {*B, E*}

**15.2  a.**   Draw an undirected graph that has four vertices and as many edges as possible. How many edges does the graph have?

   **b.**   Draw an undirected graph that has five vertices and as many edges as possible. How many edges does the graph have?

   **c.**   What is the maximum number of edges for an undirected graph with *V* vertices, where *V* is any nonnegative integer?

   **d.**   Prove the claim you made in part (c).

   *Hint:* Use induction on *n*.

   **e.**   What is the maximum number of edges for a directed graph with *V* vertices?

**15.3**   Suppose we have the following undirected graph:

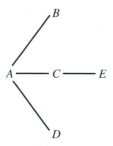

Assume the vertices were inserted into the graph in alphabetical order.

   **a.**   Perform a breadth-first traversal of the undirected graph.

   **b.**   Perform a depth-first traversal of the undirected graph.

**15.4**   Develop a high-level algorithm, based on the isConnected( ) algorithm in Section 15.5.2, to determine if an undirected graph is connected.

**15.5**   For the network given below, determine the shortest path from *A* to *H* by brute force; that is, list all paths and see which one has the lowest total weight.

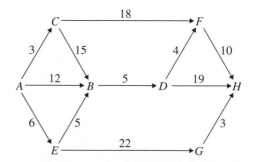

**15.6** For the network given in Concept Exercise 15.5, use Dijkstra's algorithm (getShortestPath) to find the shortest path from *A* to *H*.

**15.7** Prim's algorithm (getMinimumSpanningTree) and Dijkstra's algorithm (getShortestPath) are **greedy:** the locally optimal choice has the highest priority. In these cases, greed succeeds in the sense that the locally optimal choice led to the globally optimal solution. Do all greedy algorithms succeed for all inputs? In this exercise we explore coin-changing algorithms. In one situation, the greedy algorithm succeeds for all inputs. In the other situation, the greedy algorithm succeeds for some inputs and fails for some inputs.

Suppose you want to provide change for any amount under a dollar using as few coins as possible. Since "fewest" is best, the greedy (that is, locally optimal) choice at each step is the coin with largest value whose addition will not surpass the original amount. Here is a method to solve this problem:

```java
/**
 * Prints the change for a given amount, with as few coins (quarters, dimes,
 * nickels and pennies) as possible.
 *
 * @param amount – the amount to be given in change.
 *
 * @throws NumberFormatException – if amount is less than 0 or greater than
 *         99.
 *
 */
public static void printFewest (int amount)
{
        int coin[ ] = {25, 10, 5, 1};

        final String RESULT =
                "With as few coins as possible, here is the change for ";

        System.out.println (RESULT + amount + ":");
        for (int i = 0; i< 4; i++)
                while (coin [i] <= amount)
                {
                        System.out.println (coin [i]);
                        amount -= coin [i];
                } // while
} // printFewest
```

For example, suppose that amount has the value 62. Then the output will be

25
25
10
1
1

Five is the minimum number of coins needed to make 62 cents from quarters, nickels, dimes, and pennies.

**a.** Show that the above algorithm is optimal for any amount between 0 and 99 cents, inclusive. *Hint:* First, consider amounts less than 5 cents, then amounts greater than or equal to 5 cents but less than a dime, and so on.

**b.** Give an example to show that a greedy algorithm is not optimal for all inputs if nickels are not available. That is, if we have

```
int coins[ ] = {25, 10, 1};
...
for (int i = 0; i < 3; i++)
...
```

then the algorithm will not be optimal for some inputs.

**15.8** Ignore the direction of arrows in the figure for Concept Exercise 15.5. Then that figure depicts an undirected network. Use Prim's algorithm to find a minimum spanning tree for that undirected network.

**15.9** Ignore the direction of arrows and assume all weights are 1.0 in the figure for Concept Exercise 15.5. Use Dijkstra's algorithm to find a shortest path (fewest edges) from *A* to *H*.

**15.10** From the adjacency-list implementation of the Network class, define the removeEdge method in the UndirectedNetwork class.

**15.11** If we adopt the adjacency-matrix implementation of the UndirectedNetwork class, what interesting property will adjacencyMatrix possess?

**15.12** Give specific examples of methods to show that the adjacency-list implementation of the Network class is faster (either on average or in the worst case) than the adjacency-matrix implementation if *E* is linear in *V*.

**15.13** Give specific examples of methods to show that the adjacency-matrix implementation of the Network class is faster (either on average or in the worst case) than the adjacency-list implementation if *E* is quadratic in *V*.

**15.14** If *V* is large—say, greater than 100,000—and *E* is quadratic in *V*, which implementation of the Network class would you prefer: adjacency-list or adjacency-matrix?

**15.15** What is the major drawback to the adjacency-matrix implementation of the Network class?

**15.16** Reorder the edges in Figure 15.35 so that the solution path generated by backtracking is different from the solution path provided.

**15.17** For the project network in Figure 15.30, there were two topological orders given. Find three other topological orders. If a project network has a cycle, can its vertices be put into a topological order? Explain.

## PROGRAMMING EXERCISES

**15.1** Create a Network object with vertices *a, b, c, d,* and *e* such that an iteration over the whole network starts at some vertex v and visits the same vertices and in the same order as a breadth-first iteration starting at v and a depth-first iteration starting at v. Use the main method from Section 15.6.1 to test your hypothesis. *Hint:* Enter the vertices, in any order, and run the main method to see the ordering produced by an iteration over the whole network. Then, . . . .

**15.2** Modify Dijkstra's algorithm to find the shortest paths from a given vertex v to all other vertices in a network. Run the main method from Section 15.6.1 to test your modified version of the getShortestPath method.

**15.3** In the main method in Section 15.6.1, the getMinimumSpanningTree method is not called if the network is not connected. In that main method, comment out the line

    if (network.isConnected( ))

Run that main method to create a network that is not connected but for which the getMinimumSpanningTree method still succeeds. *Hint:* Make the network "almost" connected.

**15.4** In the Network class, develop a method to produce a topological order. Here is the specification:

    /**
     * Sorts this acyclic Network object into topological order.
     * The averageTime(V, E) is linear in E.
     *
     * @return an ArrayList object of the vertices in topological order.
     *
     */
    public ArrayList<Vertex> sort( )

*Hint:* First, construct a HashMap object, inCount, that maps each vertex $w$ to the number of vertices to which $w$ is adjacent. For example, if the Network object has three edges of the form $<?, w>$, then inCount will map $w$ to 3 (technically, to **new** Integer (3)). After inCount has been constructed, push onto a stack (or enqueue onto a queue) each vertex that inCount maps to 0. Then loop until the stack is empty. During each loop iteration,

**a.** Pop the stack.

**b.** Append the popped vertex v to an ArrayList object, orderedVertices.

**c.** Decrease the value, in inCount's mapping, of any key w such that $<v, w>$ forms an edge.

**d.** If inCount now maps w to 0, push w onto the stack.

After the execution of the loop, the ArrayList object, containing the vertices in a topological order, is returned.

## Programming Project 15.1

### The Adjacency-Matrix Implementation of the Network Class

Complete, from Section 15.6.4, the adjacency-matrix implementation of the Network class. In light of your implementation and Concept Exercises 15.12 through 15.15, give an overall comparison of the adjacency-list implementation and the adjacency-matrix implementation.

# Programming Project 15.2

## Backtracking through a Network

Given a network in which each vertex is a city and each weight represents the distance between two cities, determine a path from a start city to a finish city in which *each edge's distance is less than the previous edge's distance.*

### Analysis

Each city will be given as a String of at most 14 characters, with no embedded blanks. The first line of input will contain the start city and finish city. Each subsequent line— until the sentinel of ***—will consist of two cities and the distance in miles from the first of those two cities to the second.

There is no input editing to be done. The initial output will be the network. If there is no solution, the final output will be:

There is no solution.

Otherwise the final output will be:

There is a solution:

followed by the edges (from-city, to-city, distance) corresponding to the solution.

### System Test 1 (Input in Boldface):

Please enter the start and finish cities, separated by a blank. Each city name should have no blanks and be at most 14 characters in length.
**Boston Washington**

Please enter two cities and their distance; the sentinel is ***
**Boston NewYork 214**

Please enter two cities and their distance; the sentinel is ***
**Boston Trenton 279**

Please enter two cities and their distance; the sentinel is ***
**Harrisburg Washington 123**

Please enter two cities and their distance; the sentinel is ***
**NewYork Harrisburg 168**

Please enter two cities and their distance; the sentinel is ***
**NewYork Washington 232**

Please enter two cities and their distance; the sentinel is ***
**Trenton Washington 178**
Please enter two cities and their distance; the sentinel is ***
*****

The initial state is as follows:
{Trenton=[Washington 178.0], NewYork=[Harrisburg 168.0, Washington 232.0], Washington=[ ], Harrisburg=[Washington 123.0], Boston=[NewYork 214.0, Trenton 279.0]}

*(continued on next page)*

*(continued from previous page)*

A solution has been found:

| FROM CITY | TO CITY | DISTANCE |
|-----------|---------|----------|
| Boston | NewYork | 214.0 |
| NewYork | Harrisburg | 168.0 |
| Harrisburg | Washington | 123.0 |

**System Test 2 (Input in Boldface):**

Please enter the start and finish cities, separated by a blank. Each city name should have no blanks and be at most 14 characters in length.
**Boston Washington**

Please enter two cities and their distance; the sentinel is ***
**Boston Trenton 279**

Please enter two cities and their distance; the sentinel is ***
**Boston NewYork 214**

Please enter two cities and their distance; the sentinel is ***
**Harrisburg Washington 123**

Please enter two cities and their distance; the sentinel is ***
**NewYork Harrisburg 168**

Please enter two cities and their distance; the sentinel is ***
**NewYork Washington 232**

Please enter two cities and their distance; the sentinel is ***
**Trenton Washington 178**

Please enter two cities and a weight; the sentinel is ***
**\*\*\***

The initial state is as follows:
{Trenton=[Washington 178.0], NewYork=[Harrisburg 168.0, Washington 232.0], Washington=[ ], Harrisburg=[Washington 123.0], Boston=[Trenton 279.0, NewYork 214.0]}

A solution has been found:

| FROM CITY | TO CITY | DISTANCE |
|-----------|---------|----------|
| Boston | Trenton | 279.0 |
| Trenton | Washington | 178.0 |

*Note:* The solution to this system test is different from the solution to System Test 1 because in this system test, the Boston-Trenton edge is entered before the Boston-NewYork edge.

# Programming Project 15.3 (Heavenly Hash!)

## Determining Critical Activities in a Project Network

*Note:* This project assumes the completion of Programming Exercise 15.4.

In the Network class, develop a method to calculate the slack time for each activity in a project network. Here is the method specification:

```
/**
   * Determines the slack time for each activity in this Project Network object.
   * The averageTime(V, E) is linear in E.
   *
   * @return a HashMap object that maps each activity, that is, each
   *         edge triple <v1, v2, weight>, to the slack time for that activity.
   *
   */
  public HashMap<EdgeTriple, Double> getSlackTimes( )
```

*Hint:* First, create a HashMap object, inMap, that maps each vertex v to the LinkedList object of vertex-weight pairs <w, weight> such that <w, v> forms an edge with weight weight. That is, inMap is similar to adjacencyMap except that each vertex v is mapped to the vertices coming into v; in adjacencyMap, each vertex v is mapped to the vertices going out from v.

Then loop through the ArrayList object in topological order. For each vertex v, use inMap to calculate ET(v). (The functional notation ET(v) suggests a mapping, and earliest Time can be another HashMap object!) Then loop through the ArrayList object in reverse order to calculate LT(v) for each vertex v. Then calculate the slack time for each vertex.

## Programming Project 15.4

### Integrated Web Browser and Search Engine, Part 6

This final part of the project involves increasing the relevance count of a given Web page for each other Web page that has a link to the given Web page. For example, suppose the word "network" appears 4 times in the Web page "browser.in11" and "neural" appears 2 times. If the Web pages "home.in1", "browser.in12" and "browser.in13" have a link to "browser.in11", that indicates that "browser.in11" is more relevant than if it had no links to it. So we will increase the relevance count for "browser.in11". For simplicity, we increase the relevance count by 1 for each file that has a link to "browser.in11". So the new relevance count for "browser.in11" will be 9: 4 for "network", 2 for "neural", and 3 for having three Web pages that had links to "browser.in11".

To accomplish this change to the search engine, we need to determine, for each given Web page, the list of other Web pages that have a link to the given Web page. In other words, we need to create a directed graph in which there is an arrow from vertex *A* to vertex *B* if Web page *A* has a link to Web page *B*. For the sake of simplicity, restrict the graph to Web pages that are reachable from "home.in1" (including "home.in1" itself).

One way to accomplish this is as follows: The default constructor, as before, calls processInput ("home.in1"). Within processInput (String s), if **s** has a link to the page link and is not already in the directed graph, add to the graph and call processInput (link). After creating the graph, serialize it to "network.ser".

You will need to modify Browser.java to create the connectivity graph (as a network), and then serialize the graph to "network.ser". This should be done just once, because the connectivity graph is independent of the search string.

After "network.ser" has been created, you will need to deserialize it for your search engine. Unlike the case for "search.ser", you do not reserialize "network.ser" because the network does not change as the result of your searches.

The files home.in1, browser.in10, browser.in11, browser.in12, and browser.in13 are different from before. Network.java and VertexWeightPair.java, differ from Lab 23's versions because these versions are serializable.

You need to develop a version of Browser.java that creates network.ser, GUI BrowserListener.java, a class that implements Comparable and a serializable version of the Vertex class.

Incorporating hyperlink connectivity into a search engine was one of the innovations of Google, and the graduate students who created Google are very wealthy.

System Test 1:

(The end-user searches for "neural network")

Here are the results of the new search for "neural network"

browser.in10 10
browser.in13 9
browser.in11 9
browser.in12 7

(The end-user searches for "network")

Here are the results of the old search for "network"

browser.in11 7
browser.in10 6
browser.in13 5
browser.in12 5

(The end-user clicks on the Back button)

Here are the results of the new search for "neural network"

browser.in10 10
browser.in13 9
browser.in11 9
browser.in12 7

System Test 2:

(The end-user searches for "neural network")

Here are the results of the old search for "neural network"

browser.in10 10
browser.in13 9
browser.in11 9
browser.in12 7

(The end-user searches for "network decree")

Here are the results of the new search for "network decree"

browser.in11 8
browser.in12 7
browser.in10 7
browser.in13 6

# Java Review

This appendix is intended for those who have some background in Java programming, but would be helped by a review. ∎

## A1.1 | JAVA FUNDAMENTALS

Every Java program consists of a collection of classes. A *class* consists of variables, called *fields,* together with functions, called *methods,* that operate on those fields. A program is executed when a special method, the main method, is called by the runtime system (also known as the Java Virtual Machine). The heading of this method is fixed, as shown in the following program:

```
public class HelloWorld
{
        public static void main (String [ ] args)
        {
                System.out.println ("Hello, world!");
        } // method main
} // class HelloWorld
```

The main method in this program calls another method, println, to produce the following output to the console window:

    Hello, world!

Console output, that is, output to the console window on your monitor, is handled by the methods System.out.print and System.out.println.

## A1.2 | PRIMITIVE TYPES

A *primitive type* is a collection of values, together with operations that can be performed on those values. For example, the reserved word **int** denotes the primitive type whose values are integers in the range from about $-2$ billion to 2 billion, and whose operations are addition, subtraction, and so on. A *variable*—also called an *instance*—of type **int** is a location in computer memory that can hold one value of type **int**. The term "variable" is used because the value stored can change during the execution of an instruction. Instead of specifying the location's address, we provide an identifier (that is, a name) and the Java compiler associates the identifier with a location. For example, here is a declaration for an **int** variable whose identifier is score:

    int score;

By a standard abuse of language, we say that score is a variable instead of saying that score is an identifier for a variable. An asignment statement allows us to store a value in a variable. For example,

    score = 0;

stores the value 0 in the variable score. A subsequent assignment can change the value stored:

    score = 88;

The left-hand side of an assignment statement must be a variable, but the right-hand side can be an arbitrary *expression:* any legal combination of symbols that has a value. For example, we can write

    score = (score + 3) / 10;

If score had the value 88 prior to the execution of this assignment statement, then after its execution, score would have the value 9. Note that the division operator, /, returns the result of integer division because the two operands, 91 and 10, are both integers.

Another operator in the **int** type is %, the *modulus operator,* which returns the integer remainder after integer division. For example, 91 % 10 returns the remainder, 1, after 91 is divided by 10. Similarly, 87 % 2 returns 1, $(-37)$ % 5 returns $-2$, and 10 % 91 returns 10.

Java supports eight primitive types, summarized in Table A1.1.

**Table A1.1** | The primitive types.

| Primitive Type | Range | Size |
|---|---|---|
| int | $-2,147,483,648$ to $2,147,483,647$ | 4 bytes |
| long | $-2^{63}$ to $2^{63} -1$ | 8 bytes |
| short | $- 128$ to 127 | 2 bytes |
| byte | $- 64$ to 63 | 1 byte |
| double | $-1.7976931348623157 * 10^{308}$ to $1.7976931348623157 * 10^{308}$ (15 digits of precision) | 8 bytes |
| float | $- 3.4028235 * 10^{38}$ to $3.4028235 * 10^{38}$ (6 digits of precision) | 4 bytes |
| char | | 2 bytes |
| bool | false, true | 1 byte |

## A1.2.1  The char Type

The **char** type stores characters in the Unicode collating sequence, which includes all of the ASCII characters such as 'a', 'A', '?,' and ' ', the blank character. For example, suppose we write

    char delimiter = ' ';

Then delimiter is a variable of type char and contains the value ' '. The Unicode collating sequence also includes other—that is, non-Roman, alphabets—such as Greek, Cyrillic, Arabic, and Hebrew. The Unicode collating sequence holds up to 65,536 ($= 2^{16}$) distinct characters, but only about half of them have been assigned as of now. To include a character such as ☺ in a program, you provide an *escape sequence:* a sequence of symbols that starts with the backslash character, '\' and designates a single character. For example, the escape sequence for the smiley-face character, ☺, is '\u263A', so we can write

    char c = '\u263A';

to declare a **char** variable c and assign the smiley-face character to c.

More importantly, escape sequences are used for print control. For example, '\n' represents the new-line character and '\t' represents the tab character. The execution of

    System.out.println ("We can control\n\noutput with \tprint-control\t\t characters");

will produce output of

    We can control

    output with      print-control      characters

An escape sequence is also needed to print a double quote—otherwise, the double quote would signify the end of the string to be output. For example, the execution of

    System.out.println ("His motto was \"Don't sweat the nickels and dimes!\"");

will produce output of

    His motto was "Don't sweat the nickels and dimes!"

# A1.3 I OBJECTS AND REFERENCES

In addition to variables whose types are primitive, Java also has objects. An *object* is an instance of a class. That is, an object is a variable that has the fields of and can invoke the methods of the class. Objects are not directly declared in Java. Instead, we declare variables, called *reference variables,* that can contain the address of an object. For example, suppose we declare

    String s1;

Then s1 is a reference variable that can contain the address of a String object. If we want s to contain the address of a String object, we can initialize s by invoking the new operator:

```
s1 = new String ("halcyon");
```

The execution of this assignment statement accomplishes the following:

1. A new String object is created.
2. A constructor for the String class is called, which initializes the fields in the newly created String object so that the String object has the value "halcyon".
3. The address of the newly created String object is assigned to s1.

A *constructor* is a method that has the same name as the class, and whose purpose is to initialize an instance of that class.

Technically, s1 is a reference to a String object, but not a String object itself. This distinction is often ignored for the sake of brevity.

In addition to the above constructor, the String class also has a *default* constructor, that is, a constructor with no parameters. We can do the following:

```
String s2 = new String( );
```

The effect of invoking the default constructor is to initialize the String objects fields to represent the empty string: " ". Compare that assignment to

```
String s3 = null;
```

This assigns a special value to s3, a value that is not the address of any object.

Classes can have other methods besides constructors. For example, another method in the String class is concat. Here is the method specification (using javadoc notation):

```
/**
  * Concatenates, that is, joins this String object and a specified String object.
  *
  * @param str – the specified String object to be joined to this String object.
  *
  * @return a new String object formed by concatenating this String
  *       object with str – if str is not the empty String object. If str
  *       is an empty String object, this String object is returned.
  *
  * @throws NullPointerException – if str is null.
  *
  */
public String concat (String str)
```

In the method specification, "this String object" refers to the calling object, that is, the object that invokes the method. For example, if we have

```
s1.concat (" days")
```

Then s1 is the calling object. Well, technically, s1 is a reference to the calling object, and in the heading for the concat method, str is a reference to a String object, and a reference is returned by the method.

A *message* is the invocation of a method by an object (reference). For example, with the values of s1, s2, and s3 given earlier, here are some messages that utilize the concat method:

```
s1.concat (" days")                        // returns a reference to "halcyon days"
"in".concat ("flam").concat ("mable")      // returns a reference to "inflammable"
"in".concat ("flam".concat ("mable"))      // returns a reference to "inflammable"
s1.concat (s3)                             // throws NullPointerException
s1.concat (s2)                             // returns a copy of the reference s1
s3.concat ("days")                         // throws NullPointerException
s2.concat ("days")                         // returns a reference to "days"
```

The first of these messages shows a typical use of the concat method: to join strings together to form a larger string. The second message exemplifies that the reference returned by the message

```
"in".concat ("flam")
```

can itself be used to send a message. The third example shows that the argument may be a message. The fourth message results in NullPointerException being thrown because the argument is **null**. The fifth message illustrates the argument can be a reference to an empty string. The sixth message indicates that the calling object must be non-null, and the seventh message shows that the calling object can be an empty string.

Note that in the next-to-last message, an exception is thrown, even though this situation is not specified in the method specification. The reason the specification does not explicitly mention the illegality of having a **null** reference at the beginning of a message is that it is always illegal to have a **null** reference at the beginning of a message!

Concatenation is so frequently used, especially in output messages, that Java has endowed the String class with a concatenation operator, namely, +. For example, instead of

```
System.out.println ("Normalcy ".concat ("is recessive."));
```

We can write

```
System.out.println ("Normalcy " + "is recessive.");
```

The String operator + has fewer restrictions than the concat method. Either operand (in fact, both operands) can be **null**. For example, we can write

```
System.out.println ("Normalcy " + s3);
```

The output will be

```
Normalcy null
```

Also, either operand (but not both operands) can be of a primitive type. For example, we can write

```
System.out.println ("The highest score is " + 96);
```

The evaluation of operator + is from left to right. So if there are several applications of operator +, the result of the first application is the left operand of the second application. This is true even if the first application is for integer addition. For example, suppose we have

```
System.out.println (5 + 7 + "are the correct answers.");
```

The output will be

```
12 are the correct answers.
```

If instead we write

```
System.out.println (5 + " " + 7 + " are the correct answers.");
```

the output will be

```
5 7 are the correct answers.
```

Operator + applies to String objects: a new String object is created by concatenating the objects referenced by the operands of +, and a reference to the newly created String object is returned. Note that operator + is the only Java operator that can be applied to objects. Other operators, such as = and ==, apply to references but not to objects.

## A1.4 | THE StringTokenizer CLASS

The StringTokenizer class allows a programmer to split a string up into meaningful units, called *tokens.* For example, suppose a line of input consists of a student's name, class rank, and grade point average, separated by blanks. With the help of the StringTokenizer class's nextToken( ) method, we can store those three values into the following variables:

```
String name;

int classRank;

double gpa;
```

Because our interest in the StringTokenizer class will be as users rather than as developers, we will focus on method specifications rather than fields and method definitions. There are three widely used methods: a constructor with a String parameter, countTokens( ), and nextToken( ). Here are the method specifications:

```
/**
 * Initializes this StringTokenizer object with a specified String object.
 * The delimiters, that is, token separators, are the blank, new-line, tab,
 * carriage-return and form-feed characters.
 *
 * @param str – the String object used to initialize this StringTokenizer
 *        object.
```

```
*
* @throws NullPointerException – if str is null.
*
*/
public StringTokenizer (String str)

/**
* Counts the number of tokens still available from this StringTokenizer
* object's string.
*
* @return the number of tokens still available.
*
*/
public int countTokens ( )

/**
* Returns the next available token from this StringTokenizer object's string.
*
* @return the next available token.
*
* @throws NoSuchElementException – if there are no more tokens
*       available from this StringTokenizer object's string.
*/
public String nextToken ( )
```

The result returned by the nextToken method is a String object (strictly speaking, a reference to a String object), so a conversion is necessary if the result is to be stored in a variable of a primitive type. For example, the Double class has a parseDouble method that takes a String argument and returns a **double** value, so we can write

```
double gpa = Double.parseDouble ("3.86");
```

When parseDouble is called, there is no calling object because the effect of the method depends only on the String argument. To signify this situation, the class identifier replaces the reference to a calling object when parseDouble is called. A method that is called without a calling object is known as a **static** method, as seen in the following heading

```
public static double parseDouble (String s)
```

Every Java program includes the declaration of a **static** main method. For example, here is a main method that illustrates the above three StringTokenizer methods in concert by printing the sum of a line of test scores:

```
public static void main (String [ ] args)
{
        String line = "50 85 75 80";

        final String SUM_ANSWER = "The sum is ";
```

```
            StringTokenizer st = new StringTokenizer (line);

            int sum = 0;

            while (st.countTokens ( ) > 0)
                    sum += Integer.parseInt (st.nextToken( ));

            System.out.println (SUM_ANSWER + sum);
        } // method main
```

Any program that declares a StringTokenizer object must include information that allows that class to be used in the program. One possibility is to include the full path for the StringTokenizer class:

```
    java.util.StringTokenizer tokens;
```

A simpler way is to include an **import** directive to the compiler to make the String-Tokenizer class available to the program. To import that class, write

```
    import java.util.StringTokenizer;
```

at the beginning of the file that includes any class in which StringTokenizer is instantiated. The StringTokenizer class and many other useful classes have been grouped together into java.util, a *package,* that is, a collection of related classes. Many of the classes you declare will utilize several of the classes from java.util, so you can simply import the whole package:

```
    import java.util.*;
```

## A1.5 | CONSOLE INPUT

The treatment of console input is somewhat more complex than console output, but after a little up-front work, we will be able to store a string of input characters into a String object. Here is the set up:

```
    BufferedReader keyboardReader = new BufferedReader
                                    (new InputStreamReader (System.in));

    String line = keyboardReader.readLine ( );
```

Basically, System.in is a static constant associated with input from the keyboard (echoed on the console window), the InputStreamReader constructor allows those input bytes to be converted into Unicode characters, and the BufferedReader constructor allows the Unicode characters to be stored in a temporary location—a *buffer*—until the newline character ('\n') has been read in. Then the buffer, not including the newline character, is stored in String object, the buffer is flushed (that is, emptied), and a reference to the String object is returned. The readLine method may throw an IOException,[1] so that contingency must be either explicitly handled or, because IOException is a checked exception, explicitly propagated.

---

[1] No exception is thrown for console input, but if the BufferedReader object is associated with an input file, an exception will be thrown, for example, if the file does not exist or if an attempt is made to read past the end-of-file marker.

Here is a complete program that prints the sum of test scores read in from the keyboard; the *sentinel*—that is, the special value to indicate the end of the input—is "***".

```java
import java.io.*;

public class Scores1
{
        public static void main (String [ ] args) throws IOException
        {
                final String SENTINEL = "***";

                final String PROMPT = "Please enter a test score, or " +
                        SENTINEL + " to quit: ";

                final String RESULT = "\nThe sum of the scores is ";

                BufferedReader keyboardReader = new BufferedReader
                        (new InputStreamReader (System.in));

                String line;

                int sum = 0;

                while (true)
                {
                        System.out.print (PROMPT);
                        line = keyboardReader.readLine( );
                        if (line.equals (SENTINEL))
                                break;
                        sum += Integer.parseInt (line);
                } // while
                System.out.println (RESULT + sum);
        } method main
} // class Scores1
```

Notice that the sentinel need not be an integer. That is because the conversion of the input line to an **int** is made *after* the test to determine if the input line contains the sentinel.

Another noteworthy feature of the program is the structure of the **while** statement. The loop continues until the sentinel is read in. The execution of the **break** statement causes an abrupt exit of the loop; the next statement to be executed is the println that outputs the sum. The loop has only one entrance and one exit, and that helps us to understand the action of the loop. Also, there is only one place where the prompt is printed, and only one place where input is read.

# A1.6 | LOCAL VARIABLES

Variables declared within a method—including the method's formal parameters—are called *local variables.* For example, the following method has two local variables, n and j:

```
/**
 * Determines if a specified non-negative integer is prime.
 *
 * @param n – the integer whose primality is being tested.
 *
 * @return true – if n is prime.
 *
 */
public static boolean isPrime (int n)
{
        if (n % 2 == 0)
                return false;
        for (int j = 3; j * j < n; j = j + 2)
                if (n % j == 0)
                        return false;
        return true;
} // method isPrime
```

Local variables must be initialized before they are used. For example, suppose we have

```
public static void main (String [ ] args)
{
        int k;

        System.out.println (isPrime (k));
} // method main
```

Compilation will fail, with an error message indicating that "variable k might not have been initialized." The phrase "might not have been initialized" in the error message suggests that the compiler does not perform a detailed analysis of the method's code to determine if, in fact, the variable has been properly initialized. For example, the same error message will be generated by the following method:

```
public static void main (String [ ] args)
{
        int k;

        boolean flag = true;

        if (flag)
                k = 20;
        if (!flag)
                k = 21;
        System.out.println (isPrime (k));
} // method main
```

Clearly, if we look at this method as a whole, the variable k does receive proper initialization. But if each statement is considered on its own, no such guarantee can be made. The following slight variant is acceptable because the **if-else** statement is treated as a unit:

```
public static void main (String [ ] args)
{
        int k;

        boolean flag = true;

        if (flag)
                k = 20;
        else
                k = 21;
        System.out.println (isPrime (k));
} // method main
```

The **scope** of an identifier is the region of a program to which that identifier's declaration applies. In the isPrime method, the scope of the parameter n is the entire function definition, but the scope of the variable k is only the **for** statement. A compile-time error results if an attempt is made to access an identifier outside of its scope: for example, if we tried to print out the value of k outside of the **for** statement. This restriction of identifiers to specific code segments—and not, for example, to an entire method—promotes modularity.

## A1.7 | ARRAYS

An **array** is a collection of elements, of the same type, that are stored contiguously in memory. **Contiguous** means "adjacent," so the individual elements are stored next to each other.[2] For example, we can create an array of five String objects as follows:

```
String [ ] names = new String [5];
```

Here the **new** operator allocates space for an array of five String references (each initialized to **null** by the Java Virtual Machine), and returns a reference to the beginning of the space allocated. This reference is stored in names.

In order to specify one of the individual elements in an array, an index is used. An **index** is an integer expression in square brackets; the value of the expression determines which individual element is being denoted. The smallest allowable index is 0. For example,

```
names [0] = "Cromer";
```

will store a reference to "Cromer" at the zeroth entry in the array names.

The capacity of an array, that is, the maximum number of elements that can be stored in the array, is fixed once the array has been created. If the capacity turns out to be too small, a larger array must be allocated and the contents of the smaller array

---

[2] Actually, all that matters is that, to a user of an array, the elements are stored *as if* they were contiguous.

copied to the larger array. Also, the capacity need not be determined at compile-time. For example, we can do the following:

```
public void processInput (String s)
{
        int n = Integer.parseInt (s);

        String [ ] names = new String [n];

        . . .
```

When the processInput method is executed at run time, names will be assigned a reference to an array of n strings, all of which are initialized to **null**. An array is an object, even though there is no corresponding class. So, as suggested in Section A1.3, names may be called an "array," even though "array reference" is the accurate term.

The capacity of an array is stored in the array's length field. For example, suppose we initialize an array when we create it:

```
double [ ] weights = {107.3, 112.1, 114.4, 119.0, 117.4};
```

We can print out the capacity of this array as follows:

```
System.out.println (weights.length);
```

The output will be

```
5
```

For an array x, the value of any array index must be between 0 and x.length − 1, inclusive. If the value of an index is outside that range, ArrayIndexOutOfBounds Exception will be thrown, as in the following example:

```
final int MAX = 10;

double [ ] salaries = new double [MAX];

for (int i = 0; i <= MAX; i++)
        salaries [i] = 0.00;
```

For the first 10 iterations of the loop, with i going from 0 through 9, each element in the array is initialized to 0.00. But when i gets the value 10, an ArrayIndexOutOf BoundsException is thrown because i's value is greater than the value of salaries. length − 1, which is 9.

# A1.8 | ARGUMENTS AND PARAMETERS

In Java, the relationship between arguments (when a method is called) and parameters (in the called method's heading) is straightforward: a copy of the value of the argument is assigned to the parameter. So the argument is not affected by the method call. For example, consider the following program:

```
public class Nothing
{
        public static void main (String[ ] args)
        {
                int k = 30;

                triple (k);

                System.out.println (k);
        } // method main

        public static void triple (int n)
        {
                n = n * 3;
        } // method triple
} // class Nothing
```

The output will be 30. When the method triple (**int** n) is called, a copy of the value of the argument k is assigned to the parameter n. So at the beginning of the execution of the call, n has the value 30. At the end of the execution of the call, n has the value 90, but the argument k still has the value 30. Incidentally, the name of the parameter has no effect: the result would have been the same if the parameter had been named k instead of n.

Next, we look at what happens if the argument is of type reference. As with primitive arguments, a reference argument will not be affected by the method call. But a much more important issue is "What about the object referenced by the argument?" If the object is an array, then the array can be affected by the method call. For example, here is a simple program in which an array is modified during a method call:

```
public class Swap
{
        public static void main (String[ ] args)
        {
                double[ ] x = {5.0, 8.0, 12.2, 20.0};

                swap (x, 1, 2);

                System.out.println (x [1] + " " + x [2]);
        } // method main

        public static void swap (double[ ] a, int i, int j)
        {
                double temp = a [i];
                a [i] = a [j];
                a [j] = temp;
        } // method swap

} // class Swap
```

The output will be

12.2 8.0

In the array referenced by x, the elements at indexes 1 and 2 have been swapped.

For objects other than arrays, whether the object can be affected by the method call depends on the class of which the object is an instance. For example, the String class is ***immutable,*** that is, there are no methods in the String class that can modify an already constructed String object. So if a String reference is passed as an argument in a method call, the String object will not be affected by the call. The following program illustrates the immutability of String objects.

```java
public class Immutable
{
    public static void main (String[ ] args)
    {
        String s = "yes";
        flip (s);
        System.out.println (s);
    } // method main

    public static void flip (String t)
    {
        t = new String ("no");
    } // method flip
} // class Immutable
```

The output will be "yes". The flip method constructed a new String object, but did not affect the original String object referenced by s. Figure A1.1 shows the relationship between the argument s and the parameter t at the start of the execution of

**Figure A1.1** I The relationship between the argument s and the parameter t at the start of the execution of the method flip( ) in the class Immutable.

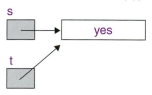

**Figure A1.2** I The relationship between the argument s and the parameter t at the end of the execution of the method flip( ) in the class Immutable.

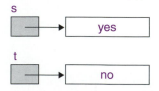

the call to the method flip( ). Figure A1.2 shows the relationship between s and t at the end of the execution of the method call.

Some built-in classes are mutable. For example, the following program illustrates the mutability of the StringTokenizer class.

```java
import java.util.*; // for the StringTokenizer class

public class Mutable
{
    public static void main (String[ ] args)
    {
        StringTokenizer tokens = new StringTokenizer ("yes no maybe");

        System.out.println (tokens.nextToken( ));
        advance (tokens);
        System.out.println (tokens.nextToken( ));
    } // method main

    public static void advance (StringTokenizer st)
    {
        st.nextToken( );
    } // method advance

} // class Mutable
```

The output from this program will be

yes
maybe

The string "no" was returned when st.nextToken( ) was called, and that call advanced the current position of the StringTokenizer object (referenced both by tokens and st) beyond where "no" is. Because of this alteration of the StringTokenizer object, the second call to println in the main method prints out "maybe".

To summarize this section, an argument is never affected by a method call. But if the argument is a reference, the corresponding object may (for example, an array object or a StringTokenizer object) or may not (for example, a String, Integer, or Double object) be affected by the call.

# A1.9 | OUTPUT FORMATTING

What do you think the output will be from the following code fragment?

```java
double grossPay = 800.40;

System.out.println (grossPay);
```

The output will not be

800.40

but rather

800.4

To get two fractional digits printed, we need to convert grossPay to a string with two fractional digits. This is accomplished by first creating a DecimalFormat object with a fixed format that includes two fractional digits, and then applying that object's format method to grossPay. The code is

```
DecimalFormat d = new DecimalFormat ("0.00");

double grossPay = 800.40;

System.out.println (d.format (grossPay));
```

The fixed format, "0.00", is the argument to the DecimalFormat constructor. That format specifies that the String object returned by the format method will have at least one digit to the left of the decimal point and exactly two digits to the right of the decimal point.

The DecimalFormat class is in the package java.text, so that package is imported at the beginning of the file in which the formatting is performed.

## PROGRAMMING EXERCISES

**A1.1** The package java.lang includes the Integer class. In that class, what is the definition of MAX_VALUE? The number 0x7fffffff is in *hexadecimal,* that is, base 16, notation. To indicate hexadecimal notation, start with "0x", followed by the hexadecimal value. In hexadecimal, there are 16 digits: 0, 1, 2, . . . , 9, a, b, c, d, e, and f. The digits 0 through 9 have the same value as in decimal, and the letters a through f have the following decimal values:

a   10
b   11
c   12
d   13
e   14
f   15

The decimal representation of hexadecimal 7fffffff is

$7*16^7 + 15*16^6 + 15*16^5 + 15*16^4 + 15*16^3 + 15*16^2 + 15*16^1 + 15$
$= 2147483647$

Similarly, the decimal value of MIN_VALUE is $-2147483648$. Hypothesize the decimal value of each of the following:

```
Integer.MAX_VALUE + 1

Math.abs (Integer.MIN_VALUE)
```

Test your hypotheses with a main method that calls the System.out.println method.

**A1.2** Suppose we have the following:

```
int a = 37,
```

```
b = 5;
```

```
System.out.println (a − a / b * b + a % b);
```

Hypothesize what the output will be. Test your hypothesis by executing a main method that includes that code. Can you find another pair of positive **int** values for a and b that will produce different output? Explain.

**A1.3** Hypothesize the output from the following:

```
System.out.println (1 / 0);
System.out.println (1.0 / 0);
```

Test your hypotheses by executing a main method that includes that code.

**A1.4** In the String class, read the specification for the indexOf method that takes a String parameter. Then hypothesize the output from the following

```
System.out.println ("The snow is now on the ground.".indexOf ("now"));
```

Test your hypothesis by executing a main method that includes that code.

**A1.5** In the String class, read the specification for the indexOf method that takes a String parameter and an **int** parameter. Then hypothesize the output from the following

```
System.out.println ("The snow is now on the ground.".indexOf ("now", 8);
```

Test your hypothesis by executing a main method that includes that code.

**A1.6** Modify the DecimalFormat constructor in Section A1.9 so that the output starts with a dollar sign and there is a comma to the left of the hundreds digit. For example, if the gross pay is 74400.00, the output will be

```
$74,400.00
```

**A1.7** Write and run a main method in which an input string is read in and the output is the original string with each occurrence of the word "is" replaced by "was". No replacement should be made for an embedded occurrence, such as in "this" or "isthmus".

**A1.8** Write and run a main method in which an input string is read in and the output is the original string with each occurrence of the word "is" replaced by "is not". No replacement should be made for an embedded occurrence, such as in "this" or "isthmus".

**A1.9** Write and run a main method in which the end user enters three lines of input. The first line contains a string, the second line contains a substring to be replaced, and the third line contains the replacement substring. The output is the string in the first line with each occurrence of the substring in the second line replaced with the substring in the third line. No replacement should be made for an embedded occurrence, in the first line, of the substring in the second line.

**A1.10** Study the following method:

```java
public static void mystery (int n)
{
        System.out.print ("For n = " + n);
        while (n > 1)
            if (n % 2 == 0)
                        n = n / 2;
            else
                        n = 3 * n + 1;
        System.out.println (", the loop terminated.");
} // method mystery
```

Trace the execution of this method when n = 7. In the same class as the method mystery, develop a main method to show that the **while** statement in the method mystery successfully terminates for any positive integer n less than 100.

*Cultural note:* It can be shown that this method terminates for all **int** values greater than 0, but it is an open question whether the method terminates for all integer values greater than 0.

# APPENDIX 2

## Mathematical Background

### A2.1 | INTRODUCTION

Mathematics is one of the outstanding accomplishments of the human mind. Its abstract models of real-life phenomena have fostered advances in every field of science and engineering. Most of computer science is based on mathematics, and this book is no exception. This appendix provides an introduction to those mathematical concepts referred to in the chapters. Some exercises are given at the end of the appendix, so that you can practice the skills while you are learning them.

### A2.2 | FUNCTIONS AND SEQUENCES

An amazing aspect of mathematics, first revealed by Whitehead and Russell (1910), is that only two basic concepts are required. Every other mathematical term can be built up from the primitives *set* and *element.* For example, an ordered pair $<a, b>$ can be defined as a set with two elements:

$$<a, b> = \{a, \{a, b\}\}$$

The element $a$ is called the *first component* of the ordered pair, and $b$ is called the *second component.*

Given two sets $A$ and $B$, we can define a *function f* from $A$ to $B$, written

$$f: A \rightarrow B$$

as a set of ordered pairs $<a, b>$, where $a$ is an element of $A$, $b$ is an element of $B$, and each element in $A$ is the first component of exactly one ordered pair in $f$. Thus no two ordered pairs in a function have the same first element. The sets $A$ and $B$ are called the *domain* and *co-domain,* respectively.

For example,

$$f = \{\ < -2, 4>, <-1, 1>, <0, 0>, <1, 1>, <2, 4>\ \}$$

defines the "square" function with domain $\{\ -2, -1, 0, 1, 2\ \}$ and codomain $\{\ 0, 1, 4\ \}$. No two ordered pairs in the function have the same first component, but it is legal for two ordered pairs to have the same second component. For example, the pairs $<-1, 1>$ and $<1, 1>$ have the same second component, namely, 1.

If $<a, b>$ is an element of $f$, we write $f(a) = b$. This gives us a more familiar description of the above function: the function $f$ is defined by

$$f(i) = i^2 \quad \text{for } i \text{ in } -2 \ldots 2$$

Another name for a function is a ***map.*** This is the term used in Chapters 12, 14, and 15 to describe a collection of elements in which each element has a unique **key** part and a **value** part. There is, in effect, a function from the keys to the values, and that is why the keys must be unique.

A ***finite sequence t*** is a function such that for some positive integer $k$, called the *length* of the sequence, the domain of $t$ is the set $\{ 0, 1, 2, \ldots, k - 1 \}$. For example, the following defines a finite sequence of length 4:

$$t(0) = \text{``Karen''}$$
$$t(1) = \text{``Don''}$$
$$t(2) = \text{``Mark''}$$
$$t(3) = \text{``Courtney''}$$

Because the domain of each finite sequence starts at 0, the domain is often left implicit, and we write

$$t = \text{``Karen''}, \text{``Don''}, \text{``Mark''}, \text{``Courtney''}$$

## A2.3 | SUMS AND PRODUCTS

Mathematics entails quite a bit of symbol manipulation. For this reason, brevity is an important consideration. An example of abbreviated notation can be found in the way that sums are represented. Instead of writing

$$x_0 + x_1 + x_2 + \cdots + x_{n-1}$$

we can write

$$\sum_{i=0}^{n-1} x_i$$

This expression is read as "the sum, as $i$ goes from 0 to $n - 1$, of $x$ sub $i$." We say that $i$ is the ***count index***. A count index corresponds to a loop-control variable in a **for** statement. For example, the following code will store in sum the sum of components 0 through n−1 in the array x:

```
double sum = 0.0;

for (i = 0; i < n; i++)
        sum += x [i];
```

Of course, there is nothing special about the letter $i$. We can write, for example,

$$\sum_{j=1}^{10} (1/j)$$

as shorthand for

$$1 + 1/2 + 1/3 + \cdots + 1/10$$

Similarly, if $n \geq m$,

$$\sum_{k=m}^{n} (k2^{-k})$$

is shorthand for

$$m2^{-m} + (m+1)2^{-(m+1)} + \cdots + n2^{-n}$$

Another abbreviation, less frequently seen than summation notation, is product notation. For example,

$$\prod_{k=0}^{4} a_k$$

is shorthand for

$$a_0 \cdot a_1 \cdot a_2 \cdot a_3 \cdot a_4$$

# A2.4 I LOGARITHMS

John Napier, a Scottish baron and part-time mathematician, first described logarithms in a paper he published in 1614. From that time until the invention of computers, the principal value of logarithms was in number-crunching: logarithms enabled multiplication (and division) of large numbers to be accomplished through mere addition (and subtraction).

Nowadays, logarithms have only a few computational applications—for example, the Richter scale for measuring earthquakes. But logarithms provide a useful tool for analyzing algorithms, as you saw (or will see) in Chapters 3 through 15.

We define logarithms in terms of exponents, just as subtraction can be defined in terms of addition, and division can be defined in terms of multiplication.

Given a real number $b > 1$, we refer to $b$ as the **base.** The **logarithm,** base $b$, of any real number $x > 0$, written

$$\log_b x$$

is defined to be that real number $y$ such that

$$b^y = x$$

For example, $\log_2 16 = 4$ because $2^4 = 16$. Similarly, $\log_{10} 100 = 2$ because $10^2 = 100$. What is $\log_2 64$? What is $\log_8 64$? Estimate $\log_{10} 64$.

The following relations can be proved from the above definition and the corresponding properties of exponents. For any real number $b > 1$ and for any positive real numbers $x$ and $y$,

> **Properties of Logarithms**
> 1.  $\log_b 1 = 0$
> 2.  $\log_b b = 1$
> 3.  $\log_b (xy) = \log_b x + \log_b y$
> 4.  $\log_b (x/y) = \log_b x - \log_b y$
> 5.  $\log_b b^x = x$
> 6.  $b^{\log_b x} = x$
> 7.  $\log_b x^y = y \log_b x$

From these equations, we can obtain the formula for converting logarithms from one base to another. For any bases $a$ and $b > 1$ and for any $x > 0$,

$$\begin{aligned}\log_b x &= \log_b a^{\log_a x} &&\text{(by Property 6)} \\ &= (\log_a x)(\log_b a) &&\text{(by Property 7)}\end{aligned}$$

The base $e$ ($\approx 2.718$) has special significance in calculus; for this reason logarithms with base $e$ are called *natural logarithms* and are written in the shorthand *ln* instead of $\log_e$.

To convert from a natural logarithm to a base 2 logarithm, we apply the base-conversion formula just derived. For any $x > 0$,

$$\ln x = (\log_2 x)(\ln 2)$$

Dividing both sides of this equation by ln 2, we get

$$\log_2 x = \ln x/\ln 2$$

We assume the function ln is predefined, so this equation can be used to approximate $\log_2 x$. Similarly, using base 10 logarithms,

$$\log_2 x = \log_{10} x/\log_{10} 2$$

The function ln and its inverse exp provide one way to perform exponentiation. For example, suppose we want to calculate $x^y$ where $x$ and $y$ are of type **double** and $x > 0$. We first rewrite $x^y$:

$$\begin{aligned}x^y &= e^{\ln (x^y)} &&\text{(by Property 6, above)} \\ &= e^{y \ln x} &&\text{(by Property 7)}\end{aligned}$$

This last expression can be written in Java as

```
Math.exp (y * Math.ln (x))
```

or, equivalently, and without any derivation,

```
Math.pow (x, y)
```

## A2.5 | MATHEMATICAL INDUCTION

Many of the claims in the analysis of algorithms can be stated as properties of integers. For example, for any positive integer $n$,

$$\sum_{i=1}^{n} i = n(n + 1)/2$$

In such situations, the claims can be proved by the Principle of Mathematical Induction.

---

**Principle of Mathematical Induction**   Let $S_1$, $S_2$, . . . be a sequence of statements. If both of the following cases hold:

1.   $S_1$ is true
2.   For any positive integer $n$, whenever $S_n$ is true, $S_{n+1}$ is true

then the statement $S_n$ is true for any positive integer $n$.

---

To help you to understand why this principle makes sense, suppose that $S_1$, $S_2$, . . . is a sequence of statements for which cases 1 and 2 are true. By case 1, $S_1$ must be true. By case 2, since $S_1$ is true, $S_2$ must be true. Applying case 2 again, since $S_2$ is true, $S_3$ must be true. Continually applying case 2 from this point, we conclude that $S_4$ is true, and then that $S_5$ is true, and so on. This indicates that the conclusion in the principle is reasonable.

To prove a claim by mathematical induction, we first state the claim in terms of a sequence of statements $S_1$, $S_2$, . . . . We then show that $S_1$ is true—this is called the *base case.* Finally, we need to prove case 2, the *inductive case.*

Here is an outline of the strategy for a proof of the inductive case: let $n$ be any positive integer and assume that $S_n$ is true. To show that $S_{n+1}$ is true, relate $S_{n+1}$ back to $S_n$, which is assumed to be true. The remainder of the proof often utilizes arithmetic or algebra.

**EXAMPLE A2.1**

We will use the Principle of Mathematical Induction to prove the following:

**Claim**   For any positive integer $n$,

$$\sum_{i=1}^{n} i = n(n + 1)/2$$

**Proof**   We start by stating the claim in terms of a sequence of statements. For $n = 1, 2, . . .$ , let $S_n$ be the statement

$$\sum_{i=1}^{n} i = n(n + 1)/2$$

1.   *Base case.*

$$\sum_{i=1}^{1} i = 1 = 1(2)/2$$

Therefore $S_1$ is true.

2. *Inductive case.* Let $n$ be any positive integer and assume that $S_n$ is true. That is,

$$\sum_{i=1}^{n} i = n(n + 1)/2$$

We need to show that $S_{n+1}$ is true, namely,

$$\sum_{i=1}^{n+1} i = (n + 1)(n + 2)/2$$

We relate $S_{n+1}$ back to $S_n$ by making the following observation: The sum of the first $n+1$ integers is the sum of the first $n$ integers plus $n + 1$. That is,

$$\sum_{i=1}^{n+1} i = \sum_{i=1}^{n} i + (n + 1)$$

$$= n(n + 1)/2 + (n + 1) \qquad \text{because } S_n \text{ is assumed true}$$

$$= n(n + 1)/2 + 2(n + 1)/2$$

$$= [n(n + 1) + 2(n + 1)]/2$$

$$= (n + 2)(n + 1)/2$$

We conclude that $S_{n+1}$ is true (whenever $S_n$ is true). So, by the Principle of Mathematical Induction, the statement $S_n$ is true for any positive integer $n$.

---

An important variant of the Principle of Mathematical Induction is the following:

---

**Principle of Mathematical Induction—Strong Form** Let $S_1, S_2, \ldots$ be a sequence of statements. If both of the following cases hold:

1. $S_1$ is true
2. For any positive integer $n$, whenever $S_1, S_2, \ldots, S_n$ are true, $S_{n+1}$ is true

then the statement $S_n$ is true for any positive integer $n$.

---

The difference between this version and the previous version is in the inductive case. Here, when we want to establish that $S_{n+1}$ is true, we can assume that $S_1$, $S_2, \ldots, S_n$ are true.

Before you go any further, try to convince (or at least, persuade) yourself that this version of the principle is reasonable. At first glance, you might think that the strong form is more powerful than the original version. But in fact, they are equivalent.

We now apply the strong form of the Principle of Mathematical Induction to obtain a simple but important result.

Show that for any positive integer $n$, the number of iterations of the following loop statement is floor($\log_2 n$):

**while** $(n > 1)$
    $n = n / 2;$

**Proof** For $n = 1, 2, \ldots$, let $t(n)$ be the number of loop iterations. For $n = 1, 2, \ldots$, let $S_n$ be the statement:

$$t(n) = \text{floor} (\log_2 n)$$

1.  *Base case.* When $n = 1$, the loop is not executed at all, and so $t(n) = 0 = $ floor $(\log_2 n)$. That is, $S_1$ is true.

2.  *Inductive case.* Let $n$ be any positive integer and assume that $S_1, S_2, \ldots, S_n$ are all true. We need to show that $S_{n+1}$ is true. There are two cases to consider:

   **a.**  $n + 1$ is even. Then the number of iterations after the first iteration is equal to $t((n + 1)/2)$. Therefore, we have

$$
\begin{aligned}
t(n + 1) &= 1 + t\,((n + 1)/2) \\
&= 1 + \text{floor}\,(\log_2((n + 1)/2))) && \text{(by the induction hypothesis)} \\
&= 1 + \text{floor}\,(\log_2(n + 1) - \log_2(2)) && \text{(because log of quotient} \\
& && \text{equals difference of logs)} \\
&= 1 + \text{floor}\,(\log_2(n + 1) - 1) \\
&= 1 + \text{floor}\,(\log_2(n + 1)) - 1 \\
&= \text{floor}\,(\log_2(n + 1))
\end{aligned}
$$

     Thus $S_{n+1}$ is true.

   **b.**  $n + 1$ is odd. Then the number of iterations after the first iteration is equal to $t(n/2)$. Therefore, we have

$$
\begin{aligned}
t(n + 1) &= 1 + t\,(n/2) \\
&= 1 + \text{floor}\,(\log_2(n/2)) && \text{(by the induction hypothesis)} \\
&= 1 + \text{floor}\,(\log_2 n - \log_2 2) && \text{(log of quotient equals} \\
& && \text{difference of logs)} \\
&= 1 + \text{floor}\,(\log_2 n - 1) \\
&= 1 + \text{floor}\,(\log_2 n) - 1 \\
&= \text{floor}\,(\log_2 n) \\
&= \text{floor}\,(\log_2(n + 1)) && \text{(since } \log_2(n + 1) \text{ cannot be an integer)}
\end{aligned}
$$

     Thus $S_{n+1}$ is true.

Therefore, by the strong form of the Principle of Mathematical Induction, $S_n$ is true for any positive integer $n$.

Before we leave this example, we note that an almost identical proof shows that in the worst case for an unsuccessful binary search, the number of iterations is

$$\text{floor}\,(\log_2 n) + 1$$

In the original and "strong" forms of the Principle of Mathematical Induction, the base case consists of a proof that $S_1$ is true. In some situations we may need to start at some integer other than 1. For example, suppose we want to show that

$$n! > 2^n$$

for any $n \geq 4$. (Notice that this statement is false for $n = 1$, 2, and 3.) Then the sequence of statements is $S_4, S_5, \ldots$. For the base case we need to show that $S_4$ is true.

In still other situations, there may be several base cases. For example, suppose we want to show that

$$\text{fib}(n) < 2^n$$

for any positive integer $n$. (The method fib, defined in Lab 7, calculates Fibonacci numbers.) The base cases are:

$$\text{fib}(1) < 2^1$$

and

$$\text{fib}(2) < 2^2$$

These observations lead us to the following:

---

**Principle of Mathematical Induction—General Form**   Let $K$ and $L$ be any integers such that $K \leq L$ and let $S_K, S_{K+1}, \ldots$ be a sequence of statements. If both of the following cases hold:

1. $S_K, S_{K+1}, \ldots, S_L$ are true
2. For any integer $n \geq L$, if $S_K, S_{K+1}, \ldots, S_n$ are true, then $S_{n+1}$ is true

then the statement $S_n$ is true for any integer $n \geq K$.

---

The general form extends the strong form by allowing the sequence of statements to start at any integer ($K$) and to have any number of base cases ($S_K, S_{K+1}, \ldots, S_L$). If $K = L = 1$, the general form reduces to the strong form.

The next two examples use the general form of the Principle of Mathematical Induction to prove claims about Fibonacci numbers.

## EXAMPLE A2.3

Show that

$$\text{fib}(n) < 2^n$$

for any positive integer $n$.

**Proof**  For $n = 1, 2, \ldots$, let $S_n$ be the statement

$$\text{fib}(n) < 2^n$$

In the terminology of the general form of the Principle of Mathematical Induction, $K = 1$ because the sequence starts at 1, $L = 2$ because there are two base cases.

1. $\text{fib}(1) = 1 < 2 = 2^1$, and so $S_1$ is true.
   $\text{fib}(2) = 1 < 4 = 2^2$, and so $S_2$ is true.
2. Let $n$ be any integer $\geq 2$ and assume that $S_1, S_2, \ldots, S_n$ are true. We need to show that $S_{n+1}$ is true (that is, we need to show that $\text{fib}(n + 1) < 2^{n+1}$). By the definition of Fibonacci numbers,

$$\text{fib}(n + 1) = \text{fib}(n) + \text{fib}(n - 1), \text{ for } n \geq 2.$$

Since $S_1, S_2, \ldots, S_n$ are true, we know that $S_{n-1}$ and $S_n$ are true. Thus

$$\text{fib}(n - 1) < 2^{n-1}$$

and

$$\text{fib}(n) < 2^n$$

We then get

$$\begin{aligned}
\text{fib}(n + 1) &= \text{fib}(n) + \text{fib}(n - 1) \\
&< 2^n + 2^{n-1} \\
&< 2^n + 2^n \\
&= 2^{n+1}
\end{aligned}$$

And so fib $(n + 1)$ is true.

We conclude, by the general form of the Principle of Mathematical Induction, that

$$\text{fib}(n) < 2^n$$

for any positive integer $n$.

---

You could now proceed, in a similar fashion, to develop the following lower bound for Fibonacci numbers:

$$\text{fib}(n) > (6/5)^n$$

for all integers $n \geq 3$. **Hint:** Use the general form of the Principle of Mathematical Induction, with $K = 3$ and $L = 4$.

Now that lower and upper bounds for Fibonacci numbers have been established, you might wonder if we can improve on those bounds. We will do even better! In the next example we verify an exact, closed formula for the $n$th Fibonacci number. A **closed formula** is one that is neither recursive nor iterative.

**EXAMPLE A2.4**

Show that for any positive integer $n$,

$$\text{fib}(n) = (1/\sqrt{5})([(1 + \sqrt{5})/2]^n - [(1 - \sqrt{5})/2]^n)$$

Before you look at the proof below, calculate a few values to convince yourself that the formula actually does provide the correct values.

**Proof**  For $n = 1, 2, \ldots$, let $S_n$ be the statement

$$\text{fib}(n) = (1/\sqrt{5})([(1 + \sqrt{5})/2]^n - [(1 - \sqrt{5})/2]^n)$$

Let

$$x = (1 + \sqrt{5})/2 \quad \text{and} \quad y = (1 - \sqrt{5})/2$$

Note that

$$x^2 = \frac{(1 + \sqrt{5})^2}{4} = \frac{1 + 2\sqrt{5} + 5}{4} = \frac{3 + \sqrt{5}}{2} = x + 1$$

Similarly,

$$y^2 = y + 1.$$

We now proceed with the proof.

**1.**  $\text{fib}(1) = (1/\sqrt{5})([(1 + \sqrt{5})/2]^1 - [(1 - \sqrt{5})/2]^1) = 1$, so $S_1$ is true.

To show that $S_2$ is true, we proceed as follows:

$$(1/\sqrt{5})([(1 + \sqrt{5})/2]^2 - [(1 - \sqrt{5})/2]^2) = (1/\sqrt{5})(x^2 - y^2)$$
$$= (1/\sqrt{5})[x + 1 - (y + 1)]$$
$$= (1/\sqrt{5})[x - y]$$
$$= (1/\sqrt{5})([(1 + \sqrt{5})/2]^1 - [(1 - \sqrt{5})/2]^1)$$
$$= 1$$

which fib(2) equals, by definition, and so $S_2$ is also true.

**2.**  Let $n$ be any positive integer greater than 1 and assume that $S_1, S_2, \ldots, S_n$ are true. We need to show that $S_{n+1}$ is true; that is, we need to show that

$$\text{fib}(n + 1) = (1/\sqrt{5})([(1 + \sqrt{5})/2]^{n+1} - [(1 - \sqrt{5})/2]^{n+1})$$

By the definition of Fibonacci numbers,

$$\text{fib}(n + 1) = \text{fib}(n) + \text{fib}(n - 1)$$

Since $S_n$ and $S_{n-1}$ are true by the induction hypothesis, we have (using $x$ and $y$)

$$\text{fib}(n) = (1/\sqrt{5})(x^n - y^n)$$

and

$$\text{fib}(n - 1) = (1/\sqrt{5})(x^{n-1} - y^{n-1})$$

Substituting, we get

$$\begin{aligned}
\text{fib}(n + 1) &= (1/\sqrt{5})(x^n + x^{n-1} - y^n - y^{n-1}) \\
&= (1/\sqrt{5})[x^{n-1}(x + 1) - y^{n-1}(y + 1)] \\
&= (1/\sqrt{5})(x^{n-1} x^2 - y^{n-1} y^2) \\
&= (1/\sqrt{5})(x^{n+1} - y^{n+1})
\end{aligned}$$

Therefore $S_{n+1}$ is true.

We conclude, by the general form of the Principle of Mathematical Induction, that $S_n$ is true for any positive integer $n$.

---

The next example establishes part 1 of the Binary Tree Theorem in Chapter 9: the number of leaves is at most the number of elements in the tree plus one, all divided by 2.0. The induction is on the height of the tree and so the base case is for single-item tree, that is, a tree of height 0.

**EXAMPLE A2.5**

Let $t$ be a non-empty binary tree, with leaves($t$) leaves and $n(t)$ elements. We claim that

$$\text{leaves}(t) \leq \frac{n(t) + 1}{2.0}$$

**Proof** For $k = 0, 1, 2, \ldots$, let $S_k$ be the statement: for any nonempty binary tree $t$ of height $k$,

$$\text{leaves}(t) \leq \frac{n(t) + 1}{2.0}$$

1. If $t$ has height 0, then leaves($t$) = $n(t)$ = 1, and so

$$\text{leaves}(t) = 1 = \frac{n(t) + 1}{2.0}$$

Therefore $S_0$ is true.

2. Let $k$ be any integer $\geq 0$, and assume that $S_0, S_1, \ldots, S_k$ are true. We need to show that $S_{k+1}$ is true. Let $t$ be a nonempty binary tree of height $k + 1$. Both left Tree($t$) and rightTree($t$) have height $\leq k$, so both satisfy the induction hypothesis. That is,

$$\text{leaves(leftTree}(t)) \leq \frac{n(\text{leftTree}(t)) + 1}{2.0}$$

and

$$\text{leaves(rightTree}(t)) \leq \frac{n(\text{rightTree}(t)) + 1}{2.0}$$

But each leaf in $t$ is either in leftTree($t$) or in rightTree($t$). That is,

$$\text{leaves}(t) = \text{leaves(leftTree}(t)) + \text{leaves(rightTree}(t))$$

Then we have

$$\text{leaves}(t) \leq \frac{n(\text{leftTree}(t)) + 1}{2.0} + \frac{n(\text{rightTree}(t)) + 1}{2.0}$$

$$= \frac{n(\text{leftTree}(t)) + n(\text{rightTree}(t)) + 1 + 1}{2.0}$$

Except for the root element of $t$, each element in $t$ is either in leftTree($t$) or in rightTree($t$), and so

$$n(t) = n(\text{leftTree}(t)) + n(\text{rightTree}(t)) + 1$$

Substituting this equation's left-hand side for its right-hand side in the previous inequality, we get

$$\text{leaves}(t) \leq \frac{n(t) + 1}{2.0}$$

That is, $S_{k+1}$ is true.

Therefore, by the general form of the Principle of Mathematical Induction, $S_k$ is true for any nonnegative integer $k$. This completes the proof of the claim.

The next example, relevant to Chapter 12, shows that the height of any red-black tree is logarithmic in $n$.

---

**EXAMPLE A2.6**

As noted in Chapter 12, the **TreeMap** and **TreeSet** classes require only logarithmic time—even in the worst case—to insert, remove, or search. The reason for this speed is that those classes are based on red-black trees, whose height is always logarithmic in the number of elements in the tree. The proof that red-black trees are balanced utilizes the general form of the Principle of Mathematical Induction.

**Theorem** The height of any red-black tree is logarithmic in $n$, the number of elements in the tree.

In order to prove this theorem, we first need a couple of preliminary results.

**Claim 1** Let $y$ be the root of a subtree of a red-black tree. The number of black elements is the same in a path from $y$ to any one of its descendants with no children or one child.

Suppose $x$ is the root of a red-black tree, and $y$ is the root of a subtree. Let $b_0$ be the number of black elements from $x$ (inclusive) to $y$ (exclusive). For example, in Figure A2.1, if $x$ is 50 and $y$ is 131, $b_0 = 1$, the number of black elements in the path from 50 through 90; 131 is not counted in $b_0$.

Let $b_1$ be the number of black elements from $y$ to any one of its descendants with no children or one child, and let $b_2$ be the number of black elements from $y$ to any other one of its descendants with no children or one child. Figure A2.2 depicts this situation.

For example, in Figure A2.1, suppose that $y$ is 131 and the two descendants of $y$ are 100 and 135. Then $b_0 = 1$ because 50 is black; $b_1 = 2$ because 131 and 100 are black; $b_2 = 2$ because 131 and 140 are black.

In general, by the Path Rule for the whole tree, we must have $b_0 + b_1 = b_0 + b_2$. This implies that $b_1 = b_2$. In other words, the number of black elements is the same in any path from $y$ to any of its descendants that have no children or one child. We have established Claim 1.

Now that Claim 1 has been verified, we can make the following definition. Let $y$ be an element in a red-black tree; we define the **black-height** of $y$, written bh($y$), as follows:

$$\text{bh}(y) = \text{the number of black elements in any path from } y \text{ to any}$$
$$\text{descendant of } y \text{ that has no children or one child.}$$

By Claim 1, the number of black elements must be the same in any path from an element to any of its descendants with no children or one child. So black-height is well defined. For an example of black height, in Figure 12.3, the black-height of 50

**Figure A2.1 |** A red-black tree of 14 elements with maximum height, 5.

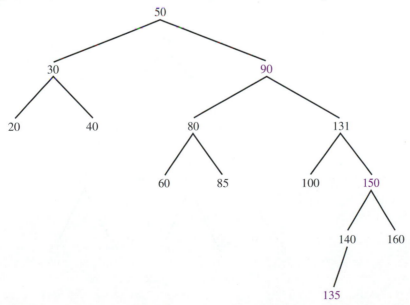

**Figure A2.2** I Part of a red-black tree rooted at $x$; $y$ is a descendant of $x$, and $z_1$ and $z_2$ are two arbitrarily chosen descendants of $y$ that have no children or one child. Then $b_0$ represents the number of black descendants in the path from $x$ up to but not including $y$; $b_1$ and $b_2$ represent the number of black elements in the path from $y$ to $z_1$ and $z_2$, respectively.

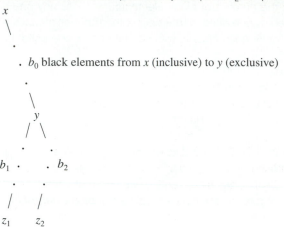

**Figure A2.3** I A red-black tree whose root has a black height of 3.

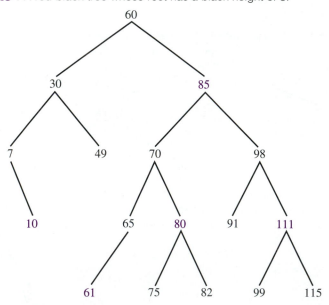

is 2, the black height of 20, 30, 40, or 90 is 1, and the black-height of 10 is 0. Figure A2.3 shows a red-black tree in which 60 has a black height of 3 and 85 has a black height of 2.

**Claim 2** For any nonempty subtree $t$ of a red-black tree,

$$n(t) \geq 2^{bh(root\,(t))} - 1$$

(In the claim, $n(t)$ is the number of elements in $t$, and root($t$) is the root element of $t$.) The proof of this claim is, as usual, by induction on the height of $t$.

**Base case** Assume that height($t$) = 0. Then $n(t) = 1$, and bh(root($t$)) = 1 if the root is black and 0 if the root is red. In either case, $1 \geq$ bh(root($t$)). We have

$$n(t) = 1 = 2^1 - 1 \geq 2^{bh\,(root\,(t))} - 1$$

This proves Claim 2 for the base case.

**Inductive case** Let $k$ be any nonnegative integer, and assume Claim 2 is true for any subtree whose height is $\leq k$. Let $t$ be a subtree of height $k + 1$.

If the root of $t$ has one child, then the root must be black and the child must be red, and so bh(root($t$)) = 1. Therefore,

$$n(t) \geq 1 = 2^1 - 1 = 2^{bh(root(t))} - 1$$

This completes the proof of the inductive case if the root of $t$ has only one child.

Otherwise, the root of $t$ must have a left child, $v_1$, and a right child, $v_2$. If the root of $t$ is red, bh(root($t$)) = bh($v_1$) = bh($v_2$). If the root of $t$ is black, bh(root($t$)) = bh($v_1$) + 1 = bh($v_2$) + 1. In either case,

$$bh\,(v_1) \geq bh(root(t)) - 1$$

and

$$bh(v_2) \geq bh(root\,(t)) - 1$$

The left and right subtrees of $t$ have height $\leq k$, and so the induction hypothesis applies and we have

$$n(leftTree(t)) \geq 2^{bh(v_1)} - 1$$

and

$$n(rightTree(t)) \geq 2^{bh\,(v_2)} - 1$$

The number of elements in $t$ is one more than the number of elements in leftTree($t$) plus the number of elements in rightTree($t$).

Putting all of the above together, we get:

$$
\begin{aligned}
n(t) &= n(leftTree(t)) + n(rightTree(t)) + 1 \\
&\geq 2^{bh\,(v_1)} - 1 + 2^{bh(v_2)} - 1 + 1 \\
&\geq 2^{bh(root(t)) - 1} - 1 + 2^{bh(root(t)) - 1} - 1 + 1 \\
&= 2 \cdot 2^{bh(root(t)) - 1} - 1 \\
&= 2^{bh(root(t))} - 1
\end{aligned}
$$

This completes the proof of the inductive case when the root of $t$ has two children.

Therefore, by the Principle of Mathematical Induction, Claim 2 is true for all nonempty subtrees of red-black trees.

Finally, we get to show the important result that the height of any nonempty red-black tree is logarithmic in $n$, where $n$ represents the number of elements in the tree.

**Theorem**   For any nonempty red-black tree $t$ with $n$ elements, height($t$) is logarithmic in $n$.

**Proof**   Let $t$ be a nonempty red-black tree. By the Red Rule, at most half of the elements in the path from the root to the farthest leaf can be red, so at least half of those elements must be black. That is,

$$bh(root(t)) \geq height(t)/2$$

From Claim 2,

$$n(t) \geq 2^{bh(root(t))} - 1$$

$$\geq 2^{height(t)/2} - 1$$

From this we obtain

$$height(t) \leq 2 \log_2 (n(t) + 1)$$

This inequality implies that height($t$) is $O(\log n)$. By the Binary Tree Theorem in Chapter 9,

$$height(t) \geq \log_2((n(t) + 1)/2)$$

Combining these two inequalities, we conclude that height($t$) is logarithmic in $n$.

This theorem states that red-black trees never get far out of balance. For an arbitrary binary search tree on the other hand, the height can be linear in $n$—for example, if the tree is a chain.

---

**Induction and Recursion**   Induction is similar to recursion. Each has a number of base cases. Also, each has a general case that reduces to one or more simpler cases, which, eventually, reduce to the base case(s). But the direction is different. With recursion, we start with the general case and, eventually, reduce it to the base case. With induction, we start with the base case and use it to develop the general case.

## CONCEPT EXERCISES

**A2.1**   Use mathematical induction to show that, in the Towers of Hanoi game from Chapter 5, moving $n$ disks from pole $a$ to pole $b$ requires a total of $2^n - 1$ moves for any positive integer $n$.

**A2.2**   Use mathematical induction to show that for any positive integer $n$,

$$\sum_{i=1}^{n} Af(i) = A \sum_{i=1}^{n} f(i)$$

where $A$ is a constant and $f$ is a function.

**A2.3** Use mathematical induction to show that for any positive integer $n$,

$$\sum_{i=1}^{n} (i \cdot 2^{i-1}) = (n-1)2^n + 1$$

**A2.4** Let $n_0$ be the smallest positive integer such that

$$\text{fib}(n_0) > n_0^2$$

1. Find $n_0$.
2. Use mathematical induction to show that, for all integers $n \geq n_0$,

$$\text{fib}(n) > n^2$$

**A2.5** Show that fib($n$) is exponential in $n$, specifically, $\Omega((1 + \sqrt{5})^n)$.

*Hint:* See the formula in Example A2.4 above. Note that the absolute value of

$$((1 - \sqrt{5})/2)^n < 1$$

and so

$$((1 - \sqrt{5})/2)^n$$

becomes insignificant for sufficiently large $n$.

**A2.6** Show that

$$\sum_{i=0}^{n} 2^i = 2^{n+1} - 1$$

for any nonnegative integer $n$.

APPENDIX 3

# Additional Features of the Java Collections Framework

## A3.1 | INTRODUCTION

The Java Collections Framework has several features beyond those encountered so far in this book. This appendix focuses on two of those features: serialization and fail-fast iterators.

## A3.2 | SERIALIZATION

Suppose we have gone to the trouble of creating a large and complex ArrayList object as part of a project. After we have used that ArrayList object in an execution of the project, we might want to save the ArrayList, on file, so that we can later resume the execution of the project without having to reconstruct the ArrayList. Fortunately, this is easily done with just a couple of statements.

How? All of the collection classes in the Java Collections Framework implement the Serializable interface that is in the package java.io. This interface has no methods, but merely provides information to the Java Virtual Machine about sending instances of the class to/from a stream. Specifically, any class that implements the Serializable interface will be able to copy any object in the class to an output stream—that is, to "serialize" the elements in the object. "Deserialization" reconstructs the original object from an input stream.

For example, suppose we have created an ArrayList object named fruits. We can create an ObjectOutputStream object and then write fruits to the FileOutputStream object fruits.ser as follows:

```java
try
{
    ObjectOutputStream oos = new ObjectOutputStream (
                                    new FileOutputStream ("fruits.ser"));
    oos.writeObject (fruits);
} // try
```

```
catch (IOException e)
{
        System.out.println (e);
} // catch
```

The ArrayList object fruits has been *serialized*, that is, is saved as a stream of bytes. The file qualifier, "ser", is an abbreviation of "serializable", but you are free to use any qualifier you want, or no qualifier. The definition of the writeObject method depends on the class of the object serialized. For example, here is the definition in the ArrayList class:

```
/**
 * Save the state of the <tt>ArrayList</tt> instance to a stream (that
 * is, serialize it).
 * The worstTime(n) is O(n).
 *
 * @serialData The length of the array backing the <tt>ArrayList</tt>
 *         instance is emitted (int), followed by all of its elements
 *         (each an <tt>Object</tt>) in the proper order.
 */
private void writeObject (java.io.ObjectOutputStream s)
                throws java.io.IOException
{
        // Write out element count, and any hidden stuff
        s.defaultWriteObject( );

        // Write out array length
        s.writeInt (elementData.length);

        // Write out all elements in the proper order.
        for (int i=0; i<size; i++)
                s.writeObject (elementData [i]);

}
```

The size of the ArrayList object is saved first, and then the length of the element Data array field, so that an array of the exact same capacity can be created when the ArrayList object is reconstructed from the file. Finally, the elements in the ArrayList object are saved to the file.

In another program, or in a later execution of the same program, we can *deserialize* fruits. To accomplish that task, we create an ObjectInputStream object to read the stream of bytes, from the FileInputStream whose path is "fruits.ser", into fruits:

```
try
{
        ObjectInputStream ois = new ObjectInputStream (
                                        new FileInputStream ("fruits.ser"));
        fruits = (ArrayList)ois.readObject ( );
} // try
catch (Exception e)
```

```
        {
                System.out.println (e);
        } // catch
```

In the readObject method, the first value read from the stream represents the size of the ArrayList object, and the next value represents the length of the underlying array, and finally, the individual elements are read, one at a time.

An object that is saved and then retrieved in another program (or later execution of the same program) is called *persistent.* In this example, the ArrayList object fruits is persistent. And the same mechanism shown above can be used to create persistent instances of any of the other collection classes in the Java Collections Framework.

You can make your own classes serializable. If all that have to be saved are fields, you needn't even define writeObject and readObject methods: the default serialization/deserialization will handle fields. In the ArrayList example above, the defaults were not enough; the length of the array elementData and the elements themselves had to be saved. That is why the ArrayList class explicitly defines writeObject and readObject methods.

For more details on serialization and deserialization, see

http://developer.java.sun.com/developer/TechTips/2000/tt0229.html

## A3.3 | FAIL-FAST ITERATORS

Once an iterator has started iterating over a collection, that collection should not be structurally modified except by that iterator. A *structural modification* is either an insertion or removal; accessors and mutators do not structurally modify a collection. First, we'll see how this prohibition against structural modification can be helpful to users, and then we'll look at how the prohibition is enforced in the Java Collections Framework.

The following main method creates a small LinkedList object. During an iteration over that object, the object modifies itself, and then the iteration continues.

```
public static void main (String[ ] args)
{
        LinkedList<String> list = new LinkedList<String>( );

        list.add ("humble");
        list.add ("meek");
        list.add ("modest");

        Iterator<String> itr = list.iterator( );
        System.out.println (itr.next( ));      // prints "humble"
        list.remove ("modest");
        System.out.println (itr.next( ));      // prints "meek"?
        System.out.println (itr.next( ));      // ???
} // method main
```

The program constructs a LinkedList object, list, of three elements. An iterator, itr, starts iterating over list. When itr calls its next( ) method, the element "humble" at index 0 is returned, and itr advances to index 1. At this point, list removes the element at index 2. The second call to the next( ) method should be flagged as illegal. Why? The element "meek" at index 1 *could* be returned, but itr should not be allowed to advance to index 2 because there is no longer an element at index 2. So what is best for the programmer is to have the error detected when the second call to the next( ) method is made, rather than having the error detected later in the program.

And that is exactly what happens. When this program was run, the value "humble" was output, and there was an exception thrown: ConcurrentModificationException. This exception was thrown when the second call to the next( ) method was made.

The idea is this: once you start iterating through a collection in the Java Collections Framework, you should not modify the collection except with messages to that iterator. Otherwise, the integrity of that iterator may be compromised, so Concurrent ModificationException is thrown. Such iterators are *fail-fast:* the exception is thrown as soon as the iterator may be invalid. The alternative, waiting until the iterator is known to be invalid, may be far more difficult to detect.

The mechanism for making iterators fail-fast involves two fields: one in the collection, and one in the iterator. We have studied six collection classes within the Java Collections Framework: ArrayList, LinkedList, TreeMap, TreeSet, HashMap, and HashSet. Each of these classes has a modCount field[1] that is initialized to 0. Each time the collection is structurally modified, modCount—for "modification count"— is incremented by 1.

The iterator class embedded in the collection class has an expectedModCount field, which is initialized to modCount in the iterator's constructor. Whenever the iterator structurally modifies the collection (for example, with a call to itr.remove( )), both expectedModCount and modCount are incremented by 1. Also, whenever the iterator object itself is modified (for example, with a call to itr.next( ) or itr.remove( )), there is a test:

```
if (modCount != expectedModCount)
        throw new ConcurrentModificationException( );
```

If modCount and expectedModCount are unequal, that means the collection has been structurally modified, but not by the iterator. Then for example, as in the program at the beginning of this section, a call to the next( ) method might advance to an element that is no longer in the collection. Instead of returning a possibly incorrect value, the next( ) method throws ConcurrentModificationException.

If, for some reason, you want to bypass this fail-fast protection, you can catch ConcurrentModificationException and do nothing in the **catch** block.

You may view the fail-fast iterator mechanism as much ado about nothing because it is unlikely that a collection being iterated over would be structurally modified except by the iterator. But Java operates in a multithreaded environment. Because a collection object can be modified by different threads, the fast failure of iterators can be very helpful.

---

[1] For the ArrayList and LinkedList classes, modCount is inherited from AbstractList. TreeMap and HashMap explicitly declare the modCount field. TreeSet and HashSet utilize the modCount field in the backing map field (an instance of TreeMap and HashMap, respectively).

# REFERENCES

ACM/IEEE-CS Joint Curriculum Task Force, *Computing Curricula 1991,* Association for Computing Machinery, New York, 1991.

Adel'son-Vel'skii, G. M., and E. M. Landis, "An Algorithm for the Organization of Information," *Soviet Mathematics,* vol. 3, pp. 1259–1263, 1962.

Albir, S. S., *UML in a Nutshell,* O'Reilly & Associates, Inc., Sebastopol, CA, 1998.

Andersson, A., T. Hagerup, S. Nilsson, and R. Raman, "Sorting in Linear Time?," *Proceedings of the 27th Annual ACM Symposium on the Theory of Computing,* 1995.

Arnold, K., and J. Gosling, *The Java Programming Language,* Addison-Wesley, Reading, MA, 1996.

Bailey, D. A., *Data Structures in Java for the Principled Programmer,* McGraw-Hill, Burr Ridge, IL, 1999.

Bayer, R., "Symmetric Binary B-trees: Data Structure and Maintenance Algorithms," *Acta Informatica,* vol. 1, no. 4, pp. 290–306, 1972.

Bentley, J. L., and M. D. McIlroy, "Engineering a Sort Function," *Software—Practice and Experience,* vol. 23, no. 11, pp. 1249–1265, November 1993.

Bloch, J., *Effective Java Programming Language Guide,* Addison-Wesley, Boston, 2001.

Collins, W. J., *Data Structures and the Standard Template Library,* McGraw-Hill, New York, NY, 2003.

Cormen, T., C. Leierson, and R. Rivest, *Introduction to Algorithms,* 2nd ed., McGraw-Hill, New York, 2002.

Dale, N. "If You Were Lost on a Desert Island, What One ADT Would You Like to Have with You?," *Proceedings of the Twenty-First SIGCSE Technical Symposium,* vol. 22, no. 1, pp. 139–142, 1990.

Dijkstra, E. W., "A Note on Two Problems in Connexion with Graphs," *Numerische Mathematik,* vol. 1, pp. 269–271, 1959.

Dijkstra, E. W., *A Discipline of Programming,* Prentice-Hall, Englewood Cliffs, NJ, 1976.

Fowler, M., and K. Scott, *UML Distilled,* 2nd ed. Addison-Wesley, Reading, MA, 2000.

Gamma, E., et al., *Design Patterns,* Addison-Wesley, Reading, MA, 1995.

Goodrich, M., and R. Tamassia, *Data Structures and Algorithms in Java,* 2nd ed., John Wiley & Sons, New York, 2001.

Gries, D., *Science of Programming,* Springer-Verlag, New York, 1981.

Guibas, L., and R. Sedgewick, "A Diochromatic Framework for Balanced Trees," *Proceedings of the 19th Annual IEEE Symposium on Foundations of Computer Science,* pp. 8–21, 1978.

Heileman, G. L., *Data Structures, Algorithms and Object-Oriented Programming,* McGraw-Hill, New York, 1996.

Hoare, C. A. R., "Quicksort," *Computer Journal,* vol. 5, no. 4, pp. 10–15, April 1962.

Huffman, D. A., "A Model for the Construction of Minimum Redundancy Codes," *Proceedings of the IRE,* vol. 40, pp. 1098–1101, 1952.

Jackson, M. A., "Principles of Program Design," Academic Press, San Diego, CA, 1997.

Knuth, D. E., *The Art of Computer Programming,* vol. 1: *Fundamental Algorithms,* 2nd ed., Addison-Wesley, Reading, MA, 1973.

Knuth, D. E., *The Art of Computer Programming,* vol. 2: *Seminumerical Algorithms,* 2nd ed., Addison-Wesley, Reading, MA, 1973.

Knuth, D. E., *The Art of Computer Programming,* vol. 3: *Sorting and Searching,* Addison-Wesley, Reading, MA, 1973.

Kruse, R. L., *Data Structures and Program Design,* Prentice-Hall, Englewood Cliffs, NJ, 1987.

Lewis, J., and W. Loftus, *Java Software Solutions: Foundations of Program Design,* 2nd ed., Addison Wesley Longman, Reading, MA, 2000.

McIlroy, M., "A Killer Adversary for Quicksort," *Software—Practice and Experience,* vol. 29, pp. 1–4, 1999.

Meyer, B., *Object-oriented Software Construction,* Prentice-Hall International, London, 1988.

Newhall, T., and L. Meeden, "A Comprehensive Project for CS2: Combining Key Data Structures and Algorithms into an Integrated Web Browser and Search Engine," *Proceedings of the 33rd SIGCSE Technical Symposium on Computer Science Education,* pp. 386–390, March 2002.

Noonan, R. E., "An Object-Oriented View of Backtracking," *Proceedings of the 31st SIGCSE Technical Symposium on Computer Science Education,* pp. 362–366, March 2000.

Pfleeger, S. L., *Software Engineering: Theory and Practice,* Prentice-Hall, Upper Saddle River, NJ, 1998.

Pohl, I., and C. McDowell, *Java by Dissection,* Addison Wesley Longman, Reading, MA, 2000.

Prim, R. C., "Shortest Connection Networks and Some Generalizations," *Bell System Technical Journal,* vol. 36, pp. 1389–1401, 1957.

Rawlins, G. J., *Compared to What? An Introduction to the Analysis of Algorithms,* Computer Science Press, New York, 1992.

Riel, A. J., *Object-Oriented Design Heuristics,* Addison-Wesley, Reading, MA, 1996.

Roberts, E. S., *Thinking Recursively,* John Wiley & Sons, New York, 1986.

Sahni, S., *Data Structures, Algorithms, and Applications in Java,* McGraw-Hill, Burr Ridge, IL, 2000.

Schaffer, R., and R. Sedgewick, "The Analysis of Heapsort," *Journal of Algorithms,* vol. 14, pp. 76–100, 1993.

Shaffer, C., *A Practical Introduction to Data Structures and Algorithm Analysis,* Prentice-Hall, Upper Saddle River, NJ, 1998.

Simmons, G. J., ed., *Contemporary Cryptology: The Science of Information Integrity,* IEEE Press, New York, 1992.

Wallace, S. P., *Programming Web Graphics,* O'Reilly & Associates, Sebastopol, CA, 1999.

Weiss, M. A., *Data Structures and Problem Solving Using Java,* 2nd ed., Addison Wesley Longman, Reading, MA, 2002.

Whitehead, A. N., and B. Russell, *Principia Mathematica,* Cambridge University Press, Cambridge, England, 1910 (volume 1), 1912 (volume 2), 1913 (volume 3).

Williams, J. W., "Algorithm 232: Heapsort," *Communications of the ACM,* vol. 7, no. 6, pp. 347–348, 1964.

Wirth, N., *Algorithms + Data Structures = Programs,* Prentice-Hall, Englewood Cliffs, NJ, 1976.

Zwillinger, D., *CRC Standard Mathematical Tables and Formulae,* 31st Edition, Chemical Rubber Company, Cleveland, OH, 2002.